A Light unto My Path

A Light unto My Path

Gettysburg Theological Studies IV

OLD TESTAMENT STUDIES IN HONOR OF JACOB M. MYERS

Edited by
Howard N. Bream
Ralph D. Heim
Carey A. Moore

Temple University Press • Philadelphia

Temple University Press, Philadelphia 19122

Published 1974
Printed in the United States of America

International Standard Book Number: 0-87722-026-3
Library of Congress Catalog Card Number: 73-85042

Contents

Preface

This Festschrift is an unusual case of poetic justice. Jacob Myers himself helped set in motion a project that has now culminated in making him its final target.

Nearly fifteen years ago, a three-man committee conceived the idea of a series, to be known as "Gettysburg Theological Studies," in honor of outstanding faculty members of the Lutheran Theological Seminary at Gettysburg. Jacob Myers supplied necessary experience and knowledge, while the junior members of the partnership, Otto Reimherr and Howard N. Bream, gladly followed his leadership. Professor Myers even contributed an article to that initial Festschrift, *Biblical Studies in Memory of H. C. Alleman*, which came out in 1960.

Two books followed later: *Theological and Missionary Studies in Memory of John Aberly* in 1965, and *Search the Scriptures: New Testament Studies in Honor of Raymond T. Stamm* in 1969.

Now the Myers name stands, on what will probably be the omega of that series, not among the editors but emblazoned in the title. And how rightly so! For while he cannot be said to have authored this book, Jacob Myers has in a real sense fathered it.

The present editors found, to their joy, that invitations to take part in this project met with enthusiastic responses. It was as if the idea of honoring J. M. Myers had been quietly germinating in the field of Old Testament scholarship, waiting for the right moment to spring up. To the busy and earnest people who took time to prepare papers, the editors here gladly record their gratitude.

The day of the unstructured Festschrift, with essays on subjects chosen more or less at random by the several authors, seems to be waning. However, in the case of this book, heterogeneity offers a means of showing the nature of Myers' influence. The wide variety of topics selected and the diverse backgrounds of the contributors fittingly reflect the breadth of viewpoint, the multiple gifts, and the manifold accomplishments of Myers himself.

A word about the occasion of the Festschrift: The editors did not plan to mark a special birthday anniversary or to give particular recognition to the fact that in 1972 Myers completed thirty years as professor of Hebrew and Old Testament literature and theology at the seminary. They simply felt that the fullness of time had come, when the harvest of years of productive toil, unattended by fanfare, deserved some fitting recognition. Thanks to the efforts of those whose articles make up the volume, and those who have supported it financially, the honor has taken form in a contribution to biblical scholarship, which is exactly what Professor Myers himself would want the most.

Nearly all the papers in this volume were written in 1970. This means that some time has passed between the time of their composition and their publication, a fact that the reader should keep in mind.

It should be noted and acknowledged that a former student of Professor Myers has presented an anonymous gift to make possible the publication of this Festschrift.

The Editors

Ralph D. Heim
Lutheran Theological Seminary at Gettysburg

Jacob Martin Myers

Every productive scholar creates his own autobiography, for he records his life and thought inevitably in his formal publications, and less tangibly, but just as importantly, he leaves his mark upon the minds and lives of his students, friends, and fellow scholars. We have chronicled below the major facts and achievements in Professor Myers' life—what he did, and when—yet these offer but the skeletal outline. To understand who he really is, how he thinks, and what he believes, one must go on to read his books and articles, and talk with those who know him personally.

Jacob M. Myers is the West Pennsylvania Synod professor of Hebrew and Old Testament language, literature, and theology in the Lutheran Theological Seminary at Gettysburg, Pennsylvania (LCA), a position he has held with great distinction since 1942. Prior to that appointment, he served the seminary, first as a lecturer in New Testament studies (1937–40) and then as instructor in the Old Testament department (1940–42). Thus his service to the seminary spans a period of more than three decades. Myers has also been a visiting professor at the Pittsburgh Theological Seminary, the Washington Theological Consortium, and the Gettysburg-Lancaster postgraduate program at York College. This briefly sets forth one facet of his life: his career in teaching.

The son of Harvey A. and Annie (nee Seiffert) Myers, Jacob Myers was born October 25, 1904, on a Pennsylvania farm in West Manchester township. Myers likes to refer to himself as a "York County Dutchman," and still dreams occasionally of buying "a little farm on which to retire." In any case, he has constantly manifested virtues highly prized in rural America: industry, simplicity of habit, friendliness, and helpfulness.

In 1926, he married Mary Helen Kimmel; they have one daughter, Helen Elizabeth Bream, and three grandchildren. No small part of their life has been invested in this growing family.

Myers prepared for college at the York County Academy, graduating in 1923. Gettysburg College awarded him the Bachelor of Arts degree in 1927 (and a Doctor of Letters in 1967) and he received the Bachelor of Divinity degree from Gettysburg Seminary in 1930. That same year he was ordained a pastor by the West Pennsylvania Synod of the United Lutheran Church in America.

His first public ministry was to Grace Lutheran Church and St. Luke Lutheran Church, which formed a multiple parish near Gettysburg. Inasmuch as this ministry did not end until 1950, it may be said that he has been pastor and teacher simultaneously for two decades—a fact which helps to explain why his scholarly work has never lost touch with the grassroots religious issues of life. Even today, he can sometimes be heard wishing for "a little—just a little—country parish again." He still preaches regularly and over a wide area as a guest pastor, and frequently addresses church groups large and small, relishing this kind of direct contact with the man in the pew.

But that he is most at home in the study is clear not only from his writings but also from the fact that over the years he has built up a magnificent personal library of several thousand volumes, many rare and precious. They are his hobby as well as his professional tools for research.

Myers' pastoral and early teaching responsibilities were always accompanied by advanced study, first at Gettysburg Seminary (STM in 1931), then at Temple University in Philadelphia (STD in 1937), and finally at Johns Hopkins University (PhD in Semitics, 1946). It was at Johns Hopkins that he came under the profound influence of Professor W. F. Albright, the man who, as Myers has frequently and gratefully acknowledged, continued to affect his scholarship most influentially over the years.

Throughout his career, Myers has been a steadily productive scholar, writing with equal skill and clarity technical works for the specialist as well as more popular books and articles for the general reader. As his bibliography shows, his latter years have brought forth more books than articles. Most of his articles, in fact, were written before he received his degree from Johns Hopkins. Recently, he has completed the manuscripts for two more volumes in The Anchor Bible, *I and II Esdras*, and is currently preparing a lengthy article on Ezra and Nehemiah for *Encyclopedia Biblica*.

Myers is a member of several professional and scholarly societies: the American Oriental Society, the American Academy of Religion, the Archaeological Institute of America, and the Society of Biblical Literature. He also belongs to the British Society for Old Testament Study, and has an honorary membership in Phi Beta Kappa.

Fortunately, research and writing have not detracted from Myers' commitment to his students. He has always felt a love for education, and, through his classes as well as personal counseling, many a future pastor has been intellectually and spiritually enriched. Myers has also been alert to discover and encourage the student who has that extra something necessary for advanced study, and to such he has given his time and attention unstintingly. As a result, he has had the personal satisfaction of seeing protégés go on to become teachers and scholars who are a credit to their mentor.

While over the years he has enjoyed the difficult task of introducing students to the history, literature, and religion of the Old Testament, Myers has always found special delight in courses which deal directly with Hebrew. Here he is in his element. He has more than once said to a colleague that he comes from those class sessions "like a bridegroom leaving his chamber." Those who know him well understand that he goes to his study early each morning with that same zeal.

Jacob M. Myers

Congratulators: Former Students and Colleagues of Professor Myers

Fred Aigner
E. Jerome Alexis
John M. Aurand
William O. Avery
Richard Carl Baker
Horst H. Bandle
Richard F. Batman
Harry F. Baughman
Robert C. Benner
George H. Berkheimer
Samuel L. Besecker
Ralph W. Birk
Kirk W. Bish
John S. Bishop
Harold Z. Bomberger
Herbert L. Bomberger
Norman L. Bortner
Marlin C. Bottiger
Ronald M. Brant
Dale S. Bringman
Sharlene Brokering
Roger E. Burtner
Marvin F. Cain
Robert C. Camac
Charles A. Chamberlin
Gerald Christianson
Clarence L. Chubb
Paul R. Clouser
Norman E. Cooper, Sr.
Charles L. DeLaney, Jr.
Winfield J. Devonshire, Jr.
Ray E. Dice
Elwood W. Dietz
Edward E. Donnald
Preston H. Dusman
Frederick J. Eckert
Paul D. Emenheiser
William W. J. Ennis
William E. Ervin, Jr.
Warren M. Eshbach
Mervin S. Eyler
Elwood S. Falkenstein
John W. Fehringer
J. Frank Fife
J. Russell Fink
John D. Foerster
Lawrence D. Folkemer
Walter F. Forker
Edward S. Frey
James R. Fuchs
Donna Y. Gardner
Helen D. Gardner

Jack R. Gardner
Richard E. Geib
J. Thompson George
Paul R. Gerschwitz
W. Kent Gilbert, III
Luther A. Gotwald, Jr.
J. W. Gouker
John M. Grissinger, Jr.
Augustus Hackmann
Glenn T. Hafer
B. John Hagedorn
J. Russell Hale
Dale W. Hallberg
John P. Harman
Charles M. Heaps
H. Lee Hebel
Donald R. Heiges
Jacob W. Heikkinen
Henry H. Heins
Marie Jensen Heins
John R. Hershberger
Howard W. Hinkeldey
Jered L. Hock
Bengt R. Hoffman
Timothy L. Hoffman
David R. Hoover
Emmanuel J. Hoover
Gerald E. Houseknecht
Daniel O. Hoy
Paul A. Jones
Nathan A. Kale
William C. Karns
Lester J. Karschner
Richard F. Kauffman
Glen B. Keidel, Sr.
Russell Ray Kerns, Sr.
Kenneth L. Kilheffer
C. Leighton King
Woodrow J. Klinger
Robert W. Koons
Edwin R. Kopp
Paul F. Kramp, Jr.
Otto Kroeger
Allen C. Lambert
James B. Lau, Jr.
John A. Leaf
Elwood H. Leister
Robert B. Logan
Robert H. Logan
Robert H. Mack
Richard E. Manning
Richard E. Martin
Robert A. Martin
Howard J. McCarney
Leon A. McCleary
Ronald H. McClung
Ted N. McGill
Eugene R. McVicker
L. Guy Mehl
George I. Melhorn
Edward G. Mertz
Dale E. Messersmith
Charles E. Miller
Howard W. Miller
Ralph H. Miller
Raymond M. Miller
Bruce K. Minor
Richard H. Mintel
Joseph Molnar, III
F. Elwood Moreland
Alton M. Motter
James A. Mummert
John H. Myers
Victor A. Myers
Robert E. Nale
C. Arthur Neal
J. Pennell Neikirk
Carol L. Nelson
Neil E. Newton
Fuad N. Nucho
Bertha Paulssen
Ernest L. Pee

Paul R. Peel
C. Wayne Peterman
John W. Pfahler
George W. Pieper
Charles A. Pollard
Donald R. Poole
Dwight F. Putman
Carl C. Rasmussen
Robert Browning Rau
Donald G. Raup
Paul L. Reaser
Otto Reimherr
Roland W. Renkel
Paul H. Rhoads
Elmer F. Rice
Robert J. Richards
Howard H. Ritterpusch
James M. Robbins
James A. Rodgers
Harold L. Rowe
Benton F. Rudisill
Clayton L. Rudolph
Dean E. Rupe
Arthur L. Ruths
Carl Sacherich, Jr.
John F. Sammel
W. Raymond Sammel
Robert G. Sander
Daniel H. Sandstedt
Donald F. Sause
Henry E. Schaefer, Jr.
David L. Scheidt
Oscar C. Schultz, Jr.
Raymond Shaheen
Lloyd E. Sheneman
Russel T. Shilling
Carl R. Simon
William M. Slee
Roy L. Sloop
Jacob M. Spangler
John R. Spangler
Henry G. Springer
Irvin F. Stapf, Jr.
Arthur R. Stees
Charles L. Stetler
M. Luther Stirewalt, Jr.
John L. Strube
Herman G. Stuempfle, Jr.
Robert W. Suder
Viggo Swensen
Clarence M. Swinn, Sr.
L. Ralph Tabor
Charles C. Talley
Lowell S. Thompson
Cedric W. Tilberg
James W. Tipton
Dennis L. Trout
Donald Lee Turley
Dean E. Tyson
Lester M. Utz
Jerome D. VanBrakle
Charles Leslie Venable
Gilson C. Waldkoenig
Roderick Wallace
Donald R. Warrenfeltz
Abdel Ross Wentz
Edwin C. Wentz
L. Stanley Whitson
Samuel E. Wicker
Gould Wickey
Raymond F. Wieder
Pierce M. Willard
C. Wesley Willson
John H. Witmer
Eric P. Wogen
Allen S. Wysocki
Arthur E. M. Yeagy
Donald R. Yost
Carol H. Youse
Edgar D. Ziegler
Morris G. Zumbrun

Abbreviations

BOOKS OF THE BIBLE

OT		*Apocryphal or Deuterocanonical*		*NT*	
Gen	Eccles	Tb	Tobit	Mt	1 Tim
Ex	Song	Jdt	Judith	Mk	2 Tim
Lev	Is	1 Macc	First Maccabees	Lk	Tit
Num	Jer	2 Macc	Second Maccabees	Jn	Philem
Deut	Lam	Wis	Wisdom of Solomon	Acts	Heb
Josh	Ezek	Sir	Sirach (Ecclesiasticus)	Rom	Jas
Judg	Dan	Bar	Baruch	1 Cor	1 Pet
Ruth	Hos	Let Jer	Letter of Jeremiah	2 Cor	2 Pet
1 Sam	Joel	Ad Est	Additions to Esther	Gal	1 Jn
2 Sam	Amos	1 Esd	First Esdras	Eph	2 Jn
1 Kings	Obad	2 Esd	Second Esdras	Phil	3 Jn
2 Kings	Jon	Pr Az	Prayer of Azariah	Col	Jude
1 Chron	Mic	S of 3 Y	Song of the Three Young Men	1 Thess	Rev
2 Chron	Nahum			2 Thess	
Ezra	Hab	Sus	Susanna		
Neh	Zeph	Bel	Bel and the Dragon		
Esther	Hag	Pr Man	Prayer of Manasseh		
Job	Zech				
Ps	Mal				
Prov					

Other Abbreviations

AASOR	*Annual of the American Schools of Oriental Research*
AB	Anchor Bible
Act Or	*Acta Orientalia*
AfO	*Archiv für Orientforschung*
AJA	*American Journal of Archaeology*
AJSL	*American Journal of Semitic Languages and Literatures*
AJT	*American Journal of Theology*
Akk	Akkadian
ANEP	*The Ancient Near East in Pictures*
ANET[2,3]	*Ancient Near Eastern Texts,* 2d ed, 3d ed.
AO	*Der Alte Orient*
AOB	*Altorientalische Bibliothek*
APAW	*Abhandlungen der preussischen Akademie der Wissenschaft*
Apoc	Apocrypha
Arab	Arabic
Aram	Aramaic
ARI[5]	W. F. Albright, *Archaeology and the Religion of Israel,* 5th ed.
ARMT	*Archives royales de Mari. Textes transcrits, traduites et commentés*
ASOR	American Schools of Oriental Research
Assyr St	*Assyriological Studies*
ATD	*Das Alte Testament Deutsch*
AV	Authorized Version
BA	*Biblical Archaeologist*
BAR	*Biblical Archaeologist Reader*
BASOR	*Bulletin of the American Schools of Oriental Research*
BAW	*Bibliothek der alten Welt*
BCE	Before the Common Era
BDB	Brown, Driver, and Briggs, *A Hebrew and English Lexicon of the Old Testament*
BHK[3]	*Biblia Hebraica,* ed. R. Kittel and P. Kahle, 3d ed.
BHS	*Biblica Hebraica Stuttgartensia,* ed. K. Elliger and W. Rudolph
Bibl	*Biblica*
Bi Or	*Bibliotheca Orientalis*
BJRL	*Bulletin of the John Rylands Library*
BKAT	*Biblischer Kommentar: Altes Testament*
BLTSG	*Bulletin of the Lutheran Theological Seminary at Gettysburg*
BS	*Bibliotheca Sacra*

BT	*The Bible Today*
B.T.	Babylonian Talmud
BW	*Biblical World*
BWANT	*Beiträge zur Wissenschaft vom Alten und Neuen Testament*
BWAT	*Beiträge zur Wissenschaft vom Alten Testament*
BZ	*Biblische Zeitschrift*
BZAW	*Beihefte zur Zeitschrift für die alttestamentliche Wissenschaft*
CAD	*Chicago Assyrian Dictionary*
CAH	*Cambridge Ancient History*
CBQ	*Catholic Biblical Quarterly*
CBSC	*Cambridge Bible for Schools and Colleges*
CD	Zadokite Document
CE	The Common Era
DBS	*Dictionnaire de la Bible, Supplement*
DJD	*Discoveries in the Judean Desert*
DSS	Dead Sea Scrolls
E	Elohist source
EA	El-Amarna
EB	Early Bronze Age
EH	*Exegetisches Handbuch zum Alten Testament*
EI	Early Iron Age
EI	Eretz Israel
ET	*Expository Times*
ETL	*Ephemerides Theologicae Lovanienses*
EvT	*Evangelische Theologie*
FRLANT	*Forschungen zur Religion und Literatur des Alten und Neuen Testaments*
FSAC	W. F. Albright, *From the Stone Age to Christianity*
G	Greek
GB	Gesenius-Buhl, *Handwörterbuch*
HALAT	W. Baumgartner, *Hebräisches und aramäisches Lexikon zum Alten Testament*
HAT	*Handbuch zum Alten Testament*
HDB	*Hastings' Dictionary of the Bible*
Heb	Hebrew
HKAT	*Handkommentar zum Alten Testament*
HQ	*Hartford Quarterly*
HTR	*Harvard Theological Review*
HUCA	*Hebrew Union College Annual*
IB	*The Interpreter's Bible*
ICC	*International Critical Commentary*

IDB	*The Interpreter's Dictionary of the Bible*
IEJ	*Israel Exploration Journal*
Interp	*Interpretation*
J	Yahwist source
JA	*Journal Asiatique*
JAOS	*Journal of the American Oriental Society*
JBC	*Jerome Bible Commentary*
JBL	*Journal of Biblical Literature and Exegesis*
JBR	*Journal of Bible and Religion*
JCS	*Journal of Cuneiform Studies*
JE	*Jewish Encyclopedia*
JJS	*Journal of Jewish Studies*
JNES	*Journal of Near* Eastern *Studies*
Jos	Josephus
JPOS	*Journal of the Palestine Oriental Society*
JQR	*Jewish Quarterly Review*
JR	*Journal of Religion*
JRAS	*Journal of the Royal Asiatic Society*
JSOR	*Journal of the Society of Oriental Research*
JSS	*Journal of Semitic Studies*
J.T.	Jerusalem Talmud
JTC	*Journal for Theology and the Church*
JTS	*Journal of Theological Studies*
Jud	*Judaica*
KAT[2]	*Kommentar zum Alten Testament*, 2d ed.
KB	Koehler-Baumgartner, *Lexicon in Veteris Testamenti Libros*
KeH	*Kurzgefasstes exegetisches Handbuch zum AT*
KHK	*Kurzer Hand-Kommentar zum Alten Testament*
KJV	King James Version
Lat	Latin
LB	Late Bronze Age
LCQ	*Lutheran Church Quarterly*
LQ	*Lutheran Quarterly*
LXX	Septuagint
M	Mishna
MB	Middle Bronze Age
MGWJ	*Monatsschrift für Geschichte und Wissenschaft des Judentums*
MIOF	*Mitteilungen des Institute für Orientforschung*
MS, MSS	manuscript, manuscripts
MT	Masoretic text
MVAG	*Mitteilungen der vorderasiatische-ägyptischen Gesellschaft*

NAB	New American Bible (Confraternity of Christian Doctrine)
NCE	*New Catholic Encyclopedia*
NEB	New English Bible
NF	Neue Folge
NKZ	*Neue Kirchliche Zeitschrift*
NS	New Series
NT	New Testament
NTS	*New Testament Studies*
OA	*Oriens Antiquus*
OLZ	*Orientalistische Literaturzeitung*
Or	*Orientalis*
OT	Old Testament
OTC	*Old Testament Commentary*, eds. H. C. Alleman and E. E. Flack
P	Priestly source
PAAJR	*Proceedings of the American Academy of Jewish Research*
PBI	Pontifical Biblical Institute
PEQ	*Palestine Exploration Quarterly*
PJ	*Palästina Jahrbuch*
Prop.	proposed reconstruction
PSBA	*Proceedings of the Society of Biblical Archaeology*
Pseudep	Pseudepigrapha
PTR	*Princeton Theological Review*

The following refer to manuscripts from Qumran, the initial number designating the cave where the manuscript was found, Q designating Qumran, and the remaining symbols designating the particular manuscript. Minor fragments of biblical books, designated by the abbreviation of the book and a small letter, are not all listed here.

1QApoc Gen	The Genesis Apocryphon
1QDM	The Words of Moses
1QH	The Hymns
1QIs^a	The St. Mark's Monastery Isaiah Scroll
1QIs^b	The Hebrew University Isaiah Scroll
1QM	The War of the Sons of Light and the Sons of Darkness
1QpHab	Commentary on Habakkuk
1QpHos	Commentary on Hosea
4QpIs	Commentary on Isaiah
1QpMi	Commentary on Micah
4QpNah	Commentary on Nahum

1QPrayers	Liturgical fragments
4QPrNab	The Prayer of Nabonidus
4QpPs37	Commentary on Ps 37
11QPsaPlea	Plea for Deliverance
1QS	Manual of Discipline
1QSa	The Rule of the Congregation
1QSb	The Blessings
4QTest	The Testimonia
RB	*Revue Biblique*
REA	*Revue des études anciennes*
REJ	*Revue des études juives*
RES	*Revue des études sémitiques*
RGG[1,2,3]	*Die Religion in Geschichte und Gegenwart*, 1st ed., 2d ed., 3d ed.
RHPR	*Revue de l'histoire et de philosophies religieuses*
RHR	*Revue de l'histoire des religions*
RQ	*Revue de Qumrân*
RSO	*Rivista degli studie orientali*
RSR	*Recherches de science religieuse*
RSV	Revised Standard Version
RTP	*Revue de théologie et de philosophie*
RV	Revised Version
SANT	*Studien zum Alten und Neuen Testament*
SAOC	*Studies in Ancient Oriental Civilization*
SPAW	*Sitzungsberichte der preussischen Akademie der Wissenschaften*
Syr	Syriac
TCL	*Textes Cuneiformes.* Musée du Louvre
TDNT	*Theological Dictionary of the New Testament*, ed. G. Kittel
ThR	*Theologische Rundschau*
TLZ	*Theologische Literaturzeitung*
Tos	Tosefta
TSBA	*Transactions of the Society of Biblical Archaeology*
TTQ	*Tübingen Theologische Quartelschrift*
TWNT	*Theologisches Wörterbuch zum Neuen Testament*
TZ	*Theologische Zeitschrift*
Ugar	Ugaritic
ÜS	M. Noth, *Überlieferungsgeschichtliche Studien*
UT	C. H. Gordon, *Ugaritic Textbook*
VAB	*Vorderasiatische Bibliothek*
vs, vss	verse, verses

VT (S)	*Vetus Testamentum (Supplements)*
Vulg	Vulgate
WMANT	*Wissenschaftliche monographien zum Alten und Neuen Testament*
WVDOG	*Wissenschaftliche Veröffentlichungen der deutschen Orient-Gesellschaft*
WZKM	*Wiener Zeitschrift für die Kunde des Morgenlandes*
YOS	Yale Oriental Series
ZA	*Zeitschrift für Assyriologie und verwandte Gebiete*
ZAW	*Zeitschrift für die alttestamentliche Wissenschaft*
ZDMG	*Zeitschrift der deutschen morgenländischen Gesellschaft*
ZDPV	*Zeitschrift des deutschen Palästina-Vereins*
ZNW	*Zeitschrift für die neutestamentliche Wissenschaft*
ZS	*Zeitschrift für Semitistik*
ZTK	*Zeitschrift für Theologie und Kirche*

A Light unto My Path

Elizabeth Achtemeier
Union Theological Seminary in Virginia

The Relevance of the Old Testament for Christian Preaching

It has become a truism to say that the Old Testament has been lost for Christian preaching in large sections of the church. One has only to participate in the life of almost any congregation to find evidence of such loss. But biblical scholars have not arrived at a consensus as to how we are to recover the lost two-thirds of our canon, and the purpose of this article is to aid in the ongoing discussion of the problem. We will put the question, first, in its historical perspective in order that we may realize just where we are. Second, we will attempt to lay the exegetical and theological basis for the Christian use of the Old Testament. Finally, we will suggest some possible methods of preaching from the Old Testament. Certainly this article makes no claim to solve all the problems. We do hope that it shows that the problems are not insoluble, and that it aids the church in proclaiming the whole Word of God which has been spoken to us.

A Historical Review

The neglect of the Old Testament in the contemporary proclamation of the Church did not come about accidentally. It is, rather, the result of specific scholarly views imposed on the Bible during the last part of the nineteenth century which are disastrously still very much alive among laymen and clergymen today. There have been efforts in the church ever since the time of Marcion to discard the Old Testament portion of the canon of course, but the modern abandonment of the Book of the Old Covenant grows largely out of the developmental, historical philosophy of Israel's history, which was finally decisively formulated by Julius Wellhausen in his *Israelitische und Jüdische Geschichte* (1894).

In Wellhausen's philosophical treatise, the history in the Old Testament was viewed as a natural development of human institutions and ideas, proceeding by its own inner dynamic and paralleling natural development and evolution in the biological world. Israel's religious life proceeded, according to Wellhausen, by stages, developing out of an early natural, spontaneous period of monolatry, through the strict monotheism of the prophets, to the cultic and legalistic religion of post-exilic Judaism.

This meant, as Wellhausen's views were elaborated (and sometimes distorted) by scholars and laity at the turn of the century, that the history of the Bible came to be viewed as a progressive development upward toward the final achievement of the highest religious ideals in the teachings of Jesus. Revelation was equated with ideas about God, and the highest ideas, represented in the teachings of the Master, superseded and made irrelevant all that had gone before them. The Old Testament became an outdated book, primitive in its earliest history, stultified by a rigid legalism in its final stages, exhibiting only in occasional teachings of the psalmists and prophets religious ideals consonant with the ethics of Jesus. It certainly had no revelatory or authoritative value for the church, and it need be heeded only insofar as it provided an historical background to the understanding of the New Testament. Largely the Old Testament was an object of study for the antiquarian, the historian of religion, the archeologist. For the man in the pew, as well as the preacher in the pulpit, it could be safely ignored.

Anyone familiar with the course of modern biblical scholarship knows that the philosophy of the historical, developmental school has now been thoroughly shattered against the rocks of form and tradition criticism, with the approval of every other branch of biblical science. The developmental view of biblical history has been abandoned, the basic formative period of the Judaic-Christian faith has been placed in Mosaic times, revelation has come to be understood in active and creative terms, and emphasis on the ethical ideals of the Bible has given way to an acknowledgment of its thoroughly kergymatic character.

What has not been provided by modern scholarship is an interpretive approach to the Bible as a whole to replace the Wellhausian consensus. For at least half a century, nearly everyone in the church agreed that the Old Testament could be abandoned. Knowledgeable churchmen now know that such abandonment is disastrous to the proclamation of the Gospel, but there is no general agreement among biblical interpreters as to just why this is so. The result is that many clergy and laymen still cling to their developmental views, uneasily refusing to abandon old safe positions for a maze of conflicting new ones.

Modern attempts to justify the authority of the Old Testament for the church have been as many as they are varied, and this article makes no attempt to review them all. Rather, we shall concentrate on some attempts which have a bearing on Christian preaching, since it is in the modern pulpit that the authority of the Old Testament is most noticeably lacking.

One of the chief advocates of the relevance of the Old Testament for Christian preaching has been Lawrence E. Toombs of Drew Theological Seminary and later of Union College in British Columbia. In a number of writings,[1] Toombs has attempted to illustrate how the relevance of the Old Testament can be uncovered for our time. The two Testaments are one, says Toombs, in their understanding of the nature of man and his needs and of the manner in which God makes himself known. Furthermore, the essence of the sermon is the invitation to participate in an existence lived in history under the demand and freely offered grace of God. The Old Testament is, says Toombs, ". . . a book of God's approach to man, and if preaching is an invitation to accept the God who comes to men, it can hardly be conceived, much less conducted, without the Old Testament."[2]

Toombs links our historical existence with that of man in the Old Testament on the basis of a common humanity: "Insofar as we of the twentieth century share with ancient man in a common humanity, his evaluations of his situation are potentially relevant to our own."[3] The task of the preacher in Toombs' method of preaching from the Old Testament is therefore to discover to what facet of the human condition an Old Testament passage was originally directed, to ask what the contemporary equivalents of such a human situation are, and then to transfigure and transform the ancient word of the Old Testament so that it will speak its authentic message to the new forms in which that human situation has found expression in the present day.[4]

In such methodology, Toombs acknowledges the relativity of man's historical existence: "The specifics of a divine demand heard in an earlier time cannot merely be transposed into the existence of another person. It must be transformed into a demand which rises from, and speaks back to, his own distinctive situation."[5] The difficulty is that Toombs has not fully understood the historical specificity of the Old Testament. The Word in the Old Testament is not directed to "humanity" in general. It is directed to Israel, a specific people who stand in a specific relation to God, and it is solely in the context of that relationship (which itself changes, as von Rad has shown) that the Old Testament Word of demand and judgment and salvation has authority. It is not only that Israel is separated from us by time and culture and language and world-view—Toombs has made allowance for that gap. It is also that she is a unique people who knows that God is with her, to judge and to redeem her, and it is this uniqueness that Toombs has not acknowledged. Indeed, even those portions of the Old Testament which seem to concern humanity in general, such as Gen 1–11 or some of the Writings, are deductions from or responses to Israel's consciousness of her election.

It is this historical specificity which forms the offense of the Bible, for both the Old Testament and the New (as we shall show) claim that God has entered into his world only in relation to a specific people. Thus the Word of the Scriptures is a Word which is spoken to that people, and unless somehow we are related to Israel, the Word is not spoken to us. As Paul puts it: "They are Israelites, and to them belong the sonship, the glory, the covenants, the giving of the law, the worship, and the promises: to them belong the patriarchs, and of their race, according to the flesh, is the Christ" (Rom 9: 4–5).

The question of the relevance of the Old Testament to Christian preaching, then, is the question of our relationship to Israel. What do we have to do with that God-met people, and what do they have to do with us? Do we in any way share in Israel's election relationship to God and therefore in the Word of judgment and salvation spoken to her?[6]

It is this historical specificity of the Old Testament Word which is recognized by Rudolph Bultmann. In his article "The Significance of the Old Testament for Christian Faith,"[7] Bultmann points to the historical, relative nature of Israel's existence and the fact that God's revelation in the Old Testament is bound to the history of that particular people:

> So far as man belongs to this people, he can take comfort in the grace of God. What God has done in this history he has done unto each individual in so far as this individual has an integral place within his people and his people's history. What God has done unto the patriarchs, what he has done unto the people when he summoned Moses, led the people out of Egypt, guided them through the wilderness, and brought them into the Holy Land, he has done even now unto each person, since this history is not past history but present, ever reactualized in the present generation of the people.[8]

But, says Bultmann, for the Christian, this concrete history of God's dealing with a specific people has now come to an end. In Christ, God's eschatological deed of forgiveness is now proclaimed and is no longer an historical account about a past event, mediated through an ethnic, national, or cultural community, but is, rather, an immediate Word which addresses each individual directly as the Word of God. Thus for the Christian, the Old Testament is no longer the Word of God or revelation. Its history "has come to an end. The old has passed away, the new has come."[9]

Seen from this standpoint, says Bultmann, the Old Testament is law for the Christian, history without grace, and, as such, it can be used in the church only for pedagogical reasons—that is, it can be used to show the nature of our existence under the divine demand. But even the concrete demands of the Old Testament are tied to Israel's specific situation, and therefore they are obsolete. The only demands of the law in the Old Testament which are still valid for us are those truly moral demands "that spring out of human relationship as such and not out of its concrete historical form."[10] These are set forth in a clear and radical way in the Decalogue and the prophets, but they are not specifically Old Testament demands as such. "They are grounded in human relationship itself, and every period finds them simply by serious reflections upon this relationship."[11] It is these demands, then, with their understanding of our existence as set under the demand of God, that can be used pedagogically to prepare us to hear the proclamation of grace in the Gospel. But such demands are not found merely in the Old Testament. There may be other sources which give the same understanding of existence.

If the Old Testament is understood as the Word of God for the church, writes Bultmann, it can only be so in the indirect sense that it mirrors our situation into which the Word of Christ is spoken. But nothing is found in it which is not already known from the revelation in Jesus Christ,[12] and the Old Testament becomes the Word of God for the Christian only when it is thus freed from its original reference to the Israelite people and their history and is understood as preparation for the Christian understanding of existence.

Bultmann thus wrestles with the historical specificity of the Old Testament Word in a far more cognizant way than does Toombs, but he is finally able to place the Old Testament's proclamation within the church only by abandoning such specificity. Its concrete demands must be turned into general moral demands, found also elsewhere, in order to serve as pedagogical tools for the church. Or its proclamation, to be the Word of God, must be understood apart from Israel and within an eschatological, ahistorical, individualistic framework, as the address of Christ to the individual now.[13] Unfortunately, this approach does violence to both Old Testament and New, since the Old Testament never understands the law as a general moral demand but only as the concrete commandment of God to its specific elected situation, and the New Testament Gospel is never divorced from its specific and historical realization in the person of Jesus Christ and, through him, in the community of the church. It is precisely Bultmann's attempt to shed the historical specificity of the biblical Word which places his work outside the biblical understanding.

In his important book *The Authority of the Old Testament*,[14] John Bright initially seems to avoid the errors of both Bultmann and Toombs. The Old Testament is related to the New, and therefore authoritative for the Christian, says Bright, by reason of the fact that it shares with the New Testament a common "pervasive, constantly present, normative" theology or structure of faith. This theology Bright characterizes under the biblical categories of election, covenant (which includes the exclusive lordship of Yahweh and his covenant demands laid upon Israel), and hope in God's future action—although Bright by no means intends this list to be exhaustive. Furthermore, although any "structure of faith" is an abstraction out of a living history, as von Rad has so cogently shown in his *Old Testament Theology*,[15] and although the language of Bright's discussion unfortunately gives the impression at times that he has completely divorced this "structure of faith" from the events of Israel's history and taken flight into a gnostic understanding of revelation,[16] he nevertheless grounds this structure in the events of the biblical history. Thus Bright has recognized that it is a common participation in an election relationship with the covenant God of Israel that binds together Israelite and Christian, Old Testament and New, and thus makes the Old Testament relevant for the proclamation of the Gospel.[17]

Bright reverses his position in his very next chapter, however, when he discusses hermeneutics and the use of the Old Testament in the Christian pulpit.[18] He recognizes that not only there is a *heilsgeschichtliche* continuity between the Testaments, but also that there is a discontinuity, which led to the Jewish rejection of Christ and to the New Testament's radical reinterpretation of Israel's faith, and this discontinuity, says Bright, can be characterized by the fact that the entire perspective of the Old Testament is B.C. But ". . . B.C. is not—theologically speaking—simply an epoch in history that ended with the birth of Christ: it is a condition of living. It is the condition of standing, whether through ignorance or by decision, outside, or not fully subject to, the messianic kingdom of Christ."[19] This, writes Bright, is more or less the condition of every man, even of the Christian, and thus, in its "B.C.-ness," the Old Testament speaks to the condition of every man. This is the "typical" element in the Old Testament, which "enables it to address modern man with immediacy." "It is typical because human nature remains essentially unchanged, and because men do find themselves in typical situations and react to circumstances, their fellowmen, and their God in typical ways."[20] In this typical "B.C.-ness," the Old Testament therefore serves a pedagogical function, mirroring the human condition and impelling man beyond the bounds of B.C. to the newness of the Gospel.[21]

It is clear that Bright is sharing here Toombs' view of a common humanity (if in a somewhat different context) and also Bultmann's view of the Old Testament as a propaedeutic to the Gospel, with the latter transformed into an eschatological, existential, individualistic understanding of existence. It is equally clear that Bright has followed both Toombs and Bultmann in their abandonment of the historical specificity of the biblical Word, for what has happened to that "structure of faith" which Bright has previously maintained to be normative for biblical theology? Where are the election and the covenant relationship, when the Old Testament speaks in its "B.C.-ness" to the "typical" human situation? The Old Testament never speaks without the presupposition of God's election relationship with Israel. Its Word is intended for a people who knows Yahweh has been with her, and surely that experience is not the "typical" condition of modern man! Thus the Old Testament remains fully alien to us, whether Christian or non-Christian, unless somehow we participate in Israel's relationship with her God. This portion of Bright's hermeneutical method falls victim to the historical specificity of the Word of God.

Brevard S. Childs of Yale has fully recognized the necessity of interpreting the Old Testament in its historical specificity, as addressed solely to an elected people, when he calls for the recovery of the canonical context in doing biblical theology.[22] The concept of a "canon," in Childs' view, has meaning only in the context of the church as that body of writing which calls forth the life of the church and continues to nourish it with the bread of life from God for each succeeding generation. Thus Childs grounds the interpretation of Scripture solidly in the elected community of faith, and it is within this community, with its whole canon, that each Testament is listened to with its historically conditioned texts. Neither Testament is sufficient in itself, for both are part of that canon which has given birth to the church itself and through which the living God continues to confront his people. Thus the Testaments stand in a two-way dialogue with one another, and both, in their decidedly different ways and in their own historical context, witness to Jesus Christ. Childs has not fully presented the exegetical basis of this canonical view of the Scriptures, and thus there is every likelihood that his position will be widely misunderstood. Nevertheless, he has correctly perceived the heart of the Old Testament hermeneutical problem.

It is precisely such faithfulness to the historical specificity of the biblical Word, such recognition that the Old Testament, as well as the New, is addressed to a specific, historical, elected people of God that will prevent the allegorizing and moralizing uses of the Old Testament so prevalent in the Christian pulpit today. Wherever one finds sermons published today, one can almost at random find the Old Testament being so misused. Only a few examples must suffice.

In a sermon entitled, "Moral Choice in a Bountiful Land," published in *The Pulpit*,[23] Dwight E. Stevenson expounds on Josh 24: 15–16 : ". . . choose this day whom you will serve, but as for me and my house, we will serve the Lord." The situation of the Israelites newly arrived in the promised land is compared to that of Americans on the frontier, and the question is raised whether we will now be conquered by the comforts of urban culture, as the Israelites were conquered by the "fertile acres of the promised land." The assumption is that the imperative of the Old Testament, addressed to the elected people of Yahweh as they partake of the fulfillment of the divine promise to the patriarchs, can somehow be generalized to apply to any pioneer people faced with the temptations of civilization. Not only is the specific historical situation of the Israelites ignored, but, more important, the whole credo of Josh 24, with its recital of God's electing acts toward the patriarchs and Israel, is ignored. Stevenson has departed from his text and its setting at the very beginning of his sermon.

The same error is found time and again in the expository sections of *The Interpreter's Bible*. For example, in commenting on Num 2: 1–34, with its description of the Tent of Meeting in the midst of the Israelite camp, Albert George Butzer moralizes, "Is it not one of our deepest needs to put the church back again at the center of the community's life?"[24] as if somehow the church could be equated with the ancient Tent of Meeting and the elected tribes of Israel with any American community. Or, in expounding the story of Joseph thrown into the pit, Gen. 37: 24, the late Walter Russell Bowie allegorized: "Joseph is thrown by his brothers into a pit—a dreadful physical fact. But morally and spiritually, too, it may often seem that the soul of man is in a pit."[25] Such abandonment of the specific historical nature of the Old Testament Word would seem amusing were it not for the fact that it is widely practiced in the American pulpit every Sunday of the year.

The point which should be emphasized, however, is that not only must the historical setting of the Old Testament be preserved in any interpretation of it, but it must be recognized that part of the historical context of the Old Testament Word is the election relationship of Israel with her God. If that relationship is abandoned, if the Word of the Old Testament is understood as addressed not to a specific, historical, elected people but to mankind in general, then the historical context of the Old Testament has been lost and its proper interpretation has become impossible. The Old Testament is understood within the context of Israel as chosen, or it is not understood at all; and the question of the relevance of the Old Testament for Christian preaching remains the question of our relation as Christians to the Old Testament people of God.

Exegetical and Theological Basis for the Christian Use of the Old Testament

As with most questions of theology, the question of our relation to biblical Israel can be answered only from the perspective of a proper understanding of who Jesus Christ is, and this perspective is given by New Testament and Old alike. One approaches Jesus Christ initially through the witness of the New Testament, but it becomes startling clear in that witness that Jesus Christ is understood by the New Testament writers to a great extent in terms of the function and role of Old Testament Israel. We can by no means indicate within the brief limits of this article all the exegetical evidence which supports that statement, but the general argument can be indicated.

The first sentence of the First Gospel proclaims that Jesus Christ is the son of Abraham and the son of David, and certainly Jesus is understood throughout the New Testament as the fulfillment of the promises given to both Abraham and David. Most evident to the church has been the fulfillment of the latter promise, with its hope of the coming of a righteous Davidic king or Messiah. Thus, the prophetic messianic pictures such as those in Is 9: 2–7 and 11: 1–9 or Zech 9: 9–11 have been most frequently referred to in the pulpit. Much less understood and utilized has been the whole theology of the Old Testament's Royal Psalms[26] in which the descendant of David who is awaited is the adopted son of God, the guarantor of Israel's relation with Yahweh, the embodiment of the people's life, the giver of righteousness and *shalom*, the mandator of Yahweh, sitting at his right hand and sharing in his cosmic rule and power. But the New Testament borrows frequently from this Old Testament picture of the ideal coming king in order to make clear just who Jesus is,[27] and the fact that it understands our Lord as the Davidic Messiah immediately binds up his life with the life of Israel, for the point of the messianic expectation in 2 Sam 7, in the Deuteronomic history of the Books of Kings, and in the Chronicler's history, as well as in the Royal Psalms, is that the covenant promise to David is the foundation stone of Yahweh's relation to Israel. It is through the Davidic king, who is the representative of the people before God, that the Royal Theology sees Yahweh as entering into relation with Israel, and the righteousness of the awaited Messiah will insure that that relation is favorable, bringing blessing and *shalom* (cf Jer 23: 5–6).

The Hexateuchal tradition, centered in the promises to Abraham, is of a totally different nature, and indeed, in the Old Testament, often stands in conscious tension with the Royal Theology. Nevertheless, the New Testament understands who Jesus is also in terms of the promises to the fathers. According to the traditions of Genesis, it is through Abraham and his descendants that Yahweh will make a new people, who will live under his righteous rule, and who will therefore suffer none of the disruptions of communal and family life which are pictured as the results of sin in the primeval history of Gen 2–11. Given to this people will be a "good land, flowing with milk and honey," to replace the good garden which mankind has lost, and in the P traditions, Israel will participate in an everlasting covenant with Yahweh, in which they will once more be Yahweh's people and he will be their God. As this new people of Yahweh, Israel will be a blessing in the midst of the earth, the community through which all nations, who now stand under the curse of God according to the primeval history, will once again find blessing.

That this promise finds its partial fulfillment in the gifts of descendants and nationhood and land and covenant to Israel[28] is quite clear in the Old Testament record. In fact, the Deuteronomic historians affirm the total fulfillment of the promise (Josh 21: 43–45). But the pre-exilic prophets announce that the fulfillment is totally reversed by Israel's rebellion: the covenant is broken, the land will be lost in the exile, Israel becomes "no people," and even her power to propagate is taken away, according to Hosea. Thus the hope for a new people, a new land,[29] a new covenant, becomes part of the eschatological hope in the prophets, as does the role of Israel as a blessing in the midst of the earth (Is 19: 24; Zech 8: 13; cf Jer 4: 2).

That which is pictured in the hope of Isaiah of Jerusalem is a new congregation of faith, which becomes the cornerstone of the new Zion and the mediator of revelation and peace to all nations (Is 28: 16; 2: 2–4), and the expectation is that through Israel all nations will come to God (cf Zech 8: 20–23; Pss. 47; 87; Zeph 3: 9) That this expectation is pushed to its most radical form in Deutero-Isaiah, then, seems quite clear, despite the long dispute over the identity of the Suffering Servant. If the Servant is meant to be identified with Israel transformed by the Spirit of God—and we think he is—the picture of the Servant's work is fully consonant with the picture given by Isaiah of Jerusalem, of whose school of tradition, in all likelihood, Deutero-Isaiah was a member. Once again Israel, the Servant, is the mediator of revelation (light) to the nations, the center from which Yahweh's *mishpat* and *torah* go out to all people (cf Is 2: 3–4; 42: 1–4). But the theology has become radically incarnational, and the covenant as well as the suffering and atoning death for sin become embodied in the person of the Servant (Is 42: 6; 49: 6; 52: 13–53: 12). At the same time, the Royal Theology with its "steadfast, sure love for David," is understood as the additional guarantee of Yahweh's favor toward his people (Is 55: 3–5).

Indeed, it can be said that the major emphases of both the Royal and Hexateuchal theologies are summed up and combined in the figure of the Suffering Servant in Deutero-Isaiah. There is the emphasis on the exodus, the wilderness time, the covenant, the good land, the new people as a blessing in the midst of the earth. But within this Hexateuchal framework, the figure of the Servant (although probably primarily a prophetic figure) borrows from the characteristic Isaianic understandings of the Messiah as the bearer of the Spirit and the bringer of righteousness and *shalom*, as well as from Isaiah's emphasis on Zion as the center of revelation, incarnated in the new congregation of faith (cf Is 40: 9; 51: 16; 52: 8–9). And the way the Royal and Hexateuchal theologies are combined by Deutero-Isaiah makes it almost impossible to separate them. Both before and after Deutero-Isaiah, the Deuteronomic historians and the Chronicler, respectively, combined the Royal and Hexateuchal theologies to some extent, the former by making the Davidic king subject to the law of Moses, the latter by modeling David after the figure of Moses, and all these traditions witness to post-exilic efforts to bring Israel's various theological complexes into a unified whole. But the fruits of these efforts in the Old Testament are largely eschatological projections into the future, hopes for Israel's future life before God.

It is in the New Testament that Israel's hope is fulfilled, and the unity toward which the Old Testament theologies strain finds its concrete historical realization in the figure of Jesus of Nazareth. He is, as we have noted, the awaited Messiah, the bearer of the promise to David. But he is clearly also the fulfillment of the promise to Abraham, not only in general terms but in terms of the concrete content of the promise. He is the one who becomes, as Israel was meant to become, the blessing in the midst of the earth (Acts 3: 25; Gal 3: 8). He is understood as the new covenant and the beginning of God's new people. Indeed, he is even identified with the promised land Israel was to inherit, her place of rest (Heb 3: 12–4: 13). But, after the manner of the Isaianic prophecies, all has become incarnational, the promises and prophetic words to Israel clothed in flesh and blood. Thus Jesus Christ is an incarnate covenant (Gal 4: 21 ff) and light to the nations and an incarnate atoning sacrifice. And his body becomes identified with Zion and its temple, as the place of revelation (Mt 26: 61; 27: 40; Jn 2: 19; 4: 21 ff; cf Heb 12: 22 ff; Rev 14: 1; 21: 22). He becomes Isaiah's cornerstone, the germ cell of the new and faithful Israel (1 Pet 2: 4 ff; Eph 2: 18-22), and all who trust in him are built into him as members of his body. At the same time, as son of David and of Abraham, he is the new

Moses in the First Gospel,[30] and in the Gospel according to John and in Acts, he is the awaited "prophet like Moses."[31]

The New Testament utilizes every tradition at its disposal to proclaim that Jesus Christ has gathered up into himself and fulfilled the role and function of Old Testament Israel, as those are understood in both corporate and individual terms, and it is in his person alone that the Old Testament finds that unity and completion of its history for which Israel had hoped. Jesus Christ means the confirmation of Israel's history, the assurance that her hope was not in vain and that her God was faithful to his Word. And certainly without the Old Testament, Jesus Christ cannot be known for who he truly is.

At the same time, Jesus Christ means the end of Old Testament Israel's history, for he replaces Old Testament Israel as God's chosen son. The unfaithful son of the Old Testament (cf Ex 4: 22–23; Is 1: 2; Hos 11: 1–9; Jer 31: 20) gives way to the faithful son of the New, and from the time of his resurrection on, the promises, the election, the covenant, the law, the Messiah, the future hope—all the traditions of Israel—can be rightly understood only in terms of Jesus Christ. In this sense, Jesus Christ is therefore the fulfillment of the prophetic words of judgment and salvation; for with his death, all the old Israel (as well as all the old mankind) dies—a judgment never fully realized in the exile of Israel—and with his resurrection, the new Israel (which is synonymous with the new mankind) lives—a consummation unrecognized and still hoped for by the Jews. Thus, at the same time that the New Testament is a summation and completion and fulfillment of the Old Testament, it is also its transformation, and it is quite true that the Christian can read the Old Testament only in the light of the New, while at the same time understanding the New Testament only with the help of the Old.

But the Old Testament still remains a strange document to the Christian and of help only in understanding who Jesus Christ is unless we go a step further and examine the meaning of the new Israel for us.

The new Israel is Jesus Christ, as we have shown. In him, according to the New Testament, the new people of God has its beginning and its life, and apart from him, there is no new people and therefore no fulfillment of the Word to Israel. But it is the proclamation of the New Testament that by faith in Jesus Christ, by trust in God's saving act in him, we too become members of God's chosen people and participate in his life. Through Christ, we enter into covenant relationship with God, and the former alienation caused by our sin is ended. We become the elected people, the redeemed people, the God-met people, with our new Moses and our Davidic Messiah. We become God's kingdom of priests and God's holy nation, set apart to be the instrument of God's purpose in the world. Especially 1 Pet 2: 9–10 and Eph 2: 11–22 make this clear:

> Remember that you were at that time separated from Christ, alienated from the commonwealth of Israel, and strangers to the covenants of promise, having no hope and without God in the world. But now in Christ Jesus you who once were far off have been brought near in the blood of Christ. (Eph 2: 12–13.)

Thus the words which were spoken to Old Testament Israel as she approached the mount of covenanting in Ex 19: 6 are in 1 Pet 2: 9 spoken to those who are "in Christ Jesus"; and in 1 Pet 2: 10, then, Hosea's promise of a new people (Hos 2: 16–23) is seen as fulfilled by the people of Christ (cf Rom 9: 22 ff; 15: 7 ff). We who were once outside the people of God have become, in Paul's words, the wild olive shoots who have been grafted onto the root of Israel (Rom 11: 17 f). In the Gospel according to Matthew, the followers of Jesus are therefore given their new law, preached from their new mount of covenanting, by their new Moses (Mt 5–7). In Mark 3: 13–19, after Jesus' rejection by the scribes and Pharisees, the twelve disciples are called up "into the hills" (the mount?) to become those who now replace the twelve tribes of Israel. And in the Gospel according to John, to cite only one example, Jesus is that bread of life which is the manna given to all who believe in him, as the manna was given to Israel in the wilderness (Jn 6). As those who are "in Christ" or who are "members of his body," to use Paul's terminology, we too become God's new people, God's new Israel in Christ, built into the "household of God," as his sons and members of his new covenant. In Christ, but in him alone, the Christian church has become the new people of God, fulfilling the Old Testament prophetic hope for the participation of all peoples in Israel. Contrary to Bultmann, the new Israel in Christ is a concrete historical entity, manifested in the historical life of the Christian church. But the national, ethnic, cultural life of the Old Testament Israel has been left behind. In fulfillment of the promise to Abraham, the new Israel in Christ has become that fellowship in which the divisions of mankind pictured in Gen 2–11 have been finally healed, and there is now one fellowship under the sovereignty of God:

> There is neither Jew nor Greek, there is neither slave nor free, there is neither male nor female; for you are all one in Christ Jesus. And if you are Christ's, then you are Abraham's offspring, heirs according to promise. (Gal 3: 28.)

In the light of this good news—that we are members of God's chosen people through our faith in Jesus Christ—for the first time the Old Testament may be seen as addressed to us, as the Word of God which is authoritative for our life. The Old Testament is addressed to the covenant people of Yahweh and is authoritative only for them, and through faith in Christ we have now become members of that people. Now the Old Testament may be our story; now its history may be our history. Now its God may be our God, and its Word may be the Word also to us. But there can be no authority in the Old Testament for us outside that covenant framework, outside the act of God in Jesus Christ which has made us members of his people. There is no possibility for us of understanding the Old Testament as the Word of God for B.C. man; no possibility of seeing the Old Testament as divine law and nothing else; no possibility of identifying the Old Testament Word with God's instruction for mankind under wrath—for the Old Testament has the possibility of becoming Word of God for us only in the context of A.D. grace, only in the context of the new covenant in the new Israel in Jesus Christ.

Homiletical Methodology

The foregoing does not mean that we abandon the historical understanding of the Old Testament. It must be understood in its historical context, as words and traditions addressed at specific times, through the witness of human speakers and writers, to the ancient Near Eastern people of Israel. As the history of ancient Israel, it tells us of our beginnings. It shows us the long and tortuous way by which God has fashioned for himself a new people. It tells us about the promises of which we have now become heirs. It makes clear how the Christian church has been created in Jesus Christ and why its creation was necessary. And that can all be read and studied as the interesting history of our beginnings, just as a United States citizen can read the interesting history of the American Revolution.

Certainly the Christian preacher has the responsibility of telling that history to his people, of proclaiming the story of what God has done in Israel. Otherwise his people will never know clearly who Jesus Christ is or even who they are as members of the new covenant people, the Christian church. And without that knowledge, the Old Testament—and, indeed, the New Testament—can never become the Word of God for the preacher's people. There must be, as the foundation of all Christian proclamation, the announcement of what God has done, and this is as true when one is preaching from the Psalms as it is when one is preaching from Genesis or the prophets. The picture of the historical people of Israel, in their historical situation before God, must be clearly implanted in the minds of the preacher and his people.

In the 1940s, it was the tendency of many in the Biblical Theology Movement to regard this first step in biblical preaching as sufficient; and during the 1950s and 1960s, it became a shibboleth throughout the church in the United States to regard biblical theology as consisting solely in the proclamation of the "mighty acts of God."[32] But the proclamation of what God has done in the history of Israel, as that is witnessed to in both Old Testament and New, lays only the foundation for biblical preaching. It has merely made it possible for the Old Testament, and, indeed, the Bible as a whole, to become Word of God for us, since it has made it clear that we are related to biblical Israel, and that our relationship is founded on our new covenant with God in Jesus Christ. Nevertheless, that whole story of what God has done, and of how we have become what we are, can remain a fully past event, having no significance for us except as etiology. It is fully possible to acknowledge that we are the new Israel in Christ without confronting the biblical story as authority for our life—as, sadly, the history of the Christian church has so frequently made clear. Toombs and Bultmann and Bright and the others in the long list of modern biblical scholars who emphasize the existentialist nature of the biblical Word are quite correct when they emphasize that biblical preaching must show the Word to be salvation and judgment and imperative for our present situation if it is to become Word of God for us. To use one of George Buttrick's colorful phrases, somehow the sermon must finally "nail the hearer to the pew." Our question is, then: How is this to be done in Christian preaching, specifically in relation to the Old Testament?

Two methods present themselves out of the biblical material itself: representation, and analogy. But, at the risk of being boringly repetitious, let it be emphasized once more that neither method has any validity except as it is used against the background of our relationship to Israel in Jesus Christ. Bultmann has used the first method, and Toombs the second, for example, but our argument has been that the foundational relationship of the Christian to Israel through Christ has not been fully understood by either of these scholars, as is the case with many others.

Martin Noth has discussed the method of re-presentation in his article on "The 'Re-Presentation' of the Old Testament in Proclamation."[33] He has correctly pointed out that in the three great annual festivals of Israel past and future events in Israel's history with her God, such as the wilderness wanderings or the exodus or the eschatological accession of God to rule,[34] as well as the giving of the law, were presented to Israel as present, contemporary happenings, which carried with them the immediate judging and saving and demanding action of God toward Israel. That is, Israel's history with God, both past and future, became contemporary, a fact of "now," for each new generation of Israelites who made their pilgrimage to the annual feasts, and this was done, Noth believes, through the cult, primarily by means of proclamation and narration but perhaps also by means of cultic drama.

That this was the case in ancient Israel is made clear throughout the book of Deuteronomy, in which seventh-century B.C. Israel is addressed as if she were the Israel of the thirteenth century B.C., still in the wilderness with Moses. Thus there is the constant emphasis on "this day" in Deuteronomy: ". . . this day you have become the people of the Lord your God" (Deut 27: 9).

> You stand this day all of you before the Lord your God . . . that you may enter into the sworn covenant of the Lord your God, which the Lord your God makes with you this day; that he may establish you this day as his people, and that he may be your God, as he promised you, and as he swore to your fathers, to Abraham, to Isaac, and to Jacob. Nor is it with you only that I make this sworn covenant, but with him who is not here with us this day as well as with him who stands here with us this day before the Lord our God. (Deut 29: 10–15; cf 5: 2–4.)

In other words, the biblical understanding of the nature of the Word is that it carries with it the action of God, not only in the past or in the future but contemporarily in the present "now." For biblical Israel in Palestine, for example, the exodus was not simply a past saving event which Israel knew to be part of its former history with God. Through the narration of the exodus story, at the Feast of Tabernacles and at Passover, the exodus event became contemporary; the Word of the exodus continued to work, exerting its influence on the present and working its redemption among those who were hearing the story anew. As von Rad has so brilliantly pointed out in *Old Testament Theology*, it was this continuing working of the Word which led to the constant reformulation and contemporizing of Israel's past traditions, and the ever new action of the past Word to Israel can be seen throughout the Old Testament in the constant updating of the past saving events and ordinances.

Basic to this phenomenon of contemporizing in the Old Testament is a dual understanding with regard to the Word of God. It is taken for granted that the Word of God is an active, effective power which creates and shapes the course of history,[35] just as it similarly works in the realm of nature. Secondly, it is assumed that a Word, spoken to a specific situation, is not exhausted in its action in that situation, but that it continues to work in the events which come after, influencing also their course. The Word of God in the Old Testament—and, indeed, in the New—is not the conveyor of knowledge, which is but a deduction from it, but the powerful action of God within the sphere of man. And always the Word is alive in the Bible (Jesus Christ is risen !), it works, it acts according to the purposes of God, it exerts its influence.

Such an understanding might seem a little farfetched to twentieth-century man were it not for the fact that we know the same phenomenon in Christian worship. For example, we gather around the Lord's table for the Last Supper, and we hear the ancient story: ". . . the Lord Jesus on the night when he was betrayed took bread, and when he had given thanks, he broke it, and said, 'This is my body which is broken for you . . .'" And by the active effective working of the Word of God (many would say, by the working of the Holy Spirit), the event of the Last Supper suddenly becomes contemporary. Suddenly, we are now there in that upper room, sitting among the disciples, hearing that one of us will betray Jesus and wondering, "Is it I?" Through the narration of the past history, the events of the Bible become present history for us, and we find ourselves confronted by the immediate action of God through them.

Thus, as members of the covenant people, when we hear a story of God's dealings with Israel from the Old Testament, in all its concrete historical detail, it can happen by the working of the Word of God that that story becomes a present event for us. It is here. The saving or judging or demanding of God, directed to our fathers in the faith, becomes an action directed immediately also to us, and we can say, in the manner of Deuteronomy, "Not toward our fathers did God act, but toward us, who are all of us here alive this day." When we hear the story of the exodus, for example, we become the ancient Israelites, waiting behind doors smeared with blood, our loins girded for flight, our kneading bowls bound in our mantles on our shoulders, and the smell of roasted lamb in our nostrils. The Word of God, spoken to ancient Israel and told once more to us, creates the situation before God of which it speaks, in our lives, and God acts through that Word not only toward ancient Israel but now toward us, the new Israel.

Thus it can happen that dramatic proclamation of the story, the retelling of the mighty acts of God, itself becomes the medium through which the Bible becomes for us Word of God and authoritative. It was precisely this phenomenon which gave the Biblical Theology Movement its great impetus during the past two decades. But because this phenomenon depends on the free grace of God, acting through his Word, it is also an experience which cannot be coerced, as the Biblical Theology Movement also discovered, somewhat to its dismay. There is no homiletical technique which will insure that the story becomes the Word of God for us. Certainly the preacher can trust that such an event will take place. He can suggest to his people that it may happen. He can, and indeed he must, through careful preparation and historical research and vividness and clarity of language, attempt to remove needless obstacles from the way of the coming Word. But in the last analysis, whether or not the biblical story becomes Word of God for us is up to God himself, a fact for which we should surely be grateful, considering our constant prideful attempts to manipulate our people and to capture God. We preachers stand under the command to proclaim the story—as Paul puts it (1 Cor 3), to plant and to water. Whether or not there is growth then depends on the Lord.

Theoretically, because the entire Old Testament is primarily concerned with the action of God toward ancient Israel, in this method of re-presentation no portion of the Old Testament should be incapable of being proclaimed as part of God's action, and in fact the church needs much more to utilize the narrative portions of the Old Testament in this fashion. There are vast areas of the biblical witness to God which have been omitted from the church's proclamation by the omission of these narratives (e.g., the many-sided views of the judging actions of God). On the other hand, there are portions of the Old Testament story in which the action of God is so obscure or in which such action is spread out over such a length of time that it becomes almost impossible to present it within the framework of the sermon. The preacher has the responsibility of carefully choosing his texts in order to tell the whole story most vividly and forcefully, but he must be equally sure that he does not omit some portions of the biblical story simply because they are distasteful to him or because he himself has not studied them sufficiently to understand what God did in them toward Israel.

Finally, in re-presenting the Old Testament, the preacher must always make clear the foundation on which the Old Testament is given to us—through God's act in Jesus Christ, which has made us the new Israel, which means ultimately that the Old Testament is never the story solely in itself, but that it is the story which finds its purpose and fulfillment and close in Jesus Christ. This foundation may simply be presented at the beginning of the sermon, and the preacher can then proceed to the exposition of an Old Testament text. But, methodologically, the preacher will most often find it necessary to utilize also a second method—that of showing the Old Testament story as the analogy of our life before God.

A great deal has been written about this method of using the Old Testament in the Christian church, largely on the basis of Gerhard von Rad's renewed use of it, and most often such a method has been called "typology." But this is a poor term, since it confuses the method with that of earlier pre-critical approaches to the Old Testament, in which the history was completely ignored, and persons, places, and things in the Old Testament were seen as standing for elements in the New Testament or in the life of the Christian. For example, in pre-critical typology, the mark put on Cain, in Gen 4: 15, was understood as standing for or as the "type" of the cross, or the figure with whom Jacob wrestled in Gen 32 was understood as in reality Christ.[36] We have something different in mind—the method of seeing that the concrete history of Old Testament Israel before God forms an historical analogy to our historical existence in Christ before God, and of therefore realizing that the Word of God addressed to ancient Israel may be similar to or the same as the Word addressed to us.

There can be no doubt that our life as Christians is remarkably similar to the life of ancient Israel in its relationship to God. Both Israel and we are redeemed through no worth of our own, delivered from slavery, and given the possibility of a new life, in a new fellowship. Both of us, in response to God's initial act of deliverance, enter into covenant with Yahweh. Both of us have covenant commandments laid upon us, at whose center is the command to love God and neighbor. Both of us have not yet entered into our final fulfillment. Both of us have the responsibility of being God's witness to the world. Both of us strain toward the ultimate goal of God's kingship on this earth. Both of us wait for God's kingdom in faith and hope, and certainty that it will come. Both of us are therefore to live as if the kingdom were already here. It is therefore clear that ancient Israel's life before God is analogous to our own, and that her history can authoritatively illumine and guide our history in Christ.

Such analogous use of ancient Israel's history is not foreign to the Bible, for both Old Testament and New themselves use such a method. When Deutero-Isaiah describes the new age, for example, he describes it as analogous to the old, with a new exodus, a new wilderness wandering, a new and universal people, just as Jeremiah has a new covenant and Ezekiel a new David. And when the New Testament describes the life in Christ, it describes it in terms of Israel, with baptism become our passage out of Egypt and the Lord's Supper modeled on the feeding in the wilderness and the event at Sinai (cf 1 Cor 10–11). There is a real correspondence between the histories of the old Israel and the new, and therefore the preacher can proclaim the Old Testament as Word of God which is meaningful also for us. We are not separated from Israel by some vast historical gap, but participate historically in the relationship with God that Israel participated in. As we have shown, we now have entered into that covenant relationship through Jesus Christ.

Whereas with the method of re-presentation the past action of God is made present in the "now," with the method of analogy the "now" becomes the "then," and as we hear the ancient words of Deuteronomy, for example, we can project ourselves back into their situation, and they can become words directed also to us, because we too are the covenant people who are now journeying from our redemption toward our final fulfillment:

> Take heed lest you forget the Lord your God, by not keeping his commandments and his ordinances and his statutes, which I command you this day: lest, when you have eaten and are full, and have built goodly houses and live in them, and when your herds and flocks multiply, and your silver and gold is multiplied, and all that you have is multiplied, then your heart be lifted up, and you forget the Lord your God, who brought you out of the land of Egypt, out of the house of bondage . . . . Beware lest you say in your heart, "My power and the might of my hand have gotten me this wealth." (Deut 8: 11–14, 17.)

It is in this context that the Old Testament can serve as a warning to us, as, indeed, the New Testament so often uses it. The continual Word is, "Harden not your hearts as in the rebellion, on the day of testing in the wilderness" (cf Heb 3–4). The Old Testament can warn us who share in Israel's situation before God not to share also her pride and unbelief and therefore not to be led into her rejection and destruction by God. But the Old Testament speaks to us in this manner not as B.C. men but as those who have been redeemed while they were yet sinners by the cross and resurrection of Jesus Christ. Our situation becomes analogous to Israel's only through the new covenant, and thus the Old Testament's warning is not "propaedeutic" or preparation for the Gospel but, rather, its consequence. There is no way the Old Testament can be understood by the Christian as merely law. It becomes part of the Christian's canon only in the prior context of grace, and we can share in the exodus experience of redemption, to cite another example, only because we have already shared in the cross of Christ.

This method of analogy once again opens the whole Old Testament to the Christian preacher, for now there is no portion of Israel's life which is without interest to us. At every point, Israel is working out the consequences of its elationship with God, and it is one of the greatest gifts of God's grace that we have been given the story of ancient Israel as the forerunner of our own. Of course all of Israel's story is culturally and historically conditioned. The commands of the law, for example, are formulated in terms of Israel's concrete historical situation. But the intention of the law—to implement the lordship of God in the communal and individual life of his chosen people—remains quite relevant to our analogous situation, and both Israel and we are given commands only because we have been redeemed. In the same manner, it is by the method of analogy that the prophetic oracles, addressed to Israel's specific historical situation, become authoritative for us. Indeed, we can say that it is often through the Old Testament that the Christian learns how to live as an elected person, and as the elected people in Christ, we are addressed by God, and therefore authoritatively, through the Old Testament.

Space does not permit the dozens of ramifications and illustrations of method which flow out of this approach to the Old Testament. Some will certainly condemn the approach as far too "Christological." Some will complain that the Old Testament is given no authority in and of itself, apart from the New Testament. Our reply is simply that we Christians should not expect it to be otherwise. Jesus Christ has lived and died and risen again, and he has told us plainly, "No one comes to the Father but by me." We should not expect to hear the Word of God from the Old Testament except through Jesus Christ. It is in him alone that the Old Testament is given to us, the new Israel. It is now through him alone that God speaks his Word to us.

Notes

1 *The Old Testament in Christian Preaching* (Philadelphia: Westminster Press, 1961); "The Old Testament in the Christian Pulpit," *Hartford Quarterly*, VIII, No. 2 (Winter 1968), 7–14; "The Problematic of Preaching from the Old Testament," *Interp*, July 1969, 302–14.

2 *Hartford Quarterly, op. cit.*, p. 11.

3 *Interp, op. cit.*, p. 303.

4 *Ibid.*, p. 304.

5 *Ibid.*, p. 308.

6 The crucial nature of this question of the relationship to Israel is posed very early, in the Yahwist's history, in the promise to Abram: "I will bless those who bless you, and him who curses you I will curse; and by you all the families of the earth shall bless themselves" (Gen 12: 3).

7 In B. W. Anderson, ed., *The Old Testament and Christian Faith* (New York: Harper and Row, 1963), pp. 8–35.

8 *Ibid.*, pp. 29–30.

9 *Ibid.*, p. 31.

10 *Ibid.*, p. 16.

11 *Ibid.*

12 *Ibid.*, p. 32.

13 It should be noted, however, that Bultmann rejects all allegorizing of the Old Testament, and insists on historical research to discover the original sense: "For if this sense were changed, then it would no longer be the Old Testament that speaks." *Ibid.*, p. 33. But it is this "original sense" of the Old Testament that Bultmann must then divorce from its original reference to the Israelite people and their history.

14 Nashville: Abingdon Press, 1967.

15 London: Oliver and Boyd, Vol. I, 1962; Vol. II, 1965. Bright is largely following

the method of Walter Eichrodt's *Theology of the Old Testament* (Philadelphia: Westminster Press, Vol. I, 1961; Vol. II, 1967).

[16] *Ibid.*, especially in the discussion on pp. 148–50.

[17] *Ibid.*, Ch. III, pp. 110–51.

[18] *Ibid.*, Ch. IV, pp. 161–212.

[19] *Ibid.*, p. 206.

[20] *Ibid.*, p. 207.

[21] *Ibid.*, p. 208.

[22] *Biblical Theology in Crisis* (Philadelphia: Westminster Press, 1970). See especially pp. 97–122.

[23] Jan. 1968, pp. 19–21.

[24] Vol. 2 (Nashville: Abingdon Press, 1953), p. 149.

[25] Vol. 1 (Nashville: Abingdon Press, 1952), p. 754.

[26] Pss 2, 18, 20, 21, 45, 72, 89, 101, 110, 132.

[27] Ps 2 is utilized in the accounts of Jesus' baptism and transfiguration, and performs a basic role in Acts 4 and 13. In addition, its language frequently echoes from Heb and Rev. Ps 110 is the most important Royal Psalm for the New Testament, being quoted or alluded to in Mk 12: 36; 14: 62; 16: 19; Acts 2, 7; Rom 8: 34; 1 Cor 15: 25; Eph 1: 20, 22; Col 3: 1; Heb 1, 2, 5, 10, 12; 1 Pet 3: 22. But Ps 18 and 132 also speak from Acts 2, as does the language of Ps 89 from Col 1: 15–20 and Heb 1: 5.

[28] In P, the emphasis is on the revelation of the *kabod Yahweh* in the tabernacle on Sinai.

[29] Cf the pictures of nature transformed and Palestine become an Eden, Is 51: 3; Ezek 36: 33–35.

[30] Thus, Matthew's picture of Jesus giving the new law on the new mount, in the Sermon on the Mount, is quite deliberate, in contrast to Luke's sermon on the plain. Cf also Paul's comparison of Jesus with the Moses of Ex 34: 29–35, in 2 Cor 3–4.

[31] Acts 3: 22–23; 7: 37; Jn 6: 14; 7: 40, 52.

[32] For an excellent discussion of the Biblical Theology Movement, see Childs, *Biblical Theology in Crisis.*

[33] Claus Westermann, ed., *Essays on Old Testament Hermeneutics*, 2d ed. (Richmond: John Knox Press, 1964), Ch. 4, pp. 76–88.

[34] Cf the Enthronement Ps 47, 93, 96–99.

[35] Cf Is 55: 10–11; Ezek 12: 28, among many examples.

[36] W. Vischer still engages in a great deal of this typological, pre-critical exegesis, despite his claim to do otherwise. See his *The Witness of the Old Testament to Christ*, Vol. I (London, 1949).

William F. Albright
Johns Hopkins University

The Lachish Cosmetic Burner and Esther 2: 12

The object to be discussed below has attracted increased attention in recent years, while it was being explained by all of us as belonging to a class of cultic objects—either pagan or Jewish or both. It turns out to be neither; the religious interpretation is entirely erroneous, and it has an easy explanation as belonging to the secular world of cosmetics and beautification of women, especially during the Persian (Achaemenian) period.

In 1944 Gertrude Caton Thompson published a series of carved incense burners at Ḥureiḍa in Ḥaḍramaut. They were of sandy limestone (refractory to heat), cuboid or slightly rectangular in vertical axis, standing on four

Before his death Professor Albright completed a first draft of the text of this paper and the first paragraph of a second draft. Had he lived, his essay would have been somewhat expanded and more completely documented. Unhappily, his footnotes, while marked in the text, consisted of cryptic marginal comments and, in some cases, more fully written notations (usually dated) on separate slips of paper placed in the file folder with the drafts of his text. I have tried to record his documentation in footnotes as fully as possible, but have succeeded only partially in reconstructing their content. In editing the first draft of the text, I have taken no liberties aside from removing minor grammatical inconcinnities, adding diacritical marks, shifting sentences to the notes, and the like. The wording of the text is wholly Albright's. I have added my corrected drawing of the inscription which reflects the material text upon which Albright and I were in full agreement. It should be noted, finally, that Albright had not seen, at the time of his preparation of the first draft, the article of Nelson Glueck, "Incense Altars," in the volume *Translating and Understanding the Old Testament: Essays in Honor of Herbert Gordon May*, eds. H. T. Frank and W. L. Reed (Nashville: Abingdon, 1970), pp. 325–29, with 13 plates. He had planned, however, to include a discussion of it in his second draft [Frank Moore Cross, Jr., December 13, 1971].

squat legs, with a shallow basin at the top, where fragrant resinous substance had been burned.[1] Miss Caton Thompson also recognized the close affinity of these objects to the similar limestone "altars" found at Gezer and published by R. A. S. Macalister in 1912,[2] but she was not aware of similar finds at Tell Jemmeh published by Flinders Petrie.[3]

In 1929 Kurt Galling published a discussion of some of the Palestinian material, in which he expressed doubt about the interpretation of these objects as altars of incense. At that time he was not yet acquainted with the South Arabian incense burners of the same general form and size and with inscriptions on the four sides listing the names of different aromatic substances (all belonging to the category of *bĕśāmîm*, "spices," mentioned so frequently in the Old Testament).[4] In his short article on "Incense Altar" in *IDB*,[5] Galling then called these objects *ḥammānîm* and accepted their interpretation as altars of incense. The identification with the pagan incense altar called *ḥammān* is, however, certainly wrong.[6]

In 1953 Miss Olga Tufnell published a cuboid chalky limestone object of the same type which had been found by J. L. Starkey in his excavation at Tell ed-Duweir (Lachish).[7] A. Dupont-Sommer published a first translation of the inscription on one side of the cuboid incense burner, in which he rendered it:[8]

1. lbnt' y[ʾ]	L'encens J[oa]
2. š bn mḥ[r]	s(?) fils de Meḥ[ir](?)
3. lyh mrʾ[šmyʾ]	à Yah, maître [du ciel]

Later that same year I published a short discussion of the text[9] in which I made some modifications in line 3 and rendered the text:

O Incense! Let Ya'osh(?)
son of Mazzer(?)
be absolved from guilt!

Five years later J. T. Milik[10] offered a new translation in which he read the letters of the inscription correctly almost throughout, rendering: "The (altar of) incense belonging to ʾIyas, son of Maḥlai of. . . ." In 1968 Yohanan Aharoni published a short discussion in his preliminary report on his own trial excavation at Lachish in the summer of 1966.[11]

In February 1969 Frank M. Cross, Jr., published a superior reading of the text of this same incense burner from Lachish, rendering as follows:[12]

1. lbnt ʾy	The incense (altar) of ʾIy-
2. š bn m[ḥ]	-yōš son of Ma[ḥ]-
3. ly hmlʾ[k]	-lī, the courie[r]

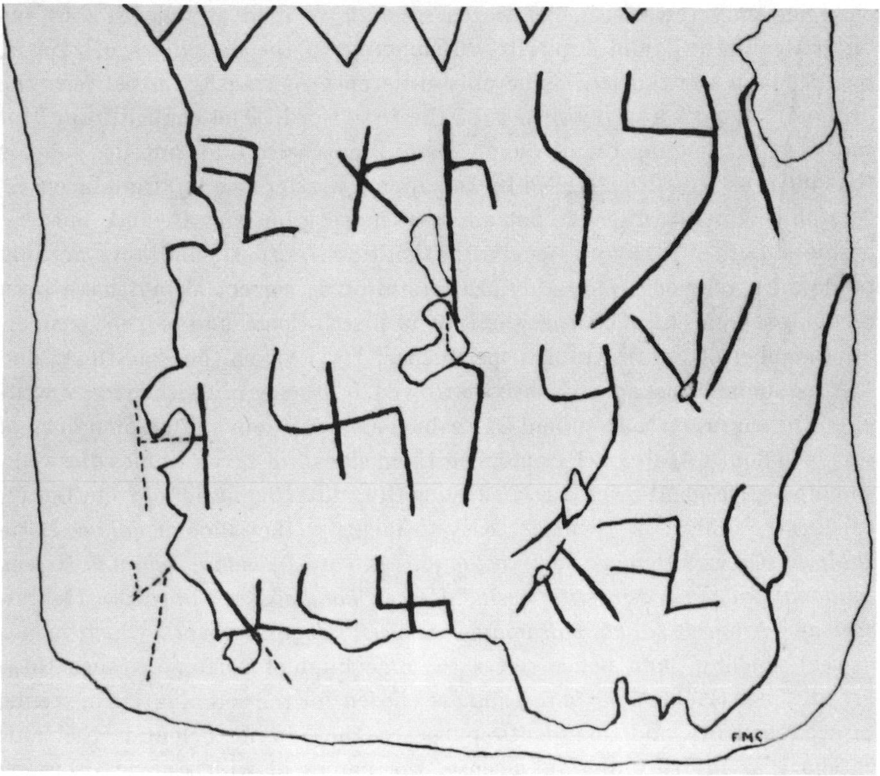

Drawing of the inscription on the Lachish cosmetic burner, by Frank M. Cross.

In a postscript to his article, Cross rejected Aharoni's reading on the same grounds which he had brought against Dupont-Sommer's interpretation.

After studying this article of Cross's, Aharoni changed his mind and proposed a new reading in a letter to me, enclosing an excellent photograph.[13] His new position was published in a Hebrew article on "The Altar of Incense from Lachish," in *Leshonenu* 45 (1970–71), 3–6. He now proposed the reading:

lbntʾ y[ʾ]	Incense - Yau-
š bn mḥ	sh son of Maḥa-
lyh mlk[š]	lyah from Lachish

Another excellent photograph of the inscription was attached to the article in *Leshonenu*. Because of the two photographs, which I have studied with great care, there seems to be no doubt that Cross's reading of the letters is correct throughout. I should, therefore, read the whole as Hebrew, changing only the division of words so that we read as follows: lbnt 'yš bn mḥly hml'[k], and translate, "Belonging to the daughters of 'Iyyōš, son of Maḥlî the courier." The only difference in translation between the proposal of Cross and my own is in the first word. The change from "Incense" to "Belonging to the daughters of" may seem odd, but the point is that all of us have been misled by the apparent reference to "frankincense." The objects in question are not altars of incense but simply spice burners, cosmetic burners; they are secular, not cultic in purpose, and have nothing to do with religion. That this interpretation is correct should have been recognized by us at once from the type of inscription found on the considerable number of South Arabian specimens,[14] from which the Palestinian and Mesopotamian types are obviously borrowed, but generally without any writing. On the numerous cuboid spice burners with four different names of spices in South Arabian characters on their sides are seven names of sweet-smelling spice plants which recur frequently, differing in detail from burner to burner.[15] Most of them are easy to identify; they include *qalam*, Latin *calamus* (Greek *kalamos*); *qust, costus* (Greek *kostos*); *ladan, ladanum* (Greek *ladanon*); *kamkam, lentiscus* "resin," (Greek *kamkamon*);[16] *ḍurwa* = Hebrew *ṣorī* and Amarna *ṣurwa, balsamum lentiscus*;[17] *ṭayyib*, a word which means "sweet-smelling" and hence refers to some kind of perfume. Since these are all spices (Hebrew *bĕsāmîm*) and are chosen for the combination of scents, insect repellents, and therapeutic purposes, they do not belong in the same category as myrrh and frankincense, the names of which never occur on these incense burners.

In short, the four spices listed on the South Arabian incense burners are rather like apothecary's labels. In no case are they recipes for religious incense as such. Their use is described very clearly by Sir S. W. Baker in his important book *The Nile Tributaries of Abyssinia* (London, 1868). A long quotation from Chapter 6 of this rare work is given by the late Dr. David I. Macht.[18] In describing the customs of the semi-nomadic Arabs of the eastern Sudan (northeast of the incense-producing areas of northeast Africa and southern South Arabia) he says that different perfumed spices such as oil of roses, oil of sandalwood, essence of the mimosa tree, essence of musk, and oil of cloves were the cosmetics most in demand by women from traveling native merchants.

> The women have a peculiar method of scenting their bodies and clothes, by an operation that is considered to be one of the necessaries of life and which is repeated at regular intervals. In the floor of the tent or hut . . . a small hole is excavated sufficiently large as to hold . . . a fire of charcoal . . . into which the woman about-to-be-scented throws a handful of various drugs. She then takes off the cloth or tope which forms her dress, and

crouches naked over the fumes while she arranges her robe to fall as a mantle from her neck to the ground like a tent. . . . None of the precious fumes can escape, all being kept under the robe, exactly as if she wore a crinoline with an incense burner. . . . She now begins to perspire freely in the hut or tent, and . . . the volatile oil from the burning perfumes is immediately absorbed [by her skin]. By the time that the fire has expired the scenting process is completed and both her person and the robe are redolent of incense with which they are so thoroughly impregnated that I have frequently smelt a party of women a full one hundred yards distant.

Baker went on to give other details, including especially a list of the characteristic perfumes used in the purification process: "ginger, cloves, cinnamon, frankincense, sandalwood, myrrh, a species of sea weed . . . from the Red Sea" and lastly "part of a shellfish brought from the southern Red Sea."

It is impossible to doubt any longer that the objects which all of us have taken to be religious in character and called altars of incense are actually quite secular and may correctly be called cosmetic burners. In fact, this very type of cosmetic incense stand may be referred to among the gifts to be given, as stipulated in the marriage contract from Elephantine, No. 15,[19] by the father of the bride to his daughter. The expression in question (line 16) reads *prks* 1, *zy ḥṣn ḥdt*, which Cowley translates "a new cosmetic box of ivory." There is no basis in Hebrew or the cognate languages for the rendering "ivory," and the word means specifically "lapful" or "bosomful." See especially Ps 129: 7. This designation would apply very nicely to a cosmetic incense burner in some more elegant material and more ornamental form than the objects we have been discussing. It is interesting to note that the date of Papyrus No. 15 in Cowley is somewhere in the third quarter of the fifth century, just about the most probable date for our inscription. The marriage contract is itself unique, since both parties are Jews, though the groom bears an Egyptian name. The latter was apparently a Persian government employee.

It is easy to understand why *Maḥlî*, name of a Levite family (often associated with the subtribe or clan of Merari), should appear as patronymic, since there was undoubtedly a high proportion of unemployed Levites among the Jewish population of Palestine after the Exile. Owing to their genealogy, they enjoyed respect in the community, but they must often have been desperately poor. The mention of the Levite family of *Maḥlî* is very interesting, since it is the first extrabiblical evidence for this particular family. The original name cannot have been **Maḥliyah*, as has been suggested, because *Maḥlî* is almost certainly a gentilic formed from the name *Maḥlah* which appears as the designation of a clan of Manasseh along with Noah,

Hoglah, Milcah, and Tirzah. Mahlah was the eldest daughter of Zelophehad in Num 27: 1, followed by the four sisters Noah, Hoglah, Milcah, and Tirzah, shown by the Ostraca of Samaria to be one of a group of clans of Manasseh settled to the southeast of the plain of Esdraelon, east of the watershed ridge on which Shechem stands.[20] The Greek Bible reads *Mool(e)i* in the passage in Num 3: 33 [MT 20] and in 1 Chron 6: 4 [MT 19]. The Lucianic text offers *Mooli* in Chronicles, and so it is evident that the Masoretic Hebrew vocalization is extremely doubtful. Num 26: 58 has among the Levite families *Hā-Libnî*, *Hā-Ḥebrōnî*, and *Hā-Maḥlî*; it is obvious that *Libnî* and *Maḥlî* are both gentilics from the towns or districts of *Libnah* and *Maḥlah*. As a matter of fact, we have Libnah listed as one of the Levite cities in both recensions of this tenth-century list.[21] It follows that the pronunciation of the name in the time of the Greek translation (third century B.C.) was something like *Mĕḥolî*, an obvious gentilic of the name Abel-meholah. Elsewhere I have pointed out that the original form of the word *mĕḥōlāh*, "dance," was something like **maḥullatu*, which would yield a normal *mĕḥōlāh* in classical Hebrew.[22] It is therefore more than probable that Abel-meholah, which is certainly on the west bank of the Jordan in the territory occupied by the five sisters Mahlah, Milcah, and so on, is perfectly suited to being the home of this particular Levite family. It stands to reason that the Levites settled in areas such as this would become refugees after the successive destructions of Samaria and Jerusalem.

The father of the daughters, whose name should probably be vocalized *ʾIyyōš* or *ʾAyyūš*, bears a name which is presumably a hypocoristic of common type from a name such as *ʾŌšiyahū*, itself shortened from *Yōšiyahū*, "Josiah," for still older *Yaʾōšyahū;* cf. *ʿIddō* for *ʿAddayah(ū)*.

The occupation of the Levite *ʾIyyōš* is clear. Since he is called *ha-malʾak*, he must have been a royal courier, an *ἄγγαρος* such as described by Herodotus and Xenophon for this same fifth century B.C. While a royal courier can scarcely have been paid very well, he was still a minor official of the Persian government and so must have enjoyed a certain amount of modest prestige. That he should have lived at Lachish, known from excavations to have been a district capital in the Achaemenian period and on an important north-south road just far enough inland to be safe from pirates and far enough from the mountains to be safe from bandits, was therefore the most natural thing in the world. We can well understand why his daughters were unmarried, since it is extremely doubtful that he had enough means of his own to provide the dowry large enough to attract suitable husbands for his daughters. That the family was poor is obvious from the fact that they were joint owners of the cosmetic incense burner and that the object itself was of poor quality.

Biblical parallels happen to be few but clear enough, on the whole. Toward the end of Is 3 the prophet follows a famous denunciation of the pride and ostentation of the daughters of Zion by saying that their elaborate use of perfumed spices (*bōsem*) will be replaced by rot (*taḥat bōsem maq*). This, however, is too early a date for the use of the South Arabic type of incense burner, and so we are left in uncertainty as to how the spices were used. In Ps 45: 8 f, where, as generally recognized, the text is somewhat poorly preserved, suggesting early oral transmission, we read in vs 9 that "therefore God will anoint thee . . . with myrrh, aloes, and cassia all thy clothes." Since the pronominal suffixes can just as well refer to the queen, as far as the consonantal text goes, this passage may refer to the elaborate perfuming practices of noble ladies.[23]

A passage neglected by recent writers is Esther 2: 12, where we are told about the elaborate conditioning treatment required of the maidens who were to become members of the harem of King Xerxes in the early fifth century (485–460 B.C.). The chosen women were put into condition with six months of oil of myrrh and six months of fragrant spices (*bĕsāmîm*). The commentators have been understandably very chary about speculating on just what this may have meant actually, but it now seems obvious that the periods of conditioning were accompanied by the extensive use of fumigation, which would have both hygienic and therapeutic value. It is, however, impossible to separate the process from the use of cosmetic incense burners of some sort, especially in view of the traditional fifth-century date.[24]

Notes

1 *The Tombs and the Moon Temple of Ḥureiḍa* (*Ḥaḍramaut*) (Oxford, 1944), Pl. XVII, and pp. 1, 3, 5.

2 R. A. S. Macalister, *The Excavation of Gezer II* (London, 1912), pp. 442–47; and *III*, Pl. CCXXV.

3 Flinders Petrie, *Gerar* (London, 1928), Pls XL, XLI, and pp. 18 f. In 1935, I also called attention to Babylonian parallels, *BASOR* 132 (1953), 46; cf Liselotte Ziegler, *ZA* NF 13 (1942), 224–40.

4 *ZDPV* 52 (1929), 246 ff.

5 Vol. II (1962), pp. 699 f.

6 For a discussion of the *ḥammān*, see W. F. Albright, *ARI*, pp. 215 f, n. 58, and references.

7 *Lachish III: The Iron Age* (Oxford, 1953), pp. 226, 358 f; Pl. 68–71.

8 *Lachish III*, pp. 358 f.

9 *BASOR* 132 (1953), 46 f.

10 *Studii Biblici Franciscani: liber annuus* 9 (1958–59), p. 334, n. 4.

11 *IEJ* 18 (1968), 163 f.

[12] "Two Notes on Palestinian Inscriptions of the Persian Age," *BASOR* 193 (1969), 21–24.

[13] Tel-Aviv, September 3, 1970.

[14] Adolf Grohmann, *Südarabien als Wirtschaftsgebiet* (Vienna, 1922), pp. 115 ff. Cf. Grohmann, *Arabien* (Munich, 1963), p. 248, n. 6.

[15] For a philological exegesis of the words in question, see N. Rhodokanakis in *Altorientalische Texte zum Alten Testament*, ed. H. Gressmann (1926), pp. 469 ff.

[16] This spice was brought from Malao in Somaliland to Arabia in the first century, according to the *Periplus of the Erythraean Sea*.

[17] Cf. Grohmann, *Südarabien*, pp. 114 f.

[18] *The Holy Incense* (Baltimore, 1928), pp. 25 f; see also E. Neufeld, "Hygiene Conditions in Ancient Israel (Iron Age)," *Journal of the History of Medicine* 25 (1970), 427 ff.

[19] A. Cowley, *Aramaic Papyri of the Fifth Century* B.C. (Oxford, 1923), pp. 44–50.

[20] On the geography of western Manasseh, and the distribution of the clans, see my discussions in "The Administrative Divisions of Israel and Judah," *JPOS* 5 (1925), 28–41; "The Site of Tirzah and the Topography of Western Manasseh," *JPOS* 11 (1931), 241–51, and the extension of these studies by F. M. Cross, "Epigraphic Notes on Hebrew Documents of the Eighth-Sixth Centuries B.C.: I. A New Reading of a Place Name in the Samaria Ostraca," *BASOR* 163 (1961), 12–14; and G. E. Wright, "The Provinces of Solomon," *EI* 8 (1967), 58*–68*.

[21] See my study, "The List of Levitic Cities," in the *Louis Ginzberg Jubilee Volume* (New York, 1945), pp. 49–73.

[22] See my comments on *mĕḥōlah*, Akk *mēlultu* (from **maḫlulatu*) in *Hebrew and Semitic Studies Presented to G. R. Driver*, ed. D. Winton Thomas and W. D. Hardy (Oxford, 1963), p. 5, n. 4. Cf also the "sons of *Maḥol*," 1 Kings 5: 11.

[23] I wish to thank N. Sarna and S. Talmon for suggestions in connection with these passages. [Albright did not specify precisely the obligation in question—FMC.]

[24] See now the Anchor commentary *Esther* by Carey A. Moore (Garden City, 1971), pp. xxiv–lx.

Robert G. Boling
McCormick Theological Seminary

"In Those Days There Was No King in Israel"

The range of problems in the exegesis of the book of Judges[1] was succinctly stated in a half paragraph by Martin Buber:

> Historical scholarship, if it replaces religious concepts with profane ones, that of the repetitive falling away from God with that of a repetitive falling to pieces of a unity of people into self-willed tribes, will recognize that the age of which the Book of Judges tells stood in a fluctuating movement between tearing-asunder multiplicity and a completion-desiring unity, and in addition probably this too, that here the principle of unity of a people and that of a faith were sustained by the same powers, by the same persons. The profane-historical transcription of the sequence "apostasy-affliction-conversion-rest" reads: "apostasy-affliction-unification-rest." But cannot it be assumed that just as at one time the believing experience of an event constituted the people, so the specific conversion to the believing experience of history again and again revived anew the power of unity in the people? That it did not prove itself strong enough gives to the Book of Judges its melancholy character, to the whole, not just to the closing section. One ought to pay attention to this character, and one will embed in it many an episode which now appears to burst strangely out of the context. How Gideon sets up an "ephod" which then becomes the centre of a service of Baal, how Jephtha offers his daughter to the God whose interpreters rebel against nothing so much as against his "Molochization," all this stands in its place with almost symbolic importance. The tradition supplied it, but he who knew how to impose selection and arrangement upon it in such a way was a great teacher.[2]

Buber proceeded in that chapter to develop an analysis in terms of two "books" of Judges—the bulk of the earlier traditions in chs 1–12 (anti-monarchical) and the later literary products in chs 17–21 (pro-monarchical)

—with the Samson cycle (chs 13–16) understood as the redactional pivot. To the inevitable question of how two such different works might be brought together without nullifying the unity and credibility of the finished book, Buber's explanation wears well:

> The balancing . . . depended upon an historical perspective which would be accepted by the readers of the book in so far as it was not already their own. This implicit view of history, which preserved the unity of the book while it enabled its two antithetical parts to be true simultaneously, one can perhaps formulate thus: Something has been attempted—about which the first part reports; but it has failed—as the last part shows. This "something" is that which I call *the primitive theocracy*.[3]

Thanks to the recent voluminous work on second-millennium treaty forms[4] and their ramifications for the reexamination of the biblical conquest traditions,[5] it now appears that the primitive theocracy was more of an institutional reality than Buber believed. It does not, however, in any way detract from the stature of his thesis to object that his analysis in Judges was too schematic and tended to obscure a much more complex redactional history, as clearly demonstrated in the studies of a number of scholars, from the earlier work of Professor Myers in *The Interpreter's Bible* to the recent work of W. Richter.[6] The latter has traced the rise of the book of Judges about as far as the methods of traditions-history can go, and we agree, in the main, with his results. Perhaps a chief contribution has been the demonstration that the term "Deuteronomic" is far too general at the present time for the material attributed to the various redactors. For reasons which will become clear in this paper, we have not adopted Richter's sigla for the several contributors to the book of Judges, but continue, instead, to argue for two main editorial efforts, updating an earlier "pragmatic framework" edition of material found in old Joshua-Judges epic sources. This allows for the closest possible correlation with questions about the growth of the larger historical work to which Judges belongs (not generally within Richter's purview), where the distinction must be drawn between "Deuteronomic" (i.e., Josianic) and "Deuteronomistic" (i.e., exilic) work on the historical traditions.

> The second edition completed ca. 550 B.C. not only updated the history by adding a chronicle of events subsequent to Josiah's reign, it also attempted to transform the work into a sermon on history addressed to the Judean exiles.[7]

While the exilic work involved only minor modifications, they were skillful modifications involving, as has recently been shown, inverted use of "holy warfare" language in the latest work on the introduction to Deuteronomy.[8] In the book of Judges, we will argue, the main "Deuteronomistic" contribution was to revive during the exile some previously neglected traditionary units, which now provide the entire book with a tragicomic framework in chs 1 and 19–21. The result is that the book of Judges, in its finished form, begins with historical Israel starting to fall apart in the wake of initial military successes (ch 1) and ends with a very delicate, persistent ideal, Israel, reunited at last in the wake of the tragic civil war with Benjamin—that is, for thoroughly incongruous reasons (chs 19–21). Any exilic updating of a work previously organized so as to climax and end with a justification of King Josiah's program (2 Kings 22–23) would of necessity sound very different, if it were to be relevant to the new context. We suspect that it is a subtle matter, indeed, that the exilic redactor is profoundly concerned with such questions as the one raised so poignantly by Psalm 137—how to sing the Lord's song in a pagan country. The exilic redactor's answer counters the disillusionment of exile; for "comedy is an escape, not from truth but from despair: a narrow escape into faith."[9]

There is a large and clear parallel in ancient Israel for the sort of exegetical activity which we claim to recognize in the final edition of Judges; it is to be seen in the poetry of the book of Job and the question of the poet's stance toward the old popular story which frames that book and Job's relation to the central concerns of the wisdom schools. In the poetry Job is anything but the model of endurance who is the center of attention in the prose story, the ideal patriarchal type who by his faithfulness enables Yahweh to win a wager. Rather, in the poetry Job is a most self-righteous man who talks himself into a dialogical stalemate. Job successfully defends the abstraction (*ʾelôah*) against all opposition, and in the process persuades himself that Yahweh (as he impulsively blurts out in 12: 7–10) is wrong about his servant Job. Job goes on, however, to be so successful against the false defenders of God that he becomes a false accuser, until at last Yahweh serves up his whirlwind (using the same "argument from nature" as did Job in 12: 7–10). Job at last gets the message, intercedes for his "comforters," and all of them are given life. It is hard to evade the impression that the poet has expanded the venerable story of Job specifically for the benefit of hard-pressed sages, thus effectively revaluing some ancient pedagogical claims, while at the same time protecting the old prose story from a possible gross misunderstanding.

The book of Job illustrates the essential difference between types of "ancient romances" as delineated for the classical world by Ben Edwin Perry.[10] The prose framework belongs to the "ideal" genre, a popular story told for popular edification and delight. But the poet has broken the story open and turned the book into an example of the "comic" genre, which was always in antiquity a much more sophisticated form, intended for more sophisticated attention.[11] The recognition of the poetic Job as a profoundly comic figure helps one to understand why there are no scripture quotations in the book,[12] except where Psalm 8 is turned inside out by the haggling of Job (7: 17–18); the story was not yet "canonical" although it was authoritative, and the poet intended to protect it from the superficial interpretation that "piety pays."

The process reflected in the growth of the book of Judges is comparable to that of the book of Job. The Josianic and Exilic redactors of Judges were confronted with collected narrative tradition that was already fixed and inviolable in all essentials. A significant difference from Job is that none of the judges (with the possible exception of Othniel in 3: 9–10) is presented as an ideal figure. Rather, they are clearly presented as historical persons whose varying Yahwistic effectiveness is evaluated in the telling of their stories. The old stories were brought together in such a way as to affirm the rule of Yahweh in the period prior to Saul and David. In themselves the stories are neither clearly anti-monarchical nor pro-monarchical (contra Buber et al.). They must be essentially pre-monarchical, but were compiled early in the monarchy as a help in understanding the new and alien political arrangements within the Yahwist state. It follows that any Josianic or exilic updating of such old epic materials, which had long since been put to historical use, would be confined mostly to the introduction and conclusion of the book.

There are three obvious exceptions. In the speech of the angel (2: 1–5), the speech of the prophet (6: 7–10), and the speech of the divine organizer of Israel (10: 11–14), we recognize intrusive elements which scholars on all hands have regarded as in one way or another "Deuteronomic." In addition to the formal continuity of the indictment speech, the clearest common denominator of these three passages is the abrupt disappointment, the unexpected reversal of pious expectations for the divine response to Israel's plea.

In 6: 7-10 the Deuteronomic prophet who arises in response to Israel's cry confronts Israel with the accusation that entangling relationships with gods of the "westerners" (Amorites in the etymological sense) explains why Israel is now repeatedly immobilized before the annual depradations of the nomadic "easterners." In 10: 11–14, using Deuteronomic logic, the divine administrator first shows how the pattern of appealing to him in hard times had become habit-forming; yet confronted with that embarrassing truth, Israelites on that occasion decided to trust Yahweh anyway and he delivered them. The third passage (2: 1–5), where an angel announces an end to the conquest though it is in fact an incomplete conquest, sits very loosely in its context; we shall deal with it below as part of the expansions of the introduction to the period. The insertion of all three passages may be assigned to the period of Josiah, whose own reforming campaigns in the north had precisely the opposite effect of a turn for the better in Judahite national fortunes. The key to the Deuteronomic contrast between the judges, on the one hand, and Joshua-David-Josiah, on the other, is the "Book of the Law" (Josh 1: 6–8).

It goes without saying that there was in the old stories of the judges an abundance of humor to be exploited by the Deuteronomic historian in the three ironic homiletical inserts to the book. Yet Josiah's successes were short-lived. An exilic edition had to be relevant to the educated leadership of folk who were once again living in a period like that of the judges—with no king in Israel. The Deuteronomic edition had prepared the way. By a profoundly comic portrayal of the last days of the judges era (chs 19–21), the final editor taught that it was time once again to affirm the high kingship of Yahweh and for every man to do what was right as he thus discerned it.

Deuteronomic Introduction (1: 1 and 2: 1–5)

Preoccupation with the etiological element explaining the placc name The Wcepers (*hab-bōkîm*) in 2: 1 by reference to "weeping" (*bōkîm*) in 2: 5 has obscured a double entendre. Why were they weeping at the beginning of the unit? Clearly the unit as it now stands presupposes the frustration of the larger plan that takes place in ch 1. Yet that chapter is scarcely direct preparation for the scene of mourning that is abruptly introduced in 2: 1. We suggest that in 2: 1 "the weepers," in the view of the Deuteronomic historian, were mourning precisely because Joshua was dead and new leadership was needed. But in the view of that historian, the legitimate resumption of effective military expansion would await the establishment of the Jerusalem monarchy, the careers of David and Josiah especially; for the judges, in the Deuteronomic view, fought only defensive wars. Thus we may suspect that in a pre-Deuteronomic version of the story the angel in 2: 1 arrived only in the nick of time, perhaps to avert an oracular response to the question of 1: 1 (or a question very much like it) at an otherwise unspecified sanctuary.

On the other hand, the fragmentary speech of the envoy (beginning with a cohortative in 2: 1b which must be rendered as past tense) makes better sense as a Deuteronomic indictment of an entire epoch for its failure precisely where Josiah succeeded—that is, in the demolition of competing altars and the avoidance of entangling alliances. Our hypothesis regarding the redactional history of 2: 1–5 gains further support from the scholarly consensus that identifies the "place" in question as Bethel, one of the two great royal sanctuaries of the old northern kingdom, both of which are completely devalued in the Deuteronomic history. The Bethel altar was demolished by Josiah (2 Kings 23: 15). The other great northern sanctuary was at Dan, and it comes in for devastating criticism in the Deuteronomic conclusion to the book of Judges, the supplementary material now found in Judges 17–18.

To summarize: though "every idiom" in 2: 1b–3 derives from an old epic source,[13] the passage sits so loosely in its context as to betray a complex redactional history. Drawn from an old source, the heavenly ambassador had announced the beginning of a new era, in response to a particular question: "Who shall go for us?" Answer: "Don't go anymore." The answer has, in turn, been reshaped as a Deuteronomic prelude to the period, anticipating the older narrative indictment of 2: 10, to be discussed in the next section of this paper.[14] The problem of certain northern oracles is central also to the stories of Micah's Levite (ch 17) and the migration of the tribe of Dan (ch 18), which will be discussed below as the "Deuteronomic" conclusion to the book.

Expansions of a Pragmatic Introduction (2: 6–3: 6)

The section begins with a repetition of Joshua's death and burial notice,[15] after the insertion of 2: 1–5, with the result that the verbs in vss 6 f must be read as past perfect ("Joshua had dismissed," etc). The death and burial notice is followed by an abrupt statement of non-alignment with Yahweh in 2: 10 (failure to "know") out of an old epic source (cf Ex 1: 8), to which the logical sequence would be vss 20–23, that is, Yahweh's wrath explicated in terms of "broken covenant." The covenantal sense of "to know," however, appears to have been widely obscured in later years, remaining alive only in Deuteronomic and prophetic circles.[16] Thus the intervening vss (2: 11–19) are in essence a Deuteronomic exegesis of what is involved in a failure to "know" Yahweh. That is, to do evil was to commit a sociopolitical offense, where Yahweh was previously acknowledged as sovereign of the universe and of the Israelite state. The invariable concomitant of not "knowing" Yahweh was to fall into the clutches of the only alternatives (vs 11), the Canaanite god and his consorts. Conversely, each new threat in the period, as well as the rise of new Israelite leadership, was soon interpreted as Yahweh's real provision for the restoration of his realm.

This is an introduction to the period as a whole; it does not imply a cyclical view of historical process. The one element in the framework formula accompanying various pericopes that might support such a view, the statement that in hard times Israelites appealed to Yahweh (3: 9, 15; 4: 3; 6: 7; 10: 10), is conspicuously absent here. The right of appeal could also be exploited (see e.g., the Amarna correspondence), as the Deuteronomic historian made explicit with his insertion of the three speeches discussed above. Here at the outset of the period nothing is permitted to detract from Yahweh's even-handed administration of the realm in the hectic period after Joshua.

Judges 3: 1–6 are especially difficult. Apparently two units are involved. Vss 1–4 are used to fix the situation in the generation after the death of the older people who had participated in the conquest. They pose a question (as at the end of ch 2). Vss 5–6 (using another list of the "remaining nations") summarize the results of the test. These units may plausibly be regarded as "Deuteronomic" and "Deuteronomistic," respectively, in view of the analysis of the remainder of the framework material.

Within the body of the book, the Deuteronomic historian was, for the most part, content to leave the preformed cycle of stories intact (except for the insertion of the three speeches), with the effectiveness of the "primitive" political arrangements fluctuating throughout the period, but finally plummeting downward to the point where Samson clearly demonstrates the need for administrative reorganization, a situation which will come to a head in the careers of Eli and Samuel (1 Sam 1–3).

Deuteronomic Conclusion (16: 1–18: 31)

What was the concluding limit to the Deuteronomic (Josianic) input into the book of Judges? Allowing that it is a fair summary of Deuteronomic intention to legitimatize the rule of Yahweh from Moses to Josiah, the climactic use of the standard judge formula in reference to Samson (15: 20) comes into sharper focus. We suggest that the pre-Deuteronomic edition had taken up only those elements of tradition which would clarify and legitimatize the use of the verb "to judge." That is precisely a sequence in which Samson at last turns to Yahweh with some sort of direct address, discovering thereby that he is going to live after all (15: 17–20). Here, significantly, there is no mention of Israelites "crying out"; rather, the problem is precisely to show Samson—given the man's reputation—as doing the sort of crying out that makes one a proper Israelite warrior and good judge material.

Against the argument that the judge formula in 15: 20 was only secondarily applied to Samson, and that his career was not within the purview of the pre-Deuteronomic work, we must emphasize the inverted use in Samson's story of so many themes in common with the other judges, but especially the Deborah-Barak material. Deborah and Barak ("Honey Bee" and

"Lightning") style themselves "lovers of Yahweh" and sing at last about erupting sunshine,[17] after securing a sign and presiding over the mobilization of the militia. Surely their story was for years retold alongside stories of the tragicomic hero whose name was "Man-of-Sun" (his last girl friend "Flirt"), and who once singlehandedly slew a lion and later discovered in the carcass a whole "congregation of honey bees" [*'ēdat debōrîm* (14: 8)], but chased them away, enjoyed the honey, and suppressed the sign. His "mother," like the "mother in Israel" in 5: 7, could have told him what it all meant, having received a privileged communication regarding the whole matter of his future. There are also the thirst of the non-hero at the death of Sisera (4: 19) and the last-minute enlistment of Samson (15: 18–19). Both clusters of stories stem from the life of the early popular militia with its perennial leadership and enlistment problems, and there seems to be no clear reason for not understanding chs 13–15 as part of the pre-Deuteronomic edition.

What sort of judge did Samson turn out to be? To the redactional activity of the Deuteronomic historian, who seldom left such questions unanswered unless his sources failed him, may be assigned the incorporation of the two Samson stories of ch 16. The incident with the Gaza girl quickly sets the stage. She was fulfilling her publicly recognized role, while the Israelite judge was not fulfilling his own publicly recognized role (16: 1–3). In the Delilah story, which follows immediately, the plot centers upon the theme of the warrior's vow.[18] This old story, in its fixed form, already served admirably the intention of the Deuteronomic historian, as it told about the tragic end of Samson, but only after the Philistines had added torment to torture and Samson had cried out for Yahweh to vindicate his rule against the torturous treatment of his judge. The historian appended a repetition of the judge formula, appropriately revised in perfect tense (only here in the book): "he *had been* judge in Israel for twenty years" (16: 31).

There had been a closely comparable situation somewhere in the north (chs 17–18). Micah is clearly introduced as self-designated head of a "Little Israel" tucked away in the hills of Ephraim. This introduction balances the earlier depiction of Manoah as a loner ("from Zorah"), head of an encampment somewhere between Zorah and Eshtaol, precise location either forgotten or unimportant (13: 2 and 25). As in the Deuteronomic supplement to Samson (ch 16), the point is made by merely appending two preformed narrative units. In the first of them (17: 1–4), the cultic opportunist's name is spelled out in full (*mîkayhû*), successfully drawing attention to its inappropriateness as a name ("Who is like Yahweh?") for a maker of "images." The second unit (vss 7–11) recounts the journey of a young aspiring

Levite to a place called Beit-Micah, where, not surprisingly, there lives a man named Micah. After vs 4 the name appears consistently in the short form. Vss 5 and 6 are, accordingly, summary and transition between pre-formed narrative units, apparently a pre-Deuteronomic narrative splice. It is here that we meet for the first time the familiar title to these notes: "In those days there was no king in Israel, and every man did what was right in his own eyes" (17: 6). It was, indeed, an ironic state of affairs to the Deuteronomic historian, and he promptly appended the story of the migration of Dan, whose very name means "judgment."[19] All that he needed to do was to pen a transition (18: 1a), repeating only the first half of our title, because he intended to show how Yahweh was in fact still king, although the local arrangements were in need of revision and, eventually, Davidic stability. To make a long story short, Dan unwittingly turns Micah into a Yahwist once again by depriving him of his "image" (18: 21–26), but goes on to complete the corrupting exploitation of a Levite and to commit one of the baldest atrocities in scripture, capping it off with the installation of Micah's confiscated abomination at Laish (renamed Dan), although "the house of God was at Shiloh" (18: 31). This abrupt conclusion, often recognized as a Deuteronomic ending in Judges, balances the introduction to the same stratum (2: 1–5), which similarly serves to devalue, from the later Deuteronomic perspective, the other famous northern sanctuary and a chief target of Josiah's reforms (see above).

It is worth noting at this point how neatly ch 18 corresponds in its essentials to the Testament of Dan in Gen 49: 16–18:

> Dan shall judge his people
> as one of the tribes of Israel.
>
> Dan shall be a serpent in the way,
> a viper by the path,
>
> that bites the horse's heels
> so that his rider falls backward.
>
> I wait for thy salvation, O Yahweh!

Deuteronomistic Conclusion (19: 1–21: 25)

Scholarly attention to the ending of the book of Judges has too often been diverted by the problem of the introduction, without seeing both of them in balance. Thus, a residual question about the *Sitz im Leben* of chs 19–21 has never been satisfactorily answered: how was this tragically inverted account of Yahwist warfare, capped off by the intra-Israelite application of the *ḥerem* to the point of nearly obliterating one tribe (ch 19–20) and another entire urban center (21: 1–14) and followed by the premeditated abduction of the Shiloh maidens (21: 15–25), supposed to be relevant to anything at all? To be sure, the account of the civil war has been recognized as an invaluable source for understanding the "amphictyonic" constitution in the pre-monarchy period.[20] Yet the problem remains that there seems to be nothing in the chapters that is edifying to a religious consciousness, whether ancient or modern.

We submit that the final chapters of Judges present a comic resolution to the chaos of the entire transitional period from Joshua to the monarchy. There are two kinds of clues to the character of these narratives. One is a series of rhetorical observations which connect with ch 1, which will be discussed in the final section of this paper. The other clue is found in the contrasting characterizations of the two Levites who are the center of attention in chs 17 and 19; this contrast is surely to be correlated with the concern for the Levitical priests in the Deuteronomic legislation, on the one hand, and Josiah's policies, on the other. For it seems clear enough that one of the most problematic aspects of the seventh-century reform had to do with satisfactory provisions in Jerusalem for Levites left unemployed by the demolition of outlying cult places. We suspect therefore that in ch 19 the disaster of 587 B.C. has unleashed a most surprising bit of "Levitical criticism."

The Levite of ch 19 is already well established, and his trouble begins when his concubine goes home to Bethlehem. Thus, he is introduced in striking contrast to the aspiring young Levite from Judah who had accepted employment at Micah's place (ch 17). The inversion of narrative elements is here a redactional key; after feasting at his father-in-law's expense for the better part of a week, the Levite of ch 19 got a late start one afternoon. Unlike Micah's Levite, he was not about to take his chances just anywhere, especially in Jerusalem. Rather, he intended to capitalize on the Israelite law of hospitality, even if it meant that he must trust himself to the Benjaminites (for their reputation, see especially 3: 12–30). In response to his protest about the gang-style rape and murder of his concubine, the tribe of Benjamin was very nearly wiped out.

The model for this story, as often noted, is the old story of Lot, where the local inhabitants complain, "This fellow came to sojourn and he would play the judge" (Gen 19: 9).

Thus the last Levite to appear in the judges book sets himself up as judge and rallies "all Israel." The only other place in the book where "all Israel" appears explicitly is in the sequel to the account of Gideon's suppression of the nomads (presented in 8: 18 as a personal vendetta), where he piously declines their offer of kingship but demands, instead, the makings of an elaborate ephod (8: 22–26). That is, he demanded the trappings of judge, inasmuch as the ephod had tightly bound to it the "judicial breastplate" (Exod 28 and 39). And "all Israel went whoring" after Gideon's ephod (8: 27). The bias of this pericope is perhaps another Deuteronomistic contribution.

In ch 20, Israel is again united, but for mostly odd reasons. A clear signal to the "comedy of correctness" is the opening enquiry in 20: 18, "Which of us shall go out first to attack the Benjaminites?"[21] Nowhere in the sources is there any evidence that oracular means were used to assign particular field obligations (on 1: 1, see below). The captains had, except on rare occasions which took everybody by surprise (Joshua at Ai; David in 2 Sam 5: 23), to devise their own strategy. Moreover, we may understand that the oracle was programmed to answer only the question that was asked; and orderly enquiry before battle called for a prior question. Not "Who shall go first?" Rather, "Shall we go or not?" (2 Sam 2: 1; 5: 19; 1 Kings 22: 6, 15; cf. I Kings 12: 24). It was Yahweh's prerogative alone to declare war.

We may thus understand the narrative integrity of two severe drubbings in ch 20; it was only after they got their questions in the right order and at the proper place of enquiry (before the ark of the covenant) that victory was to be expected (20: 27 ff). What a tremendous cost, this old-style Israelite unity! The narrative admits of no compassion toward the concubine. And when the possibility of reconciliation with Benjamin is at last at hand, the *ḥerem* is revived (except for 8: 22–28, the first hint of that institution since ch 1) against Jabesh-Gilead for not sending in the expected quota of troops (21: 11). Only tardily had the combatants recognized that they were on the point of permanently rupturing the inviolable twelve-tribe organization. The ancient institutions of the Yahwist war would no longer suffice.

It is difficult, if not now impossible, to regard these chapters as anything more or less than an exilic narrator's artful elaboration, out of the historical memory and an archaic source recounting the tragic civil war with Benjamin.

How had Israel survived? The Deuteronomistic conclusion shows how they had at last used their heads. The council of elders had thought up the kidnapping of desirable maidens at Shiloh. The implication of the fact that Shiloh's location must be described is that the venerable amphictyonic center was not much visited by the Yahwists anymore (so that the insertion would not do exegetical violence to the picture of Elkanah as an exceptional Yahwist in 1 Sam 1). The elders will explain that no law has been violated: the elders did not take them and the kinsfolk did not grant them. 'Twas sheer grace!

"In those days there was no king in Israel. Every man did what was right in his own eyes" (21: 25). And so, by implication, can the exiled believer, and maybe better, thanks to the memory. According to Deuteronomy, Moses had presented such a mode of decision making as being appropriate prior to the conquest (Deut 12: 8), which had meant to the Deuteronomic historian that it was most inappropriate on at least one occasion following the conquest (Judg 17: 6); but it was now in order where the pre-conquest conditions once again prevailed. Israel was to do it again—make a new beginning.

Deuteronomistic Introduction (1: 2–36)

Recognition of the conclusion of Judges as comedy that is yet profoundly Yahwist in its affirmation suggests a new point of entry to the bulk of ch 1. The question of the character of ch 1 has been effectively obscured by the scholarly suspicion that it presents a more reliable "minority report" to the normative conquest tradition that is preserved in the book of Joshua. Proponents of this view, however, have never succeeded in making intelligible how this could begin "after the death of Joshua," in light of 2: 8. While the theory of the reliable minority report has been effectively refuted by G. Ernest Wright as being unable to accommodate the archeological data,[22] the redactional integrity of ch 1 has never been satisfactorily explained.

We propose that 1: 2–36 is a redactor's attempt to provide a fresh perspective on the indictment in 2: 1–5 and the chaotic chain of events to follow. This would explain why the selection of materials in ch 1 involves doublets with Joshua 15 as well as otherwise unattested traditions. It aims to show how the situation worsened after Joshua's death, until the master plan for economic reform was at last thwarted (vss 27-35).

The key to the final edition of the introduction is, in this view, the incongruity between the answer "Judah shall go" and the question about leadership for offensive warfare in 1: 1, an incongruity which harmonizes very well with the exaggerated caricature of civil war in ch 20, where we find the same response to a similar inquiry (20: 18). In this manner, the exilic redactor affirmed, through a tragicomic narrative, how the recent demise of Judah was the end result of a process of divine discipline that had been initiated by Yahweh's will for the well-being of his people.

The only alternative to such an approach to the problem of ch 1 would be to assume that the redactor knew nothing about traditions associating historical Joshua with reforms in land tenure (which, in light of the last half of the book of Joshua, we find almost inconceivable), or else that the redactor set out most unsuccessfully to counter such traditions (which we find implausible). Rather, in his use of older materials, he set out to frame the earlier "Deuteronomic" edition of the book of Judges with material that shows Israel virtually "on the ropes" by the end of ch 1 and painfully but surely reassembled in chs 20 and 21.

If "tragicomic" is a fair description of the final frame of Judges, then the problem of doublets between Joshua and Judges 1 is posed in a new way, for there is no clear indication of an early (that is, pre-exilic) combination of the multifarious traditionary pieces that now make up Judges 1. We suspect that the bulk of the combining and grouping of these old units stems from the same redactor as do the final chapters, where the purpose is not merely to chronicle the past but to affirm the present rule of Yahweh in the midst of chaos.

Judah sets the pace in 1: 2–7, as it will again in ch 20. In 1: 8–9, after the initial success, we are prepared for great things but are brought up short by the campaign against Debir. While our attention is momentarily arrested by Achsah (vs 15), we are presented with the peaceful performance of some Kenites for contrast (vs 16). Then the account of Judah's plundering resumes, capped by the (ironic?) summary in vs 19.[23]

Will Ephraim and Manasseh do better? Not much. There is a place in the Hittite country to this very day called Deception (*lûz*, "to turn aside," with devious or crafty intent), commemorating a piece of conquest by treachery. Manasseh, Ephraim, Zebulun, Asher, and Naphtali are all charged specifically with failure to carry through reforms in land tenure. Finally, as in the earlier Deuteronomic edition, there was Dan, who could not expand into the plain because of the "westerners" there.[24]

Ch 1 ends with Israel in complete disarray, thus anticipating the angel's response (2: 1–5) to the premature question (1: 1).

The conclusion appears inescapable that this final redactor has indeed been taught by the Deuteronomic preoccupation with reversals of Israelite expectations (clearest in 2: 1–5; 6: 7–10; and 10: 10–16). The last of these had made the point that crying out to Yahweh in time of crisis had become habit forming. Yet, confronted with that embarrassing truth, they decided to trust him anyway, and he delivered them. What had been true in Jephthah's day is regarded at last as truer than ever.[25]

Notes

[1] It is a privilege to be able to present this essay to Professor Myers, whose fine "Introduction" and "Exegesis" of the Book of Judges in *IB*. vol. II (1953) appeared just in time to help whet my appetite, as a seminarian, for critical biblical studies and to set the basic guidelines for the investigation leading to this paper.

[2] M. Buber, *Kingship of God*, 3d ed., tr. Richard Scheimann (1967), p. 68.

[3] *Ibid.*, p. 83.

[4] From the pioneering studies by G. E. Mendenhall, "Ancient Oriental and Biblical Law," *BA* 17 (1954), No. 1, 26–46, and "Covenant Forms in Israelite Traditions," No. 2, 49–76 (reprinted as *Law and Covenant in Israel and the Ancient Near East* [Pittsburgh: The Biblical Colloquium, 1955], and again in *BAR* III [1970] pp. 3–53), to the excellent summary and synthesis by D. R. Hillers, *Covenant* (Baltimore, 1969).

[5] Again, beginning with the pace setting work of Mendenhall, "The Hebrew Conquest of Palestine," *BA* 25 (1962), 66–87, reprinted in *BAR* III (1970), 100–20. See the summary and evaluation by J. L. McKenzie, *The World of the Judges* (Englewood Cliffs, N.J., 1966), pp. 95–98.

[6] *Die Bearbeitungen des "Retterbuches" in der deuteronomischen Epoche.* Bonner Biblische Beiträge 21 (1964).

[7] F. M. Cross, Jr., "The Structure of the Deuteronomic History," *Perspectives in Jewish Learning*, vol. III (1968), p. 19.

[8] W. L. Moran, "The End of the Unholy War and the Anti-Exodus," *Bibl* 44 (1963), 333–42.

[9] Christopher Fry, "Comedy," in *The New Orpheus*, ed. Nathan A. Scott (New York, 1964), p. 286.

[10] *The Ancient Romances* (Berkeley, 1967).

[11] Fry regards the book of Job as "the great reservoir of comedy." *Op. cit.*, p. 288.

[12] On the importance of the absence of scriptural quotations from Job, see W. F. Albright, *Yahweh and the Gods of Canaan* (Garden City, 1968), pp. 260–61, who relates the language of Job to the non-Israelite coast of Palestine, where culture was Phoenician but the population was certainly in part Israelite. Thus there is no need to regard the poetry of Job as exilic or later in order to discern a comparable redactional context.

[13] M. Weinfeld, "The Period of the Conquest and of the Judges as Seen by the Earlier and the Later Sources," *VT* 17 (1967), 95, who overlooks the idiom "my covenant" in vs 1b.

[14] The final answer to the question of 1: 1—"Judah"—is marked by its repetition in 20: 18 as a redactor's *inclusio*, drawing the bulk of ch 1 into the latest editorial stratum of the book, to be discussed in the final sections of this paper.

[15] Cf Josh 24: 29–31. Only the sentence order is revised in Judg 2: 7–9, yielding a movement more appropriate to the introduction of the new epoch. The literary device of "repetitive resumption" has been studied in great detail by S. Talmon, who recognizes here a recurring literary device by which independently self-contained units were incorporated into narrative texts. Among numerous examples discussed in meetings of the Biblical Colloquium (November, 1970), Talmon included also Judg 15: 20 and 16: 31; the latter passage he regards as the contribution of the redactor of ch 16 (see below). These two examples of the repetitive resumption in Joshua-Judges also illustrate another of Talmon's observations; the redactor, when he repeats, frequently inverts elements (2: 6–9) or revises slightly (the form of verb in 15: 20 and 16: 31).

[16] H. Huffmon, "The Treaty Background of Hebrew *Yādaʿ*," *BASOR* 181 (1966), 31–37.

[17] 5: 31, which, it appears from the singularity of the verse, was all that they sang in the narrative source, prior to the insertion of the archaic song which now fills the chapter. For the argument that names are of the essence in such narrative art, see L. Alonzo-Schökel, "Erzahlkunst im Buche der Richter," *Bibl* 42 (1961), 143–72. For the theo-

political referent of the verb "to love" (*'hb*), see W. L. Moran, "The Ancient Near Eastern Background of the Love of God in Deuteronomy," *CBQ* 25 (1963), 77–87.

[18] As argued by Blenkinsopp, *JBL* 82 (1963), 65–76. It is not, however, merely a matter of a "broken" vow. For it is only after Samson's lighthearted recommendation of several sorts of magic that he finally tells her the truth. Yet he cannot have regarded it as the truth or he never would have told her. The Nazirite's haircut publicly symbolized his demobilization or retirement (Num 6: 13–20)—that is, Yahweh at last allowed Samson to be dishonorably discharged. The Philistines, for their part, also bungled it, for the only way to stop a man's hair from growing was to kill him. Samson could reenlist, upon proper application. Thus the theme is not so much the "broken" vow as it is the vow which was not taken seriously until it was too late.

[19] M. Noth, "The Background of Judges 17–18," in *Israel's Prophetic Heritage*, ed. B. W. Anderson and W. Harrelson (New York, 1962), pp. 68–85, has argued convincingly that the scandalous tone of the story is to be understood as polemic from the royal Israelite sanctuary of Dan (thus originally pre-Deuteronomic polemic), established by Jeroboam I, polemic concerned to discredit the old Danite tribal shrine. The story thus reflects a prehistory. See also A. Malamat, "The Danite Migration and the Pan-Israelite Exodus-Conquest: A Biblical Narrative Pattern," *Bibl* 51 (1970), 1–16. The story in Judg 18 is explained by Malamat as "a sort of diminutive model of a campaign of inheritance, which pattern appears on the national scale in the Exodus and Pan-Israelite conquest cycles." This story will in turn be exploited by the author of ch 19–20, where we will see Israel doing everything right, but over-doing it. Only at the end of the book are things at last done simply for the right reason (21: 25).

[20] M. Noth, *The History of Israel*, 2d ed., tr. P. R. Ackroyd (1960).

[21] The text of the battle narrative is notoriously difficult. Professor Myers found it impossible to decide between evidence of "sources" and "midrashic expansions" (*op. cit.*, pp. 814 ff). We have concluded that most of the problems can be traced to variants in oral transmission. See provisionally our notes in *VT* 16 (1966), especially 293–95. All that is finally necessary to apprehend narrative integrity in such an artificial depiction of military operations is to read the first *bêt 'ēl* (20: 18) as a reference to the Mizpah sanctuary (and not "Bethel"), a possibility that John Gray now considers entirely plausible; see *Joshua-Judges-Ruth* (London, 1967), p. 241.

[22] "The Literary and Historical Problem of Joshua x and Judges i," *JNES* 5 (1946), 105–14.

[23] Vss 20–21, and probably vs 10, are plausibly understood as marginal annotations that have been drawn into the text.

[24] Cf use of "Amorites" in 6: 7–10, discussed above. 1: 36 seems to be a copyist's query based on a misunderstanding of the preceding use of "Amorite" in its original sense.

[25] The hypothesis of the redactional expansion of an old Joshua-Judges epic source in three main phases ("pragmatic," "Deuteronomic," and "Deuteronomistic") correlates well with the otherwise baffling conclusion of the book of Joshua, which also seems to end twice. Josh 24 recapitulates the great convocation at Shechem, where Joshua presides over a covenantal affirmation by all the tribes that have thus far participated in the Yahwist revolution in Canaan. The documentary basis for the chapter is a very old one, and many scholars see in it a reflection of the definitive emergence of the specifically Israelite amphictyony. The chapter leaves the matter of success or failure in the new experiment an open question: Will you or will you not maintain the covenant constitution? What is affirmed through the lively narrative depiction of negotiation and ratifica-

tion in ch 24 now has eloquent hortatory preparation in ch 23. But that chapter, as Joshua's "Farewell Address," is complete in itself; it is a preformed unit which has been inserted in such a way that the last two chapters of Josh are most inefficiently redundant. The most striking thing about the farewell speech is its negative expectation for the survival of the federation, spiraling downward to a devastating conclusion: "If you break the covenant . . . you will quickly vanish from the good land he has given you" (Josh 23: 16). This chapter clearly reflects Deuteronomic eloquence; yet, from the standpoint of the question about redaction, it fits best the period in which the prophecy had been fulfilled.

Howard N. Bream
Lutheran Theological Seminary at Gettysburg

Life without Resurrection: Two Perspectives from Qoheleth

The fact that J. M. Myers has often spoken of Ecclesiastes as his favorite biblical writing, plus a strong attraction to this member of the megilloth felt by the present writer, influenced the choice of topic for this contribution to the Myers Festschrift.

The paper will focus on two important aspects of the thought of the book of Ecclesiastes, hereafter called Qoheleth, and will relate them to similar attitudes that appear in the New Testament. The passage of time between the writer of this ancient book of wisdom and the first century A.D. saw a marked spread and development of beliefs concerning resurrection. Few would deny that the doctrine of the resurrection was basic to both Pharisaic Judaism and early Christianity. This paper does not attempt to trace the history of the doctrine of resurrection. The goal is, rather, to examine two main points in Qoheleth with respect to his outlook on life, in the context of his negative attitude toward belief in resurrection. Then we shall turn to the New Testament, where essentially the same viewpoints are present, but now standing in the context of resurrection faith.

The initial point to come under attention is Qoheleth's realism with respect to conjecture about the fate of the dead. The teachings of Jesus and Paul will then be examined for evidence of a similar outlook.

The second perspective from Qoheleth is a positive appreciation of this present life. Here too, we will look at the New Testament for signs of expression of a similar discernment of immanent good. To maintain such an attitude along with belief in a resurrection was necessary if Christians were to have a sense of proportion between eschatological expectations and values available here and now.

Tempting as it is to seek the origins of the belief in resurrection, the writer views that quest as off limits for the purposes of this paper. Nor does he intend to raise questions about the validity of the doctrine. We shall aim, instead, toward concentrating on the two aspects of Qoheleth's wisdom mentioned above, because they convey meaningful truth to those who have come after him under the sun.

Resurrection in the Old Testament Outside Qoheleth

The Old Testament, as has been pointed out many times, typically thought of a form of survival in Sheol, a sort of non-life existence. Possibly this concept rested on the common-sense observation that after the heart stops beating, the body remains and influences of the personality also persist. However that may be, the idea of a sort of shadow survival in Sheol is far removed from the later concept of a general resurrection from the dead.

There are, to be sure, in some Psalms, especially 16 and 71, what might deserve the description "intimations of immortality."[1] While such passages show the kind of faith that gave to belief in resurrection its deepest meaning, they fall far short of formulating it. They are at most faint rays of light before the dawn.[2]

When we talk about belief in resurrection, what is in mind is the full-blown conviction that the dead will be raised. We must observe the distinction between real belief that this will happen and the mere imaginative idea of the dead coming back to life. Just as men imagined that humans could fly long before the idea became a reality, so the thought of a return from the grave was abroad much earlier than general acceptance of it as a future event.

For instance, the Israelites wrote poetically of a figurative sort of resurrection when they pictured sickness or distress as descending to Sheol or experiencing death (Pss 88; 18: 4, 5; 116: 3; 143: 7) and correspondingly viewed deliverance as being redeemed from the pit, or place of death (Pss 116: 8; 103: 4; 30: 3; Job 33: 30; Jon 2: 7). This feature of the Hebrew poetic vocabulary has received much attention, and needs only to be noted here.[3]

The book of Job goes beyond the psalmists, in vividness and suggestiveness. In a passage reminiscent of the realistic pessimism of Qoheleth, Job's mind dwells on the irresistible and arbitrary power of God which summarily topples the plans of short-lived man. Despair drives Job to fantasy, and he calls on God to hide him temporarily from his anger in Sheol, that place of no return, and then to remember him and release him:

If a man dies
can he live again?
I would wait out all the time of my enlistment
until my replacement should come.
You would call
and I would answer;
you would yearn
for the one whom your hands have made. (Job 14: 14 f)

But Job quickly moves from this breathtaking thought, so tentatively expressed that one hesitates to call it a hope, back to the older view of the finality of death. As the book continues, he demands, and at last receives, answer and vindication from God in this life before dying an old man and full of days (Job 42: 17).

We have in the book of Ezekiel an allegory that describes a mass resurrection with striking profusion of detail. The passage (Ezek 37: 1–14) provides the basis for the Negro spiritual "Dry Bones," which, with a literalness entirely in keeping with Ezekiel, musically tells of the rearticulation of the skeletons bone by bone from foot to head. Of course this still lies in the realm of symbolism. Ezekiel was really predicting restoration of the nation from exile in Babylon to new life in Palestine, the homeland.[4]

Less prolix and also less obviously allegorical is the reference to a resurrection of the people in Is 26: 19:

Your dead ones will live,
their corpses will rise
—awake and rejoice
O sleepers in the dust—
for your dew
is a dew of purest light,
and earth
will bring forth alive
those reposing there.

The dating of Is 24–27 remains uncertain. Clear indications are simply lacking, and nothing is gained by being dogmatic. In any case, we can see from the context that while the language specifically refers to resurrection, there is no real clue as to whether it is meant to be understood literally. Fortunately, a decision on this point is not necessary for the purpose of this paper. We need only observe that the language of resurrection is here, without resolving its ambiguity.

While it is not a certainty that the passage in Isaiah just quoted poetically refers to a national reawakening, there is a fantasy in Jeremiah that unmistakably describes the Babylonian exile:

Nebuchadrezzar, king of Babylon,
has devoured me,
he has finished me off,
he has held me up like an empty dish;
he has swallowed me up
like a sea monster;
he has filled his belly
with my choice parts;
he has thrust me out. (Jer 51: 34)

And I [Yahweh] will see to Bel in Babylon
and draw forth from his mouth
what he has swallowed. (Jer 51: 44)

Here Hebrew imagination has depicted the dismal fate of exile in quite different terms from the allegory of the dry bones in Ezekiel. Inventiveness such as this cautions us against assuming too easily that the language of resurrection, as in Is 26: 19, always had a literal intent.

To be sure, instances of the resurrection of individuals do occur in the Old Testament, as in the New (Heb 11: 35). Both Elijah (1 Kings 17: 17–24) and Elisha (2 Kings 4: 17–37) restored the dead to life. But these miracles did not confer immortality. Those who had been raised would at some time go to Sheol, as all men were expected to do.

Only one passage in the Old Testament—Dan 12: 2—presents the resurrection hope in a prediction of an actual event connected with a coming eschatological deliverance of the chosen people. Dating from about 167 B.C., this prophecy came from one of those pious Jews who resisted to the death the ruthless attempt of their Hellenistic Syrian ruler Antiochus IV (175–163 B.C.), to stamp out Judaism in Judah. Possibly the pressure of extreme crisis impelled faith to lay hold of belief in a real, large-scale resurrection of the dead. It fell short of envisaging a universal resurrection of all mankind. Fortunately for us, the writer of Daniel was quite explicit on this point. He expected some to arise to everlasting life (*ḥayye ʾolam*), while others would arise to everlasting reproach and repugnance.

The writer of Daniel looked beyond the well-known individual exceptions to the rule of death that appear in the Old Testament to a return of many at the end of present history. Yet his brief statement, specific as it was, left room for later diverging ideas to develop. It lacked the authority of dogma.

Qoheleth probably originated before the Maccabean revolt of about 168 B.C. and the book of Daniel.[5] Because the written evidence from the Old Testament for views on resurrection or immortality is so tenuous, we cannot identify the form in which Qoheleth encountered them. However, he had a clear perspective on the subject of death and survival. To this, the first of the two subjects of this paper, we now turn.

Qoheleth on Life After Death

With respect to life after death, Qoheleth's thinking was an interaction between ideas current in his day and his own empirical observations and deductions. His realistic bent of mind led him to accept death as inevitable and final. However, he denied neither God's existence nor action, holding that man's wisdom is just great enough to realize its own limits, which fall far short of fathoming God's purposes. Qoheleth derided any trust in some form of survival of the individual in society, for instance as a memory among the living. He also abstained from trying to see what may lie beyond the grave, asking, characteristically, Who knows?

Inevitability of Death

Desire for eternal life permeated the ancient world long before the emergence of the Hebrew nation. Its presence in Israel is evident from the J account in Gen 3, the Hebrew version of the denial of immortality to man:

> And the Lord God said,
> "See, man has become like one of us,
> knowing good and evil.
> And now, lest he reach out his hand
> and take also from the tree of life
> and eat
> and live forever" (*le olam*)—
> So the Lord God sent him
> out of the garden of Eden. (Gen 3: 22, 23a)

While the writer of this passage implicitly recognized the desire of men for eternal life, and presents the tantalizing thought that it once lay within man's grasp, he categorically ruled out the possibility forever. This fits with the preceding account in Genesis of the Lord's judgment that man must return to the dust from whence he had come (Gen 3: 19).

Qoheleth agreed fully with this tradition. In the following passage, he reaffirms that man's destiny is to return to dust:

> For the lot of the sons of men
> and the lot of the animal
> are the same;
> as one dies, so does the other.
> And they all have the same spirit;
> so the superiority that man has over the animal
> is nothing—
> it is all a delusion.
> They are all headed for the same place;

they all came from the dust
and they all return to the dust. (Eccles 3: 19 f)

Of course Qoheleth's observation is hardly original. But the acceptance of death colored his attitude toward life. And his matter-of-fact attitude led him to avoid speculations about the fate of the dead, as we shall see.

SHEOL

Qoheleth used the word "Sheol" just as it appears throughout the Old Testament, to refer to the shadowy nether realm of the dead:

Take part energetically
in everything that you find to do.
For there is no activity
  no thinking
  no knowledge
  no wisdom
in Sheol,
and that is where you are going. (Eccles 9: 10)

He mentions Sheol only this once, and in a completely negative way. With reference to the fate of all men and of animals, he seems to employ a substitute phrase in two other passages (with identical Hebrew wording) which may be translated "they are all headed for the same place" (3: 20; 6: 6). Apparently Qoheleth had no interest in Sheol, and since he was a keen observer and certainly knew of the colorful traditions concerning it (see, for examples, 1 Sam 28; Is 14: 9–20; Ezek 31, 32), he seems to have ignored it intentionally. It was simply the state of death, empty of all the positive qualities which make up life. One might also say that, beyond the fact that Sheol was the place of the dead, Qoheleth's observations took him little farther than believing that there is no knowledge there (9: 10).

RESIDUAL INDIVIDUAL IMMORTALITY ON EARTH

According to popular thinking, often expressed in Jewish writings (Prov 10: 7; 13: 22; Job 18: 15–19; Wis 4: 1; Sir 30: 2–6; 37: 26; 39: 9–11; 40: 19; 41: 13; 44: 8–15), the righteous and wise individual enjoys a sort of survival on this earth in what he leaves behind at death, especially his name and his family. Qoheleth shot this hope full of holes, using his own observations for ammunition:

And I saw that nothing is better
than that man should enjoy his activity
for that is his inheritance;

for who can enable him to see
how things will be after him? (Eccles 3: 22)

For the remembrance of neither the wise man nor the fool
is perpetual.
because in the days that follow them
all will be forgotten,
and so the poor wise man
perishes along with the fool. (Eccles 2: 16)

With extensive illustrations and with terse sayings, Qoheleth repeatedly drove home his point (6: 12; 7: 14; 9: 5). No one can control what happens after his death. Let no one comfort himself with the thought that his family will persist, his wealth endure, or his plans mature. Death barricades the future against all human wishes and desires.

WHAT HAPPENS TO THE INDIVIDUAL?

Just as death seals off knowledge of the future on earth from those whom it takes away, so it prevents those on earth from seeing what befalls those who have died:

Who knows whether the spirit of the sons of men
rises upward on high
while the spirit of the animal
descends downward to the earth? (Eccles 3: 21)

This sounds much as if Qoheleth were arguing against some sort of theory of survival. We have seen that statements on this subject in the Old Testament are few and uncertain, and that Dan 12: 2, dating from about 167 B.C., offers the first unmistakable example of resurrection faith. If he was indeed refuting a current idea, Qoheleth does not bother to describe it.

Qoheleth went just as far as the facts allowed. He had learned from his own observation that men and animals alike undergo death and physical dissolution. But what about the nonmaterial factor, the spirit? This, he says, remains a question. However, Qoheleth did accept that man is a working combination of an earthly element—dust—and an enlivening power—the spirit.

When the Lord delivered judgment on man in Gen 3: 19, he condemned him to return to the dust. Nothing was said about the spirit in man.[6] The silence about the spirit may well be intentional, although one should not make too much of the fact that it is passed over in this passage. However, a later passage, the difficult Gen 6: 3, does deal with the matter of the spirit:

And the Lord said
"My spirit shall not abide[7]
in man forever,
inasmuch as he is flesh;
so his days shall be
one hundred and twenty years."

Surely it is significant that in this case as well as in Eccles 3: 21 the only clear fact is that man shall not keep the spirit forever. No clue indicates what happens to the spirit, except that when the Lord calls it "my spirit" here the inference seems to be that he will reclaim it.

The later passage in which Qoheleth speaks of the dissolution of man at death needs to be understood in the light of Genesis:

And the dust returns
to the earth as it was before,
and the spirit returns
to God, who gave it. (Eccles 12: 7)

Here he poetically describes man's death in terms of the separation into dust, and spirit, the divine vital force. That is a remarkably open-ended description, and, in the light of Qoheleth's respect for facts and his refusal to speculate, we may accept it as expressing Qoheleth's realistic agnosticism about what happens at, and after, death. He stuck with the evidence. The Lord gives the spirit, and the Lord takes it away. Qoheleth left the matter where it belongs: in the hands of the Lord.

THE LIMITS OF KNOWLEDGE

Qoheleth understood very well that the human mind can form concepts opposed to reality or beyond testing. His own experience taught him that life is full of mystery, and that man asks questions without being able to understand the answers. One of his most important insights is that wisdom recognizes the human mind's limitations as well as its potential:

When I bent my mind to the knowledge of wisdom
and the observation of the pursuits
which are carried on in the earth
—for indeed day and night
His eyes do not shut in sleep—
then I observed all the activity of God,
and saw that man is not able
to grasp the activity
which goes on under the sun;
however man works at investigating it,
he cannot comprehend it. (Eccles 8: 16, 17)

Qoheleth could utter the words "all the activity of God," but he found it simply impossible to grasp the manifold details included in that divine activity. It is like seeing the stars at night or looking at the sands of the sea and trying to count them—a feat beyond the power of man, though not of God (Ps 147: 4; Jer. 33: 22)

Not only are God's actions too vast in number to be grasped by the human mind, their nature in itself is baffling.

> Just as you do not understand
> how the spirit comes into the bones
> in the pregnant womb,
> so you do not understand
> the activities of God,
> who is active in all things. (Eccles 11: 5)

God brings life in the womb by his spirit, and he, in some way or other, takes it at death (Eccles 12: 7). But both the beginning and the end of human existence lie veiled in the secrecy of God's incomprehensible wisdom.

This, then, is the first perspective from Qoheleth. Within the context of a faith in God, he accepted the fact of death as the end of life, a step into the unknown. Both the giving of life and the ending of life are part of the manifold activity of God which extends beyond the power of man's mind to probe.

QOHELETH'S PERSPECTIVE AS SEEN IN THE THOUGHT OF PAUL AND JESUS

Both the early Christian Church and pharisaic Judaism made the resurrection a pivotal article of faith.[8] In this they took a step from which Qoheleth held back. But while the concept of the resurrection of, or from, the dead won acceptance, those who held it differed widely on the details of the event. And since it lies in the future, the resurrection must always be an object of faith rather than of sight.

To apply the perspective of Qoheleth's realism to resurrection faith means to accept the concept but to make no claim of knowledge about the various specific features of that momentous event that will attend it when it happens. These are undisclosed mysteries. We turn now to see how, according to the record of the New Testament, Paul and Jesus shared the wisdom of Qoheleth in this respect.

Paul argued vehemently for the factuality of the resurrection, particularly because for him the resurrection of Christ had become of crucial importance. However he pragmatically relied on the evidence, passed on to him through tradition, that Christ had first appeared to Peter, to the twelve, to more than five hundred believers, to James, and to "all the apostles." Furthermore, his own life had undergone a radical transformation because he himself had been confronted by the risen Lord—an experience which Acts tells three times (9: 1–9; 22: 6–11; 26: 12–20). Paul places the resurrection of Christ, attested by the eyewitnesses mentioned above, including himself, at the beginning of his long chapter on resurrection, 1 Cor 15. In the following passage, he closely links the resurrection of the dead, the resurrection of Christ, and salvation:

> If Christ is proclaimed to have risen from the dead,
> how can some among you say
> that there is no resurrection of the dead?
> If, indeed, there is no resurrection of the dead,
> Christ was not raised either.
> But if Christ was not raised,
> then our proclamation is void of truth
> as is our faith.
>
> We are then also found to be false witnesses of God,
> because we have testified about God
> that he raised Christ,
> whom he did not raise
> if in fact the dead are not raised.
>
> But if Christ was not raised,
> your faith is worthless;
> you are still saddled with your sins.
> It also follows that those who fell asleep in Christ
> have perished.
>
> If our hope in Christ is limited to just this life,
> we are the most pitiful men in the world. (1 Cor 15: 12–19)

Paul could hardly have been more radical about the importance of the resurrection. He did not, however, specify in full the ingredients that will constitute the event. In response to objections to the idea of a resurrection of the physical body, he did say that those who are raised will be changed and will have spiritual bodies instead of their present ones:

> But some one will say,
> "The dead will be raised? Just how?
> With what sort of bodies
> will they come back?"
>
> You simpleton, what you sow
> will not germinate
> unless it dies first.
> And what you sow—

well, it is not the bodily form
that it will have in the future
at the time when you sow it,
but a bare grain—
whether it happens to be wheat
or one of the others.

But God decides what
bodily form to give it,
and for each of the seeds
there is its own particular body. (1 Cor 15: 35–38)

Applying this to the case of the human body, Paul went on to say:

It is sown a physical body,
it is raised a spiritual body;
if there is a physical body
there is a spiritual one too. (1 Cor 15: 44)

Of the resurrection bodies, Paul said that they will be incorruptible, glorious, strong, and immortal (1 Cor 15: 42 f). Yet by means of the analogy between the change in appearance of the plant from the seed that was sown and the change in the body that is to be raised from our present ones, the apostle strongly suggests that God alone knows just what the new, changed spiritual bodies will be like. We can know that we will be changed. We know that we must pass through death to that change. But beyond the general terms just cited, Paul does not reveal the how or what of the change. That is up to God. At this point, Paul has the same realistic perspective that Qoheleth had. He did not go beyond the evidence, or his trust in the power of God, for the sake of answering questions which arose from curiosity or doubt.

Nor, on the evidence of the Gospels, did Jesus himself disclose information about the resurrection or conditions pertaining to it, beyond the famous saying that in the resurrection there is neither marrying nor being married (Mk 12: 25). Even in this case, Jesus was not discoursing to his disciples on the subject of resurrection, but gave his statement as an answer to the Sadducees who were arguing that there is no resurrection. When they proposed the absurd situation of a woman who had lived as wife with seven brothers in succession, and asked whose wife she would be in the resurrection (Mk 12: 18–23), Jesus disposed of their trick question without going into lengthy teaching about the subject. The fact that the most explicit sayings from Paul and Jesus on resurrection came as answers to objections to belief in the resurrection deserves our notice. Neither of the two was, as far as our evidence goes, concerned with delving into the secrets of the beyond. They believed in the resurrection but trusted in the power of God rather than an explanation tailored to human specifications.

The parable of the rich man and Lazarus (Lk 16: 19–31) may seem on the surface to offer new revelation of the intermediate state between death and the general resurrection. But deeper reflection shows that it is not so. Jesus, as he usually did in his teaching, was employing familiar ideas of his time[9] to convey teaching to those who heard him about their life on earth before death. The conclusion to the teaching seems to warn us away from seeking support for resurrection faith by direct revelation. For when the rich man asks that Lazarus go back to earth to warn the rich man's brothers, he is told that if his brothers will not believe on the strength of the witness of Moses and the prophets, they will not believe even if one comes back from the dead.

The very paucity of Jesus' teaching about the life hereafter left a vacuum which inevitably attracted curiosity and led to the introduction of strange ideas. The statement in Acts 1: 3 that Jesus appeared to the disciples for forty days after the crucifixion, speaking to them about the kingdom of God, provided an opportunity for later writers to supply their own versions of what Jesus said during that period. A number of apocryphal works, often gnostic in tendency, offer accounts of private revelations attributed to Jesus. Their divergence from the New Testament tradition and from each other betrays their inauthenticity.[10]

The early Church, then, faced the future with a firm faith in the resurrection, but without detailed information from either Jesus or Paul on the matter. Many questions were unanswered. Here is where Qoheleth's pragmatic realism seems to have been echoed by both Jesus and Paul. While they were not agnostic about the resurrection, as Qoheleth had been, they nevertheless rested their faith on the power of God rather than on explanations which by the very nature of the case must always be speculative.

The Second Perspective: God Desires Man to Find the Goodness of Life Now

Although Qoheleth had no hope for life beyond the grave, he did find positive values to be a present potential. With the same clear-eyed realism that he applied to theories of survival, he sifted the axioms and values that he perceived men guiding themselves by. He concluded that in their folly men overcapitalize the worth of riches, fame, and pleasure. They strive to heap up, to hold on to, to control, and thereby to find satisfaction in what they conceive to be the good things of life. All this he labeled vanity, or emptiness (NEB), or futility (Berkeley version), or vapor (Scott, in *Anchor Bible*)

(2: 1–11; 18–23; 4: 7, 8; 5: 10, 11, 13–17; 6: 1–7, 11, 12; 8: 9, 11; 9: 1–3, 11, 12).[11] Life yields its treasures only to those who in wisdom accept and use with enjoyment what God gives them, ever conscious that the quality of life depends on how it is lived:

> I know that there is nothing better
> than to be joyful
> and get the most out of life.
> Whenever a man eats and drinks
> and gets satisfaction from all his toil
> it is a gift from God. (Eccles 3: 12 f)
>
> Go ahead and eat your bread with pleasure
> and drink your wine with gladness;
> since before you ever do them
> God looks with favor
> on these activities of yours. (Eccles 9: 7)
>
> Experience life to the full
> with the wife whom you love
> all the days of your fleeting life
> which he has given you under the sun;
> for that is your destined reward from life
> and from the toil in which you engage
> under the sun. (Eccles 9: 9)[12]

Qoheleth was advocating neither seeking pleasure for its own sake nor trying to satisfy oneself with physical or material things. His own experiments had shown him that this is folly (2: 1–11). Here he gives his mature view that the wise man balances active participation in life with an appreciation of its immediately apprehended, and transitory, goodness. Qoheleth, it seems, had learned to accommodate himself to the limits of the range of action and time allotted him by God, within which he found the best advice to be, "Take part energetically in everything you find to do" (9: 10). Echoes of this perspective are heard in the New Testament.

Qoheleth's Perspective Seen in the New Testament

The New Testament reflects eager expectancy of the day of the Lord. Writer after writer reminds his audience that the eschaton looms on the horizon of history.[13] While the eschatological passages of the New Testament fail to agree on the precise nature and sequence of all the components connected with the one great event—the eschaton—they apparently expected that Christ would return and gather his own, both those then still living and those who had died (1 Cor 15: 23, 24, 51, 52; 1 Thess 4: 13–17; Rev 20:

4; Mk 13: 26, 27; Acts 1: 11). The ordinary course of history would be interrupted by divine intervention, and a new order would begin (2 Pet 3: 10–13 f).

In view of the anticipated shortness of time left before the eschaton, and the futility of human efforts to perpetuate business as usual in the face of the coming radical change, what did the present have to offer the Christian of the first century? Passing years quickly brought about positive answers to that question.

THE RISEN CHRIST DWELLS IN HIS BELIEVERS

Without ever giving up hope for the future great day of the Lord, the New Testament points to an immediate fellowship with Christ here and now:

> For where two or three
> come together
> invoking my name
> I am there
> among them. (Mt 18: 20)

The same thought occurs at the end of the first Gospel:

> Go then and make disciples
> of all the nations . . .
> And hear this!
> I am with you
> through all the days
> until the end of the world. (Mt 28: 19, 20)

The gospel of John places in the context of the discourse at the Last Supper Christ's assurance that after his death he will return to his disciples while they are still on earth:

> I will not abandon you
> like orphans;
> I will come to you.
> Just a little while longer
> and the world will see me no more,
> but you will see me
> because I am alive
> and you will be alive.
> At that time you will realize
> that I am in my father
> and you are in me
> and I am in you . . .
> He who loves me

will be loved by my father,
and I will love him
and show myself to him. (Jn 14: 18–21)

BELIEVERS NOW ENJOY FRUITS OF THE SPIRIT

So evident is this fact to the writers of the New Testament that it is mentioned here briefly because proof is hardly necessary. It has, however, great importance for our line of thought.

In Acts, the Spirit is given at baptism (Acts 2: 38) and by the laying on of hands (Acts 8: 14–17; 9: 17). Paul, who did not always keep clear the distinction between the risen Lord and the Spirit (2 Cor 3: 17; Rom 8: 2), at one point lists this inventory:

The fruit of the Spirit is: love, joy, peace,
patience, generosity, goodness,
faith, humility, self-control. (Gal 5: 22 f)

Indeed, the gifts of the Spirit proved to be something of an embarrassment of riches to the Corinthians, to whom Paul had to send rather lengthy instructions concerning the proper attitude toward them (e.g., 1 Cor 12).

A WEALTH OF SHARED RELATIONSHIPS AND POSSESSIONS OPEN TO BELIEVERS

The book of Acts reports that:

all the believers
stuck together
and shared everything;
they sold both their livestock
and their goods
and made distribution
to each according to his need. (Acts 2: 44, 45)[14]

This practice of togetherness and sharing evidently lies back of a striking speech of Jesus to Peter in the gospel of Mark. After Peter had pointed out that the disciples had given up everything to follow him, Jesus replied:

There is no one who has left home
or brothers or sisters
or mother or father or children
or fields
on account of me and the gospel
without getting back
a hundred times over

in this present time
homes
and brothers and sisters
and mothers and children
and fields
—with persecutions—
and in the world to come,
eternal life. (Mk 10: 29 f)

While much more could be said on the subject of what was immediately available to Christians in the interim between the first and second comings of Christ, what has been adduced suffices, I hope, to make clear that what distinguished the Christian from the nonbeliever was not just resurrection faith and a future orientation connected with that faith but a very present difference in the quality of life experiences. The Christian already enjoyed fellowship with his risen Lord; he possessed, at least potentially, charismatic gifts; and he lived in a support system of family concern that included both his bodily needs and his emotional needs.

To put the situation in another way, the Christian was already living by, and participating in, the values of eternity. He did not need to wait or to deprive himself of what mattered most to him. Qualitatively, he already had eternal life (Jn 5: 24; 14: 6; 17: 3). His present relationships—with Christ, the Spirit, and the community—were, indeed, established in this worldly sphere, but partook of eternal values and were of infinite worth.

The second perspective of Qoheleth, then, reappears in the New Testament. The Christian awaiting the eschaton already lived in eternity, but in such a way that he experienced it within the limits God has drawn. He could strike a balance between engagement in present activities and his hope for the future. The need of such a perspective remains to this day.

Notes

1 See W. Eichrodt, *Theology of the Old Testament* (trans. by John Baker; Philadelphia: Westminster, 1967) II, pp. 520–22; E. Jacob, *Theology of the Old Testament* (London: Hodder and Stoughton, 1958), pp. 308 f).

2 M. Dahood finds reflection of belief in resurrection and immortality in some forty Psalms, in his commentary on Psalms in the Anchor Bible. See especially his remarks in *Psalms III 101–150* (AB; New York: Doubleday, 1970), pp. xli–lii. Bruce Vawter, "Intimations of Immortality and the Old Testament," *JBL* 91 (1972) 158–71, presents a searching critique of Dahood's philological method and his conclusions. (Vawter's article appeared too late for use in the writing of this present article. It includes a valuable appreciation of the Hebrew view of life, under God, in this world.) A characteristically well-balanced discussion of the subject of what lies beyond the grave in OT thinking appears in H. H. Rowley, *The Faith of Israel* (London: SCM Press, 1956); see especially pp. 153 f and 170–75.

[3] See, for example, A. R. Johnson, *The Vitality of the Individual in the Thought of Ancient Israel* (Cardiff: University of Wales Press, 1949), pp. 94 f. Also, J. Pedersen, *Israel* (Copenhagen and London: 1926) I–II, pp. 466–70; and C. Barth, *Die Errettung vom Tode in den individuellen Klage- und Dankliedern des Alten Testaments* (Zollikon: Evangelischer Verlag, 1947), pp. 11–17.

[4] For a poetic conjunction of exile and descent into Sheol, see Is 5: 13 f.

[5] An excellent discussion of the problem of the date of the book of Ecclesiastes stands in R. Gordis, *Koheleth: The Man and His World* (New York: Bloch, 1955), pp. 63–68; for bibliography of a general nature, see R. B. Y. Scott, *Proverbs, Ecclesiastes* (AB; New York: Doubleday, 1965), pp. 207 f.

[6] The term "Sheol" does not occur in Genesis until the Joseph saga, Gen 37: 35.

[7] E. A. Speiser, in *Genesis* (AB; New York: Doubleday, 1964), p. 44, translates the Hebrew *ydwn* as "shield"; his reasons are given in an article in *JBL* 75 (1956), 126–29. This is hardly the place, nor am I expert enough, to argue cogently on the basis of linguistics; however, I cannot resist thinking that perhaps the person or persons responsible for the Hebrew text of Gen 6: 3 may also have been less than expert linguists with respect to Akkadian, and have used *ydwn* to mean "dwell" anyway. Certainly the contrast between "spirit" (*ruaḥ*) and "flesh" (*bśr*), as well as the limitation set on man's life, imply that the spirit will be withdrawn, and man will die; for the contrast of flesh and spirit, cf Is 31: 3; for the connection of spirit and life, see Gen 6: 17 (P), where God announces that he is bringing the flood "to destroy all flesh in which is the breath (*ruaḥ*) of life." A. R. Johnson, *op. cit.*, has an excellent discussion of the meanings of *ruaḥ*, pp. 26–39. On Gen. 6: 3, see also H. Gunkel, *Genesis* (7. Auflage; Göttingen: Vandenhoeck and Ruprecht, 1966), pp. 57 f, who thinks it probable that this verse refers to the spirit of life given men by God, and that God's purpose is to limit the duration of man's life to one hundred and twenty years.

[8] A. Oepke, *TWNT* I, 370; R. Gordis, *op. cit.*, pp. 33 f.

[9] See W. O. E. Oesterley, *The Gospel Parables in the Light of Their Jewish Background* (New York: Macmillan, 1936) pp. 203–11; Strack-Billerbeck, *Kommentar zum Neuen Testament aus Talmud und Midrasch* (München: Beck, 1924) II, pp. 222–33.

[10] For information about some of these writings and English translations of some of the texts, see Hennecke-Schneemelcher, *New Testament Apocrypha* (Eng. trans. ed. R. McL. Wilson; Philadelphia: Westminster, vol I, 1963; vol II, 1965) I, pp. 82–84; 243–48; 250–59; 314–31; 486–503; II, pp. 663–83.

[11] Qoheleth's pet expression *hbl* is too rich to submit to translation by a single English equivalent. W. E. Staples has written a fine article, pointed out to me by J. M. Myers, entitled "The 'Vanity' of Ecclesiastes" *JNES* 2 (1943), 95–104.

[12] Cf Eccles. 5: 18–20.

[13] Examples: "You see the day approaching" (Heb 10: 25); "The coming of the Lord is at hand" (Jas 5: 8); "See, the judge stands at the gates" (Jas 5: 9); "The end of all things is at hand" (1 Pet 4: 7); "I am coming shortly" (Rev 2: 16; 3: 11; 22: 7, 12, 20); "The kingdom of heaven (or God) is at hand" (Mt 3: 2; Mk 1: 15; Lk 10: 9, 11; cf also Rom 13: 11 f; 1 Cor 7: 29; 10: 11).

[14] Cf Acts 4: 32–5: 11; also 1 Tim 6: 17: "To those endowed with the riches of this world, direct this charge: 'don't become haughty, nor trust confidently in ephemeral wealth, but in God, who offers everything to us richly for our enjoyment.'"

Harry M. Buck
Wilson College

Worship, Idolatry, and God

O God! if I worship Thee in fear of Hell,
burn me in Hell;
and if I worship Thee in hope of Paradise,
exclude me from Paradise;
but if I worship Thee for Thine own sake,
withhold not Thine Everlasting Beauty![1]

Worship, particularly when viewed as the expression of a heart overflowing with the love of God, has been praised in virtually all religious traditions. In the Hebrew-derived traditions—Jewish, Christian, Muslim—the caveat of the Q Document is echoed again and again: "You shall worship the Lord your God, and him only shall you serve."[2] Hence there is an instinctive positive reponse to this *ṣūfī* lady's prayer with its evident sincerity. Instinctive reactions can, nonetheless, be misleading.

In the cultures in which many of us have been reared, propriety and good taste dictate that a good person will profess a belief in God, worship him regularly in church or synagogue, and lead a moral life. Of those who conform to this minimum standard, few questions are asked; those who depart from any portion of it will find little reckoned to their credit. When support for this popular notion is sought in the Bible, however, few passages appear to echo the oft-repeated injunction, "Bow the knee and become religious."

The first element of the standard may have little religious importance, as the author of the Epistle of James clearly perceived—"You believe that

The author wishes to thank Robin Roome for valuable assistance in developing this article.

God is one; you do well. Even the demons believe—and shudder" (Jas 2: 19)—suggesting that belief in God per se does not mark one as necessarily better than a demon. Throughout the Bible, faith, not simple belief, is emphasized; and faith and belief can never be equated. Faith is the opposite of unconcern, not of disbelief. Disbelief is the opposite of belief, yet faith embraces both. This point is rarely appreciated by those who, with their security slipping from them, ask, "But you do believe in God, don't you?" A bland "yes" that considers the implications of neither the term "God" nor the term "believe" reassures them; a thoughtful response, seeking more precise content for either term, frequently proves unnerving.

The third element in the series may be largely a product of community judgment, inasmuch as "moral" must be understood at least in terms of its etymology—from *mos, moris* ("manner, custom, habit"). So-called "moral" behavior can hide a heart of stone, and the prophets of Israel habitually directed their barbs not against the ungodly but against the practitioners of conventional religion and morality (cf Amos 4: 1–6; 5: 21–27; Jer 7). The middle third of the conventional description, however, is the focus of this paper: the worship of God and its correlate, the prohibition of the worship of idols.

Professor Myers, to whom this volume of essays is being offered, delighted in challenging many current views. Shibboleth after shibboleth came under his prophetic scrutiny. This essay therefore attempts to apply some of the same rigor—although not necessarily at all the same beliefs—to the criticism of popular views of belief, worship, and morality as the essence of man's duty before the Almighty.

Worship: Value Structure and Deference

Current English usage tends to equate worship with an attitude or feeling. Friedrich Schleiermacher's speech on "The Nature of Religion" turned on "perception, feeling and activity,"[3] and his stress on the internal nature of the religious experience has profoundly influenced our religious legacy. Dictionary definitions of the word "worship" stress such synonyms as "honor," "intense love," "admiration," and the like, linking it with words like "awe" and "adoration." Its etymology, however, is via Middle English *worschip*, from Anglo-Saxon *weorthscipe*, clearly expressing a value judgment. Any object of worship must therefore appear higher on an individual's scale of values than some object that is not worshiped. Worship then implies a commitment to what is regarded as of highest value. In this sense, everyone worships if he has ever taken the trouble to reject a lower value for a higher one. Whether it accords with any conventional definition or not, whatever a person will sacrifice all other values for is his God.

Thus it would seem appropriate to urge that only what is truly God be worshiped and, as the *ṣūfī* lady sang, for his own sake, not for fear of hell or for hope of paradise; for either of these would make hell or pardise of greater "worth" than God, and hence the object of worship. The religious question, according to H. N. Wieman, then emerges: "What ultimate commitment will deliver me from the false and superficial level of life and enable me to live myself out to the full with whatever struggle and suffering and courage and ecstasy this may involve?" But that such commitment implies anything like a conventional "belief in God" was refuted by Wieman, who went on to say: "The word 'God' is irrelevant to the religious problem *unless* the word is used to refer to *whatever in truth* operates to save man from evil and to the greater good *no matter how much this operating reality may differ from all traditional beliefs about it.*"[4] Hence, the highest value one knows is his object of worship, and if it is a matter of ultimate concern, that object is his god.[5]

BODILY POSTURE

To understand worship either as an emotional state or as commitment to a value structure reflects an interiorization and modernization never implicit in ancient forms, despite the Anglo-Saxon derived meaning of the word in English. Outside the Anglo-Saxon tradition, a different usage appears. In Zen Buddhism, for example, the normal word corresponding to "worship" is a verb meaning simply "to sit." In Hindu meditative practices, the word used means "to sit down to." When we divorce our thinking from the interiorization that characterizes much of modern religious thought, worship shows itself as something done far more than as something felt, thought, or valued. When, for example, a Japanese worshiper presents himself before a Shinto shrine, he first washes his hands in a prescribed manner and then stands before the shrine's closed doors, bowing his head and clapping his hands. What does it stand for? "Clap! Clap!" That's what it stands for; that's what it is.

The "service" of worship is again something done, typically as a dramatic representation of an archetypal event, presented as a perpetual *da capo* to re-present the saving event being recalled.[6] The service is neither mere history nor mere drama; it is a dramatic remembrance, recollection, or reminder (*anamnesis*). Costume and mask play their roles, abstracting the officiant so that only "the minister" or "the priest" remains. As the assigned roles of the liturgy are acted out, the personalities of the worshiper and the officiant are sublimated to the powers they represent.

In the Hebrew scriptures, which are the special concern of this essay, only three words are commonly rendered into English as "worship." In connection with the "worship" of the Queen of Heaven, Jeremiah (44: 19) uses *'āṣaḇ* ("pained, grieved, thwarted," by extension "to worship"), but this may be a spurious reading, and it is omitted in the RSV. In Daniel, the word is typically *sāḡaḏ*, with *l*[e] ("fall down," "prostrate"). But the most important term is *šoḥoh* ("bow down"), implying a usage similar to the essential meaning of "worship" in other Eastern spiritual systems. *Šoḥoh* is something done, whether felt or not. It need not be used with an object.

> When Gideon heard the telling of the dream and its interpretation [i.e., of the tent destroyed by the barley cake], he worshiped. (Judg 7: 15)
>
> [After receiving news of the destruction of his family] Job arose, and rent his robe, and shaved his head, and fell on the ground, and worshiped. (Job 1: 20)
>
> And Moses made haste to bow his head toward the earth, and worshiped. (Ex 34: 8)
>
> The whole assembly worshiped. . . . And they sang praises with gladness, and they bowed down and worshiped. (2 Chron 29: 28, 30)

When the word does have specific reference, God or YHWH is not normally the object, although the Second Isaiah foretells the "worship" of YHWH's suffering servant (Is 49: 7); however, the real meaning of this passage is the vision of other nations bowing low before Israel.

The act of worship (bowing) is an automatic response in the presence of power, or else it is an auspicious act performed for its own sake. After the death of David's first child by Bathsheba, following a period of fasting and intercession,

> David arose from the earth, and washed, and anointed himself, and changed his clothes; and he went into the house of YHWH, and worshiped; he then went to his own house. (2 Sam 12: 20)

When Naaman was to be cured of his leprosy, he also worshiped, without the specification of any object of the verb (2 Kings 5: 18); when a wife was finally found for Isaac, "the man bowed his head and worshiped YHWH" (Gen 24: 26—J); and when Samuel and Saul split over Saul's failure to annihilate all the Amalakites, "Saul worshiped YHWH" (1 Sam 15: 31). These last two instances would seem to negate our principles, but closer inspection shows that in both cases the construction of the Hebrew sentence is literally, "worship *toward* YHWH." The parallelism expressed in "bow the head and worship" confirms the meaning (cf Ex 4: 31; 12: 27), and the conception of worship as an important act to be pursued in its own right can be seen in such an illustration as the case of Abraham, who "said to his young man, 'Stay here with the ass; I and the lad [Isaac] will go yonder and worship'" (Gen 22: 5—E). In the temple and out of it, worship implies primarily a prostration, a bowing. Elkanah, father of Samuel, went up to the temple to worship and sacrifice (1 Sam 1: 3), and Samuel himself worshiped before YHWH in the Temple (1 Sam 1: 19, 28). The theophany to Joshua may be as instructive an incident as any. While reconnoitering Jericho before the siege, Joshua met the commander of YHWH's army in a vision, "and Joshua fell on his face to the earth, and worshiped, and said to him, 'What does my lord bid his servant?' And the commander of YHWH's army said to Joshua, 'Put off your shoes from your feet.'" (Josh 5: 14; cf Num 22: 22 and 2 Kings 6: 17.)

DEFERENCE

On the other hand, the act of worship, *šoḥoh*, may have an external reference because it is usually performed with reference to the presence of power before which man defers. When cultic worship is performed, worshiper and priest are both depersonalized, and the act itself becomes the bearer of power and the reintegrator of life:

> . . . in the cult the actual agent is not man nor the human community, but sacred Power, whether this is merely the sacred common element or a sacred will. In worship, therefore, "to do," "to act," is always sacramental. Something different and something more is done than what is actually performed: things are manipulated to which man himself is not superior; he stands *within* a sacred activity and not above this. He does not govern, that is to say, but serves.[7]

A worshiper at shrine, mosque, church, or temple may be as little aware of the nuances of theology as a native speaker cares about the fine points of grammar. Nonetheless, he feels compelled to practice his devotion in certain prescribed ways that show due deference to the object of his faith: to bow, to prostrate, to gaze, perhaps to touch, to kiss, or to share food or drink. On a sophisticated level, intellectual assent or understanding of what is being done may be expected, but the actions themselves are not so much expressions of value structures as they are the spontaneous, physical expressions of the urge to do something in the presence of power, either to submit to it or to appropriate it. Power is apprehended in many ways. Stephen did mighty works because the power of God was poured out on him (Acts 6: 8), and Peter, likewise full of the power of God, caused a lame man to walk (Acts 3: 6). By deferring before the power, the worshiper may lay claim to it. Hence, in classical Roman Catholic theology, grace is a measurable substance that can be dispensed by the Church. A benediction is not merely sweet words—nor is a malediction simply an insult—but the conveyance of power, the power of God, for good or for ill.

All these ideas are present in the Bible in some measure, and herein its universal character is revealed. But the distinctive features of the Bible appear when it is seen that these universal ideas are not controlling. Man deferring before God seeks to be either his slave or his master, for deference can be a form of control fully as much as a form of submission. Certainly the Bible contains its share of men who have attempted to be God's masters as well as those who have groveled before him, but the dominant note throughout Hebrew scriptures is the presentation of man neither as God's master nor as God's slave but as God's interpreter:

> When the prophets discovered the living God, they discovered at the same time the life of man as a free, responsible, *human* person. . . . The prophet is one who stands in God's presence, and having listened to him, speaks to man on his behalf.[8]

No Gods Before YHWH

When Muhammad proclaimed, "There is no god [*al lah*] except God [*Allah*]," he was scarcely more insistent than the Deuteronomist who phrased the first Commandment as "You shall have no other gods before me [lit. 'face' or 'presence']" (Deut 5: 7). This verse and those that follow deserve careful reading. The commandment is "You shall *have* no other gods" except YHWH, and "You shall not *make* for yourself a graven image . . ." and "you shall not *bow down* [*šoḥoh*] to them" (Deut 5: 8, 9). Significantly, the word for "worship" is bracketed with idols and not with YHWH. Also, the command concerning YHWH is a prohibition, something not to be done before his face, not a demand that something be done.

NOT TO BOW DOWN TO THEM

Hebrew scriptures say little about worshiping before God, and even less about "worshiping God," but they are unequivocal in prohibiting the worship of anything that is not God. The horror of making a gesture of obeisance to anything that is not God obsesses many biblical writers.

According to the Deuteronomist, the cardinal sin was the worship of false gods. His strictures are well known:

> If you forget YHWH your God and go after other gods and serve them and worship them, I solemnly warn you this day that you shall surely perish. (Deut 8: 19)

> Take heed lest your heart be deceived, and serve other gods and worship them. (Deut 11: 16)
>
> But if . . . you will not hear, but are drawn away to worship other gods and serve them, I declare to you this day that you shall perish. (Deut 30: 17–18)

And there is the unequivocal, ringing statement of the Decalog:

> You shall have no other gods before me [lit. "before my face"]. You shall not make for yourself a graven image, or any likeness of anything that is in heaven above, or that is on the earth beneath, or that is in the water under the earth; you shall not bow down to them or serve them; for I YHWH your God am a jealous God. . . . (Deut 5: 7–9)

Deut 17: 3 and 29: 26 also warn against serving and worshiping alien gods. Deuteronomic literature abounds in such strictures (cf 1 Kings 9: 6; 9: 9; 11: 33; 16: 31; 22: 53; and parallel material in 2 Chron 7: 19, 22; 32: 12). Even the book of Jeremiah contains an indictment that must have come originally from deuteronomic circles (Jer 16: 11).

But to what were the Deuteronomists objecting? Were they conducting a kind of celestial beauty contest, propagandizing for the worship of their favorite deity, YHWH, instead of the god Baʿal of their Canaanite neighbors? Not really. The commandment not to worship Baʿal is not equivalent to the command to worship YHWH; two entirely different frames of references are involved. From the days of Elijah, it was no longer possible for any thinking person in the mainstream of Hebrew tradition to equate YHWH with the forces of nature on which the life of the world depends. On Mount Horeb, Elijah was confronted by an earthquake, wind, and a fire, but YHWH was not in them (1 Kings 19). These mighty manifestations of nature were followed by a "still small voice," and, contrary to popular exegeses of this verse, YHWH was not in the voice either. When the phenomena of nature were silenced, Elijah became conscious of the presence of the living God—a God whose life is in no way dependent upon the world in which he works, who can be neither represented nor worshiped in any of the conventional ways common to human religions.

This scene marks the turning point in Israel's religion, a clear expression of the otherness of God. A confrontation of the living God does not call for contemplation but for hearing his voice and obeying. No wonder the deuteronomic editor saw in Elijah's experience a parallel to that of Moses, the great leader whose faithful obedience and courageous faith gave birth to the community of Israel. Moses' obedience was given a new significance by this action of Elijah. Other prophets followed. Isaiah taunts him who worships the work of his own hands (Is 2: 8), and promises that in the days of righteousness to come "men will cast forth their idols of silver and their idols of gold, which they made for themselves to worship" (Is 2: 20). Jeremiah condemns the worship of the work of one's own hands (Jer 1: 16), warning those who "go after other gods to serve and worship them" (Jer 13: 10; 25: 6; cf 22: 9). Micah sees a day when man shall no longer bow down to images (Mic 5: 13), and the Second Isaiah sets forth the ludicrous situation of a goldsmith making a god and then falling down and worshiping it (Is 46: 6).

Not only do biblical writers condemn the worship of man-made objects, including Aaron's golden calf (Ex 32: 21–35; cf also Ps 106: 19–22), special venom is reserved for the worship of heavenly objects. The fall of Samaria came about, so they said, "because they worshiped the hosts of heaven" (2 Kings 17: 16–18) and, possibly in reaction to Manasseh's worship of the hosts of heaven (2 Kings 21: 9, 21), Deuteronomy contains stern prohibitions, saying of the stars, they are "things which YHWH your God has allotted to all the peoples under the whole heaven" (Deut 4: 19). Against the worship of anything in the heavens above (cf 2 Chron 33: 3; Jer 8: 2; Ezek 8: 16), it is urged, "You shall worship no other god, for YHWH, whose name is Jealous, is a jealous God" (Ex 34: 14—J).

Deuteronomy and many other books of the Hebrew scriptures breathe a spirit of confidence, but in the face of such certainty, some questions intrude. That most of the writers whose works are preserved in the Old Testament consistently oppose idolatry, who can deny? That they understood what they were condemning, who can confidently affirm? That they really practiced what they preached, who, in the face of the evidence, can convincingly demonstrate?[9]

The first of these caveats is obvious. Deuteronomy speaks for the dominant community when it legislates:

> If a prophet arises among you, or a dreamer of dreams, and gives you a sign or a wonder, and the sign or wonder which he tells you comes to pass, and if he says, "Let us go after other gods," which you have not known, "and let us serve them," you shall not listen to the words of that prophet or that dreamer of dreams. . . . But that prophet or that dreamer of dreams shall be put to death, because he has taught rebellion against YHWH your God, who brought you out of the land of Egypt, and redeemed you out of the house of bondage. . . . (Deut 13: 1–5)

Such severe penalties may indicate widespread disregard of this principle in non-deuteronomic circles. That the Deuteronomists understood what they were condemning or that they lived consistently with their preaching is not so easy to demonstrate.

A basic question emerges: What, then, is an idol? Without raising this question to a larger frame of reference, answer is impossible. Collectively, the god-figures of the world project into a cosmic setting man's search for salvation—that is, the transformation of his existence. The salvation sought for is usually presented in the recollection (*anamnesis*) of a narrative (*Geschichte*) which depicts the life of the gods. Functionally, gods—whether in India, Greece, Canaan, or Israel—are not so much independent entities as they are projections of man's search for significance and meaning. An idol, Erich Fromm notes, "represents the object of man's central passion: the desire to return to the soil-mother, the craving for possession, power, fame, and so forth."[10] The idol, then, is the reification or objectification of our basic needs, the consecration of a portion of human power and human value.

That is to say, an idol exists in order to be worshiped because it functions precisly as the projection of a value, a *weorth.* Contrary to the too-limited perception of deuteronomic books, idols are not *things.* They are not objects that represent deities, nor are deities identical with the objects. Idols represent unifying forces around which life can be structured, and by offering a symbolic sacrifice, one is saying of the value represented by the idol, "This is worth more than that." Idols are not things, and idolatry is not belief—at least not in any simple sense. The idol is valorization of a portion of human power and of humanity's basic drives; idolatry is a means of living harmoniously with that power and exploiting it to serve human ends.

What are some of these basics? The need for food and shelter and, in most climates, clothing. The need for satisfying human relations, including meaningful sexual union. The drive for power, including accumulation of possessions and power over other people. Indeed, the list is endless, for veneration of idols is veneration of certain means of obtaining whatever is designated as the good life, including the nation-state, the flag—a totemic emblem—ideals of economics, or even particularly strong attitudes about the proper length of skirts or hair.

There are positive values associated with the worship of idols, and Old Testament writers did not always realize that they had fallen prey to the same tendencies they fought vigorously to avoid. Because they misread what they were condemning, considering the idol itself as a god, the Deuteronomist isolated himself from the thought world about him. Yet, no biblical writer could deny human nature. Man must consecrate his powers, and it may be argued that it is healthier to recognize certain basic drives and venerate them intelligently than to suppress them. "More than one hundred years ago," Richard Rubenstein writes,

> Heine warned that the rejected gods of the Teutons slumbered but had not died. When Thor awoke with his mighty hammer, there would be played out on the European scene a catastrophe which would make the French Revolution seem like child's play. We have lived through that drama. The grandeur of the Torah is that it never permitted a comparable split within the Jewish psyche. The priests of ancient Israel wisely never suffered Jahweh entirely to win his war with Baal, Astarte and Anath. That is why Jews were never Puritans, cut off from their inner life and the powers of the earth which engendered it. Paganism was transformed, but not entirely done away with in Judaism. In the redemption of the first born son . . . for example, the murderous quality of paganism was deflected, but its essential insight into the hostility between the generations was retained. . . . In the twentieth century, we have learned much concerning the futility of repression in personal matters. The Torah instinctively and intuitively understood this long ago in religious matters . . . . It understood the paradoxical truth that one can best overcome atavisms and primitivisms, in so far as they are destructive, by acknowledging their full potency and attractiveness and channeling their expression to eliminate their harm.[11]

Biblical literature, then, seems ambivalent in that in the midst of its harsh condemnation of idols, it does not entirely do away with idolatry—indeed, the Bible itself is a kind of idol—but it warns over and over against the absolutizing of a relative. This is what is meant by the prohibition against bowing down to that which is not God. "You shall *have* no other gods. . . . You shall not *make* a graven image. . . . You shall not *bow down*" to what is not an object of ultimate concern (Deut 5: 8, 9). Jewish rituals, as they were later formulated, reacted to the tragic existence man experiences as he is caught up in the swirl of the world's uncontrollable powers. By subconsciously incorporating some of the basic apprehensions of the Canaanites into their ritual, Israel expressed the deep-seated need of men to objectify their powers and consecrate them so that benefit rather than harm would result.

> It came out of disguise when least expected. In sacrificial offerings of the Temple services as well as in *kashruth*, Jews were enjoined to return the blood of the slaughtered animal to the earth before consumption of the rest of the animal was permitted. Is this not one of the oldest offerings made by man to thank and appease their cannibal Earth-mother? By offering Earth the blood, in which the soul was found, it was hoped that the rest of the animal would be permitted.[12]

In the broadest sense, some veneration of idols is inevitable. Danger strikes when the idol becomes the end of the search, and here the biblical injunction breaks through with new force. True religion will always be iconoclastic. In this regard, even the weapons of the biblical writers used to smash idols can themselves become idols if they arrest the process of denunciation of the gods.

NOT TO HAVE ANOTHER GOD

By prohibiting the worship of Ba'al, the Bible did not offer as an alternative simply a command to bow down to YHWH. Although there are prescriptions for the proper mode of making sacrificial offerings, the word "worship" (*šoḥoh*) does not appear in the priestly legislation of Leviticus or Numbers. What, then, is involved?

Worship of idols—perhaps worship itself—reifies the spiritual dimensions of man's response to reality. By objectifying a value and bowing down before it, a worshiper transfers his own passions and qualities to the object, improverishing himself to strengthen his shadow. What he worships is not even himself but the shadow of himself. Such a worship experience is stifling, limiting, and growth-inhibiting. "Man, trying to be like God," says Fromm,

> is an open system, approximating himself to God; man, submitting to idols, is a closed system, becoming a thing in himself. The idol is lifeless; God is living. The contradiction between idolatry and the recognition of God is, in the last analysis, that between the love of death and the love of life.[13]

Israel's prophets, however, were quick to see that an idolized god remains an idol. When anything is made the object of intense concern, so that it admits no rival, it becomes an idol, even if that intense concern be sanctioned in the name of YHWH or of Jesus Christ. The mere addition of such a name cannot insure that the policy sanctioned thereby is not another projection of selfish ideals. The Deuteronomist and the Chronicler recoil in horror at the report of Hiel of Bethel, who "built Jericho" and "laid its foundation at the cost of Abiram his first-born, and set up its gates at the cost of his youngest son Segub" (1 Kings 16: 34), a common practice designed to insure the security and permanence of such a construction or, at the report of the ritual slaughter of infants, to appease the hungry earth deities so that the nation can survive. Yet these activities were performed in good faith, with the best of motives, to secure compelling power for the preservation of a social order. From a phenomenological point of view, the mass sacrifice of a nation's sons on a distant battlefield in order to oppose an alien ideology considered demonic differs only in that the present slaughter is more widespread and devastating than that of the Hebrews or of the Canaanites. That it is performed in the name of God against "godless" forces means only that a shadow of the living God has been invoked as the sanction for an idolatrous worship.

The Prohibition of Idols

It is evident that the prohibition of idols in its essential and radical form includes a prohibition against idolizing God. The commands "You shall have no other gods," "you shall not make for yourself a graven image," and "you shall not bow down to them," are not convertible into "You shall have YHWH, make a graven image of him, and prostrate yourself before it. "The demand in Deut 5: 8 is negative; its obverse comes in the following chapter:

> Hear, O Israel, YHWH is our God, and YHWH only;
> and you shall *love* YHWH your God with all your heart, and
> with all your soul, and with all your might. (Deut 6: 4)[14]

The positive commandment is not to *worship* YHWH but to *love* him with the totality of one's self. The commandment continues, "You shall *fear* the Lord your God; you shall *serve* him. . . ." (Deut 6: 13).[15] Love, fear, serve—these are commanded; worship is not.

Prophetic Israel sensed the futility of placing faith in worship. The following examples are typical:

> What to me is the multitude of your sacrifices?
> says the Lord;
> I have had enough of burnt offerings of rams
> and the fat of fed beasts;
> I do not delight in the blood of bulls,
> or of lambs, or of he-goats.
> When you come to appear before me,
> who requires of you
> this trampling of my courts?
> Bring no more vain offerings. . . . (Is 1: 11–13*a*)

> Because Ephraim has multiplied altars for sinning,
> they have become to him altars for sinning. . . .
> They love sacrifice;
> they sacrifice flesh and eat it;
> but the Lord has no delight in them. (Hos 8: 11, 13)

> Come to Bethel, and transgress;
> to Gilgal, and multiply your transgression;
> bring your sacrifices every morning,
> your tithes every three days; . . .
> for so you love to do, O people of Israel,
> says the Lord God. (Amos 4: 4, 5)

> For thus says the Lord to the house of Israel:
> Seek me and live; but do not seek Bethel,
> and do not enter into Gilgal or cross over to Beersheba. (Amos 5: 4, 5)

> I hate, I despise your feasts,
> and I take no delight in your solemn assemblies.

Even though you offer me your burnt offerings and cereal offerings,
  I will not accept them
and the peace offerings of your fatted beasts
  I will not look upon.
Take away from me the noise of your songs;
  to the melody of your harps I will not listen.
But let justice roll down like waters,
  and righteousness like an ever-flowing stream. (Amos 5: 21–24)

But man did worship God, and fully as stringent as their strictures on the worship of false gods were the prophets' condemnation of false worship of the true God. To the passages cited above, we may add:

> Thus says YHWH-Sebaoth, the God of Israel: "Add your burnt offerings to your sacrifices, and eat the flesh. For in the day that I brought them out of the land of Egypt, I did not speak to your fathers or command them concerning burnt offerings and sacrifices [cf the Priestly projection of cultic demands]. But this command I gave them, "Obey my voice, and I will be your God and you shall be my people; and walk in the way that I command you." (Jer 7: 21–23)

Throughout the Hebrew scriptures, the closest construction to a command to worship YHWH can be seen in the paranetic section describing the fall of Samaria in the deuteronomic 2 Kings 17: 36, "You shall fear the Lord. . . .You shall bow yourselves (from *šoḥoh*) to him, and to him you shall sacrifice." There is also 1 Chron 16: 29:

Ascribe to the Lord the glory due his name;
  bring an offering and come before him!
Worship the Lord in holy array;
  tremble before him all the earth.

Although virtually no English translation makes this fine distinction, the Hebrew text contains the preposition *l*^{e}, and a more accurate translation would be "worship *before* YHWH" or "worship *toward* YHWH." The Chronicler parallels Ps 29: 2, "Worship the Lord in holy array" (RSV). English translations of the Psalms are misleading because it would appear that many of them use the proper name of YHWH as an object of the verb "worship." But translators tend to ignore the preposition *l*^{e}. If it were translated, Ps 96: 9 would read, "Worship before YHWH in holy array," and so with the remaining references from the Psalms:

5: 7: I will worship toward thy holy temple in the fear of thee.

22: 27: . . . all the families of the nations shall worship before him [i.e., YHWH] [following LXX] or before thee [Heb].

22: 29: [Heb 28] . . . before him [lit. "before your face"] shall bow all who go down to the dust.

45: 11:	Since he is your lord, bow to him.
86: 9:	All the nations . . . shall come and bow before thee, O Lord. . . .
95: 6:	O come, let us worship and bow down [the parallelism makes the meaning absolutely clear], let us kneel before YHWH our maker.
97: 7:	All gods bow down [worship] before him.
99: 5:	Extol YHWH our God; worship at his footstool.
99: 9:	Extol YHWH our God; worship at his holy mountain.
132: 7:	Let us worship at his footstool.
138: 2:	I bow down toward thy holy temple.

Psalm 81: 9 commands that the people shall not bow down to a foreign god.

To be sure, worshipers are commanded to bring their sacrifices to YHWH and set them before him (sometimes "before his face"; cf Lev 3: 1; 1 Kings 8: 62; Deut 12: 6–7). Yet, these acts also refer simply to a bodily action or posture. Significantly, even in those passages that condone or even command a sacrificial action, its performance at the place where YHWH's presence can be felt and his saving actions recollected is what is asked.

A striking example comes in connection with the deuteronomic directions for the celebration of the Festival of the First Fruits, an agricultural festival reinterpreted in the light of the deuteronomic Exodus theology. The worshiper was directed to take "some of the first of the fruit of the ground" to the shrine, where the priest would take the basket and "set it before the altar of YHWH your God." The one who brought the offering was then to recite the famous formula about the wandering Aramaean, whereupon he would set the gift down "before YHWH your god, and worship before YHWH your God" (Deut 26: 1–10 *et passim*). The command is literally "to set it before the face of YHWH your God and to prostrate yourself before the face of YHWH your God" (cf Is 66: 23), but even here, strictly speaking, the command is not simply: Worship YHWH. That the essential reference is to the posture of the body is confirmed in the Yahwist account of the giving of the Torah, when YHWH commanded Moses, "Come up to YHWH, you and Aaron, Nadab, and Abihu, and seventy of the elders of Israel, and worship afar off" (Ex 24: 1).

What, then, is it that YHWH desires if not worship? Included in most of the demands not to worship false gods is the prohibition against serving them as well (cf Deut 4: 19, 28; 17: 3, 28, 36; Josh 23: 7; Jer 5: 19; 11: 10; 25: 6; and others). Service is an important part of the God-man relationship, particularly when it is noted that YHWH has commanded man to serve him (cf Deut 6: 13; 10: 12; Josh 22: 5; 1 Chron 28: 9; Ps 2: 11; and others). Is "serve" identical to "worship?" Hardly, else the two terms would appear consistently in synonymous parallelism. Instead, the commandment is not to *worship* or to *serve* other gods but to *serve* YHWH.

In this context, "serve" refers to doing the will of God, obeying him in human affairs. The demand for obedience grows out of the covenant relationship, resulting from the free choice of a free God who called his people to himself. Service has nothing to do with the ritual prostration that is worship. Instead, it refers to a life style based on three principles: justice, love, and fellowship with God.

Man is set in the world in a relationship of responsible stewardship, to till the earth, not to plunder it (Gen 2: 15), and as the sense of the free but interdependent relationship between man and God grows throughout the history of Hebrew religion, the demands laid on man are more and more those that deal with his whole life style, his relations to the world in which he has been set and to the persons with whom he must live. The act of obeisance is irrelevant because man is not God's slave. The magic of sacrifice is likewise abhorrent because man cannot be God's master. In biblical—especially prophetic—thought, man is God's interpreter, responsible with him for the earth and its inhabitants.

What Does the Lord Require?

Attention has focused on the Torah commandments in Deut 4 and 5, but more prominent in the liturgy of Judaism is a passage from Micah:

> . . . what does the Lord require of you
> but to do justice, and to love kindness (mercy),
> and to walk humbly with your God? (Mic 6: 8)

To *do*, to *love*, to *walk*. These words are important and so are their objects: *justice* and *mercy*.

The primary requirement is to "do justice" (Heb *mîšpāṭ*), a total ethical demand requiring a total commitment to truth. The covenant with YHWH does not maintain itself, nor can it be influenced, by any amount of prostrations; it can be maintained only by *mîšpāṭ*. *Mîšpāṭ* is not simple obedience but a quality of genuineness and authenticity in all human relationships. Throughout the history of the covenant, the priests were charged with teaching *mîšpāṭ*. Finally, the Servant of Second Isaiah was glorified because of his ability to give himself on behalf of others and thus establish *mîšpāṭ* in the earth.

In addition to doing justice, man is commanded to love mercy (*ḥeseḏ*). This word seems particularly at home in the prophecies of Hosea, where it is the quality of a loving relationship between man and God. Both *ḥesed* and *mîšpāṭ* are necessary to a genuine relationship with God, and this is what he demands. This commandment is to love mercy, not simply to love God.

Then, instead of commanding man to bow low, prostrate himself before God, Micah urges, "Walk humbly with your God." This humility has its own dignity. The life style based on justice, love, and fellowship demands that man "let justice roll down like waters, and righteousness like an overflowing stream" (Amos 5: 24). To love mercy includes the demand of love: to love your neighbor as yourself (Lev 19: 18, cf Mk 12: 31 and parallels). A man will act with *mîšpāṭ* if motivated by *ḥesed*. He can then walk with God, a relation which is both the source and the result of the first two of Micah's requirements. Nothing more is necessary.

NOTES

[1] Prayer of Rābi'a, a woman *ṣūfī* (Muslim mystic) in A.D. 801 (185 A.H.), quoted in A. J. Arberry, *Sufism* (London: George Allen & Unwin, 1950), p. 42.

[2] Mt 4: 10 = Lk 4: 8. However, it is not written, "You shall worship . . ." as Q has stated the case, but, "You shall fear the LORD your God; you shall serve him, and swear by his name" (Deut 6: 13). "Worship" is substituted for "fear," and "only" is added after "him" in the Temptation Narrative.

[3] Cf Friedrich Schleiermacher, *On Religion: Speeches to Its Cultured Despisers* (available as a Harper Torchbook, TB 36, New York: Harper and Brothers, 1958). Schleiermacher, whose *Speeches* appeared in 1799, marked a turning point in Protestant theology, perhaps even the beginning of "modern theology."

[4] Henry Nelson Wieman, *Man's Ultimate Commitment* (Carbondale: Southern Illinois University Press, 1958), pp. 11–12.

[5] Cf Paul Tillich, *Biblical Religion and the Search for Ultimate Reality* (Chicago: University of Chicago Press, 1955).

[6] Cf G. van der Leeuw, *Religion in Essence and Manifestation* (London: George Allen & Unwin, 1938), ch. 53.

[7] *Ibid.*, 53, 1.

[8] Harry M. Buck, *People of the Lord: The History, Scriptures, and Faith of Ancient Israel* (New York: The Macmillan Company, 1966), p. 322.

[9] Yehezkiel Kaufmann, "The Bible and Mythological Polytheism," *JBL* LXX/3 (September, 1951), 135–48, develops a similar position.

[10] Erich Fromm, *You Shall Be as Gods* (New York: Holt, Rinehart and Winston, 1966), p. 43.

[11] Richard Rubenstein, "The Meaning of Torah in Contemporary Jewish Theology," *JBR*, XXXII/2 (April, 1964), 121–22.

[12] *Ibid.*, p. 123.

[13] *Op. cit.*, p. 44.

[14] RSV marginal trans., alt.

[15] Emphasis added. Cf the use made of this passage in Lk 4: 8. The additional commandment, "swear by his name," has been omitted from this quotation as its reference is again negative: not to swear by the name of an idol.

Edward F. Campbell, Jr.
McCormick Theological Seminary

The Hebrew Short Story: A Study of Ruth

For a Hebrew literary production of a mere four chapters and eighty-five verses, the state of whose text is quite sound and the vocabulary of which is fairly simple, the book of Ruth nevertheless contains a striking set of engrossing problems. While accorded relatively little space in studies of Old Testament theology or in the comprehensive literary introductions, it has called forth a volume of special study which appears disproportionate to its importance. As a part of the Old Testament canon, it is in some ways unique; like a lost maverick, it wanders around in the canonical order of the Old Testament looking for its proper niche, whether after Judges, or at the beginning of the Kethubim, or in any one of the first six positions in that grouping, or even in the tenth position of the eleven. No consensus has been reached as to its date of composition or, indeed, as to whether one should properly speak of a single date of composition. Now that the popular handbooks have rather commonly hit upon the post-exilic period, three prestigious German commentaries have appeared recently (Hertzberg, Gerleman, and Rudolph)[1] all of which place it in the pre-exilic period. On another front, there is a broad range of disagreement concerning the historical value of the data it presents, and a veritable mare's nest of criteria, both valid and invalid, has been assembled which claim to pertain to both date and authenticity. To add to the catalog, one notes the oft-cited observation that, set, as it claims to be, in the period of the Judges, it displays a tranquillity of scene which contrasts with the turbulence described in the book of Judges. Then again, it is noted that the proper names in the narrative can be shown to be genuinely Israelite and many pre-Israelite, but the question remains whether the story now employs them out of deference to historical tradition or in some clever allegorical sense.

When it comes to the content of the story, a new crop of queries arises: Why do the legal affairs, so vitally and carefully portrayed in the book, not accord more directly with laws and customs described in the Deuteronomic and Holiness codes? Why, if Naomi seems so specifically to understand the principle of levirate marriage (as her words in 1: 11–12 indicate), does she take so long to hit upon the thought of a possible marriage for Ruth in Bethlehem? And then, how does the story want us to understand what is portrayed at the threshing floor? What is the connection, then, between the law of levirate marriage and the law of land redemption? How many different senses of the term *gô'ēl/g^{e}'ullah* are there in the narrative after all? Where, by the way, did Naomi come by the field she now wishes to sell at the beginning of chapter 4? There has been no previous mention of it, and one might be led to wonder why the two widows are so desperately poor if Naomi holds title to some land. Should Ruth have to glean elsewhere in that case? Where did Boaz learn about Naomi's plan to sell the field so as to be able to use it as the "counter in the game" played out at the city gate? If Naomi knew Boaz was a kinsman, why did she not know about the closer kinsman? Surely she knew her husband's relatives in a little place like Bethlehem. Even if she was not sure of the matter, one pleasant afternoon spent with that talkative gaggle of women who met her at her homecoming would have brought her up to date, would it not? And why do these neighborhood women apparently function as the ones to bestow the name Obed on Ruth's child—a name that does not even fit the carefully prepared context—when in all other instances in the Old Testament it is the parents who name their children?

There are more such questions, and, as is perfectly well known, there are adequate answers to many of them, ingenious suggestions available for others. What would seem to be a prior set of questions to all these content questions, and a prior set of questions pertinent to some of those dealing with date, canonical placement, historical value, is just what kind of a writing is this, how did it come into being and what is its aim.

It is here that one senses the importance of some of the materials of the newer literary criticism which is making itself felt in the study of biblical literature, especially in the area of the artistic prose of the *Gattungen* known as the *novelle*, the anecdote, and the tale. In a very real sense, the task is one begun and left somewhat unfulfilled by Hermann Gunkel, but now considerably sharpened by literary comparisons to materials relatively far afield from Near Eastern comparative texts. A milestone is surely Erich Auerbach's *Mimesis*, especially its first chapter; another landmark study is that of Ben Edwin Perry on *The Ancient Romances*, published in 1967. Useful from another angle is A. B. Lord's fascinating *The Singer of Tales* (1960). James Muilenberg has explored several facets of the issue; for Ruth itself, key studies are those of L. Alonso-Schökel,[2] Werner Dommershausen,[3] and Stephen Bertmann.[4] Also not to be forgotten is Paul Humbert's artistic article from 1938.[5]

Gunkel's judgments in his long Ruth article, included in *Reden und Aufsätze* (1913), are the basis for his entry on the book of Ruth in the first edition of the *RGG*, and are changed in only one important way—to which we shall return—in the second (1930) edition of *RGG*.[6] For him, the Ruth story was almost the perfect example of an artistic tale, a poetic popular saga, a *novelle*. As such, its primary—and really its sole—aim was to entertain. In this he was strongly seconded by Hugh Gressmann,[7] who placed special stress on the non-historical character of the story. Both men were following the lead of Goethe's classic description of the book as a fine little idyll; they heard Goethe's insistence that the story be taken as a whole and, further, that it be taken within its wider context in the overall framework of biblical religion. Gunkel's excellent description of the book's careful structure into four discrete scenes with transitional interludes has become more or less standard, as have many of his observations about the internal artistry of the scenes. Less binding upon subsequent scholarship but nevertheless still impressive in its conviction is his insistence that there is no clearly discernible *Tendenz* which would allow the book to find its *Sitz im Leben* somewhere in Israelite culture as a protest paper or a propaganda document, but, at least among the most recent commentaries, that claim has reasserted itself.

In two directions, however, Gunkel's papers led into more controversial areas. The first was his attempt to rank the Ruth story on the basis of some rather intangible factors into a chronological scheme. Thus the very quality of the art was seen as a mark of lateness; only a person with a deep *Seelenleben* could produce it, and that meant relative lateness and growing sophistication. The poetic features for Gunkel, here as elsewhere in his writings, meant late and developed artistry. Only after these factors were cited, did linguistic considerations augment the argument, together with attention to the antiquarian note in 4: 7. On the other hand, there were marks of personal naïveté in the depiction, and that, combined with certain customs relatable to the history of Israelite law, kept him from moving so late as into the time when Tobit or the other Apocryphal narratives were composed. Indeed, the lack of self-consciousness about Ruth's foreign origins joined these psychological and cultural historical factors to lead Gunkel in 1913 to a seventh-century date. There is something quite important about the combination of factors he employed to arrive at his conclusion, and probably also something quite suggestive in the fact that in his 1930 article he dropped any attempt to assign a date.

This leads to the other problematic area. Bound closely to Gunkel's assessment of the date and place in the literary development was a brief treatment of the literary pre-history of the book. Here he listed Genesis 38 as in some sense a precursor, predictably noting that the Tamar-Judah story, while offering related, and even in some ways identical, circumstances, was a much rougher and coarser story and therefore of course earlier. Going further afield, and without drawing chronological conclusions, Gunkel brought in as a literary precursor the Egyptian Isis-Osiris story, noticing certain motif resemblances. He pursued that even further, back into the *Brüdermärchen* of Egypt. The final judgment of Gunkel's lengthy treatment in *Reden und Aufsätze* was, then, that the Israelite story had recast an ancient *Märchen*, in which wizardry and magic played a dominant role, by substituting the human institution of levirate marriage as the means by which an Israelite would overcome a similar set of problems. Israel's appropriation of an old and hoary motif was accomplished by the application of the dictates of her own high and pure religion, which would expel certain elements in story material derived from polytheistic cultures.

A most interesting development in Gunkel's 1930 *RGG* article, and the one major change from the earlier article, is his sketching in of an analysis of stages of development in the story which eventually became the Ruth story. In the back of one's mind one finds the question whether the need for time for these developments to take place is one reason why Gunkel gave up his attempt to assign a date to the finished product. In 1930 Gunkel could adopt the hypothesis that there existed a stage in the story when Naomi was the sole feminine protagonist and that this stage was the one which offered the transition from the old *Märchen* motif to the Israelite adaptation. It was Naomi who bore a child to carry on her dead husband's name, and she did this by inveigling a relative to sire the child. A later stage placed Ruth beside Naomi, so that the motif of the wise, old, crafty woman could make its appearance and Ruth could become the type of the young, obedient, and faithful woman. Again, Gunkel's notion of development obtrudes, from a simple to a more complex plot, and we have in the earlier stage something much closer to the Genesis 38 narrative.

I have taken this long to summarize what may be quite familiar to many because I suspect it stands at the fountainhead of streams which have run off in all directions. Thus, in carrying out motif research, a spate of what in many instances are bizarre conjectures have beclouded Ruth research. Two of the most striking are those of W. E. Staples (followed up by Herbert

Gordon May)[8] and of Margaret Crook.[9] The first of these finds a Bethlehem cult legend behind the Ruth story, and leads into a miasma of fertility cult, ritual prostitution, and game playing with the allegorical meanings of names which makes one's head swim and, more important, bids fair to make of biblical material in general a literature which would cause the exegete to throw up his hands in despair. Miss Crook's proposal is more down-to-earth, but is almost completely uncontrolled by hard evidence, since it divides into two stages (the Old Story and the Second Telling) the fundamental ingredients of the book in a quite arbitrary way, and then finds a convenient polemic use for the Second Telling in the occasion of Athaliah's accession, since Athaliah is "everything that Ruth is not." I do not want to stir forgotten memories of a rejected past here, but only to raise the first inklings of a rather fundamental question: Do we in fact have any justification for assuming that stories in ancient Israel must have a ladderlike set of pre-final-form stages which will link the stories to all their possible predecessor ingredients? Be it noticed that such an assumption has a great deal to say about the elements of creativity and the control exercised by tradition, two factors about whose balance we need to be a great deal more careful than we have often been, whether in the study of biblical stories like Ruth or in the much more central study of such matters as the growth of the Pentateuch.

Let us, then, turn to a far more sober and attractive attempt to explore the question of antecedents in relation to Ruth. When Jacob Myers published his important study, *The Linguistic and Literary Form of the Book of Ruth*, in 1955, he succeeded, at least in the early part of the book, in keeping two things in balance—namely, his appreciation for the extremely fine prose form of the book, and his observation of the poetic character of much of its contents, not only in the conversations and speeches of the book but also in the idiom of the prose itself. The isolation of the poetry, however, led to a further set of conclusions which opened the door to speculation about a process of literary development. A poetic nucleus was assumed and therefore a poetic precursor, and a new chain of development was posited which proposes that Ruth was perhaps an old nursery table passed on for a long period of time in oral form and "finally reduced to writing shortly after the exile."[10] The oral form was poetry, and the written form was prose, with poetic remnants protruding through the final prose form. It would seem, however, that Myers' conclusion abandoned an earlier affirmation—namely, that the prose is classic and fine in its style and, indeed, that it sounds most like the kind of prose in which the J and E Pentateuchal narratives appear.

One fears, then, that somehow the prose is nothing but the end, the fixing point of a long oral poetic process. Perhaps sensing the problem, George

Glanzman[11] proposed some nuances to Myers' thesis that began by adding another stage in the literary activity. First, there was a poetic tale, probably of non-Israelite origin, borrowed by the Israelites, perhaps from the Canaanites. (It is worth noting that this first of Glanzman's stages has at least two substages.) Glanzman, then, has this oral poetic tale put into prose, further "Israelitized" with the law and custom of the times, in the ninth or eighth century. The final stage is a post-exilic refurbishing which puts it into its final form. Glanzman's conjecture concerning the oldest form of the story is that it was an entertaining story of human devotion of daughter-in-law for mother-in-law, with the subsequent reward of finding a loving husband. A footnote suggests Glanzman's tentative approval of the idea that the original story ended at the threshing floor with the consummation of marriage. It is interesting to see how the ingredients of Glanzman's first stage are really the core of the story as we have it, so that subsequent stages call only for embellishments, expansion by greater precision of detail, and the particular application of Israelite theological terminology to already present motifs. This is a long distance separated from the proposal of Staples and quite different from that of Gunkel.

But it leaves a signal question unanswered: Why was the story "reduced" to prose? The shift away from the position of late-nineteenth-century scholarship, which saw poetry as a sophisticated and late product of a developing culture, to the twentieth-century position, which sees it as the early and dominant form of oral transmission of traditional material, has placed the study of poetry in the forefront. Studies such as that of Robert C. Culley,[12] building on the work of Parry and Lord, have shown even more dramatically than before how stock poetic formulas can make for ease of memory across long periods of time. But the result should not be to leave prose an undesirable end product, the unhappy result of the need to write things down. Baldly stated, it can simply be asked why poetry, when it came time to write down oral tradition, would not be written as poetry. So we still have to account for prose narrative of the kind we have in Ruth, and it does not seem to me satisfactory to claim that it became prose only upon writing.

This is where the lead of Ben Edwin Perry is worth following. Perry is working with a particular literary form—that of the ancient Greek romance—a literary form noteworthy not so much for quality of style or content but, rather, for its difference in style and purpose from other literary material of its own time and the period just before it. While the romance contains many familiar motifs of both myth and history, it is usually somewhat maudlin and sentimental; indeed, Perry is wry enough to note that many a student of classical literature would be struck by its giving an impression of modernity, since the genre reads like the text for a modern historical novel being prepared for a movie treatment.

Perry claims to have begun on his studies of the romances by attempting to explain their existence and origin on the basis of antecedents in previous classic literature and to make use of motif research in charting the development of the new literary form. The operative assumption, which he describes as dominating the field at least in the first half of the twentieth century, was that a series of successive stages would link various genres of literature in which the same motifs, events, personages, and even formulas appear. The conclusions Perry comes to, however, embody quite a different stance, one, by the way, with which he now claims most classical literary critics would agree in principle if not always in practice. I believe they should become more operative in biblical literary criticism as well, although there too they may be agreed to in principle. Perry confesses to having failed "to understand what the real forces are that create new literary forms. Such forms, I am convinced, never come into being as the result of an evolutionary process taking place on the purely literary plane, but only as the willful creations of men made in accordance with a conscious purpose . . . to satisfy the new spiritual or intellectual needs and tastes that have arisen in a large part of society in a given period of cultural history."[13] So to speak, new occasions teach new duties and develop new forms. To quote Perry once more: "One form does not give birth to another . . . . Historiography, for example, cannot become romance without passing through zero, that is, through the negation of its own *raison d'être*, the thing which defines it as historiography."[14] This does not mean of course that motifs do not persist and exercise effect, but it clearly warns that the presence of a fairy-tale, or mythic, or epic motif in a story will say very little about intermediate stages in transition from one type of literature to another; indeed, the very existence of intermediate stages is called seriously into doubt. What purports to be historical or looks to be an authentic historical datum in a romance cannot be judged one way or the other as to authenticity on the basis of its presence in the new form, but will have to be tested by some external evidence. Let me close this conversation with Perry's thesis with one summary quote: "The analogy of biological evolution is false and misleading in the realm of literary history, because it ignores the human will and capacity to create new forms at frequent intervals in response to its own spiritual or intellectual needs."[15] Notice here the emphasis upon the special creativity of the author of the new form. This would seem to be a very important help in resolving the question of why poetic epic would become prose story in biblical materials, and an excellent corrective on much *Gattungsforschung* and even more on Redactions-criticism in contemporary biblical study.

Lest all this seem old hat, I at least note that, for Myers, it was possible to write in his conclusion to the study of the literary form of Ruth that, in its final form, it was the "work of an exilic or early post-exilic writer . . . [who] in a sense was a literary editor; in no sense may his story be regarded as a new artistic creation any more than that the stories and poems of JE, Joshua, Judges, and Samuel were the creation of the men who first wrote them down."[16] Far as this insistence goes to protect the essential integrity of the process of oral transmission, I feel it does not properly account for the truly remarkable *prose* artistry which such literary creations as the book of Ruth display, and it has to be rethought in some rather fundamental ways.

Now let it be admitted that we have in the Old Testament at least two major instances in which we possess both poetic and prose presentations of the same event: in Judges 4 and 5, and in Exodus 14 and 15. It would be beyond the scope of this study to enter into comparison between poetry and prose in these two instances so as to see how well the prose version or versions succeed in reflecting the poetic predecessor. There are some rather important differences, however, in content, emphasis, and purpose. But it is not at all clear that one can make a transfer from those two cases to the instances of Ruth and its literary confreres. The Exodus and Judges examples cited relate to key and crucial events in the catalog of *magnalia Dei* in Israelite literature, for one thing, while Ruth does not. Neither does another excellent example of the same literary genre as Ruth—namely, the prose narrative of the book of Job. As Myers has for Ruth, so Nahum Sarna has for Job[17] posited an epic-poem substratum which belongs to an earlier stage of the present narrative. Both these instances—Ruth and Job—display remarkable and exceedingly attractive literary style and structure much as they stand, and should be accounted for, in my opinion, differently.

Here it is proposed, then, with others including Albright and Cassuto,[18] that there existed in Israel a style of artistic prose which was not the stepchild of any other style, and was used to express literary forms which were not the stepchildren of any other forms. The Hebrew short story is a distinct and discrete form, with its own ground rules, its own puposes, its own range of content (which could be quite varied, by the way, and could include much valuable historical information), and its own style. Included in it were rhythmic elements which are characteristic of the style and probably at least partially mnemonic in purpose. As examples we can include a number of the patriarchal narratives, especially Genesis 24 and 38; the Joseph story; a number of the Judges narratives, including, for example, Judges 3: 15–29 (the Ehud-Eglon episode) and Judges 4; Ruth (minus only its last five verses); and the Job prose story. Quite probably these stories in rhythmic prose had an oral period in that style, and their writing down came not at the end of a process of poetic transmission but at the end of a period of oral transmission in more or less their present rhythmic prose style. Their content, while varied, includes a combination of a certain kind of concern about rather typical people doing rather mundane things which nevertheless turn out to have rather significant results. Their purpose is both entertaining and edifying; it seems too that such narratives are peculiarly Israelite in that the scene of human life where very ordinary human events and figures function is also the scene where God works. And so, while the stories can have all the fun and delight and pathos and violence of common human existence, they also have the dimension of seriousness.[19]

The form of the Israelite short narrative story had a long history. Aage Bentzen,[20] who could find only Esther and Judith as comparative writings to Ruth, at least succeeded in pointing to two exemplars of the end of its period of existence, and he might have added Tobit and Susanna. Here I tread softly because legendary themes are very prominent in Tobit especially, and any distinctions between the group I am seeking to isolate and the legend may begin to disappear here. For that matter, it is difficult to decide where to put the story of Jonah in all this.

Now in bringing Perry's work into the discussion, I did not intend to equate ancient Greek romance and the Israelite short story. Certain features of Perry's analysis have quite general application, and a few are specifically pertinent. The biggest problem I see remaining would seem to be to find an occasion when new demand combined with new creative impulse to produce the new form.

Gerhard von Rad has proposed that the Joseph narrative be considered a *novelle*, and a quite sophisticated one at that; he has placed it in the tenth century and linked it to the wisdom movement.[21] Interestingly enough, von Rad has gotten himself caught on some of the same problems that Myers and Sarna have, except that he has the thoroughly grounded documentary hypothesis with which to contend. I believe R. N. Whybray[22] has succeeded in placing von Rad in a very tight position by challenging him to resolve two things in his theory: one, that the Joseph story is a carefully crafted, magnificently worked-out whole; and the other that it has J and E components. Whybray feels that von Rad makes a better case for the creativity and uniqueness of the story than he does for the existence of J and E ingredients, the seams between which have been so smoothly caulked as to have virtually disappeared from sight. The problem here is quite analogous to our problem with the literary pre-history of Ruth, and persuades me that the issue of posited pre-histories is by no means a closed one.

I would propose that the new occasion for the development of the Israelite short story is the early monarchic period, and that the new need was compounded of a relatively sophisticated nation, rapidly growing in its sophistication, wanting a somewhat less austere type of instruction and edification than the sort of thing going on in the court, where emergent institutions of kingship and prophecy demanded heady theologizing about Davidic covenant and charismatic messenger from the great king. Wisdom appears also to have been a courtly phenomenon for the most part, and only if wisdom as a movement can become more popular than it is usually described as being, could it be the locus for the edifying Israelite short story. The material of our genre is popular—it is folksy. It concerns the commonplace and God's relation to the commonplace. Following the lead of several other commentators, I suspect it often included in its earlier stages a theology of the working of God from the shadows, such as characterizes the Joseph narrative, Ruth, and, in its rather special way, the prose narrative of Job. Indeed, it would not surprise me if the genre got its start a little earlier, in the Judges period, at a time when several recent studies have proposed that the patriarchal narratives took their form. For Ruth itself, I see little difficulty in positing a tenth-century date for its present form in all essential aspects minus only the last five verses. That is where Gerleman places it on the basis of a quite different line of argument,[23] and it is not totally incompatible with the reasoning of Rudolph[24] and Hertzberg.[25]

It will be necessary further, however, to posit a Hebrew "singer of tales,"[26] and for him we have little evidence beyond the existence of his product. It is striking that we know as little about Israelite common life—village life, let us say—as we do, but Ruth itself may be an indicator of the context in which the tale teller functioned. His it was to entertain and edify at the village gate; his it was to portray in popular terms the critical issues of the day—for example, international affairs. His it was to bring the court to the people, even perhaps to tell them of their king's humble origins. If I can have Jonah back, his it was to portray what a prophet is (here with a bow to Martin Buber, who gives the tale of Jonah a far more important role to play than simply a propaganda white paper addressed to post-exilic nationalism).[27] Such a function may suggest the existence of *Tendenzen* in the short rhythmic stories, but the propaganda element is really very light, if it is present at all. If *Tendenz* there exists in Ruth, it may possibly be the old one Goethe first suggested with a slight twist—namely, that of giving David an interesting and impressive set of forebears one of whom, amazingly enough, was a foreigner. The sooner *that* is said, the better; in this connection, perhaps the story shares with the Court History of David in its openness, candor, and unabashedness.

It will not have escaped attention that I have rather badly blurred the distinction between historical narrative and the short narrative tale. That cannot be avoided. The prose style is really very similar. And from what has been said, the presence of a varying amount of historically accurate information in one of the short stories is entirely possible—indeed, in Israel, very likely; however, the proportion cannot be decided by any fixed rule. In Judges 4, the proportion is probably quite high. In Ruth, the proportion is probably higher than sometimes maintained, certainly higher than Gressmann would have allowed. The point has often been made that a purely fictional story is hardly likely to succeed in giving David a Moabite great-grandmother if he did not indeed have one. For that reason, I see no cogency to Eissfeldt's argument to remove 4: 17b from the original story as a late addition.[28] In fact, I rather doubt that we can draw a clean and clear line between historical narrative and the short story genre here proposed. If the date I have proposed can possibly be sustained, I would even hazard the observation that there is not that much difference between this genre and that of what most agree is the first great piece of Israelite historical writing —namely, the Court History of David. I suggest that the major difference is not so much a matter of form or style but of audience. The story was for popular consumption, and was crafted to reach that audience.

Let me now turn to exploring the craft of the book of Ruth more closely to demonstrate two things: that it is a highly creative literary masterpiece, even as Goethe and Gunkel claimed it to be; and also that it has a purpose of combining just those issues I mentioned earlier, of the joy and pathos of Israelite common life with the serious purpose of God, who governs from the shadows. Indeed, for the purposes of Old Testament theology, I would maintain that the author uses his artistry—in this case, by employing key words—to correlate God's will and human action so inextricably as to make each of the main protagonists the servant of God to the other.

L. Alonso-Schökel[29] has done a most interesting job of lining out the artistry of the Israelite storyteller in an analysis of two episodes in the prose of Judges. He has noted, in studies of the Ehud-Eglon story in Judges 3 and of the Deborah-Baraq-Yael story in Judges 4, the various ways in which even such subtle matters as the rhythm and pace of the story carry the action forward or retard it. He notes that inversion of the order of events can serve to delay an action and maintain suspense. Contemporaneity of action can occur so that the hearer or reader can sense how important it is that several things are happening concurrently to prepare for a critical climax. These factors all relate to the special kind of time and tempo that belongs to good storytelling, and such sensitivity to timing can be abundantly illustrated in the Ruth narrative. The very structure which Gunkel described so well

—whereby swift strokes of the brush establish the situation in the introduction and in the transitions, while the main scenes move at a much more leisurely pace—is a comprehensive indicator. No words are used that are unnecessary in the introduction, precisely because the pace is so fast, and therefore the hearer of the tale must take cognizance of such an apparently unimportant group of four Hebrew words as "and they dwelt there about ten years." These are ten years of childless marriage, and ten years when property ownership back in Bethlehem can become scrambled, and ten years during which Naomi can reach the age when she can have no more children. But these are ten years which do not require ten words to describe, because that is not where the action must lie.

On the other hand, the scene at the threshing floor and the scene at the city gate need some protraction, for they are full of good-hearted and rather robust suspense. The storyteller gets Ruth to the threshing floor in 3: 6, but must have her wait, as it were, while Boaz eats and drinks and has his heart get merry and goes to lie down in the corner of the threshing floor. The hearer is waiting with her; this maneuver is no joke, and it has to be brought off correctly. Likewise, the scene at the city gate is one which is suspenseful. As a whole, this scene, as well as the previous surprise announcement that there even exists a nearer kinsman, is an example of the familiar retarding motif of good storytelling; but, even within that scene at the gate, the lengthy style of the speeches of Boaz serves to draw out the tension.

However, the storyteller is not toying with us. It is important that Boaz get right to this business. While Ruth is talking with her mother-in-law at the end of chapter 3, the storyteller signals a quick pace to Boaz's action by using contemporaneity. I take the beginning of 4: 1, *ûbō'az 'ālâ*, as indicative by its word order not only of a change in subject but of a corresponding action to Ruth's departure from the threshing floor.

The timing and tempo of the story, then, are striking evidence of its artistry. Alonso-Schökel also calls attention to the way in which precision of detail and color makes for vividness at those moments when vividness is required. Again, there is more to such parts of an Israelite story than just the barely necessary words. Several examples suggest themselves as places where the story's camera eye rests languidly on a momentary vignette. Thus the scene of the leave-taking in Moab where twice the women stop to weep and much must be made of the argument to persuade at least Orpah to stay at home. Thus the splendid portrayal of the little meal at the midday break in the fields, where Ruth is asked to join the others and to dip her morsel in the *homeṣ*—whatever that really is—and receives the special heap of parched grain which is sufficient not only for herself but also for a supply to be taken home to her mother-in-law. There is purpose to all this, as the storyteller evokes the character of the personages and binds them together, but there is just good storytelling also. Consider as another example here the detail of 3: 3, where Naomi instructs Ruth in the preparations for her visit to the threshing floor, "Wash yourself, and anoint yourself, and put on your raiment."[30]

Vividness and color are employed where they are most needed, and it is interesting to contrast the instances cited (to which must be added the vivid scene at the city gate) with what might after all be thought of as the whole point of the book—namely, the birth of the baby. Five swift syntactical units and the whole business is over: "And Boaz took Ruth, and she became his wife, and he went in to her, and Yahweh gave her conception, and she bore a son." That's all! This may be the point of all that has gone before, but the fun, the tension, the pathos, the excitement have been in getting the hearer or reader there! And besides that, the storyteller needs to get on to wrap up one more important matter which is yet to come.

The storytelling techniques so far described have hinted at another technique of immense importance both in the book of Ruth and in the prose style of Hebrew tales in general. It is the technique of repetition and, most especially, of the repetition of key words. This technique operates in two ways, both short-range and long-range. Muilenberg got a good start on this rhetorical device in 1953,[31] but he confined his examples almost exclusively to poetry per se. He wrote of repetition as a style technique: "It serves, for one thing, to center the thought, to rescue it from disparateness and diffuseness. . . . Repetition serves, too, to give continuity to the writer's thought; the repeated word or phrase is often strategically located, thus providing a clue to the movement and stress of the poem."[32] This judgment can be transferred to the artistic prose which confronts us. Hertzberg, in his *ATD* commentary, had already pointed out how the verb *šûb* dominates the first chapter of the book with its twelve occurrences.[33] Now Werner Dommershausen,[34] of the Catholic theological faculty at Tübingen, has pointed out an entire series of *Leitworte* which bind each of the scenes in the Ruth book together. With some ingenuity but also a good deal of sagacity, he has shown that oftentimes these key words take strategic position so as to emphasize certain points. In chapter 1, for example, *šûb* manages, by its pattern of appearance, to underscore the basic tension; who will return whence? Orpah and Ruth to their country, Naomi to hers? By the time we reach verse 22 and Ruth is returning with Naomi, the question of the significance of Ruth's leaving Moab and returning to Judah has become quite an important issue. For chapter 2, Dommershausen establishes the verb *lqṭ*, "to glean," as a binding key word; and also the reminder that Ruth is a Moabitess, which occurs three times; and the phrase "to find favor in the eyes of someone," which appears in Ruth's hope in verse 2, her bewilderment in verse 10, and her expression of gratitude in verse 13. His analysis suggests a carefully worked-out structure to all this, so that Ruth's discovery of favor from Boaz grows as her success in gleaning grows, while all the time one is reminded that this is a foreigner to which this is happening. The high spot of that emphasis is the neat stylistic device of the word play in 2: 10: "Why do I find favor in your eyes?" *lᵉhakkîrēnî weʾānōkî nokrîyāh.*

For chapter 3, one key term is *gōren*, "threshing floor," but it, like *lqṭ* in the preceding chapter, really only sets the stage. For Dommershausen, the chapter depends on the repetition of *škb* in the first half of the chapter and of *gʾl* in the second half. Here the rhetorical effect is heightened by the double implication of the verb *škb*, since it can mean "to prostrate oneself at the feet of one in a gesture of petition," and it can mean "to sleep with," "to have sexual intercourse." Apparently Dommershausen was not inclined to follow up on the rather too frequent appearance of the verb *ydʿ*, "to know," and its derivatives or the potentially dangerous meaning of the term "to uncover the feet," which occurs in verses 4 and 7. But I have meant to be emphasizing that our author knew what he was doing with his story, and a combination of terms like this must be taken with the utmost seriousness. Entertainment and edification in Hebrew storytelling, especially when closely bound to the common life of real, if typical, men and women, do not turn squeamish at the last minute. The situation at the threshing floor is told as it is, precisely because it would have had a quite different outcome with different people from this remarkable threesome with whom the story is dealing. Every bit of the suspense is intended. But the audience has been led to realize that in chapter 2 Boaz and Naomi both have Ruth's best interest very much at heart and that both approve of her modesty and fidelity. Now the storyteller presents the conditions for the acid test. It is hard to believe that his propensity to entertain and edify would not include his compelling his hearer to participate in a decision bound up in the suspense at the threshing floor. And with the decision quickly made, the drama of the story shifts from a focus upon sleeping to a focus upon redeeming.

In chapter 4, Dommershausen sees the key words as *gʾl* and *qnh*, and they carry the action to its climax until, in one master stroke in 4: 14–15, the author has the *gôʾēl* born to Ruth become the means of returning (restoring) the soul of Naomi (using the hiphil of the prominent word of chapter 1, the verb *šûb*).

Nevertheless, Dommershausen has by no means exhausted the importance of the key-word technique in the style and structure of Ruth. There is another group of terms which stand out not because of their frequency but precisely because of their infrequency and yet their appearance at absolutely crucial points. It is surprising how rarely they have been noticed and used for interpretation of the purpose of the Ruth book.[35] They occur exclusively in the speeches of the protagonists, and especially in blessings, sentences expressing approval, and sentences designing strategy. Perhaps the most striking is the word *kānāp*. At the peak of the scene in the field in chapter 2, when Ruth has prostrated herself in wonder at Boaz's feet and asked why he would take notice of her, a mere foreigner, he explains that he has heard of her faithfulness in leaving home to accompany her mother-in-law. He then expresses the ceremonial wish for her: "May Yahweh recompense your deed and may your payment be in full from Yahweh the God of Israel under whose wings you have come to seek refuge." The picture of Yahweh's wings has had sufficient ventilation to be familiar, but it is striking to find another meaning for that same term appear in 3: 9, when Ruth, upon identifying herself at the threshing floor, then implores Boaz to "spread your wings over your handmaid." Yahweh's wings, Boaz's wings. Boaz is to fulfill for Ruth, by marriage, what the hope in chapter 2 had related to Yahweh.

Similarly with the term *mᵉnûḥāh* in 1: 9. Naomi wishes for her two daughters-in-law that they find rest in the house of a new husband. But when we reach 3: 1, by which time the artful mother-in-law has seen a plan developing, her question is, "Have I not been seeking for you rest (*mānôaḥ*) which will serve you well?" In this case also, the wish connected to Yahweh's activity becomes fulfilled by the human protagonist.

A similar pattern revolves around the use of the term *ḥesed*. In 1: 8, again as a part of Naomi's blessing to the two girls, she wishes for them: "May Yahweh do with you *ḥesed* just as you have done with the dead and with me." Already here *ḥesed* is a two-way street. Then, in 2: 20 occurs a verse with a slight residue of ambiguity in it, as Naomi expresses a blessing on Boaz when she learns of the largesse with which Ruth has come home from her first day of gleaning: "Blessed be he before Yahweh who has not abandoned his *ḥesed* with the living and the dead." Nelson Glueck, in his word study of *ḥesed*,[36] hazarded the claim that the relative clause refers here to Boaz and not to Yahweh, calling upon 2 Samuel 2: 25 for support for the syntax. That would be almost too good to be true for my thesis here, but, frankly, I doubt its validity. *Ḥesed* here is probably Yahweh's work. But in 3: 10, Boaz blesses Ruth before Yahweh because she has made her latter *ḥesed* even better than her former in not going after younger men.

There is yet another. In the sad and angry lament of Naomi in the last verses of chapter 1, when she finds a sympathetic audience and pours out her indictment against God and tells her erstwhile colleagues to call her *Mara* from now on, she wails, "I went off full but Yahweh has brought me back empty (*rêqām*)." In Ruth, the mood is not simply idyllic and tranquil, for here is one of our protagonists giving vent to one of the most characteristic of the possible stances of man before God in the Old Testament. God is the one who has brought her back empty, and the hearer of the story will hardly have forgotten that wail when he comes upon 3: 17: "These six measures of barley he has given me because he said to me you must not return *rêqām* to your mother-in-law."

These leading and guiding terms cannot be there by accident. Every one of them relates a key theological theme to the action of God and to the action of the human figures who dominate the story. For Wilhelm Rudolph, it is important, as it has been for other commentators, to insist that the key figure in the story of Ruth is not Ruth, or Naomi, or Boaz, but God.[37] God is there quietly guiding the course of events, seeing to it that "by chance" Ruth comes to Boaz's field, that on just that day Boaz pays a visit to the field, that after ten years of barrenness in Moab, Yahweh at once grants Ruth conception of a son in Bethlehem. Rudolph's emphasis is important so far as it goes, but it is not all that the storyteller wants to portray. He also wants to have his hearer explore the interpenetration of divine *ḥesed* and human *ḥesed*, of divinely granted *rest* and the *rest* a scheming old lady and a nicely perfumed young woman can bring about with a little strategy. He wants us to realize that refuge under God's wings is connected to the perpetuation of the name of a dead and childless husband by marriage to a kinsman. In a way, for our storyteller, the analogy between men's activity and God's activity runs counter to the way most of us would want to speak of the major themes in Old Testament theology. It is more or less axiomatic to assert that one understands Old Testament God talk by running the analogy from the best of human behavior to a description of how God acts. But oddly, for our book, the analogy runs the other way. Men and women here are to act after the analogy of how God acts. Theological terms of special power, especially the term *ḥesed*, have become so charged theologically that they can become normative for human behavior with new and extra expectations beyond what normal human behavior might call for. In the book of Ruth, normal, sensible, good human behavior is exercised quite well by Orpah and by the unnamed relative, who could do a lot but could not take on too much. In the final analysis, Humbert, in the essay cited in note 5, may have had the most important thing to say about all this—that the book of Ruth is a book about *ḥesed*, especially if that term is understood with all the fullness and power it really has in

Old Testament thought, that it is more than what is to be expected in the normal contractual relation.

Let me try to summarize the working room I have sought to create for the book of Ruth. It is proposed that it is an exemplar of a particular literary form in Israel, and a classic example at that. Indeed, it is virtually the only example which has not had at least some tampering done with it which has sought to build it into another unity, or to break it open for a new and different purpose (such as presumably happened to Job), or to broaden its impact by adding another *Gattung* (as presumably happened to Jonah).[38] This literary form has a special artistic prose which has much in common with certain straight poetic features; it shares this special Hebraic prose, however, with other literary *Gattungen.* This prose was memorable, and may well have had a period of oral transmission. As a new literary form, it shows its own high level of distinctive creativity, and the motifs or names or vignettes or historical information which it may have borrowed are transformed in the new genre, not simply developed along evolutionary lines.[39] Let me be clear, now, that such a description does not preclude the entire onomasticon coming from the Late Bronze age; in Ruth and Job, the majority of the names doubtless do, as a matter of fact. Nor does it preclude old customs from being included as a part of the story. But the author was a creative teller of tales, making his own way. I have had to call for a hypothetical guild of such storytellers operating probably outside the main city centers and engaged in both entertainment and edification on the popular level. I have claimed that these storytellers were masters of their art, or at least those were whose works have come down to us. They structured their works beautifully with certain memorable features which not only impressed their audience but made their stories maintain their structure through sometimes long periods of time. With the examples of their art which survived, various things could be done, by the Deuteronomic historian, by the poet of Job, and, in the case of Ruth, by some late annalist who felt he needed to add a genealogy. But in Ruth, we have one of the most pristine examples of one of the most delightful forms the Old Testament knows.

Notes

1 H. W. Hertzberg, *ATD,* 9 (1953), 255 ff; Gillis Gerleman, *BKAT* XVIII/1 (1960); Wilhelm Rudolph, *KAT*², XVII/1 (1962).

2 L. Alonso-Schökel, "Erzählkunst im Buche der Richter," *Bibl* 42 (1961), 143–72.

3 Werner Dommershausen, "Leitwortstil in der Ruthrolle," *Theologie im Wandel: Festschrift zum 150-jährigen Bestehen der katholisch-theologischen Fakultät an der Universität Tübingen, 1817–1967* (Munich and Freiburg, 1967), pp. 394–407.

[4] Stephen Bertmann, "Symmetrical Design in the Book of Ruth," *JBL* 84 (1965), 165–68.

[5] Paul Humbert, "Art et leçon de l'histoire de Ruth," *RTP*, NS 26 (1938), 257–86.

[6] *RGG*[1], Vol. V, cols. 106–8; *RGG*[2], Vol. IV, cols. 2180–82.

[7] Hugo Gressmann, *Die Anfänge Israels* (*Die Schriften des Alten Testaments*, I.2) (1914), pp. 284–87.

[8] W. E. Staples, "The Book of Ruth," *AJSL* 53 (1937), 145–57; Herbert G. May, "Ruth's Visit to the High Place at Bethlehem," *JRAS* (1939), 75–78.

[9] Margaret B. Crook, "The Book of Ruth: A New Solution," *JBR* 16 (1948), 155–60.

[10] Jacob M. Myers, *The Linguistic and Literary Form of the Book of Ruth* (Leiden, 1955), p. 43.

[11] George S. Glanzman, "The Origin and Date of the Book of Ruth," *CBQ* 21 (1959), 201–7.

[12] Robert C. Culley, *Oral Formulaic Language in the Biblical Psalms* (Toronto, 1967).

[13] Ben Edwin Perry, *The Ancient Romances* (Berkeley, 1967), pp. 9 f.

[14] *Ibid.*, p. 10.

[15] *Ibid.*, p. 12.

[16] Myers, *op. cit.*, p. 64.

[17] Nahum M. Sarna, "Epic Substratum in the Prose of Job," *JBL* 76 (1957), 13–25.

[18] W. F. Albright, *ARI*[5] (Anchor Edition), 21 f; U. Cassuto, *A Commentary on the Book of Genesis* I (1961), 7–17, esp. p. 11, although the argument here applies to the style of Genesis 1 particularly. See also Hermann Gunkel, "Genesis" *HKAT*, 8th ed., 1969), pp. xxvii f, translated in *The Legends of Genesis* (New York, 1964), pp. 37 f.

[19] It is delightful to note that theological writing about joy or play can observe that seriousness and joy are not opposites but in some sense correlative. See Johan Huizinga, *Homo Ludens* (Boston, 1955), pp. 44–45, for example, where the opposite of play and joy is earnestness, which takes itself too seriously—a trap the Bible rarely falls into!

[20] Aage Bentzen, *Introduction to the Old Testament* I (1952), 240.

[21] Gerhard von Rad, "The Joseph Narrative and Ancient Wisdom," in *The Problem of the Hexateuch and Other Essays* (New York, 1966), pp. 292–300.

[22] R. N. Whybray, "The Joseph Story and Pentateuchal Criticism," *VT* 18 (1968), 522–28.

[23] Gerleman, *op. cit.*, p. 10.

[24] Rudolph, *op. cit.*, pp. 26 ff.

[25] Hertzberg, *op. cit.*, p. 257.

[26] Cf Gunkel, *op. cit.*, p. 41.

[27] Martin Buber, *The Prophetic Faith* (Harper Torch edition: New York, 1960), p. 104.

[28] Otto Eissfeldt, *The Old Testament: An Introduction* (New York and Evanston, 1965), pp. 479 f; but see "Wahrheit und Dichtung in der Ruth-Erzählung," *Sitzungsberichte der Sächsischen Akademie der Wissenschaft zu Leipzig, Phil.-hist. Kl.*, 110, 4 (1965), 23–28.

[29] *Op. cit.*, note 2 above.

[30] The Lucianic group of Septuagint manuscripts adds here "rub with unguent"; while this may simply be a variant which found its way from the margin into a conflate text, there are a few hints of genuine readings from a slightly fuller alternate textual tradition in the Septuagint and Old Latin of the book of Ruth. Discussion of this issue will have to await the volume on Ruth in the Anchor Bible series.

[31] James Muilenberg, "A Study in Hebrew Rhetoric: Repetition and Style," *VT(S)* 1 (1953), 97–111.

[32] *Ibid.*, p. 99.

[33] *Op. cit.*, p. 263.

[34] *Op. cit.*, note 3 above.

[35] This study was substantially complete when D. F. Rauber independently pointed to several of these devices in an article which calls for the same kind of reevaluation which this paper advocates. Apparently, Rauber sensed many of the stylistic devices without resort to Hebrew, which underscores their obvious character. See his "Literary Values in the Bible: The Book of Ruth," *JBL* 89 (1970), 27–37.

[36] Nelson Glueck, *Ḥeṣed in the Bible* (Cincinnati, 1967), pp. 41 f.

[37] *Op. cit.*, p. 33.

[38] See recently George M. Landes, "The Kerygma of the Book of Jonah," *Interp* 21 (1967), 3–31.

[39] Albright uses the word "transform" in *ARI*^{5}, p. 21, a term which is in accord with the thesis here propounded and would, I suspect, please Perry.

Harold L. Creager
Lutheran Theological Southern Seminary

The Divine Image

Man has always been curious about himself. This has led to many speculations about his origin and to varied views about his essential nature. The first chapter of Genesis presents a view which, although apparently simple, is profound, challenging, and richly suggestive.

The Biblical Background

"God said, 'Let us make man in our image, after our likeness.' . . . So God created man in his own image" (Gen 1: 26 f). Taken strictly, this simply indicates the *fact* of similarity to God. But it is a natural extension of language to use "image" for the *content* of the similarity, that in which the likeness consists, the constituent qualities or powers in man which have some resemblance to aspects of God's being.

This does not say that men are God's image, as one Egyptian text did. Paul's statement, "Man . . . is the image and glory of God" (1 Cor 11: 7), certainly cannot be taken literally. Man is far from the infinite, exalted majesty of God's glory; the meaning may be that man can glorify God. Likewise, some modification is to be seen concerning image—perhaps that man has resemblance to God. And it is quite inadmissible to say: "There is a little bit of God in man," or "Man is a mingling of dust and deity," or anything of the sort—as has been done. God is God, and man is man; and never does the Bible hint at any slightest identifying of the two or any disregarding of their essential separateness or any confused thinking about man as a part of God.

Whether "image" is to be understood literally or figuratively has been much discussed. In most of its sixteen occurrences in the Old Testament, *ṣelem* has the basic etymological meaning of a "material image"—for example, Num 33: 52; 1 Sam 6: 5. But sometimes it was used figuratively for a "mere empty semblance." Thus in Ps 39: 6, RSV has "Man goes about as a shadow"; and in Ps 73: 20, "their phantoms." In Ezek 23: 14, it refers to painted pictures; and while this does indicate outward appearance, it is not a solid physical substance. Therefore there is no a priori necessity to see a physical body as the significance here.

The word rendered "likeness" (*d*[e]*mût*) usually indicates resemblance in lexternal appearance. But it is also used figuratively for any sort of simiarity—for example, "tumult . . . as of a great multitude" (Is 13: 4); "they have venom like the venom of a serpent" (Ps 58: 4); the "as" and "like" represent this word. The two words "image" and "likeness" have essentially the same meaning in the Genesis passage. This is a clear instance of the synonymous parallelism that is such a frequent characteristic of the Hebrew Bible.

It is scarcely possible that the author simply referred to man's physical body, and said it resembled that of God. The statement that man was created in the likeness of God points in two directions. On the one hand, it indicates man's great difference from all other creatures on earth. On the other, it looks in the direction of God, and specifies that man's unique and distinctive quality lies in a certain similarity to God. In neither direction is a physical reference at all probable. The major differences between man and the animals are not merely physical. And in Deuteronomy, which most scholars recognize as antedating the Priestly material to which Gen 1 belongs, it had been indicated that God has no physical form (Deut 4: 12, 15). Anthropomorphic references to God's eye, hand, mouth, and so on are obviously figurative. And temporary manifestations in theophany are no evidence for a permanent bodily form. Sexual differentiation also militates against physical similarity to God; "male and female" is added after the words, "in the image of God" (Gen 1: 27). Even if the writer here may have had some background of a primitive myth or legend which ascribed a physical body to God, it seems clear that he reinterpreted or transcended it. It is possible, however, that the special aspects of man's body were included as a subordinate factor, though not the essential meaning; both the anthropomorphic expressions about God and the fact of the Incarnation show clearly that the human body is not alien or antagonistic to God.

Although one must always seek the original meaning of biblical statements, it is a serious question whether we are absolutely limited to the ideas the original writer had. This involves the conception that is held of the processes of inspiration and revelation. When God seeks to communicate truth, he not only offers revelation but also enables man, at least in some degree, to receive it and to express it in words. But it seems that man often gets only a partial understanding of a great idea toward which God leads him. Thus it is scarcely possible that either Abram or the writer comprehended the full impact of God's gracious words recorded in Gen 12: 1–3. A valid and valuable meaning would be evident at once; but God intended a much richer significance, which would ultimately be realized. Compare also what was said by and about Caiaphas in Jn 11: 49–52.

Basic in this discussion is the conviction that, although the writer of Gen 1 probably did not completely comprehend the ideas embodied in the words he used, we are not restricted to the limited insights which he had. Rather, we can seek the great realities to which his words point; or, to put it another way, we should seek the truth which God meant and toward which he was leading the writer.

Our understanding of man's creation in the divine likeness therefore depends on our understanding of the nature of God. The fact of basic significance here is that God is a personal Being—not an abstract power, not a set of ideas, not an automatic source of rewards and retribution, not a mechanical source or center of energy, not an "it." Fundamental in this personal quality is self-consciousness. Whatever translation is accepted in Ex 3: 14, the self-consciousness of God is obvious. This is true of course in varying degree all through the Bible. This personal nature of God, moreover, manifests itself in many activities and relationships; the personal quality of the actions implies the personal quality of the Actor. This does not exclude the possibility that in some way God is superpersonal, so infinitely beyond human comprehension or imagination that even the most profound philosophic efforts cannot fathom the ultimate and total reality of his nature. But it does say that God is at least personal, that his nature definitely includes the various positive qualities and powers that characterize a personal being.

We therefore conclude that the likeness to God which characterizes man is essentially in the realm of personal quality. Before looking at specific details, we should note two general considerations in this connection.

The Bible does not explicitly analyze the nature of man. But it does say much about what man does and can do—thus implying a great deal about his nature. Therefore our study looks basically at capacities and powers, either actual abilities or inherent potentialities; and we are justified in seeking, from these significant clues, an understanding of the essential nature of man which is their necessary background. This approach emphasizes a dynamic conception, not a merely passive or static one. But of course there must be an existent something that has the capacities and powers.

Man has a group of characteristics, above the mere physical level, which differ markedly from those of other earthly creatures. These characteristics have such a closeness of relationship among themselves, such an inner coherence, that they clearly seem to belong together and to constitute a unified whole; it is in this totality that the essential nature of the human person is to be found. Most of these qualities and functions have distinct similarity to some which God has revealed as being characteristic of himself. Therefore, in the absence of any specific biblical definition of the content of meaning in the phrase, "the image of God," it is reasonable to think that God intended us to see the higher or personal nature of man as a whole and in its various details as being indicated thereby.

Distinctive Powers

From the functional standpoint, the fundamental aspect of the human person, and therefore of the divine image, is what may be broadly designated as the *psychological powers.* They are the essential prerequisite for the other six main aspects that will be surveyed—in fact, for all personal life.

Basic is the capacity for self-consciousness, the deep sense that "I am I," with clear differentiation from all else and with at least a considerable recognition of individual factors. As noted above, this is characteristic of God. A small degree of it is found in the higher animals. But in its profound richness and fullness, it is distinctive of persons.

The intellectual powers of thinking and reasoning function in many areas—for example, in perceiving cause and effect and extensive details of other relationships, in recognizing and classifying similarities and differences and far-reaching influences, in gaining and organizing astonishing amounts of information, in piercing below surface appearances and characteristics to inner reality, and in planning methods to achieve desired results. In Hos 6: 4, even God seems thus to seek an effective procedure: "What shall I do with you, O Ephraim?" (or, "What *can* I do?") Obviously these powers reach far beyond direct contacts, both in space and in time; for people can gain information and understanding concerning matters in distant locations, can project probabilities and expectations into the distant future, and can construct plans with reference to such remote things.

Language is an important factor in this. Unless ideas get expressed in words, they are vague and of little value; and only in words can they be communicated to other people. Words are essential also for identifying factual matters and for sharing information on them. In the Bible, God frequently speaks—in contrast to the idols, which "have mouths, but do not speak" (Ps 115: 5). The fact that parrots, for example, can learn to pronounce a few words, rather mechanically, or that dolphins have some system of intercommunication, does not really detract from the distinctive importance of language for people.

Closely associated with linguistic ability is the capacity for abstract thought. This appears in religious concepts, such as sin, holiness, piety, and in a great variety of other ideas, such as gratitude, wealth, illusion, grandeur. It is seen also as men develop theories, trace out implications, reach logical conclusions, make mathematical calculations, and engage in many other areas of mental activity.

Another noteworthy power is the comprehension of values. Various levels of value are found in various relationships, experiences, achievements, and qualities. It is important to recognize values, to appreciate them, and to discriminate between the greater and the lesser, and thus to be ready to "seek first" the higher values (cf Mt 6: 25–33). The capacity for such thoughtful discernment of values is a significant aspect of the divine image—even though men often fail to get the true divine viewpoint or to evaluate accurately.

Without attempting to catalog all areas of intellectual powers, we should at least note the capacity for imagination, especially in the basic meaning of that term—getting clarity and pictorial vividness of conceptions; constructing mental images; also such imperfectly understood matters as mental telepathy and extrasensory perception.

The emotional qualities of persons are very significant. The higher animals can feel something of anger, of affection, and probably of pleasure. But feelings in people have a vastly deeper and richer quality, as well as a much broader variety. And emotional attitudes can be felt with reference to people with whom one has never had any direct contact; the outreach of both love and hate is potentially worldwide.

The powers of will are sometimes considered the most specific characteristic of persons. This involves the making of choices and determination and persistence in accomplishing chosen purposes. Here again, the transcending of space and time is noteworthy. Purposes can be formulated and actions undertaken or projected on a comprehensive social scale, and with reference to matters at great physical distance and far off in the future. Also to be noted here is the ability to strive for achieving the higher values, both for oneself and for others. This includes such efforts as those to gain fuller knowledge, to develop finer qualities of character, to grow in richness of fellowship with God, to deepen friendships, and to promote righteousness and peace. Man's will reaches its noblest expression in harmonizing with God's will.

Much discussion has been given to the "freedom" of the will. Actually this is not a good term to use; for the will is not an irresponsible, irrational something, independent of the other factors in the person, which makes a more or less blind stab at doing something. The will is the personal self acting in certain areas. There is a large degree of self-determination, or at least the capacity for it; this is true in spite of various limitations, both from strong outside influences and from inner defects. Thoughts, feelings, and desires tend to express themselves, to carry over into action. But this is not automatic. And if there is any conflict between various such influences, there is not a sort of mechanical struggle between them, with the strongest winning out. On the contrary, the person decides—wills—which particular motive or influence shall be given dominant place and shall express itself in action. Of course some persons (with a "weak" will) yield rather easily to various human influences, without aggressively asserting an independent choice; but others (with a "strong" will) vigorously assert and exercise the dominating power of personal choice, even against strong influences in an opposite direction. Testimony to the reality of such choosing is found in the constant personal consciousness that it would have been possible to act otherwise than was done in numerous and varied situations. And the Bible speaks frequently of important choices deliberately made, or called for—for example, Deut 30: 19; Josh 24: 15, 22; Is 56: 4; Lk 10: 42; Acts 17: 30.

Although the functional powers had to be surveyed first, the most profoundly significant aspect of human beings, when viewed qualitatively, is the unique capacity for *knowing God and having personal relationship with him*. Almost surely no mere animal can even have any idea of God—much less have conscious fellowship with him. The divine-human fellowship works in both directions. It involves revelation from God to man, the bestowing of various spiritual gifts and blessings, and God's calling of man into love and loyalty to him. On man's part, it involves prayer, worship, faith, devotion, aspiration, obedience. Man can even be God's friend (2 Chron 20: 7; Jas 2: 23). Man is one whom God loves, and who is destined (if he will accept it) for salvation through faith in Christ and for full spiritual communion with God. He finds his true self only in a free response to God.

Not only can there be intelligent communication between God and man but also God can establish both individual purposes and purposes of history in connection with man, and can work out such purposes in and through man. Man can be personally confronted with God's purposes and demands, and can make some sort of intelligent response to them. There is interaction; when God acts in human affairs, man is not a mere pawn that is shoved but can participate meaningfully in what is done. Thus man not only has responsibility to God but also can cooperate with God.

The third highly significant aspect of persons is the *moral quality.* In God himself, this appears in establishing standards of righteousness, in acting in accordance with such standards, and in seeking to promote them among men. In man, it appears in conscience and some related functionings. Three areas of this ethical concern and activity are to be noted.

Conscience is, first of all, moral understanding, a functioning of the intellectual powers in the moral area. It is knowledge or opinion—whether accurate or imperfect—about right and wrong. There are many sources of such moral ideas. Basic for the Christian is the Bible, especially the teachings of Jesus and the Ten Commandments. Contributions come from teachings by parents and others, opinions of friends, ideas found in books and other reading, radio and TV, observation of the consequences of actions, and the results of social experience as expressed in custom, public opinion, and civil law, as well as reflective thinking on problems of right and wrong. Thus men come to recognize the reality of right and wrong, the fact that moral distinctions exist. And they can get both a conception of some general principles of the nature of right and wrong—of what they ought to do and ought not to do—and a set of ideas concerning the moral quality of various kinds of actions.

On such bases men form moral judgments with reference to individual problems or issues, and have the equipment to make (more or less) intelligent moral choices. The efforts at discriminating evaluation often are necessarily directed not at positive evil or good but at trying to decide which of two or more possible lines of action would produce the larger good. One's moral conceptions get applied also in evaluating the rightness or wrongness of the actions of others. This may not be exactly conscience—which deals, at least primarily, with moral aspects of one's own life—but it is part of this whole moral capacity. All this is unique for persons: an animal may learn that certain acts bring praise or reward, others bring censure or punishment—but that is far from a recognition of moral quality.

The second function of conscience is the moral imperative or dynamic. It is the sense of urgency that one ought to do the right and not do the wrong—a sense of duty and of obligation, constraining one to follow the conclusions reached by the moral understanding, to refrain from yielding to any blandishments and allurements that might come from possibilities that are deemed improper or unworthy, and to strive to accomplish the purposes that have been chosen. There is also the urgency to choose the greater good rather than the lesser, and to persevere in achieving it, in spite of the greater cost that may be entailed—either greater effort required or greater sacrifice of what may seem desirable and may actually have real but minor value. Probably to be classified here also is the sense of concern about injustices and various sufferings endured by others, with the urge to do something to relieve or to help. Of course there is no compulsive power in these areas, but strong influence is exerted.

Various motives for obedience to the moral judgments that are reached may be adduced to strengthen this urgency—for example, the fact of God's will; grateful appreciation for God's goodness; the inherent rightness of right and wrongness of wrong; the beauty of love and kindness and the repulsiveness of evil; a sense of personal responsibility for one's conduct; the valuable results, to self and to others, from doing right; the disvalues from doing wrong, including the danger of suffering or punishment and the failure to attain worthy goals; good examples set by admired people, especially Christ; and warnings from bad examples. This sense of urgency often goes beyond the individual and reaches out to others, both to lead them to take moral issues seriously and to stimulate motivating influences in them.

In God there is probably never any struggle between tendencies to do good and to do evil, for "God cannot be tempted with evil" (Jas 1: 13). There are a few hints that God may consider actions that are improper or evil, but rejects them—for example, "How can I give you up! How can I make you like Admah!" (Hos 11: 8). But in general, since moral standards arise from and express his very nature, it would seem he does good automatically. Also, he is active to exert influence on men to choose and do the good and to avoid evil—both by direct commands and by various other motivations. The Spirit of God works to guide, inspire, and strengthen man in the good way and to dissuade from evil—for example, see Neh 9: 20; Ps 143: 10; Ezek 36: 27; Gal 5: 22 f. Man only very imperfectly reflects God's moral dynamic.

The third area of the functioning of a person in this realm is the moral judiciary. Conscience passes judgment on what has been done or left undone—either to condemn and give a sense of guilt and shame or to approve and give a feeling of satisfaction (cf Rom 2: 15). Such passing of judgment (just as the other moral functionings) reaches beyond oneself, to commend or to censure the actions of others. This third function also reinforces the second one; it becomes an influence in making succeeding choices rightly, and strengthens the urgency to persevere in the good.

The popular saying that conscience is the voice of God is scarcely accurate with reference to gaining moral ideas or condemning evil; at best, there would seem to be a sort of echo of God's voice, or concurrence with it. The idea is somewhat more probable in the urging of obedience. All three functional areas have similarity to God's moral activity; but man often does not succeed in reaching the divine moral realities.

The idea has sometimes been advanced that the divine image means—or originally meant—moral and spiritual perfection. This is not said in Genesis, and almost surely is not implied. The absence of sin is not the same as moral perfection, which includes developed positive virtue. And the fellowship with God, though pictured as intimate at times, does not seem to have been full and complete. Even if the original state of man had included moral perfection—a special high quality associated with the basic fact of personal quality which was then lost—this was not the essential of the divine image. The New Testament references to the truly spiritual likeness to God which is the result of his saving grace (for example, Eph 4: 24; Col 3: 10) obviously say nothing about what man was as originally created. Available evidence indicates that man was endowed in creation with moral capacity, not moral perfection.

The fourth major aspect of man to be noted lies in the *social area*—the capacity for friendship and for sharing in mutual interests and activities with other persons. It would be possible to combine this with the second general area noted above (capacity for fellowship with God) under a general idea of interpersonal relationships; but the divine-human and the interhuman have significant differences, and each is important, so that it seems preferable to consider them separately. Just as God has active relations with persons (both human and angelic), so the divine image involves important relations with others.

Human social relationship is on a much higher level than such gregariousness and cooperation as are found, for example, in a hive of bees, a hill of ants, or a herd of elephants. It is distinctly different from any group organization of animals, in that it includes a more profound quality of conscious fellowship, without the need for physical propinquity, and planned activities on a vastly broader scale. In addition to the richness of the male-female and other family relationships, there are important community and national aspects and a great many significant associations in terms of specialized interests.

Men have responsibilities to their fellowmen as well as to God. God confronts us with them. They are ones whom God loves and for whom Christ died and rose again. We are to recognize and give careful attention to the divine image which characterizes all humans, and act appropriately, not only in matters of right moral conduct in dealing with them but also in feelings of respect for them, in kindly fellowship, and in active help.

Of the several distinctive aspects of man, the Bible makes most explicit mention of *supremacy over nature*. "Fill the earth and subdue it; and have dominion . . . over every living thing" (Gen 1: 28). "Thou hast given him dominion over the works of thy hands; thou hast put all things under his feet, all sheep and oxen . . ." (Ps 8: 6 f). This is sometimes considered a result of the creation in the divine image rather than a part of its essence. But certainly such supremacy is characteristic of God himself; and so it seems appropriate to classify it as a real aspect of the divine image. Control over animals is stressed in both Bible passages just noted; but the language is general enough to be much more inclusive. This properly covers a multitude of factors in ordinary human life, as well as the whole vast realm of scientific achievement.

An important aspect closely related to the foregoing is *creativity*. God is always emphasized as Creator. Does man share in this power? In the absolute and primary sense, it is only God who creates; and in the Bible, only he is spoken of as creating. But in a secondary sense, this power has been conferred on man. It is found in three areas.

The first area is procreation, the producing of new human lives: "God said, 'Be fruitful and multiply'" (Gen 1: 28). Various characteristics in parents often reappear in children; and this is thought not to be entirely the result of postnatal influences. Thus there seems to be effective human participation in producing not only the body of a child but also the personality. Some believe that each individual self is a direct creation by God; and this is partly supported by Jer 38: 16. But inasmuch as even the body of an infant is said to be formed by God (for example, Job 10: 8; Jer 1: 5), all that can be taken as certain is that the ultimate power is God's; it is quite conceivable that he has delegated the actual direct exercise of this power to man. And the theory of traducianism is probably more widely held than is direct creationism—that is, that in the act of propagation, the soul, as well as the body, is produced by human instrumentality.

The second area in which human action is commonly called creative is art. Writers are said to create characters in novels and to create poetry; painters create pictures with new and distinctive qualities; sculptors create statues; architects create novel structures.

The third creative area is scientific invention, with the devising of new instruments and gadgets that have wonderful potencies. We seem to have no better word than "create" to designate such achievements that are characterized by newness.

There is one more distinctive and significant aspect of man that belongs in this analysis—the capacity for *immortality*. But that will be considered in the following main section.

The Inner Personal Self

Occasional reference has already been made to the idea of the inner self. This crucial concept needs to be further considered. The materialistic idea has often been advanced that the varied activities of man are merely the more or less mechanical functioning of a biological-neurological organism, that man is just a bundle of reactions. But certainly there must be something that has adequate ability to react in the unique ways, a being with appropriate quality to have and to exercise the various special capacities and powers. Many actions, attitudes, and relationships of which only persons are capable have been noted above; and this implies that the actor is a distinctively personal being, far above a mere organization of psychophysical systems.

There is some value—but also some danger—in designating this personal being as a personality. This word is used with a variety of significances. There is the loose popular use for the degree of charm and attractiveness or of energy and forcefulness that a person has. Closely allied is a somewhat broader view of the particular individuality of a person, including such things as temperament, special interests and capabilities, habits, and traits of character. Such uses tend to divert attention from the deeper conception that a personality is a spiritual entity with distinctive powers and capacities of a personal sort. Because of such possibilities of confusion, it is probably better to use a term such as the "personal self" or the "inner self" for this more profound idea.

For this inner self, the word "heart" is sometimes used. The Hebrew words for "heart" occur eight hundred and fifty times in the Bible; the Greek word about one hundred and fifty times. Almost always these words actually refer to the mind and thought, the desires and the will, the moral character and conscience, the emotions, or the inner man in general—for example, Jer 31: 33; Mt 5: 28; Mk 7: 6; Lk 6: 45. Sometimes the writers may have used the word literally, thinking that the psychological functions operated through the physical organ. But this seems impossible in some passages; for example, no surgical operation is contemplated when God says, "I will take out of your flesh the heart of stone and give you a heart of flesh" (Ezek 36: 26). The same is true in the command, "Circumcise the foreskin of your heart" (Deut 10: 16). And no physical ill is involved in a "broken heart" (Ps 51: 17). In such passages, the completely figurative use, referring to the personal self, is inescapable. Even when the physical organ may have been thought of as seat or instrument, the emphasis is clearly on the personal self that functioned through it. And references to

God's heart must be entirely personal and spiritual in meaning, with no implication of anything physical—for example, Jer 3: 15; Acts 13: 22.

Attention must be given also to the word "soul." Sometimes objection is made to a religious use of this word, because undesirable associations from Greek philosophy may cling to it. But it is a prominent biblical word, occurring in RSV over two hundred times in the Old Testament and over fifty times in the New Testament. The picture is somewhat complicated by the fact that both the Hebrew *nephesh* and the Greek *psuchē* often have other meanings, such as "life," or "person," or various psychical powers or activities. So "my soul" may simply be "I myself," and often "soul" is to be understood as indicating a psycho-physical totality. But by no means is this always the case. Undoubtedly it sometimes means the moral center, the inner or spiritual self, with no reference whatever to the body—for example, "The law of the Lord is perfect, reviving the soul" (Ps 19: 7); "he whose soul is not upright in him" (Hab 2: 4). In fact, a few times the soul is put in specific contrast to the body. "Shall I give . . . the fruit of my body for the sin of my soul?" (Mic 6: 7). "Do not fear those who kill the body but cannot kill the soul" (Mt 10: 28). The statements in Jas 1: 21 and 1 Pet 1: 9 about saving the soul certainly refer to the inner personal self and carry no associated implication about the body. That the word came to be used of the spiritual self appears also in the references to God's soul in at least seventeen passages in the Old Testament—for example, in Ps 11: 5, "his soul" refers to God; and God says "my soul" in Lev 26: 30; Jer 12: 7. The term points emphatically to the personal being of God, certainly with no implication that a physical body is involved.

Because of possible ambiguity and confusion in the significance of soul and personality, "spirit" is a better word for the inner self—as often in the Bible—for example, "Blessed is the man . . . in whose spirit there is no deceit" (Ps 32: 2); "What person knows a man's thoughts except the spirit of the man which is in him?" (1 Cor 2: 11). The spirit is contrasted with the body, even spoken of as independent of it—for example, ". . . for the destruction of the flesh, that his spirit may be saved" (1 Cor 5: 5); "The dust returns to the earth as it was, and the spirit returns to God who gave it" (Eccles 12: 7). Some Greek influence is possible in this last statement. But there is at least a partial parallel in the word of Jesus as his body was dying on the cross—soon to be placed in the tomb: "Father, into thy hands I commit my spirit" (Lk 23: 46). Similar is Stephen's word, as recorded in Acts 7: 59. Also, in view of the prominence of the Spirit of God, speaking of man's spirit emphasizes his close relationship with God.

There is further support, if any is needed, for the distinct recognition of the inner self: "Thou desirest truth in the inward being" (Ps 51: 6); "I will put my law within them" [literally, "in their inward part"] (Jer 31: 33). Even God says, "My heart [literally, "my inward parts"] yearns for him" (Jer 31: 20; and cf, similarly, Is 63: 15). Certainly God was not thought of as having physical viscera, although that was the basic meaning of the word used in these last two passages; the supposed (human) seat of emotion had become an established symbol for the personal self.

From all this it is evident that the reality of the inner spiritual self, distinct from the body, was recognized and expressed in the Bible, even though not with perfect clarity and precision of language or with complete consistency; where unity is emphasized, it is a functional unity. The essence of the divine image is in this inner personal self.

The question may well be raised here whether infants, and idiots, have the divine image. When we think in terms of powers, either as actually functioning or as latent capacities, rather than of positive existing qualities, it is obvious that infants have the divine image. They are persons, with an inner spiritual self that can develop—they do not just gradually become persons. As for idiots, certain unfortunate conditions cause the inherent capacities to remain in a permanently undeveloped state in this life; but they are still persons, with an inner spiritual self. They too have the divine image.

With this background, the implications for the future may now be considered. Although there is some variation in the biblical evidence, the preponderant testimony indicates conscious survival. There are two alternative views. A very few passages, coming from a spirit of skepticism or hopeless discouragement, suggest annihilation (Job 7: 21; Ps 39: 13). However, so far as the wicked are concerned, it is inconceivable that a personal self would cease to exist at physical death and, then, that a righteous and loving God would perform what would amount to a new act of creation to produce a personal being, at the time of resurrection, in order to consign him to eternal suffering for the sin of one who formerly existed. Almost equally difficult is the idea of a new person inheriting the blessings promised to the godly.

There are several references to death as a sleep—for example, Dan 12: 2; Jn 11: 11–13; 1 Thess 4: 13–15. Also, there are a few statements that the dead have no knowledge, no experience of God, and therefore probably no consciousness (for example, Ps 6: 5; Eccles 9: 10); these are in terms of the semi-heathen idea of Sheol—a cheerless, sorrowful situation. And some scholars consider such statements determinative, and believe that between death and resurrection people are in a sort of coma—unconscious, dormant, inert.

But there are other passages that point strongly in the opposite direction. The significant message given several times in the Old Testament is that the basic blessedness of fellowship with God will continue. It is said of Enoch that he "walked with God; and he was not, for God took him" (Gen 5: 24); obviously "he was not" means he was not on earth, he was gone—not that he ceased to exist. Apparently he went directly to a fuller fellowship with God. The same is true of Elijah (2 Kings 2: 11). The outburst of faith in Job 19: 26 is noteworthy: "Then without my flesh I shall see God" (this is the most probable translation of a difficult and possibly corrupt passage). The climax is in Ps 73: 23 f: "I am continually with thee . . . afterward thou wilt receive me to glory." Briggs, Fleming James, Oesterley, Terrien, Weiser, and other commentators see here the conscious survival of the person, a richer fullness of fellowship with God, a true life after death. Two other noteworthy passages in the Psalms transcend the popular idea of Sheol. The writer of Ps 49: 15 believed that God either would take him directly to himself, instead of letting him go to Sheol, or else would quickly deliver him from there. And Ps 139: 8 has the unique idea that God is in Sheol as well as in heaven, so that even there one would not be cut off from his presence. Conscious survival appears also apart from this faith in God. In the strange picture in Is 14: 9 ff, at least kings (not all of whom, surely, would be godly) are shown as speaking. Obviously none of these are subsequent to resurrection.

The New Testament has equally significant teachings. We note first the events of the Transfiguration: Moses and Elijah talked with Jesus. Later Jesus said that God is "God . . . of the living" (Mk 12: 27); and since he is the God of Abraham, Isaac, and Jacob, they are living. The parable of Dives and Lazarus (Lk 16: 19–31) —though certainly we need not take all details literally—would have no point whatever if there were no continuing conscious personal existence for both the godly and the ungodly. Jesus said to the penitent thief, "Today you will be with me in Paradise" (Lk 23: 43)—obviously alive and conscious. The preaching to "the spirits in prison" (1 Pet 3: 19) almost surely was before the resurrection of Jesus; and of course those who heard him were conscious. Paul says, "To depart and be with Christ . . . is far better . . . [than] to remain in the flesh" (Phil 1: 23 f). This is important testimony to the distinction between the body and the personal self as well as to the continuation of the latter in conscious fellowship with Christ. This clearly points to immediate experience after death, not to a future resurrection situation; so also all these references. But none of them exclude or contradict a future resurrection, with an enriching transformation for the godly.

It is understandable that there is some opposition to using the word "immortality." This is partly because it has been contaminated by Greek philosophic speculations. Also, God "alone has immortality" (1 Tim 6: 16).

This, however, is to be understood as meaning that deathlessness is inherent only in God. But God can bestow this on man. In the New Testament this endowment is mentioned specifically only for Christians: "When the mortal puts on immortality . . . death is swallowed up in victory . . . God gives us the victory through our Lord Jesus Christ" (1 Cor 15: 54, 57; cf also 2 Tim 1: 10). It seems that here immortality has practically the same rich significance as eternal life—that is, not merely existence beyond this earthly life, but the blessed condition promised to those who are in Christ by faith. It is not said whether this bestowal of immortality is at resurrection or previously.

On the whole, even though the word "immortality" has some New Testament use, it is probably better to avoid the difficulties and possible ambiguities that it raises (either of mere philosophical humanism or of the glorious eternal life and of timing) by using some expression (as partly suggested already) such as "the continued conscious existence of the personal self under the power of God." The Bible has no specific statement of how the ungodly are caused to continue existing—it just shows the fact, as has been noted above with reference to Dives, the kings in Is 14, and the spirits in prison; the term "immortality" is not applied to them.

There is no evidence that any subhuman creature has any life beyond this earthly life in the flesh. If one would assume that some animals do, it would be practically impossible to find a reasonable line of demarcation between those that do and those that do not. But it seems that all human beings have this capacity; and so it is to be seen as being included in the divine image.

The Importance of This

The basic message in the creation story is echoed several times in the Bible. The divine image is mentioned twice more in Genesis—in 5: 1 and 9: 6. Probably Job 32: 8 refers to it. It is specifically stated in 1 Cor 11: 7 and Jas 3: 9. Most special is Ps 8. Someone has said that this is Gen 1 set to music—even though the distinctive words are not used.

These passages show that the divine image is a continuing reality and permanent value for mankind. There have been some attempts to limit it to the original creation and to claim that it was lost when man fell into sin—especially by those holding the view (rejected above) that it meant moral perfection. But both New Testament statements just mentioned indicate it as a present fact. Men *have* the divine image—they did not only previously have it. The essence of the divine image was not lost in the fall. It was damaged but not destroyed—defaced but not effaced. All the various powers and functions were, indeed, weakened and perverted—spiritual, moral, psychological. But the basic reality remains, with the various capacities that make human life uniquely significant.

The divine image is the foundation of the whole religious philosophy about man. Herein lies the distinctive quality of human life. It is the basis of man's dignity and value, and also of his responsibility. It is this that both enables man to receive spiritual salvation and makes him worth saving. It makes his life here meaningful, and makes possible the outreach to continued and increased significance beyond this life.

The ethical powers that have been noted are essential for any real morality. This requires that choices of action can be made by exercising a rational and responsible volition. The person must not be a victim of determinism, with actions predetermined and completely controlled by inheritance, by previous experiences, by any material or psychic mechanism of absolute causation, or by any other compulsive force. Neither may a person be of such a nature that there would simply be blind, erratic, irresponsible, arbitrary actions according to mere whim or impulse or caprice, without intelligent purpose or motivation and regardless of previously established and existing character. Thus the whole range of psychical powers, and their specialized application in conscience, are needed. Also, for the higher levels of good, both the relationship with God and the social outlook are necessary. Thus extensive areas of the divine image are important for the proper moral functioning.

As this divinely given dignity of human nature is more clearly recognized, it becomes a valuable stimulus both to nobler effort and worthier living by the individual and to finer relations with others.

Mitchell Dahood, SJ
Pontifical Biblical Institute, Rome

Chiasmus in Job: A Text-Critical and Philological Criterion

Failure to appreciate the chiastic word order may account for Otto Eissfeldt's[1] unsatisfactory translation of *UT*, 51: VII: 37–39:

wyʿn aliyn bʿl
ib bʿl lm tḫš a:b
lm tḫš nṯq dmrn b:a′

Und es hob an Aliyan Baal:
Ihr Feinde Hadads, warum meidet(?) ihr,
warum meidet(?) ihr die Waffe Demarus?

In the second and third cola, the position of *lm tḫš* suggests a chiastic arrangement; this means that disputed *nṯq dmrn* should be the close semantic counterpart of *ib bʿl*, "O foes of Baal!" in an a:b:b:a′ sequence:

And Puissant Baal replied:
O foes of Baal, why do you flee,
why do you flee, O assailants of Demarous?

Since it is now apparent from *UT*, 2001: 7–8, that *dmrn* is an epithet of *bʿl*—and that is the point[2] Eissfeldt wanted to make—it becomes very probable that the one remaining uncertain word, *nṯq*, is a synonym of *ib*, "foes." Eissfeldt interprets *nṯq* as the noun *Waffe*, but the apparent chiastic parallelism of *nṯq dmrn* and *ib bʿl* suggests that *nṯq* are persons, hence to be parsed as a qal participle of *nṯq*, from which derive Ugar *nṯq*, "weapon," "ballista," "missile," and Heb *nēšeq* or *nešeq*, "weapons," "missiles." When *nṯq dmrn* is rendered "assailants of Baal," the verb *tḫš* can be identified with Heb *ḥûš*, "to hasten, make haste, flee."

The hypothesis proposed in this paper may be stated thus: when the poet uses the chiastic word order, the synonymy of the parallel members tends to be stricter than when the order is not chiastic.[3] It bids fair to alleviate the ambiguity in numerous verses of the book of Job; in several verses (e.g., 34: 6) it elicits sense for the first time. To bring out more clearly the chiastic structure of the original, the translations will be very literal, hewing to the Hebrew word order as closely as English idiom will permit.

Job 21: 9 may be chosen as the first example because it focuses the problem sharply:

bottêhem šālôm mippāḥad	a:b
w^e^lō' šēbeṭ '^e^lô^a^h ʿ^a^lêhem	b′:a′

In their houses is prosperity without fear,
and the rod of God is not upon them.

Uncertainty touches only the first colon; the phrase *bottêhem šālôm mippāḥad* may be parsed either in the light of Job 5: 24, *w^e^yādaʿtā kî šālôm 'oh^o^lekā*, "You shall know that your tent is safe" (RSV), or, in view of its immediate counterpart, *w^e^lō' šēbeṭ '^e^lô^a^h ʿ^a^lêhem*, "and the rod of God is not upon them," a nominal sentence consisting of a subject and prepositional phrase. If we assume a similar nominal sentence in the first colon and a chiastic arrangement of the entire verse, then ambivalent *bottêhem* answers to prepositional *ʿ^a^lêhem* both in function as well as in sound. Hebrew grammars and lexica admit the wide prepositional use of *bêt* when in the construct state—that is, it need not be preceded by the preposition *b^e^*.[4] A close parallel is Prov 15: 6, *bêt ṣaddîq ḥōsen rāb*, "In the house of the just man is much treasure," where the apparatus of *BHK*[3], "l c Targ *b^e^bêt*," may safely be ignored.[5] Equally to be declined are proposals to emend *šālôm* to *šāl^e^mû* on the authority of LXX, Syr, and Vulg (so Siegfried, Duhm), or to *šālw* (Houbigant), or to *š^e^lēwîm* (Perles).

The assonance of parallel *bottêhem*, "in their houses," and *ʿ^a^lêhem*, "upon them," suggests that in the preceding verse (Job 21: 8) *lipnêhem*, "in front of them," was intended to balance assonant *l^e^ʿênêhem*, "before their eyes." Hence the *athnach* of MT should be advanced from *ʿimmam* to *lipnêhem* and Job 21: 8 be read and scanned as follows:

zarʿām nākôn lipnêhem	a:b:c
ʿammīm (MT *ʿimmām*) (*w^e^*) *ṣe'^e^ṣā'êhem l^e^ʿênêhem*	b′:a′:c′

Their progeny is settled in front of them,
vigorous is their offspring before their eyes.

In MT the line seems overlong, and *BHK*[3] suggests either the deletion of *lipnêhem* or the transfer of *'immām*, repointed *'ammām*, to the second colon. When, however, *lipnêhem* and *le'ênêhem* are seen to balance each other, the chiastic arrangement of the remaining four words comes into view. Since *zar'ām*, "their progeny," obviously pairs with *ṣe'eṣā'êhem*, "their offspring," one may conclude that uncertain *'mm* chiastically answers to participial *nākôn*, "settled." Accordingly, vocalize as plural adjective *'ammīm* from the root **'mm*, "to be vigorous, sagacious."[6] Consonantal *'mm* would then be another instance of *scriptio defectiva*, so characteristic of the text of Job.[7]

Job 6: 15	*'aḥay bāgedû kemô nāḥal*	a:b:c
	ka'apîq neḥālîm ya'abōrû	c':b'

My brothers have been treacherous as a wadi,
like a source of wadis they have vanished.

The ambivalent word here is *ya'abōrû*. Is its subject *'aḥay*, "my brothers," as understood by KJV, "My brethren have dealt deceitfully as a brook, *and* as the stream of brooks they pass away," or is it *neḥālîm*, "wadis," as construed by RSV, "My brethren are treacherous as a torrent bed, as freshets that pass away," and by NEB, "But my brothers have been treacherous as a mountain stream, like the channels of streams that pass away." The latter construction assumes a relative clause with the relative pronoun unexpressed—no problem in the elliptical style of Job—whereas the chiastic position of the synonymous middle members suggests that the verbs are also chiastically arranged, with *'aḥay*, "my brothers," the subject of both verbs. It may be noted in passing that the *qtl/yqtl* sequence of verbs follows Canaanite practice (here both verbs refer to the same past time),[8] and the *kemô/ka* parallelism reflects the balance of *km/k*, witnessed in such texts as *UT*, 51: IV: 51.

Job 8: 5	*'im 'attāh tešaḥēr 'el 'ēl*	a:b:c
	we 'el šadday titḥannān	c':b'

If you will seek after El,
and to Shaddai make supplication.

Since piel *šiḥēr* elsewhere always governs the accusative, some scholars have proposed either the emendation of first-colon *'el* to *'et* (cf. *BHK*[3]) or its deletion.[9] Others who retain *'el* tend to explain it on the analogy of *dāraš 'el*, "to seek after,"[10] but a more immediate explanation is prompted by the chiastic ordering of the verse. To make the chiasmus with *'el šadday* perfect, the author chose a construction that would yield *'el 'ēl*. Here then would be an instance where the appreciation of Job's chiastic style proves text-critically valuable.

Job 11: 14	*'im 'āwen beyādekā harḥîqēhû*	a:b:c
	we'al taškēn be'ōholekā 'awlāh	c′:b′:a′

If iniquity is in your hand, put it far away,
and permit no evil to dwell in your tent.[11]

Consonantal *tškn* lends itself to two interpretations. Though MT construed it as hiphil *taškēn*, the ancient versions read it as qal *tiškōn*. The application of the stylistic principle of chiasmus sustains MT hiphil *taškēn* against qal *tiškōn* of the ancient versions. Since the line is apparently patterned in an a:b:c::c′:b′:a′ sequence, hiphil *taškēn* makes an apter counterpart to hiphil *harḥîqēhû*, "put it far away," than does qal *tiškōn*, which involves a shift from the second person of the first colon to the third person in the latter half of the verse. This shift partially obscures the chiastic pattern.

Job 12: 10	*'ašer beyādô nepeš kol ḥāy*	a:b:c
	werûaḥ kol bāšār 'ōšō (MT *bešar 'îš*)	c′:b′

That from his hand is the soul of every living being,
and the spirit in all flesh is his gift.

Proposed in 1965, and confirmed by a reading from Qumran,[12] the reading is further sustained by the stylistic observation that when the order is chiastic, the synonymy tends to be stricter. In the present instance, this means that consonantal *'š* should semantically balance *beyādô*, "from his hand," a balance that is realized when it is vocalized *'ōšō* and derived from *'wš*, "to give, donate," a well-documented root,[13] witnessed in Ugar *ušn*, "gift." MT *'îš* would thus have stemmed from an original defectively written *'š*, which, on the basis of Arab *'awsu*, "gift," and Ugar *ušn*, "gift," I would now vocalize as *'ōšō*, to balance *yādô*, and to avoid two accents falling on two successive syllables; see below on Job 41: 7.

Job 13: 12	*zikrōnêkem mišlê 'ēper*	a:b
	legabbê ḥōmer gabbêkem	b′:a′

Your maxims are ashen aphorisms,
indeed defenses of clay your defenses.

Since the order of the two cola is chiastic, one may infer that the syntactic elements in each colon are similar. The first colon is a nominal sentence consisting of subject and predicate. One thus looks for a predicate followed by a subject in the second colon. These emerge when *l*^{e} of *l*^{e}*gabbê* is construed as the emphatic *lamedh*,[14] "indeed," frequent in nominal sentences, rather than as the preposition.[15]

Job 15: 18	*ʾ*^{a}*šer ḥ*^{a}*kāmîm yaggîdû*	a:b:c
	w^{e}*lōʾ kiḥ*^{a}*dûm ʾ*^{a}*bôtām* (MT *kiḥ*^{a}*dû mēʾ*^{a}*bôtām*)	c′:b′

What wise men have told,
and their fathers did not conceal from them.

The chiastic positioning suggests that second colon *ʾ*^{a}*bôtām* should be the subject of the second colon, just as *ḥ*^{a}*kāmîm*, "wise men," is the subject of the first colon. This becomes possible when prepositional *mē* of MT *mēʾ*^{a}*bôtām* is attached to the preceding word, as has long been suggested, and parsed as the dative suffix. In the two transitive[16] verbs *yaggîdû* and *kiḥ*^{a}*dûm* one notices the *yqtl-qtl* sequence commented upon in connection with Job 6: 15.

Chiasmus and dative suffix likewise characterize Job 31: 16:

ʾim ʾemnāʿēm ḥēpeṣ (MT *ʾemnaʿ mēḥēpeṣ*) *dallîm*	a:b:c
w^{e}*ʿênê ʾalmānāh ʾ*^{a}*kalleh*	c′:b′

If I have withheld the poor's desire from them,
or the eyes of the widow caused to fail.

Since *ʿênê ʾalmānāh*, "the eyes of the widow," is the direct object, it would seem that its chiastic counterpart *ḥēpeṣ dallîm*, "the poor's desire," should also be the direct object. By attaching the preposition *mē* of *mēḥēpeṣ* to the preceding verb and parsing it as the prospective dative suffix, we obtain the desired direct object. Moreover, the verb *mānaʿ*, "to withhold," elsewhere governs the accusative of the thing desired, e.g., Job 22: 7, *ūmērāʿēb timnaʿ lāḥem*, "and from the hungry you withheld bread," or the accusative of the person refused, e.g., Num 24: 11, *m*^{e}*nāʿ*^{a}*kā yhwh mikkābôd*, "Yahweh has refused you glory." The dative suffix of *ʾemnāʿēm*, "(If) I have withheld from them," recalls Job 15: 18, *kiḥ*^{a}*dûm*, "did (not) conceal from them."

Job 17: 7	*wattēkah mikkaʿaś ʿênî*	a:b:c
	wîṣūray kaṣṣēl kālū-mī (MT *kullām*)	c′:b′:a′

Dimmed with sorrow is mine eye,
and my limbs like a shadow are wasted.

The evident chiasmus of the line points to the desirability of a verb in consonantal *klm*. This stylistic observation lends support to the suggestion of N.M. Sarna[17] that *kālū* plus enclitic *mem* be read for MT *kullām*. I would vocalize *kālū-mī*, to produce assonance with *ʿênî* and to even the syllable count at 8: 8.

Job 19: 14	*mimmennî ḥādᵉlû qᵉrôbāy*	a:b:c
	ūmᵉyuddāʿay šᵉkēḥûnî	c′:b′:a′

From me have fallen away my close friends,
and my kinsmen have forgotten me.

With the transposition of *mimmennî* from the end of vs 13 to the beginning of vs 14, the syllable count of vs 13 becomes 7: 7 and that of vs 14 evens at 9: 9. What is more, in vs 14 an a:b:c::c′:b′:a′ chiastic pattern, so characteristic of Job, comes to light; it consists of prepositional phrase: verb:subject:: subject:verb: pronominal suffix.

Job 20: 6	*ʾim yaʿᵃleh laššāmayim mšy* (MT *śîʾô*)	a:b:c
	ʾô rōʾšô lāʿāb yaggîᵃʿ	c′:b′:a′

If his statue should rise to heaven,
or its head to the clouds reach up.

The unexplained hapax legomenon *śîʾô* presents the chief difficulty in this verse. The chiastic word order bespeaks a close semantic bond between c and c′. The LXX reading, *a toû tà dôra*, indicates that they had *šay*, "present," (Ps 68: 30; 76: 12) in mind. Another possibility assumes an instance of a shared consonant[18] whereby the final *mem* of *šāmayim* also serves as the initial consonant of *mš*, "statue," a well-attested noun in the Phoenician inscriptions[19] and probably identifiable in 2 Kings 23: 12. The suffix of *mšy* would parse as the third person singular suffix *-y*, as in Phoenician, a stylistic variant to the normal suffix of *rōʾšô*.[20] Of course, the picture that comes to mind is that of Dan 3: 1: "King Nebuchadnezzar made an image of gold, ninety feet high and nine feet wide."

Job 26: 5	*hārᵉpāʾ îm yᵉḥôlālû-mī*	a:b
	tēḥat (MT *mittaḥat*) *mayim wᵉšôkᵉnêhem*	b′:a′

The Shades writhe in pain,
dismayed are the waters and their dwellers.

A. C. M. Blommerde[21] has correctly seen that MT *mittaḥat* conceals the verb needed chiastically to balance *yᵉḥôlālû*, "writhe in pain." When *mī* is attached to the first-colon verb as the enclitic, consonantal *tḥt* can be parsed as the niphal third feminine singular *tēḥat* followed by the plural subjects understood collectively. Compare Ezek 32: 30, which juxtaposes the roots *ḥll* and *ḥtt* that are juxtaposed here. The emergent chiasmus and the 9: 9 syllable count tend to preclude the various emendations and reconstructions that have been hitherto proposed.[22]

Job 28: 2 *barzel mē'āpār yuqqāḥ* a:b:c
wᵉ 'eben yᵉṣûqā (MT *yāṣûq*) *nᵉḥûšāh* b':a'

Iron is taken from ore,
and from smelted rock, bronze.

To elicit a coherent statement from this couplet, the critic must recognize, first, the use of a double-duty preposition, with *'eben*, "rock," sharing the preposition of synonymous *mē'āpār*, "from ore." Second, he must see in consonantal *yṣwq* defective spelling for feminine *yᵉṣûqā* that modifies feminine *'eben*. For similar instances, compare Job 20: 26; 28: 14, 21.

Job 32: 14 *wᵉlō 'e'ᵉrōk* (MT *lō' 'ārak*) *'ēley* (MT *'ēlay*) *millîn* a:b:c
ūbᵉ'imrêkem lō' 'ᵃšîbennû c':b':a'

I shall not marshal against him your arguments,
and with your words I shall not rebut him.

From the chiastic position of *millîn* and *'imrêkem*, the textual critic may assume that unintelligible MT *lō' 'ārak 'ēlay* is the close semantic counterpart to *lō' 'ᵃšîbennû*, "I shall not rebut him." The reading *lō 'e'ᵉrōk 'ēley*, based on no consonantal changes of the text, provides the desired counterpart. To be sure, one may read *lō'*, invoking the practice of shared consonants, but since the negative particle in Ugaritic is simply *l*, the reading *lō* may stand. Consonantal *''rk 'ly* must then answer to *'ᵃšîbennû*, "I shall rebut him"; this becomes possible when the suffix of *'ly* is parsed as the Phoenician third person singular *-y*. Thus the suffix of *'ēley* balances the accusative suffix *-ennû* of *'ᵃšîbennû*. For other instances of *'el*, "against," compare Job 9: 4; 15: 13, 25, 26. Suffixless *millîn*, "your arguments," shares the suffix of synonymous *'imrêkem*, "your words."[23]

Job 34: 6 *'al mišpāṭî 'ᵃkuzzāb* (MT *'ᵃkazzēb*) a:b
'ānûš ḥiṣṣî bᵉlî pāša' b':a'

Despite my honesty I am declared a liar,
wounded by his arrows though sinless.

BDB, p. 754b, recognizes *'al*, "despite, notwithstanding," here and in Job 10: 7, but *GB*[17], p. 586b, rightly adds Job 16: 17. Here it may be noted that failure to grasp this nuance may underlie the defective understanding of Job 23: 2, *gam hayyôm m^{e}rî śîḥî yādî kāb^{e}dāh ʿal ʾanḥātî*, "Especially today my complaint is bitter; his hand [suffix of *yādî* is third singular] is heavy despite my groaning." Compare NEB, "My thoughts today are resentful, for God's hand is heavy on me in my trouble."[24]

Since *ʿal mišpāṭî*, "despite my honesty, " and *b^{e}lî pāšaʿ*, "though sinless," evidently pair off, *ʾkzb* and *ʾnwš ḥṣy* must be mutually elucidated. MT passive *ʾānûš* points to the passive vocalization *ʾ^{a}kuzzab*, "I am declared a liar,"[25] namely, by Yahweh. Accordingly the suffix of *ḥṣy*, to be pointed either as singular *ḥiṣṣî*, "his arrow," or plural *ḥiṣṣey*, "his arrows," should refer to Yahweh. This analysis thus links our verse to Job 6: 4, *ḥiṣṣê šadday ʿimmādî*, "Shaddai's arrows are toward me," and Job 16: 14, "His shafts encompass me, he pierces my entrails without pity."

Job 36: 3 *ʾeśśāʾ dēʿî l^{e}mērāḥôq* a:b
ūl^{e}p ʿ^{a}lî ʾettēn ṣedeq b′:a′

I bring my knowledge from afar,
and from my Maker I present the truth.

The similarity of *ʾeśśāʾ* and *ʾettēn*, both from *primae nun* verbs, bespeaks the chiastic structure of the verse. And since *l^{e}mērāḥôq*, as in Job 39: 29, signifies "from afar," *l^{e}* of *l^{e}pōʿ^{a}lî* carries the force of "from," as so often in Ugaritic. Cf UT, 68: 12–13, where *l*, "from," is parallel to *l*, "from," as here.[26] The precise force of the hapax legomenon phrase *ʾettēn ṣedeq* must be inferred from its chiastic parallelism with *ʾeśśāʾ dēʿî*, whose meaning is tolerably clear. In *dēʿî* and *ṣedeq* we have the breakup of a composite phrase signifying true knowledge.[27]

Job 36: 12 *w^{e}ʾim l ʾ yišm^{e}ʿû*
b^{e}šelaḥ yaʿ^{a}b rû a:b
w^{e}yigw^{e}ʿû bib^{e}lî dāʿat b′:a′

But if they do not obey,
the Channel[28] they cross,
and expire in Unknowing.

In his study of this passage, N. J. Tromp[29] recognizes the a:b::b′:a′ structure of the verse but hesitates to accept *b^{e}lî dāʿat* as a poetic epithet for Sheol. He renders the final colon, "And they die for lack of knowledge." But he fails to notice that the translation and exegesis of our verse are bound up with the preceding verse:

ʾim yišm^{e}ʿû w^{e}yaʿ^{a}bōdû
y^{e}kallû y^{e}mêhem baṭ ôb
ūš^{e}nêhem bann^{e}ʿîmîm

If they obey and serve,
they pass their days in happiness,
and their years in comfort.

Here the consequence of obedience is expressed by two terms that are strictly parallel and synonymous: *ṭôb* and *n*ᵉ*ʿîmîm.* In vs 12 the consequence of disobedience is presumably stated in strictly parallel and synonymous terms: *šelaḥ* and *b*ᵉ*lî dāʿat.* The basic thesis of this paper, that the chiastic pattern bespeaks an even stricter synonymy, excludes Dhorme's and Tromp's explanation of *b*ᵉ*lî dāʿat* as giving the cause of their death. The cause of their death is *ʾim lōʾ yišm*ᵉ*ʿû*, "if they do not obey," not ignorance. Vs 10 plainly states, "He opened their ear for instruction and warned them to draw back from evildoing"; so it seems improbable that two verses later death would be ascribed to ignorance.

This translation and interpretation are sustained by comparison with Job 14: 20–21, which collocate the two motifs of Channel and Unknowing: "You overwhelm him, he passes away forever; you change his visage and send him across the Channel (*t*ᵉ*šall*ᵉ*ḥēhû*). His sons are honored, but he never knows (*lōʾ yēdāʿ*); they are disgraced, but he perceives not."[30]

Job 37: 3 *taḥat kol haššāmayim yišrēhû* a:b
*w*ᵉ*ʾôrô ʿal kan*ᵉ*pôt hāʾāreṣ* b′:a′

Beneath the whole heaven it flashes,[31]
and his lightning is upon the corners of the earth.

In the dispute over the meaning of the hapax legomenon *yišrēhû*, the stylistic observation regarding the chiastic wording sustains the definition of *šrh* (Ugar *šrh*), "to flash," since its chiastic counterpart is *ʾôrô*, "his lightning."

Job 39: 6 *ʾ*ᵃ*šer śamtî ʿ*ᵃ*rābāh bêtô* a:b:c
*ūmišk*ᵉ*nôtāyw m*ᵉ*lēḥāh* c′:b′

I made the wilderness his home,
and his dwelling the salt flats.

The chiastic parallelism with singular *bêtô*, "his home," shows that *mišk*ᵉ*nôtāyw*, though plural in form, is to be understood as singular in meaning.[32] The apparatus of *BHK*³ recommends the insertion, *metri causa*, of *ʾereṣ* before *m*ᵉ*lēḥāh* in the second colon, but the strict chiastic balance of three-syllabled *ʿ*ᵃ*rābāh*, "wilderness," and three-syllabled *m*ᵉ*lēḥāh*, "salt flats," discountenances such an insertion. What is more, the current 9: 8 syllable count and the fact that *ūmišk*ᵉ*nôtāyw* can bear two accents render such an addition unnecessary.

Job 39: 8 *yātûr* (MT *y^etûr*) *hārîm mir'ēhû* a:b
w^e'aḥar kol yārôq yidrōš b':a'

He roams the hills as his pasture,
and for anything green he searches.

The longstanding practice of reading verbal *yātûr* for nominal *y^etûr* of MT is upheld by the resultant chiasmus with verbal *yidrôš*.[33]

Job 41: 7 *ga'^awāh '^apîqê māginnîm* a:b
sāgûr ḥôtām ṣūrō (MT *ṣār*) b':a'

His back[34] rows of shields,
enclosed by a seal[35] his dorsum.

Once the chiasmus is recognized, it becomes probable that consonantal *ṣr* should be identified with Ugar *ẓr*, "back, dorsum."[36] The vocalization *ṣūrō* instead of *ṣūr* is adopted to avoid two accents falling on two successive syllables, the same procedure as above at Job 12: 10. The chiastic parallelism of *ga'^awāh* and *ṣūrō* thus recalls the straight balance between *'^aṣāmāyw*, "his bones," and *g^erāmāyw*, "his gristles," in Job 40: 18. *Scriptio defectiva* in the original will account for MT *ṣar* as against revowelled *ṣūrō*; since it is a *mediae waw* root, it would appear as *ṣwr* in normal Hebrew orthography.

The recognition of chiasmus in Job proves valuable in reducing the number of options in equivocal texts. In some verses, it can even prove decisive. The MT (as well as the ancient versions which, though checked, were rarely cited for lack of space) betrays a limited appreciation of this element of Job's style.

Notes

1 *Bi Or* 26 (1969), 182–83.

2 A point also made in my *Ugaritic-Hebrew Philology* (Rome, 1965), p. 55.

3 In *Ugarit-Forschungen* 1 (1969), 24–25, the writer has applied this hypothesis to *UT* 49: I: 22–24; 1 Aqht: 114–15; 77: 38–39, and 'nt: III: 23–25.

4 H. Bauer and P. Leander, *Historische Grammatik der hebräischen Sprache des Alten Testaments*, p. 217a; *BDB*, p. 109a; W. Baumgartner, *HALAT*, p. 119b. It may be noted here that the same usage appears in Ugaritic, underlining the close syntactic relationship between Ugaritic and Hebrew; see *UT*, §§ 10.4; 11.8.

5 See M. Dahood, *Proverbs and Northwest Semitic Philology* (Rome, 1963), p. 33.

6 For the Ugar-Heb attestation of this root, see Dahood, *Psalms I* (AB), pp. 112–13, 283–84, 286; *Psalms II* (AB), pp. xxiii, 93, 231, 316, 348, 368; *Psalms III* (AB), pp. xxxi, 68, 116; H. J. van Dijk, *Ezekiel's Prophecy on Tyre* (*Ez. 26, 1–28, 19*): *A New Approach* (Rome, 1968), pp. 4–10, 100–101; A. C. M. Blommerde, *Northwest Semitic Grammar and Job* (Rome, 1969), pp. 122–23. Particularly relevant for the present purpose, since it collocates two of the roots in our verse, is Ps 89: 22, *yādî tākîn 'ammô*, "My hand shall supply his power," as read and translated in *Psalms II* (AB), pp. 309, 316.

[7] Cf. D. N. Freedman, "Orthographic Peculiarities in the Book of Job," *Eretz Israel* 9 (1969), 35–44.

[8] For a list of examples from the Psalter, consult Dahood, *Psalms III* (AB), pp. 422–23.

[9] Thus Georg Fohrer, *Das Buch Hiob* (*KAT*; Gütersloh, 1965), p. 184, writes, "'Nach' ist zu streichen, da *šḥr* den Akkusativ nach sich zieht."

[10] *Mutatis mutandis*, the observations on Job 8: 5 also obtain in Job 15: 25.

[11] Though plural in form, *'ōholekā*, being the name of a dwelling, is singular in meaning. See below on Job 39: 6. This usage is well documented in Ugaritic and in Hebrew; consult *UT*, § 13.17; Dahood, *Ugaritic-Hebrew Philology*, p. 37; *Psalms III* (AB), p. 384. This principle applies also in Job 37: 8, to be discussed below. Hence Fohrer's comment (*Hiob*, p. 222) on our passage, "mit zahlreichen Versionen ist das Singular *b'hlk* statt Plural zu lesen," must be disallowed. The collocation of *yādᵉkā*, "your hand," and *'awlāh*, "evil," in this verse echoes their juxtaposition in *UT*, 127: 32, *šqlt bġlt ydk*, "You have let your hand fall into evil."

[12] See Dahood, "Ugaritic *ušn*, Job 12, 10 and 11QPsᵃPlea 3–4," in *Bibl* 47 (1966), 107–8.

[13] F. M. Cross, Jr., presents fully the evidence in *BASOR* 184 (1966), 8–9; see also *BASOR* 193 (1969), 23, and Dahood, *Psalms III* (AB), pp. 61–62, 128.

[14] As recognized by, among others, C. Brockelmann, *Hebräische Syntax* (Neukirchen, 1956), § 31a, p. 28.

[15] Compare the prepositional explanation given by S. R. Driver and G. B. Gray, *The Book of Job* (*ICC*; Edinburgh, 1921), II, 83, "*lgby ḥmr gbykm* = '*become* bosses of clay,' the *l*, as often, denoting *transition into*, usually with a verb, as *śm*, *ntn*, *hyh*, etc., but occasionally in poetic and late Hebrew without one, as Mic 1: 14; Hab 1: 11, Zech 4: 7; Lam 4: 3." But in all these texts the *lamedh* can more convincingly be explained as emphatic rather than as prepositional; cf F. Nötscher, *VT* 3 (1953), 372–80.

[16] Needlessly rendered as passives and in brackets by *NEB*:

> [what has been handed down by wise men
> and was not concealed from them by their fathers].

[17] Some Instances of the Enclitic *-m* in Job," *JJS* 6 (1955), 108–10, esp. 110.

[18] The most recent study of this orthographic practice being that of W. G. E. Watson, "Shared Consonants in Northwest Semitic," *Bibl* 50 (1969), 525–33, with full bibliography. In a paper read at the annual national meeting of the American Oriental Society in Baltimore, 16 April 1970, S. Gevirtz applied this principle to good effect in Gen 49: 3, *yeter rš't* (MT *śᵉ'ēt*) *wᵉyeter 'ōz* (MT *'āz*), "an excess of authority and an excess of power." The resultant parallelism of *rš't* and *'z* matches that of Phoenician Karatepe III: 6, *rš' t n'mt 'z 'dr*, "good authority and mighty power." [See S. Gevirtz, "The Reprimand of Reuben," *JNES* 30 (1971), 87–98.—Reader's note.]

[19] See C. F. Jean and J. Hoftijzer, *Dictionnaire des inscriptions sémitiques de l'ouest* (Leiden, 1965), pp. 168–69.

[20] Jeffrey H. Tigay, "Psalm 7: 5 and Ancient Near Eastern Treaties," *JBL* 89 (1970) 178–86, has unwittingly confirmed the existence of the third singular suffix *-y* by his observation that Ps 7: 5 *ṣôrᵉrî* should mean "his enemy" because it is parallel to *šôlᵉmî*, "my ally." On p. 182 he correctly renders vs 5, "If I repaid my ally with treachery and rescued his enemy . . .", but needlessly emends *ṣôrᵉrî* to *ṣôrᵉrô*, claiming scribal confusion of *wāw* and *yōd*. But this emendation is ruled out because it destroys the rhyme of the three syllables of *šôlᵉmî* with the three syllables of *ṣôrᵉrî*! That Hebrew, like Phoenician, possessed the third singular suffix *-y* steadily gains new adherents; e.g., L. Sabottka, *BZ* 12 (1968), 242; C. van Leeuwen, *Nederlands Theologisch Tijdschrift* 24 (1969), 140; L. Gorssen, *ETL* 46 (1970), 298.

[21] *Northwest Semitic Grammar and Job* (Rome, 1969), p. 103.

[22] Among them, those proposed by Lynn Roy Clapham, "Sanchuniaton: The First Two Cycles," a thesis presented to the Department of Near Eastern Languages of Harvard University, December 1969, p. 74. Clapham scans these verses: *hrp'ym yḥwllw mtḥt mym/šknyhm ʿrym mšʾl ngdw/ʾyn kswt lʾbdwn*, "The Rephaim writhe from beneath the waters/Their inhabitants the 'Watchers' from Sheol before Him/There is no cover for the deceased."

[23] For a list of double-duty suffixes in the Psalter, see Dahood, *Psalms III* (AB), pp. 429-34.

[24] Since the *NEB* is so freewheeling, one cannot readily reconstruct the Hebrew underlying their translation. Compare also their version of Job 34: 6, "He has falsified my case; my state is desperate, yet I have done no wrong," where *ʾkzb* is emended to *ykzb*, with no explanatory note that the text has been altered.

[25] Whereas, in the words of Elihu, Job considered himself just: *ʿal ṣadd*^{e}*qô napšô mēʾ*^{e}*lōhîm*, "because he considered himself just before God."

[26] For further details, consult Blommerde, *Northwest Semitic Grammar and Job*, p. 125.

[26] On *ṣedeq*, "the truth," in Prov 12: 17, see W. A. van der Weiden, *Le Livre des Proverbes: Notes philologiques* (Rome, 1970), pp. 100–101.

[28] For this definition of *šelaḥ*, see the full discussion, with bibliography, by N. J. Tromp, *Primitive Conceptions of Death and the Nether World in the Old Testament* (Rome, 1969), pp. 147–51.

[29] *Ibid.* p. 150.

[30] Compare Is 5: 13–14, where *b*^{e}*lî dāʿat* "Unknowing," occurs in a *Wortfeld* teeming with names for the nether world.

[31] The ending of the singular verb *yišrēhû* can be parsed as the archaic indicative ending found in Ugaritic. Blommerde, *Northwest Semitic Grammar and Job*, p. 15, cites other examples in Job and pertinent bibliography.

[32] This poetic usage is discussed above in connection with Job 11: 14.

[33] It has long been observed that the proper understanding of this verse sheds light on Prov 12: 26:

> *yātūr mirʿēhû* (MT *yātēr mērēʿē, hû*) *ṣaddîq*
> *w*^{e}*derek r*^{e}*šāʿîm tatʿēm*
> The just man roams his pasture,
> but the path of the wicked leads them astray.

Contrast *NEB*: "A righteous man recoils from evil, but the wicked take a path that leads them astray." That *mirʿēhû*, "his pasture," and *derek*, "path," are a congenial parallel pair may be argued from Is 49: 9: *ʿal d*^{e}*rākîm yirʿû ūb*^{e}*kol š*^{e}*pāyîm marʿîtām*, "Near the paths they shall pasture, and upon all the bare heights shall be their pasture." Thus the parallelism in repointed Prov 12: 26 may in turn be cited against the adoption of 1QIs^{a}, which reads in 49: 9, *ʿl kwl hrym*, "upon all hills," for MT *ʿal d*^{e}*rākîm*, "near the paths."

[34] On *gaʾ*^{a}*wāh*, "back," see Dahood, *Bibl* 45 (1964), 398–99.

[35] I am indebted to Ms Tiqva Frymer for this translation of *sāgûr ḥôtām*.

[36] Dahood, *Psalms II* (AB), p. 361, collects the evidence for biblical *ṣûr*, "back." To the texts listed there, Job 19: 24 *baṣṣûr* may have to be added. The traditional translation "upon the mountain/rock" introduces a new element that ill accords with the imagery of the preceding three cola. Perhaps we should translate Job 19: 24: "With iron stylus upon lead may they be inscribed upon it (*baṣṣūr*, literally "upon its back," as in Job 22: 24) forever."

Karl Elliger
University of Tübingen

Dubletten im Bibeltext

Gemeint ist das Stichwort der Überschrift nicht im strengen Sinne des zweimaligen Vorkommens ein und desselben Spruches, Liedes oder noch grösseren Abschnittes, wofür etwa Prv $10_1 = 15_{20}$, $10_{2b} = 11_{4b}$ oder Ps 14 = 53, Ps 18 = 2 Sa 22 oder die Chronik im Verhältnis zum deuteronomistischen Geschichtswerk Beispiele wären. Gedacht ist auch nicht an jenes spezifisch deuterojesajanische Stilmittel, das Köhler "Doppelung" genannt hat, den zweimaligen Gebrauch des gleichen Wortes in der gleichen Form unmittelbar hintereinander, der sofort durch den Anfang 40_1 "Tröstet, tröstet" illustriert wird. Es geht vielmehr um eine die Textkritik beschäftigende Erscheinung, bei der ein Ausdruck erst sekundär durch einen anderen gleichen oder ähnlichen Sinnes ergänzt ist, wohl um ihn in irgendeiner Weise zu erklären und deutlicher zu machen. So ist etwa Jes $51_{17.22}$ das Wort *kôs* "Becher" nach fast einstimmigem Urteil "explikative Glosse" zu dem Hapaxlegomenon *qubbaʿat* "Kelch." Aber das ist bekanntlich nicht der einzige Fall. Lassen sich alle diese Fälle unter der Bezeichnung "Glosse" begreifen? Was bedeutet die Bezeichnung eigentlich? Handelt es sich wirklich nur um Bemerkungen, die erst dem eigenen Nachdenken von Schreibern entsprungen und von diesen allererst zu Papier gebracht worden sind? Oder steht dahinter der ganze weithin mündlich verlaufende Prozess der Tradition und der Exegese, der obendrein verschieden aussah in den verschiedenen Gebieten der jüdischen Gemeinde? Zur Erkenntnis

Dr. Elliger in his introduction says that he presents this offering to the festive collection honoring Professor Myers, aware that its technical nature and modest limits stand in contrast with his warm feelings toward the one being honored, who through CARE packages helped the writer and his family through extremely difficult times following World War II.

dieses Prozesses lohnt es sich, der Erscheinung der Dubletten, die sich nicht nur in 𝔐,[1] sondern zuweilen unabhängig von 𝔐 auch in den Versionen findet, einmal nach ihrer sicherlich verschiedenen Motivation und Zielsetzung nachzugehen. Im Rahmen des vorliegenden Beitrages soll das Problem nicht grundsätzlich und erst recht nicht in extenso erörtert werden. Das muss jüngeren Kräften überlassen bleiben. Ich darf mich begnügen, das Problem an ein paar Beispielen aufzuzeigen, wie sie sich mir bei der Arbeit für meinen Dtjes-Kommentar präsentiert haben. Auch ein Beitrag, der infolge der Eigenart seines Stoffes am ehesten einem trockenen Grase gleicht, darf hoffen, in dem Blumenstrauss, der dem Jubilar von seinen Kollegen überreicht wird, seinen bescheidenen Platz auszufüllen. Jedenfalls aber steht diese Trockenheit und Bescheidenheit in keinem Verhältnis zu den herzlichen Gefühlen des Dankes, die der Autor dem Geburtstagskinde entgegenbringt, nicht zuletzt dafür, dass es mit seinen CARE-Paketen ihm und seiner Familie geholfen hat, die Katastrophe vor einem Vierteljahrhundert durchzustehen.

Begonnen sei mit ein paar Beispielen aus Jes 41. In v 17a werden die beiden Anfangswörter *hʿnyym whʾbywnym* gewöhnlich für Varianten gehalten, wobei man der ersten den Vorzug gibt. In der Tat ist eine der beiden Bezeichnungen für die "Armen" überschüssig, wie das Metrum, das in dem ganzen Verheissungswort 17–20 durchgehend der Doppeldreier ist, einwandfrei ausweist. Es ist auch sicher richtig, das Wort *ʾbywnym* auszuscheiden, wofür wiederum ein einleuchtender Grund beizubringen ist: Dtjes gebraucht *ʾbywn* nie, dagegen *ʿny* noch dreimal (49_{13} 51_{21} 54_{11}). Aber ebendeshalb sollte man nicht den Begriff "Variante" gebrauchen, der im Prinzip doch wohl die Gleichwertigkeit einschliesst. Der Sachverhalt wird allein durch die Formulierung in BHK, BHS getroffen: additum. Dafür ist wohl auch die Lage in 𝔔ᵃ bezeichnend, wo das isolierte *hʾbywnym*—die Kopula fehlt!—noch nicht in den Verband des ursprünglichen Satzes aufgenommen erscheint. Damit erhebt sich die Frage, wie der Zusatz zu erklären ist. Hat nur ein Psalmwort das andere angezogen? Warum dann gerade hier und anderswo nicht? Sollte hier nicht ein Beispiel dafür vorliegen, wie spätere Generationen das in früheren Zeiten ergangene Wort Gottes auf sich bezogen, aktualisierten? Die *ʿnyym* waren bei den Propheten die sozial Schwachen, in den Psalmen dann allgemein die irgendwie in Not Geratenen, oft mit dem religiösen Unterton der nun die Rettung allein von Gott Erwartenden. In nachexilischer Zeit trat die religiöse Komponente innerhalb des Begriffes immer mehr in den Vordergrund, die soziale entsprechend in den Hintergrund. Die "Armen" waren die "Frommen." Womöglich noch einseitiger verlief die Entwicklung bei dem verwandten Begriff der *ʾbywnym*, der geistlich bedürftigen Stillen im Lande. Wahrscheinlich ist die Aufnahme dieses Titels in den Text ein Akt der Auslegung, der das Verständnis der *'nyym* als der geistlich Armen sicherstellen soll, und signalisiert zugleich die allegorische Auslegung der gesamten Verheissung nicht auf die Stillung des wirklichen Durstes der Exilierten auf ihrem beschwerlichen Rückmarsch durch die heisse, baumlose Steppe, sondern auf die Erfüllung der jeweiligen religiösen Sehnsüchte der Frommen. Ein Beispiel dieser Auslegungsweise liefert dann 𝕿. Hier geht zwar die Allegorisierung nicht so weit, dass Wasser und Bäume nicht bleiben, was sie sind. Aber sie begleiten jetzt die Heimwege der verschiedensten Diasporagruppen "aus (ihren Aufenthaltsorten) unter den Völkern." So erhört Jahwe das Gebet der Heimatgemeinde, "der Armen und Glücklosen (*'nwtny' wḥšyky'*), die nach Belehrung trachten, wie einer nach Wasser dürstet . . . , deren Geist vor Pein verschmachtet" (vgl. v 17a).

Etwas anders liegt der Fall in v 15a. Auch hier handelt es sich wahrscheinlich um eine Dublette, jedenfalls dann, wenn *ḥrwṣ* nicht als adjektivisches Attribut "geschärft" oder "einschneidend"—vgl. 𝕲 *aloōntas*, 𝖁 triturans—anzusehen ist, sondern mit den meisten Neueren als Substantivum. Überall sonst (Jes 28_{27} Am 1_3 Hi 41_{22}) erscheint das Wort in substantivischer Bedeutung "Dreschschlitten," wobei der Vergleich mit dem mit "spitzesten Scherben" besetzten und den Schlamm breit drückenden Bauch des Krokodils Hi 41_{22} besonders instruktiv ist. *mwrg*, das ausser hier nur noch 2 Sa 24_{22} = 1 Chr 21_{23} belegt ist, ist kein anderes Instrument, jedenfalls in der Hauptsache auch aus Holz, das zum Opferfeuer dienen kann. Wieder zeigt das Doppeldreiermetrum—v 14a ist ein rhythmisch gleichwertiger Sechser—des Heilsorakels 14–16, dass v 15a um eine Hebung überfüllt ist. 𝕾 bietet nur das eine Wort **grgr'** "Dreschschleife." Daraus ist freilich der Schluss nicht unbedingt sicher, dass sie nur ein Wort auch in der Vorlage fand. Aber dann hat 𝕾 zumindest gewusst, dass die beiden Wörter dieselbe Bedeutung haben. Vermutlich steht dieses Wissen auch dahinter, wenn 𝕿 die beiden Substantiva durch die Steigerung "starker Dreschschlitten" (*mwrg ḥqyp*) übersetzt. Aus allem Bisherigem ergibt sich, dass eins der beiden Wörter sekundär ist und dass es höchstwahrscheinlich das zweite ist, das hinzugefügt worden ist. Wie erklärt sich der Fall? Offenbar liegt er ähnlich wie bei dem oben in der Einleitung schon zitierten *kws/qb't*. Dort soll ein ungebräuchlicher Ausdruck durch den gebräuchlichen, hier ein älterer—1 Chr 21_{23} ist aus dem altüberlieferten Kapitel 2 Sa 24 nur abgeschrieben—und daher allmählich unbekannter Ausdruck durch den später geläufigen ersetzt werden. Man mag an eine Glosse denken. Aber sollte dahinter nicht gottesdienstliche Übung sichtbar werden, die beim und für den Vortrag der Texte solche Dubletten schuf aus dem Streben, sich ihrer Gegenwart verständlich zu machen?

Es ist kein Wunder, dass die Erscheinung der Dubletten auch in den Versionen auftritt. Zunächst seien aus 𝔗 zwei Beispiele vorgeführt, in denen der Übersetzer offensichtlich zwei verschiedene Deutungen oder Lesarten eines hebräischen Wortes kennt, die er nun beide in seiner Übersetzung unterbringt. Jes 41_{7a} geht es um das letzte Wort *p'm*. Nach dem Zusammenhang muss ein Werkzeug gemeint sein, mit dem jemand "schlägt," wie ein anderer "mit dem Hammer glättet." Die Versionen haben meist das Wort nicht verstanden, d.h. zwei von ihnen vertreten eine Tradition, die *p'm* im übertragenen Sinne nimmt und als eine Art Zeitbegriff auffasst. 𝔊 übersetzt *pote*, 𝔙 tunc temporis, beide trennen es von v a; 𝔊 zieht es überdies zum Folgenden. 𝔖 lässt es aus; aber auch *α'* hat nur geraten: (*sun katelaunonta*) *kathodon*, auch *σ'*, obwohl er der Sache schon näher kommt, wenn er das Objekt von v a*β* mit *ton akmoneutēn* (von *akmōn* "Amboss") wiedergibt. Das Richtige findet sich bei *θ'*: *ton sphurokopon* "den Hammerschläger." Denn wie im Griechischen *sphura* "Hammer" und *spuron* "Knöchel am Fuss, Ferse, Fuss überhaupt" zusammenhängen, so kann offenbar auch im Hebräischen *p'm* nicht nur den "Fuss," sondern gelegentlich nach der Gestalt auch den "Hammer, Schlägel" bezeichnen, zumal schon im Ugaritischen diese Bedeutung belegt zu sein scheint. Bestätigt wird diese Bedeutung nun von 𝔗, aber in eigenartiger Weise. 𝔗 übersetzt die zweite Hälfte von v 7a*β* (*'t-hlm p'm*) durch *'m dmṭmh bqrns'* "zusammen mit dem, der da schlägt mit dem Schlägel" und fährt mit *zmn'* "zur (gegebenen) Zeit" fort, ehe es den Text von v 7b bringt. 𝔗 übersetzt also *p'm* doppelt: zuerst mit "Schlägel," dann mit "zur Zeit," und zwar verbindet es das Letztere genau wie 𝔊 ihr *pote* mit dem folgenden Satz: "zur rechten Zeit sagt er von der Lötung: . . . ." Schwerlich ist eine der beiden Übersetzungen freie Erfindung. Die erste ist noch bei *θ'* belegt, die zweite, sogar in der gleichen Form der Verbindung mit v b, noch bei 𝔊 und 𝔙. Offenbar handelt es sich um zwei verschiedene Auslegungstraditionen, deren keiner 𝔗 den Abschied geben möchte. So verteilt der Übersetzer, vielleicht nach Auslegungsregeln seiner Zeit, gar nicht ungeschickt die beiden Möglichkeiten auf zwei verschiedene Sätze and kann beiden gerecht werden.

Der andere Fall einer Dublette in 𝔗 betrifft Jes 41_{25b}. Diesmal bezieht sich die Doppelung nicht auf die Auslegung eines Wortes, sondern ist das zugrundeliegende Wort selbst offenbar schon in verschiedener Gestalt überliefert. Es handelt sich um das den Stichus einleitende *wyb'*. Die Vokalisation in 𝔐 als 3.m.sg.impf.qal ergibt keinen Sinn. Die alten Übersetzer haben sich zu helfen versucht, indem sie die Form als Plural nahmen mit *sgnym* als Subjekt—so 𝔊 und 𝔖, und sie befinden sich dabei in der Gesellschaft von 𝔔ᵃ, die *wybw'w* schreibt—oder als Hiphil mit *sgnym* als Objekt—

so 𝔙. Als geglückt sind diese Versuche nicht anzusehen, ebensowenig der moderne von R. Amiran (Sepher N. H. Tur Sinai, 1960, 97 f.), wenigstens den Konsonantenbestand zu retten durch die Annahme einer einfachen Metathesis von ʾ und *s*, als habe der ursprüngliche Text gelautet *wybs ʾgnym*, wobei *ʾᵃgannîm* die "Zuber" bedeuten soll, in denen der Töpfer seinen Ton stampft. An *sgnym* ist nichts auszusetzen. Dass der Fehler allein an dem ʾ liegt, das an der Stelle eines ursprünglichen *s* steht, hat schon Johannes Clericus erkannt. Die weit überwiegende Meinung der Forscher geht dahin, dass der Text ursprünglich *wᵉyābôs* oder *wᵉyābus* oder auch *wayyābos* lautete; vermutlich fiel das *s* durch Haplographie aus und wurde der Rest im Blick auf das vorhergehende *wyʾt* zu *wybʾ* ergänzt. Der Zeuge, auf den schon Clericus sich beruft, ist 𝔗. In der Tat setzt 𝔗 *wybs* voraus, aber nicht nur *wybs*, sondern zugleich das *wybʾ* von 𝔐. 𝔗 bietet *wyyty wydws slṭwny* (*ʿmmyʾ*) "und er kommt und zertritt (die Herrscher der Völker"). *wyyty* entspricht dem *wybʾ* von 𝔐. Sollte *wydws* in 𝔗 freie Zutat sein und nicht mindestens auf die übliche Exegese von *wybʾ* zurückgehen? Wahrscheinlicher ist, dass auch die ursprüngliche Lesart *wybs* noch bekannt war. Zugleich aber wollte oder musste 𝔗 auch die von 𝔐 bezeugte schlechtere Lesart respektieren, wobei die Frage offenbleibt, ob dieser Respekt sich nur aus dem Alter der Lesart oder bereits aus der Heiligkeit des Textes erklärt.

Dubletten wie in 𝔗 gibt es auch in 𝔊; dafür zwei Beispiele wieder aus Jes 41. V 28aα übersetzt 𝔊: *apo gar tōn ethnōn idou outheis*. Der Anfang entspricht gewiss nicht dem *wʾrʾ* von 𝔐. Dieses steckt vielmehr in dem *eis odon*, mit dem 𝔊 den vorhergehenden Vers schliesst, ob man *wʾrʾ* nun mit Ziegler zu *lᵉʾōraḥ* verlesen sein lässt oder mit Torrey an eine innergriechische Verderbnis *ei eidon*→*eisidon*→*eisodon* denkt. Woher stammt dann das in 𝔊 unmittelbar folgende *apo gar tōn ethnōn*? Hat 𝔊 es frei ergänzt, um ein Gegenstück zu ihrem *kai apo tōn eidōlōn* = *wmʾlh* v aβ und ein Beziehungswort für ihr *autōn* zu haben? Nun wird *wʾrʾ* von vielen für eine entstellte Textform gehalten; und es lässt sich nicht leugnen, dass das *wmʾlh* in v aβ nach einem korrespondierenden *mʾlh* in v aα ruft. Sollte 𝔊 von diesem ursprünglichen Text in seiner Vorlage wenigstens noch den Anfang *m* = *apo* erkannt haben? Sie böte dann, wenn auch in entstellter Form, die Dubletten *wʾrʾ* und *mʾlh*, von denen nur die zweite Form Anspruch auf Originalität erheben kann.

Zum Schluss sei noch eine Dublette in 𝔐 hinzugefügt, die in der bisherigen Literatur kaum gewürdigt worden ist. Gemeint ist $45_{8b\alpha}$. Hier liegen nicht die Reste zweier paralleler Halbstichen eines Doppeldreiers wie v a und b$\beta\gamma$ vor, so dass man je eine Hebung zu ergänzen hätte, wie Duhm und die Älteren, auch Haller und Mowinckel annehmen. Es handelt sich überhaupt nicht um zwei Halb- oder Teilstichen, ob man sie nun als eine Zeile bzw.

Doppelzeile beisammen lässt (zuletzt Steinmann 1957 [anders 1960], Penna, Westermann, BHS) oder sie auf das Vorhergehende und Folgende verteilt (Fohrer) oder auch allein mit dem Folgenden verbindet (North, McKenzie). Vielmehr bildet v b*α* einen einzigen, dem v b*β* sachlich und metrisch parallelen Halbstichus mit ursprünglich nur einem Verbum. Das hat schon Volz erkannt, Steinmann 1960 ist ihm gefolgt; und das lässt sich durch die Betrachtung der Textüberlieferung erhärten. Fest steht in allen Versionen *ʾrṣ* als Subjekt, auch das Wort *yšʿ* wenigstens in 𝕲 𝕾 𝔙, ob es nun als Objekt (𝕲 *eleos*, 𝔙 salvatorem) oder als weiteres Subjekt (𝕾 *pwrqnʾ* "Erlösung") verstanden wird. Nur 𝕿 hat statt *wyprw-yšʿ* den Satz *wyyḥwn mythyʾ* "und die Toten sollen lebendig werden," eine eigenwillige Interpretation, die freilich ebenfalls keinen anderen Text als 𝔐 voraussetzen dürfte. Die Differenzen beginnen bei den Verben. Beim zweiten hat 𝕿 offenbar die Kopula und den Plural in seiner Vorlage gelesen. Sicher haben die Kopula, übersetzen aber das Verbum im Singular 𝕾 (*wnsgʾ* "und viel werden soll") und 𝔙 (et germinet), während die ursprüngliche 𝕲 gar nichts hat und erst die Handschriften der Origenes- und teilweise der Lukian-Rezension, ferner die Catenengruppe, freilich auch die alexandrinische Gruppe *kai blastēsatō* "und sie soll sprossen lassen" bieten, immerhin auch nur den Singular and das Verbum von einem Stamm, der sonst immer der hebräischen Wurzel *prḥ* entspricht. 𝕾 übersetzt neutrisch, 𝔙 wie die spätere 𝕲 aktivisch. Dabei könnte man bei 𝕾 noch an eine Form von der Wurzel *prh* als Vorlage denken und mit einigem guten Willen sogar die Wahl des Wortes **sg**ʾ "viel werden" auf den Plural *wyprw* zurückführen, mit dem 𝕾 fertigwerden musste. Aber bei 𝔙 versagt diese Auskunft; die Erde als Subjekt setzt eine 3.f. des Prädikats voraus, und germinare trans. "sprossen lassen, hervorbringen" mit Objekt ist etwas anderes als "fruchtbar sein" und erst recht "fruchtbar machen" und entspricht dem Kausativ von *prḥ*, nicht von *prh*. 𝔙 mag durch 𝕲 beeinflusst sein, wie denn Hieronymus in seinem Kommentar v b*α* nach 𝕲 zitiert als "germinet terra et oriatur misericordia." Daraus geht mindestens so viel hervor, dass Hieronymus einem *wyprw* oder auch *wypr* seiner Vorlage misstraute, welch letzteres (*wᵉyēper*) jedoch nach Haller, Budde, Köhler, und zuletzt Westermann, BHS gerade der ursprüngliche Text sein soll, während Torrey wie schon Grätz, Perles, Cheyne und wieder Kissane *wyprḥ* statt *wyprw* für ursprünglich halten.

Was das erste Verbum in v b*α* betrifft, so ist die Konsonantenfolge *tptḥ* durch 𝕾 𝕿 𝔙 bezeugt, aber nur von 𝕿 als Qal = 𝔐, von 𝕾 (*ttptḥ*) und 𝔙 (aperiatur) als Niphal verstanden. 𝕲 übersetzt *anateilatō* "sie soll aufsprossen lassen". Das griechische Wort gibt oft das hebräische *ṣmḥ* wie sofort in v b*β*, sechsmal auch *prḥ* wieder, aber niemals sonst *ptḥ*. Es dürfte kaum einem Zweifel unterliegen, dass 𝔊 hier *tapriaḥ* gelesen hat. Und das ist offenbar der ursprüngliche Text, der in 𝔐 nur zu *tptḥ* verlesen ist. 𝔊 bietet auch insofern das Ursprüngliche, als sie vor *yšʿ* kein weiteres Verbum kennt und *yšʿ* als Objekt fasst, so dass ein glatter Parallelismus zu v bβ in die Erscheinung tritt. Das *wyprw* von 𝔐 ist weiter nichts als jenes *tprḥ*, das nicht als Korrektur von *tptḥ* erkannt wurde vielleicht, weil es zwischen den Zeilen auch schlecht geschrieben stand, so dass die sonderbare Pluralform herausgelesen werden konnte, in deren *w* sich immerhin noch einer der senkrechten Balken das *ḥ* erhalten hat. Dass aus dem *t* ein *wy* wurde, erklärt sich leicht daraus, dass das Wort für das Prädikat zu *yšʿ* gehalten wurde. Aber 𝔙 (germinet) hat noch die volle Form *tprḥ* gekannt und sie richtig als Hiphil, wenn auch nicht als Korrektur von *tptḥ* erkannt. Und schliesslich bezeugt auch 𝔔ᵃ hier die Wurzel *prḥ*, wenn auch in der schon auf das vermeintliche Subjekt *yšʿ* zugeschnittenen Form *wyprḥ*. Im übrigen hat 𝔔ᵃ sich den anscheinend (durch Korrektur?) verschmierten oder sonstwie verderbten Anfang des v bα auf seine Weise zurechtgelegt: *hʾmr lʾrṣ* “der da sagt zur Erde,” worauf folgt: *wyprḥ yšʿ*. Als ursprünglicher Text ergibt sich: *tapriaḥ ʾereṣ yešaʿ*, zu dem sich der offenbar als paralleler Halbstichus gedachte v bβ aufs Beste fügt, während v bα als Abschluss des ganzen Liedes v 8 für sich steht. Interessant ist, dass in 𝔔ᵃ der Schluss des v 8 von *yḥd* ab fehlt, so dass dort auf den Doppeldreier 8a ein Sechser folgt. 𝔔ᵃ stellt ein eigenes, späteres Stadium des Schicksals des Textes von v bα dar, 𝔊 das Anfangsstadium. 𝔐 ist das Ergebnis einer Entwicklung, an deren Anfang die Verlesung oder Verschreibung des *tprḥ* zu *tptḥ* stand. *tprḥ* wurde irgendwann wieder dazugeschrieben, aber dann als Dublette nicht mehr erkannt und geriet, zu *wypr(w)* entstellt, als selbständige Parallele in den Text.

Notes

[1] Die Sigla sind die in BHS (Biblia Hebraica Stuttgartensia) gebräuchlichen.

Abstract of “Doublets in the Text of the Bible”

The aim of this essay is to call attention to a phenomenon in the text of the Old Testament in which one expression is supplemented by another which has the same or similar meaning and which is probably intended somehow to explain or clarify the first.

An example appears in Is 51: 17 and 51: 22, where in each case the word *kôs* (cup) is followed by *qubbaʿat* (bowl), a hapax legomenon which is generally agreed to be an explicative gloss.

But can all such cases be understood as glosses? And just what does this term really mean? Is it indeed only a matter of notes originating in the thinking of the scribes who first wrote them down? Or is there behind it the whole long process of the oral transmission of the tradition and exegesis, which assumed differing forms in the various areas of the Jewish community?

To understand this process, it is necessary to investigate doublets in the versions as well as in the Masoretic text in order to discover their obviously different motivations and purposes. This study has space to consider only a few examples which were observed in the author's work on his commentary on Deutero-Isaiah.

Is 41: 17 begins with the phrase *hāʿaniyîm wehāebyônîm* (the poor and the needy) of which the second part (the needy) is properly understood to be an addition rather than a variant. While in the prophets *ʿānî* (poor) designated primarily a weak social position, in the Psalms it often has the connotation of one who looks only to God for help, and after the exile came to assume the meaning of "the pious." The second term, "needy," also carried strong religious overtones, the connotation being the spiritual want of those in the land who wait quietly for the Lord. It was added here to emphasize the allegorical interpretation of the first term, and to make sure that it would not be taken to be literal, physical poverty.

Is 41: 15a, "Behold, I have made you a *môrag* (threshing sledge) *hārûṣ*, has another doublet. Most recent interpreters take the second word to be a later term for "threshing sledge" that gradually displaced the first, older noun. While it may be considered a gloss, it reflects the practice of adding more recent words during the reading of a biblical text in religious services with the aim of making the older language understandable to the audience.

There are also doublets in the versions. From the Targum, two cases may be cited which illustrate how the translator apparently knew two different meanings or readings of a Hebrew word and used both of them.

The last word of Is 41: 7a, *pāʿam*, is translated in the Targum as the last word of verse 7a to mean "hammer," and then again, at the beginning of verse 7b, to mean "at the (right) time." Evidence from the Septuagint, Vulgate, and Syriac indicates that there were two different traditions of translation, both equally valid, which the Targum retained in this manner, perhaps according to traditional rules of translation of the time.

The second doublet occurs in Is 41: 25b, where, according to a preponderance of scholarly opinion, the text originally began with *weyābôs*, or *weyābus*, or even possibly *wayyābos*, instead of *weyābōʾ*, as it now stands. The Targum reads, "and he comes and treads down (the rulers of the peoples)." This presupposes both the Hebrew word now in the text, which was changed probably by scribal error, and the original reading in one of the forms just mentioned. The Targumist respected the altered reading of the text before him, but also was likely familiar with the older, correct form and retained it in his translation too.

Doublets may also be detected by means of the Septuagint, two of which may be mentioned here. The beginning of Is 41: 28 in the LXX seems not to reflect the present reading, *w*ᵉ*'ēre'* (and I look), but a *mē'ēlleh* (from these), which may have stood there originally but later dropped out. The first of these two Hebrew words is considered by many to have been corrupted. In some form it apparently stood behind the last two Greek words in 41: 27, while the *mē* of the lost *mē'ēlleh* accounts for the first word of 41: 28, *απο*, in the LXX.

The second example stands in Is 45: 8b, which RSV translates, "let the earth open, that salvation may sprout forth, and let it cause righteousness to spring up also; I the Lord have created it."

LXX translates 8b as follows:

let the earth cause mercy [its translation of "salvation"]
to sprout forth [reading the hiphil *taphriaḥ* instead of the qal *tiphtaḥ* now in MT]
and let it cause righteousness
to sprout forth at the same time [its translation of "also"];
I am the Lord who created you.

Originally MT had "let the earth cause salvation to sprout forth (*taphriaḥ*)," as the LXX witnesses. When at some time or other "open (*tiphtaḥ*)" displaced "cause to sprout forth (*taphriaḥ*)" as the first verb in 8b, the latter was written following it as a doublet, so that the text would have read "let the earth open, and cause salvation to sprout forth." At a later time, however, *taphriaḥ* was no longer recognized as a doublet for *tiphtaḥ*, and was changed to the present *w*ᵉ*yipr(û)*, "that salvation may sprout forth," thus becoming an independent parallel in the text to the preceding *tiphtaḥ*.

(This abstract was made by H. N. Bream.)

Donald M. C. Englert
Lancaster Theological Seminary

Bowdlerizing in the Old Testament

A recent reading of Noel Perrin's *Dr. Bowdler's Legacy*[1] and its chapter on bowdlerizing the Bible led me to pursue a subject which had been lying dormant in the back of my mind since my studies for my doctoral dissertation.[2] Thomas Bowdler (1754–1825) was an English editor of an expurgated edition of Shakespeare. He went on from there to the King James Bible and other examples of English literature. His activities led to the verb "to bowdlerize"—"to expurgate by removing or modifying passages prudishly considered immodest."[3] While Bowdler has given his name to a common literary device, it was already widely practiced long before his time in the Hebrew text of the Old Testament.

My initial inquiry had begun with the text of 2 Sam 12: 14: ". . . thou hast given great occasion to the enemies of the Lord to blaspheme" (KJV). The Hebrew text does not permit this translation, as if a causative form of the verb were there. The verbs—infinitive construct and perfect—are both Piel. To be sure, there are some Hebrew verbs which have a causative meaning in the Piel; for example, *mālē* Qal, "to be full"; Piel, "to fill"; and *kālâ* Qal, "to be complete"; Piel, "to complete." But the Piel of *nā'aṣ* never has the meaning of "cause to blaspheme."

The text as it stands can be translated only as "because you have greatly blasphemed the enemies of the Lord," which makes no sense in this context. The solution was noted by C. D. Ginsburg,[4] that the word *'yby* "enemies of" was inserted by a scribe to absolve David of Nathan's harsh judgment "you have greatly blasphemed the Lord."

A similar act of the scribe may have occurred in 2 Sam 12: 9. Here Nathan's condemnation of David is "wherefore hast thou despised the commandment of the Lord?" One could argue that David's act of adultery with Bathsheba and his subsequent legalized murder of her husband constituted "despising the word [or commandment] of the Lord." But I would suggest that the original indictment by Nathan may well have been "wherefore hast thou despised the Lord?" and that this sacrilegious idea was softened by a scribe who inserted the word *dbr*. It is interesting that Theodotion omitted the word.

Another form of bowdlerizing in the MT is the use of euphemisms for genital organs. In Gen 24: 2–3 Abraham commands his servant, "Put your hand under my thigh and I will make you swear." The servant is to touch the scrotum of Abraham, much as we put our hand on a Bible to be sworn as a witness in court. Here was the whole future of Abraham's seed to ensure the servant's carrying out the command. Is it a coincidence that in Latin *testis* means both "scrotum" and "witness"?

In Is 6: 2 we are told that the seraph in the prophet's vision used two wings "to cover his feet." From the use of the word "feet" elsewhere as a euphemism, it is likely that the seraph was covering his genitals. Other examples would include Is 7: 20 where "hair of the feet" means "pubic hair," and Ruth 3: 4, 7 where the young widow's "uncovering the feet of Boaz" may mean "exposing his genitals." In Ex 4: 25 Zipporah's act in casting her son's bloody foreskin at Moses' "feet" may mean "touching his genitals."

Deut 11: 10 *whšqyt brglk* "and waterest it [the land] with thy foot" (KJV) has been a puzzle to the commentators. "As far as we know, most of the machines used in lifting water into irrigation ditches were not run by the foot."[5] Could it be that the Hebrew workers turned aside in their labors to perform a natural function, much as millions of farm laborers before them and since have done? Thus "water with thy foot" may mean "to urinate."

It is well known that elsewhere in the Old Testament the MT bowdlerizes its descriptions of natural functions. In Judg 3: 24 Eglon, king of Moab, is said to be "covering his feet" *msyk hw' 't-rglyw* when he was evidently relieving himself. Similarly, in 1 Sam 24: 3, Saul was "covering his feet" (RSV "went in to relieve himself"). A less certain case is that in which natural functions may have been intended by the euphemism "gone aside." In Esther 7: 7, King Ahasuerus "rose up in wrath and went into the palace garden," leaving his vizier, Haman, alone with the young queen. Perhaps the king had had too much wine at the feast, which necessitated his hasty departure from the scene.

Another euphemism for "genitals" in the Old Testament is "nakedness." In Gen 9: 22 Ham is cursed for seeing his father's nakedness. Some commentators[6] have suggested that the severity of the curse on Ham was due to his having committed an unnatural act with his father, for which the MT used a euphemism. Elsewhere (Lev 18: 6 ff) "carnal knowledge" is similarly bowdlerized by the expression "to uncover the nakedness of."

The Babylonian Talmud[7] suggests another example. In Is 62: 4 "and your land Married" (MT *bᵉʻûlah,* the passive participle from the verb *bāʻal,* "to possess as a husband") is possibly alluding to the sexual act in which the land is impregnated by the rain, as the husband upon the wife.

Another example of euphemism can be seen in Ezek 16: 17, where the text *ṣalmê zākār,* literally "images of flesh [or men]," has been translated in the RSV "and with them has played the harlot." Could this coarse language of the prophet mean that the women were using dildoes?

Dr. Bowdler was not alone in his desire to clean up the Bible, Shakespeare, Burns, and other works of English literature. In 1952, there appeared the *Olive Pell Bible,*[8] published by Mrs. Pell at her own expense. A vegetarian, she took out of the Bible all mention of the eating of meat, as well as of sex and violence. It sold fairly well, a commercial publisher took over the book, and it is still in print.

Notes

1 Perrin, Noel, *Dr. Bowdler's Legacy: A History of Expurgated Books in England and America.* New York: Atheneum, 1969.

2 Englert, Donald M. C., *The Peshitto of Second Samuel* (*JBL,* monograph series, vol. 3). Philadelphia: Society of Biblical Literature and Exegesis, 1949.

3 *The Random House Dictionary of the English Language.* New York: Random House, 1967.

4 Ginsburg, C. D., *Introduction to the Massoretico-Critical Edition of the Hebrew Bible.* New York: KTAV, 1966: "That this is an official alteration is attested by Rashi, one of the most illustrious Jewish expositors of the middle ages and the most faithful depository of the ancient traditions. He emphatically declares, 'This is an alteration due to the reverence for the glory of God,'" p. 364.

5 *IB,* II, p. 404.

6 Speiser, E. A., *Genesis* (AB). Garden City: Doubleday, 1964, p. 62. Also von Rad, G., *Genesis.* Philadelphia: Westminster Press, 1961, p. 133.

7 Ta'anit 6b.

8 Pell, Olive, ed., *The Olive Pell Bible.* New York: Crown (undated).

Edwin D. Freed
Gettysburg College

Some Old Testament Influences on the Prologue of John

During my days as a seminary student, it was Dr. Myers who impressed upon me the importance of a knowledge of the Old Testament for a proper understanding of the New. Ever since that time I have frequently been grateful for the wisdom Dr. Myers imparted in the classroom and my subsequent association with him as a friend. I am delighted to have this opportunity to contribute to a volume of essays in his honor.

Although influence from the OT upon a writer of the NT may be seen most clearly, perhaps, in his direct quotations, frequently the language and thought of a NT writer show familiarity with the OT more indirectly through allusion and paraphrase. This is especially true of the writer of the Fourth Gospel.

As I have shown elsewhere,[1] in his formal quotations the author of John, like most NT writers and the sect of Qumran, shows a preference for Isaiah and the Psalms. Quotations in John are sometimes combined and/or conflated, as, for example, in 6: 31 and 12: 15. In several places, one can detect influence on the thought of John from an OT passage or passages in addition to the one specifically quoted, as in 6: 45 and 7: 37 f. Sometimes a quotation may show influence also from the Qumran Scrolls, as, for example, in 7: 37 f. And some quotations or their contexts show acquaintance with the Synoptics or the Synoptic tradition—for example, 2: 17; 13: 18; 19: 28 f, 36 f.

I should like to suggest that when the writer of the Prologue composed his verses presenting Jesus as the Light, he was influenced primarily by the poetic eschatology of Is 60: 1–3, 5, 19, especially by vss 1–3. He may also have been influenced by one or more of the passages from the Psalms quoted below, especially 36: 9 (10), where the symbols of life and light associated with God are brought together. In Jn 1: 4, both life and light are applied to Jesus and even in the same order. The writer of the Prologue was very probably influenced by the passage from Qumran quoted below, which is the closest parallel from the Dead Sea Scrolls yet known to any passage in the NT (cf Jn 1: 3). This influence coincides with that from Qumran elsewhere in the Gospel. And acquaintance with the Synoptic tradition at several points is also apparent.

Is 60: 1–3, 5a, 19cd

1 Arise, give light, for your light has come;
and the glory of the Lord shines forth over you.

2 For, behold, the darkness shall cover the earth,
and thick darkness the peoples;
but over you the Lord will shine forth,
and his glory will be seen over you.

3 And nations shall walk by your light,
and kings by the brightness of your shining.

5 Then will you see and be bright [or shine or be radiant].

19 The Lord will be to you a light everlasting,
and your God will be your glory.

Ps 36: 9 (10)

For with you is the fountain of life;
in your light shall we see light.

Ps 56: 13 (14)

That I may walk before God in the light of life

Ps 27: 1

The Lord is my light and my salvation

1QS 11: 11

And by his knowledge everything was brought into being;
and all things that are were established by his thought;
and apart from him it is not done.[2]

The theme of Is 60 may be stated thus: "The light of God's glory revealed for all to see" (cf Is 40: 5). The first three verses are an introductory strophe to a chapter of prophecy complete in itself. While darkness covers the rest of the world, the light of Yahweh's glory dawns upon Jerusalem, and the nations are attracted to it.

For John, the darkness of the end of the age has settled upon the earth. But the light of salvation, so long promised yet so long expected in vain, has finally come. Jesus is "a light everlasting" (Is 60: 19 f), "the light of life" (Ps 56: 13[14]; Jn 8: 12), the light which the darkness could not overcome (Jn 1: 5). Jesus, as the eschatological and ethical Light of the world, came to save men from the darkness of sin and death (cf Jn 3: 19–21; 8: 12; 9: 5; 11: 9 f; 12: 35 f, 46). What more fitting introduction to his Gospel could there be than a poem about Jesus as the Light?—as my reconstruction here given and supported later clearly shows.

Jn 1:3–14

Strophe 1

6 There was a man,
sent from God,
whose name was John.

7 He came for a witness,
to bear witness to the light,
that all might believe through him.

8 He was not the light,
but [came] to bear witness to the light.

Strophe 2

9 The light, the true one,
that gives light to every man,
was coming into the world.

3 All things came into being through him,
and apart from him nothing has come into being.

4 In him was life,
and the life was the light of men.

5 The light shines in the darkness,
and the darkness has not overcome it.

10 He was in the world,
and the world was made through him,
but the world did not know him.

11 He came to his own,
but his own did not receive him.

Strophe 3

12 But as many as received him,
to them he gave power to become children of God,
to those who believe on his name.

13 They were born not of blood,
nor of the will of the flesh,
nor of the will of man,
but of God.

Strophe 4

14b And we beheld his glory,
glory as of a unique Son from the Father.

The vocabulary common to the passages cited, especially Is 60 and the Prologue, is obvious. Not so obvious, however, are certain *ideas* common to Is 60 and the Prologue:

1. Pervading eschatological mood.
2. Repetition of the word "come" (Is 60: 1, 4bc, 5d, and Jn 1: 7, 8 [understood], 9, 11).

3. Antithesis between light and darkness.
4. Light prevails.
5. Presence of a believing community (Jerusalem in Isaiah; "those who believe on his name" in Jn 1: 12 = "we" in 1: 14).
6. Acceptance or belief is not universal (cf Is 60: 7 ff, 12 and Jn 1: 11 f). There is a contrast between Jerusalem and the world in Isaiah; in John, between the world and those receiving the Light and believing.
7. Use of "name" for the person ("the name of the Lord your God" in Is 60: 9; "believe on his name" in Jn 1: 12).
8. Idea of glory; but whereas it is central in Isaiah, light is central in John. In Isaiah, it is the glory of Yahweh, but of Christ as the Light in John, a natural transference for the writer, as elsewhere in the Gospel (cf also ἐγώ εἰμί). But in both cases, it is a glory that is "seen."
9. The verbs *'ôr* and *r'h* occur in Is 60: 1 f. In the LXX, both are translated either with φαίνω or φωτίζω. The latter occurs in the LXX of Isaiah only in 60: 1, 19. Both words appear in the Prologue; the former in 1: 5, the latter in 1: 9. The fact that φωτίζω occurs nowhere else in the Gospel seems to indicate influence from Is 60: 1 f in the Prologue.
10. A "coalescence of the external and physical manifestation with spiritual revelation is a central feature of the poet's eschatological representation."[3] Although the writer of the Prologue wants the reader to know that the Light came in human form, spiritual overtones are apparent.[4] "It is a mistake, therefore, to divorce the literal and material from the symbolic and spiritual. The external and internal manifestations of Yahweh's presence and his eschatological and redemptive deeds belong together."[5]
11. "The poet employs all the resources of terminology, repetition, word order, and grammatical construction to portray the glory of the Lord's self-manifestation."[6] Again an apt description of the Johannine poet as well.

Upon examination of the Prologue certain observations seem important. Light (φῶς), not Word (λόγος), is the dominant theme of vss 3–13 and 14b. Whereas the word λόγος occurs only four times in vss 1–14, three of which are in the first verse, the word φῶς is used six times in vss 4–9. Moreover, λόγος does not appear anywhere else in the Gospel with the same meaning—namely, in a christological sense. In the whole NT λόγος is used as a title for Jesus only twice, both in Johannine writings (1 Jn 1: 1; Rev 19: 13). Although Jesus never applied the title Logos to himself, he did apply the symbols light and life to himself: "I am the light of the world" (8: 12); "As long as I am in the world, I am the light of the world" (9: 5); "The light is with you for a little while longer" (12: 35; cf also 12: 46). The themes of light and darkness, with Jesus as the Light, are an inherent part of the rest of the Gospel.

The dominance of the λόγος concept in the Prologue has been grossly exaggerated. And since Light, not Word, is the dominant idea, we have a Phōs (light) poem or hymn. But how, then, does this Phōs poem fit in with the rest of the Prologue (1: 1 f, 14a, 15–18) and the Gospel as a whole?

In the opinion of some scholars, the Prologue serves as a rather thorough introduction or summary or outline for the Gospel, and stands in a close relationship to it. According to others, the Prologue is scarcely related to the body of the Gospel, and thus represents an effort on the part of someone to express the coming of Jesus in Hellenistic terms in a way that would appeal to Greek readers.[7]

There is a wide range of opinion with respect to which verses comprised the original form of the Prologue. Of the cross section of scholarly opinions cited by Brown, all "regard vss. 6–8, and 15 as secondary additions; and many would add vss. 9, 12–13, 17–18. The only general agreement is on vss. 1–5, 10–11, and 14 as parts of the original poem."[8] Before presenting my own proposal, I should like to discuss here two of the more recent and perceptive studies on the Prologue.

J. A. T. Robinson on the Prologue

J. A. T. Robinson[9] presupposes the literary unity of the Gospel on purely stylistic grounds, including both Prologue and Epilogue as the work of a single hand, though not written at one sitting. According to Robinson, there is "no clear line demarcating" the Prologue from the body of the Gospel, and it is difficult to determine the thought and poetic structure of the Prologue. The most obvious difficulties are vs 15—the rudest interruption—and the change of subject beginning with vs 6. The differences in subject and rhythm have "prompted numerous reconstructions . . . of what has been called a 'Wisdom hymn' or 'Logos ode.'" Robinson finds "little evidence for" and "much presumption against" such a hymn being pre-Johannine or even non-Christian in origin, taken over from Mandaeans, Alexandrians, or Gnostics. "Nor does it even fit the facts to presuppose an independent Logos poem previously composed by the same author and then forced into uneasy union with the narrative of his Gospel. It is more as though in the Prologue the themes of the Gospel are played over beforehand, as in the overture to an opera."

I am in substantial agreement with most of what Robinson says up to this point. The last sentence of the above paragraph is particularly apt, but it is even more valid if the primary feature of the Prologue is a Phōs poem and not a Logos hymn. Robinson himself notes that λόγος never recurs in the Gospel as a title, that "the dominant Christology of the Gospel is . . . 'the Christ, the Son of God,'" and that certain connections, such as "the most markedly 'metaphysical' language of the Gospel" (3: 13) and the distinction between τὰ ἄνω and τὰ κάτω (3: 31), which some see as Platonic, are missing just where one might expect to find them. He also says that "in the central affirmation of the Prologue . . . 'the Word became flesh' . . . the usage of the key terms is subtly different from that of the Gospel as a whole" (cf 1: 14; 6: 14; 3: 6). For the terminology of the Word becoming flesh, we must look not to the Gospel but to the Epistles of John, in such places as 1 Jn 4: 2; 2 Jn 7; and 1 Jn 1: 1.

Noting the parallels between 1 Jn 1: 1, 2 and Jn 1: 14, 4, 2, Robinson suggests that the opening of 1 Jn "represents the first sketch for the Prologue," and that the Prologue, as well as the Epilogue, belongs to the period during which the Epistles were written. The Prologue is, therefore, "a definite addition—more like a preface to a second edition—setting the original work in a new context." The Gospel "once began—as it ended—differently." While the original ending of the Gospel is preserved in 20: 31, its original beginning cannot be reconstructed with certainty. Robinson defends the thesis that the Prologue consists "not (as has usually been suggested) . . . of a poem with prose additions, but . . . an original narrative opening around which a poetic structure (with its own prose commentary) has subsequently been built."

Starting with the poetic or rhythmic meditation portion first, Robinson says that vss 1, 3, 4, 5, 10, 11, and 14 represent the material common to the reconstructions of J. Weiss, C. Cryer, C. F. Burney, J. H. Bernard, H. C. Green, and R. Schnackenburg.[10] Other verses, not so clearly poetic but dependent theologically upon the rhythmic meditation, are 2, 12, 13, 14b, 16, 17, 18. After the prose portion is detached, we are left with vss 6–9, 15, and 19, which possibly constituted the original opening of the Gospel.

If the Prologue was written after, not with, the Gospel as an addition to it, then, according to Robinson, two consequences follow: one for the historical setting of the Gospel, and the other for its theology.

First, "the Logos theology belongs to the *environment* of the Gospel rather than to its *background*." The environment "in and for which the Gospel was published was one of Greek-speaking Diaspora Judaism, but . . . the background of the author and his tradition was Aramaic-speaking Palestinian Judaism." The Logos hymn could be the product of Palestinian Judaism or more probably of Diaspora Judaism, even perhaps of Hellenism. Although Robinson does point out that "one of the most interesting correspondences in the Qumran literature is in fact with John i. 3," he says that the Qumran Scrolls provide no parallel to the Logos theology.

Second, the history of the Gospel "has its own primacy, the facts are sacred—and the theology is given only in, with and under it. This is made crystal clear in the opening verses of the first Epistle, and the Prologue restates it by insisting upon the centrality of the Word made flesh."

It is clear that throughout his discussion, as in discussions of the Johannine Prologue by other scholars in general, Robinson is primarily concerned with the Logos, "the centrality of the Word." It is precisely this point, I think, which has to be seriously reconsidered.

In the course of his discussion, Robinson lists themes common to the Prologue and the rest of the Gospel:

The pre-existence of the Logos or Son
In him was life
Life is light
Light rejected by darkness
Yet not quenched by it
Light coming into the world
Christ not received by his own
Being born of God and not of flesh
Seeing his glory
The only-begotten Son
Truth in Jesus Christ
No one has seen God, except the one who comes from God's side

I should like to point out, first of all, that the list is "impressive," to use Robinson's term. But it is impressive to me because of the centrality of the Light and the things associated with it, not the Logos. In fact, the only reference to the Logos (first theme) should not be included, not just for the reason that the title Logos itself appears nowhere in the Gospel—to say nothing of its pre-existence—but because the pre-existence of the Son is not stated in the Prologue. And all the other comparisons are equally valid, or even more so, when made with Christ as the Light.

Following the suggestion of B. T. D. Smith, Robinson says there may be "a deliberate correspondence between the *structure* of the Prologue and that of the Gospel":

Christ as the agent of (the new) creation (1: 3 = 1: 35–4: 42)
Christ as the life of the world (1: 4 = 4: 43–6: 71)
Christ as the light of the world (1: 4 f = 7: 1–9: 41)
He came to his own and his own received him not (1: 10 f = 10: 1–12: 50)
But to all who believed in his name he gave power to become children of God (1: 12 f = 13: 1–20: 29)

Here again Light, with the things associated with it, not Logos, may be taken as predominate. In line one, presumably Christ as Logos is "the agent of (the new) creation," since Jn 1: 3 is given as the reference from the

Prologue. But Christ is nowhere the agent of creation in 1: 35–4: 42. It is very important to notice here that the Christ through whom the world was made (vs 10) is characterized in vs 9 as "the true light," not as the Logos. While it is not explicitly stated elsewhere in the Gospel that Christ as the Light—or under any other title, for that matter—is the agent in creation, at least a "new creation" may be taken as implied in such passages as 6: 33; 8: 12; 9: 5 (with the whole story of the healing of the blind man); 11: 9 f, 25 f (the raising of Lazarus); and 12: 35 f, 46. Better yet, perhaps, are those passages about Jesus working—as, for example, in 4: 34; 5: 17–36; 10: 25–38; 14: 10–12; 17: 4.

Joachim Jeremias on the Prologue

More recently, Joachim Jeremias has produced a chapter on the Prologue to John.[11] He begins with an observation with respect to the sentence structure. "The Prologue is constructed by means of parallelism, the pairing of similarly sounding clauses, constituting a kind of call and response—perhaps echoing the alternation between precentor and congregation." He adds: "The Prologue, as everyone knows today, is a powerfully contrived song, an early Christian religious poem, a psalm, a hymn to the Logos Jesus Christ" (p. 72).

Thus Jeremias also calls the poetry of the Prologue a Logos-hymn, so the Logos remains as the center of his attention. According to Jeremias, the hymn is divided into four strophes: (1) the Logos of God (vss 1–5); (2) the witness pointing to him (vss 6–8); (3) the fate of the Logos in the world (vss 9–13); and (4) the confession of the believing community (vss 14–18).

Notice here that much of what Jeremias takes as applied to Jesus as the Logos could more aptly be applied to him as the Light. In the second strophe, John the Baptist came "to bear witness to the Light" (1: 7), not to the Logos, which is totally consistent with the portrayal of the Baptist elsewhere in the Gospel. In 5: 35, "light" is used with reference to the Baptist who, as in 1: 7, is thought of as bearing witness to Jesus: "John has borne witness to the truth . . . . He was a burning and shining lamp, and you were willing to rejoice for a time in his light"; and in the context of 5: 33–36, the Baptist is presented as inferior to Jesus, as in other places in the Gospel.

In the third strophe, what is described is the fate of the Light, not of the Logos, in the world (1: 9–13). The antecedent of everything that is stated in vss 10–13 is "the true light . . . that was coming into the world" (vs 9). In this strophe, things are also in perfect harmony with passages elsewhere in the Gospel. At two places in the Gospel, there is reference to Jesus as

Light having come into the world, once probably in the words of the writer, though perhaps in the words of Jesus (3: 19), once definitely in Jesus' words (12: 46). These two passages confirm the translation in 1: 9—that is, taking *ἐρχόμενον* with *φῶς* instead of *ἄνθρωπον*.

Even in the fourth strophe, "the confession of the believing community" should be thought of as directed toward "the unique Son," rather than toward the Logos. In vs 15, "John bears witness to him" (Son, as antecedent) finds a parallel in 1: 34: "And I have seen and I have borne witness that this is the Son of God." At other places the Baptist is said to bear witness to Jesus, but never to him as the Logos (cf 1: 32 f; 3: 26; 5: 33). Whereas the term Logos never appears elsewhere in the Gospel, the words "unique Son" (1: 14b) occur in 3: 16.

The descriptions which Jeremias uses to summarize the strophes seem much more appropriate if the Prologue is considered as a Phōs poem rather than as a Logos hymn. Taken in this way, all the verses of the Prologue (3–13, 14b) except 1 f, 14a, and 15–18 are entirely consonant with the Gospel.

Jeremias observes that in the Prologue there is a kind of poetry well known in Hebrew literature—"a skilful elaboration of the synthetic form, namely climactic parallelism (step-parallelism). It is so named because every line takes up a word of the preceding line, as it were lifting it up a step higher." In the Prologue, it appears in 1: 4 f, 1: 14b, and 1: 16:

> In him was *life*,
> and the *life* was the *light* of men.
> And the *light* shines in the *darkness*,
> and the *darkness* has not comprehended it.
> We have beheld his *glory*,
> *glory* as of the only son from the Father,
> *full* of *grace* and truth,
> and from his *fulness* have we all received *grace* upon *grace*.

"This climactic parallelism is the dominating formal feature of the Prologue." Jeremias points out the lack of climactic parallelism in some verses (12b, 13, 14–16). Only by taking the words "full of grace" from vs 14a and connecting them with vs 16, omitting vs 15, can he obtain a climactic parallelism in vss 14–16.

> This observation corresponds to another one. Whereas the climactic parts of the Prologue differ in their vocabulary from the Fourth Gospel (such important words as "the Logos," "grace and truth," even "grace," do not recur outside the Prologue), the non-climactic insertions betray the language of the Fourth Evangelist himself (vv. 6–8, 12b–13, 15 and, perhaps, 17–18).

This has led to the commonly accepted conclusion that we must distinguish between the original Prologue (*Urprolog*) and the Evangelist's comments about it. The *Urprolog* is of Christian origin and was "one of the hymns sung at the daily Eucharist . . ." (pp. 73–75).

According to Jeremias, the Christian origin of the Logos hymn is certain because it was one of many in the NT exalting Christ, including Phil 2: 6–11; Col 1: 15–20; 1 Tim 3: 16; and 2 Tim 2: 11–13, of which Phil 2: 6–11 is most nearly like the Christ hymn in Jn 1. "They are *Heilsgeschichte in Hymnenform.* This literary genre . . . comes from the Old Testament." The Logos hymn of John replaces the birth narratives of Matthew and Luke, but on a more exalted note (pp. 75 f, 78 f).

The Prologue as a Phōs (light) Poem

Several observations with respect to Jeremias' view should be noted. First of all, in the poetic verses which Jeremias sets off, Light is the dominating feature. There could scarcely be better evidence for the nucleus of a Phōs poem in the Prologue than that fact. Moreover, the italicized words (italics are his), with the exception of the ones in the last two lines, are among those which occur most frequently in the Gospel. So Jeremias' statement that "the climactic parts of the Prologue differ in their vocabulary from the Fourth Gospel" is correct only for the words which he takes from vss 1, 14a, and 16 f. Precisely because the vocabulary of all verses, including the climactic parts, except 1 f, 14a, and most of 15–18, *does* coincide with that of the Gospel is a major reason for concluding that vss 1 f, 14a, and most of 15–18 were probably not written by the author of vss 3–13, 14b, and the rest of the Gospel.

If it be granted at this point that Light, not Logos, is the dominant feature of the Prologue, then surely it is clear that the Logos idea has been overworked. I have suggested that the author of John, under the influence of a combination of OT passages, especially Is 60: 1–3, 5, 19, the Qumran Scrolls, and the Synoptic tradition, composed the Prologue as an introduction to his work. As in the case of many introductions, I believe his was composed after the completion of the Gospel. I also think that it originally comprised most, if not all, of vss 3–13 and 14b, and that the idea of the Logos (vss 1 f and 14a) was not a part of it. We can omit the Logos passages —and, as I will establish later, they are the only ones we can omit—without losing a single concept or theme of the Gospel.

On the other hand, the missing connection between Prologue and Gospel which Robinson points out—"the pre-existent Son of man who descends from heaven to return thither"—does not seem to be serious. As I have shown elsewhere,[12] "Son of man" in John is only a literary variation for the Son, Son of God, and Jesus, and not a distinct theological concept. Although not as vividly or explicitly stated as in vss 1 and 14a, the pre-existence of Jesus may be implied from the language of vs 9—"the light . . . was coming into the world"—in the same way as from similar language elsewhere in the Gospel, rather clear statements of which are in 3: 19; 6: 51; 8: 58; and 12: 46. With the idea of pre-existence in 1: 9 and 14b, compare especially 16: 26–30, and notice the similarity of language and thought. Whether or not pre-existence is implied in 14b, it seems more appropriate to associate glory—"glory as of a unique Son from the Father"—with the concept of Jesus as the Light, as we have done, than with that of the Logos. In 17: 1–5, as in 1: 14b, glory is associated with the Son, and there it is the glory of the Son which was pre-existent (cf 17: 22). In 17: 24, as in 1: 14b, it is glory which is "beheld." Moreover, the Light and Son (of God) are synonymous in the Gospel in 3: 16–21. The connection between Prologue and Gospel is clear.

One of the difficulties which arises from including vss 1 f, 14a, (15), and 16–18 in the original Prologue is that certain terms, including such theologically important ones as *λόγος* ("word," used as a title), *σκηνόω* ("dwell"), *χάρις* ("grace"), *πλήρωμα* ("fullness"), *πλήρης* ("full"), and *ἐξηγέομαι* ("declare," "make known"), occur there but nowhere else in the Gospel. Besides these, the preposition *πρός*, in the phrase *πρὸς τὸν θεόν* in vss 1 and 2, is used nowhere else in the Gospel with the same meaning. In strong contrast, the only word in vss 3–13 and 14b which does not appear elsewhere in the Gospel is *φωτίζω* (1: 9) which, as I have said, may indicate influence from Is 60: 1 f. And many words, such as "life," "light," "darkness," "witness" (both the verb and the noun), "believe," "world," "come," "know," "receive" (two different words in 1: 11 f), "to be born," "will," and "glory," are key words, occurring again and again.

The Gospel as we now have it has two "endings" (20: 30 f and 21: 24 f); it appears to have two "beginnings" as well (1: 1 ff and 1: 6 ff). When one restricts the Prologue to vss 3–13 and 14b, then vss 6–8 become the natural beginning. In spite of the fact that most scholars regard vss 6–8 as secondary additions, I believe these verses are original with the Gospel writer.

Some scholars have noted that 1: 6 is a natural opening for a historical narrative and have called attention to parallels in the OT, such as Judg 13: 2 and 1 Sam 1: 1. It is, indeed, likely that the author used the OT in 1: 6 and in exactly the same way as in some other places in the Prologue and Gospel.

In having vss 6–8 first, there is no interruption in the sequence of thought. Moreover, the language and thought of the verses themselves are entirely consonant with the writer's portrayal of the Baptist as inferior to Jesus at every turn (cf 1: 19–37; 3: 23–30; 4: 1; 5: 33–36; 10: 40–42). In contrast to the Synoptists, the writer in the Prologue is consistent with the rest of his Gospel by always referring to the Baptist as John, never as "the Baptist." I have already indicated that in Jn 5: 35 the term "light" is used with reference to the Baptist and that he bears witness to Jesus.

Robinson shows parallels between Jn 1: 6 and opening lines in the Synoptics (Mk 1: 4; Lk 1: 5; 3: 1 f). I should like to note, further, that in Jn 1: 6 the Baptist is introduced as "a man sent from God." In Jn 3: 28, the Baptist thinks of himself as being sent: "I was sent before him" (i.e., Christ). In both of these passages, the writer shows affinity with Mk 1: 2: "Behold, I send my messenger before your face." Thus it appears that the writer of John, like that of Mark, began his story of Jesus by introducing the Baptist as his forerunner (cf Jn 1: 15–34 and 3: 28). With the witness of the Baptist in the beginning of the Gospel, the sequence in 1: 19 ff is in no way disturbed.

At this point, perhaps, some comment on the poetic and rhythmic character of the Prologue should be made. The nature of much of the poetry seems to me still to be an open question. Almost all agree that most of vss 14–18 is basically prose, and many would also include some of vss 9–13 in that category. Vs 2 is difficult to fit into any poetic arrangement. While some verses do not precisely fall under any form of Hebrew poetry, there seems to be a certain rhythmic quality about them which I have tried, maybe unsuccessfully, to bring out in the translation.

The content of my proposed arrangement of the Prologue is an effective introduction or prelude which easily blends in with the rest of the Gospel. I have already indicated a number of things in it consistent with the rest of the Gospel. We turn now to additional ideas and themes and style of writing in the Prologue consonant with the Gospel.

The strophe about John (1: 6–8) is the writer's equivalent of the Synoptists' introduction of the Baptist. In addition to the parallels already noted, compare Mt 3: 1: "In those days came (*παραγίνεται*) John the Baptist" with Jn 1: 7: "He came for a witness." There is also the same kind of parallel between Jesus as the Light "coming into the world" in Jn 1: 9 and the Synoptists' introduction of Jesus to the world: *καὶ ἐγένετο ἐν ἐκείναις ταῖς ἡμέραις ἦλθεν Ἰησοῦς ἀπὸ Ναζαρέθ* (Mk 1: 9; cf Mt 3: 13). In the same way, the statement in the Prologue about Jesus as the Light coming into the world reflects the Synoptists' view that Jesus' coming was regarded as the fulfillment of OT prophecy: "The people sitting in darkness saw a great light, and upon those sitting in the region and shadow of death a light has arisen" (Mt 4: 15 f, quoting Is 9: 1 f); compare also: "A light for a revelation to Gentiles and glory of your people Israel" (Lk 2: 32 and Is 42: 6; 49: 6). All this coincides with the writer's knowledge and use of the Synoptics elsewhere in the Gospel when using OT sources as well.[13]

In NT thought, it was not the long-expected Logos that had come but the Light. That theme is repeated in the Gospel of John several times (3: 19; 11: 9; 12: 35 f, 46). Moreover, Jesus' followers are exhorted to believe in him so that they may become "sons of light" (12: 36)—an expression well known from the Dead Sea Scrolls (e.g., 1QS 1: 9; 3: 24; 1QM 1: 1, 3; and *passim*; cf Lk 16: 8; Eph 5: 8; 1 Thess 5: 5). I am familiar with the phrase "sons of light" (cf above), but I know of no place in either the Bible or the Dead Sea Scrolls where the expression "sons of the Word" occurs.

When vss 3–5 are placed after vs 9, then Jesus as the Light, not as the Logos, is their antecedent. Such an arrangement is quite defensible for the following reasons. To regard the Light as the agent in creation in vs 3 is justifiable on the basis of vs 10, where the writer of the Prologue states in a different way a point he had made earlier. (This kind of repetition and variation of language is one of the most characteristic features of the Johannine style.[14]) Moreover, in the Fourth Gospel, Jesus as the Light and Giver of light is also the Life and Giver of life (cf many passages from 3: 16–17: 3). The sentence, "In him [i.e., the Light] was life," is confirmed by the reference to Jesus as "the Light of life" in 8: 12, the latter itself being an OT expression (cf Ps 56: 13 [14]; Job 33: 30); so also 5: 26: "For as the Father has life in himself, so he has granted to the Son also to have life in himself."[15]

The theme of light and darkness, with the antithesis between the two but with the light not being overcome, is well known in John (cf 3: 16–12: 46). As in Is 60 and the Qumran Scrolls (for example, 1QS 3: 18–25; 4: 9–14; 1QM 13; 15: 9 f), so in the Prologue and Gospel the light is both eschatological and ethical.

The idea of Jesus coming into and being in the world, with some not knowing or receiving him, recurs in the Gospel: "I have come in the name of my Father, and you do not receive me" (5: 43); "If you had known me, you would have known my Father also" (14: 7). See also 4: 44; 8: 28; 13: 1; 15: 18; 16: 3; and many other places for Jesus' rejection by the Jews. On the other hand, those who believe in Jesus have a special relationship with him and receive special privilege, such as becoming "children of God" (1: 12) or "sons of light" (12: 36; cf also 3: 15–18, 36; 5: 24; 6: 35, 40, 47; 11: 25 f, 40; 14: 12–17). The expression "believe on his name" (1: 12) is consistent with usage elsewhere in the Gospel (2: 23; 3: 18).

Vs 13 also has its counterpart in the Gospel: "That which is born of the flesh is flesh, and that which is born of the spirit is spirit" (3: 6; cf 3: 3); and "It is the spirit which gives life; the flesh does not do any good in any way" (6: 63). The obvious antithesis between these verses and 6: 51–58 (where the bread which came down from heaven and gives life to the world is Jesus' flesh) need not concern us here, since variation of thought, even to the point of contradiction, is an inherent part of the writer's style.[16]

The glory and glorification of Jesus are among the main themes of the Gospel. Jesus' glory was pre-existent (12: 37–41), was currently evident through his works (2: 11; 11: 4), and, though already observed, was still anticipated in the future (12: 20–23). A combination of two or three of these ideas occurs in 12: 20–33; 13: 30–32; 17: 1, 4f, 10, 22, 24). Jesus' ultimate glorification came through the crucifixion and/or resurrection (in addition to the above, cf 7: 39; 12: 16; and 2: 22). Compare "glory as of a unique Son from the Father" (1: 14b) with "and do not seek the glory from the only God" (5: 44). Just as the glory of the Son is associated with that of the Father in 1: 14b, so it is in 5: 44 and most of the above passages also.

After one has compared the ideas of the Prologue and Gospel, the fact remains that the only idea in the Prologue which has no counterpart in the Gospel is Jesus as the Logos. Certainly this fact is crucial to any argument for a Logos hymn. On the other hand, when one takes the Prologue as a Phōs poem, then all the ideas which are there associated with Jesus as the Light recur as basic themes of the Gospel.

It remains only for us to point out some basic similarities in style between Prologue and Gospel. The following are some examples:

Synonymous words or expressions within the same sentence or context (many times in Gospel): *πάντα δι' αὐτοῦ ἐγένετο . . . ὁ κόσμος δι' αὐτοῦ ἐγένετο* (1: 3, 10); *οὗτος . . . ἐκεῖνος* (1: 7; both words, especially the latter, are favorites of the Gospel); *ἄνθρωπος . . . ἀνήρ* (1: 9, 13; same words in 6: 10); *τὰ ἴδια . . . οἱ ἴδιοι* (1: 11); and *παρέλαβον . . . ἔλαβον* (1: 11 f).

ἵνα with finite verb as telic, instead of *τοῦ* with infinitive: *ἵνα μαρτυρήσῃ* (1: 7; especially frequent in Gospel).

Preposition *εἰς* with accusative to denote purpose: *εἰς μαρτυρίαν* (1: 7; 9: 39; cf 3: 11).

Words with double meanings: *καταλαμβάνω* (1: 5; cf 3: 3, 7, 31; 3: 8; 3: 20; 8: 28; 12: 32, 34).

Καί adversative (1: 5; 17: 1).

Elliptical use of *ἀλλ' ἵνα* (1: 8; 9: 3; 11: 52).

γεννάω and *ἐκ* (1: 13; 3: 5; 6: 1; 8: 41; cf 3: 3, 7).

Casus pendens: *ὅσοι δὲ ἔλαβον αὐτόν, ἔδωκεν αὐτοῖς* (1: 12) and *ὃς ἦν μετά σοῦ . . . ᾧ σύ* (3: 26).

εἰμί in imperfect with participle in present (1: 9; 2: 6; 3: 23; 10: 40).

πιστεύω and *εἰς* with accusative (1: 12; very frequent in Gospel but rare elsewhere in NT).

Pronominal subject of verb sometimes expressed, sometimes not (1: 7 f, 11; many times in Gospel).

ἐγένετο ἄνθρωπος . . . ὄνομα αὐτῷ Ἰωάννης (1: 6) and *ἦν δὲ ἄνθρωπος ἐκ τῶν Φαρισαίων, Νικόδημος ὄνομα αὐτῷ* (3: 1)

Καὶ ἡ σκοτία αὐτὸ οὐ κατέλαβον (1: 5) and *ἵνα μὴ σκοτία ὑμᾶς καταλάβῃ* (12: 35; this passage confirms the translation "overcome" in 1: 5).

Climactic parallelism:

In him was life,
and the life was the light of men (1: 4).
And you will know the truth,
and the truth will make you free (8: 32).
I am the good shepherd,
the good shepherd gives his life for the sheep (10: 11; cf also 11: 25; 16: 7).

Because of the writer's technique of repeating his main themes with variations throughout the Gospel, no outline of the structure of his composition can be wholly accurate. There is bound to be some overlapping of ideas in any proposed outline, but I believe that the following comparative outline of the structure of the Prologue and Gospel, in which only the second part overlaps the first to any significant degree, is not a wholly inaccurate one:

Strophe 1: The superiority of Jesus to John the Baptist (1: 6–8 = 1: 19–5: 47).

Strophe 2: Jesus' work of giving light and life to the world rejected by the world (1: 9, 3–5, 10 f = 3–12).

Strophe 3: Jesus' withdrawal from the world into the company of those who did receive him (1: 12 f = 13–16).

Strophe 4: Jesus' ultimate glorification and exaltation through his death and resurrection (1: 14b = 17–20[21].

As valid as any other I have seen proposed, this structural outline of the Gospel comes little short, it seems to me, of confirming my arrangement of the Prologue as something more than the mere figment of my imagination.

I submit that the evidence presented here warrants these conclusions: After the body of the Gospel was completed, the author wrote the Prologue to serve as an introduction or prelude to his entire composition. It is a creative, succinct composition, and was comprised originally of poetry and rhythmic prose dealing with Jesus as the Light. Like many other passages of similar length in the Gospel, it shows acquaintance with and influence from the OT, Qumran, and the Synoptic tradition.

The original poetic and rhythmic section consisted of vss 3–13 and 14b, most likely, though not necessarily, in the order we have given them—that is, 6–8; 9; 3–5; 10–13; 14b. The Prologue conceived as a Phōs (light) poem is entirely consonant with the Gospel, and serves as a genuine introduction to its basic content and structure.

There may have been a Logos hymn, fragments of which may be extant in vss 1 f, 14a, and some or all of vss 15–18. But since vss 1 f, 14a, and most of 15–18 (particularly with respect to vocabulary) are not consonant with the rest of the Gospel, they are best regarded as supplied by a later hand.

In strong contrast to the original Prologue in vss 3–13 and 14b and the rest of the Gospel, where we do find parallels from a number of sources, there has as yet been no true parallel to the Logos theology provided from any source, Palestinian or Hellenistic Judaism or any other known to me. This can only mean, it seems to me, that some editor(s), seemingly unfamiliar with the basic vocabulary of the Gospel, in an effort to make the Gospel appeal to readers in an environment different from the one in which it was originally written, wrote an introduction (vss 1 f) and a conclusion (vss 14a and some or all of 15–18) to the Phōs (light) poem to tie the whole in with 1: 19 ff, and probably rearranged the verses in between.

The relationship between the Gospel and First Epistle of John, including the relationship between the prologues of each, still remains an enigma. The "obvious and striking" parallels which Robinson sets out (p. 123; the ones involving Jn 1: 4 seem a bit forced) may all be accounted for by the view of C. H. Dodd proposed more than thirty years ago, assuming, of course, that the author of the First Epistle was familiar with the Gospel in a form very similar to the one we have:

> I conceive the First Epistle of John . . . to have been written by an author who was quite possibly a disciple of the Fourth Evangelist, and certainly a diligent student of his work. He has soaked himself in the Gospel, assimilating its ideas and forming his style upon its model. He sets out to develop, commend and apply certain of these ideas to meet the particular needs of the situation.[17]

The view of Dodd is for me a preferable alternative to that of Robinson. But in view of the likenesses and differences between the two writings, I must confess that neither view is completely satisfactory to me. Unfortunately, however, I have no better solution to offer.

Notes

1 See my *Old Testament Quotations in the Gospel of John* (Leiden: E. J. Brill, 1965), especially pp. 127–30.

2 Passages from the OT are translated from the MT by me. For Is 60, there are no substantial differences among MT, LXX, or 1QIs[a]. In general, the language of the Prologue is closer to MT than to LXX. Cf also Is 9: 1: "The people that walk in darkness have seen a great light . . . a light shines over them"; and Is 2: 5; 42: 6; Job 29: 3; 33: 28, 30. I am not unaware of possible influence on the writer of the Prologue also from Jewish wisdom literature (or even Philo), an influence also apparent in some formal quotations in Jn (1: 23; 7: 37 f; 17: 12), such as Prov, Wis, Sir, Bar, and others, as J. R. Harris (*The Origin of the Prologue to St John's Gospel* [Cambridge: University Press, 1911]) and others

have shown. The general reader will find convenient summaries of such influences in R. E. Brown, *The Gospel According to John i–xii* in *AB* (New York: Doubleday, 1966), 29, pp. 519–24, and William Barclay, *The Gospel of John* (Philadelphia: Westminster Press, 1956), I, pp. 2–14.

[3] With reference to Isaiah, so James Muilenburg, "The Book of Isaiah" in *IB* (Nashville: Abingdon Press, 1956), V, p. 698.

[4] The humanity of Jesus in neither the Prologue nor the Gospel is dependent upon the vivid "The Word became flesh." Comparison of Jesus with the Baptist, Jesus' coming into the world and to his own, and his being received or not are sufficient to establish Jesus' humanity in the Prologue.

[5] So Muilenburg of Isaiah (*ibid.*).

[6] *Ibid.*

[7] See the treatment of the Prologue with a summary of views and bibliography in R. E. Brown, *op. cit.*, pp. 1–37.

[8] *Ibid.*, p. 21.

[9] "The Relation of the Prologue to the Gospel of St John," *NTS* 9 (1962–63), 120–29.

[10] For references see Robinson, *ibid.*, p. 126.

[11] "The Revealing Word" in his book, *The Central Message of the New Testament* (New York: Scribners, 1965).

[12] See my "The Son of Man in the Fourth Gospel," *JBL* 86 (1967), 402–9.

[13] See my *Old Testament Quotations in the Gospel of John* for comments on 1: 23; 7: 42; 12: 13, 15, 39 f; 19: 24.

[14] See my "Variations in the Language and Thought of John," *ZNW* 55 (1964), 167–97.

[15] Such a rearrangement in the Greek text causes no grammatical problems. Placing vss 3–5 after vss 6–9 causes no problems with the grammar because the use of αὐτός as a personal pronoun in every instance can be taken as a neuter in agreement with its antecedent φῶς. However, placing vss 10–12 after vss 3–5 may result in a shift in gender to a masculine accusative pronoun (αὐτόν) with a neuter antecedent (φῶς). But this shift may already be made in the Greek text as it now stands since the subject antecedent of vs 10 is by no means clear and could presently be taken as τὸ φῶς. So αὐτόν in vs 10 would already represent a shift in gender to a masculine personal pronoun with a neuter antecedent. But our rearrangement requires such a shift in gender by reading the present αὐτόν (translated "him" in vss 10, 11, and 12) instead of the normally expected αὐτό with a neuter antecedent such as το φῶς (as in vs 5). At any rate, it should be observed that, if one reads vss 10–12 after vs 9, as in the present text, or after vs 5, as in our suggested rearrangement, the shift in gender is entirely consonant with the style of the writer in at least two passages elsewhere in the Gospel. In 14: 26 and 15: 26 the neuter antecedents τὸ πνεῦμα τὸ ἅγιον and τὸ πνεῦμα τῆς ἀληθείας are followed by the masculine demonstrative ἐκεῖνος, presumably because the writer thought of the spirit in personal terms (see J. H. Bernard, *The Gospel According to St. John* [*ICC*] [New York: Scribners, 1929], II, pp. 499 f and C. K. Barrett, *The Gospel According to St John* [London: S.P.C.K., 1955], p. 402). Obviously in the text as it now stands the writer has thought of the Light in personal terms. So our rearrangement is entirely in keeping with both the letter and spirit of the text of the writer both in the Prologue and elsewhere (cf, for example, also 16: 13 f; 1 Jn 5: 6). These arguments, though perhaps not entirely convincing to some, seem to me much more preferable than the simpler suggestion to emend the text from αὐτόν to αὐτό in vss 10-12.

[16] See note 14.

[17] C. H. Dodd, "The First Epistle of John and the Fourth Gospel," *BJRL* 21 (1937), 30.

David Noel Freedman
University of Michigan

Strophe and Meter in Exodus 15

Continuing discovery and publication of Canaanite cuneiform tablets, current research into the language and forms of early Hebrew poetry, and recent contributions to the elucidation of the poem in Ex 15 have recommended further reflections on and reconsideration of certain aspects of this national victory song. We are primarily concerned with the strophic structure of the poem and the associated problem of metrical analysis. Other questions will be dealt with incidentally in the course of the discussion. Throughout, the presentation mentioned above will be assumed.[1]

In dealing with questions of strophe and meter, two opposing principles or assumptions must be reckoned with: 1) that in all likelihood the poem has not been transmitted to us precisely in the form in which it was composed, and that changes, some deliberate, some accidental have occurred in the course of transmission; 2) that strophic and metrical or rhythmic structures must be derived or established from the text as we have it, since it would be methodologically untenable to emend the text in the interests of a certain metrical or strophic structure or to base such a structure on an emended text.

In practice, then, if the results are to be at all convincing or persuasive, it is necessary to have a well-preserved text, with a minimum of difficulties in readings and meanings. It should be sufficiently long so that clear-cut patterns or structures can be determined. Then, presumably, if such patterns emerge from the analysis of the preserved materials, minor deviations, anomalies, or inconsistencies could be regarded as the result of accidental change in the process of copying and possibly corrected. At the same time, there must be compelling reasons for regarding the deviations as errors, and not as deliberate variations from the established scheme and therefore part of it. The following study is an attempt to analyze a representative piece of Hebrew poetry in a good state of preservation to determine whether strophic and/or metrical patterns exist, and to recover them so far as the evidence permits.

The existence of a strophic structure in this poem may be regarded as highly probable if not virtually certain. The single most important clue has been provided by Professor James Muilenburg in his recent study of Exodus 15.[2] He has correctly identified certain lines which serve a purpose similar to refrains and act as dividers or buffers between the strophes of the poem. They relate closely or loosely both with what precedes and what follows, but stand apart both in form and in content from the strophes themselves. They share certain formal characteristics which distinguish them from the rest of the poem, thus confirming the view that they are deliberately placed to serve as structural markers.

The lines to be considered are vss 6, 11, and the latter half of 16. All three follow a pattern of partial repetition familiar from Ugaritic poetry and a number of Biblical poems. This pattern is usually characterized as abc/abd, in which the first two elements of each colon are identical while the third is different. Variations occur, such as abcd/abef or abc/abd/efg, where the final colon repeats the thought of the preceding cola but uses different words. A well-known example of the last variety, based on a Ugaritic prototype, is to be found in Ps 92: 10:[3]

kī hinnē ʾōyᵉbēkā yahwē	For behold your enemies, Yahweh
kī hinnē ʾōyᵉbēkā yōʾbēdū	For behold, your enemies will perish
yitpārᵉdū kol - pōʿᵃlē ʾāwen	May all image makers be scattered

The Canaanite precursor goes as follows:

ht ibk bʿlm	Behold your enemies, Baal
ht ibk tmḫṣ	Behold, you shall smash your enemies
ht tṣmt ṣrtk	Behold, you shall destroy your foes

Other examples are scattered through the Psalter, especially Ps 29 (cf Ps 96: 1–2, 7–8); Ps 77: 17. The Song of Deborah, similar in many other respects to this victory ode, also contains numerous examples of this pattern: Judg 5: 3, 5, 6, 7, 12, 19, 21, 23, 24, 27, 30. The lines in Ex 15 follow:

6	ymynk yhwh	By your right hand, Yahweh[4]
	nʾdry bkḥ	resplendent among the powerful
	ymynk yhwh	By your right hand, Yahweh
	trʿṣ ʾwyb	you have shattered the enemy

11	my kmkh	Who is like you
	b'lym yhwh	among the gods, Yahweh?
	my kmkh	Who is like you
	n'dr bqdš	resplendent among the holy ones
	nwr' thlt	Awesome in praises
	'śh pl'	worker of wonders?
16^2	'd y'br	While your people
	'mk yhwh	pass over, Yahweh
	'd y'br	While your people,
	'm - zw qnyt	whom you purchased, pass over

It is to be noted that only these three lines have the repetitive pattern described. A possible exception is vs 3, with the repetition of *yhwh*, but the similarity is vague and limited, and the metrical structure is significantly different. Furthermore, in each of these refrains or dividers, the name Yahweh appears (twice in 6, once each in 11 and 16^2), whereas it appears nowhere in the material bounded by them (vss 7–10, 12–16^1). To complete the picture, it appears twice in vs 3 and twice in vss 17–18. It also occurs in vs 1 (and 21), which may have had a function similar to that of the dividers. The abbreviated form *Yah* occurs in vs 2, which, however, stands outside the strophic pattern, and requires special comment.

Returning to the repetitive lines (6, 11, 16^2), we observe that vss 6 and 16^2 are in couplet form, while vs 11 is more elaborate, having a third element in the form of participial phrases in apposition with *n'dr* and modifying *yhwh*. Thus the three refrains or dividers form the skeletal structure on which the poem is built.

It is in the shape of a triangle or pyramid, with the two regular refrains forming the base, and the more elaborate central refrain at the apex.

If we examine the material between Refrains A (vs 6) and B (vs 11), we find that it falls naturally into two parts, dividing at vs 9. This division is strictly in accordance with the content, though there is a corresponding shift in mood and rhythmic movement as well. Vss 7–8 deal with the violent storm and its effects both on the enemy (vs 7) and the sea (vs 8). With vs 9 we have a sharp break, since the poet goes back to an earlier stage of the story, picking up the action with the enemy's decision to pursue, overtake, and conquer. The fate of the enemy described in vs 10, which echoes vss 4–5 (and 1), stands in stark contrast to the glorious and greedy expectations expressed in the preceding verse.

If we turn to the material between Refrains B (vs 11) and C (vs 16^2), we find that it also falls structurally into two parts, though the disjuncture between the sections is not as sharp as in the preceding strophe. We find the break between vss 14 and 15; it is signalized by the particle *'az*, which introduces the second part of the strophe. Vss 15–16 pick up and elaborate the theme of vs 14, the terror of the nations at the demonstration of Yahweh's power.

According to this analysis, each strophe consists of two stanzas or half-strophes: vss 7–8 and 9–10; vss 12–14 and 15–16[1]. Closer inspection indicates that each of these stanzas consists of five units or bicola, organized in clusters of two or three units, forming couplets and triads. Thus Stanza B in the first strophe consists of a triad (vs 9) and a couplet (vs 10); Stanza B of the second strophe has the same structure—a triad (vs 15) and a couplet (vs 16[1]). Stanza A of Strophe II has a similar structure, with a triad (vss 12–13) and a couplet (vs 14). Although vs 12 stands somewhat apart, so far as content is concerned, it is structurally very similar to 13a and b. Turning to Stanza A in the first strophe, we find a more difficult situation. It is clear that vs 7 constitutes a couplet, its component units being parallel in content and structure. The same is true of 8b and c, which is a couplet containing parallel units. How does the unit 8a fit into the overall pattern? So far as content is concerned, it clearly belongs with 8b and c (cf *n'rmw mym / nṣbw . . . nzlym / qp'w thmt*; the opening phrase, *wbrwḥ 'pyk*, applies to all three clauses). But structurally it is more closely related to 7a (and b): cf *wbrb g'wnk / wbrwḥ 'pyk*. Note also that the metrical pattern of vs 7 is 4:4 (or 2:2 / 2:2) and 8a is the same, while the pattern in 8b and c is, in all likelihood, 3:3.

It is to be observed, however, that the syllable count in vs 7 is 12:12 (or 6:6/6:6), while in 8a, it is 10 (6:4); 8b and c have a count of 9:9. In view of the fact that the other three stanzas have the triad first, followed by the couplet, we may conclude that the intended pattern in the first stanza was the same, but that content does not always follow form (as is true in a different sense in vs 12 and also, to some extent, with respect to the stanza division between vss 14 and 15).

On the basis of the foregoing discussion, we may represent the strophic structure of the central section of the Song of the Sea schematically as follows:

Refrain	A	(6)	4:4	or	(2:2/2:2)
Strophe	I	(7–10)			
	A	7	4:4		(2:2/2:2)
		8	4		(2:2)
			3:3		
	B	9	4:4:4		(2:2/2:2/2:2)
		10	4:4		(2:2/2:2)

Refrain	B	(11)	4:4:4 or	(2:2/2:2/2:2)
Strophe	II	(12–16[1])		
	A	12	4	(2:2)
		13	4:4	(2:2/2:2)
		14	3:3	
	B	15	4:4:4	(2:2/2:2/2:2)
		16[1]	4:4	(2:2/2:2)
Refrain	C	16[2]	3:3	

As already observed, the stanzas all have the same basic pattern, consisting of a triad followed by a couplet; the principal variation between Stanzas A and B (in both strophes) is that the concluding couplet in A is 3:3, while in B it is 4:4 (or 2:2/2:2). We note a similar pattern in the refrains: A and C are couplets, while B is a triad; A and B have the pattern 4:4(:4) or 2:2/2:2(/2:2), while C is 3:3. It may be added, however, that the analysis depends upon construing *mīkāmōkā* in vs 11 as 2, and *ʿad - yaʿᵃbōr* in vs 16 as 1. In other words, the difference between 2:2 or 4 and 3 may not be significant. While on the subject of stress or accent counting, a comment may be in order concerning the controversy over whether the prevailing meter is 4 or 2:2. In my judgment, both characterizations are valid, but for different purposes. With respect to the content of the lines in question, there is rarely if ever any parallelism between the two cola; thus 4:4 (and 3:3) is the appropriate designation to indicate the parallelism in content between lines: for example, 7a/7b, 8b/8c, 9b/9c, 13a/13b, 15a/15b/15c.

To designate such 4 stress lines as 2:2 on the basis of content would be unwarranted. However, there is often a caesura in the middle of such a line, and some indication of it in notation would be appropriate, for example, 7a (after *gʾwnk*) and 7b (after *ḥrnk*), 9b (after *šll*) and 9c (after *ḥrby*). So long as the distinction is recognized, either or both sets of figures may be used: for example vs 15 can be designated 4:4:4 according to content, and 2:2/2:2/2:2 structurally; the last line (15c) poses a problem, since *kōl* is normally taken with *yšby knʿn* as part of a construct chain. While Masoretic punctuation encourages the division after *kōl*, we may remain hesitant. However, it may be better to take *kōl* adverbially and to compare *nāmōgū kōl* with *ʾāz nibhᵃlū* as parallel constructions (i.e., verb plus emphatic adverb). Because of uncertainties in any stress-counting system and an inescapable element of subjectivity in deciding doubtful cases, and in order to reflect certain detailed poetic phenomena more precisely, I have opted for a syllable-counting system. Since there are many more syllables than accents in a line, the element of subjectivity is reduced (i.e., a disagreement over a count of nine or ten syllables is less important than one over two or three accents), and we have a more sensitive instrument for measuring the length of lines or cola.

There are additional complications since MT hardly reflects the actual pronunciation of words at the time of composition. The question of the length of syllables as well as the number of syllables can hardly be settled in the present state of our knowledge, and allowance must therefore be made for some variation in counting. Furthermore, the poet himself could take advantage of variations in current usage for metrical or rhythmic purposes, and syllables might be elided, or shortened, or lengthened in accordance with the exigencies of the verse. For example, we know that case and verbal endings which existed in older forms of the language were largely lost by the time of Moses and certainly by the time of composition of even very early Hebrew poetry. Nevertheless, case endings have been preserved in certain instances (cf vs 16, *ʾymth*), we believe for metrical reasons.[5] We may speculate further that in some instances such case endings, originally incorporated into the poem, have, in the process of transmission, been dropped or lost since their function was not recognized. We can document such developments with regard to other archaic features (like enclitic *mem*)[6] which were used deliberately by the poet for metrical and other stylistic reasons but which were edited out of the text by modernizers and revisers.

In attempting to determine the approximate time length of a line, it is necessary to consider not only the number of syllables but their length as well. Vowel quantity is a notoriously difficult question in the analysis of classical Hebrew, especially since the artificiality of the Masoretic vocalization is most apparent at this point. Nevertheless, a schematic representation on the basis of a hypothetical *Ursprache* would be equally bad or worse, since the language was already far along in the history of its development when biblical poetry was composed. Striking an appropriate balance is both the goal and the problem, since we do not have adequate controls for the period in question; and we must always recognize the liberty of the poet in using materials of different age and provenience to suit his purposes. The treatment of short vowels is a particularly thorny and difficult subject: some were lengthened, others reduced, still others elided, and a few remained as they were. MT illustrates all these changes, but when and under what conditions did they take place? Consider segolate nouns, which are regularly vocalized as having two syllables. Originally or at an earlier time, they were monosyllabic; but at a still earlier time, they had case endings; and in some words, it is difficult to see how they could have been pronounced as a single syllable. It may be that the process reflected in MT was a sort of compensation for the loss of the final syllables provided by case endings (note that the monosyllabic form is normally retained before pronominal suffixes). The same problem faces us with regard to diphthongs. For the most part, these were contracted in the north of Israel, and the syllable count is not thereby affected. But in the south, they were retained, and at some later date many of these were resolved into two syllables (e.g., *mayim* <*maym*). When? We know too that there were both long and short forms of the pronominal suffixes (e.g., *kā* and *-k* for 2 m.s.).[7] MT, for the most part, has standardized the long form, but is this true for the twelfth century B.C., or the tenth, or whenever the poem was written? My impression is that the poet was free to make choices among available forms, and did so according to the requirements of the poem, including metrical considerations. Individual problems will be considered as we work through the poem verse by verse.

With all these possible variations to consider, it may be said that the metrical pattern derived by syllable counting emerges with a regularity which matches that of the stress-counting system and, in some cases, improves upon it. On the whole, our poem is so well preserved that any metrical system will work and work well. In a third possible counting system, we attempt to take into account the difference between long and short vowels and between open and closed syllables. To apply this method, we simply count all the vocables in a colon, whether consonants or vowels, and then add one for each long vowel (taking a long vowel as having twice the value of a short vowel):

	Open Syllable	*Closed Syllable*
Short vowel	2	3
Long vowel	3	4

By using several systems simultaneously, we can check and confirm our results.

Proceeeding from the main body of the poem, with its strophes, stanzas, refrains, or dividers (vss 6–16), we turn to the immediately adjacent materials both before and after. The concluding stanza, vss 17–18, is balanced by a corresponding introduction, vss 3–5. More particularly, vs 18 forms an *inclusio* with vs 3. It is Yahweh the warrior, whose martial exploits are celebrated in the poem, who is also the eternal king. We may therefore recognize the parallel structure of these opening and closing stanzas (which together form an inclusive strophe like those in the body of the poem), but in reverse order. Thus vss 3 and 18 complement or balance each other. Similarly, vs 4ab is balanced by 17bc—4:4 (or 2:2 / 2:2) in both cases. That leaves 5 to match 17a. Neither seems to scan with any regularity, but they are roughly similar in length and make adequate sense as they are.

Leaving the details to later discussion, we may conclude that each stanza has five units distributed as follows:

vs 3	4 (2:2)	17	2:2(?)
4	4:4(2:2/2:2)		4:4(2:2/2:2)
5	3:3(?)	18	4(2:2)

Comparison with the stanzas of the main strophes indicates that these opening and closing stanzas belong to the same or a similar pattern, but with greater variation. Thus the introduction (vss 3–5) conforms to the A stanzas of Strophes I and II with a triad (the first element, vs 3, standing somewhat apart, as vs 12 in II A), 4:4:4 (or 2:2 / 2:2 / 2:2), followed by a couplet 3:3 (vs 5 could be taken as 2:3; the syllable count is 8:10, which may be a legitimate variant of the pattern reflected in vs 8bc, 9:9, or 14, 8:8). With regard to the final stanza, if we compare vss 17–18 with IB (9–10) and IIB (15–16), then we might identify vs 17 abc with the opening triad, and vs 18 as a truncated form of the closing couplet. But, in view of the connection between vs 18 and vs 3, we should perhaps look for a closing triad (to match the opening triad of vss 3–4), which we find in 17bc and 18 (the reign of Yahweh affirmed in 18 is predicated on the building of the divine throne and temple in 17). That leaves 17a, which ought to have come out as 3:3 to match vs 5 (or, on the analogy of I and IIB, 4:4). As the text stands, 17a looks like an anomalous and unbalanced 2:2, but it can hardly be anything else.[8] The syllable count is roughly 9:6, which balances rather cleverly with vs 5: 8/10 (but which could also be counted as 7/9). Thus we would have completely complementary stanzas forming an envelope for the body of the poem.

It remains to consider vss 1 and 2. Vs 2 may properly be regarded as an Exordium or personal introduction by the precentor, in this case, the "Moses" figure. It is only in vs 2 (cf discussion of *ʾšyrh* in vs 1; the suffix with *ʾdny* in vs 17 is purely formal) that the poet speaks in the first person; clearly this section stands by itself from a formal or structural viewpoint as well. It may have constituted the liturgical prologue to the singing of the Song of the Sea in the sanctuary or temple.

Finally, there is the opening line, which is repeated with slight variation as the Song of Miriam in vs 21. The form in vs 1 with *ʾšyrh* belongs to the same pattern as the Song of Deborah (Judg 5: 3), where the subject also is "I." The form in vs 21 with *šīrū* is a choral antiphon sung by Miriam and the women in response to the larger poem. Since the longer poem is already supplied with dividers, it would be difficult to position this refrain except at the beginning and end of the poem. It may well be that in liturgical performances the precentor began with vss 1–2 as the Exordium. Thus the opening and closing verses (1 and 21) form an *inclusio*, as indicated by the arrangement in MT, and with additional information as to how this device functioned in a liturgical setting: with precentor and chorus.

The form of this refrain is unlike those in the body of the poem, though the general metrical pattern is characteristic: 4:4 or 2:2 /2:2. Concerning the unity and overall symmetry of the poem, there should now be considerably less doubt than there has been. We suggest a date for the original poem in the twelfth century B.C., and attribute its final liturgical form to the worship in Jerusalem under David and Solomon.

Text and Translation

1	6	ʾašīrā la yahwē	I will sing of Yahweh	2
	5	kī gaʾō gaʾā	that he is highly exalted	2
	5	sūs warōkibō	Horse and its charioteer	2
	4	ramā bəyām	he hurled into the sea	2

Exordium (Proem)

2	7	ʿozzī wazimrat(ī) yāh	My mighty fortress is Yah	3
	7	wayəhī lī līšūʿā	He has become my Savior	3
	7	zē ʾēlī waʾanwēhū	This is my God whom I admire	3
	11	ʾelōhē ʾabī waʾarōmimenhū	My father's God whom I extol	3

Opening

3	6	yahwē ʾīš milḥamā	Yahweh—that man of war	2
	4	yahwē šimō	Whose name is Yahweh	2
4	8	markabōt parʿō waḥēlō	Pharaoh's chariot army	3
	4	yarā bəyām	He cast into the sea	2
	6	wamibḥar šalīšēw	And his elite officers	2
	6	ṭubbaʿū bəyam sūp	Were drowned in the Reed Sea	2
5	8	tihōmōt yakassiyūmū	The Abyss covered them	2/3
	10	yaradū bəməṣōlōt kəmō-ʾābn	they went down into the depths like a stone	3

Refrain (A)

6	5	yamīnka yahwē	By your right hand, Yahweh	2
		neʾdōrī bəkōḥ	resplendent among the mighty	2
	5	yamīnka yahwē	By your right hand, Yahweh	2
	4	tirʿaṣ ʾōyēb	you shattered the enemy	2

Strophe I

A

7	6	wabərōb gaʾōnka	Through your great majesty	2
	6	tahar(r)ēs qāmēka	you destroyed your foes	2
	6	tašallaḥ ḥarōnka	You sent forth your anger	2
	6	yōʾkilēmō kəqaš	it devoured them like stubble	2

8	6	wabərūḥ ’appēka	By the blast of your nostrils	2
	4	ne‘ramū mēm	the waters were heaped up	2
	9	niṣṣabū kəmō-nēd nōzilīm	The waves mounted as a bank	3
	9	qapa’ū tihōmōt bəlib-yām	The depths churned in the heart of the sea	3
B				
9	4	’amar ’ōyēb	The enemy boasted	2
	4	’erdop ’aśśīg	"I'll pursue, I'll overtake	2
	5	’aḥallēq šalāl	"I'll seize the booty	2
	6	timla’ēmō napšī	my gullet will be filled with them	2
	4	’arīq ḥarbī	"I'll bare my sword	2
	6	tōrīšēmō yadī	my hand will dispossess them"	2
10	6	nasåpta bərūḥka	You blew with your breath	2
	4	kissamō yām	the sea covered them	2
	6	ṣalalū kə‘opərt	They sank like lead	2
	5	bəmēm ’addīrīm	in the dreadful waters	2

Refrain (B)

11	4	mī-kamōka	Who is like you	2
	5	bə’ēlīm yahwē	among the gods, Yahweh?	2
	4	mī-kamōka	Who is like you	2
	4	ne’dār bəqōdš	resplendent among the holy ones	2
	5	nōrā’ təhillōt	Fearsome in praises	2
	3	‘ōśē pil’	worker of wonders?	2

Strophe II

A				
12	6	naṭīta yamīnka	You stretched out your hand	2
	5	tibla‘ēmō ’ārṣ	the netherworld swallowed them	2
13	7	naḥīta bəḥasdika	You led in your kindness	2
	5	‘am-zū ga’ālta	the people whom you redeemed	2
	7	nēhalta bə‘ozzika	You guided them with your might	2
	6	’el nawē qodšeka	to your holy habitation	2
14	8	šama‘ū ‘ammīm yirgazūn	The peoples trembled when they heard	3
	8	ḥīl ’aḥaz yōšibē palašt	Anguish seized the inhabitants of Philistia	3
B				
15	4	’āz nibhalū	Indeed, the generals	2
	5	’allūpē ’ədōm	of Edom were unnerved	2
	4	’ēlē mō’āb	Shuddering gripped	2
	5	yō’ḥəzēmō rā‘d	the chiefs of Moab	2
	4	namōgū kōl	The kings of Canaan	2

	5	yōšibē kənāʿn	collapsed completely	2
16	5	tappīl ʿalēhem	You brought down on them	
	6	ʾēmāta wapaḥda	dreadful terror	
	6	bəgadōl zərōʿka	Through your great arm	2
	5	yiddammū kaʾābn	they were struck dumb like a stone	2
			Refrain (C)	
	8	ʿad-yaʿbōr	While your people	2
		ʿamməka yahwē	passed over, Yahweh	2
	8	ʿad-yaʿbōr	While your people,	2
		ʿam-zū qanīta	whom you purchased, passed over	2
			Ending	
17	4	tabīʾēmō	You brought them in	(3 or 4)
	(6)	[ʾel gəbūl qōdšəka]	(to your sacred territory)	
	5	watiṭṭaʿēmō	You planted them	3 or 4
	6	bəhar naḥlātəka	in your hereditary mountain	
	6	makōn ləšibtəka	The dais of your throne	2
	5	paʿalta yahwē	Yahweh, you made	2
	5	miqdāš ʾadōnay	Your sanctuary, Lord	2
	6	kōninū yadēka	your hands created	2
18	4	yahwē yimlōk	Yahweh has reigned	2
	5	ləʿōlām waʿed	from everlasting to eternity	2
		. . . .		
21		šīrū la yahwē	Sing of Yahweh	2
		kī gaʾō gaʾā	that he is highly exalted	2
		sūs warōkibō	Horse and its charioteer	2
		ramā bəyām	he hurled into the sea	2

General Comments

The received Hebrew text has been followed throughout the proposed reconstruction; the few very slight changes in readings adopted are almost all matters of vocalization, and are defended in the notes to the text. With regard to the vocalization, we have attempted, with more courage than prudence perhaps, to reproduce cultivated Hebrew speech of the twelfth to the tenth centuries B.C. The basis for this representation is inevitably MT, which remains our best source for Hebrew pronunciation in spite of its late date and artificial character. Next in order of importance are the Ugaritic tablets, which offer a partial vocalization of a closely related Canaanite dialect; their great value lies in their antiquity, since this material antedates the classical period of Hebrew poetry (fourteenth to the thirteenth centuries B.C.), and therefore offers an important corrective to MT. Then there are transcriptions of Canaanite words in a variety of languages, beginning with Egyptian texts of the second millennium, including the Amarna letters and other Akkadian transliterations, and extending to the LXX, the famous second column of the Hexapla, and other late sources.

In our transliterations we have endeavored to represent both long and short vowels. With regard to so-called tone-long vowels, we assume that in most cases short vowels under the accent were lengthened but that unaccented syllables were not (i.e., so-called pretonic lengthening). With regard to short vowels, we employ the symbol "ə" to indicate any short vowel concerning the quality of which we are uncertain (it may be *a*, *i*, *u*, or a variation of these: *o*, *e*). It often reflects MT vocal *shewa*, but we wish to leave open the question of which vowels were slurred over or elided in actual speech. We have accepted the Masoretic vocalization of 2 m.s. forms of the perfect form of the verb and the suffixes attached to nouns and verbs (with final *a*, except that we regard the vowel as short, not long), even though the consonantal text reflects a tradition in which these final vowels were not pronounced. We believe that the longer forms were preserved in cultivated literature, especially poetry of the classical period.

The vocalization of so-called segolate nouns poses a problem, since forms like *'ereṣ* and *melek* are secondary, the earlier pronunciation being *'arṣ-* and *malk-*. Originally the nouns had case endings which facilitated pronunciation in some instances, so it may be that with the loss of case endings, the process which resulted in segolate forms was initiated. If this assumption is correct, then there would be no perceptible effect on the meter: for example, *'arṣu* → *'ereṣ* (two syllables each). Nevertheless, the available evidence shows that the monosyllabic forms persisted for a long time and were recognized as such. The same considerations apply to the matter of diphthongs. In Ugaritic, Phoenician, and North Israelite, the diphthongs *ay* and *aw* were regularly contracted to *ê* and *ô*. In Southern Israelite (Judahite) as in Aramaic and classical Arabic, the diphthongs were preserved; in MT, they are often resolved into two syllables—for example *mayim* ← *maym* (→ *mēm* in the northern dialect). If we accept the vocalization of the northern dialect as normative, it is on the view that the earliest literature of Israel was composed and transmitted in northern circles, and that under the influence of Canaanite-Phoenician royal culture the court of David or Solomon adopted this mode of expression. There is no significant metrical difference between the northern and southern forms; even if we were to follow MT as is, instead of a reconstructed vocalization, we would secure essentially the same results. We wish to emphasize the flexibility of the language, the variety of forms (long and short) available to the poet, and his prerogative as a poet to vary his choices depending upon the requirements of a given line. We may add a note about the use of the definite article; the article as such does not occur in the poem, which is strictly in accord with the pattern of Ugaritic poetry (and presumably Canaanite poetry in general). It is presupposed here and there in the vocalization of MT (e.g., *bayyām*, vss 1, 4; *bakkōaḥ*, vs 6; *kaqqaš*, vs 7; *baqqōdeš*, vs 11), but the doubling of the initial consonant of the word is doubtless artificial, and can safely be disregarded. It is to be noted that neither *ʾēt* nor *ʾᵃšer*, which are elements of Hebrew prose usage, occurs in the poem—another indication that the text has been remarkably well preserved from contamination by prosaic additions or substitutions.

Notes on the Verses

Verse 1

ʾašīrā: Lit. "Let me sing." This form is to be compared with *šīrū*, "Sing!" in the parallel passage vs 21. Note the use of the same word *ʾāšīrā* in the Song of Deborah (Judg 5: 3) in a more elaborate construction. The verse in Judges supports the view that the preposition *l* before Yahweh is to be rendered "of, about" rather than "to." In Judg 5: 3, the poet is singing to the "kings/potentates" about Yahweh, the God of Israel. Cf also the opening line of the Aeneid: *arma virumque cano.*

sūs warōkibō. MT should be translated: "horse and its charioteer" rather than "horse and its rider." As Ex 15: 19 and 14: 9 (cf 14: 6, 7) make clear, the reference is to chariotry not cavalry. Vs 4 confirms that the poet had in mind the officers as well as the horse-drawn chariots.

The line is usually scanned as a couplet or double bicolon, and schematized as 4:4 or 2:2 / 2:2. Structurally, the main division occurs after *gaʾō gaʾā*, while there are secondary pauses after *yahwē* and *rkbw*, so that either or both analyses can be justified. But it is important to note that there is no parallelism of content either within half-lines or between them. The thought proceeds in consecutive fashion; the verse can be taken as a summary of the content of the poem which follows, especially the first part. The syllable count is as follows: 6:5 / 5:4. The parallel verse, 21, has 5:5 / 5:4. In accordance with the syllable-value system proposed above, we obtain these results: For vs 1, the first bicolon would have the following count: 13 + 3 = 16 (or: 2 + 3 + 3 / 2 + 3 + 3 = 16) for the first colon (the parallel line, vs 21, would have a value of 11 + 3 = 14, or 3 + 3 / 2 + 3 + 3 = 14). The second colon would be: 10 + 3 = 13 (or 3 / 2 + 3 / 2 + 3 = 13). The second bicolon would have the following count: 11 + 3 = 14 (or 4 / 2 + 3 + 2 + 3 = 14) for the first colon; 9 + 2 = 11 (or

2 + 3 / 2 + 4 = 11) for the second colon. The totals for vs 1 would be 16 + 13 = 29 and 14 + 11 = 25; for vs 21, 14 + 13 = 27 and 14 + 11 = 25. The general pattern is standard throughout the poem.

Verse 2

ʿozzī wazimrāt yāh, Lit. "My strength and fortress is Yah." The following points may be noted. The first person suffix is to be understood with *zmrt*; the text can be explained in one or more of several ways: the suffix of *ʿzy* is to be taken with *zmrt* as well (double-duty suffix); the *yod* at the beginning of "Yah" is to be understood as also representing the suffix at the end of *zmrt*. This was an epigraphic device which obviated the necessity of writing the same letter twice in succession. In early orthography, the *yod* of the first person suffix would not have been written. That the suffix was at least understood if not actually pronounced is demonstrated by the reading of the Samaritan Pentateuch (*zmrty*), along with some MSS of MT. The second proposal seems most attractive to us, and we have adopted it. Further, we take the two words as an example of hendiadys: "Yah is my mighty fortress."[9] Concerning the form *yāh*, it does not occur in other early poems and its usage here may be questioned; or else the whole verse may be regarded as late.

wayəhī lī lyšwʿh, Lit. "He belongs to me for salvation." The use of f.s. abstract nouns to represent concrete objects or persons is well attested in the Psalter; and in particular, *yšwʿh* is used often of Yahweh with the meaning, "Savior."[10]

wʾnwhw . . . wʾrmmnhw. The *waw* before the verb in each case is emphatic, not conjunctive.

With regard to the meter, the situation is not so clear. Normally vs 2a would be scanned as 3:3, but it is also possible to read it as 3:2, 2:3, or 2:2, depending on how the combination *zmrt yh* is construed in the first colon and *wyhy-ly* in the second. Syllable counting is similarly subject to differing interpretations, but the total is larger and the net variation therefore less important. Thus MT has 6 syllables for the first colon, while our preferred reconstruction comes to 7. The second colon, following MT, has 7 syllables (if we take the *shewa* in *wyhy* as vocal; if we regard the *shewa* as silent, then the total is 6). On the other hand, MT has elided a syllable in *līšūʿā* < *ləyəšūʿā*; the longer form may still have been in vogue when the poem was composed, or the poet may have preferred it here. In that case, the total could be 8. Averaging the differences, and assuming that the two cola were meant to balance, we emerge with a proposed 7:7 syllable count, acknowledging that it is approximate but insisting that it is not likely to be more than one syllable off:—that is, 6–7 / 6–8 represents the maximum range.

By following the vocable system already described, the first colon in MT would have a count of 16 vocables plus 3 long vowels = 19 (or by syllables, 3 + 3/ 2 + 3 + 4/ 4 = 19). However, according to our reconstruction, the total would be 17 + 3 = 20 (or 3 + 3 / 2 + 3 + 2 + 3 / 4 = 20). The second colon in MT would have a count of 14 + 5 = 19 (2 + 2 + 3 / 3 / 3 + 3 + 3 = 19). If we restore the elided syllable in *lyšwʿh*, the count would be 16 + 4 = 20 (or 2 + 2 + 3 / 3 / 2 + 2 + 3 + 3 = 20). If we regard the *shewa* in *wyhy* as silent, the total would be 18. The pattern can be described as follows 2a—19–20 / 18–20. The variation in each case is about the same, but its net importance has diminished. However we describe the mathematical ratios, we can say that the two cola balance—that is, they were meant to be said or sung in the same time.

Turning to vs 2b, we find a more complex situation. The meter would probably be regarded as 3:3, though the first colon could with much justice be counted as 2 by taking *zh ʾly* as one stress, while the second is so much longer that 4 would seem more appropriate (taking *ʾrmmnhw* as 2). Syllable counting serves to clarify the situation by pinpointing the discrepancy between the two cola; the first has 7 syllables, the second 11. Nevertheless, the cola balance; only in each case, the second term is considerably longer than the one it matches: *ʾlhy ʾby* || *ʾly* and *wʾrmmnhw* || *wʾnwhw*. Even the addition of *zh* to the first colon (it also serves the second: This is my God . . . / This is my father's God . . .) does not completely redress the imbalance. It would have been a simple matter to switch the verbs of the two cola and produce an exact syllabic balance (9:9); but presumably the poet preferred to overbalance the bicolon as in the preserved text, thus producing a sequence with 2a as follows: 7:7 / 7:11. Since this stanza is outside the body of the poem, and no other material conforms to it in content, it is impossible to say whether this is a deliberate pattern or not, or whether some corruption has occurred. Since the text makes good sense, and poetic parallelism is maintained, we should assume that the pattern is deliberate, and that the poet (presumably for melodic or rhythmic reasons) chose a 7:11 pattern against the normal or expected 9:9. That an unbalanced bicolon is a legitimate variation of the normal balanced variety can be established without difficulty from the corpus of early Israelite poetry. For example, in the Lament of David over Saul and Jonathan, 2 Sam 1: 20, we read:

20a	ʾl tgydw bgt	Do not announce it in Gath
	(w)ʾl tbśrw bḥwṣt ʾšqlwn	Do not proclaim in the streets of Ashkelon
20b	pn-tśmḥnh bnwt plštym	Lest the daughters of the Philistines rejoice
	pn-tʿlznh bnwt ()ʿrlym	Lest the daughters of the uncircumcised exult

The balance between the cola of 20b is clear and regular. It would normally be taken as 3:3; by syllable counting, we have 9:10 for MT, and if we drop the definite article before *ʿrlym* as a prosaic addition, we would have an exact equivalence at 9:9. In 20a, we have good parallelism in content but a serious imbalance in meter. It could be construed as 2:3 or 3:4, but hardly as 3:3, which would be expected on the basis of 20b. Syllable counting only serves to emphasize the imbalance. Following MT, we have 6:11 (or if we read the *waw* before *ʾl-tbśrw*, following the versions and some Hebrew MSS, the second colon would be 12). The ratio is approximately 1:2, though the poet could easily have achieved a more balanced bicolon by switching words or supplying a parallel term for *ḥwṣt* in the first colon.[11] Presumably he preferred to overbalance the line. The point we wish to make is that the total of the two cola of 20a, 6 + 11 (12) = 17 (18), is roughly the same as 20b, 9 + 9 (10) = 18 (19). Therefore we can say that an unbalanced bicolon, 6:11 (12), can legitimately be paired with a balanced one, 9:9 (10), or, more simply, that the unbalanced or overbalanced bicolon is a legitimate tool in the Israelite poet's arsenal.

Returning to Ex 15: 2b, if we use the vocable system of counting, we come out with 15 + 5 = 20 (or syllabically: 3 / 3 + 3 / 2 + 3 + 3 + 3 = 20) for the first colon, and 23 + 5 = 28 (or 2 + 3 + 3 / 2 + 3 / 2 + 2 + 3 + 2 + 3 + 3 = 28) for the second.

OPENING

Verse 3

This verse establishes the theme of the poem: Yahweh the invincible warrior. Throughout the poem, emphasis is placed on Yahweh's warlike prowess, his overwhelming power in nature and battle, and his enduring total sovereignty. With vs 18, it forms an *inclusio*, or envelope, within which the action of the poem develops. It may be noted that the form and order of the words are very similar to the Shema in Deut 6: 4, which is also deceptively simple and resists adequate analysis and interpretation:

Deut 6: 4	yhwh ʾlhynw /	yhwh ʾḥd	6:4
Ex 15: 3	yhwh ʾyš mlḥmh /	yhwh šmw	6:4

They share the same metrical structure, which is 2:2 (or 3:2), or 6:4 by syllable count. The vocable count is 18:11, apparently an unbalanced bicolon, but it is difficult to establish the pattern, since the expected parallelism is lacking. The balancing bicolon in vs 18 is also 2:2 (syllable count 4:5, vocable count 13:14) but without parallelism; it is a single continuous sentence.

Verse 4

There is widespread agreement among scholars that this verse is metrically unbalanced; and on the basis of metrical considerations, it is generally suggested that *wḥylw* be dropped from the first colon of 4a, since as it stands, the metrical pattern appears to be 3:2 / 2:2, which is not consistent with the prevailing 2:2 meter of the poem. The following considerations may be urged against such a conclusion, apart from the total lack of textual evidence for such an emendation: Assuming that the analysis is correct, would a variation in the prevailing pattern be automatic proof of later editorial tampering? Has the poet no freedom to vary his style deliberately? But in fact, the analysis is less than convincing. Thus it is to be noted that what parallelism in content there is in the verse is between the bicola 4a and 4b and not within them. Within the bicola, we have at most a caesura, the placement of which may vary somewhat from line to line. When the larger groupings are compared, there would still appear to be a discrepancy according to a stress system of analysis: 5/4. But in actuality, there is a very good formal balance as well as in content between the half-verses. Thus each has 5 content words and, perhaps more to the point, each consists of 12 syllables. The count by cola is as follows: 4a: 8/4; 4b: 6/6. In other words, the 8/4 division in the first bicolon is a perfectly legitimate variant of the "normal" 6/6 arrangement in the second bicolon. The conclusion therefore would be that *wḥylw*, far from being otiose, is necessary to the metrical balance. There would be a major imbalance if it were omitted. It should be added that the phrase at the beginning of 4 should be taken as hendiadys: Pharaoh's military chariots, or chariot force, rather than as a reference to both chariots and the rest of the army. The prose description in 14:7, 17, 28 sufficiently explains the situation. The vocable count is $19 + 4 = 23$ (or: $3 + 2 + 4 / 3 + 3 / 2 + 3 + 3 = 23$) for the first colon of 4a, and $9 + 2 = 11$ (or: $2 + 3 / 2 + 4 = 11$) for the second colon. For 4b, the count is as follows: $15 + 2 = 17$ (or: $2 + 3 + 3 / 2 + 3 + 4 = 17$) for the first colon, and $15 + 2 = 17$ (or: $3 + 2 + 3 / 2 + 3 / 4 = 17$) for the second colon. The total for 4a is 34, and for 4b is also 34. It may be said with some confidence that the verse as it has been transmitted divides into two half-verses of exactly equal length.

Verse 5

This verse also appears to be unbalanced, the metrical pattern being apparently 2:3, though 5a could be construed as 3 and 5b as 4. In any case, the second half-line is perceptibly longer than the first. Following MT, we have a syllable count of 3 + 4 or 5 (depending upon whether the *shewa* with *samek* is regarded as vocal or not) for 5a; 5b has 10 syllables in MT; a syllable has been elided in *bmṣwlt*, and so one syllable could be added to the total; on the other hand, the final word, *'āben*, was originally monosyllabic, so that one could be subtracted. The range could have been between 9 and 11; thus 10 is a satisfactory average. Our provisional conclusion is that we have an unbalanced bicolon of 18 syllables divided 8/10. It is to be compared with the bicolon 8bc, which also has 18 syllables, divided 9/9, or with vs 16cd, which in MT is a bicolon of 18 syllables, divided 9/9. It could also be compared with 2b, which totals 18 syllables, divided 7/11. The vocable count follows: 5a: $18 + 4 = 22$ ($2 + 3 + 4 / 2 + 3 + 2 + 3 + 3 = 22$); 5b: $23 + 5 = 28$ ($2 + 2 + 3 / 2 + 2 + 3 + 4 / 2 + 3 / 5 = 28$).

REFRAIN (A)

Verse 6

The metrical pattern is 2:2 / 2:2. From the syllabic point of view, there is some question about the proper count for *ymynk*, which may be considered 3 or 4 depending on whether the vowel after *nun* was elided or not. It is barely possible that the extra syllable was counted in one bicolon and not in the other, for metrical reasons. The preservation of the archaic infinitive form *ne'dōrī* may also have a metrical basis among other reasons. The syllable count would then be: 6a: 5:5, 5:4. The vocable count is: 6a: $12 + 2 = 14$ ($2 + 4 + 2 / 3 + 3 = 14$) for the first colon, and $12 + 3 = 15$ ($3 + 3 + 3 / 2 + 4 = 15$) for the second; 6b: $12 + 2 = 14$ for the first colon, and $11 + 2 = 13$ ($3 + 3 / 3 + 4 = 13$) for the second. The apparent discrepancy between $6a^2$ and $6b^2$ could be corrected, if desired, by reading the plural *'ōyᵉbīm* with LXX against MT *'ōyēb*. This would produce 5 syllables and 15 vocables in exact parallel with 6a; the inclusion of the archaic *ī* ending on *n'dr* seems to suggest that the poet required a fifth syllable in that colon. Other emendations in $6b^2$ are possible, such as adding the modal ending to the verb or the case ending to the noun. It must also be recognized that there may have been a slight shift in the rhythm corresponding to the shift in content from the first colon of each half-line to the second.

STROPHE I

Verse 7

The structure of vs 7 is fairly intricate, and deserves extended comment. The initial impression is that the second bicolon (7b) interprets and elaborates on the central element in the first—namely, the destruction of the foes. Further to be noted is the close parallel between $7a^1$ and b^1 in which the terms *g'wnk* and *ḥrnk* not only complement each other but rhyme; the means of destruction is the majestic anger of Yahweh. We must in fact combine these cola to get at the intention of the poet. The term *rb* applies as well to *ḥrn* as to *g'wn*; so also *tšlḥ* must extend to *g'wn*, since it governs *ḥrn*. These are symbolically the weapons or armed messengers whom Yahweh sends out to perform the act of punishment. The presentation here reflects two important themes of Canaanite myth: the messenger gods who perform the will of the sovereign deity, and the personified weapons of the god in his battle against the foe. The term *g'wn* may be the symbol of sovereignty of the king of the gods, the royal mace which is used to smash (cf Ps 58: 7, "Knock their teeth out of their mouths"), while *ḥrn* represents the sword which devours the foe as flames consume stubble. The association of anger with fire, and of both with the sword, is so standardized that the poet needs only to hint at the combination in his allusive statement to evoke all three images. It may be added that the verse is highly figurative in the context, since so far as we are aware there was no battle, no fire, no sword—only watery death. But these phrases point to the unique majesty of the king of the gods and his special prerogatives.

The meter of vs 7 is 2:2 / 2:2. The syllable count is as follows: 7a: 6 or 7 (depending on whether the original vowel after *n* in *g'wnk* was still pronounced or elided at the time of the poet; presumably he could have chosen either pronunciation. The initial *waw* is probably emphatic rather than conjunctive. / 6 (I suggest that we read **taharris* → *tᵉhārēs* [Piel instead of Qal; cf Ex 23: 24], to match the emphatic *tᵉšallaḥ* of the next bicolon. So far as MT is concerned, it does not affect the syllable count, which remains 3, though we may question whether the *ḥatef-pataḥ* was pronounced in forms such as *tahᵃrōs* in classical Hebrew.) 7b: 6 or 7 (*ḥrnk* presumably had the same vocalization as *g'wnk*, and could be taken as 3 or 4 syllables) / 6. We may conclude that the syllable count for this couplet was normalized at 12:12, as in vs 4. The vocable count is as follows: 7a: 14 + 2 = 16 (or: 2 + 2 + 4 / 2 + 4 + 2 = 16) for the first colon; 14 + 2 = 16 (2 + 3 + 3 / 3 + 3 + 2 = 16) for the second colon. 7b: 15 + 1 = 16 (2 + 3 + 3 / 2 + 4 + 2 = 16) for the first colon; 13 + 3 = 16 (3 + 2 + 3 + 3 / 2 + 3 = 16) for the second colon.

Verse 8

As already mentioned, 8a seems to belong structurally with vs 7: 8a is to be scanned as 2:2 or 4, like 7ab, while 8b and c are 3:3. At the same time, its content clearly connects with 8bc. The first colon of 8a, *wbrwḥ 'pyk*, while structurally similar to the first colon of 7, actually governs the whole of 8, thus serving a triple function. Clearly too, *n'rmw mym* is parallel to *nṣbw . . . nzlym* and *qp'w thmt*. Furthermore, 8a has 10 or, at the most, 11 syllables (depending on the count for *mym*), while 7 is consistently 12 in both parts, and 8b and c are 9. Thus we may say that 8a serves as a transition from 7 to 8bc sharing features with both preceding and succeeding couplets.

As indicated, the meter of 8a is 2:2; syllabically, the count is 6 (we do not count the *pataḥ* furtive in *rūaḥ*; it was either not pronounced or not considered significant) / 4 or 5 (we vocalize the verb *neʿramū*, but this does not affect the count; with respect to *mym*, it is much more likely that the diphthong was preserved (*maym*) or contracted (*mēm*) rather than resolved, as in MT (*mayim*). The pattern is to be compared with vs 3. The vocable count is as follows: $8a^1$: 14 + 2 = 16 (2 + 2 + 4 / 3 + 3 + 2 = 16); $8a^2$: 10 + 2 = 12 (3 + 2 + 3 / 4 = 12); note that MT here has 12 + 1 = 13 (3 + 2 + 3 / 2 + 3 = 13). It will be observed that $8a^1$ conforms exactly to the pattern of the cola in 7 in all three systems, but that $8a^2$ does not. We may note a limited example of chiasm in 8bc. In 8b, we have after the verb a prepositional phrase followed by the subject; in 8c, the order of prepositional phrase and subject is reversed. Since this device became very popular in Hebrew poetry, it is interesting to observe its relatively modest role in this early poem.

The meter of 8bc is apparently 3:3, in contrast with the more common 2:2 / 2:2. The syllable count is 9:9; and the vocable count is 21 + 5 = 26 (or: 3 + 2 + 3 / 2 + 3 + 4 / 3 + 2 + 4 = 26) for 8b; and 21 + 4 = 25 (or: 2 + 2 + 3 / 2 + 3 + 4 / 2 + 3 + 4 = 25) for 8c.

STROPHE I B

Verse 9

Various poetic devices are employed in this verse. Notice should be taken of the alliterative pattern at the beginning of the verse (the first five words begin with *aleph*, perhaps as an onomatopoeic way of evoking the clatter of horses and chariots). Connected with this is the repetition of first person forms throughout the triad: four imperfect 1 s. forms of the verb, and three 1 s. pronominal suffixes attached to nouns, making 7 in all (cf Ps 74: 13 ff, in which the pronoun *ʾt* is repeated 7 times to symbolize the divine assault on the seven heads of the sea dragon).[12] In the balancing triad vss 12–13, 2 m.s. forms are used for God, by contrast with the enemy. There are four perfect forms of the verb, and four pronominal suffixes of the 2 m.s. attached to nouns, making 8 in all. Perhaps the sequence 7:8 familiar in Ugaritic and Hebrew poetry is deliberate in this case. The metrical scheme in vs 9 is 2:2 / 2:2 / 2:2. The syllable count produces 4/4 = 8; 5/6 = 11; and 4/6 = 10. With this should be compared the similar triad, vs 15: 9/ 9/ 9. The vocable count produces the following results: 9a: 10 + 2 = 12 (or: 2 + 3/ 3 + 4 = 12) for the first colon; 12 + 2 = 14 (3 + 4 / 3 + 4 = 14) for the second colon; 9b: 13 + 2 = 15 (2 + 3 + 4 / 2 + 4 = 15) for the first colon; 14 + 3 = 17 (3 + 2 + 3 + 3 / 3 + 3 = 17) for the second colon; 9c: 10 + 2 = 12 (2 + 4 / 3 + 3 = 12) for the first colon, and 12 + 5 = 17 (3 + 3 + 3 + 3 / 2 + 3 = 17) for the second colon.

In defense of MT, *tml'mw* and *twryšmw* with 3 m.pl. suffix, against LXX which apparently does not read them, it may be pointed out that the poet had a special interest in using the archaic form of the suffix. Including the cases under discussion, it occurs exactly seven times with imperfect forms of the verb, and in patterns which can hardly be the result of accident:

7	yō'k^{e}lēmō	15	yō'ḥ^{a}zēmō
9	timlā'ēmō	17	t^{e}bī'ēmō
9	tōrīšēmō	17	tiṭṭā'ēmō

12 tiblā'ēmō

The single occurrences in vss 7, 12, and 15 all refer to actions against the Egyptians (7, 12) and the other nations (15). The forms in 7 and 15 match (Qal imperfect 3 m.s.) even with respect to vocalization (*pe aleph* verbs with initial *ō*). The subject in each case is an abstract noun; whereas the object varies from the Egyptians in the first case to the Moabites in the second: Yahweh's anger devours the former, while trembling seizes the latter.

The paired verbs in vss 9 and 17 have the Israelites as the object. In the former, it is the enemy who threatens them with conquest and annihilation: "my gullet will be filled with them, my hand will conquer them." In the latter, it is Yahweh who brings them into the land and plants them there. The first pair have 3 f.s. verbal prefixes, whereas the latter have 2 m.s. prefixes (the poet has taken advantage of the fact that these are homonymous forms—both represented by *t*). In each pair there is a Qal form and a Hiphil form, balanced chiastically.

9	(Q)	tml'mw	tb'mw	(H)	17
9	(H)	twryšmw	tṭ'mw	(Q)	17

Verse 10

In content, vs 10 is very similar to vs 5; in form and meter, 10a closely resembles 8a and 3, while 10b corresponds to the pattern of vss 4 and 7. The basic meter is 4:4 (or 2:2 / 2:2), but 10a is measurably shorter than 10b. Thus the syllable count in 10a is: 6 (reading *brwḥk* as three syllables): 4 (note that in *ksmw* the final *yōd* of the root has been elided, contrary to the practice in vs 5, where it has been preserved, *yksymw*; in our judgment, metrical considerations figure in the choice of the poet). In 10b, the count is: 6 (reading *kʿprt* as three syllables against MT, since the ending was originally monosyllabic—*part* or *pirt*): 5 (reading *mym* as *maym* or *mēm* instead of MT *mayim*). The syllable count is thus 10:11. The vocable count is 10a:14 + 1 = 15 (or: 2 + 3 + 2 / 2 + 4 + 2 = 15) for the first colon, and 10 + 2 = 12 (or: 3 + 2 + 3 / 4 = 12) for the second; 10b: 14 + 2 = 16 / (or: 2 + 2 + 3 / 2 + 3 + 4 = 16) for the first colon and 13 + 3 = 16 (or: 2 + 4 / 3 + 3 + 4 = 16) for the second.

REFRAIN (B)

Verse 11

Another instance of partial chiasm is to be noted (cf vs 8). After the initial interrogative expression, we have a prepositional phrase followed by the vocative form Yahweh in the first colon. In the second colon, however, the corresponding vocative, *nʾdr*, is followed by the prepositional phrase. With regard to the prepositional phrases, we may point to the m.pl. form *ʾlym* in the first colon, which is balanced by an abstract (or collective) singular form *qdš* in the second, a poetic device which occurs frequently in the Psalter. It may be added that in prose the two words would naturally be combined: "the holy gods," as in the Phoenician inscription of *Yḥymlk* from Byblus.[13] In similar fashion, *nʾdr* (here the Niphal participle m.s.) is linked to *yhwh*—that is, "Yahweh, the resplendent."

From the metrical point of view, the structure seems to be 4:4:4 (or 2:2 / 2:2 / 2:2) as was the case in vs 6. However, in each bicolon a case can be made for 3 stresses (depending on how we analyze *my-kmkh*, or whether we take *ʿśh plʾ* as a single unit in 11c), as is true presumably of vs 16cd, which also serves as a divider. The syllable count is somewhat easier to manage, though some variation is possible. Vs 11a: 4/5; 11b: 4/4 or 5 (depending on whether we read *bqdš* as 3 with MT, or 2 on the basis of an earlier monosyllabic pronunciation *qudš-*); 11c: 5/3 or 4 (if we read *plʾ* with MT we have 4 syllables for this colon, but 3 if we revert to an earlier monosyllabic form. In the latter case, however, it seems likely that the case ending would have been retained if the final *aleph* of the root was to be pronounced at all—that is, *pilʾi* or *pilʾa*). Our judgment is that the triad consisted of bicola of 9, 8, and 8 or 9 syllables. The vocable count is as follows: 11a: 8 + 2 = 10 (3 + 2 + 3 + 2 = 10) for the first colon, and 12 + 3 = 15 (or: 2 + 3 + 4 / 3 + 3 = 15) for the second; 11b: 10 for the first colon, and 12 + 2 = 14 (3 + 4 / 2 + 5 = 14) for the second; 11c: 12 + 3 (omitting the *aleph* at the end of *nwrʾ* from the count) = 15 (or: 3 + 3 / 2 + 3 + 4 = 15) for the first colon, and 8 + 2 (counting either the final *segol* or the final *aleph* of *plʾ* but not both) = 10 (or: 3 + 3 / 4 = 10).

As has been pointed out, the refrain in vs 11 is longer and more elaborate than the ones in vss 6 and 16 which follow a similar pattern. In the present case, the third bicolon picks up the participle in 11b (*n'dr*), and expands on the theme of the fear-inspiring, wonder-working Deity. Thus *nwr'* is parallel to *n'dr*, and *'śh pl'* partakes of the same numinous quality. By thus concentrating on the unique splendor of Yahweh, in contrast with other divine beings, and his mighty works, the poet here reaches the climactic point in his composition. Standing at the center and apex of the poem, it relates equally to both strophes: the God described in vs 11 is equally responsible for the victory at the sea and for the triumphant march to the Holy Land. By being less specific than the other refrains, which relate directly to the theme of their respective strophes (i.e., vs 6 focuses on the powerful right hand of Yahweh by which he wreaked destruction on the enemy; vs 16 speaks of the passage of the people of Yahweh into the promised land), vs 11 serves them both as center and fulcrum.

STROPHE II

Verses 12–14

Vss 12–13 form a triad of bicola, in which the first (vs 12) recapitulates the content of the first half of the poem, while the latter two carry the story from that point. The destruction of the Egyptian host is the necessary condition and presupposition of the march through the wilderness, so that the association of these ideas in a single unit is entirely in order. If that were insufficient to convince, then the word patterns in the three bicola provide additional evidence of their purposeful combination in the plan of the poet: thus each bicolon begins with a perfect form of the verb (2 m.s.); the verbs form an alliterative sequence—*naṭīta, naḥīta, nēhalta*—and each verb is followed by a noun with the 2 m.s. suffix: *ymynk, bḥsdk, b'zk*. While 13ab are more closely related in content, 12 clearly belongs to the same scheme.

The structure of Strophe II is essentially the same as that of Strophe I, though there are some minor variations. That structure has already been discussed and defended. At the same time, there is a contrasting movement in the two strophes, toward and away from the central point in vs 11. Thus we may expect to find certain points of contact between Part A of Strophe I and Part B of Strophe II, and similarly between Part B of Strophe I and Part A of Strophe II, reflecting a certain chiasm in the whole pattern of the poem and cutting across the purely structural lines.

Vs 12 serves as a connecting link between the two strophes, and constitutes an admirable parallel to 10a, providing a sequence of synonymous terms in the same order:

10a	nšpt brwḥk ksmw ym	You blew with your breath The sea covered them
12	nṭyt ymynk tblʿmw ʾrṣ	You stretched out your hand The netherworld swallowed them

Vs 13, however, correlates well with the opening couplet of Strophe I, vs 7. Just as the theme of vs 7 is the destructive violence of Yahweh against his enemies, so in vs 13 emphasis is placed on the constructive care and guidance of his own people. The twin instruments of military punishment in vs 7, *gʾwnk* and *ḥrnk*, are balanced by Yahweh's protective agents in vs 13, *ḥsdk* and *ʿzk*. The imperfect verbs *thrs* and *tšlḥ* are matched by the perfect forms *nḥyt* and *nhlt*, while in the subordinate clauses we have *yʾklmw* balanced by *zw gʾlt*. It is not yet clear what distinction, if any, is to be drawn between perfect and imperfect forms in early Hebrew poetry; it is clear that they are interchangeable so far as tense is concerned, and it may be that the poet's choice is purely stylistic. (Note the alternations between perfect and imperfect, or vice versa, in vss 5, 12, 14, 15, 17.) From the point of view of the poet, it can be argued that all the action of the poem (vss 4–17) is in the past, or at least that there is no warrant for supposing that any of the verbs are necessarily in the future tense.

There is also a correlation between vss 12–13 and vs 9. In vs 9, the enemy boasted, and his boasting was made emphatic by the repetition of the first person singular forms no fewer than seven times. Now in vss 12–13, we have the counter to man's boasting—namely, God's action. In this triad, the second person singular used of Yahweh is repeated eight times, thus confirming the old adage that man proposes but God disposes.

Metrically, the structure of vss 12–13 is 4:4:4 (or 2:2 / 2:2 / 2:2). The syllable count has some slight uncertainties but is fairly regular: 12: 6 or 7 (depending on whether we vocalize the shewa after *n* in *ymynk*; originally there was a connecting vowel here, but it ultimately was elided) / 5 or 6 (if we follow MT in the pronunciation of *ʾrṣ*, then the count is 6; if we read it as a monosyllable, it is 5). The minimum total for the verse is 11. The count in 13 is as follows: 13a: 7 (in this case we cannot avoid reading some vowel after *d* in *bḥsdk*) / 5; 13b: 7 (we also need a vowel after *ʿz* in *bʿzk*) / 6. The vocable count is as follows: 12: 13 + 2 = 15 (or: 2 + 3 + 2 / 2 +4 + 2 = 15) for the first colon, and 13 + 3 = 16 (or: 3 + 2 + 3 + 3 / 5 = 16) for the second. Vs 13a: 15 + 1 = 16 (or: 2 + 3 + 2 / 2 + 3 + 2 + 2 = 16) for the first colon, and 12 + 2 = 14 (or: 3 + 3 / 2 + 4 + 2 = 14) for the second. Vs 13b: 16 + 1 = 17 (or: 3 + 3 + 2 / 2 + 3 + 2 + 2 = 17) for the first colon, and 14 + 1 = 15 (or: 3 / 2 + 3 / 3 + 2 + 2 = 15) for the second. On this method of reckoning, the triad of bicola balances out satisfactorily, with the total for 13a and b (30 + 32) coming out exactly double that of 12 (31).

With regard to the two bicola of vs 13, we wish to point to an interesting example of combination or enjambment. To begin with, we have closely parallel first cola: *nḥyt bḥsdk* / *nhlt bʿzk*, though, strictly speaking, *ḥsd* and *ʿz* complement rather than duplicate each other. A form of hendiadys is indicated here: "your mighty *ḥesed*" or "your merciful strength." For the rest, we have two separate objects—one direct, the other indirect—which are not parallel at all but are in sequence. They are meant to be taken together as the objects of the verbs, which are themselves synonymous. If we were to write the verse as prose, we could bring out the intended sense as follows: "You led / guided in your powerful kindness the people whom you redeemed, to your holy habitation." Thus we have in vs 13 three types of material distributed between the cola: synonyms, *nḥyt* // *nhlt*; complements or combinations which belong together but are often divided between cola in poetry: *bḥsdk*—*bʿzk*, cf *bʾlym*—*bqdš* in vs 11; supplements or sequences, *ʿm-zw gʾlt* and *ʾl-nwh qdšk*. Vs 14 concludes Part A of Strophe II. Part B is then an elaboration of this verse; in a similar way, Part B of Strophe I is an elaboration of vs 7 in Part A. The metrical pattern is presumably 3:3, though 4 is a possibility for the second colon (it depends on how the first two words, *ḥyl ʾḥz*, are treated). The syllable count is 8/8 (counting *plšt* as 2 syllables rather than 3 with MT). The vocable count is as follows: 14a: 20 + 3 = 23 (or: 2 + 2 + 3 / 3 + 4 / 3 + 2 + 4 = 23), and 14b: 20 + 4 = 24 (or: 4 / 2 + 3 / 3 + 2 + 3 / 2 + 5 = 24).

STROPHE II B

Verse 15–16ab

While structurally parallel to vss 9–10 (Part B of Strophe I), which also consist of a triad and couplet in that order, this stanza has very interesting affinities with Part A of Strophe I, thus reflecting the contrasting movement toward and away from the central point of the poem. In this case, in a chiastic arrangement, vs 15 corresponds to the triad 8abc, while 16ab corresponds to vs 7, thus providing a closing sequence to match the opening sequence in vss 7–8. While the subject matter of vs 15 corresponds more closely to that of vs 9 (i.e., the enemy or foreign nations) and there is a striking contrast between the boastful words of the "enemy" in 9 and the horror-struck silence of the "foreigners" in vs 15 as a result of the intervening action of Yahweh, there are other factors which link 15 and 8. Thus we have three synonymous nouns, the subject of the action in each triad: *mym*, *nzlym*, *thmt* in 8, and the compounds *ʾlwpy ʾdwm*, *ʾyly mwʾb*, *yšby knʿn* in 15. Then there are two Niphal perfect forms of the verb in each triad, along with one *Qal* form. There are partial chiasms in both triads: *kmw-nd nzlym* // *thmt blb-ym* in 8 and *nbhlw 'lwpy 'dwm* // *'yly mw'b y'ḥzmw . . . nmgw . . . yšby kn'n* in 15. Both triads express Yahweh's complete control over nature (8) and nations (15), which serve as instruments in the achievement of his purpose.

Vs 16ab is structurally parallel to vs 10, and there is a certain similarity of content. Both describe the completion of Yahweh's work with respect to the "enemy" (10) and the "nations" (16). There are also resemblances to vs 7, but this is not surprising in view of the similarity in content and form of 7 and 10. Thus the reference to *'ymth wpḥd* reminds us of *g'wn* and *ḥrn* in vs 7 as well as the *mym 'dyrym* of vs 10, while in 16b *bgdl zrw'k* evokes *brb g'wnk* of 7 as well as *brwḥk* of 10; *ydmw k'bn* is reminiscent of *y'klmw kqš* structurally if not strictly according to content, and *ṣllw k'prt* of vs 10; cf also *yrdw . . . k'bn* in vs 5.

Metrically the stanza scans as a triad (vs 15) 4:4:4 (or 2:2 / 2:2 / 2:2) and a couplet (16ab) 4:4 (or 2:2 / 2:2). The problem of 15c has been discussed; in all likelihood we should read *kl* as an adverb modifying *nmgw* rather than as a pronoun in the construct chain with *yšby kn'n* (note the parallels *'lwpy 'dwm* and *'yly mw'b* with two words each). The syllable count is as follows: 4:5 / 4:5 vocalizing *r'd* as monosyllabic (rather than as bisyllabic as in MT) / 4:5 counting *kn'n* as two syllables against three in MT. The parallel triad, vs 9, does not offer much help in deciding the question, since its bicola range from 8 to 11. Presumably the normal figure would be 27 for the triad and 9 for each member. The vocable count follows: 15a: 10 + 2 = 12 (or: 4 / 3 + 2 + 3 = 12) for the first colon, and 12 + 3 = 15 (or: 3 + 3 + 3 / 2 + 4 = 15) for the second; 15b: 9 + 4 = 13 (or: 3 + 3 / 3 + 4 = 13) for the first colon, and 12 + 4 = 16 (or: 3 + 2 + 3 + 3 / 5 = 16) for the second colon (MT would be 13 + 4 = 17); 15c: 9 + 3 = 12 (or: 2 + 3 + 3 / 4 = 12) for the first colon, and 12 + 3 = 15 (or: 3 + 2 + 3 / 2 + 5 = 15) for the second (MT would be 13 + 3 = 16).

The syllable count in 16ab is as follows: 16ab: 5/6 (depending upon how we read *pḥd*; if we follow MT or read *paḥda*, with the accusative case ending to match *'ymth*, then the total would be 6; if we reduce *pḥd* to its monosyllabic state, the figure would be 5); 16b: 6/5 (with regard to the first colon, the figure can be as low as 5 or as high as 7, giving an adequate mean of 6). MT *bigdōl* reflects the elision of a syllable in the phrase which more originally read *bəgadōl*; on the other hand we should elide the *ḥatef pataḥ* after *'ayin* in *zrw'k*. Eliminating both vowels, we would have 5 syllables; counting both, we would have 7. In the second colon, we vocalize *'bn* as a monosyllable in accordance with the older pronunciation. We parse *ydmw* as Niphal imperfect of *dmm* reading *yiddammū*.

The vocable count is as follows: 16a: 13 + 2 = 15 (or: 3 + 4 / 2 + 3 + 3 = 15) for the first colon, and 13 + 2 = 15 (or: 3 + 3 + 2 / 2 + 2 + 3 = 15) for the second; 16b: 14 + 2 = 16 (or: 2 + 2 + 4 / 2 + 4 + 2 = 16) for the first colon (MT would be 17); and 14 + 2 = 16 (or: 3 + 3 + 3 / 2 + 5 = 16) for the second (MT would be 17).

REFRAIN (C)

Vs 16cd is the third refrain or divider, and closes off the main part of the poem with an explicit reference to the passage of Israel into the Holy Land, thus recapitulating the second strophe (cf vs 13 especially).

The meter is apparently 3:3. The syllable count is as follows: 16c: 8, since we do not read the *ḥatef pataḥ* in *yʿbr*, against MT 16d: 8. The vocable count is as follows: 16c: 21 + 2 = 23 (or: 3 / 3 + 4 / 3 + 2 + 2 / 3 + 3 = 23; MT would be 24); and 16d: 20 + 3 = 23 (or: 3 / 3 + 4 / 3 / 3 / 2 + 3 + 2 = 23; MT would be 24). These totals may be compared with those for vss 14, 11, 8bc, and 5.

THE CLOSING

Vss 17–18 constitute the closing section, comparable in structure with vss 3–5, which constitute the opening. The two together form a strophe comparable to the regular strophes in the body of the poem, and thus enclose the main part of the poem. Each consists of five units. For the opening, vs 3 is the initial unit, while the corresponding unit in the closing is the final bicolon, vs 18. In similar fashion, vs 4 constitutes the "long" couplet following the initial unit (4:4 or 2:2 / 2:2); and vs 17bc in the closing, following in reverse order, corresponds to this unit in the opening. It also is 4:4 (or 2:2 / 2:2). That leaves vs 5 to match 17a. Since 5 is somewhat irregular, it should not surprise us to find 17a also a bit abnormal. The latter appears to be 2:2 (though unbalanced), while 5 seems to be 2:3 (though 3:3 or 3:4 is also possible). The syllable count for 17a would be 9/6 (counting *nḥltk* as 4 syllables in place of MT *naḥ^{a}lāt^{e}kā* which has 5, or a possible *naḥlatka* with 3. Vs 5, on the other hand, was unbalanced in the other direction, and is now counted 8/10. It is possible to reduce each colon by one and produce 7/9, which would counterbalance approximately vs 17a 9/6. The vocable count for 17a is as follows: 19 + 5 = 24 (or 2 + 3 + 3 + 3 / 2 + 3 + 2 + 3 + 3 = 24) for the first colon, and 14 + 1 = 15 (or: 2 + 3 / 3 + 3 + 2 + 2 = 15) for the seond colon. At the same time, the minimum count for vs 5 would be 20 and 26, showing that there is still a considerable discrepancy.

The real question is whether we are entitled to divide 17a after *wṭṭ'mw*, thus placing the two verbs in the first colon and the prepositional phrase in the second. There is no other division like it elsewhere in the poem (9a hardly qualifies), and normally we would read the colon as follows:

wtṭ'mw bhr nḥltk	Indeed you have planted them in the mountain you possess

This would provide us with the 3-stress colon indicated by comparison with 5b, while the syllable count of approximately 11 corresponds well with the 10 or 11 of 5b. That leaves the first colon somewhat short with only *tb'mw*, and we must suppose then that something has fallen out. If 5a is to serve as a guide, then only one word (plus preposition) is to be supplied (e.g., *'el 'ereṣ* or the like). However, if we disregard such precise indications, we may be helped by having recourse to Ps 78: 54, where the same verb is used in a closely parallel context:

wyby'm 'l-gbwl qdšw	And he brought them into his holy territory
hr-zh qnth ymynw	The mountain which his right arm created.

We would therefore be inclined to add *'el gəbūl qōdšeka* to the first colon of 17a, thus balancing the bicolon and producing a 3:3 meter to correspond to the strophic structure of the poem as a whole, and the opening stanza in particular. The syllable count would be 10 for the first colon, and 11 for the second. The vocable count would be 23 + 4 = 27 (2 + 3 + 3 + 3 / 3 / 2 + 4 / 3 + 2 + 2 = 27) for the first colon, and 25 + 3 = 28 (2 + 3 + 2 + 3 + 3 / 2 + 3 / 3 + 3 + 2 + 2 = 28) for the second. The second colon of 17a corresponds exactly to 5b (also 28), while the first is somewhat longer than 5a.

However we deal with vs 17a, there can be no question that the "mount of inheritance"—that is, Yahweh's own portion—is the promised land of Canaan, which is the earthly counterpart of the heavenly mountain on which Yahweh dwells. Whether any particular mountain or range is meant is dubious though doubtless after the establishment of the temple in Jerusalem, Mount Zion was understood to be the point of reference. In the light of 17a, the meaning of 17b and c can be clarified: the "dais of your throne" (17b) and "your sanctuary" (17c) refer to the same "mount of inheritance," and specify the divine palace and throne which Yahweh himself has fashioned. These are, in the first place, the heavenly prototypes in which Yahweh dwells, and, second, describe the sacred territory which Yahweh has claimed for himself. The language is mythopoeic and therefore inexact, but it cannot refer to any existing earthly sanctuary, since all these have been made by human hands not God's. Both tabernacle and temple were regarded as human achievements, albeit based on plans provided by God and in imitation of the heavenly abode of the Deity. But what is described here is a work of God, his heavenly palace-sanctuary. His corresponding earthly abode is the Holy Land, into which he has now brought his people. There, as in heaven, he shall reign eternally.

The metrical pattern of 17bc is 4:4 (or: 2:2 / 2:2), while the syllable count is for 17b: 6/5, and for 17c: 4 or 5 (the reading *yhwh* has strong textual support, and is most likely more original than *'dny*) / 6. The vocable count is as follows: 17b: 14 + 1 = 15 (or 2 + 4 / 2 + 3 + 2 + 2 = 15) for the first colon, and 12 + 1 = 13 (or: 2 + 3 + 2 / 3 + 3 = 13) for the second; 17c: 13 + 2 = 15 (or: 3 + 4 / 2 + 3 + 3 = 15) for the first colon (if we read *yhwh* instead of *'dny*, then the count is reduced to 13); and 12 + 3 = 15 (or: 3 + 2 + 3 / 2 + 3 + 2 = 15) for the second.

Vs 18 closes the poem, forming an *inclusio* with vs 3 as already mentioned. It is a single bicolon of 4 beats or 2:2 meter. The syllable count is 4/5, and the vocable count is as follows: 18a: 11 + 2 = 13 (or: 3 + 3 / 3 + 4 = 13) for the first colon, and 12 + 2 = 14 (or: 2 + 3 + 4 / 2 + 3 = 14) for the second.

On the basis of the transmitted text, we believe that a strong case can be made for the essential unity of the poem in Exodus 15. A repeated pattern of strophes and stanzas, marked off by refrains, in a determinate metrical structure has been demonstrated for the main part of the poem vss 3–18. The Exordium, vs 2, may have been attached in order to provide the proper liturgical framework for presentation of the poem in public worship (by a prophetic or royal representative). Concerning vss 1 and 21, we suggest that they constituted an opening and closing refrain similar to the other dividers which set off the major sections of the poem. Structurally vss 1 and 21 are very much like vs 6 (2:2 / 2:2; syllable count 10:9, which is the same as vs 21); and they share the practice of the dividers in using the name Yahweh.

The main body of the poem falls into two parts (vss 3–10, and vss 12–18). The principal theme of the first part is the victory of Yahweh over the Egyptians at the Reed Sea. The principal theme of the second part is Israel's march through the wilderness and passage into the promised land under the guidance of the same Yahweh. Thus Yahweh the warrior, who annihilates his foes, is identified with Yahweh the redeemer, who saves his people and establishes them in their new homeland. The themes are linked causally. It is the victory at the sea which permits the people of God to escape from bondage; and it is through his devastating display of power that Yahweh overawes the other nations who might otherwise block the passage of the Israelites. Thus the one mighty action produces two notable results: the destruction of the enemy; and the intimidation of the other nations, who are paralyzed by fear and cannot obstruct the victorious march of the Israelites or their successful entry into the Holy Land. At one stroke therefore the Egyptians "went down into the depths *like a stone*" and the other nations "were struck dumb *like a stone.*" Neither could interfere with the realization of the divine plan—to release the slaves and establish them in a new land.

The refrains carry the same content as the opening and closing. The first of these (vs 6) emphasizes the mighty hand of Yahweh in dealing death to the enemy, while the third (vs 16) speaks of the passage of Yahweh's people into the Holy Land. The victory at the sea is Yahweh's alone, and it makes possible the passage of the people. The second refrain stands at the center of the poem, and is an elaborate apostrophe on the incomparability of Yahweh. It serves to link not only the two major parts of the poem but also the thematic statements at the beginning and end: vs 3, Yahweh the warrior, and vs 18, Yahweh the king who will reign over his people.

The strophes develop in detail the thematic statements concerning the victory at the sea and the passage of the people. Thus Strophe I deals with specific aspects of the victory over the Egyptians. Part I (vss 7–8) treats of Yahweh's overwhelming rage and the violent storm with which he stirs up the sea. The stage is set for the appearance of the antagonist. Part II (vss 9–10) shows the enemy in all his boastful folly (vs 9). He is already gloating over the spoils, gorging himself on his prey, when the raging sea breaks over his head, and he sinks like lead in the dreadful waters (vs 10). Act one has ended.

The second strophe presents the aftermath, Israel's march through the wilderness and entry into the promised land. The theme is mentioned in the first part (vs 13), to be repeated and expanded in the closing section of the poem. This part closes with a reference to the effect of the victory at the sea on the other nations: When they heard, they trembled; terror seized them (vs 14). The second part of the strophe (vss 15–16) develops this interest in detail: Overwhelmed by divine fear and dread, they are benumbed, and watch helplessly as the people cross over into the promised land, Yahweh's own possession.

While we do not expect a poem, especially in the mythopoeic tradition, to record historical experience soberly and in sequence, we can use it, with caution, to recover a historical tradition. Since the poem comes from the twelfth century in all likelihood, its relative proximity to the events which it celebrates makes it a prime witness, if not to the events themselves, then at least to the effect produced on the people of Israel by them. In this connection, both what is said and what is omitted (in contrast with the prose traditions concerning the victory at the sea and the entry into the land) are of special interest. With regard to the episode at the Reed Sea, the poet focuses on the storm at sea and the drowning of the Egyptian chariot force. By contrast, nothing is said of the passage of Israel on dry ground, or in fact of Israel at all in connection with the event. The only passage of which the poet is conscious or that he mentions is the crossing into Canaan (vs 16cd).

With regard to the entry into the promised land, the poet speaks of Yahweh's guidance and protection and at some length of the total paralysis of the nations, which enabled Israel to enter without opposition. Nothing at all is said of the battles with those peoples or of the victories by Moses and Joshua over them which are described in detail in the prose narratives.

According to the poet, only one battle counted, and one victory, at the sea; that was enough to permanently disable Egypt and at the same time terrify the other nations into complete passivity. The victory was total—and totally Yahweh's. Israel contributed nothing then or later, except to march under divine guidance. While the poet's view is essentially the same as that of the bulk of biblical writers, historians, and prophets, it is radically stated, and suggests a certain background or orientation on the part of the poet, to which the views of Isaiah or Hosea may be compared. But perhaps we should not press a poet too far in any particular direction.

One fairly certain result of the analysis of this poem is the establishment of a strophic structure. The poem has been organized into a regular pattern of strophes and stanzas, with divisions marked by refrains. Opening and closing stanzas form an envelope in which the body of the poem is encased. An Exordium or Proem introduces the whole. We have also suggested a role for vss 1 and 21.

Within this larger framework, an attempt has been made to describe the internal metrical pattern of the stanzas and strophes. Following the commonly accepted stress- or accent-counting system, we arrive at the following scheme:

Introduction (vs 1b):	2:2		2:2
Exordium (vs 2):	3:3		3:3
Opening (vss 3–5):			
3	2:2		
4	3:2		2:2
5		3:3	
Refrain (A) (vs 6):	2:2		2:2

Strophe I (vss 7–10):				
A (7–8)				
	7	2:2		2:2
	8		2:2	
			3:3	
B (9–10)				
	9	2:2	2:2	2:2
	10		2:2 2:2	
Refrain (B) (vs 11):		2:2	2:2	2:2
Strophe II (vss 12–16ab):				
A (12–14)				
	12		2:2	
	13	2:2		2:2
	14		3:3	
B (15–16ab)				
	15	2:2	2:2	2:2
	16ab		2:2 2:2	
Refrain (C) (vs 16cd):			3:3	
Closing (vss 17–18):				
	17		2:2 (or 3:3)	
		2:2		2:2
	18		2:2	
Conclusion (vs 21b):		2:2		2:2

According to this scheme, the prevailing metrical pattern is a bicolon 2:2 (or simply a colon of 4). It occurs separately as a unit, as well as in couplets and triads: Units: vss 3, 8a, 12, 17a, 18; Couplets: 1b, 4, 6, 7, 10, 13, 16ab, 17bc; Triads: 9, 11, 15. A variant pattern is 3:3, which occurs in vss 5, 8bc, 14, 16cd. We have the apparently anomalous 3:2 in 4a, and a possible 2:3 in 5, as well as a peculiar situation in 17a, but each of these is susceptible of explanation (see Notes).

The Strophes consist of two stanzas each, while the stanzas are made up of several units. IA (7–8) consists of two couplets with a transition link between them: the first couplet has bicola of 2:2, and the link is a bicolon with the same pattern. The closing bicolon is 3:3. The parallel stanza, Strophe IIA (12–14), has the same units in different order: an opening bicolon 2:2, followed by a couple of bicola 2:2, and a closing bicolon 3:3. The B stanzas, on the other hand, have a slightly different structure. They consist of a triad 2:2 / 2:2 / 2:2 followed by a couplet 2:2 / 2:2.

The refrains show some variation: vss 1 and 21, as well as vs 6, are couplets: 2:2 / 2:2; vs 16cd is a bicolon 3:3; vs 11 is a triad 2:2 / 2:2 / 2:2. Each of these types is attested in the Strophes.

The opening and closing stanzas have a structure similar to that of the Strophe stanzas: the opening (vss 3–5) begins with a bicolon, followed by two couplets, the first 2:2 / 2:2, the second 3:3 (similar to IIA). The closing (vss 17–18) begins with a bicolon 2:2, continues with a couplet 2:2 / 2:2, and ends with another bicolon 2:2. As it stands, it is somewhat anomalous, since it does not conform to any of the patterns so far noted. The difficulties in the analysis of 17a have been discussed, and we have proposed an emendation which results in a 3:3 pattern.

The Exordium (vs 2) consists of a quatrain 3:3 / 3:3, but its structure is by no means symmetrical. This pattern is otherwise unattested in the poem.

On the face of it, the patterns exhibited in this schematic presentation are sufficiently regular to show that some metrical structure is inherent in the poem. Its precise nature remains elusive, however, because the analysis is rather flexible, not to say loose. The categories tend to be broad and indefinite, and the terms rather vague, referring to a number of diverse items. In other words, such a scheme conceals more than it reveals, and the image of symmetry and regularity it presents may be inexact, indicating more consistency than is actually present. At the same time, it may fail to indicate more intricate patterns that may be present.

In the search for a more precise method of reflecting the actual meter of Hebrew poems, we have turned to syllable counting and even vocable counting (in order to make allowance for open and closed syllables, as well as the length of vowels). Not that we imagine that the Hebrew poets used such a method or were even aware of numerical ratios and equivalences in their poetic composition, but we are convinced that a strong sense of rhythm permeated poetry that was composed to be sung, and that men and women marched and danced to these songs. In fact, Ex 15 is a victory march, as both the contents and the prevailing 2:2 or 4:4 meter indicate. In marching rhythms especially, unaccented syllables must be reckoned with as well as accented ones. It is in an effort to deal with more of the phenomena and more accurately reflect the actual state of affairs that we have employed these methods alongside the more familiar stress system. It may be that such effort is wasted because of our lack of controls (of vocalization of the words and ignorance of ancient Israelite musical patterns) or because the poetry is simply not amenable to such detailed analysis. But it is worthwhile to set the evidence down and then to draw conclusions, if any. On the whole, the two proposed systems agree with each other very well and generally with the stress system, only adding detail and occasionally clarifying a hazy or erroneous impression of the actual meter before us.

Turning to the material at hand, we find the following in Strophe IA:

	A	*S*	*V*
7a	2:2	6:6	16:16
b	2:2	6:6	16:16

8a	2:2	6:4	16:12
b	3	9	26
c	3	9	25

The corresponding stanza in Strophe IIA:

	A	*S*	*V*
12	2:2	6:5	15:16
13a	2:2	7:5	16:14
b	2:2	7:6	17:15
14a	3	8	23
b	3	8	24

While the accent scheme shows no variations between the stanzas, both the syllable and vocable count do, and thus reflect the attested differences in the structure of the stanzas as well as their resemblances. The initial couplet of IA (vs 7) is shown to be absolutely symmetrical in both S and V. At the same time, 8a is shown to vary distinctly from the pattern of 7 although also designated 2:2. It is clearly shorter, and in fact close to 8bc with which it belongs, though the latter are 3:3. The balance between 8b and c is strongly attested in S and V.

In IIA, the initial bicolon (vs 12), which differs in content from the couplet in vs 13, is nevertheless structurally very similar. Both S and V bear this out, so that we have a triad in pattern if not in content. The symmetry of the concluding couplet (3:3) is borne out in S and V. Taking the stanzas as a whole, we have: for IA: 12:12 / 10 / 9:9; a total of 52 syllables; for IIA:11 / 12:13 / 8:8, also a total of 52 syllables, thus demonstrating that the stanzas are of equal length. The V count shows: IA, 32:32 / 28 / 26:25, for a total of 143; IIA, 31 / 30:32 / 23:24, for a total of 140. The discrepancy is well within the margin we must allow for possible variations in vowel length and pronunciation at the option of the poet, to say nothing of our limited knowledge of the state of the language at the time of composition.

The second stanzas of Strophes I and II may be described as follows:

Strophe IB	*A*	*S*	*V*
9a	2:2	4:4	12:14
b	2:2	5:6	15:17
c	2:2	4:6	12:17
10a	2:2	6:4	15:13
b	2:2	6:5	16:16
Strophe IIB			
15a	2:2	4:5	12:15
b	2:2	4:5	13:16
c	2:2	4:5	12:15
16a	2:2	5:6	15:15
b	2:2	6:5	16:16

While the A system shows an unbroken line of 2:2 bicolon, both S and V point to a break between the triad (vss 9 and 15) and the following couplet (vss 10 and 16ab). The former are shorter, averaging 9 syllables; the latter are longer, averaging 11 syllables. The pattern for the stanzas as a whole is: IB: 8: 11:10 / 10:11, for a total of 50; IIB: 9:9:9 / 11:11 = 49. The vocable count shows for IB: 26:32:29 / 28:32 = 147; for IIB: 27:29:27 / 30:32 = 145. Taking the Strophes as a whole, we have for I : S = 102, V = 290; for II: S = 101, V = 285.

Turning to the opening and closing stanzas, we find:

	A	*S*	*V*
Opening			
Vs 3	2:2	6:4	18:11
4a	3:2	8:4	23:11
b	2:2	6:6	17:17
5a	3(?)	8	22
b	3	10	28
		52	147
Closing			
Vs 17a	2:2	9:6	24:16
b	2:2	6:5	15:13
c	2:2	5:6	15:15
18	2:2	4:5	13:14
		46	125

The peculiaritics and difficulties of both the opening and closing have already been discussed. With regard to the opening, the irregularities in the metrical count under A are resolved in S and V. As a whole, the opening conforms to the pattern of IA and IIA. The syllable count is 10 / 12:12 / 8:10 = 52; the vocable count is 29 / 34:34 / 22:28 = 147.

For the closing, if we accept 17a (2:2) as a legitimate variant of the expected 3:3, we have the following totals: S: 15 / 11:11 / 9 = 46; V: 40 / 28:30 / 27 = 125. If, however, we restore 17a, as suggested above, the totals become:

	A	*S*	*V*
Vs $17a^1$	(3)	(10)	(28)
$17a^2$	3	11	28

The revised count would be: S: 10:11 / 11:11: 9 = 52; V: 28:28 / 28:30 / 27 = 141.

The totals for the group would be:

	S	*V*
Opening	52	147
Closing	46 (52)	125 (141)
Total	98 (104)	272 (288)

The Refrains present the following pattern:

		A	*S*	*V*
	(1b)	2:2	6:5	16:13
		2:2	5:4	14:11
A	(6a)	2:2	5:5	14:15
	(6b)	2:2	5:4	14:13
B	(11a)	2:2	4:5	11:15
	(11b)	2:2	4:4	11:14
	(11c)	2:2	5:4	15:10
C	(16c)	3	8	23
	(16d)	3	8	23
	(21b)	2:2	5:5	14:13
		2:2	5:4	14:11

Taking the Refrains together as a structural unit, we have the following totals:

	S	*V*
Vs 1b	11:9 = 20	29:25 = 54
6	10:9 = 19	29:27 = 56
11	9:8:9 = 26	26:25:25 = 76
16cd	8:8 = 16	23:23 = 46
21b	10:9 = 19	27:25 = 52
Total	100	284

It is interesting to note that the total is equivalent to that of the other strophes:

	S	*V*
I	102	290
II	101	285
Opening and closing	98 (104)	272 (288)
Refrains	100	284

The Exordium (vs 2) presents the following pattern:

	A	*S*	*V*
Vs 2a	2	7	20
2b	2	7	19
2c	3	7	20
2d	3	11	28
Total		32	87

We may combine vss 1 and 2, as was done at some point in the history of the poem, to form a preliminary stanza: the various counts would be: S:32 +

20 = 52; V:87 + 54 = 141. S is thus approximately the same as S for the opening, Strophes IA, IIA, and our reconstructed closing stanza. The similarity is superficial, however, and the pattern of vss 1–2 remains uncertain. Possibly we should construe it as a couplet 2:2 / 2:2 followed by a transitional line 2:2, which leads into the closing bicolon, 3:3. The pattern would resemble that of Strophe IA, in which we have an opening couplet 2:2 / 2:2 followed by a transitional line, 2:2, which connects with a closing couplet, 3:3. The unbalanced final line of vs 2 (S, 7:11) can be compared with vs 5 (S, 8:10), also read as 3:3.

As a check on our statistical analysis, and to test the view that almost any syllable counting system will produce the same comparative results providing that it is applied consistently, we can substitute the figures derived from rigorous adherence to MT, both text and vocalization. The results show no significant change from the patterns already observed.

Introductory	*S*	*V*
Refrain (1b)	6:5	17:15
	5:4	14:13
Exordium (2)	6:7	19:19
	7:11	20:29
Total	51	146
Opening (3–5)		
3	6:4	19:11
4a	8:4	23:13
b	6:6	18:17
5a	7	20
b	10	29
Total	51	150
Refrain (A) (6)	6:5	16:16
	6:4	16:13
Total	21	61
Strophe IA		
Vs 7a	6:6	17:17
b	6:6	17:17
8a	6:5	17:13
b	9	26
c	9	26
Total	53	150
Strophe IB		
9a	4:4	13:14
b	5:6	16:18
c	4:6	13:18
10a	7:4	19:13
b	7:6	18:17
Total	53	159

Refrain (B)		
11a	4:5	12:16
b	4:5	12:16
c	5:4	15:11
Total	27	82
Strophe IIA		
12	6:6	18:18
13a	7:5	19:16
b	7:6	19:16
14a	8	25
b	9	26
Total	54	157
Strophe IIB		
15a	4:5	12:15
b	4:6	13:17
c	4:6	13:16
16a	5:6	15:17
b	6:6	17:17
Total	52	152
Refrain (C)		
16c	4:5	11:14
d	4:5	11:15
Total	18	51
Closing		
17a	9:7 (10)	25:17 (28)
	(12)	(31)
b	6:5	17:15
c	5:6	16:17
18	4:5	13:15
Total	47 (53)	135 (152)
Concluding Refrain		
21b	5:5	14:15
	5:4	14:13
Total	19	56

Summary and Comparison

	S		*V*	
	MT	Prop.	MT	Prop.
Exordium (1–2)	51	52	146	140
Opening and Closing	98 (104)	98 (104)	285 (302)	272 (288)
Strophe I	106	102	309	290
Strophe II	106	101	309	285
Refrains	105	100	309	284

It is apparent that the variations introduced into MT with respect to pronunciation aad vocalization tend to cancel each other out, and that the ratios and proportions tend to remain constant. Thus all the stanzas fall within the range of 51–54 syllables in MT, which is precisely the theoretical range postulated by the possible sequences of long and short lines: that is, 3 short lines with 27 syllables, and 2 long ones with 24 syllables, making a total of 51; or 3 long lines with 36 syllables, and 2 short ones with 18, making a total of 54. The Strophes total S = 106, and V = 309, while the sum of the opening and closing stanzas is S = 104 and V = 302 (as reconstructed; as the text stands, the totals are S = 98 and V = 285). The Exordium also comes within the limits indicated at S = 51 and V = 146.

To summarize, we suggest that the poem exhibits two basic line lengths: one of approximately 12 syllables (sometimes 11, rarely 13) normally construed as 2:2; the other usually of 8 or 9 syllables (occasionally 10) and construed as 2:2 or 3. These are the basic building blocks used by the poet and ingeniously arranged in pairs or triads to produce a dramatic work of art. Designating the lines S and L, we can diagram the poet's structural pattern for the poem as follows:

Opening Refrain (1b)	S : S
Exordium (2)	S : S
	S : L
Opening (3–5)	S
	L : L
	S : S
Refrain (A) (6)	S : S
Strophe IA (7–8)	L : L
	S
	S : S
IB (9–10)	S : S : S
	L : L
Refrain (B) (11)	S : S : S
Strophe IIA (12–14)	L
	L : L
	S : S
IIB (15–16b)	S : S : S
	L : L
Refrain (C) (16cd)	S : S
Closing (17–18)	(S : S) ?
	L : L
	S
Closing refrain (21b)	S : S

In our opinion, all three systems of analysis (A = accent; S = syllable counting; V = vocables) contribute to an appreciation of the metrical patterns; of the three, S seems to be the most useful and flexible.

A few words about the date of the poem may be in order. The standpoint of the author is some time after the settlement in the Holy Land, when it would be possible to speak of a general occupation of the country. Hence the earliest date of composition would be the twelfth century B.C. Very likely the period of the United Monarchy would provide us with an adequate *terminus ad quem*. Certain details may help us to fix the date more exactly. The omission of the Ammonites from the list of nations in vss 14–15 (if it is not a happenstance owing to the exigencies of stanza construction) reflects an accurate knowledge of the political situation in the thirteenth and twelfth centuries, when only Moabites and Edomites were in that region. Later traditions, as reflected in the Deuteronomic writings, were confused on this point. Such a datum would tend to support an earlier date for the poem, or at least indicate that the author had access to reliable, presumably early historical traditions. On the other hand, the inclusion of Philistia in the list points in another direction. If the word is part of the original composition, then it reflects the hegemony established by the Philistines in the Holy Land beginning in the twelfth century. The author imagines that the Philistines were already settled in the land and, in fact, in control of much of it at the time of the wilderness wandering. He has apparently telescoped events and reversed the sequence of Israelite and Philistine entry into the land of Canaan. We must place the poem subsequent to the Philistine invasion and conquest. All the data suggest that the poem in its original form was composed in the twelfth century. Its nearest companion in form and style is the Song of Deborah, universally recognized to be a product of the same period.

We may add that the evidence of vocabulary, grammar, usage, poetic structures, and poetic devices is all inconclusive. There are numerous archaic features, correctly used, in the poem; they are certainly not inconsistent with an early date, but they do not prove it. The knowledge of many archaic elements of the language persisted in Israel, and some of them show up even in comparatively late materials. Until more refined methods are developed, and more exact information concerning poetry writing in Israel is acquired, we must rely on impressions and the few historical references and details which appear.

Notes

1 This paper is intended a a supplement to and revision of the joint article, "The Song of Miriam," *JNES* 14 (1955), 237–50, by Frank M. Cross, Jr., and me. Among recent articles on the subject, the following may be noted: B. S. Childs, "A Traditio-Historical Study of the Reed Sea Tradition," *VT* 20 (1970), 406–18; G. W. Coats, "The Traditio-Historical Character of the Reed Sea Motif," *VT* 17 (1967), 253–65; and "The Song of the Sea," *CBQ* (1969), 1–17; Cross, "The Song of the Sea and Canaanite Myth," *JTC* 5 (1968), 1–25; N. Lohfink, "Das Siegeslied am Schilfmeer," *Das Siegeslied am Schilf-*

meer (1965), pp. 103–28; J. Muilenburg, "A Liturgy on the Triumphs of Yahweh," *Studia Biblica et Semitica* (1966), pp. 233–51; D. A. Robertson, *Linguistic Evidence in Dating Early Hebrew Poetry* (University Microfilms, 1970; Yale University dissertation, 1966); P. C. Craigie, "An Egyptian Expression in the Song of the Sea (Exodus XV 4)," *VT* 20 (1970), 83–86; "Psalm XXIX in the Hebrew Poetic Tradition," *VT* 22 (1972), 143–51.

[2] *Studia Biblica et Semitica*, pp. 237 ff.

[3] M. Dahood, *Psalms II*, *AB* (1968), pp. 335, 337.

[4] While the verb *trʿṣ* may be interpreted as either a 3 f.s. or 2 m.s. form, I think it preferable to take Yahweh as the subject; *ymynk* would then be a dative of means.

[5] D. N. Freedman, "Archaic Forms in Early Hebrew Poetry," *ZAW* 62 (1960), 101–7. See also my "Prolegomenon" in G. B. Gray, *The Forms of Hebrew Poetry* (1972), pp. vii–lvi.

[6] Cross and Freedman, "A Royal Song of Thanksgiving—II Sam 22 = Psalm 18," *JBL* 72 (1953), 26 and fn. 41 for discussion of the parallel texts, II Sam 22: 16 = Ps 18: 16.

[7] See the discussion of these and similar forms in Cross and Freedman, *Early Hebrew Orthography* (1952), pp. 65–68.

[8] The problem is discussed in some detail and a solution proposed at a later point in this paper.

[9] E. M. Good, "Exodus XV 2," *VT* 20 (1970), 358–59.

[10] Dahood, *Psalms III*, *AB* (1970), pp. 411–12; examples occur in Pss 28: 8, 68: 20, and 88: 2.

[11] Cross and Freedman, *Studies in Ancient Yahwistic Poetry* (1950), pp. 45, 48 fn. *a*, for the suggested emendation. Since then it has been proposed independently by S. Gevirtz, *Patterns in the Early Poetry of Israel* (1963), pp. 83–84. A similar emendation has also been adopted by W. Holladay, "Form and Word-Play in David's Lament over Saul and Jonathan" *VT* 20 (1970), 157–59.

[12] Dahood, *Psalms II*, p. 205.

[13] W. F. Albright, "The Phoenician Inscriptions of the Tenth Century B.C. from Byblus," *JAOS* 67 (1947), 156–57.

Stanley Brice Frost
McGill University

The English Bible

The custom that colleagues and former students of a teacher greatly beloved and highly esteemed should organize the production of a Festschrift to honor his name and to signalize his contribution to their discipline and profession is one of the happiest traditions that attach to scholarship. In the age of the anti-hero, when the leading literary figures of the day draw men small and mean, and when the role of the humanities, from the theater of the absurd to the distortions of the visual arts, is apparently to denigrate man and all his achievements, it is good to find the custom still healthily maintained among scholars of acknowledging the stature and contribution of one of their fellows and of proclaiming by a collection of essays on the subjects of their discipline their admiration and affection for him. Those of us who have known Jacob M. Myers chiefly by his writings recognize our indebtedness to him, and I as one of those am appreciative of the opportunity to join with his nearer colleagues and friends to salute a scholar for whom affection on his home campus is worthily matched by the high regard which his contributions to Old Testament studies have won for him throughout the wider ecumene of the biblical disciplines.

Since Professor Myers has recently made a notable contribution[1] to a series which required of him that he become in no small way a biblical translator, I offer some comments on the present position with regard to the Bible in English translation. Some of the paragraphs are taken, with the permission of the editor, more or less directly from an article on the same general subject but in a rather more popular style which recently appeared in the *Queen's Quarterly*.[2]

It is a remarkable fact that the beginnings of the English Bible mark the beginnings of the English language itself, and that in all the developments, from the heterogeneous dialects of the Nordic invaders of Britain to the homogeneous world language of today, the English Bible has very fairly kept pace, and indeed has often led the way.

Beowulf is a truly splendid epic but, like the other few heroic poems of its kind, it belongs to the old pagan world of the time before either the Nordic peoples or their dialects had been fused into the new dynamic unity. Because of its typically oral character and the sparseness of the written remains, we are left largely to guess at the range and versatility of the literary tradition from which the poems come. They are the last few evidences of a culture which has passed away. But the nine precious lines of Caedmon's Creation Hymn, even if we now possess them only in the Latin translation, and the tradition of Bede's Gospel of John in the Northumbrian dialect, point to the new literary tradition which was to grow and increase into the immensely rich repository of the English language in many centuries and in many lands. The achievements of Shakespeare, Scott, and Yeats have been enhanced by Longfellow and Eugene O'Neill, and are now being further enriched by West African songwriters, Maori poets, and Eskimo novelists—all in the one common speech. The Bible in English, which was there at the beginning of it all, has not only played a major role both in the diffusion and in the development of the language but is even today making new and vigorous contributions to its strength and well-being in all parts of the world. The King James Version in the past and the Bible in Basic English in the present have been major influences to ensure that the local versions of pidgin English should remain simply what they are, and that Standard English should maintain itself fairly well as one and the same the world over. "Poetry," said John Wesley, "is the handmaid of Piety." For the English language, the Bible has repaid that service many times over.

The tradition that began with Caedmon and Bede and went on to Alfred the Great and his laws can be documented from at least the end of the ninth century. The translation known as the Vespasian Psalter, dating from about that time, gives us an example of the Kentish dialect; North Mercian is evidenced by the almost contemporary gloss to the Harewood Gospels. Northumbrian is supplied by another gloss, that to the Lindisfarne Gospels; West Saxon is well represented by the half-dozen or more Gospel manuscripts dating from the early tenth century through to the end of the twelfth. Indeed, the considerable West Saxon works of Abbot Aelfric (c. 955–1020), both in the instance of his biblical translations and in his freer compositions such as the Homilies, illustrate the growing maturity of a language which had become richly expressive. Since during the twelfth and thirteenth centuries English was in a period of eclipse as a result of the Norman invasion, there is naturally little direct evidence of fresh translations, but at least some copying of Anglo-Saxon manuscripts continued. Margaret Deanesly,[3] who is concerned to stress the lack of a complete English Bible before the time of Wycliffe, nevertheless mentions the Psalterium Triplex of Eadwine, which was compiled about 1120 and included an Anglo-Saxon as well as Norman-French and Latin versions. She also mentions that while the earliest manuscripts of the verse paraphrases of Genesis, Exodus, and Daniel, popularly attributed to Caedmon but more probably the product of a folk tradition, are to be assigned to the tenth century, the latest are to be assigned to the middle of the thirteenth.[4] The resurgence of English as a consequence of the Hundred Years' War is first testified by the writings of Richard Rolle (1300–1349), whose Middle English Psalter achieved a considerable circulation. So also, though to a lesser degree, did the somewhat later Psalter of William of Shoreham. But Richard's Psalter was in the Northern dialect, and William's in the West Midland. The literary significance of the Lollard Bible, which appeared in the last quarter of the fourteenth century, was that for the first time a work in English was assiduously copied and actively promulgated in all parts of the country, so that the language of London and the East Midlands had an opportunity to reach up into Yorkshire and the North[5] and as well as down into Somerset and the West. It is fair to say that while Chaucer and his peers gave Middle English its literary standards and its self-confidence among the upper classes, the Lollard Bible did as much if not more for its coherence and unification in all strata of society. From the beginning through to the emergence of Modern English in the fifteenth century, in all the major developments such as the liberation from gender, the reduction of inflections, the evolution of the tenses, and the great enrichment of vocabulary, the tradition of the Bible in English marched with the linguistic progress, recording the new developments, and sometimes pointing the way ahead.

William Tyndale, therefore, brilliantly fresh and original in the field of translation as we know him to have been, was nevertheless the heir to a tradition already rich, and in the choicest phrases of the Reformer, the attentive ear can from time to time detect echoes of his Lollard predecessors, Nicholas of Hereford and John Purvey.[6] Even so, the beginning of the story of "The English Bible" proper clearly belongs to Tyndale, and from his time until our own the story is really the narrative of the successive revisions which his splendid version underwent. Coverdale's Bible, the Great Bible, the Geneva Version, the Bishops' Bible—they were all Tyndale revised, and the King James Version itself owed more to Tyndale than to any of the revisers. It has been calculated that of the King James Version, at least two-thirds is clearly attributable to Tyndale.[7] While Miles Smith was formally referring to the Bishops' Bible when he said that the aim of the revisers was to make not a bad version good but, rather, a good version better, it was really of Tyndale's work that he was speaking. Thus it was basically one and the same work, "The English Bible," that appeared in those successive editions from 1525, the date of Tyndale's first New Testament, through to 1611, when the King James Version finally appeared.

The influence of the King James Version upon the growth and development of English language and culture, both at home and in the many distant lands to which trade and empire dispersed the island speech, has been much observed and often commented upon. The King James Bible, more than any other work, has been the arbiter of style for many centuries wherever English has established itself. In his essay, "The Noblest Monument of English Prose," John Livingstone Lowes has aptly written: "Its phraseology has become part and parcel of our common tongue—bone of its bone and flesh of its flesh. Its rhythms and cadences, its turns of speech, its familiar imagery, its very words, are woven into the texture of our literature, prose and poetry alike."[8] This might be thought too extravagant a judgment, but when we reflect how much more at ease we are with the King James Version than with the language of its "Translator's preface to the Reader" (which was the normal prose style of the day), or consider the difference between the sermons of Latimer, who was not influenced by this version, and the writings of John Bunyan, who was, we begin to recognize how its simplicity of style and force of language have impressed themselves upon us all.

Nevertheless, even after the King James Version had, by its own sheer excellence, driven from the field all its competitors, including even the doughty Geneva Version, which had been the Bible of Spenser, Shakespeare, and the Pilgrim Fathers, and which had effectively taken Standard English into the popular life of Scotland,[9] it did not reign for the next three and a half centuries altogether unchallenged. As early as the time of the Commonwealth, a Quaker named Robert Gell, published *An Essay toward the Amendment of the Last English Translation*, in which he asked that a new and better version should be undertaken. It is significant that John Wesley placed Gell's treatise upon the reading list of his itinerant preachers, and that he himself issued a revised version of King James along with his *Notes on the New Testament*. But not even Wesley, successful editor, plagiarizer, and publisher that he was, could disturb the serene rule of the King James Version in Britain, in North America, and, indeed, wherever the English language was spoken and read. As Adam Clarke, the great orientalist of the early nineteenth century, remarked: "While the common translation is authorized by Law, and has alone dictated salvation for nearly two hundred years, the majority of the people will not readily admit that it can be easily mended; or that any attempt to do this can be wholly destitute of danger to the cause of Divine Revelation." As is well known, the King James never was "by law appointed." The familiar words "Appointed to be read in Churches," which still appear on British printings and which have given the version its other surrogate, the Authorized Version, were simply transferred from the Bishops' Bible and its predecessors, notably the Great Bible of Thomas Cromwell, and were never formally justified either by royal license or by an Act of the Convocations of the Church of England. This circumstance reminds us that a version lives or dies by popular acceptance or neglect, and that the edicts of authorities, ecclesiastical or lay, do not have much influence on the matter.

The Revised Version of 1885[10] is a case in point. By the latter half of the nineteenth century, the pressure for a more accurate and a more modern rendering had become very strong, and it was undertaken in Britain by resolution of the Convocation of the Province of Canterbury of the Church of England in 1870, but the revision was governed by some very stringent rules. The work was to be not a new translation but a revision of King James, and the revisers bound themselves to make changes only by a two-thirds vote and, moreover, to employ only such words as were established in the language in the seventeenth century, unless it was clearly apparent that no appropriate word of that period was available. It is not surprising therefore that the version which emerged was a very conservative revision, and that a great deal of its best work was to be found in the marginal notes, to which were consigned those proposals which gained a simple majority of support but which failed to win two-thirds approval. An American company of revisers, invited to participate in the task, was a little more adventurous, so that the edition of the Revised Version published in the United States in 1901 as the American Standard Version differed from the English edition in a number of small particulars, but more particularly in substituting "Jehovah" for the traditional "the Lord."

Cautious as the revision was, the furore it caused was immense. One of the most vehement critics in England was Dean Burgon of Chichester, a fundamentalist of extreme views, who assailed the new version in the *Quarterly Review* in the most vehement terms: "that most unfortunate production," "the grossest literary imposture of the age," "insufferable pedantry," "impertinent priggishness." These are but a few of the phrases which the outraged Dean allowed himself, so that the *Leeds Mercury* was moved to remark: "In a series of what would be called in anyone but a dignitary of Church impudent assumptions, the Dean pours forth a good array of ecclesiastical Billingsgate."[11] However, the final outcome was that the version was warmly welcomed by scholars and largely ignored by the great mass of Bible readers on both sides of the Atlantic. They continued unperturbed to read and quote the King James Version.

Thus, the effect of the Revised Version was to emphasize the need for a more thoroughgoing revision rather than to supply that need, and this was further increased by the appearance of a number of notable private versions, the best known being the second version of James Moffatt (1913), the *Holy Scriptures According to the Masoretic Text* (Jewish Publication Society of America, 1917), the *American Translation* of Goodspeed and Powis Smith (1923 and 1927; Apocrypha, 1938), and the version of J. B. Phillips (1947; complete New Testament, 1958). All these have their virtues, but none could be thought of as taking the place of the King James Version as "The English Bible." Plans for a further revision of the American Standard Version were set on foot in the United States as early as 1937, but owing to the incidence of World War II, they had to be carried to completion by United States and Canadian scholars without very much participation by the scholars of other countries. The new version was designated the Revised Standard Version. The New Testament appeared in 1946, the Old Testament in 1952, and the Apocrypha in 1957.

The Revised Standard Version may fairly be described as a remarkable success. It accomplished what it set out to do, which was to continue the tradition of "The English Bible," but in such a way as to commend the old version to a new age. It is of course open to criticism on many smaller points, but is guilty of perhaps only one major fault: it tends to be conservative in well-known and much-loved passages, but once off the comparatively narrow and well-beaten path of popular passages, it becomes much more ready to call a spade a spade and not disguise it under some ecclesiastically dictated euphemism. A case in point is Is 53, where *ḥly* is still translated "grief," and "sickness" is left to the margin, presumably because "the Suffering Servant" is widely held to be a christological prophecy and there is no tradition of disease in the story of Jesus. Therefore tradition has dictated that the trait must be obscured in translating the Isaiah passage. On the other hand, in a book like Zechariah we notice a much greater readiness to forsake the Masoretic Text and to accept readings from the Greek or Syriac or even conjectural amendments. Perhaps in the revision of a classic, this practice is not altogether indefensible; the version has made whole passages in the prophets or in the epistles intelligible as they never were in the King James, and it has done so without ruthlessly wounding susceptibilities in "best-loved passages." Certainly, until quite recently, the Revised Standard Version was the one version other than the King James which was read in churches, meditated upon in the home, and almost universally quoted by scholars. In 1965, the British hierarchy of the Roman Church gave its imprimatur to a Roman Catholic edition, and the Revised Standard Version thereby became the one ecumenical version to bridge the Protestant-Catholic divide.[12] More than any other version it deserves to rank as "The English Bible" of the twentieth century.[13]

The Revised Standard Version New Testament had hardly appeared, however (and certainly had had no time to prove its worth), before a movement was begun in Scotland for a new British translation. After thirteen years of concerted effort, the translators appointed by the combined non-Roman Catholic churches in Britain produced their New Testament in 1961. What was distinctive with regard to this version was that it broke with four hundred and fifty years of history, and gave us not a further revision of "The English Bible," the Bible of Tyndale, Coverdale, Geneva, and King James, and of the Revised Standard Version, but an entirely new translation. The old familiar cadences of a leisurely, mannered style were abandoned, and a modern, taut prose was substituted. This is very apparent if we take a well-known passage (Mt 11: 28-30) and read it first in the King James, then in the Revised Standard and finally in the New English Bible:

KJ	Come unto me, all ye that labour and are heavy laden, and I will give you rest. Take my yoke upon you, and learn of me; for I am meek and lowly in heart: and ye shall find rest unto your souls. For my yoke is easy, and my burden is light.
RSV	Come to me, all who labour and are heavy-laden, and I will give you rest. Take my yoke upon you, and learn from me; for I am gentle and lowly in heart, and you will find rest for your souls. For my yoke is easy, and my burden is light.
NEB	Come to me, all whose work is hard, whose load is heavy; and I will give you relief. Bend your necks to my yoke, and learn from me, for I am gentle and humble-hearted; and your souls will find relief. For my yoke is good to bear, my load is light.

The King James and the Revised Standard are undoubtedly the same work, but in the new translation the whole feel of the passage is different. The new style tends to be rather broken, staccato, and even in narrative portions it does not flow very easily. One gets the impression that each phrase has been individually translated but that no one has gone over the whole to make of the phrases a continuous, flexible unity. In the Epistles, this may be almost an advantage, for one often gets the impression from the Greek that the writers, particularly Paul, thought in spurts and expressed themselves in sudden phrases. But in the narratives of Acts and the Gospels, this lack of stylistic continuity is a distinct loss. It makes itself severely apparent if one reads, for example, the story of the walk to Emmaus (Lk 24) first in King James and then in the New English Bible. In Britain, as one would expect, the New Testament version was somewhat uncritically accepted, and has gained fairly wide acceptance; but in North America and in the English-speaking world generally, it has been given a cordial rather than an enthusiastic reception. Whether the New English Bible as a whole would prove a serious rival to the Revised Standard Version on the world-wide stage could not be known until the appearance of the Old Testament and Apocrypha. For this we have had to be patient for almost another decade, but the long-awaited volume appeared in March 1970, and we can begin to make at least preliminary judgments.

Before we do so, there are two other developments which have to be noted. First, a modest, untrumpeted translation of the New Testament was put out in 1968 by the American Bible Society, in paperback and with charming line drawings interspersed in the text, under the title "Good News for Modern Man: Today's English Version." The translator was Robert Bratcher and the line drawings are by Annie Vallotton. The Preface states that the intention was to meet the need of people everywhere who use English as a means of communication: "Today's English Version of the New Testament attempts to follow, in this century, the example set by the authors of the New Testament books, who, for the most part, wrote in the standard, or common, form of the Greek language." It has proved brilliantly successful. Everyone who uses it for either private or public reading is struck by its simplicity, its directness, and its vitality. Even those who have long accustomed themselves to the New Testament in Greek have a sense of fresh acquaintance with passage after passage, and are led to suspect that the impact of this version upon them is something very like the impression which the original writings made upon those to whom they were first addressed. Like the King James Version, "Today's English Version" bids fair to establish itself by its own sheer worth.

One small point is that this "common English" translation naturally eschewed "thou's" and "thee's." In the New Testament, the Deity is addressed relatively seldom, and this change of style was interesting but not revolutionary. But then also in 1968 there appeared the Jerusalem Bible. This is indeed a notable translation in many respects. Its progenitor is La Bible de Jérusalem, so called because it was prepared by scholars of the French Dominican Bible School in Jerusalem. They availed themselves not only of the very best assistance of modern scholarship but also of that new-found enthusiasm for the Bible which *aggiornamento*, both before and since Vatican II, has engendered throughout the Roman Church. This splendid French version then became the inspiration and guide for a new Roman

Catholic Bible in England. This version, also called "The Jerusalem Bible," not only dispenses with "thee" and "thou," in the Old Testament as well as in the New, but it also boldly returns to the Divine Name "Yahweh" instead of employing the surrogate "the Lord," by use of which translators for over two thousand years have reverently avoided the use of the Divine Name. Thus what we have heard for centuries as "O Lord, our Lord, how excellent is thy name in all the earth!" becomes:

> Yahweh, our Lord,
> how great your name throughout the earth!

It is in the Psalms that the Jerusalem Bible scintillates. For example, the King James grandly but somewhat obscurely proclaims: "For lo, the kings were assembled, they passed by together. They saw it, and so they marvelled; they were troubled and hasted away." This becomes in the Jerusalem Bible:

> There was a rallying, once, of kings,
> advancing together along a common front;
> they looked, they were amazed,
> they panicked, they ran!

No more graphic conveyance of an irrational, fear-inspired rout is possible. Not only in the Psalms but throughout both Testaments, this is a very readable, attractive, and thoroughly commendable version of the Bible in the best literary style of our own day. At one bound, the Roman Church in England has overcome the shame of centuries and has produced a Bible which can afford comparison with the very best that the Protestant world has to offer.

The appearance of the Old Testament and Apocrypha of the New English Bible was therefore, in view of what had gone before, an event of very considerable importance. British biblical scholarship has for a century been rivaled only by the German tradition for erudition, perceptiveness, and freedom from conservative constraints. The new version comes from a tradition enriched by mature scholarship, literary sensitivity, and informed popular interest. These scholars were men trained by George Adam Smith and Arthur Samuel Peake, and their literary sensitivity had been tuned by Robert Louis Stevenson and Gerard Manley Hopkins, and played upon by T. S. Eliot, Christopher Fry, and Winston Churchill. The omens were surely set for a truly great translation.

It is impossible to review the Bible as one would any other work. Its vastness, variety, and familiarity all combine to defeat the attempt. What one can do is to take soundings; to choose a number of passages which have made their mark in previous translations, and to turn hopefully to others which have struck home in the Hebrew or the Greek but which have hitherto failed in translation. A version has to be lived with for many years before its strengths and weaknesses can be fully known. But there are some immediate reactions to this New English Bible which can be formulated. For instance, the decision to retain the older form of second-person address may have been defensible in 1946, but in 1970 it strikes one as sheer anachronism. It is not merely that "thou" belongs to a special outdated language of "religion only" but also that the whole use of auxiliary verbs is involved. In order to avoid "thou castedst" one writes "thou hast cast" and the style straightway becomes less taut. This is not so noticeable in prose narratives, in which the new version acquits itself fairly though not outstandingly well, but it shows up at once in poetical passages. Compare Ps 104, for example, from the New English Bible with the Jerusalem Bible's rendering:

NEB Thou hast spread out the heavens like a tent,
and on their waters laid the beams of thy pavilion;
who takest the clouds for thy chariot,
riding on the wings of the wind;
who makest the winds thy messengers
and flames of fire thy servants;
thou didst fix the earth on its foundation
so that it never can be shaken;
the deep overspread it like a cloak,
and the waters lay above the mountains.

JB You stretch the heavens out like a tent,
you build your palace on the waters above;
using the clouds as your chariot,
you advance on the wings of the wind;
you use the winds as messengers
and fiery flames as servants.
You fixed the earth on its foundations,
unshakeable for ever and ever;
you wrapped it with the deep as with a robe,
the waters over-topping the mountains.

It is manifestly unfair to build overall judgements on a single passage. The present writer can only say that the literary success of the second passage as compared with the awkwardness of the first has up to this point in his reading seemed to him to be representative of the two versions. "Thou didst fix" is bad enough, but "Thou it was who didst fashion my inward parts" (Ps 139: 13) is surely unforgivable.

Is 52–53 (to take another sampling) is in important details very questionable as an accurate translation, and as a whole very difficult for public reading; even for private reading, the passage emerges as irritatingly staccato in its flow of ideas. Here are the verses which Handel has made so familiar, as they appear in the Revised Standard and in the New English versions:

RSV He was despised and rejected by men;
a man of sorrows, and acquainted with grief;
and as one from whom men hide their faces
he was despised, and we esteemed him not.
Surely he has borne our griefs,
and carried our sorrows,
yet we esteemed him stricken,
smitten by God and afflicted.

NEB He was despised, he shrank from the sight of men,
tormented and humbled by suffering;
we despised him, we held him of no account,
a thing from which men turn away their eyes.
Yet on himself he bore our sufferings,
our torments he endured,
while we counted him smitten by God,
struck down by disease and misery.

The first translation has a rhythm derived from the King James, which the second wholly lacks. Nor do finer points of greater accuracy compensate for this loss. "Grief" in the second line of the RSV has, as we have seen, long been recognized as needing to be rendered by "disease." Why, then, does the NEB sidestep the difficulty by using the less direct word "suffering," and then gratuitously introduce "disease" into the last line? Some of the individual phrases in the chapter cannot readily be derived from the Hebrew at all: "after all his pains he shall be bathed in light" (vs 11) appears to be an example of sheer invention.[14] The whole passage emerges as an uneven mixture of doubtful innovations and cautious conservatism.

When one further discovers that in the NEB not only is "the Lord" retained in the old style but that in crucial passages like Ex 3 and 34 "Jehovah" unblushingly makes its reappearance, one is reluctantly forced to conclude that this version is neither of our age nor for our age. In view of the twenty and more years of devoted labor, dedicated to this task by scores of scholars who stand in the finest traditions of linguistic and literary skills, this is a truly tragic conclusion at which to arrive. One wants desperately to be able to hail this version as a superb achievement. Honesty compels us to say that it is very doubtful whether, like its great predecessor, the King James Version, the New English Bible will drive all its competitors off the market by virtue of its own sheer excellence.

The year 1970 will nevertheless clearly be remembered as a vintage year for the Bible in English, for in the late fall of that year a second major venture reached completion and was published in its entirety. The New American Bible is the product of the Catholic Biblical Association of America and is sponsored by the Bishops' Committee of the Confraternity on Christian Doctrine. The translation was undertaken in response to the Papal Encyclical *Divino Afflante Spiritu* (1943), and the work was begun as early as 1944. In span of years, the parallel with the NEB is very close, but the publishing history has been quite different. The Confraternity New Testament had been issued in 1941, and this was a revision of Douai-Rheims-Challoner. Thus, although it took cognizance of the Greek text, it was essentially a translation of the Vulgate. But the 1943 Encyclical gave a new status in the Roman communion to the original language versions behind the Vulgate, and the Catholic Biblical Association charged with responsibility for the Confraternity Bible turned to the Old Testament in Hebrew and Aramaic with a new zest. *Genesis to Ruth* was published in 1952, *Job to Sirach* in 1955, *Isaiah to Malachi* in 1961, and *Samuel to Maccabees* in 1969. The New American Bible of 1970 consists of these parts of the Confraternity Old Testament (the first three having been revised, the first of them to the extent of a new translation of Genesis) together with an entirely new version of the New Testament based on the twenty-fifth edition of the Nestlé-Aland Greek Text but with reference also to the United Bible Societies' 1966 text. The work is issued by a number of publishers in various styles. The typical edition published by the St. Anthony Guild Press includes an appendix of textual notes relating to the original languages, while the Catholic Press edition is a more ecclesiastical version, printing the sayings of Jesus in red and including such features as a charming modern version of the Jesse Tree. The scholarship of the New American Bible is beyond reproach. Full advantage has been taken of the latest Dead Sea Scroll discoveries and of the more recent advances in New Testament textual criticism. The version dispenses with the archaic form of second person address, and achieves a strong, taut rendering of poetry, as, for example, in the book of Psalms. In a passage such as Deut 5, we notice one or two noncurrent words and phrases—such as "I enjoin on you," "goods of all sorts which you did not garner," "wonders, great and dire,"—but for the most part it is a straightforward, clean, and effective version which is well calculated to encourage biblical studies by both laity and clergy in the Roman communion. In some of the Old Testament narrative passages, the unaffected style is particularly effective. Here, for example, is part of the story of Elisha and the Shunammite woman in 2 Kings 4: 18–24:

> The day came when the child was old enough to go out to his father among the reapers. "My head hurts," he complained to his father. "Carry him to his mother," the father said to a servant. The servant picked him up and carried him to his mother; he stayed with her until noon, when he died in her lap. The mother took him upstairs, and laid him on the bed of the man of God. Closing the door on him, she went out and called to her husband, "Let me have a servant and a donkey. I must go quickly to the man of God, and I will be back." "Why are you going to him today?" he asked. "It is neither the new moon, nor the sabbath." But she bade him good-bye, and when the donkey was saddled said to her servant, "Lead on! Do not stop my donkey unless I tell you to."

The urgency of the distraught mother comes through very clearly, and the simple force of the Hebrew is conveyed with great fidelity.

In the New Testament, the style is more consecutive, less staccato than in the NEB, largely because of a greater readiness to use conjunctions, participial phrases, and subordinate clauses. This shows itself in a narrative like that of the Parable of the Wise and Foolish Virgins:

NEB When that day comes, the Kingdom of Heaven will be like this. There were ten girls who took their lamps and went out to meet the bridegroom. Five of them were foolish and five prudent; when the foolish ones took their lamps, they took no oil with them, but the others took flasks of oil with their lamps. As the bridegroom was late in coming they all dozed off to sleep. But at midnight a cry was heard: "Here is the bridegroom! Come out to meet him." With that the girls all got up and trimmed their lamps.

NAB The reign of God can be likened to ten bridesmaids, who took their torches and went out to welcome the groom. Five of them were foolish, while the other five were sensible. The foolish ones in taking their torches, brought no oil along, but the sensible ones took flasks of oil as well as their torches. The bridegroom delayed his coming, so they all began to nod, then to fall asleep. At midnight, someone shouted, "The groom is here! Come out and greet him!" At the outcry, all the virgins woke up and got their torches ready.

There can be little doubt that in many small ways the American is linguistically more conservative then the British. "Can be likened" is not so idiomatic as "will be like"; "torches" is not so common on either side of the Atlantic as "lamps"; and, a little further on, "dealers" is more formal than "shop"—though an American would of course say "store." The difference between the two reveals itself even more clearly in the argumentative passages of Paul's letters, as at the beginning of Rom 8:

NEB The conclusion of the matter is this: there is no condemnation for those who are united with Christ Jesus, because in Christ Jesus, the life-giving law of the Spirit has set you free from the law of sin and death. What the law could never do, because our lower nature robbed it of all potency, God has done: by sending his own Son in a form like that of our own sinful nature, and as a sacrifice for sin, he has passed judgement against sin within that very nature, so that the commandment of the law may find fulfilment in us, whose conduct, no longer under the control of our lower nature, is directed by the Spirit.

NAB There is no condemnation now for those who are in Christ Jesus. The law of the Spirit, the spirit of life in Christ Jesus, has freed you from the law of sin and death. The law was powerless because of its weakening by the flesh. Then God sent his son in the likeness of sinful flesh as a sin offering, thereby condemning sin in the flesh, so that the just demands of the law might be fulfilled in us who live, not according to the flesh, but according to the spirit.

The British version is more effective, more communicative (and in this particular passage more consecutive in literary style) than the American, simply because it gets away from the original Pauline sentence structure and concentrates on getting the ideas across—but it lays itself open to the charge of being interpretative and paraphrastic, which the members of the Catholic Biblical Association were particularly concerned to avoid. Since they were producing a public version, one to be used in the liturgy as well as in the home, they were right to be sensitive on this point. And the American decision to use modern English second-person forms of address more than compensates for its greater linguistic conservatism in lesser matters.

The overall significance of the NAB lies, in the present writer's opinion, in three major considerations. First, the Confraternity took advantage of the 1943 Encyclical to get back to the original languages. The domination of the Roman Church by the Vulgate has at last been broken. The gyrations of Ronald Knox in trying to argue the case for the Vulgate as the proper basis of translation for the Bible in English now appear quite ludicrous. Thus the great gulf between Roman and Protestant biblical scholarship has been bridged. Even the small but important fact that the NAB uses the common forms of Old Testament names reinforces this happy new situation. Second, the inclusion of such familiar Protestant names as Frank Cross and J. A. Sanders in the list of translators is a reminder that Catholic and Protestant scholars now work with identical views as regards the canons of the art of translating. The third is a point which was already strongly made by the appearance of the Catholic edition of the Revised Standard Version—that there is no longer any justification for a threefold division of the Canon into Old Testament, Apocrypha, and New Testament. The Old Testament does include Sirach, and Wisdom, and Tobit, and Maccabees, and the rest; and "The English Bible" should now clearly exhibit this fact.

The end of the matter, then, is this: we have just completed a remarkable century of biblical translation. It was in February 1870 that the resolution for the revision of the King James Version was moved in the Convocation of Canterbury, and this led to the English Revised Version and the American Standard Version, and these, in turn, to the Revised Standard Version, the Jerusalem Bible, the New English Bible, and the New American Bible. The long reign of the King James Version has been ended in all the major communions. To read publicly the King James Version of 2 Cor 5: 11–6:2, a truly noble passage, has become impossible, because we do not know what intonations to employ, since we no longer know what the translators were trying to say—whatever it was, they did not say it. But we still do not have a version which can replace the King James everywhere in the English-speaking world. The version which comes nearest to this is the Revised Standard Version in its Catholic edition. But the unity of the English language and the possession of one English Bible have gone together since the time of Wycliffe—with, it should be added, special thanks to Challoner. The next stage of the present task is surely, then, already in sight: it is to complete our own century of translations with a new version "not justly to be excepted against" (as Miles Smith said when he introduced the King James Version) in any land or in any church. This would fittingly crown our own century of translation, just as the 1611 version crowned and fulfilled the labors of the sixteenth century. With the present splendid but competing versions to hand, the councils of churches in Canada, the United States, Australasia, and Great Britain should call upon the churches of the English-speaking world to set a new generation of scholars to work in Australia, New Zealand, Africa, India, in the Caribbean, Britain, North America—wherever English is spoken,—to produce a new version which should not be Catholic or Protestant (nor, in the Hebrew Scriptures, Jewish) but common to us all. It would be based not on the Vulgate but the original languages: it would contain not the Jewish-Protestant Canon but the larger, richer Canon of the Vulgate, and it would be rendered into not British nor American but World Standard English, for the benefit of all.

For whether we live in Boston, Massachusetts, or Boston, Lincolnshire, in London, Ontario, or London, England, in Bridgetown, Barbados or Melbourne, Australia, whether we are Christian, Jew, or Gentile, we are all, by virtue of being English-speaking, culturally the descendants of Adam and Eve. As a result we draw a bow at a venture, we cherish the apple of our eye, we seek the pearl of great price, and we know full well that we are our brother's keeper. The Bible will never again in the future influence the culture of the English-speaking peoples as it has done in the past, and perhaps it is well that it should not. But we who are the inheritors of this great tradition, stretching from Caedmon and Alfred the Great to S. H. Hooke, C. H. Dodd, Luther Weigle, Louis Hartman, and others who are happily still with us, should not now let the tradition dissipate into merely regional versions. "The English Bible" is, apart from the English language itself, probably the strongest cultural link which unites all English-speaking peoples; thus, in a world which is fast becoming one technologically, the unity of religious and literary culture takes on a new and greater significance. It must not be only our scientists who have symbols in common. Moreover, splendid and remarkable as the new versions are, none of them has all the virtues; they can all gain immeasurably from each other. We ought therefore to put our minds to the task afresh; for no man, not even a biblical translator, having once put his hand to the plow, can afford to look back until the task is fully accomplished. And this side of the Kingdom of God, that will never be.

Notes

[1] *I and II Chronicles, Introduction, Translation, and Notes*, AB, New York: Doubleday, 1965.

[2] "The Lively Oracles," *Queen's Quarterly* 77 (Autumn 1970), 333–48.

[3] *The Lollard Bible*, Cambridge, England, 1920, pp. 139–40, 143–45. (For the earlier period, cf the same writer's *Sidelights on the Anglo-Saxon Church*, London, 1962).

[4] Cf also R. W. Chambers, "On the Continuity of English Prose," an Introduction to Harpsfield's *Life and Death of Sir Thomas Moore*, London: Oxford University Press, 1932, pp. xci–xcii.

[5] There is some indirect evidence that it also circulated in Scotland. A Lowland Scots version was prepared as late as the beginning of the sixteenth century, but it appears never to have circulated because it was overtaken by the appearance of printed versions of Tyndale's New Testament, which thus also took over the role of introducing Standard English into Scotland—which was, it should be remembered, still politically and socially a very separate country from England. The Bible in Standard English was for centuries one of the strongest cultural links between the two. Cf Deanesly, *Lollard Bible*, p. 359, and the reference below to the Geneva Version.

[6] Cf C. C. Butterworth, *The Literary Lineage of the King James' Bible*, Philadelphia, 1941, pp. 46–47.

[7] Cf B. F. Westcott, *A General View of the History of the English Bible*, 3d ed. rev. by H. A. Wright, London, 1905, p. 158.

[8] *Essays in Appreciation*, Boston, 1936.

[9] The Geneva Version was officially accepted by the General Assembly of the Kirk (1560) and was the first Bible to be printed in Scotland (1579). Cf F. F. Bruce, *The English Bible*, London, 1961, pp. 91–92.

[10] New Testament, 1881; Old Testament, 1885; Apocrypha, 1895; American Standard Version, 1901.

[11] *William F. Moulton: A Memoir*, by W. Fiddian Moulton, with a chapter, "Biblical Work and Opinions" by James Hope Moulton, London, 1899, pp. 101–2. Billingsgate is both the name of the great London fish market and also of the strong language used by its porters.

[12] The same edition was authorized for use in the United States by the imprimatur of Cardinal Cushing in May 1966. Cardinal Cushing also contributed a foreword to the American edition of the Catholic RSV.

[13] The principles underlying the revision are given in two pamphlets: "An Introduction to the Revised Standard Version of the New Testament," 1946; and "An Introduction to the Revised Standard Version of the Old Testament," 1952. Cf Luther Weigle, "English Versions since 1611," in *The Cambridge History of the Bible: The West from the Reformation to the Present Day*, ed. S. L. Greenslade, Cambridge, England, 1963. Dean Weigle was Chairman of the Revision Committee.

[14] The explanation for much of the translation of the passage is to be found in G. R. Driver's contribution to *In Memoriam Paul Kahle* (eds. M. Black and G. Fohrer, Berlin, 1968) entitled "Isaiah 52: 13–53: 12; The Servant of the Lord." The article proposes many brilliant linguistic theories and not a few conjectural emendations. Whether they should have been accepted to the degree that they have in NEB is very questionable.

Henry Snyder Gehman
Princeton Theological Seminary

Peregrinations in Septuagint Lexicography

In the year 1755, there appeared in London in two volumes folio a monumental work, in which "lexicography" is defined as "the art or practice of writing dictionaries." On the same page a "lexicon" is described as "a Dictionary; a book teaching the significance of words." We can hardly say that there is anything unusual in these two explanations. The meaning of "lexicographer," however, is expressed in more vigorous terms: "A writer of dictionaries; a harmless drudge that busies himself in tracing the original, and detailing the signification of words." In this manner, Samuel Johnson describes himself as well as a number of plodding men who had preceded him in lexicography and those who have been making dictionaries ever since his day. In the year 1756, however, there was published a smaller work, abstracted from the folio, in which a lexicographer, "a writer of dictionaries," is called "a harmless drudge," without any qualifying relative clause. Perhaps everyone who works in lexicography has to accept this characterization of himself as "a harmless drudge," for it is only by unremitting toil that anything can be accomplished in enterprises of this nature.

As the basis for a Septuagint lexicon, it is necessary, in the first place, to have an adequate word list. In this connection may be mentioned Konrad Kircher, who was born in Augsburg, and served as a pastor in Donauwörth and later at Jaxthausen. Apparently be had scholarly interests, and he dedicated seven years to a work known as *Concordantiae Veteris Testamenti Graecae Ebraeis Vocibus Respondentes Polychrēstoi* (Frankfurt, 1607). In this concordance, the Hebrew words are arranged in alphabetical order, and under each are found the various Greek expressions with citations. A Greek *Index Alphabeticus* was included so that the Greek words could be found in the concordance. The impetus, however, for LXX lexicography in the Western world may be ascribed to Abraham Tromm, who was born at Groningen, Netherlands, in 1633. His most famous work was *Concordantiae Graecae Versionis Vulgo Dictae LXX Interpretum, cujus voces secundum ordinem elementorum sermonis Graeci digestae recensentur, contra atque in opere Kircheriano factum fuerat. Leguntur Hic Praeterea Voces Graecae pro Hebraicis redditae ab antiquis omnibus Veteris Testamenti Interpretibus, quorum non nisi fragmenta extant, Aquila, Symmacho, Theodotione et aliis, quorum maximam partem nuper in lucem edidit Domnus Bernardus de Montfaucon.* The drudgery of Tromm, however, did not immediately come into print. The approval of the theological faculty of Groningen was given November 17, 1710, but then for seven years the work lay dormant. Later, in a brief note dated July 4, 1717, he explained the delay in publication and shortly afterward wrote the preface at Groningen, July 24, 1717. Finally the Concordance in two tomes folio was published at Amsterdam and Utrecht in 1718. (Volume I consists of 1008 pages and a lexicon to the Hexapla of 70 pages and an index of scriptural references; vol. II contains 716 pages and an index of Hebrew and Aramaic words of 134 pages.) At that time, Tromm was eighty-four years of age, and two years later he died. Apparently the study of biblical languages had done him no harm.

This leads us to Johann Christian Biel, who was born at Braunschweig in 1687. After having studied at Leipzig and Rostock, he took up theology for one year at Helmstädt. His most important work was *Novus Thesaurus Philologicus sive Lexicon in LXX et Alios Interpretes et Scriptores Apocryphos Veteris Testamenti*, but his labors were not destined to reach the press during his lifetime. After all this drudgery, he died in Braunschweig in 1745 at the early age of fifty-eight. His work, however, was taken up by Esdras Heinrich Mutzenbecher, a pastor who was born at Hamburg in 1744. Under his editorship, the lexicon was published in three parts at The Hague in 1779–80. Mutzenbecher died at Oldenberg in 1801, when he was only fifty-seven years of age.

Next on the scene appeared Johann Friedrich Schleusner, who was born at Leipzig, January 16, 1759, and studied at the university of his native city. He had a rather remarkable career. At the age of twenty-four, he was the morning preacher at the University Church in Leipzig. In 1785, he was called to Göttingen, where as *professor extraordinarius* he lectured on the exegesis of the Old and the New Testaments as well as on dogmatics and homiletics. In 1790, he was named *ordentlicher Professor* and in 1795, he became *Probst* of the *Schlosskirche* and *ordentlicher Professor* of theology at the University of Wittenberg. At the time of his death in that city on

February 21, 1831, he was the director of the royal *Predigerseminar*, the second incumbent in that position.

Biel had relied entirely upon his predecessor Tromm, whose misunderstandings and errors he faithfully transmitted. In Biel's work, many words were lacking; the connection of words in phrases was ignored, and textual criticism was neglected. Consequently, it was as an object of gratitude that Schleusner determined, first of all, to prepare a supplement to the lexicon of Biel. Beginning in 1784 and continuing for a decade, he published his various investigations of the vocabulary of the LXX, including the Apocrypha and the Hexaplaric fragments. In his researches, he studied classical usage and also employed the lexica of Suidas (tenth century A.D.) and Hesychius (fifth century A.D. ?) as well as ecclesiastical dictionaries, such as the famous one of Johann Casper Schwyzer (Suicerus), *Thesaurus Ecclesiasticus e Patribus Graecis* (Amsterdam, 1682). He also made improvements and additions to Montfaucon's edition of Origen's *Hexapla*. These extensive studies eventually came to a climax in his lexicon: *Novus Thesaurus Philologico-criticus sive Lexicon in LXX et Reliquos Interpretes Graecos ac Scriptores Apocryphos Veteris Testamenti* (Leipzig, 1820–21). In his introduction, Schleusner makes reference to his collating the rough and undigested mass of variants—or even errors—assembled by Holmes. He calls his labors: "*in me molestum ac taediosum negotium*" ("a business annoying and tedious to me"). Without knowing the term, he refers to himself as "a harmless drudge."

The lexicon of Schleusner still has great value for LXX studies, and cannot be ignored as an antiquated piece of work. Under each entry, he places the Hebrew (or Aramaic) roots or words in alphabetical order, provided he is not dealing with the Apocrypha, and defines the Hebrew and Aramaic and the corresponding Greek words. Often he makes some critical observations or explains how the translator came to his interpretation. He may suggest what word the translator read in the Hebrew text or how he treated his original. He often displays an uncanny insight into problems and interpretations, but the remarkable thing is that, with all his extensive theological interests and duties, he was able to compose the lexicon at all. It is written in Latin, the universal language of scholarship at that time. Unfortunately, in the present age, when many students of divinity have little Greek, less Hebrew, and no Latin, it remains for some a sealed book.

Even though we do not have a modern lexicon to the LXX, we cannot say that we are without help. The *Concordance* to the LXX, edited by E. Hatch and H. A. Redpath (Oxford, 1897–1906), enables the student to assemble the evidence for the translation of a certain Hebrew or Aramaic word or root in various books of the OT. Accordingly, it can often take the place of a LXX lexicon. Occasional help in meanings can be found in the notes of F. Field's edition of the *Fragments of Origen's Hexapla* (Oxford, 1875). Naturally we can find a great deal of aid in Liddell and Scott's *Greek Lexicon* (new ed.; Oxford, 1940; Supplement, 1968), but frequently it is unsatisfactory. Once in a while definitions are available in E. A. Sophocles, *Greek Lexicon of the Roman and Byzantine Periods* (B.C. 146–A.D. 1100) (Boston, 1870), but generally the student turns away in disappointment.

Since the Greek of the LXX represents the *koinē* of the third to the first century B.C., we cannot ignore the evidence of the papyri, and in this connection we have F. Preisigke, *Wörterbuch der Griechischen Papyrusurkunden* . . . (Berlin, 1925–31), and numerous word lists in various publications of papyri. Occasionally help is found in J. H. Moulton and G. Milligan, *The Vocabulary of the Greek Testament Illustrated from the Papyri and Other Non-literary Sources* (London, 1914–29). Since the LXX had a definite influence upon the language of the NT, we cannot ignore NT lexicography. In this connection mention should be made of G. Kittel, *Theologisches Wörterbuch zum NT* (Stuttgart, 1935—); W. Bauer, *Griechisch-Deutsches Wörterbuch zu den Schriften des Neuen Testaments und der übrigen urchristlichen Literatur* (5th ed., Berlin, 1958), and the English translation by W. F. Arndt and F. W. Gingrich, published by the University of Chicago Press. Further useful tools are W. F. Moulton and A. S. Geden, *A Concordance to the Greek New Testament* (Edinburgh, 1897), and A. Schmoller, *Handkonkordanz zum griechischen Neuen Testament* (8th ed., Stuttgart, 1949). Occasionally a non-classical usage in the LXX may be represented in the Church Fathers, and in this case some help is available in G. W. H. Lampe, *A Patristic Greek Lexicon* (Oxford, 1961–68). The lexicon of Hesychius gives numerous suggestions, and from time to time Suidas should be consulted.

There are times, however, when it is necessary to compare the LXX with MT in order to arrive at a reasonable interpretation. This is especially true when the idiom of the LXX is quite Hebraic, but this does not justify us in calling without qualification the vernacular of the LXX a Jewish-Greek dialect. As a result of his studies the writer has come to the conclusion that the *Vorlage* of the Greek translators was closer to MT than the emendations of various commentators and the notes in the *Biblia Hebraica* of R. Kittel would lead us to think. The LXX contains many literalisms, and some of these may imply that the Greek interpreters had a high regard for the exact letter, and some of the crudities of rendering may have such an origin. Yet surprisingly we often meet in the same verse or adjacent verses both literalism and extreme freedom of translation; at times, in observing this phenomenon, the reader of the LXX is reminded of the swing of a pendulum from one end of the arc to the other. Sometimes it appears that the interpreter was working under a tension between literalism and freedom of rendering. In this way, a certain balance of approach was maintained by the translator, but in this connection we should always observe the atmosphere of freedom in the LXX. We have good reason to believe that what the interpreters had in mind was to reproduce the sense of the original, even though they often were not facile translators. There are difficulties of rendering from one language to another, and this is an obstacle that the Alexandrian translators continually had to face.

For a number of years the writer conducted seminars on the LXX and LXX lexicography, and accordingly he began to compile a dictionary of LXX Greek. For some years with his graduate students he was able to make substantial progress on his venture, and most of the work compiled is now on microfilm and deposited in the Speer Library of the Princeton Theological Seminary. Unfortunately, however, for reasons of age he was forced to retire, and in consequence of having no students his work has been severely retarded. Beginning at this point we shall consider various phenomena of the vocabulary of the LXX as samples of what confronts the lexicographer,[1] but for reasons of space the range of citations will have to be limited.

Obviously there is no need of discussing words whose meaning follows normal classical usage or of considering transliterations and proper names. A number of words, however, may be chosen which reflect the character of the LXX vocabulary. In treating various words in their LXX sense, we have, moreover, to bear in mind that "the Seventy" were pioneers in biblical translation. The Greek language had to be adapted to express a realm of thought foreign to Hellenic culture and the Greek religion, and consequently the translators had to mold the language to express the concepts of the OT; in many instances, this involved them in introducing vestiges of Hebrew syntax into Greek, in using Greek words in a Hebraic sense, and in giving to certain vocables connotations which they did not have before. Generally, however, such a transformation or extension of the Greek vocabulary was not unreasonable and, in many instances, was developed under semantic principles.

The following survey of examples gleaned from the writer's collection of LXX words will consider some which represent a literalistic rendering, some which have received a Hebrew sense, and, finally, a few which have made a contribution to our religious vocabulary. In case the MT and the LXX chapter and verse numbers differ, those of the Greek are put in parentheses or brackets.

First may be considered a case where the translator misunderstood the root and produced a rendering which makes sense to the reader without violating the Greek idiom. Such a word is *marturion* ("testimony," "witness"), which is used to render *mô'ēd* (from the root *y'd*), "appointed time or place," "meeting." In interpreting *'hl mw'd* as *ē skēnē tou marturiou,* the translator derived the word from the root *'wd,* which in Hiphil means "testify," "bear witness." The instances of this translation are so numerous, especially in the Pentateuch, that there is no need to cite examples. It is important, however, to observe that in Ex 30: 36 the two Hebrew roots *y'd* and *'wd* occur in two adjacent phrases: *lpny h'dt b'hl mw'd* ("before the testimony in the tent of meeting"); in Greek, this appears as *apenanti tōn marturiōn en tē skēnē tou marturiou.* Apparently the interpreter saw in these two words only the root *'wd,* and it seems probable that here he did not intend to give *marturion* the Hebrew sense of "meeting." This usage, moreover, is found also in Joshua and Chronicles. In 1 Kings 8: 4, however, we twice have the expression *skēnōma tou marturiou,* but this hardly involves a change of interpretation, even though it be the sole instance of this combination.

In this connection should also be considered *marturion,* when it is not dependent upon *skēnē.* ——— 1 Sam 9: 24, *ky lmw'd šmwr-lk* ("for unto the appointed time hath it been kept for thee"): *oti eis marturion tetheitai soi.* ——— 13: 8, *šb't ymym lmw'd 'šr šmw'l* ("seven days according to the set time that Samuel had appointed"): *epta ēmeras tō marturiō ōs eipen samouēl.* ——— vs 11, *lmw'd hymym* ("within the days appointed"): *en tō marturiō tōn ēmerōn.* ——— 20:35, *lmw'd dwd* ("at the time appointed with David"): *eis to marturion daueid.* These four citations from 1 Sam evidently are cases of what was intended to be a literalistic translation resting, nevertheless, upon a misunderstanding of the root. It may, however, be asked whether here the interpreter had meant to give the noun *marturion* the Hebrew meaning "appointed time or place," "meeting," or whether he did not understand the word. On account of the consistent usage of *marturion* in the Pentateuch in the sense of "witness, testimony," it is possible that the translator did not fully understand the word, and rendered it mechanically or in traditional fashion; in other words, he let it go at that, and was satisfied with what he had accomplished in having made what appeared to him a literal rendering. Sometimes, in fact, it is necessary to compare MT with the Greek in order to understand the LXX.

From this, we may proceed to instances where Greek words received a Hebrew meaning.

ikanos ("sufficient," "adequate")

Under this word may be cited a Hebrew idiom found in the Origenian addition, 1 Sam 18: 30, *wyhy mdy ṣ'tm* ("and it came to pass as often as they went forth"): *kai egeneto aph ikanou exodias autōn.* The same idiom occurs in 2 Kings 4: 8, *wyhy mdy ʿbrw ysr šmh lʾkl-lḥm* ("and it came to pass that, as often as he passed by, he turned in thither to eat bread"): *kai egeneto aph ikanou tou eisporeuesthai auton exeklinen tou ekei phagein.* In both instances, through a literalism, the phrase *aph ikanou* assumed a Hebrew meaning it does not have in classical Greek.

potos, o ("drinking bout," "carousal")

In a literalistic rendering, this word is used to translate *mšth* ("feast," "banquet"). Different individuals made a *mšth* ("feast"): Abraham (Gen 19: 3); Pharaoh (Gen 40: 20); Samson (Judg 14: 10, 12, 17); Nabal (1 Sam 25: 36); David (2 Sam 3: 20); Solomon (1 Kings 3: 15); Esther (Esther 1: 9; 6: 14); Ahasuerus (Esther, 1: 5; 2: 18); the sons of Job (Job 1: 4–5). Qoheleth (7: 2[3]) says, "It is better to go to the house of mourning than to the house of *mšth* (*potos*)." Jeremiah (16: 8) was not to go to the house of *mšth* (*potos*). In all these passages, the literal meaning of the Hebrew root is reproduced, and *potos* receives a Hebrew coloring and has to be understood in the sense of "feast."

pronomē,ē ("foraging", "foray"; pl. "foraging parties," "plunder," "booty," "store," "provision")

In 1 Kings 9: 15 [also A] (10: 23, B), the narrative reads: "And this is the account of the *ms* [forced labor], which Solomon levied." In Greek *ms* is rendered *pronomē*; thus goes the Greek: *autē ēn ē pragmateia tēs pronomēs.* Clearly in this case, *pronomē* signifies the same as Hebrew *ms*; it has received a Hebrew meaning. It may be that the translator made the subtle suggestion that the corvée was a form of plunder. Yet this may not be entirely original, for Hesychius defines *pronomia: ta opheilomena tō axiōmati ē ē ek tōn nomōn exousia.* Apparently he recognizes in the expression an obligation of services to the state. At any rate, it is not necessary to assume that the translator read *habbaz* instead of *hammas.*

prostithēmi

Among its meanings is "add," and this signification adequately expressed the sense of *ysp* ("add"). A few examples by way of illustration may be drawn from the Pentateuch. For the Qal, cf Lev 22: 14, *wysp ḥmšytw ʿlyw* ("he shall add the fifth part of it unto it"): *kai prosthēsei to epipempton autou ep auto.* Cf also Lev 27: 13, 15, 19, 27. ——— Num 32: 14: *lspwt ʿwd ʿl ḥrwn ʾp-yhwh* ("to add still further to the fierce anger of YHWH"): *prostheinai eti epi ton thumon tēs orgēs kuriou.* ——— Deut 19: 9, *wyspt lk ʿwd šlš ʿrym* ("then thou shalt add three cities more for thee"): *kai prosthēseis sautō eti treis poleis.* The Niphal also is used in this sense: cf Ex 1: 10, *wnwsp gm-hwʾ ʿl-šnʾynw* ("they add themselves," i.e., "join themselves unto our enemies"): *prostethēsontai kai outoi pros tous upenantious.* For the adding of an inheritance, cf Num 36: 3–4, where *prostethēsetai* represents the Niphal of *ysp.*

A few examples of the Hiphil may also be cited: Gen 30: 24, *ysp yhwh ly bn 'ḥr* ("may YHWH add to me another son"): *prosthetō o theos moi uion eteron.* ——— Lev 5: 16, *w't-ḥmyštw ywsp ʿlyw* ("and the fifth of it [that is, of its value] he shall add to it"): *kai to epipempton prosthēsei ep auto.* Cf also Lev 5: 24 [6:5].

From this literal meaning of *prostithēmi*, it was easy in Hebrew fashion for the verb with a dependent infinitive to express repetition in the sense of "again." This usage is found in the Qal in a number of passages in which *prostithēmi* has assumed the Hebrew sense of repetition; when MT has the adverb *ʿwd*, it is represented by *eti.* ——— Gen 8: 12, *wl'-ysph šwb 'lyw ʿwd* ("and she [the dove] did not return to him anymore"): *kai ou prosetheto tou epistrepsai pros auton eti.* ——— 38: 26, *wl'-ysp ʿwd ldʿth* ("and he knew her again no more"): *kai ou prosetheto eti tou gnōnai autēn.* For a similar usage to render the Qal of *ysp*, cf Lev 26: 18; Num 11: 25, without dependent infinitive; 32: 15; Deut 5: 22[25]; 20: 8.

The verb *ysp* denoting repetition, however, in the Pentateuch has more examples of the Hiphil than of the Qal. The following may in this connection be cited: Gen 4: 2, *wtsp lldt* ("and again she bore"): *kai prosethēken tekein.* ——— 4: 12, *l'-tsp tt-kḥh lk* ("it shall no longer yield to you its strength"): *kai ou prosthēsei tēn ischun autēs dounai soi.* For a similar usage in Genesis, cf 8: 21; 18: 29; 37: 8; 44: 23. In Gen 25: 1, the verb *ysp* is followed by the *waw* consecutive and the imperfect tense: *wysp 'brhm wyqḥ 'šh* ("and Abraham took another wife"); in this case, the Greek sentence starts with the participle: *prosthemenos de Abraam elaben gunaika.* In both languages, the sense of "another" is implied in the sentence. For a similar construction, cf Gen 38: 5.

This sense of repetition in the Hiphil expressed by *prostithēmi* is found also in Ex 8: 25[29]; 9: 28, 34; 11: 6; 14: 13; Num 22: 15, 19, 25; Deut 3: 26; 13: 12[11]; 17: 16; 18: 16; 19: 20; 28: 68. In Num 22: 26, *wywsp ml'k-yhwh ʿbwr* ("and the angel of YHWH went further") is thus rendered: *kai prosetheto o aggelos tou theou kai apelthōn.* In Ex 10: 28, there is a negative, *hšmr lk 'l-tsp r'wt pny* ("take heed to thyself, do not see my face again"): *proseche seautō eti prostheinai idein mou to prosōpon.* In this case the LXX does not render the negative, but evidently it is felt in the context in the verb *proseche.* The negative is found, however, in two minuscules, in the Syro-Hexaplar, and in the Bohairic (*vid.*). In Ex 5: 7, MT has the root *'sp* for *ysp: l' t'spwn ltt tbn lʿm*; here, however, the Samaritan text writes *twsypwn*:

("ye shall no more give the people straw"): *ouketi prostethēsetai didonai achuron tō laō.*

In Judg 2: 3, a variant reading is indicated by the *hypolemniscus* (⁒), which is not represented in the MT: *ou prosthēsō tou metoikisai ton laon on eipa/tou exolethreusai* ("I will not again resettle [or, deport] the people whom I determined to destroy utterly"). It may also be noted that the Hebraic use of *prostithēmi* occurs in the NT, and accordingly is an example of the importance of the LXX for the vocabulary and syntax of NT Greek.

In connection with *prostithēmi* for *ysp* may be investigated *sph* ("snatch away"; intransitive, "come to destruction or to an end"); in Syriac, however, *sp' means* "collect," "heap together," while in Jewish Aramaic, the root signifies "collect," "disappear." Two examples of the Qal may be cited: Num 32: 14, *lspwt ʿwd ʿl ḥrwn ʾp-yhwh* ("to add still more to the fierce anger of YHWH"): *prostheinai eti epi ton thumon tēs orgēs kuriou.* ——— Is 30: 1, *lmʿn spwt ḥṭʾt ʿl-ḥṭʾt* ("in order to add sin to sin"): *prostheinai amartias eph amartias.* In both cases, however, it has been proposed to read *sepet* (from *ysp*) instead of *s^epôt.* Apparently the LXX gave the root *sph* this rendering by association with *ysp*, unless the translators knew one of the Aramaic meanings.

In Amos 3: 15, however, a different problem confronts us: *wspw btym rbym* ("and the great [or many] houses shall come to an end"): *kai prostethēsontai eteroi oikoi polloi.* In the context of the LXX, this can mean: "And shall be added [to destruction] many other houses," unless we assume the possibility that the verb received a Hebrew connotation.

This brings us to the Niphal of *sph.* ——— 1 Sam 12: 25, *gm-ʾtm gm-mlkkm tsphw* ("ye shall be swept away, both ye and your king"): *kai umeis kai o basileus umōn prostethēsesthe.* In the context there is a reference to a calamity, and accordingly the Greek may signify: "both ye and your king shall be handed over, or added [to destruction]." Obviously the verb in this context has received a Hebrew sense. A similar usage is found in 1 Sam 26: 10, *wnsph* ("and he be swept away, or perish") *kai prostethē.* This verse refers to a battle, and the Greek means the same as the Hebrew; perhaps there is a semantic development from "being added or delivered [to destruction]" to "to be swept away." Such a meaning is also encountered in 1 Sam 27: 1, *ʿth ʾessāpeh ywm-ʾḥd byd-šʾwl* ("I shall now be swept away, or perish, one day by the hand of Saul"): *nun prostethēsomai en ēmera mia eis cheiras saoul.* In this example, the difficulty apparently is eliminated through the preposition *eis*: "Now I shall be deliverd one day into the hands of Saul." In this case, the sense of the Greek is clear.

The Hebrew root *ʾsp* ("gather") is also rendered literally by *prostithēmi*, and when the Niphal signifies that a deceased person is gathered to his people, there is no problem; for example, Abraham in Gen 25: 8, *wy'sp 'l-'myw* ("and he was gathered to his people"): *kai prosetethē pros ton laon autou.* For other examples of this usage, cf Gen 25: 17; 35: 29; 49: 29, 33; Num 20: 24, 26; 27: 13; 31: 2.

While the root *'sp* has a basic connotation of "gather," it also developed the sense of "gather and take away," "remove," "withdraw," and, finally, "destroy." In this connection should be noted Judg 18: 25, *w'spth npšk wnpš bytk* ("and thou lose thy life with the lives of thy household"): *prosthēsousin psuchēn* [*sou*, A] *kai tēn psuchēn tou oikou sou.* Here the Greek verb obviously has the Hebrew meaning "destroy." A similar interpretation is met in 1 Sam 15: 6, *pn-'spk 'mw* ("lest I destroy you with him"): *mē prosthō se met autou.* In such passages, it may at times be difficult to understand the Greek without making a comparison with the Hebrew text.

In connection with this usage of *prostithēmi* having this Hebrew meaning of *'sp* should be observed a few cases of *sunagō* which has assumed a Hebrew signification. ——— 1 Sam 14: 19, *'sp ydk* ("withdraw thy hand"): *sunagage tas cheiras sou.* In line with this interpretation may also be considered *aposunagō* as a rendering of *'sp.* ——— 2 Kings 5: 11, *w'sp hmṣr'* ("and recover the leper"): *kai aposunaxei to lepron* ("he will remove the leprosy"); in vss 3, 6, 7 the verb *aposunagō* means "to remove" a person from his leprosy—that is, to cure him of leprosy.

Finally, it should be noted that in Sir 14: 4, the verb *sunagō* is employed in two senses in the same verse: *mwn' npšw yqbṣ l'ḥr* ("he that withholdeth from himself, gathereth for another"): *o sunagōn apo tēs psuchēs autou sunagei allois* ("he that withholdeth from himself, gathereth for others"). In this passage the first Greek verb has received a Hebrew sense, while in the second instance the Greek meaning has been retained.

skēptron, to ("staff," "stick")

As a translation of the Hebrew *šbṭ* ("rod," "staff"), the LXX follows normal Greek usage. In Hebrew, *šbṭ*, however, also means "tribe," and this sense has been adopted by the LXX. ——— 1 Sam 2: 28, *mkl-šbṭy yśr'l* ("from all the tribes of Israel"): *ek pantōn tōn skēptrōn Israēl.* ——— 9: 21, *mqṭny šbṭy yśr'l* ("of the smallest of the tribes of Israel"): *tou mikrou skēptrou phulēs Israēl.* In this verse, *šbṭ* is represented also in the second sentence by *skēptron.* ——— 10: 19, *lšbṭykm* ("by your tribes"): *kata ta skēptra umōn.* ——— 10: 20, *kl-šbṭy yśr'l wylkd šbṭ bnymn* ("all the tribes of Israel, and the tribe of Benjamin was taken"): *panta ta skēptra Israēl kai kataklēroutai skēptron Beniamein.*

In vs 21, *skēptron* represents *šbṭ*, while *eis phulas* stands for *lmšpḥt* (pl., Q). For further examples of *skēptron* as a rendering of *šbṭ*, cf 1 Sam 15:

17; 1 Kings 8: 16; 11: 13, 31, 32, 35, 36; 12: 20–21. While this usage does not occur in the NT, it is found in some of the Patristic writers.

sumphōneō ("be in harmony," "make an agreement")

This verb is used in Gen 14: 3 to render *ḥbr* ("unite," "be joined"): *kl-'lh ḥbrw* ("all these joined forces"): *pantes outoi sunephōnēsan.* While this may be regarded as a free translation of *ḥbr*, in this case *sumphōneō* has a Hebrew meaning: "to join forces." The development of this military sense can easily be comprehended in the context.

sunaptō ("join together," "connect," "approach," "make contact")

This verb is employed to render the Hebrew *dbq*, which in the Hiphil developed the sense "pursue closely," which led to the meaning "overtake." ——— 1 Sam 14: 22, *wydbqw gm-hmh 'ḥryhm bmlḥmh* ("they followed hard after them in the battle"): *kai sunaptousin kai autoi opisō autōn eis polemon.* ——— 31: 2, *wydbqw plštym 't-š'wl* ("and the Philistines followed hard upon [or overtook] Saul"): *kai sunaptousin allophuloi tō Saoul.* ——— 2 Sam 1: 6, *wb'ly hpršym hdbqhw* ("and the horsemen pressed hard upon him"): *kai oi ipparchai sunēpsan autō.* In these cases, *sunaptō* received the Hebrew sense of *dbq*, and should be rendered "pursue closely," "overtake."

sunechō ("hold or keep together," "enclose," "compass," "constrain")

Hebrew *ṣwr* means "confine," "shut up," and "besiege." An example of the sense of "besiege" occurs in 1 Sam 23: 8, *lṣwr 'l-dwd w'l-'nšyw* ("to besiege David and his men"): *sunechein ton Daueid kai tous andras autou.* In this case, *sunechō* represents *ṣwr*, from which it has taken over a Hebrew shade of meaning. In the context, however, such a semantic development is easy to understand.

suniēmi

From the literal meaning "bring together," "set together" came that of "perceive," "observe," "understand." This verb, however, under the influence of Hebrew can have another development in LXX Greek.

As a translation of *śkl* in the Qal ("be prudent," "circumspect"), it may also signify "deal wisely," "prosper," "have success." One such example is found in a Hexaplaric addition in 1 Sam 18: 30, *śkl dwd mkl 'bdy š'wl* ("David had more success than all the servants of Saul"): *sunēken Daueid para pantas tous doulous saoul.* Obviously the Greek verb here has the same meaning as its Hebrew counterpart.

In the Hiphil, the root *śkl* means "consider," "ponder"; from this is derived the sense "have insight, or understanding"; then it has the signification "act circumspectly or prudently," whence it finally denotes either "to prosper" or "to deal wisely."[2] ——— Deut 29: 8 [9], *lmʿn tśkylw ʾt kl-ʾšr tʿśwn* ("that ye may cause to prosper, or deal wisely in, all that ye do"): *ina sunēte panta osa poiēsete* ("that ye may bring to a successful conclusion, or cause to prosper, all that ye will do"). ——— Josh 1: 7, *lmʿn tśkyl bkl ʾšr tlk* ("that thou mayest have success whithersoever thou goest"); vs 8, *wʾz tśkyl* ("and then thou shalt have success"): *ina sunēs en pasin ois ean prassēs . . . kai tote sunēseis.* ——— 1 Sam 18: 5, *bkl ʾšr yšlḥnw šʾwl yśkyl* ("whithersoever Saul sent him, he had success"): in a Hexaplaric addition, *en pasin ois apesteilen auton Saoul sunēken.* ——— 18: 14, *wyhy dwd lkl-drkyw mśkyl* ("and David acted wisely" or "was successful in all his ways"): *kai ēn Daueid en pasais tais odois autou suniōn.* It should be noted that the LXX, like MT, uses the participle. ——— 18: 15, *wyrʾ šʾwl ʾšr-hwʾ mśkyl mʾd* ("and when Saul saw that he was very successful"): *kai eiden Saoul ōs autos suniei sphodra.* ——— 1 Kings 2: 3, *lmʿn tśkyl ʾt kl-ʾšr tʿśh* ("that thou mayest cause to prosper, that thou mayest prosper in" or "that thou mayest deal wisely in all that thou doest"): *ina sunēseis a poiēseis* ("that thou mayest bring to a successful conclusion, or cause to prosper, whatever thou wilt do"). ——— 2 Kings 18: 7, *bkl ʾšr-yṣʾ yśkyl* ("whithersoever he went forth, he prospered"): *en pasin ois epoiei sunēken.* ——— Is 52: 13, *hnh yśkyl ʿbdy* ("Behold, my servant shall prosper, or deal wisely"): *idou sunēsei o pais mou.* ——— Jer 23: 5, *wmlk mlk whśkyl* ("he shall reign as a king and prosper, or deal wisely"): *kai basileusei basileus kai sunēsei.* From these examples, it is obvious that the verb *suniēmi* took on a Hebrew connotation in the LXX.

sunteleia, ē

This noun has a number of meanings, of which only two need to be cited in this connection: "completion," "completed action."

In 1 Kings 6: 25 (24) the two cherubim had *qṣb ʾḥd* ("one form"). Since the verb *qṣb* means "cut," "cut off," we can understand how the noun *qeṣeb* developed the signification of "form" from "to cut." At any rate, in this passage *qṣb ʾḥd* is rendered *sunteleia mia*, and in the context is to be interpreted in the Hebrew sense: "one form." To explain this usage, we may start with the verb *sunteleō* ("bring to an end, complete") and one connotation of *sunteleia* ("completion"). We may postulate this semantic development: "completion" can be understood as "final shape," or "form." At any rate, *sunteleia* has assumed the Hebrew meaning "form" in this passage.

sōzō (in the passive, "to be saved from death, kept alive, preserved"; "to come safe to a place")

In the Niphal, *mlṭ* signifies "slip away," "escape," "be delivered." In a number of passages, where the Niphal of *mlṭ* is rendered by *sōzō* in the passive, it may be difficult to determine whether the verb means "to be delivered" or "to escape," since the two senses inevitably blend into each other. In many cases, however, the translator gave *sōzō* the connotation of "escape"; but first should be investigated instances where the regular Greek meaning may have been used in a free translation; these may be designated as borderline cases, where the concept of "escape" and "deliver oneself" are equally good. ——— 1 Sam 19: 12, *wybrḥ wymlṭ* ("and fled and escaped"): *kai ephugen kai sōzētai.* ——— vs. 18, *wdwd brḥ wymlṭ* ("now David fled and escaped"): *kai Daueid ephugen kai diesōthē,* (*esōthē,* A). ——— Esther 4: 13, *'l-tdmy bnpšk lhmlṭ* ("think not with thyself that thou shalt escape"): *mē eipēs seautē oti sōthēsē monē.* ——— Job 1: 15 and 16, *w'mlṭh rq-'ny lbdy* ("and I only am escaped"): *sōtheis de egō monos ēlthon.* ——— Is 20: 6, *w'yk nmlṭ 'nḥnw* ("and how shall we escape?"): *kai pōs ēmeis sōthēsometha.* ——— Jer 32[39]: 4, *l' ymlṭ myd hkśdym* ("and shall not escape out of the hand of the Chaldeans"): *ou mē sōthē ek cheiros tōn chaldaiōn.* ——— 34[41]: 3, *w'th l' tmlṭ mydw,* ("and thou shalt not escape out of his hand"): *kai su ou mē sōthēs ek cheiros autou.* ——— 38[45]: 18 and 23, *w'th l'-tmlṭ mydm* ("and thou shalt not escape out of their hand"): *kai su ou mē sōthēs.*

In passages, however, where motion is implied or a destination is indicated, the Hebrew meaning of "escape" is obvious in the Greek verb. ——— Gen 19: 17, *hmlṭ 'l-npšk . . . hhrh hmlṭ* ("escape for thy life . . . escape to the mountain"): *sōzōn sōze tēn seautou psuchēn . . . eis to oros sōzou.* ——— 1 Sam 27: 1, *'yn-ly ṭwb ky hmlṭ 'mlṭ 'l-'rṣ plštym* ("there is nothing better for me than that I should escape into the land of the Philistines"): *kai ouk estin moi agathon ean mē sōthō eis gēn allophulōn.* ——— 1 Kings 18: 40, when the prophets of Baal were seized, Elijah said *'yš 'l-ymlṭ mhm* ("let not one of them escape"): *mētheis sōthētō ex autōn.* ——— 19: 17, in connection with slaying by Hazael and Jehu, *hnmlṭ mḥrb hz'l . . . whnmlṭ mḥrb yhw'* ("let him that escapeth from the sword of Hazael . . . and him that escapeth from the sword of Jehu"): *ton sōzomenon ek romphaias Azaēl . . . kai ton sōzomenon ek romphaias eiou.* ——— 20[21]: 20, *wymlṭ bn-hdd mlk 'rm 'l-sws wpršym* ("and Benhadad, king of Aram, escaped on a horse with horsemen"): *kai sōzetai uios Ader basileus Surias eph ippou ippeōs.* ——— 2 Kings 19: 37, *whmh nmlṭw 'rṣ 'rrṭ* ("and they escaped into the land of Ararat"): *kai autoi esōthēsan eis gēn Ararath.* ——— 2 Chron 16: 7, *'l-kn nmlṭ ḥyl mlk-'rm mydk* ("therefore is the host of the king of Aram escaped out of thy hand"): *dia touto esōthē dunamis Surias apo tēs cheiros sou.* ——— Jer 41[48]: 15, *nmlṭ bšmnh 'nšym mpny ywḥnn wylk 'l-bny 'mwn* ([and Ishmael] "escaped from Johanan with eight men and went to the Ammonites"):

esōthē sun oktō anthrōpois kai ōcheto pros tous uious Ammōn. ——— 48[31]: 19, *š'ly-ns-wnmlṭh* ("ask him that fleeth and her that escapeth"): *kai erōtēson pheugonta kai sōzomenon* ("and ask him that is fleeing and him that is escaping"). ——— Ezek 17: 18, in referring to Zedekiah, *l' ymlṭ* ("he shall not escape"): *mē sōthēsetai*; in this case "escape" and "be delivered" are very close in meaning, but in the context the sense seems to be "escape."

trissos, -ē, -on ("threefold")

In 1 Kings 9: 22 occurs the combination *śryw wšlšyw* ("his princes and his captains"). This verse is not represented in the Old Greek, but in the Origenian addition of this passage introduced from Aquila we have the words *archontes autou kai trissoi autou.* In the context *trissoi*, which is a literalistic rendering of the plural of *šlyš*, has to mean "officers," "adjutants," or "captains," as in Hebrew. In 2 Chron 8: 9, the plural of this noun is rendered *dunatoi*; this shows that the translators knew what the Hebrew word signified. In 2 Kings 11: 10, *tous trissous* is a case where either a copyist or the translator misread *hšlṭym* as *hšlšym*, and so this cannot be considered in this connection.

The problem, however, may be different in the book of Ezekiel, where *trissos* seems to mean "pertaining to a leader," or "distinguished." In Ezek 23: 23, *šlšym wqrw'ym* has been interpreted "officers and warriors," "captains and counselors," and "captains and men of renown." In Greek, this has been rendered *trissous kai onomastous*, a literalistic translation; this may be understood as "distinguished and notable ones." This takes us back to vs 15 in the same chapter: *mr'h šlšym klm*, which means literally: "the appearance of officers [captains], all of them." Here the Greek reads: *opsis trisse pantōn*, which may be rendered "a distinguished appearance of all," or "an officerlike look of all." This signifies that they all looked distinguished, or had an appearance like that of officers. In these passages, the LXX gave *trissos* a sense it did not have in Greek literature. In fact, the Greek in this usage would be hardly intelligible without a comparison with MT.

In connection with the expression "forever" has to be considered the root *nṣḥ*, which means "be preeminent," "enduring"; in post-biblical Hebrew, it developed the sense "be victorious," "win," "prevail"; in Judeo-Aramaic and Syriac, it signifies "be brilliant, distinguished," "conquer," "triumph." Hebrew *nēṣaḥ* denotes "eminence," "continuance," "everlastingness," "perpetuity," whence the phrase *lnṣḥ* signifies "forever" and is rendered (1) *eis telos*, Ps 9: 7. ——— (2) with a negative: *eis ton aiōna*, Is 28: 28; Jer 50: 39 [27:39]; *eis ton aiōna chronon*, Is 13: 20; 33: 20. In Is 57: 16, in a parallelism with a negative, *l'wlm* is rendered *eis ton aiōna* and *lnṣḥ, dia pantos*. In Ps 49[48]: 20, which has a negative, *'d-nṣḥ* is interpreted *eōs aiōnos.*

At this point may be considered *eis nikos* ("forever"). In this connection should be cited 2 Sam 2: 26, *hlnṣḥ t'kl ḥrb* ("shall the sword devour forever?"): *mē eis nikos kataphagetai ē romphaia.* ——— Job 36: 7 *wyšybm lnṣḥ* ("and he setteth them forever"): *kai kathiei autous eis nikos.* ——— Amos 1: 11, *w'brtw šmrh nṣḥ* ("and he kept his wrath forever"): *kai to ormēma autou ephulaxen eis nikos.* ——— 8: 7, *'m-'škḥ lnṣḥ kl-m'śyhm* ("surely I will never forget any of their deeds"): *ei epilēsthēsetai eis nikos panta ta erga umōn.* ——— In Zeph 3: 5, we have *kai ouk eis nikos adikian*, for which no Hebrew is extant. ——— Is 25: 8, *bl' hmwt lnṣḥ* ("he will swallow up death forever"): Aquila and Theodotion render *lnṣḥ, eis nikos.* ——— In Is 34: 10, *lnṣḥ nṣḥym* ("forever and ever") is rendered by Aquila and Theodotion literalistically *eis nikos nikeōn.* ——— Lam 5: 20, *lmh lnṣḥ tškḥnw* ("wherefore dost thou forget us forever?"): *ina ti eis nikos epilēsē ēmōn.* Finally, in Jer 3: 5, in a parallelism, *l'wlm* in the first member is rendered *eis ton aiōna*, while *lnṣḥ* is translated literally *eis nikos.* This passage decides the meaning of *eis nikos* as "forever."

This study of *nikos* leads to the NT, 1 Cor 15: 54: *katepothē o thanatos eis nikos*, which is the rendering by Theodotion of Is 25: 8. The LXX interpreted *lnṣḥ* by *ischusas*, but both Aquila and Theodotion translated it *eis nikos.* In this case, Saint Paul quotes Theodotion. In the context of the Epistle to the Corinthians, it appears that the standard English translation has to be retained: "Death is swallowed up in victory." Yet at the same time, we may consider a double entendre in the passage and bear in mind the OT interpretation by Theodotion: "Death is swallowed up forever." At any rate, in the LXX as a rendering of *lnṣḥ*, the phrase *eis nikos* in the sense of "forever" is well established.

This selection of words from a large accumulation extending over a number of years in the writer's files shows some of the situations that confront a lexicographer of the LXX. It must be admitted that the Alexandrians have not only left problems for the philologist and the lexicographer but, in one instance, they were the source of a difficulty transmitted to later translators and unwittingly laid a basis for future controversy: Is 7: 14, where with the article *'lmh* (*puella nubilis, mannbares Mädchen*, "marriageable young woman," and even a young women until the birth of her first child) was rendered *ē parthenos.* This rendering, however, can be defended, since in classical Greek *parthenos* may mean "girl," "maiden," as well as "virgin," and the term was applied even to a young woman who was not a virgin (e.g., *Iliad* II, 514). If the Alexandrian translators had chosen *neanis*, as did Aquila, Symmachus, and Theodotion later on, no trouble would have been bequeathed to future generations; but the Vulgate rendered it *virgo*, and the interpretation "virgin" followed in the AV and the RV.

In the RSV, even though the text reads "a young woman," there is a note in the margin: "or *virgin*," which may continue to confuse the exegesis of the passage for some readers.

At last, however, we may depart from lexicography in the narrow sense and make some reference to the influence of the vocabulary of the LXX upon the English Bible and the religious language of the present day. In this connection should be considered the Greek work for "church." It is difficult to bring out in English the exact shade of meaning of Hebrew *qhl* ("assembly," "convocation," "congregation"), and probably the closest approach to the interpretation of this politico-religious term is the German *Gemeinde*. At any rate, in translating *qhl* by *ekklēsia*, the LXX furnished the word for "church" in the NT. Furthermore, in rendering *leḥem happānîm* and *leḥem hammăʿreket* by *oi artoi tēs protheseōs*, an interpretation was available for the *panes propositionis* of the Vulgate. Thus Luther had a basis for his translation *die Schaubrote*, whence English *shewbread*.[3]

Finally, two more examples will be chosen, and both are theological. The first is Hebrew *kappōret*, which is translated in the AV, RV and RSV as "mercy seat," a rendering going back to Tyndale, who was influenced by Luther's *Gnadenstuhl*. In Ex 25: 17[16], *kprt* is translated by *ilastērion epithema*, which means literally "propitiatory cover"; in other words, *epithema* is an attempt at a literal rendering, while *ilastērion* gives the noun theological content. This is the only case, however, where the two words are used together; in the other instances *epithema* is omitted and *ilastērion* becomes a substantive, which then by itself signifies "mercy seat" or "propitiatory."

In conclusion, whether we are conscious of it or not in referring to the OT and the NT, we are using a term which owes its origin ultimately to the LXX. A discussion of the word "testament" involves Greek *diathēkē*, of which it is a translation. The Hebrew word *bryt* ("covenant"), when used of an agreement between men, involves the mutual acceptance of contract obligations. Between God and man, however, a covenant involves a free promise from the divine side and the undertaking of obligations on the human side; thus, while the idea of mutuality is involved, God remains on the higher level.

When the OT was translated into Greek, there was a difficulty of rendering *bryt*. The Greek word *sunthēkē* ("compact," "agreement," "contract," "treaty") might have suggested that God and his people were on the same plane in the covenant. Accordingly, the Alexandrians chose *diathēkē* ("disposition of property by will," "will," "testament") as the translation of *bryt* ("covenant"). It cannot be said, however, that this was a purely arbitrary meaning assigned to *diathēkē* by "the Seventy", since *diathēkē* contains the concept of "arrangement," and the sense of "agreement" or "covenant" may be found even in classical Greek (cf Aristophanes, *Birds*, 440–41). But in the rendering of *bryt* by *diathēkē*, the place of God on the higher level was preserved, and furthermore the idea of mutuality was retained. The testator makes the will, but his heirs are bound by law to carry out its provisions. Accordingly, *diathēkē* makes clear the two concepts: the covenant was God's free promise, and those who receive his gifts are on their part obligated to carry out the conditions he has imposed. In this sense, *diathēkē* signifies "covenant" and should be so understood; the idea of "testament," however, was not lost.

From the LXX this usage of *diathēkē* was taken over into the NT, and when the NT was translated into Latin, *diathēkē* was rendered literally *testamentum*, whence English "testament." In the NT, accordingly, "testament" is synonymous with "covenant," except in Heb 9: 16–17. In this connection, moreover, there must be recognized the double sense of *diathēkē* in Heb 9: 15–20. In vss 16–17, however, "testament" cannot be explained as "covenant," while in the other verses it should be so interpreted. On the other hand, in vss 16–17, the sense of "testament" cannot be avoided, and the word will have to be retained.

When the NT was formed, it was called *ē kainē diathēkē* ("the New Testament," or "the New Covenant"), since it contains the documents that attest God's new covenant with his new covenant people, the Church. How long the term was in vogue before its literary use in this sense, we cannot determine. Consequently from this usage the Scriptures inherited from Israel were called by Christians (2 Cor 3: 14) *ē palaia diathēkē* ("the Old Testament"). We must credit "the Seventy" not only with freedom in their rendering *diathēkē* but also with imagination. That one word found its way into a new body of documents, to which it eventually gave the name; from this usage in the NT it rebounded to the original source to apply itself as a name of the Hebrew Scriptures. Now Jews as well as Christians speak of "the Old Testament." After all, we must admit that terminology can be quite convenient, and whether the layman be aware of it or not, the plodding Alexandrian translators, who knew Hebrew, Aramaic, and Greek have bequeathed the word "testament" to an age when many students of theology resist the study of the original languages of Scripture.

Notes

[1] Cf in this connection articles by the writer: "A Note on I Sam. 21: 13(14)," *JBL* 67 (1948), 241–43; "The Theological Approach of the Greek Translator of Job 1–15," *JBL* 68 (1949), 231–40; "Exegetical Methods Employed by the Greek Translator of I Samuel," *JAOS*, 70 (1950), 292–96; "The Hebraic Character of Septuagint Greek," *VT* 1 (1951),

81–90; "Hebraisms of the Old Greek Version of Genesis," *VT* 3 (1953), 141–48; "Some Types of Errors of Transmission in the Septuagint," VT 3 (1953), 397–400; "Greek Versions of the OT," *Hastings' Dictionary of the Bible*, rev. ed. (1963), pp. 347–54; "Rambles in Septuagint Lexicography," *Indian Journal of Theology* 14 (1965), 90–101; "Adventures in Septuagint Lexicography," *Textus*, Annual of the Hebrew University Bible Project, V (1966), 125–32; "The Septuagint", under "Versions," *The New Westminster Dictionary of the Bible* (1970), pp. 971–75.

[2] In the Hiphil, the concept "to deal wisely" contains the implied consequence of success. The verb, however, does not express success alone, but success which is the result of wise provision. No single English word can express the full idea inherent in the Hebrew; cf S. R. Driver, *Notes on the Hebrew Text . . . of the Books of Samuel* (2d ed., Oxford, 1913), p. 149.

[3] In Ex 25: 30 [29], *lḥm pnym* is rendered *artoi enōpioi*; in Neh 10: 34[33], *lḥm hm'rkt* is translated *artoi tou prosōpou*.

Robert Gordis
Temple University and the Jewish Theological Seminary

Love, Marriage, and Business in the Book of Ruth: A Chapter in Hebrew Customary Law

Ḥesed and *Ḥokhmah* in Ruth

For two millennia, the book of Ruth has charmed readers by its idyllic beauty. Goethe described it as *das lieblicheste kleine Ganze das uns episch und idyllisch ueberliefert worden ist.* In this charming tale, the tragedies of life are muted, being bathed in a gentle melancholy, with evil being virtually nonexistent. The *Midrash* succinctly epitomizes the book as a tribute to the practice of loving-kindness (*gemilūt ḥasādīm*).[1] The word *ḥesed* in biblical Hebrew has been rendered by a variety of terms: "goodness," "kindness," "favor," "love," and most commonly by "loving-kindness." Recently, translators have sought to approximate its essence more closely in the rendering "steadfast love."[2] As the book of Ruth makes clear, *ḥesed* includes a broad spectrum of family piety, friendship, loyalty, and love, both Divine and human. Within the confines of this small book, *ḥesed* represents the basic attribute of God in dealing with his creatures, which Naomi invokes for her daughter-in-law (1: 8) and of which she finds evidence in Boaz's kindness to Ruth (2: 20). It is the quality that Boaz praises in Ruth's turning to him rather than to younger and more attractive men (3: 10). When this loyalty is suffused by deep emotion, it becomes virtually

It is a privilege to extend warmest felicitations and best wishes to Professor Jacob M. Myers on the occasion of his sixty-eighth birthday, and to join with his colleagues, students, and admirers everywhere in paying tribute to his distinguished career as a biblical scholar and teacher. Because of Professor Myers' lifelong interest in Ruth, which found expression in his monograph *The Linguistic and Literary Form of the Book of Ruth* (Leiden, 1955) I am happy to contribute this paper to the Festschrift being issued in his honor.

identical with love, as in the formula of betrothal in Hos (Hebrew) (2: 21–22): "And I will betroth you to me forever; I will betroth you to me in righteousness and in justice, in steadfast love and in mercy. I will betroth you to me in faithfulness; and you shall know the Lord." So too, in the words of his spiritual descendant Jeremiah (Jer 2: 2): "Go and proclaim in the hearing of Jerusalem, Thus says the Lord, I remember the devotion (*ḥesed*) of your youth, your love (*'ahabhat*) as a bride, how you followed me in the wilderness, in a land unsown."[3] At its ultimate, *ḥesed* represents the blending of man's love and loyalty toward God (Hos 6: 6). It is characteristic of the gentle and relaxed atmosphere of the book of Ruth that the verb *'āhabh* does not occur; all the passion may have well dwelt in Boaz's breast. It is *ḥesed*, steadfast loyalty, faithful love, that Ruth feels for her mother-in-law, which she then manifests toward Boaz and which impels her to seek refuge under the wings of the God of Israel (2: 12).

That *ḥesed* triumphs over the tragedies of life in the book of Ruth is due to another highly prized virtue in ancient Israel, that of *ḥokhmah*. The old tradition which places the book of Ruth after Judges is of course self-explanatory. The opening phrase, as well as the entire background of the tale, associates the events with the period of the Judges.[4] However, as we have suggested elsewhere, the present position of the book within the Hagiographa is not accidental. Its precise place among the five Megillot, after the Song of Songs, is of course due to its position in the synagogue liturgy as the reading for the Feast of Shavuoth.

However, its position in the Hagiographa generally is, I believe, thoroughly justified by the fact that the Hagiographa is basically the repository of Wisdom Literature.[5] This includes both the lower, conventional *ḥokhmah*, which sought to inculcate the practical qualities needed for success in life, and the higher, speculative *ḥokhmah*, which wrestled with the ultimate issues of human existence, the purpose of creation, the goals of human life, the nature of death, the inaccessibility of truth, and—above all—the agonizing problem of evil. The book of Psalms is a great collection of religious poetry, most of which was chanted at the Temple service with musical accompaniment. Both the composition and the rendition of the Psalms in worship required a high degree of that technical skill which is *ḥokhmah*. Moreover, in point of content, many Psalms (like 37, 49, 112, 128) have close affinities with the proverbial lore of the Wisdom teachers. The Song of Songs is included, not merely because it is traditionally ascribed to King Solomon, the symbol and traditional source of Hebrew Wisdom, but because these songs, whether sung at weddings or at other celebrations, were also a branch of technical song. It may also be that the Song of Songs entered the Wisdom collection because it was regarded as an allegory of the relationship of love subsisting between God and Israel. From this point of view, it would be a *māšāl*, the basic literary genre of *ḥokhmah*, which means "allegory" and "fable" as well as "proverb." The book of Daniel, the wise interpreter of dreams, obviously is in place among the Wisdom books.

The chanting of Lamentations required a special expertise described as *ḥokhmah* (Jer 9: 16). The three closing books of the Bible, which survey history from Adam to the Persian period, are really parts of one larger work, Chronicles-Ezra-Nehemiah. It is possible that they owe their position in the Hagiographa to the fact that they serve as an appendix to the Bible as a whole. It is also possible that Chronicles (with its adjuncts) is regarded as an appendix to Psalms, since one of its principal concerns is to describe in detail the establishment of the musical guilds and priestly orders in the Temple in Jerusalem.

The books of Ruth and Esther are narratives, showing how *ḥokhmah* operates and succeeds in human affairs. They belong to the same genre as the Joseph saga in Genesis. The same kind of practical wisdom that helped Joseph rise to power and influence was utilized by Mordecai and Esther to save their people, and was displayed by Naomi and Ruth on the more limited stage of domestic affairs. Without Naomi's practical wisdom, which Ruth obeyed, the young woman would not have come to the attention of Boaz; and without his shrewdness during the transaction with the kinsman, he would not have been able to marry her.

Frequently described as an idyll, the book of Ruth is by no means a simple tale. Its apparent simplicity has often prevented a full appreciation of its high literary artistry.[6] It has also served to obscure the complexity of the problems the book contains.

The Purpose and Date of Ruth

There is a wide disparity of views regarding the background of the book. It has been suggested that Ruth is a polemic against the exclusion of Moabites from the community of Israel, which is enjoined in Deut 23: 4. More often, the book has been described as a tract against the campaign of Ezra and Nehemiah to exclude mixed marriages from the post-Exilic Jewish community,[7] and contrariwise, as a possible defence of their policy.[8] But nothing could be further removed from the polemic spirit than the irenic tone of our book. It is this characteristic which also rules out the possibility of its being propagandistic in any sense. It does not agitate for the enforcement of the duty of levirate marriage,[9] even if the transaction in Chapter 4 be regarded as an instance of this rite. It does not preach benevolence toward the heathens,[10] for, be it noted, Ruth accepts the faith of Naomi long before any kindness is shown her in Bethlehem. It surely cannot be construed as a protest against intermarriage or indiscriminate proselytization.[11] That the book praises the piety of Ruth[12] and her loyalty as a widow[13] may be true, but this can scarcely be regarded as its purpose. Naomi may share the honors of being the heroine of the book with Ruth,[14] but this too supplies no purpose for the book.

It has been suggested that the function of Ruth is to supplement the account in 1 Sam 22: 3, which informs us that David sought a refuge for his parents in Moab, by supplying him with a Moabite ancestry in that country.[15] But even for those, who, like the present writer, regard the genealogy at the end of the book as integral to it and possessing a good claim to authenticity, this idea plays no part in the book and hardly qualifies as its purpose. Finally, the theory, propounded a few decades ago, that we have here a liturgical text of a fertility cult centered in Bethlehem,[16] has few, if any, defenders today. By a process of elimination, we are therefore left virtually only with the view that the book of Ruth is a story told for its own sake.[17] This conclusion does not necessarily rule out the possibility that there may have been an authentic tradition of David's being partly descended from Moabite stock.

Divergences with regard to dating are of course common in all biblical research.[18] Talmudic tradition assigns the book to the authorship of Samuel.[19] It has been variously assigned to the early Monarchy,[20] to the period between David and the Exile,[21] to the days of Hezekiah,[22] to the Exilic period,[23] and to the post-Exilic age.[24] In spite of this wide disparity of views, I am convinced that the lines of evidence converge on the period from the middle of the fifth to the early fourth century B.C.E.

The testimony from language and style must be used with caution.[25] On the one hand, the classic style of the book includes such formulas as *kh y'śh Yhwh ly wkh ysyp* (1: 17) and *'glh 'znk* (4: 4). The popular speech probably preserved such older forms as the second person singular of the imperfect with *Nun* (originally the energeticus) *tidbāqîn* (2: 8, 21), *tēd'în* (3: 18)[26] and the archaic form of the second person feminine of the perfect with *Yod*, *wyrdty* (3: 3) and *wškbty* (3: 4).[27] The Divine name *šdy* (1: 20) is ancient, but it reappears frequently in Job.

On the other hand, there are such late locutions as *wyś'w lhm nšym* (1: 4; cf 1 Chron 23: 22), where the older classic idiom was *lqḥ 'šh* (Gen 4: 4; 6: 2; 11: 14; Deut 24: 1). We may note also the use of *'syt* in the meaning "to spend (time)" (2: 19), which occurs biblically only in Eccles 6: 12 but is common in Rabbinic Hebrew, as is the root *'gn* "to be chained" (1: 13).[28]

In Mishnaic Hebrew, the *tertiae Aleph* verbs coalesce with *tertiae Yod*, under the influence of Aramaic. The orthography and vocalization of 2: 9

reflect this tendency.[29] *mrglwt* (3: 4, 7, 8, 14) occurs elsewhere only in Dan 10: 6, but the parallel form *mr'šwt* is early (Gen 28: 11, 18; 1 Sam 19: 13,16).

Elsewhere, we have called attention to the four categories of Aramaisms in biblical Hebrew and the care that must be exercised before invoking them as evidence of late dating.[30] However, it is clear that a large concentration of Aramaisms, as in Ps 139, does point to the post-Exilic period, when Hebrew writers knew and used Aramaic, the *lingua franca et scripta* of the Middle East from the sixth century B.C.E. onward. This concentration of Aramaisms does obtain in Ruth. *Hlhn*, "therefore" (1: 12), occurs in Dan 2: 6, 9; 4: 24 (*lāhēn*). The verb *tśbrnh*, "hope" (1: 13), is an Aramaism (*śbr*) occurring only in such late passages as Is 38: 18; Ps 104: 27; 119: 116, 166; and Esther 9: 1. The *Piel* (4: 7) *lqym*, "attest, confirm," is a clear Aramaism, occurring only in Ezek 13: 6, Ps 119: 28, 106; Esther 9: 21, 27, 31, 32. On the other hand, the root *lpt*, "twist turn" (3: 8), which appears in biblical Hebrew in Job 6: 18, cannot be invoked, since it occurs also in Judg 16: 29.

There is only one adequate explanation for these superficially contradictory phenomena, the occurrence of both early and late Hebrew usages in Ruth: the author was a late writer who was consciously archaizing and using colloquial speech, in order to give an antique flavor to his narrative, which he set in the period of the Judges.

Substantive considerations agree with the linguistic evidence for a post-Exilic date for Ruth. The author finds it necessary, from the vantage point of a later period *wz't pnym byśr'l* (4: 7), to explain the use of the sandal for the transfer of rights and obligations. Moreover, the period of the Judges is pictured as idyllic and peaceful, a situation radically at variance with the conditions of war, cruelty, and insecurity realistically reflected in the book of Judges. More specifically, Moab is no longer an actual enemy on the borders of Israel, as was the case during most of the pre-Exilic period, including the age of the Judges (cf Judg 3: 13 ff; 11: 15 ff; 1 Sam 12: 9).

It is admittedly difficult to fix a precise date for the book within the Second Temple period. A *terminus post quem* may be found in the fact that there is no echo of the agitation or of the activity associated with Ezra and Nehemiah, for which the date of 444 B.C.E. is generally assigned, though the problems of Ezra chronology are massive and perhaps insoluble.[31] This consideration would bring the time down to the second half of the fifth century. A *terminus ante quem* may be advanced with greater assurance. There is no echo in Ruth of the widespread upheavals in the Middle East caused by the incursion of Alexander the Great into western Asia (334 B.C.E.) and no trace of Hellenistic influence, either in style or in substance.

The book would seem to emanate from a period of relative tranquility, such as the post-Exilic Jewish community experienced under Persian suzerainty. Above all, the spirit of universalism and broad humanity which the book breathes belongs to the same spiritual climate as do the book of Jonah and the great masterpieces of wisdom literature, Job and Ecclesiastes.

As is often the case, the evidence is cumulative in character rather than decisive in detail. All in all, the most appropriate *Sitz im Leben* for the book of Ruth is the early Second Temple period, when the Jewish community enjoyed a substantial measure of autonomy under the Persian rule, about 450–350 B.C.E.

Ruth and the Levirate

Neither the problem of the purpose of the book nor its date, important as these questions are, is crucial to understanding the narrative itself. There are, however, two major difficulties in the closing chapter which fundamentally affect our comprehension of its contents. In Rowley's words, "Unexpectedly we find Naomi possessed of land, and we are left to guess how it came into her possession, and what had happened to it during the years of her sojourn in Moab. . . . That the story of Ruth's marriage must be linked with the question of levirate marriage is generally agreed, though this is clearly not strictly a case of levirate marriage, since Boaz is not a brother-in-law or levir."[32]

It is to these two basic problems that we should like to address ourselves: the nature of the transaction involving Boaz and his unnamed kinsman, and the role of Naomi in these negotiations.

Undoubtedly, many scholars and probably most readers have linked the events in Ruth, Chapter 4, to the levirate, regarding it as a rather unorthodox instance of the rite. When, however, the details of Ruth are compared with the biblical law in Deut 25: 5–10 and with other pertinent data, it becomes clear that there is virtually no similarity between them.

In Deuteronomy, the rite is obligatory upon "brothers dwelling together." Here, both Boaz and his kinsman are such distant relatives that the possibility of the levirate does not occur to Naomi, even in the extremity in which she finds herself upon her return from Moab.

In Deuteronomy, the emphasis is upon "perpetuating the name of the dead man in Israel" by the birth of a son to his widow, and there is no reference to the transfer of property. In Ruth, the transaction revolves basically around the "redemption" of property, while the concomitant marriage and the support of Ruth and her future offspring are secondary considerations. Nor can this be dismissed as part of Boaz's strategy vis-à-vis the kinsman. For even in Boaz's official avowal of his acceptance of the obligation, the property transaction is primary, and the marriage to Ruth is secondary:

> Then Boaz said to the elders and all the people, "You are witnesses this day that I have bought from the hand of Naomi all that belonged to Elimelech and all that belonged to Chilion and to Mahlon. Also Ruth the Moabitess, the widow of Mahlon, I have bought to be my wife, to perpetuate the name of the dead in his inheritance, that the name of the dead may not be cut off from among his brethren and from the gate of his native place. You are witnesses this day" (4: 9–10)

In Deuteronomy there is a clear stigma attaching to the brother who does not fulfill his duty as a *levir*. The elders therefore seek to persuade the recalcitrant brother-in-law (vs 8). If they fail, the widow "pulls his sandal off his foot and spits in his face" (vs 9). His family is henceforth called "the household of the cast-off sandal" (vs 10). In Ruth, we have a straightforward business transaction without the shadow of any discredit falling upon the kinsman when he declines to participate.

"The pulling off of the sandal" in Deuteronomy (*wtḥlṣ nʿlw*) and "the drawing off of the sandal" in Ruth (*šlp ʾyš nʿlw wntn lrʿhw*) (4: 7), which seems at first glance to represent an identical act, are totally different in both instances.

First, a different verb is used in each instance: *ḥalaṣ* and *šalaph*. Technical terms are not used indiscriminately.

Second, in Deuteronomy, it is the widow who draws off the shoe of her recusant brother-in-law. In Ruth, it is the unwilling kinsman who draws off his own shoe and transfers it to his fellow relative who does undertake the obligation.

Third, in Deuteronomy, the widow's removal of her brother-in-law's shoe is a symbolic representation of the cutting of the link binding her to him. On the other hand, in Ruth, the act of removing one's own shoe is a general procedure, commerical in character, as is clearly indicated: "Now this was the custom in former times in Israel concerning redeeming and exchanging: to confirm a transaction, the one drew off his sandal and gave it to the other, and this was the manner of attesting in Israel" (4: 7). Evidence from such varied cultures as those of India,[33] Egypt[34] and the Nuzi texts,[35] as well as the biblical passages, Ps 60: 10; 108: 10, demonstrate that the interpretation given in Ruth is valid. The shoe symbolizes power and authority, and its use in a transaction marks the transfer of some right and obligation from one party to another.[36]

Fourth, in Deuteronomy, the woman plays a central role in the rite. In Ruth, there is no evidence that Naomi or Ruth was present at all. In fact, the reference to them in third person suggests that they are absent; they surely do not participate in the proceedings.

Fifth, that we are not dealing with the levirate, even in its broadest sense, in Ruth is clear from Boaz's statement in 3: 10: "May you be blessed by the Lord, my daughter; you have made this last kindness greater than the first, in that you have not gone after young men, whether poor or rich." In the levirate, the obligation falls upon the male relative, primarily the brother, and the woman has no freedom of choice whatsoever. Here, Boaz expresses his gratitude to Ruth for preferring him to younger and presumably more attractive swains whom she might very well have married.

Finally, these far-reaching differences between the levirate in Deuteronomy and the transaction described in Ruth become even more impressive when we seek to relate the latter to the origin and purpose of the levirate in general and to its history in Israel in particular. As is well known, the levirate is one of the most widely diffused aspects of marriage custom in primitive and ancient society, one that is to be met with in Indo-European, Semitic, and Melanesian culture areas.[37] Anthropologists have suggested that it is a survival of polyandry or that it is a consequence of ancestor worship. These factors may have played a part in the levirate in other cultures, but there is not the slightest evidence for these elements as factors in Israel.

It is possible that in some societies the levirate rite may have reflected the concept of the woman as being part of the family property, so that she is inherited by the dead man's kinsman along with his estate. This is emphatically not the case in Israel. The active role played by the woman in the levirate in Deut 25 militates against this view of the woman as a passive chattel being passed from hand to hand. The only reason for the rite assigned in Deuteronomy is "to perpetuate his brother's name in Israel" (Deut 25: 7). On the other hand, it is noteworthy that the child born to Ruth, Obed, is called the son of Boaz (4: 21) and not of Mahlon, Ruth's first husband.

There is one more general consideration that supports these arguments against identifying the transaction in Ruth with the levirate. Contemporary scholarship has legitimately veered away from postulating unilinear lines of evolution in the history of human culture and institutions. In the case of the levirate in Israel, however, a clear process of development can be traced from our earliest biblical sources to the post-talmudic period, each step being marked by a consistent tendency to contract the rite and limit its exercise until it is virtually eliminated.

The first, and indeed the only, instance in the biblical narrative of the levirate is the highly unconventional encounter of Tamar and Judah (Gen

38). The narrative, which is assigned by Higher Criticism to the J Source, and is generally dated in the ninth or eighth century B.C.E., clearly reflects a very ancient tradition. When Tamar is twice widowed of Judah's sons, Er and Onan, Judah refrains from giving his third son, Shelah, to her in marriage. Tamar then decides upon extreme measures. Disguising herself as a harlot, she waits upon the highway, encounters Judah, and becomes pregnant by him. When her pregnancy is revealed some three months later, Judah is prepared to have her publicly burned for her sin. However, she discreetly lets Judah know that he is the father of her child, to which Judah responds: "She is more righteous than I, inasmuch as I did not give her to my son Shelah" (Gen 38: 26).

There are two features in this familiar story that need to be underscored:

First, the rite of the levirate is here not limited to brothers, but extends to other kinsmen, including a father-in-law. Were this not the case, Perez and Zerah, the twins that are born her, would have been the illegitimate offspring of an incestuous union and would have been excluded from "the community of JHWH" (Deut 23: 3), instead of being honored eponymous heads of Judahite clans (1 Chron 2: 4 ff; 4: 1; 9: 4; 27: 3; Neh 11: 4 ff; Num 26: 20; Josh 7: 1; 18: 24; 22: 20). In the Middle Assyrian Laws (sec. 33), the marriage of a childless widow to her father-in-law is explicitly permitted. The extant tablets date from Tiglath Pileser I (twelfth century B.C.E.), but the laws may go back to the patriarchal period (fifteenth century B.C.E.). It is a reasonable inference that the obligation first fell upon a brother, but the lacuna in the text makes this less than certain.[38] In the Hittite Laws (sec. 193), the obligation to marry the dead man's widow falls successively upon his brother, his father, and his nephew.[39]

Second, the fulfillment of the levirate rite is obligatory, and brooks of no exception. Hence, Judah's failure to have Shelah marry Tamar justifies Tamar's extreme measures, even if it includes an act of public immorality and sexual license which would normally be stigmatized as incest (Lev 18: 15; 20: 12). That marrying the widow is an obligation is clear in the Hittite Laws and is apparently the case also in the Middle Assyrian Laws.

The next stage of the levirate in Israel that we are able to document from our limited sources is described in Deut 25. Deuteronomy is generally dated shortly before the discovery of the Book of the Covenant in the Temple during the eighteenth year of Josiah (2 Kings 22), in the year 621.[40]

In Deuteronomy, the rite has now been considerably constricted.[41] It is now limited to "brothers dwelling together," with no hint that the obligation also falls upon other, more distant relatives. Moreover, even for the brothers, *yibbum* no longer is obligatory, though it is clearly the preferred procedure. A brother may avoid the duty, if he is willing to be exposed to a measure of public indignity and have his family carry some stigma, the severity of which we cannot judge.

The next stage in the history of the rite may be documented in Leviticus in the Holiness Code, usually assigned to the sixth century B.C.E. It takes the form of the total prohibition of the marriage of a woman to her brother-in-law (Lev 18: 16; 20: 21).

This thoroughgoing contradiction between Leviticus and Deuteronomy did not escape the vigilant eyes of the talmudic rabbis. The theological problem they solved by declaring that both ordinances were revealed simultaneously: *ʿrwt ʾšt ʾḥyk lʾ tglh* "the nakedness of your brother's wife you shall not uncover" (Lev 18:16) and *ybmh ybʾ ʿlyh* "her brother-in-law shall come in to her" (Deut 25: 5) were both pronounced in one divine utterance *bdbwr ʾḥd nʾmr* (*Palestinian Talmud*, *Nedarim*, Ch 3, 5). The legal antinomy they met by establishing the prohibition in Leviticus as the general principle, applicable during the brother's lifetime, and by declaring the levirate to be the one specific exception, applicable only when a man leaves a childless widow after his death. The Samaritans[42] and the early Qaraite authorities[43] solved the contradiction by ordaining (and permitting) the levirate only in the case of a *betrothed* woman whose husband had died, but forbidding the rite to a *married* woman. Thus, they avoided the possibility of a violation of Lev 18: 16. In the Laws of Manu, the *levir* was permitted to approach the childless widow only once, until a child was born—a different practice for meeting the same dilemma.[44]

It may be, as many scholars have maintained, that the talmudic reconciliation of both passages is in conformity with the original intent of the law and that the two passages were not opposed to each other. On the other hand, the resolution may represent a reasoned effort by the Rabbis at harmonizing two originally distinct and contradictory biblical laws which they regarded as equally binding.

A striking example of this harmonizing procedure is to be found with regard to the biblical laws of the tithe. In Num 18: 21–24, the tithe is a tax imposed upon the Israelite farmer for the exclusive benefit of the Levite. In Deut 14: 22–27, the tithe was to be spent by the farmer upon himself and his family, "in the place which God would choose to settle his name upon" (14: 14); only on the third year was the tithe to be left "at the gate," so that the landless Levite as well as the stranger, the orphan, and the widow might eat and be satisfied (Deut 14: 28–29). The clear-cut contradiction between Numbers and Deuteronomy was resolved by the rabbis through the creation of a complex system of double tithes.[45] The Jewish farmer was required to set aside two tithes each year: during the first, second, fourth, and fifth years of the sabbatical cycle, *maʿăśēr rišōn* "the first tithe" went to the Levites and *ma'āsēr šēnī* "the second tithe" was to be consumed by the farmer and his family in Jerusalem. In the third and sixth years of the sabbatical cycle, *ma'āsēr rišōn* still went to the Levites and *ma'āsēr 'ānī* "the tithe of the poor" was to be made available to the needy.

To revert to the levirate, if the prohibitions in Leviticus are regarded as overriding the Deuteronomic levirate law, there is a clear and direct line of development of the rite from the ineluctable obligation in Genesis, through the preferred procedure in Deuteronomy, to its total prohibition in Leviticus. If, on the other hand, the prohibition in Leviticus is interpreted as being restricted to the lifetime of the brother, while the levirate remains operative after his death, the next stage in its history is to be sought in the post-biblical period.

In Rabbinic Judaism, the recognition of personal desires and the play of human likes and dislikes affecting both the brother-in-law and the widow increasingly came to the fore. The Mishnah declares: "*Yibbum* took precedence over *ḥaliṣah* in earlier times when men were concerned with fulfilling the Divine commandment. But now, that men are not concerned with fulfilling the Divine commandment, *ḥaliṣah* takes precedence over *yibbum*."[46] Undoubtedly, the rarity of polygamy, even in talmudic times, also militated strongly against the practice of *yibbum*, since most adult men were married.

All the resources of Rabbinic hermeneutics were mobilized to limit and, where possible, to prevent the consummation of the levirate.[47] On the basis of the phrase *ky yšbw 'ḥym yḥdw* (Deut 25: 5) "when brothers dwell together," the Talmud excludes half brothers on the mother's side as well as a younger brother born subsequent to the death of the widow's husband.[48] Even more revelatory of the Rabbinic attitude is the broad interpretation given the biblical phrase "*wbn 'yn lw*" (Deut 25: 8). Quite at variance with the general practice in Rabbinic exegesis, *bēn* is construed broadly to mean "child," and not merely "son," and the phrase understood "if he left no offspring." Hence, if the dead man has an illegitimate child or a daughter or a grandchild, the brother-in-law is forbidden to marry the widow.[49] Similarly, the LXX renders *bēn* in Deut 25 by *sperma*, "seed," thus encompassing both male and female offspring and limiting the rite to a totally childless widow. The LXX rendering demonstrates that this restrictive process is substantially older than the later Mishnaic limitation.

In the tenth century, the *taqqānāh* of Rabbi Gershom Ben Judah of Mainz (born 960) and his synod forbade polygamy for European Jewry, so that henceforth *ḥaliṣah* became the only permissible mode of procedure in Western countries. *Yibbum* continued to be permissible only in Muslim countries, where polygamy was not prohibited.[50]

In sum, it is clear that the transaction in Ruth cannot be integrated into any stage of the history of the levirate in Israel. We have already noted above the substantial discrepancies between the transaction of Ruth and the law in Deuteronomy. The task becomes totally impossible in the post-Exilic period, when the practice of the levirate was increasingly restricted both by law and by custom. We conclude that the marriage of Ruth to a distant kinsman cannot be regarded as an instance of *yibbum*.

The Redemption of the Land

It is true that as a result of the transaction in the closing chapter of the book, Ruth is married to Boaz, and that this goal undoubtedly was uppermost in his mind. But the negotiations themselves revolve around property which belonged to Elimelech, the acquisition of which by a kinsman (*ge'ūlāh*) would entail support for the destitute feminine members of his family—his widow Naomi, and her nubile daughter-in-law Ruth.

This redemption of land was of course only one of the functions of the *gō'ēl*. The execution of blood vengeance on behalf of a murdered member of the family or clan (Num. 35: 9 ff; Deut 19: 1 ff) had been progressively restricted by the establishment of the cities of refuge. This process of attrition of the blood-avenging function was undoubtedly accelerated by the establishment of the Hebrew monarchy with its own organs of justice. What remained for the *gō'ēl* was the more pacific duty of preventing the alienation of land from the family. This function survived longer, since it did not compete with the structure of government. Yet, it too ultimately disappeared with the erosion of tribal distinctions and the later weakening of group solidarity. This process went hand in hand with the emergence of a new sense of individualism in the closing days of the Monarchy and in the Exilic and post-Exilic periods.

When the institution of land redemption was in force, a man suffering economic distress had four courses of action open to him:

First, he might seek out a kinsman and ask him to buy his landholdings directly from him, thus preventing its alienation from the family. He stood a better chance of repossessing it later if it was in the hands of a relation. Second, he might sell the land to an outsider and later appeal to a kinsman to "redeem" it by repurchase. Third, he might sell the land and later "redeem" the land from its alien owner himself. Fourth, if none of these methods was available to him, the impoverished seller could wait until the Jubilee Year, and it would revert to him without payment.

The second precedure is described in Lev 25: 25: "If your brother becomes poor, and sells part of his property, then his next of kin shall come and redeem what his brother has sold." The third procedure is described in Lev 25: 26–27: "If a man has no one to redeem it, and then himself becomes prosperous and finds sufficient means to redeem it, let him reckon the years since he sold it and pay back the overpayment to the man to whom he sold it; and he shall return to his property." The fourth possibility is set forth in Lev 25: 28: "But if he has not sufficient means to get it back for himself, then what he sold shall remain in the hands of him who bought it until the Year of Jubilee. In the Jubilee it shall be released, and he shall return to his property."

The extent to which these regulations were actually operative in character is not our present concern. In this connection, it should be noted that the Edict of *Ammisaduqa* and other Mesopotamian sources concerning the remission of debts, the freeing of slaves, and the reversion of landholdings suggest that the biblical laws may not have been merely utopian.[51]

It should be noted that only the last three procedures, all set forth in the Holiness Code in Leviticus, are, properly speaking, instances of redemption, that is to say, the restoration to its original owner of land sold to an outsider. The first procedure, which does not involve either the removal of the land from the possession of an alien purchaser or its restoration to its original owner, is not an instance of redemption, and is therefore not included in the laws of *ge'ulah* in Leviticus.

An examination of the biblical root *gā'al* makes it clear that its basic meaning is "the restoration of an object to its primal condition."[52] In the ordinances of the Jubilee (Lev 25), as has been noted, *ge'ūlāh* represents the process of restoration to the *status quo ante.* Since a kinsman was charged with this obligation, the participle *gō'ēl* develops the secondary meaning of "relative" pure and simple (Ruth 2: 20; 3: 9, 12) and is a synonym for *mōda'* (2: 1), and the verb gets the meaning "act the kinsman's role" (3: 13).

The root *gā'al* is frequently associated with the Exodus from Egypt (Ex 6: 6; 15: 13; Ps 75: 2: 77: 16: 78: 35; 106: 10), representing the return of Israel to its earlier condition of liberty. Deutero-Isaiah uses the root to describe Israel's restoration from Exile (Is 43: 1; 44; 23: 48: 20; 52: 9). It is applied to the promise of God to redeem man from death by restoring him to the status of the living (Hos 13: 14; Ps 103: 4; Lam 3: 58).

When Job curses the day of his birth (Job 3: 5), he prays: *yg'lhw ḥšk wṣlmwt,* "May darkness and gloom redeem it." There is more than a trace of irony in Job's use of the verb "redeem"; he is referring to the recapture of the day by the primordial darkness and chaos out of which the light emerged at Creation. Similarly, the *gō'ēl haddam,* "blood avenger" (Num 35; Josh 20: 3, 5; Deut 19: 8, 12; 2 Sam 14: 11), redresses the cosmic balance upset by the pouring out of innocent blood.

In Job's famous affirmation of faith *w'ny yd'ty g'ly ḥy*, "I know that my *Gō'ēl* lives," both nuances are to be found. Earlier he had wished that his cause could be adjudicated by an impartial arbiter (*mōkhiaḥ*, 9: 33). He then moves forward to the conviction that the witness prepared to testify on his behalf (*'ēdh, sahadh*, 16: 19) is already on hand in the heavens. In his crescendo of faith, Job now declares that he has more than an arbiter or even a witness—he has a *gō'ēl*. God is his kinsman who will defend him against injustice; he is his redeemer who will restore him to his earlier, far happier state.

The first of the four procedures outlined above is documented in our biblical sources as well, in Jer 32: 8 ff. It is clear that the transaction described in Jeremiah is not an example of land redemption, but rather of land purchase by a kinsman to keep the land of a distressed relative from being sold to an outsider. The prophet is visited by his cousin Hanamel, who says to him: *qnh n' 't śdy 'šr b'ntwt ky lk mšpṭ hg'wlh lqnwt*, "Buy for yourself my field that is in Anathoth, because the obligation-right of redemption by purchase is yours." Or, more fully in vs 8, *ky lk mšpṭ hyršh wmšpṭ hg'wlh*, "for the right of inheritance and the obligation of redemption is yours." As a kinsman, Jeremiah has the obligation to redeem the land if it is being sold to an alien, and he has the right of inheritance after Hanamel's death. As the ensuing narrative makes clear, Jeremiah does not "redeem" the land from an outsider; he purchases it directly from Hanamel, pays him for it, and prepares the papers attesting to the sale. He does not return the field to Hanamel, which would have been the case had Jeremiah purchased it from an "outside" buyer. The term used throughout is *qānāh: qnh lk* (vs 8), *spr hmqnh* (22: 11, 12, 14). The prophet's purpose is clearly indicated in vs 15: *'wd yqnw btym wśdwt wkrmym b'rṣ hz't*, "Houses, fields, and vineyards will yet be sold in this land." The Jeremiah incident is a bona fide example of the first procedure open to a farmer threatened with loss of his land to an outsider—its sale to a kinsman.

The situation in Ruth is completely different. When Naomi and Ruth return from the fields of Moab, they are completely destitute, and therefore Ruth goes out into the fields to glean with the poor. There is not the slightest indication that Naomi possesses any land, fertile or otherwise, available for sale from the past or that she has acquired any before or since her return, as Rowley seems to imply in his statement, "Then unexpectedly we find Naomi possessed of land, and we are left to guess how it came into her possession, and what had happened to it during the years of her sojourn in Moab."[53] Rowley has evidently overlooked the clear statement that the land had belonged to Elimelech (4: 3) and his sons (4: 9). It has also been proposed that Naomi was merely the executor or the trustee for the successors to the legal heirs.[54] The idea has been advanced that Naomi had property from her own family, which Elimelech had administered during his lifetime.[55] Another suggestion is that Elimelech had willed Naomi a life contract in the property.[56] But if Naomi were a landowner, or even the administrator of land, no matter what the circumstances, she would be guilty of greed and deception in sending her foreign-born daughter-in-law to glean in the fields among the poor. To turn the force of this argument, it has been suggested that the property was too slight to support Naomi and Ruth,[57] or that Naomi was unaware that she had property,[58] but neither suggestion finds the slightest support either in the letter or in the spirit of the book—Naomi is totally destitute.

Moreover, as our analysis of the root makes clear, the term *gā'al* (4: 6) could not properly be applied to the purchase of land *from Naomi* by her kinsman. Nor, indeed, is there any indication that she receives any money in the transaction or even that she is present at the proceedings.

The crucial verse 4: 3: *ḥlqt hśdh 'šr l'ḥynw l'lymlk mkrh n'my hšbh mśdh mw'b* is rendered by LXX: "And Boaz said to the kinsman: 'The portion of the field which was our brother Elimelech's which was given to Naomi [*ē dedotai noemin*] returning out of the land of Moab.'" This rendering seeks to achieve two purposes: if offers the "explanation" that Naomi received the land as a gift, and eliminates the difficulty of her "having sold" (*mkrh*) any land. However, LXX cannot possibly represent the original Hebrew. Aside from its complete graphic divergence from MT, the sentence in LXX is grammatically defective since it has no principal clause. It cannot therefore be described as a successful solution of the substantive difficulty. The LXX rendering is, in a word, a midrash. Peshitta translates the verse: "The portion of the field of our brother Elimelech, Naomi sold me." This preserves the perfect of the verb, to be sure, but gratuitously adds an all-important pronoun and omits the remainder of the verse. Even this radical procedure does not solve the difficulties either of the text or of the incident being narrated. For obviously at this point in the proceedings Boaz has bought nothing!

How is the perfect tense of *mkrh* to be construed? Many scholars vocalize it *mōkrāh*, but the change is unnecessary. We suggest that the perfect serves to affirm the act in the present, being similar in psychological motivation to the perfect of prophetic certitude.[59] The verb *mkrh* means "she is definitely selling" (cf 4: 5). Instances of this use of the perfect in a legal-commercial context occur in the transaction between Abraham and Ephron (Gen 23: 11): *hśdh ntty lk*; and 23: 13: *ntty ksp hśdh*.

I suggest that what Naomi is disposing of is the obligation-right to redeem the land which originally had belonged to her husband and her sons. Under the pressure of the famine which finally drove him and his family out of his native land, Elimelech would surely have disposed of all his holdings before leaving for Moab. Consequently, Naomi upon her return is completely without means. In view of the death of her two sons, she is the only living heir of Elimelech. As such, she has the right to redeem the alienated property of her husband by repurchasing it from its buyers. However, lacking any resources of her own, she is unable to do so. What she therefore does is to call upon her kinsman to "redeem" the land by repurchasing it from its present owners. At first, the unnamed kinsman is willing to expend some of his financial means on the redemption, because the cost will be balanced by the increased landholdings he will henceforth possess. But Boaz then informs him that the obligation will also include the marriage and support of Ruth, with the probability that she will bear children, who will then claim the land that had originally belonged to Elimelech. The kinsman will have expended some of his money, with no permanent addition to his land holdings. He now declares himself unable to proceed with the redemption, "lest he impair his own inheritance," which he is guarding for his children. The kinsman then removes his shoe in order to confirm his transference of this obligation-right to Boaz, the next of kin. Boaz willingly accepts these obligations both vis-à-vis Elimelech's former holdings as well as vis-à-vis Ruth, undertaking her support and that of the children that will be born to her as well as of Naomi, who is part of the household (4: 16).

In order to place the transaction in perspective, it is important to recognize that by the side of the official codified family laws laid down in the Pentateuch there was a body of customary law often quite different in spirit and substance. Evidence for this customary law, affecting the status and rights of women, is growing, and the subject deserves careful study and analysis.

Our extant biblical law codes give no indication that a woman possessed such legal rights as land redemption. But the point need not be labored that in ancient times, as in our own, codified law, particularly in such areas as the rights of women, lagged behind life and custom. According to the Book of the Covenant (Ex 21: 7–11), a woman was virtually rightless, being under the power of her father until her marriage and subsequently under the authority of her husband. Any vow she took could be abrogated by her father or her husband (Num 30: 6, 9). She had no rights of inheritance, since only sons shared in the estate of their father (Deut 21: 15 ff). If a betrothed girl was caught in adultery, her execution was mandatory, with no provision for forgiveness or reconciliation with her husband (Deut 22: 20 ff). Manifestly, the penalty for a married woman could be no less (Lev 20: 10).

The records of biblical life that have come down to us, however, disclose that, notwithstanding these legal liabilities, women were by no means chattels in the hands of the males but vital personalities to their own right. The gallery of sharply etched, powerful characters among the women includes Sarah and Rebecca, Rachel and Leah, Deborah and Abigail, Bath-Sheba and Esther. If nothing else, the ability to make family life a heaven or a hell, to which the Proverbist refers time and again (Prov 21: 9, 19; 25: 24; 27: 15), placed substantial power in women's hands. As the Rabbinic dictum puts it, "A woman carries her weapons in her own person" (*'šh kly zynh 'lyh*).[60]

Even in codified biblical law, a few breaches in the rightlessness of women are discernible. When Zelophehad died without male issue, his daughters were given the right to inherit from him, though, to be sure, a special Divine dispensation was required (Num 27: 1–11). A widow or a divorced woman could not easily be made totally subservient to her father again, as the law of oaths makes clear (Num 30: 10).

According to customary law, as distinguished from the official codes, women enjoyed a substantially higher status. The marital tragedy of Hosea, however interpreted, makes it clear that a woman guilty of adultery could be forgiven and restored to her husband's home (Hos 1, 2, 3, esp. 2: 16 ff; 3: 3). This attitude is entirely congruent with the fact that Hosea is the first figure in history to insist on a single standard of sexual morality for both sexes: "I will not punish your daughters when they play the harlot, nor your brides when they commit adultery; for the men themselves go aside with harlots, and sacrifice with cult prostitutes, and a people without understanding shall come to ruin" (Hos 4: 14).

The "woman of valor" in Proverbs, who undoubtedly belonged to the upper levels of society, engaged in buying and selling, and did not content herself with her household duties (Prov 31: 14). Job, after his restoration, gives his daughters an inheritance "among their brothers" (Job 42: 15). The Elephantine papyri document the elaborate business activities of the redoubtable, thrice-married property owner Mibtahiah, daughter of Mahseiah.[61]

It is one of the major achievements of talmudic law that it substantially extended the rights of women, particularly in the areas of marriage, divorce, and property.[62] The final step was taken in the post-talmudic era, when the synod of Rabbi Gershom of Mainz made the consent of the wife mandatory when the husband issued a divorce.[63]

The most radical extension of women's rights, the power to initiate a divorce, has not become normative in traditional Judaism, at least not yet. But there is mounting evidence that at various periods and in different communities a woman was able to demand and receive a divorce when she found her marriage intolerable. This right seems to have been widespread in the Elephantine Jewish colony of the fifth century B.C.E.[64] It also held true of Palestine in at least three different periods. This is clear from a second-century text found in Muraba'at,[65] from the Palestinian Talmud a few centuries later,[66] and from at least three documents in the Cairo Genizah, dating from the tenth or eleventh century.[67] This virtual equalization of the sexes with regard to divorce, which contravenes the clear intent of Deut 24: 1, was achieved either by a special prenuptial arrangement,[68] or by the court's compelling the husband to issue the divorce,[69] or by the rabbis' annulling the marriage retroactively by invoking their fundamental authority in domestic law.[70]

To revert to Ruth, it is reasonable to assume, on the basis of the data adduced, that, in the late biblical period at least, when there were no male survivors a woman would inherit from her husband and succeed to his rights and privileges. Naomi inherited no land from her husband and sons—only the right to redeem the family property that her husband had sold. Because she is unable to exercise this right, in view of her poverty, she transfers (*mkrh*) this obligation-right to her nearest kinsman. When he declines, Boaz, a somewhat more distant relative, accepts (*qnty*) this obligation-right, which brings him Ruth as a wife. His subsequent redemption of the land from the original purchaser from Elimelech, is not described in the book, because it is Ruth who is the focus of interest.

The verbs *mākhar*, "sell," and *qānāh*, "buy," must therefore carry a special nuance of their basic meaning "sell" and "buy." In our context, *mākhar* means "to transfer the obligation-right of redemption" and *qānāh* "to accept, acquire the obligation-right of redemption." It is this power which the kinsman transmits to Boaz by taking off his sandal and giving it to Boaz. The practice of a buyer's taking hold of some movable object (*m^{e}talt^{e}lin*) like a cloth-band or kerchief to confirm the transfer of property (*qabbalat qinyan*, lit. "the acceptance of ownership") is operative in Rabbinic law to the present day.[71]

This special usage of the verbs *mākhar* and *qānāh* cannot now, as far as I know, be attested elsewhere in our extant sources. The fact is perhaps explicable by the fact that we have very few descriptions of commercial transactions in biblical times. However, partial analogies for this usage may be found. The verb *mākhar* is used in a noncommercial context to "hand over to enemies" (Deut 32: 30; Judg 2: 14; 3: 8, 4: 2, 9, 10; 7; 1 Sam 12: 9; Is 50: 1; Ezek 30: 12; Ps 44: 13), a sense which embodies the nuance of "transfer," which we postulate for Ruth 4: 3. In Mishnaic Hebrew, the *Qal* of *qānāh* means "acquire," and the *Hiphil*, *hiqnah* means "to cause to acquire—empower to acquire." Thus, *'šh hqnw lw mn hšmym* (*B. Kethubot* 82a) "Heaven gave him the power to acquire a wife," *'yn 'dm mqnh dbr šl' b' l'wlm* (*B. Baba Metzia*) "A man cannot empower the sale of something not yet in existence." *lyhwh h'rṣ wmly'h 'l šm šqnh whqnh wšlyṭ b'ylmw* (*B. Roš Hašānāh* 31a) "The earth is the Lord's and its fullness—because He acquired it and empowered its inhabitants to take possession and He rules in His world."[72] The verb *mākhar* in Ruth is equivalent to the Mishnaic *hiqnāh* "cause, empower to buy." For this meaning, we may also note the Aramaic root *zbn*, which in the *Pe'al* means "buy" and in the *Pa'el* has a causative sense, "cause to buy, hence, sell."

What we have in Ruth is therefore a classic tale from the Silver Age of biblical literature that tells a moving story of a distant and idealized past. The transaction described is not an instance of the levirate, but a genuine example of the redemption of land, which had been sold under the stress of economic want to an outsider. The land is redeemed and restored to the family by a kinsman who finds his reward in the love and devotion of the destitute woman whom he has befriended and sheltered.

Notes

1 Cf *Midraš Ruth Rabbah* 2: 14: "This scroll is concerned neither with the laws of purity or impurity, of permitted or forbidden actions. Why, then, was it written? To teach you how great is the reward for the practice of loving-kindness." Cf also *Midraš Leviticus Rabbah* 34: 8.

2 Cf Nelson Glueck's well-known study, first published in German in 1927, translated into English by A. Gottschalk under the title, *Hesed in the Bible* (Cincinnati, 1967).

3 *Ḥesed* is used for "love" even in its transitory and superficial sense, as in Hos 6: 4: *mh' 'šh lk 'prym mh' 'śh lk yhwdh whsdkm k'nn bqr wkṭl mškym hlk*, "What shall I do with you, O Ephraim? What shall I do with you, O Judah? Seeing that your love is like a morning cloud, like the passing dew of the morning." For *wekaṭṭal* in MT, read the construct *ûkṭal*. On *maškîm*, lit. "rising (time), morning," cf the usage in post-biblical Hebrew: M. Bikkurim 3: 2: *wlmškym hmmwnh 'wmr*, "In the morning the official says." This usage occurs also in *Seder Olam* (ed. Marx), p. 31, and *Damascus Scroll* (S. Schechter, *Zadokite Sect*, p. 10), and see R. Gordis in *Sepher Tur-Sinai* (Jerusalem, 5720-1960), p. 158.

4 This tradition is found in the LXX and in the versions dependent upon it and is reflected in the talmudic statement: "Samuel wrote the book bearing his name, Judges and Ruth" (B. *Bathra*, 14b).

5 Cf R. Gordis, "The Bible as a Cultural Monument" (in L. Finkelstein, *The Jews*, New York, 1949), p. 809, now in idem, *Poets, Prophets and Sages* (Bloomington, 1970, p. 34), and in *Koheleth: The Man and His World* (New York, 1955), p. 18 f.

6 For an excellent recent treatment of the literary motifs in Ruth, cf D. F. Rauber, "Literary Values in the Bible: The Book of Ruth," in *JBL* 89 (1970), 27–37.

7 So Berthold and Graetz, who are followed by Bertholet, Cornill, Meinhold, Hempel, and many moderns.

8 Suggested as a possibility by H. H. Rowley, "The Marriage of Ruth" in *The Servant*

of the Lord and Other Essays on the O.T. (London, 1952), p. 164. This important paper, rich in bibliographical references, will henceforth be cited as RMR.

[9] So S. R. Driver, A. Kahana (*Peruš Mada'i*), *ad loc.*

[10] So S. R. Driver.

[11] S. J. J. Slotki in Soncino Bible, *Five Megillot* (London, 1946), p. 39a.

[12] So Humbert.

[13] So Gunkel.

[14] So Haller, *Die Fünf Megillot* (Tübingen, 1940), p. 2.

[15] So Budde, Oettli.

[16] Cf W. E. Staples in *AJSL* (1937), 147–57.

[17] So R. H. Pfeiffer, *Introduction to the OT* (New York, 1941), p. 719; O. Eissfeldt, *The OT: An Introduction* (New York, 1965), p. 480 f.

[18] See the useful conspectus of views in RMR, p. 164, n. 1, and the OT Introductions of Driver, Pfeiffer, and Eissfeldt.

[19] Cf B. *Baba Batra*, 14b, cited in n. 4 above.

[20] So Keil, Wright, Albright, and Myers.

[21] So Wright, Oettli, Driver, Fischer, Haller, and Kaufmann.

[22] So Davidson, Reuss.

[23] So Ewald, Jepsen.

[24] So Wellhausen, Bertholet, Cornill, Steuernagel. The fourth century is preferred by Jouon, Meinhold, Sellin, Oesterley-Robinson, Eissfeldt, Pfeiffer.

[25] In his careful study of the language of our book, *The Linguistic and Literary Form of the Book of Ruth* (Leiden, 1955), pp. 8–32, Jacob M. Myers concludes that Ruth belongs to the period of the early Monarchy. He categorizes the language as belonging "to the same broad category as JE in the *Pentateuch*, *Joshua*, *Judges*, *Samuel* and *Kings*" (p. 32). Our reasons for being unable to accept this view are indicated in the body of this paper.

[26] Thus, by the side of the early *tštkryn* I Sam 1: 14, note the later *tthmqyn* Jer 31: 21, and *thylyn* Is 45: 10.

[27] On these forms, which occur not only as *Kethibh-Qere* readings but in the MT with no variants, and the implications of this fact for the Masorah, see Gordis, *The Biblical Text in the Making* (Philadelphia, 1937), pp. 101 ff; augmented edition (New York, 1971).

[28] Thus *rby sm'wn š'šh šlš 'śrh šnh bm'rh*, "R. Simeon, who spent thirteen years in the cave" (*Midraš Tehillim* on Ps 17: 14) and often. On *'gwnh*, lit. "chained," the technical term for a deserted wife who has not received a religious divorce (*gēt*) from her husband, cf B. *Gittin* and often.

[29] In spite of this usage and other linguistic phenomena adduced in the text, W. F. Albright declares "Neither vocabulary nor syntax suggests any Aramaic influence in the writer's [sc. of Ruth] Hebrew" (in his review of R. H. Pfeiffer's *Introduction to the Old Testament* in *JBL*, 61 [1942], 124). Even if Aramaic influence be discounted in this instance, the well-attested tendency of *tertiae Aleph* forms to become *tertiae Yod* in "late" OT and Middle Hebrew (cf e.g., B. Margulis in *JBL* 89 [1970], 300, n. 14) would still point to a later rather than to an earlier date for Ruth. The current tendency to deny altogether the existence of Aramaisms in biblical Hebrew is an overreaction to the earlier propensity to exaggerate their extent. It has happened in the history of biblical scholarship more than once that the pendulum has swung from one to the other extreme. What is obviously needed is a balanced position. A fuller discussion of the tendency toward *tertiae Yod* forms instead of *tertiae Aleph* would also need to reckon with the problems of Biblical orthography and the evidence of Mishnaic Hebrew.

[30] See our discussion of the four categories of Aramaisms, real and alleged, in *The*

Book of God and Man: A Study of Job (Chicago, 1965), pp. 161–63, 334, and "On the Methodology of Biblical Exegesis" in *JQR* vol. 61, 1970, 93–118.

[31] Cf Rowley's summary of the various views in "The Chronological Order of Ezra and Nehemiah," *op. cit.*, pp. 131–59.

[32] See RMR, p. 163.

[33] Cf R. T. H. Griffith, *The Ramayan of Valmiki* (1915), p. 265 f.

[34] Cf J. Scheftelowitz, *Archiv für Religionswissenschaft* 18 (1915), 255.

[35] Cf E. R. Lacheman in *JBL* 56 (1937), 53 ff; E. A. Speiser, in *BASOR* 77 (1940), 15 ff, who adduces Akkadian evidence and argues for the use of the shoe to validate special transactions. It may be added that the reason for the use of the shoe to confirm a transfer of property was probably a practical one. In ancient society, men possessed few movable objects that could be used to symbolize a transaction. The only article of major clothing was the garment worn by day and used as a covering by night (Ex 22: 25–27; Deut 24: 11), which could obviously not be removed in public. Hence, the sandal was used. In Rabbinic Judaism, acquisition was validated by taking hold of a scarf (*qinyān 'agabh sūdār*). This practice is still in vogue, in the validation of the Kethubbah "marriage contract" at weddings and at *m^e^khīrat ḥāmeṣ*, the fictive "sale of leaven" before Passover, the possession of which is forbidden to householders by Rabbinic law.

[36] On the other hand, the passage in Amos 2: 6: *ʿl-mkrm bksp ṣdyq w'bywn bʿbwr nʿlym* (see also 8: 6) which is often cited in this connection (so Speiser, *loc. cit.*) is not an instance of this usage. Note that the *naʿalāyîm* are not the instruments but the object of the evildoers' activity. It is important to note: a) the parallelism in Amos, b) the textual evidence from 1 Sam 12: 3: *w'ʿlm ʿyny bw* (cf LXX, which read *wnʿlym ʿnu by*), c) the Hebrew text of Ben Sira 46: 19 *kpr wnʿalm* (cf *Pešitta*, "ransom and bribe" as well as d) the use of the noun *nʿlmym* in the Qumran Thanksgiving Scrolls (Tablet XIII, 1.3) and Ps 26: 4; on the basis of this evidence, we have postulated a noun *naʿalām*, "bribe," lit. "covering, hiding material," in all these passages. In Amos 3: 6; 8: 6, read: *ʿl-mkrm bksp ṣdyq w'bywn bʿbwr nʿlm*. Note the parallel with *ksp*. In 1 Sam 12: 3, read: *wmyd my lqhty kpr wnʿlm*. In Ben Sira, read similarly: *kpr wnʿlm*. See R. Gordis, "*Naʿalam* and Other Observations on the Ain Feshka Scrolls," in *JNES* 19 (1950), 44 ff. In Ps 26: 4 and in the Thanksgiving Scrolls, the plural *nʿlmym* is a synecdoche for "men of bribes"; cf the parallelism with *mty šw'*. The form *naʿalām* is a *Nun*-preformative noun, derived from the *Niphal*. On this formation, cf the biblical form *naptûl* (Gen 30: 8) and see Ges.-Kautzsch, *Grammatik*, 28 ed. sec. 85, par. 49. The form is more common in Mishnaic Hebrew, as, e.g., *naḥtôm*, "baker" (B. *Baba Batra* 20b.), *nḥšwl*, "crushing wind" (B. *Baba Kamma* 116b.), cf also *nṣph, nyṣoq, ndbkh*, and see M. H. Segal, *Diqduq Lešon Hamišnah* (Tel Aviv, 5696–1936), sec. 129. The existence of feminine *Nun*-preformative nouns in Mishnaic Hebrew such as *nibrešet* and *nibrekhet* suggests that in Ps 37: 38 *nkrth* may also be a noun meaning "destruction," similarly in Prov 15: 6 *wbtbu't ršʿ nʿkrt* "but for the income of the wicked, there is destruction" (note the Beth).

[37] On the levirate in general, cf E. Westermarck, *The History of Human Marriage* (5th ed., New York, 1922), vol. 3, pp. 207–20, 261–63. On the biblical institution, cf J. G. Frazer, *Folklore in the OT*, vol. 2, pp. 266–303; D. Jacobson, *The Social Background of the OT* (Cincinnati, 1942), pp. 290 ff; T. H. Gaster, *Myth, Legend, and Custom in OT* (New York, 1969), pp. 447 ff. For the levirate in post-biblical Judaism, cf L. M. Epstein, *Marriage Laws in the Bible and the Talmud*, (Cambridge, 1942).

[38] Cf T. J. Meek in *ANET*, p. 182, who supplies in brackets the crucial words, reading: "[If] she has no [son, her father-in-law shall marry her to the son] of his choice . . . or, if he wishes, he may give her to her father-in-law."

[39] Cf A. Goetze in *ANET* p. 196b; E. Neufeld, *The Hittite Laws* (London, 1951), p. 55. It is worth noting that there is no explicit reference here to the widow's childlessness. This is, however, probably the circumstance to which the levirate applied. On the other hand, it is possible that the levirate marriage in these Middle-East cultures was concerned not with "preserving the name of the dead man" but with economic factors, either providing for the widow's maintenance or, as would be more likely, with retaining her as property within the circle of the family. See E. M. MacDonald, *The Position of Women as Reflected in Semitic Codes of Law* (Toronto, 1931), pp. 45, 63 ff, who stresses the element of property in the levirate, as do other writers.

[40] The considerably earlier date we assign to the composition of Deuteronomy (the evidence for which we hope to present shortly) does not affect the development of the levirate discussed in the text. The later date proposed by some scholars would not militate against the relative antiquity of the rite. See also n. 41.

[41] Thus, Rowley correctly observes that Deuteronomy "reflects a limitation of something that was once wider in Israel, as is clear from the other duties of the *gōʾēl*" (RMR, p. 170).

[42] The Talmud (B. *Kiddušin*, 7b; B. *Yebamot*, 6: 1) explains that the Samaritans arrived at their conclusion by treating *hḥwṣh* in *lʾ thyh ʾšt-hmt hḥwṣḥ lʾyš zr* (Deut 25: 5) as an adjective modifying *ʾšt*: "hence a woman outside, not yet living in his house, i.e., a betrothed woman." They then interpret the passage to mean that this category of woman, i.e. a betrothed woman, may not be married to a stranger (but must marry her brother-in-law), but a woman "inside," living in his house, i.e., a married woman, may be taken by a stranger (and must not marry her brother-in-law). The Samaritan Targum renders *hḥwṣh* as *brʾyth* "one outside." The Talmud interprets *hḥwṣh* similarly, as a reference to a betrothed woman. It therefore requires *yibbum, both* for an engaged and for a married woman (*B. Yeb.* 13b).

[43] So Benjamin ben Moshe of Nehawend (ca 830), Joseph ben Jacob Qirqisani (tenth century), and Elijah Bashyazi (ca 1420). Later Qaraite practice permitted the levirate only to cousins of the dead husband. Other authorities forbade the rite, even in the case of a betrothed woman. For a succinct summary of Samaritan and Qaraite views, see J. D. Eisenstein, *Osar Yisrael*, vol. 5, p. 47.

[44] Cf W. Max Müller, *The Sacred Books of the East* (1886), vol. 25, p. 335.

[45] Cf the Mishnah tractates *Maʿaserōt* and *Maʿasēr Šēnī* for the detailed provisions.

[46] M. *Bekhorot* 1: 7.

[47] The great variety of views in the Talmud cannot be set forth here. For a conspectus of these views, associated with the biblical text, cf Barukh Halevi Epstein, *Torah Temimah,* (New York, 1922), vol. 5, pp. 384–404. One classic statement cited in the Babylonian and the Palestinian Talmud will suffice: (*Tosefta*, *Yebamot*, Ch 6; B. *Yebamot* 39b; 109a; J. *Yebamot* 13: 2). "Abba Saul says: He who marries his sister-in-law for the sake of her beauty or because of desire, or any other ulterior motive [*Tosefta*—for the sake of property], is guilty of incest and I am inclined to regard the offspring as illegitimate. The Sages say, "The Biblical statement 'her brother-in-law shall come into her' means no matter what the circumstances or the motive."

[48] *B. Baba Batra*, 109b.

[49] Cf Barukh Halevi Epstein, *op. cit.* p. 386, n. 52, who calls attention to this unusually broad interpretation of *bēn*.

[50] Levirate marriage is forbidden by the Franco-German school of Tosafists like Rabbi Jacob ben Meir Tam (1100–1171), the grandson of Rashi (1040–1105). The levirate is permitted by Rabbi Isaac ben Jacob Al-Fasi of North Africa (1013–1103), Maimonides

(1135–1204), and Rabbi Asher ben Jehiel (1250–1328), who lived in an Islamic environment.

[51] For the fullest text of the *Edict of Ammisaduqa* (seventeenth century B.C.E.), cf J. J. Finkelstein in *ANET*, Supplement, (Princeton, 1969), pp. 526–28. This is the most extensive document extant dealing with the proclamation of an act of "equity" (Sumerian *nig. si. sa.*, Akkadian *mišarum*) by a Babylonian king, a practice in vogue at the accession of a king to the throne and on succeeding intervals of seven or more years. Ammisaduqa, the tenth ruler of the Hammurabi dynasty, ruled from 1641 to 1626 B.C.E. Finkelstein, who cites other, less complete references to this usage in Near Eastern texts, speaks of *mišarum* as encompassing "the remission of debts and the reversion of land-holdings to their original owners" (*op. cit.*, p. 526a). It may be noted that the Edict of Ammisaduqa is very detailed only with regard to the remission of debts, but is much less explicit on the freeing of those sold into slavery for debt. I am unable to find any reference in the Edict to the restoration of land to the original owner. Nor is there an enunciation of any cosmic religious principle, such as is set forth in Lev 25: 23.

It is noteworthy that the differences in the degree of attention given in Mesopotamia to the various features of the *mišarum* have their parallel in biblical and post-biblical experience. The principle of the remission of debts (Deut 15: 1 ff) during "the year of release" was operative as late as the Second Temple Period. Its observance created grave economic problems in the more advanced, urbanized society which required access to credit. Hence, Hillel's *taqqānāh* of the *prosbūl* (first century C.E.), (M. *Shebiith* 10: 2, 3), which utilized a legal fiction to make it possible to collect unpaid debts after the *šemittāh*. On the other hand, Rabbinic tradition declares that the biblical provision for the restoration of land in the Jubilee Year was not enforced after the early exile of the Trans-Jordanian tribes of Reuben, Gad, and half of Manasseh (*Sifra*, *Behar* II, 3) or thereafter, during the Second Temple (B. *Arakhin*, 32b.).

[52] After the paper was completed, I was pleased to find that D. Daube, in *Studies in Biblical Law* (Cambridge, 1944; reprint edition New York, 1969), pp. 39–62, who treats the role of the *gō'ēl* in detail, presents a similar interpretation of the primary meaning of the root *gā'āl*.

[53] *Op. cit.*, p. 163.

[54] So E. Neufeld, *Ancient Hebrew Marriage Laws* (London, 1944), pp. 240 f.

[55] So J. A. Jepsen, *Theologische Studien und Kritiken*, 108 (1937–38) 419 ff; and W. Caspari, *Neue Kirchliche Zeitschrift*, 19, (1908) 115 ff.

[56] So, apparently, Rowley, *op. cit.*

[57] S. M. Burrows in *JBL* 59 (1940), 448.

[58] So Haller, *ad loc.*

[59] So also Haller. On this usage, cf S. R. Driver, *A Treatise in the Use of the Tenses in Hebrew* (Oxford, 1892), pp. 17 f, sec. 13 f.

[60] B. *Yebamot* 115a.

[61] See E. Sachau, *Aramäische Papyrus und Ostraka* (Leipzig, 1911) and A. Ungnad, *Aramäische Papyrus aus Elephantine* (Leipzig, 1911) for the texts discovered earlier; and for those found later, E. G. Kraeling, *The Brooklyn Museum Papyri* (New Haven, 1953). From the extensive literature we cite M. L. Margolis, *The Elephantine Documents* (*JQR*, 12 [1912], 419–43); and B. Porten, *Archives from Elephantine* (Berkeley and Los Angeles, 1960), who treats of Mibtahiah's life and career in pp. 235–63.

[62] On the content and development of talmudic law with regard to women and the family, cf L. M. Epstein, *The Jewish Marriage Contract* (New York, 1927): *Marriage Laws in the Bible and the Talmud* (Cambridge, 1942); L. Finkelstein, *Akiba: Scholar,*

Saint, and Martyr (New York, 1936), L. Finkelstein, *The Pharisees*, 3d ed. (Philadelphia, 1962), and see vol. 2, p. 837, n. 52. For the post-talmudic period, cf. A. H. Freimann, *Seder Qiddušin Unesuin* (Heb) (Jerusalem, 5705=1945).

[63] Salo W. Baron, *A Social and Religious History of the Jews* (New York, 1958), vol. 6, pp. 135 f.

[64] Cf B. Porten, *op. cit.*, pp. 209 f, 261 f for the divorce formula in Elephantine and its relationship to other evidence for this practice.

[65] For this as yet unpublished document, see P. Benoit, J. T. Milik, R. de Vaux, *Discoveries in the Judean Desert II* (Oxford, 1961), p. 108.

[66] Cf J. *Ketubot* 30b, v, 8; also J. *Ketubot* 31c, VII, 6; and see L. M. Epstein *The Jewish Marriage Contract* (New York, 1927), pp. 197 ff.

[67] Cf the brief discussion of these texts and their implications in M. A. Friedman, *Bittul Hanesu'in 'al pi Baqqašat Ha'išah*, "The Termination of a Marriage on the Wife's Request," in *Ha'arets*, Oct. 1, 1968, p. 19, and his more extensive treatment of the subject in *PAAJR*, 1969, pp. 29–55.

[68] This was an optional procedure practiced in Palestine, according to the Palestinian Talmud.

[69] The formula used to validate the practice was: *kwpyn 'wtw 'd šy'mr rwṣh 'ny*, "The husband is placed under duress until he says 'I am willing!'" (B. *Yebamot* 106a.)

[70] The far-reaching principle laid down in the Talmud is: *kl hmqdš 'd't' drbnn mqdš*, "Whoever marries does so by the authority and consent of the Sages." (B. *Kethubot* 3a.)

[71] Cf n. 35 above.

[72] Cf Rashi *ad loc. klwmr qwng wmqnh*, "He acquires and transmits the right to it." Jastrow: "He gave His creatures possession of His world."

Delbert R. Hillers
Johns Hopkins University

Observations on Syntax and Meter in Lamentations

The Hebrew Verbless Clause in the Pentateuch, by Francis I. Andersen,[1] is an exceptionally significant step forward in Hebrew syntax. Andersen reaches important new conclusions concerning word order in verbless clauses, showing that varieties of word order are associated with differences in the semantic relation between subject and predicate, in the relation of a clause to other clauses, and so on. The study is commendably explicit and thorough; all the verbless clauses in the Pentateuch are studied and classified.

Andersen's monograph is therefore a good basis for comparative study of syntax. The present investigation is devoted to the book of Lamentations, a work which may claim interest because it is datable within rather narrow limits, in the view of most scholars, and because it is very widely acknowledged to be poetry and to exhibit a particular meter, labelled "Qinah meter" by Budde, in its first four chapters. In the first part of this paper, the verbless clauses in Lamentations are compared with those of the Pentateuch as classified by Andersen in his recent monograph. In the second part, the order of postverbal elements in verbal clauses are compared with the patterns of order in Genesis, as classified by Andersen in an unpublished work.[2] The intention is to find answers to these questions: Are there differences in the syntax of this poetic work as compared with a large body of mostly prose material? If the poetic text departs from the norm, does it do so in conformity with a particular metrical or rhythmic pattern?

Verbless Clauses in Lamentations

The present writer has attempted to follow Andersen's model as closely as possible in separating "verbless clauses" from other types. Sentences with quasi verbal elements such as *yēš* and *ʿôd* have not been included.[3] In addition, some strings that are possibly verbless clauses have been omitted as being too dubious textually to permit analysis. These are 1: 12a (*lôʾ* . . . *derek*); 2: 4a*b* (*niṣṣāb yᵉmînô*). 4: 13 is understood as joined to 4: 14; in any case, it is not a verbless clause, since it does not apparently contain any predication. In 3: 19 and 3: 26, certain emendations would yield verbless clauses, but other solutions to the textual problems might also be proposed; so these examples have not been included. In the following cases, where there is no textual problem, strings have been omitted as not constituting clauses, since they do not seem to contain a subject and predicate: 2: 15c (*kᵉlîlat yôpî māśôś lᵉkôl hāʾāreṣ*); 3: 23 (*ḥᵃdāšîm labbᵉqārîm*); 4: 15 (*ṭāmēʾ*).

Two related problems arise in poetic lines where parallelism is present. First, in parallelism, a verb may be expressed in the first colon and omitted from the second. The second colon is then formally "verbless," but is not so in sense, since the verbal predicate must be understood also in the second colon; or else the whole line is to be read as a single verbal clause of unusual structure. On this basis, 5: 2 (*bāttēnû lᵉnokrîm*) and 1: 20 (*babbayit kammāwet*) have been omitted; the latter is also suspect textually. 5: 3 (*ʾimmôtēnû kᵉʾalmānôt*) is problematic: should one supply a form of *hāyāh* as in the first colon? This example has been included as a verbless clause here. The second problem arises where a poetic line can be interpreted either as one verbless clause with a compound element or as two separate clauses, assuming ellipsis of some element or elements in the second. The three lines of this sort have all been interpreted here as containing two verbless clauses.

There are thirty-one verbless clauses in Lamentations. Almost all agree with the rules as stated by Andersen. The following exemplify his rule 1, that the order is S(ubject)-P(redicate) in clauses of identification, where both S and P are definite: 2: 15c; 2: 16c; 3: 1; 3: 24; 3: 63. In 3: 24 (*ḥelqi Yhwh*), however, it is difficult to be certain as to which is subject and which is predicate.

Rule 3, that the order is P-S in a clause of classification, where P is indefinite relative to S, is exempllfied in 1: 22*ca*; 2: 13c; 3: 10 (twice); 3: 25 (twice); 4: 7b. Rule 5, that the order is S-P when the predicate is a participle, is exemplified in 1: 4 (four times); 1: 11 (twice). Five other verbless clauses in Lamentations are of the sort where P is a prepositional phrase, for which no rules as to normal order are framed by Andersen (see pp. 49–50 of his monograph): 1: 9a; 2: 9b; 3: 62; 5: 3; 5: 16.[4]

One example is clearly abnormal (though not unparalleled in Andersen's corpus), a case where a participial predicate precedes the subject: 1: 21a (*kî ne'enāḥāh 'ānî*). Possible explanations for such abnormal ordering are given by Andersen on page 48 of his book.

One other verbless clause calls for special comment: 1: 18 (*ṣaddîq hû' Yhwh*). This might be taken as a sentence of classification, with normal order (P-S): "He, Yahweh, is righteous." But if so, one must take *hû'* to be the subject, and *Yhwh* as in apposition to *hû'*. The only parallel for such an unusual apposition seems to be Ezek 33: 8, and it is neither exactly the same as the present case nor beyond question textually. An alternate analysis would be to take *ṣaddîq* as the subject, resumed by the pleonastic pronoun *hû'*. On this line, one would also have to assume that *ṣaddîq*, though without the article, is definite, since it is almost equally unparalleled for an indefinite subject to be resumed by a pleonastic pronoun.[5] The line would mean: "The righteous one [in this issue] is Yahweh, because I [the other party] defied his command." Perhaps Lamentations at this point preserves older poetic practice, in which the definite article is seldom used; note that *ṣaddîq* is the first word in a stanza that must begin with *ṣādê*. A rather close parallel is Is 9: 14: *zāqēn ûneśû' pānîm hû' hārô'š wenābî' môreh šeqer hû' hazzānāb*, "[The] elder and [the] honored man is the head / And [the] prophet who teaches falsehood is the tail." If this latter analysis of Lam 1: 18 is correct, the clause fits Andersen's rule 2, according to which a pleonastic pronoun comes before the predicate in a clause of identification.

To sum up, Andersen's description proves to fit word order in the verbless clauses of Lamentations very well. There is no evidence that the author or authors practiced any greater freedom than did the writers of the Pentateuch. Though the body of clauses for comparison is small, it does contain examples of all the principal rules in Andersen's study.

The Order of Sentence Elements Following the Verb in Lamentations

In many verbal sentences in Hebrew, two or more sentence elements follow the verb. These may be an independent pronoun serving as subject, a nominal subject, a nominal direct object, and so on. In a portion of his unpublished work *Studies in Hebrew Syntax*, Andersen has tabulated the order of these sentence elements relative to each other, and gives a matrix showing the order normally followed.[6] Only a small percentage of sentences depart from this normal order. It is to be hoped that Andersen will soon publish a study of the Hebrew verbal sentence; in advance of that, the present writer will cite certain of the data from Andersen's work for comparative purposes, since there is no similar body of tabulated data available and since, as the reader will readily see, the evidence cited is factual and not dependent on any particular theory as to Hebrew syntax.

In Genesis, where a verb is followed by both a nominal subject (NSubj) and a prepositional phrase modifying the verb (PrPh), the nominal subject precedes. This is true in 115 of the 122 examples in the book. Where a verb is followed by a nominal direct object (DObj) and a prepositional phrase, the direct object precedes. The pattern is followed in ninety-two of 103 sentences in Genesis.

In Lamentations there are thirty-two verbal sentences with a nominal subject and a prepositional phrase following the verb. In twenty-one of these, the order is the one normally found in Genesis: V-NSubj-PrPh.[7] In eleven, the order is the opposite: V-PrPh-NSubj.[8] Though several of the sentences are rather difficult and hence uncertain, the general picture is clear: a much higher proportion of sentences—about one-third of the total—show abnormal order than is true in Genesis.

A similar picture is presented in the second case. There are twenty-six verbal sentences in Lamentations in which both a nominal direct object and a prepositional phrase follow the verb. In fifteen cases, the order is that normally found in Genesis: V-DObj-PrPh.[9] In eleven cases, the abnormal order occurs: V-PrPh-DObj.[10] Though the order of other sorts of postverbal elements might also be tabulated, the number of examples in Lamentations seems too small to permit any conclusions. The above two types are the most common, and occur sufficiently often to show a marked contrast to the situation in Genesis.

Andersen's tabulation for Genesis showed that verbal sentences with more than two postverbal sentence elements follow the same pattern as those with two, though there was a somewhat higher proportion of sentences with abnormal order (345 of 409 exhibited normal patterns). In Lamentations, only seven of twenty-four sentences of this sort show "normal" order, while seventeen are abnormal.[11] In Genesis, the nominal subject ordinarily precedes the nominal direct object, and the latter precedes any adverbial prepositional phrase which is present. Most of the sentences from Lamentations which are classified here as abnormal show some departure from this pattern.

One hypothesis which suggests itself almost inevitably is that these syntactic abnormalities in Lamentations have to do with meter. The whole book is poetry, and ever since K. Budde's "Das hebräische Klagelied" (1882),[12] most scholars have recognized that the dominant metrical form in Lamentations chapters 1–4 is a line in which the second of two parallel cola is shorter than the first, whether one prefers to call this a Qinah verse, a "fiver" (Fünfer),[13] or a "brachycatalectic" line of some sort.[14] Though not all the lines are of this type, many are. Even though the norms of this kind of verse have not been defined with any great precision, it may be possible to determine whether or not some clear relation between meter and syntax exists. Specifically, we may ask whether the poet adopts abnormal order only or primarily when the meter demands it—that is, to achieve the unbalanced line characteristic of chapters 1–4.

This seems not to be so. Of the eleven cases of the abnormal order V-PrPh-NSubj, five[15] constitute only a single poetic colon, not a whole line, and therefore the Qinah meter seems unaffected even if the elements are reversed. Thus, for example, 2: 9a, *tābᵉʿû bāʾāreṣ šᵉʿāreyhā* seems to work just as well if we make it **tābᵉʿû šᵉʿāreyhā bāʾāreṣ*. In four other examples (1: 6a; 2: 20c; 2: 22b; 3: 31), which cover a whole poetic line, metrical relations do not seem to be disturbed if we change to normal prose order, thus 2: 20c: *ʾim yēhārēg bᵉmiqdaš ʾᵃdônāy kôhēn wᵉnābîʾ* goes well as **ʾim yēhārēg kôhēn wᵉnābîʾ bᵉmiqdaš ʾᵃdônāy*. Only in two cases of eleven would the normal prose order seem difficult from the standpoint of Qinah meter: 1: 1b and 1: 16b.

Similarly, eight of the eleven cases of the unusual order V-PrPh-DObj would seem metrically acceptable if the normal prose order were restored. Five of them comprise only a single colon (2: 4c; 2: 6a [textually very uncertain]; 3: 16; 3: 29; 3: 53), and the others (2: 5c; 2: 6c; 2: 7b) would still give a Qinah verse if the postverbal elements were transposed. Only 2: 2b; 3: 13; and perhaps 2: 3a seem rather difficult metrically if transposed.[16]

It is of course possible that greater refinement of our metrical conceptions would show a correlation between metrical form and the order of postverbal sentence elements, but the evidence gathered here does not show any apparent relation. Though we must conclude that the author or authors were freer in this aspect of syntax than were the writers of Genesis, we cannot readily explain their practice as related to meter. One factor can be singled out, however, as involved in a good many cases of abnormal ordering. This is the tendency, already noted by Andersen with reference to Genesis,[17] to put markedly long elements last, regardless of syntactic function. Compound elements also tend to stand last.

Of the twenty-two examples of abnormal order cited above, the following nine sentences illustrate this tendency: 1: 1b; 1: 16b; 2: 2b; 2: 3a; 2: 5c; 2: 6c; 2: 7b; 2: 20c; 3: 13. A preference for putting long or compound postverbal elements last in the sentence is especially noticeable in sentences with three or more postverbal elements. Note, for instance, 2: 1b: *hišlîk miššāmayim ʾereṣ tipʾeret yiśrāʾēl*, where the long direct object is put last. Compare 2: 6b: *šikkaḥ Yhwh bᵉṣiyyôn môʿēd wᵉšabbāt*. The compound direct object is last, whereas in normal prose order the prepositional phrase *b^eṣiyyôn* would be last. In a similar way, this tendency is observable in 2: 1a; 2: 3b; 2: 10c; 2: 15a; 2: 16a; 2: 18b; 2: 19b; 2: 21a; 3: 44; 3: 46; 3: 55; 4: 10b. Though judgment in this sort of question is inevitably somewhat subjective, it does seem that this type of patterning emphasizes the caesura in these lines, and also yields a second colon which is sufficiently long to fit the common metrical pattern of the poems. This seems especially clear in the four cases of V-PrPh-DObj-NSubj (2: 10c; 2: 15a; 2: 16a; 3: 46), where placing the subject last strongly emphasizes the division of the line into cola.

Notes

1 *JBL* Monograph Series, Vol. XIV (New York and Nashville, 1970).

2 "Studies in Hebrew Syntax," unpublished Ph. D. dissertation, Johns Hopkins University, 1960. I am grateful to Professor Andersen for permitting me to make reference to this work.

3 Andersen, *Hebrew Verbless Clause*, p. 23, para. 10, does not include *'ayyēh*, "where?" in the list of quasi verbals, or in the list of interrogatives he gives elsewhere. On the basis of form, it presumably belongs with the quasi verbals; hence Lam 2: 12*ab* is not included here.

4 The proper classification of *'ôy*, "Woe!" is uncertain to me. On the basis of Prov 23: 29, where it is clearly a nominal, I have understood it to be the noun subject of a verbless clause in 5: 16.

5 In Prov 10: 18 and 28: 24, however, a formally indefinite subject is resumed by *hû'*.

6 See *Studies in Hebrew Syntax*, Table V, pp. 308–11.

7 1: 3a; 1: 5a; 1: 6b; 1: 10a; 1: 12c; 1: 17a; 1: 20b; 1: 22a; 2: 5a; 3: 18; 3: 39; 3: 48; 3: 50; 3: 54; 4: 1b; 4: 6a; 4: 7a; 4: 8b; 4: 9a; 4: 14a; 4: 19a.

8 1: 1b; 1: 6a; 1: 16b; 2: 9a; 2: 11a; 2: 20c; 2: 22b; 3: 17; 3: 31; 4: 8a; 5: 15.

9 1: 13a; 2: 1c; 2: 4a; 2: 8b; 2: 9c; 2: 10c; 2: 15b; 3: 1; 3: 9; 3: 27; 3: 56; 4: 11b; 4: 18a; 5: 9; 5: 21.

10 2: 2b; 2: 3a; 2: 4c; 2: 5c; 2: 6a; 2: 6c; 2: 7b; 3: 13; 3: 16; 3: 29; 3: 53.

11 Normal: 1: 11b; 1: 14c; 1: 15b; 1: 17c; 2: 19c; 3: 41; 4: 4a. Abnormal: 1: 15a; 2: 1a; 2: 1b; 2: 3b; 2: 6b; 2: 10c; 2: 15a; 2: 16a; 2: 18b; 2: 19b; 2: 21a; 2: 22a; 3: 44; 3: 46; 3: 52; 4: 10b; 4: 17a.

12 *ZAW* 2, 1–52.

13 E. Sievers' term, *Metrische Studien I: Studien zur hebräischen Metrik*, Erster Teil (Leipzig, 1901), pp. 116, 120–23.

14 So already J. Ley, *Grundzüge des Rhythmus, des Vers- und Strophenbaues in der hebräischen Poesie* (Halle, 1875), pp. 51–53. He also used the term "elegiac pentameter." Similarly, G. Hölscher, "Elemente arabischer, syrischer und hebräischer Metrik," *BZAW* 34 (1920), 98–101; and S. Mowinckel, "Zum Problem der hebräischen Metrik," *Festschrift für Alfred Bertholet* (Tübingen, 1950), pp. 391–93.

15 2: 9a; 2: 11a; 3: 17 (textually uncertain); 4: 8a; 5: 15.

16 Sentences with normal order include some that apparently must have this order to fit the meter—e.g., 1: 3a,—and (more commonly) some that could just as well have had the reverse order—e.g., 3: 18.

17 *Studies in Hebrew Syntax*, pp. 373–79; 400-401.

Herbert B. Huffmon
Drew University

Exodus 23: 4–5: A Comparative Study

The Book of the Covenant, Ex 20: 22 through 23: 33, is not a polished legal document bringing together in careful and standardized language a variety of materials. Rather, the diversity within the Book of the Covenant is quite clear. The *mšpṭym* (Ex 21: 1 through 22: 16) and Ex 23: 13–19 and 23: 20–33 are fairly cohesive, and may be separated out. The primary portion remaining—Ex 22: 17 through 23: 12—is usually regarded as somewhat of a potpourri, and the commentators remark on intrusive verses and redactional activity. In this last-mentioned portion, we find a collection of diverse materials, variously expressed, but centering on special concerns of a markedly religious and humane character. Concern for the poor is promoted, and justice is raised above special interests.

Among the humane laws, Ex 23: 4 5 in particular are very striking. They stand out in the humane laws because of their formulation as casuistic rules in the style of the *mšpṭym*, being introduced by *ky* (cf Ex 21: 1, 7, 14, 18, 20, 22, 26, 28, 33–34, 35, 37; 22: 4, 5, 6, 9–10, 13, 15), in contrast with the casuistic rules introduced by *ʾm* (Ex 22: 24, 25–26; cf Ex 20: 25) outside Ex 21: 1 through 22: 16. Also, the language in Ex 23: 4–5 is rather special. The reference to the other party as "your enemy" (Ex 23: 4) or as "the one who hates you" (Ex 23: 5) immediately indicates that we are not dealing with a cautious, dispassionate legal draftsman. These terms for legal parties are far removed from the normal usage in the Old Testament or ancient Near Eastern legal collections. Such terminology is restricted to very special circumstances. It is no surprise that the analogous rules in Deut 22: 1, 4 describe the other party with the much less colorful term "your brother." Ex 23: 4–5 are provocative in their wording. They do not merely derive from justice in the gate, but boldly and deliberately express in casuistic form a deep-going moral concern. The distinctive content of the two verses further indicates their special nature. Moreover, their contrast with the common-law tradition of England and America is rather intriguing.

> *ky tpgʿ šwr ʾybk ʾw ḥmrw tʿh hšb tšybnw lw*
> If you come across a straying ox or ass belonging to your enemy, you must return it to him. (Ex 23: 4)

There are a number of laws about straying stock animals. Frequently, as Ex 22: 4 probably indicates, the concern is about the damage that stray animals might do to the crops and the fields or vineyards. Since the finder of a stray animal would commonly discover it on his own land, recovery for any damage done might be expected to be the primary concern of the law. This is what we find in the Laws of Hammurapi, Nos. 57–58, and in the Hittite Laws, No. 107.[1] As for the common law, Roscoe Pound points out that "it is a general doctrine of the common law that the keeper of an animal of any kind which is likely to do harm to the land of others if it strays, is liable although not even negligent and although the animal may have been released by a trespassing stranger, for trespass on another's land and for damage done to the land or to the person or property of the landowner."[2] Indeed, whereas Hittite custom (Hittite Laws, No. 79) permitted stray oxen to be worked for the remainder of the day, before being returned —a form of distraint—more drastic penalties were permitted in early English law. For example, in the laws of the Anglo-Saxon King Ine (late seventh century A.D.) we find that "if . . . any beast breaks hedges and wanders at large within, since its owner will not or cannot keep it under control, he who finds it on his cornland shall take it and kill it. The owner [of the beast] shall take its hide and flesh and suffer the loss of the remainder."[3] This early law permits vengeance against the stray animal. Subsequently, the emphasis is on liability for damage done.[4]

Where an instance of known ownership is stated, the concern of the law tends to be that of misappropriation or conversion of lost property. As in Deut 22: 1–3, a finder is normally not entitled to appropriate for himself a stray animal of known ownership.[5] In Hittite law (Nos. 45, 71), a stray is handed over to the king, assigned to the finder, or returned to its owner if known, much as in older English law.[6] Yet it is interesting to note that whereas stress may be placed on the duty to return, as in Deut 22: 3 and the Hittite Laws, the common law does not acknowledge a duty to find. The finder is entitled to ignore the goods that he discovers, and has no duty to return something of which he has taken no custody.[7] When a rule clearly states that the stray belongs to the finder's enemy, as in Ex 23: 4, it is easy to see that there would be a strong temptation to ignore the stray animal and thereby increase the injury to its owner. It is not every man who would pass up "coals of fire" to help his enemy.

The use of the term "enemy" in the biblical law is especially interesting. This term, as far as legal statements—especially casuistic statements—go, is otherwise very restricted in use. It is not surprising to find it in the laws regulating warfare (Deut 20: 1, 3, 4, 14; 21: 10; 23: 10, 14). It may also be appropriate in the law of homicide (Num 35: 23), where intent is so important and, in the presumption of the law, "enemies" are not accidentally killed.[8] But the term "enemy" does not seem to belong in a law concerning stray cattle. Its use in Ex 23: 4 is deliberate, however. Specifying the other party as "your enemy" is a means of giving a sharper moral and emotional focus while obscuring the strictly legislative focus. The provocative formulation of the rule emphasizes that the finder has strict duties to *all* members of the community—even his enemy, the man who is so at odds with him that serious bodily injury to the finder would be presumed not to be accidental.[9] The stray stock animal cannot be ignored, but must be returned, whoever his owner may be.

As Cassuto emphasizes, the unusual formulation is a way of expressing "this, needless to say that"—that is, if you return your enemy's stray, it goes without saying that you would return your friend's or that of a mere acquaintance.[10] Also, it goes without saying that you would return something of greater value. Realizing this point—that the rule is intended as a basis for generalization rather than as the statement of a particular case—it becomes obvious that Ex 23: 4 is actually very carefully formulated, a rule that may well convey the real intent of the law more dramatically and more effectively than the less colorful and more cautious formulation in Deut 22: 1.[11] Ex 23: 4 focuses on the weakest link in the system of justice, the instance when the temptation to do less than justice is at its strongest. Those who pass this test will not fail others.

The Book of the Covenant reflects a small, village–farming community, a community in which one might well be acquainted with the neighbor's animals, the oxen and the asses so important to him. In a small community it is "prudent and reasonable" to assume that personal feelings, rather than legal principles, will frequently affect one's relations with his neighbors. In Ex 23: 4 (and 5), that emotional quality is ably countered by using the emotional term "enemy." In this seemingly imprudent formulation, one may actually see a more effective approach to expressing and impressing certain legal rules. From some points of view, ancient Israel here surpassed the traditional legal draftsmanship of the ancient Near East.

ky-tr'h ḥmwr śn'k rbṣ tḥt mś'w wḥdlt m'zb lw 'zb t'zb 'mw
If you see an ass belonging to someone who hates you, lying down under its load, you shall desist from leaving (it) to him; you must arrange (it) together with him. (Ex 23: 5)

This verse presents a number of translation problems, as is well known. In view of the very common pattern, *'zb* plus object plus *l* indicating an indirect object, it seems best to assume an ellipsis of the object in verse 5a.[12] In vs 5b, it seems best to retain the MT and to translate *'zb* with the aid of Old South Arabic *'ḏb*, "restore (in whole, to former condition),"[13] and Ugaritic *'db* (**'ḏb*), "prepare, arrange," used for preparing or putting on the trappings of a jenny ass.[14] Biblical Hebrew also offers some support for such a translation.[15] Admittedly, one does not expect a play on words in a legal text, but it can be avoided only by a gratuitous emendation, such as, following Bochart, *'zr t'zr*, "you must help." Perhaps also it should be stressed that *rbṣ* consistently refers to animals lying down at rest or at ease, and that the parallel with Balaam's ass, which "laid down beneath" him (Num 22: 27) because an angel of God was blocking the path, indicates that the animal may be on the ground voluntarily as well as involuntarily.

The incident of an ass lying down under its load must have been fairly common. If the animal is not kept moving, it is likely to just lie down; it may even roll around a bit, which usually means some repacking. The surefooted ass may even stumble at times and have difficulty getting back up. If the cinch rope is not tightened properly, if a hitch loosens, if the trail is steep and a breeching strap and/or breast collar is not used (properly), if the pack animal gets excited and starts running—if any of these accidents happen, the pack may be lost or the ass may be pulled down by a shifted load.[16] Yet normally, pack animals are not left to meander along by themselves, but are accompanied by the driver or owner. If the animal should be down, the driver is presumably at hand, able to give assistance. Indeed, the assumption of Ex 23: 5—and the clear wording in Deut 22: 4—is that the owner is at hand.

A further consideration is the kind of load than an ass might carry. One of the smaller asses, the burro, used as a pack animal in the American West, normally carries a pack or payload of between 75 and 100 pounds. The "black asses" used in the Old Assyrian caravan trade were stronger, and probably carried a payload of 150 to even 200 pounds.[17] It is not clear whether the ass in Ex 23: 5 is like the burro or more like the "black ass." But even assuming the stronger animal, a 200-pound load is not particularly heavy, nothing like the 600 pounds that a pack camel can handle. One experienced man can load an ass by himself without too much difficulty, though it is much easier and faster with two people. If the pack animal is down and unable to get up because of the pack, which may have shifted, it may well be a different situation. The owner could, without additional help, unload the animal and get it back up. Given time, he could also reload the pack. Another person would be a big help, however, if only in holding and calming the obviously frightened animal. With two people, it might be possible to avoid the tedium of unloading and reloading; and even if that were necessary, it could be done much more quickly. But the second person, except in unusual circumstances, would not be a matter of life or death for the ass, and he would rarely be unexpendable to the owner.[18]

The commentators differ as to the nature of the aid. First of all, they generally point to the owner of the beast as the beneficiary—that is, a concern for his property. Another view is that this rule is directed toward the prevention of cruelty to animals, the main goal being the release of the pack animal.[19] Second, the issue is whether the animal is only helped to get back on its feet[20] or whether the load is also repacked or rearranged.[21] It is important to bear in mind that, at least in most circumstances, one man could release the animal. Cassuto is surely right in arguing that the aid—primarily for the animal's owner—extends to seeing to it that the pack animal is not only back on its feet but also properly loaded.

Apart from maritime law, the Anglo-American common-law tradition does not acknowledge a general duty to rescue or render assistance. Pound states that "so long as one has not caused the peril and there is no relation, one who merely fails to come to the aid of another [person] who is even in extreme peril and even if it would involve no danger, incurs no liability."[22] As otherwise put by Gregory, "it is clear at common law that nobody has to lift a finger—let alone spend a dime and dial a phone number or actually render aid—to help a stranger in peril or distress."[23] Gregory cites an interesting case that somewhat parallels the ass lying under its load:

> Consider what happened when something called a safety guard non-negligently fell from the front of a trolly car onto a trespassing pedestrian drunkenly asleep on the right of way. This safety guard eventually crushed the life out of him. Had the car backed up, it would have relieved the deceased of this pressure. But the Alabama court said the trolly crew were no more required to remove this safety guard than a casual bystander would be. The only danger of liability would be if the crew, in moving the victim, *did* something negligently that caused him harm. Under this view it would behoove the company—financially, at least—to leave things exactly as they were until the victim expired.[24]

Although various Continental codes know a duty to rescue or give assistance under various circumstances,[25] the common law does not.[26]

In Ex 23: 5, the rule stipulates that one has a duty to render assistance to "the one who hates you." Again, this is a curious way of formulating a legal rule and one that has no parallel in Near Eastern "codes." "Hating" is an attitude of interest to the law in special circumstances, such as legal separation from wife,[27] family,[28] or political community,[29] and the law of homicide with its interest in intent. In Israel, the cities of refuge were not open to a person who had "hated" the person killed.[30] A killing that involved "hatred" (*śn'h*) or "enmity" (*'ybh*) was first-degree murder and permitted no leniency.[31] That means that the duty to give assistance concerns assistance even to the person who might be led by his passion to kill you and, if so, could not gain the protection of a city of refuge.

Of course Ex 23: 5 is another example of "this, needless to say that."[32] The principle is exemplified in a twofold way, however. First, if you are under a duty to assist "someone who hates you," you are certainly obligated to aid someone who is indifferent to you or who loves you. Second, if you are obligated to give assistance in a situation where there normally is no particular threat or peril to the pack animal—assuming that the driver or owner is at hand—let alone to the person "who hates you," you surely must give aid to someone—or some stock animal, presumably—who actually is in peril.

These two provocatively worded rules in Ex 23 are, from a certain point of view, masterpieces. Within a small community where people had some acquaintance with each other, these formulations which strike the jurist as oddities might well be more effective than the usual legal draftsmanship. At any rate, Ex 23: 4–5 is not inferior to Deut 22: 1–4, and it is not inferior to the common-law tradition of our own country. And in view of the didactic role that law admittedly plays,[33] the very careful draftsmanship of Ex 23: 4–5 is worthy of serious consideration.[34] These laws are aimed at the weakest link in the just society. In a similar way, Jesus exhorted his listeners to "love your enemies and pray for your pursuers," for even scoundrels look out for their friends. If you have regard for even your enemy's interests, that is nigh to perfection.

Notes

1 For a convenient translation of the Near Eastern "codes" cited in this study see *ANET*. References are by paragraph number. In the laws cited here, note that sheep are specifically mentioned. Sheep of course are particularly damaging.

2 R. Pound, *Jurisprudence* (St. Paul, 1959), Vol. V, pp. 335–36.

3 Quoted in Glanville L. Williams, *Liability for Animals* (Cambridge, 1936), p. 9. Williams comments (p. 10) that "as late as 1387 it was said to be the custom of Canterbury that, if pigs were found wandering in it, their owner was on the first occasion bound over; the second and third times he was fined fourpence, and the fourth time the pigs were killed by the bailiffs and given to the hospice of the poor." Williams sees here the ancient rule of vengeance being watered down.

[4] See Williams, *op. cit.*, pp. 9–10, 127.

[5] This is true under both the Roman law and the common law; see W. W. Buckland and A. D. McNair, *Roman Law and Common Law: A Comparison in Outline*, 2d ed. rev. by F. H. Lawson (Cambridge, 1965, corrected reprint), pp. 357–58. The stray may be distrained until such time as payment is made for the damage done, but that is not conversion; see W. Blackstone, *Commentaries on the Laws of England*, vol. III, Chap. 1.

[6] Blackstone, *op. cit.*, Vol. II, Chap. 26–27.

[7] See W. E. Baldwin, ed., *Bouvier's Law Dictionary* (New York, 1928), p. 415a, s.v. "finder."

[8] See below, on the cities of refuge.

[9] H. Cazelles, *Études sur le code de l'alliance* (Paris, 1946), p. 88, specifies that the enemy is a private enemy, and takes that to mean a neighbor with whom one is having a (legal) dispute. Although the enemy presumably comes from within the Israelite community, he is not merely a person with whom the finder is having a dispute. Litigation does not normally lead to murder. E. Gerstenberger, *Wesen und Herkunft des "apodiktischen Rechts,"* *WMANT* 20 (1965), 30, recognizes the juristic peculiarity of the wording, but takes it to refer to the correct conduct toward one's personal enemy.

[10] U. Cassuto, *A Commentary on the Book of Exodus*, trans. I. Abrahams (Jerusalem, 1967; Hebrew orig., 1951), p. 297. See also S. R. Driver on Ex 23: 4–5 (*CBSC*) for a similar observation. This is a principle of basic importance. The failure to appreciate this technique in the case of Ex 23: 3, e.g., even by S. R. Driver, leads to curious results; see Driver's commentary, *ad loc.* As has often been pointed out, legal reasoning is primarily reasoning by analogy, seeing the application of generalized rules. Holmes tells of "a Vermont justice of the peace before whom a suit was brought by one farmer against another for breaking a churn. The justice took time to consider, and then said that he had looked through the statutes and could find nothing about churns, and gave judgment for the defendant." O. W. Holmes, Jr., "The Path of the Law," in *The Holmes Reader*, ed. J. J. Marke (New York, 1955), p. 80. Biblical commentators are sometimes like the Vermont justice.

[11] It therefore is not correct to regard the terminology of "your brother" as widening or broadening the application of Ex 23: 4, as do, e.g., S. R. Driver (*ICC*) and G. E. Wright (*IB*) in their commentaries on Deuteronomy, *ad loc.*, and G. Beer (with K. Galling) in his Exodus commentary (*HAT*), *ad loc.* Cf. M. Noth, *Exodus* (*ATD*), *ad loc.*, who finds the prescription directed against the extralegal relationship with an enemy or opponent. The point, however, is to bring even those relationships within the law, as Noth seems to acknowledge; see O. Procksch, *Theologie des AT* (Gütersloh, 1950), p. 115.

[12] See Carl Brockelmann, *Hebräische Syntax* (Neukirchen Kreis Moers, 1956), pp. 126, 136–37; R. J. Williams, *Hebrew Syntax: An Outline* (Toronto, 1967), sec. 584.

[13] K. (C.) Conti Rossini, *Chrestomathia arabica meridionalis epigraphica* (Rome, 1931), pp. 202-3.

[14] Herdner, No. 4 (II AB; Gordon, No. 51), iv. 7, 12; translation by H. L. Ginsberg in *ANET*, p. 133.

[15] For discussion see Cassuto, *Or*, NS 7 (1938), 282, and *Exodus*, p. 297; C. H. Gordon, *Or*, NS 21 (1952), 123; E. Vogt, *Bibl* 33 (1952), 160; and M. Held, in *Studies and Essays in Honor of A. A. Neuman*, ed. M. Ben-Horin, B. D. Weinryb, and S. Zeitlin (Leiden, 1962), p. 283, n. 8, who points to other possible examples in Hebrew.

[16] The parallel law in Deut 22: 4 involves a somewhat different situation. Unless the ass and the ox are improperly joined here, the picture is that of a draft animal fallen down in the roadway, not of a pack animal which is lying down, fallen or otherwise. Whether or not a prudent man would join in an attempt to raise or lift up an ox is another matter.

Cazelles (*op. cit.*, p. 88) is doubtless right in suggesting that the Deuteronomic redactor no longer understood Ex 23: 5.

[17] See the discussion by H. Lewy in *RSO* 39 (1964), 186, 192, and in *CAH*, rev. ed., vol. I, Chap. xxiv, secs. vii–x (Fasc. 40; Cambridge, 1965), p. 21.

[18] For a discussion of the burro as a pack animal, see David R. Brower, ed., *Going Light: With Backpack or Burro* (San Francisco, 1951), pp. 108–41. I owe this reference to N. Q. Hamilton.

[19] S. R. Driver emphasizes that the beast is preserved from harm (*CBSC, ad loc.*), a point that is generally admitted for Deut 22: 4.

[20] See the commentaries by A. Dillmann (*KeH*, 1897^3), H. Holzinger (*KHK*), C. F. Keil (*Biblical Commentary on the OT*, ed. C. F. Keil and F. Delitzsch, trans. J. Martin), *inter alia*.

[21] Cassuto, *Exodus*, p. 297. This is also the understanding in the Mishnah (*Baba Metzia*, 2.10), with certain restrictions.

[22] Pound, *op. cit.* (n. 2), Vol. I, p. 215.

[23] Charles O. Gregory, "The Good Samaritan and the Bad: The Anglo-American Law," in *The Good Samaritan and the Law*, ed. J. R. Ratcliffe (Garden City, 1966), p. 24. The relationships that create a duty to help are restricted in number.

[24] Gregory, *op. cit.*, p. 26. Cf the remarks in the same volume by J. P. Dawson (p. 63).

[25] A number of contributions in the volume edited by Ratcliffe (n. 23) survey the situation.

[26] Maritime law, even in common-law countries, differs. Perhaps this is because of the obvious dangers of the sea and the clear knowledge that all who venture on it may face similar predicaments; perhaps also because of the influence of different legal traditions. The United States Code provdes that "the master or person in charge of a vessel shall, so far as he can do so without serious danger to his own vessel, crew, or passengers, render assistance to every person who is found at sea in danger of being lost; and if he fails to do so, he shall, upon conviction, be liable [for fine and imprisonment]," as cited by Gregory, *op. cit.*, p. 40, n. 50. Note also the provision in the "International Convention for the Safety of Life at Sea" (1948), which states that "the master of a ship at sea, on receiving a signal from any source that a ship or aircraft or survival craft thereof is in distress, is bound to proceed with all speed to the assistance of the persons in distress, informing them if possible that he is doing so." See L. Waller, in the Ratcliffe volume (n. 23), p. 153, n. 32.

[27] In the law of divorce, see Deut 21: 15–17; 22: 13 ff; 24: 1–4; see also the Laws of Hammurapi, No. 142 (n. 1, above).

[28] See the Laws of Hammurapi, No. 193.

[29] See the Laws of Eshnunna, No. 30, and the Laws of Hammurapi, No. 136. This separation brings with it a loss of rights.

[30] Deut 4: 42; 19: 4, 6, 11; Josh 20: 5.

[31] Num 35: 20 ff. Note that the language of Ex 21: 12–14 is more satisfactory to the jurist, who is more interested in actions than in emotions.

[32] Cassuto, *Exodus*, p. 297. See n. 10, above.

[33] See the comment by Louis Waller in the Ratcliffe volume (n. 23): "There is general agreement today that the criminal law has a strong didactic purpose. It serves to teach, in its own terrible fashion, the canons of right and wrong to the community" (p. 141).

[34] It is clear that the formulation of these rules is designed more to educate the public than to inform the learned legal community. But one must recognize the difficulties involved in expressing positive duties in casuistic forms. Note the close resemblance to the formulations for maritime law cited above (n. 26), especially the "International Convention." The Exodus rules in question may well have had their locus in priestly instruction.

George M. Landes
Union Theological Seminary

Creation Tradition in Proverbs 8: 22–31 and Genesis 1

It is somewhat surprising to discover that scholarly treatments dealing with a more or less detailed comparison between Prov 8: 22–31 and Gen 1 are virtually nonexistent. To be sure, in the massive literature on Gen 1, there are occasional allusions to Prov 8: 22–31; while in the somewhat less numerous studies on the latter, there are also sporadic references to specific points in Gen 1. But apparently nowhere has anyone concentrated on examining these two literary units in relation to one another. Presumably this is because even a superficial study of them turns up more obvious differences than points of contact, so that the effort of closely comparing them would not seem to be a very fruitful or appropriate enterprise. Hence, though in 1914 Morris Jastrow asserted rather categorically that in Prov 8 "the description given of Creation may be regarded as a poetical paraphrase of the account of Creation in Genesis,"[1] few scholars—including Jastrow himself—have bothered to demonstrate the validity of such a statement through a searching comparative analysis of the two texts. Perhaps what would seem to be a scholarly consensus in this respect is correct: except for drawing upon some common resources of ancient Near Eastern creation tradition, Prov 8 and Gen 1 diverge quite radically from each other in form, style, purpose, and certain matters of content. Nevertheless, it is the underlying contention of this paper that these two passages deserve a more careful comparative study than has hitherto been given them, not because their acknowledged differences are deemed any less striking or significant but because what points of contact between them do exist merit greater attention and more thorough evaluation than they have previously received, while the results of the comparative analysis do suggest certain implications for the understanding of each that are not clear when they are studied in isolation. The limitations of time and space imposed on the preparation and length of this study have precluded the present writer from undertaking the most comprehensive type of examination needed, but perhaps the basic data can be set forth here, leaving the treatment of some of the more complex issues and problems raised for a later investigation.

At the outset, it is important to be clear about the distinctive differences between Prov 8 and Gen 1, as the proper background against which to distinguish and analyze their similarities and mutually informing conceptions. With regard to *form*, Prov 8: 22 ff serves as the final strophe of a three-strophe poem which Aage Bentzen has perhaps correctly characterized as a poetic allegory.[2] Its predominant poetic unit is the bicolon (the principal exceptions are vss 29–30, which are tricola), with a 3 + 3 meter and synonymous parallelism. Gen 1 of course is a prose narrative or story, and though Cassuto[3] is probably right that it goes back to an original poetic prototype (a fragment of which is most clearly seen in the section on the creation of man, 1: 27–28), the subsequent prose form has sufficiently modified the verse structure of the poetic original so that it is no longer possible to reconstruct the verse units or discern their metrical patterns,[4] except in 1: 27–28 and possibly at several other points where poetic reminiscences seem to be present (in 1: 2, 5, 16, and in the refrains . . . *wyhy ʿrb wyhy bqr ywm* . . . and *wyrʾ ʾlhym ky-ṭwb*. But even here, what parallelism is noticeable is not of the most archaic type—that is, synonymous.[5] The *Sitz im Leben* for the form of Prov 8: 22 ff was presumably the same as for the nine discourses in Prov 1–7—the teacher-pupil relationship, in which the hearer would be instructed in the nature, function, value, and origin of wisdom. The *Sitz im Leben* for Gen 1 is more difficult to ascertain with any assurance. Its original setting was perhaps cultic, celebrating not only the Creator-God and his creation works, but also the climactic event of the cessation of creation activity, which Israelite tradition related to the institution of the sabbath. All efforts, however, to persuade us that Gen 1 represents the later reworking of a cultic liturgy used in the Temple on the occasion of some kind of Yahwistically baptized Hebrew New Year's festival fall short of convincing evidence or proof.[6] Whether in its present form Gen 1 ever served a nonliturgical purpose outside its context in the Genesis traditions is impossible to say. It is not inconceivable that it may have been used to instruct about the peculiarly Israelite conception of God's creation activity in vivid contrast to that manifest in the Canaanite milieu. But there is little clear evidence to show that Gen 1 was ever used (and hence perhaps redacted) by the wise men in the pursuance of their pedagogical interests. Unlike Prov 8: 22 ff, Gen 1 is largely devoid of specific wisdom motifs and terminology, though there are places where it is possible some wisdom influence may lie in the background. We shall return to that matter toward the end of this study.

An examination of *language and terminology* in Prov 8: 22 ff leaves the impression that it is somewhat more archaic, with a richer diversity of expression than is found in Gen 1. To be sure, there are not many rare or unusual words in Prov 8: 22 ff, and few, if any, indisputable remnants of old Canaanite grammatical features. But several words do point to older usages. Three of these occur in the opening verse: *qnny*, where the meaning "to beget, produce, create," would seem to be earlier than the much more common "to buy, acquire, possess"[7]; *drkw*, which probably should not be related to *derek*, "way", but to Ugar *drkt*, "dominion, authority" (unless Dahood[8] is correct that we should read this as a verb form, and even so, in accordance with his interpretation, the meaning would be rare); and *qdm* in the sense of a divine appellative, "the Primeval One" (so Dahood), which accords well with the parallelism in vs 22, though the usual understanding of "before" cannot be ruled out. In vs 23, there would seem to be two old usages: *m'wlm* makes good sense construed as a divine appellative, "the Eternal One" (again following Dahood[9]), particularly if *m'z* is made the first word of the second bicolon, as seems stylistically and metrically preferable to the MT division; the verb *nskty*, if the Masoretic pointing is correct, refers to a creation by "outpouring," apparently a very archaic idea in the ancient Near East,[10] though used only here in that sense in the Old Testament.[11] If *nkbdy-mym* in vs 24 should stand for an original *nbkm-ym* or *nbky-mym*, we would clearly be dealing with an old expression referring to the primordial waters, well known from Ugaritic.[12] *Bhkynw* (vs 27) is probably best understood in light of Ugaritic-Phoenician *kwn*, "to be"; only here it is in the *Hiph'il*, "to bring into being."[13] Finally, Albright would seem to be correct in viewing *'mwn* (vs 30) as a Canaanite reminiscence.[14]

By contrast with Prov 8: 22 ff, the vocabulary of Gen 1 is much more typically classical Hebrew and less varied. Though it agrees with Prov 8 in using certain words,[15] none of the rarer forms mentioned above occur in Gen 1.[16] It is true that Gen 1 has some rare forms of its own that do not appear in Prov 8: 22 ff, but they are not quite so numerous.[17] The vocabulary referring to similar actions or things tends to be more variegated in Prov 8: 22 ff than in Gen 1. For example, the former employs ten different verbal roots to indicate creation (*qnh, nsk, ḥwl, tb', 'śh, kwn, ḥqq, 'mṣ, 'zz*, and *śym*), while Gen 1 has basically only three (*br', 'śh*, and *hyh*, though perhaps *bdl* should be added, since it is the verb used with the distinctive creation act of separating between light and darkness). Prov 8: 22 ff and Gen 1 thus agree only in the use of one of these verbs (*'śh*), and even here the object(s) of the verbal action is (are) different. Strikingly, the root *br'* occurs nowhere in Prov 8: 22 ff, while it is used four times in Gen 1 (as is *'śh*). In the terminology indicating what is created—the constituent elements of the world and the cosmos—Prov 8: 22 ff and Gen 1 are in basic agreement on the following: *thwm, mym, šmym, ym, 'rṣ*, and possibly *'dm* (though no explicit Creation vocabulary is used with *'dm* in Prov 8: 31). Prov 8: 22 ff, however, has one or more synonyms for several of these words: for *thwm: thmwt, m'ynwt, nbkm-ym* or *nbky-mym, 'ynwt*; for *šmym: ḥwg, šḥqym*; for *'rṣ: ḥwṣwt, 'prwt tbl, tbl 'rṣw*. Gen 1 uses *rqy'* for *šmym* and *ybšh* for *'rṣ*. In Prov 8: 22 ff, eight objects receive mention as being created which are not specified as such in Gen 1: *ḥkmh, m'ynwt, hrym, gb'wt, ḥwṣwt, 'prwt, tbl, ḥwg 'l-pny thwm, mwsdy 'rṣ*. Of these, perhaps only *ḥkmh, hrym, gb'wt*, and *mwsdy 'rṣ* should be understood as not covered by another expression in Gen 1. On the other hand, Gen 1 describes the creation of six things not so indicated in Prov 8: 22 ff: light, plants, heavenly bodies, marine life, animals, and man. Prov 8: 22 ff also omits any mention of the primordial darkness, and hence of the separation of light and darkness. Another interesting terminological difference is in the name of the creator-God: for Prov 8: 22 ff, it is the personal name Yahweh, mentioned only once (vs 22), together with perhaps two appellatives, *qdm* (vs 22) and *'wlm* (vs 23), while for Gen 1, it is always 'Elohim, mentioned twenty-seven times.[18] The terminological differences between Prov 8: 22 ff and Gen 1 are, of course, due not simply to variant origins and sources of creation tradition but also to the different purposes for which each document was composed, and to that we now turn.

The purpose of Prov 8: 22 ff within the entire poem of chapter 8 would seem to embody three basic points: 1) the priority of wisdom's creation in relation to all other creation activity by Yahweh (8: 22–26); 2) the presence of wisdom in the time when all other creation events took place (8: 27–30a); and 3) the constant joy of God in wisdom and wisdom's reciprocal delight in God and in the world (8: 30a–31). It follows from this that Prov 8: 22 ff does not seek to be a creation story in poetic form; nor does it necessarily reflect a full account of Yahweh's creation activity. Thus, it should not be judged by what it omits in relation to Gen 1. The latter, on the other hand, does intend to give a more comprehensive account of creation. It is interested in the origin of the cosmos and each of its fundamental constitutive elements. But it wants to say something not only about *what* was created—including its ordering and goodness—but also about *who* is the Creator—including the mode of his creating and the relationship between himself and what he creates. In light of these differences in purpose, it is easier to account for the differences in content between the two passages. Thus, in order to accomplish his purpose, the poet of Prov 8: 22 ff does not need to include such creation events as light, its separation from darkness, the making of the heavenly bodies and of all the forms of life from plants to man, while the author of Gen 1, on his part, had no compelling reason to say something about the creation of wisdom, or to add such details as the topographical features of hills, mountains, and fields, or such cosmic elements as the foundations of the earth. But though these differences do exist, and cannot be discounted, it is instructive to look at those points where certain affinities occur between Prov 8: 22 ff and Gen 1, and and to probe their implications.

Affinities between Prov 8: 22 ff and Gen 1

THE NATURE OF CREATION EVENTS

Though Prov 8: 22 ff is not a creation story like Gen 1, it does mention certain creation events. Verse 22–26 speak of the cosmic and world situation *before* creation of the heavens and the earth—that is, when only wisdom had been created. Though creation events are mentioned here as having not yet occurred, it is doubtful that the author intended the order in which he mentions them to correspond with the order of their later occurrence. In vss 27–29 he speaks of creation events, not still to come but as having already happened: the bringing into being of the heavens and the placing of the vault on the surface of the circumambient ocean that surrounds and is beneath the earth (vs 27); the strengthening of the vault of heaven above and of the sources of the Deep below (vs 28)[19]; setting limits for the sea beyond which it is not to pass (vs 29a); and carving the subterranean mountains, the pillars upon which the flat disk of the earth rests (vs 29b).

Gen 1 would seem to tie in with two of these events: the making of the *rqyʿ* or heavenly vault (1: 6–8), and the gathering of the waters into one place (1: 9–10). They occur together in the same order as in Prov 8: 27–29, though their respective descriptions are quite different. Whereas in Prov 8: 27, the *šmym* are "brought into being" (*hkyn*), in Gen 1: 7, God "makes" (*wyʿś*) the *rqyʿ* which will be subsequently named *šmym* (1: 8). To be sure, the *rqyʿ* is one of those elements which God creates by fiat: *yhy rqyʿ*, but this does not preclude additional divine activity in "making" and "separating." Thus Prov 8: 22 ff agrees with Gen 1 that the heavens involved more than the divine fiat in their creation, but they diverge in the terminology used to describe the divine activity. Prov 8: 22 ff and Gen 1 also agree that creation of the heavenly vault at the same time involved some action with regard to the already existing primordial waters. In both texts, these waters are conceived as below the vault, though the Genesis passage is quite explicit that they are both below *and above* the vault—it is the vault itself that separates the waters above from those below. The Proverbs text may also presuppose the same conceptuality, but it is not explicit. Certainly the inscribing of the circle on the surface of *thwm* suggests the preparation for the placing of the circular heavenly vault on the waters that surround the earth (which is perhaps still thought of as uncreated, or at least hidden within the waters, as in Gen 1: 9). The fact that this vault needs to be strengthened or steadied (*b'mṣw*) "from above" (*mm'l*) is perhaps meant to suggest that the waters above it are quite powerful, so that what is to keep them back must be strong or steady. But how does this relate to *b'zwz 'ynwt thwm*? Scott's translation in the Anchor Bible[20] gives the impression he thinks these words may refer to the creation of the sources of the Deep ("and made the mighty fountains of the abyss"), but this is problematical in light of 8: 27b, in which *thwm* is already in existence. Perhaps it means that when the Deep had to bear the whole weight of the heavenly vault, with the waters above pressing down upon it, it had to be strengthened in order to support the vault. This would seem to be the best interpretation in the context. Prov 8: 29a should possibly be connected with Gen 1: 9, where action with respect to the waters below the heavens is described. Again the terminology is somewhat different, but the basic idea may be the same. In Gen 1: 9, the lower waters are to be gathered into one gathering (or place), which clearly implies limitation. Moreover, these waters receive the name *yammîm*, which is quite close to *layyām* in Prov 8: 29a. The meaning of the following words, *wmym l' y'brw-pyw*, is somewhat difficult, but clearly they reinforce the idea of limitation and control. If Dahood's translation is followed ("lest the waters should cross its edge"),[21] the "limit" or "edge" of the sea would presumably be the earth or "dry land" of Gen 1: 9, where it is the purpose of the gathering of the waters into one area to cause the dry land to appear. In light of this, it is perhaps significant that the next words in Prov 8: 29 refer to the carving of the "foundations of the earth"—that is, making the necessary preparations so that the earth can be fixed above the subterranean waters of the Deep. Thus Prov 8: 29b would envision the creation of the earth after the limitation imposed upon the sea, just as in Gen 1: 9–10.

THE MODE OF CREATION ACTIVITY

As already pointed out, Prov 8: 22 ff employs a great many more verbs than does Gen 1 to describe God's creative work. They agree in the use of *'śh*, though not explicitly in the object of this verb. In Prov 8: 26, the object is *'rṣ*, while in Gen 1, there are four objects: *rqy'* (1: 7), *šny hm'rt hgdlym* (1: 16), *ḥyt h'rṣ* (1: 25), and *'dm* (1: 26). Though *'rṣ* is not among any of these, it is perhaps implicit in Gen 1: 31, *wyrʾ ʾlhym ʾt . . . kl-ʾšr ʿśh.* Thus Prov 8: 22 ff and Gen 1 are in agreement that creation does involve direct and mediate divine activity. All the other verbs used in Prov 8: 22 ff reinforce this, though the images are quite varied and more precise in some respects than those contained or conveyed in *brʾ*, *ʿśh*, and *hyh* of Genesis. Thus we have "begetting" or "creating" (*qnh*), emanation or outpouring (*nsk*), birth (*ḥwl*), planting (*ṭbʿ*), inscribing (*ḥqq*), strengthening (*ʿzz*), (*ʾmṣ*), setting (*śym*), and carving (*ḥqq*). Quite distinct in Gen 1 is the conception of creation by divine fiat or command, or by fiat accompanied either by God's activity ("making", *wyʿś*) or by some created element participating in furthering the creative process. Light is the only thing in Gen 1 described as created by fiat alone (1: 3). Darkness, the sky, earth, seas, heavenly bodies, and man are all created by fiat *plus* some divinely instigated type of activity, described by the verbs *bdl* (for darkness), *ʿśh* (for the heavenly vault, luminaries, and man), *qwh* (for the waters), and *brʾ* (for the sea monsters and man). In the creation of plant and marine life, God is assisted by *hʾrṣ* (1: 11) and *hmym* (1: 20), respectively. Even with regard to animal life, *hʾrṣ* seems to play a mediating role (1: 24). For the creation of man, God apparently first consults or deliberates with his divine council (1: 26), though it is not clear that they assist in bringing man to existence. If the motif of *ḥkmh* had been in Gen 1, even implicitly, one might conclude, in light of one possible interpretation of the role of *ḥkmh* in Prov 8, that the subject of *nʿśh* could refer to 'Elohim and wisdom, or to the presence of wisdom personified among the members of God's council. However, with no mention or even allusion to *ḥkmh* in Gen 1, this interpretation is ruled out.

But this raises the question of what role or function *ḥkmh* has in Prov 8: 22 ff. In vss 22–29, it is clear that *ḥkmh* is present and existing when the creation of the cosmos takes place. It is not obvious that *ḥkmh* assists or in any way executes the divine will with respect to the creation events.[22] Though this may be what the author wanted understood, particularly in view of Prov 3: 19, it is also possible that only the existence, as against the participation, of wisdom in creation is all that was intended to be emphasized. The crux is the interpretation of the disputed *ʾmwn* in 8: 30a. If *ʾmwn* means "craftsman, architect, wizard," or the like, and is to be construed as identifying wisdom's role in creation, then the problem is solved. Here we would have explicit indication of wisdom's active functioning in creation. But if Dahood is right,[23] and *ʾmwn* is to be understood as an appositive related to the suffix on *ʾṣlw* referring to God, then wisdom's presence but passive role would seem to be all that is meant. I am inclined toward the latter interpretation, agreeing with Dahood that if the former were meant, the expression and arrangement of words would most likely be different.

However, if *ḥkmh* does assist Yahweh in creation, then its role is somewhat in line with *ʾrṣ* and *hmym* (and perhaps the other members in the subject of *nʿśh* in 1: 26) in Gen 1.

CREATION AND THE PRIMORDIAL WATERS

To my knowledge, there is no text in the Old Testament which speaks directly of God's creation of the primordial waters (*thwm*, *thwmwt*). Prov 8: 22 ff comes closest when it states quite explicitly (8: 24) that there was a time "when there were no deeps" (*thwmwt*), and then in 8: 27–28 speaks of *thwm* as existing, the implication being that subsequently the subterranean waters were created, presumably prior to the heavens. In Gen 1, the creation of *thwm* is not described as a part of God's creative activity in relation to the world. It is already assumed to be in existence, along with darkness and *hʾrṣ* in the state of *thw wbhw*, in Gen 1: 2. All these are "givens" when God begins to create the heavens and the earth.[24] The negative formulations in Prov 8: 24, 26 are rightly compared to similarly cast statements in several of the ancient Near Eastern creation traditions,[25] but in contrast to this type of formulation in Prov 8: 22 ff and the ancient Near Eastern creation texts, Gen 1: 2 is not negative in form, even though it may be somewhat in meaning. It is asserted there not what *hʾrṣ* was *not* but what it *was*—that is, *thw wbhw*. Admittedly, *thw wbhw* bears a negative connotation by implication, in that it describes *hʾrṣ* in its pre-creation form of darkened desolation or gloomy waste—certainly negative qualities—but it is only by implication and not by a formal, direct negation. There may also be a question as to how negative darkness was considered to be by the Gen 1 author, for it is not radically changed or destroyed in creation, but simply limited and incorporated into the temporal structure of the world as night. With respect to *thwm*, its existence in the pre-creation situation is simply assumed, without any overt perjorative connotations. Nothing is said about its origin or of conditions before its existence. The only hint of a possible negative note is in the presence of the *rwḥ ʾlhym*, "soaring" or "hovering" over *hmym*, where the image is either of the eagle or the hawk circling its prey, thus possibly suggesting some hostility,[26] or of the eagle teaching its young to fly by forcing it out of the nest into the air (as in Deut 32: 11). The hostility or conflict motif fits well with those Old Testament passages where Yahweh is depicted as entering into combat with the mighty waters, often personified as Rahab or Leviathan. The word *thwm* does not appear in any of these texts, but we do find *mym* in parallelism with *thwm* in Ps 104: 6–7, and we find the plural form of *thwm* in a passage alluding to the act of gathering the waters in Ps 33: 6–7. Is Gen 1: 2 intentionally alluding to the motif of God's conflict with the rebellious waters, or is the idea simply of God's control and authority over the waters for the purpose of utilizing them in creation? Since we perceive no other clues to suggest the writer may have had in mind the more violent conceptuality, it is perhaps better to adhere to the second interpretation—that is, God's moving above the waters in the power of his direction and ordering. Significantly, quite in contrast with the Babylonian conception, where Ti'amat is slain and annihilated before the cosmos is created, the biblical picture never portrays the destruction of the waters or of *thwm*, but only their control and ordering by Yahweh *within* the created cosmos, which, interestingly, is in keeping with Egyptian creation tradition.

THE MOTIF OF PRIORITY IN CREATION

I am unaware of any creation tradition within Israel or elsewhere in the ancient Near East which refers to an absolute beginning—that is, a beginning of *all* things, including the gods. Thus, in the Old Testament, when *r'šyt* is used temporally, it never indisputably means "in the beginning" with reference to either the beginning of time or creation. It follows that in Prov 8: 22 and Gen 1: 1, *r'šyt* and *br'šyt*, respectively, should not be rendered "in the beginning." From the context in Prov 8: 22 ff, it seems clear that *r'šyt* means "first" or "foremost," indicating that *ḥkmh* was the first thing to be created, even before the cosmos. This does raise a problem with *drkw* if the latter is not to be construed verbally (with Dahood), but it is not insuperable. If *drk* means "power, authority," then *r'šyt drkw* would presumably be something like "the first [manifestation] of his [Yahweh's] power [or authority]," maintaining the idea of priority. This understanding seems to fit the context of Prov 8: 22 quite satisfactorily, and also causes no problems when compared with Gen 1: 1, even though the idea there is somewhat different. Before dealing with that, however, we should mention one other text which does appear to be in tension with Prov 8: 22 if translated as just indicated, and that is Job 40: 19. This passage is the closest parallel in terminology to Prov 8: 22, though it deals not with the creation of *ḥkmh* but of *bhmwt*, the primordial beast. In vs 15, the writer says Yahweh made *bhmwt* but he amplifies this in vs 19 by adding: *hw' r'šyt drky-'l*, which the RSV translates: "He is the first of the works of God." Here, however, as in Prov 8: 22, it is likely that *drk* is better connected with the word meaning "power, dominion, sovereignty," so that the translation should be: "He is the first [manifestation or example] of the divine power [dominion or authority]." In 1952, Dahood translated this passage: "He is the finest manifestation of God's power."[27] Marvin Pope[28] renders: "He is a primordial production of God," which is the most neutral rendition, but not without its difficulties. The Jerusalem Bible has: "He is the masterpiece of all God's work," admitting in a footnote that the translation is conjectural. If one opts for the priority of *bhmwt* in creation here, then the text clearly opposes Prov 8: 22 (unless of course Scott[29] and others are right and vs 22 is not really speaking about the creation of wisdom by God, but only of his possession of it). It would seem unlikely there were two traditions in circulation among the wise men with regard to what God had created first: on the one hand, wisdom; on the other, *bhmwt*. Given such a choice, it is doubtful they would have assigned preeminence to anything but *ḥkmh*. I am inclined to think that, in view of the whole context of Job 40: 19, *r'šyt* should probably be translated much as Dahood has done. Hence, *bhmwt* would not necessarily be Yahweh's first created work, but the finest example of his creative power or dominion (cf vs 19b, "but his Maker must threaten him with the sword"), and consequently imply nothing as to his priority in the whole creative process. Or it is possible that *bhmwt* was thought of simply as the first creature subdued or held in check by God. There is nothing in the context of this passage which forces us to interpret *bhmwt* as a male counterpart of *thwm*, and the Hebrew myth with which he was originally connected may have had nothing to do with a creation story. The setting in which *bhmwt* is described actually presupposes the earth's creation, for it speaks of the mountains which provide food for him, of his natural habitat among lotus plants and trees, reeds, marshes, willows, brooks, and even the river Jordan! Hence this mythological material may have come from a tradition dealing with a post-creation relationship between Yahweh and *bhmwt*.

In Gen 1: 1, *br'šyt* is used differently from *r'šyt* in Prov 8: 22. The opening of Genesis does not speak of what God created first of all—that is, what he created *before* the heavens and the earth (though this is probably implicit in Gen 1: 2)—but of what he created first when he began to create the cosmos —light. Hence, there is no tension between (*b*) *r'šyt* in Gen 1: 1 and Prov 8: 22, though in both texts the word is used to indicate a priority—in each case, a different priority—and to emphasize that there was creation activity prior to the creation of the heavens and the earth. This is of course only implicit in Gen 1: 1–3, more explicit in Prov 8: 22 ff.

THE MOTIF OF JOY IN CREATION

Prov 8: 22 ff concludes on a threefold note of joy: God's constant delight in the wisdom he has created; wisdom's equally perpetual joy in God's presence; and wisdom's rejoicing in the world and mankind (8: 30–31). There is no clear point of contact here with Gen 1, where the motif of joy, if present at all, is considerably more subtle. One may perhaps detect it in the reiterated divine approval of what has been created: "And God saw how good it was . . ." (1: 4 etc.); "And God saw everything he had made, and found it very good" (1: 31). And perhaps too it was understood as the predominant emotion prevailing when God ceased creating and blessed and sanctified the seventh day. But no verbs or nouns directly indicating joy occur in Gen 1, so that the motif is not as obvious as in Prov 8: 31 or Job 38: 7 ("Where were you when I laid the foundation of the earth . . . when the morning stars sang together and all the sons of God shouted for joy?"). Moreover, it would appear that the theme of divine joy in creation in Prov 8 is limited to joy in wisdom, not in the whole creation.

Genesis 1 and Wisdom Creation Traditions

Though Gen 1 is traditionally assigned to the Priestly stratum of literary material in the Pentateuch, there is no compelling demonstration that the priests actually composed this story themselves or even left their unmistakable literary marks upon it.[30] This raises anew the question about the literary origin and composition of Gen 1, which, I regret, cannot be undertaken here. It has sometimes been suggested, however, that Gen 1 shows certain affinities to wisdom traditions about creation and to other features characteristic of wisdom interests, and so it is legitimate to ask whether the origin of Gen 1 should not be traced to the literary activity of the wise men. Comparison with Prov 8: 22 ff, however, as well as with wisdom traditions about creation in the Psalter and in Job, does not appear to lend very strong support for such an hypothesis. Both Gen 1 and the wisdom creation texts draw upon common ancient Near Eastern sources for some of their conceptions, but neither seems to be more directly related to one another. Our study of Prov 8: 22 ff in particular has not left the impression that this passage was composed under the influence of Gen 1 or vice versa. The failure of Gen 1 to make any mention at all of *ḥkmh* or of its function in creation encourages the doubt that this narrative came directly from the hands of the wisdom scribes. Yet, are there any evidences of indirect wisdom influence on Gen 1? It is possible that the two types of plant distinctions made in 1: 11–12 (*dšʾ ʿśb mzryʿ zrʿ lmynhw ʿṣ ʿśh pry ʾšr zrʿw-bw lmynhw*) go back to the kind of observations and classifications associated with the activity of the wise men, though I know of no wisdom text where this specific division is made. A more general relationship to the wise men has been pointed out in the lists of natural phenomena and constituents of the cosmos which one finds in wisdom literature. In his monograph on Gen 1, Werner Schmidt has studied these in relation to the initial creation story, and concluded that there is no convincing case to be made for thinking that the order and arrangement of the created universe and what is named as its constituent elements go back in detail to any of the wise men's *Listenwissenschaft*.[31]

Moreover, there is very little in the language, style, and purpose of Gen 1 that suggests any clear ties with the wisdom movement. But is it possible that some of the traditional elements in Gen 1 came into Israel through Canaanite-Phoenician sources with which the wise men were particularly familiar?[32] There are a number of Canaanite-Phoenician reminiscences in Gen 1 that possibly point in this direction. For example, in Gen 1: 2, *bhw* is probably a mythological recollection of the old Phoenician goddess Baau, known from Philo as quoted by Eusebius (*Praep. Evang.* I, 10: 7), but going back originally to the work, now lost, of Sanchuniaton.[33] Baau was a night goddess, who, according to Phoenician myth, united with the east(?) wind to produce the first human creatures. It is possible also that *tnynm* in Gen 1: 21 reflects a Canaanite-Phoenician background, since the singular form *tnyn*, referring to some kind of huge marine creature, occurs a number of times in Old Testament poetic passages, and seems related to the Ugaritic figure of the same name (*tnn*). Did *thwm* likewise come into Israel through Canaanite-Phoenician intermediaries? Ugaritic *thm* appears to be used in the same way in Hebrew—that is, always with the meaning Deep(s), and rarely, if ever, personified, as is the Mesopotamian goddess Ti'amat. Other clues to Phoenician influence might possibly be:[34] 1) The use of *ky* in the refrain, *wyrʾ ʾlhym ky ṭwb*, to mean "how" rather than "that," a usage with good examples attested at Ugarit, as well as in the Amarna letters and Mari texts;[35] 2) the use of *mrḥpt* in Gen 1: 2, attested in the Ugaritic Dan'el texts;[36] 3) the enclitic *mem* in 1: 9, if *miqwēmî* is the correct vocalization of *mqwm*;[37] 4) the so-called *waw compaginis* in *hytw-ʾrṣ* of 1: 24, certainly an archaic poetic feature which probably represents an original Canaanite **hayyatu 'arṣi*; 5) the employment of the heptaemeron structure for the whole narrative, a literary device found some seven times in the Ugaritic mythological texts as well as in the Gilgamesh Epic.[38] Significant Phoenician contact and influence upon Israel had certainly begun by the tenth century B.C., and continued down to about the sixth century, when Israelite literary materials coming from this period show the largest number of Ugaritic points of contact. Both Prov 8 and Gen 1 contain clues that suggest Phoenicia as a source for their common traditions. Even the evidence for an ultimate Egyptian conceptuality underlying a number of features in Gen 1 may have come through Phoenicia rather than directly from Egypt. From the standpoint of poetic verse form, Prov 8 would appear to be the older, and quite conceivably could go back to the tenth century for its original composition. Gen 1 too may go back just as far in its initial poetic form, but even its prose rendition should probably not be dated later than the seventh century B.C.[39]

In conclusion, I would say Gen 1 and Prov 8: 22 ff probably have a common heritage in specifically Canaanite-Phoenician traditions about creation, mixed with other ancient Near Eastern traditions which came into Israel through a Phoenician alembic. Within Israel, the composition of Gen 1 and Prov 8: 22 ff was by different circles, the latter most clearly from the wise men; the former, though perhaps ultimately redacted by the priests, goes back in both its putative poetic and its present prose form to literary artists whose identity still remains obscure and problematic.

Notes

[1] Jastrow, M., *Hebrew and Babylonian Traditions* (New York, 1914), p. 125.

[2] Defining "allegory" as he does—as a series of metaphors which are often personifications of inanimate things or abstract ideas. See his *Introduction to the Old Testament* (Copenhagen, 1958), Vol. I, p. 180. B. Gemser, on the other hand, thinks the *Stilform* is reminiscent of the *Schöpfungshymnus* (cf *HAT*, *Sprüche Salomos* [Tübingen, 1963], and in his new commentary on the book of Proverbs, William McKane would appear to agree with him (*Proverbs: A New Approach* [Philadelphia, 1970], p. 352).

[3] Cassuto, U., *A Commentary on the Book of Genesis, Part I: From Adam to Noah,* translated by I. Abrahams (Jerusalem, 1961), pp. 8, 10 f.

[4] In the way, for example, that Jacob Myers has shown can be done for the book of Ruth. Neither Bruno (*Die Bücher Genesis-Exodus: eine rhythmische Untersuchung* [Stockholm, 1953]) nor Sievers, earlier (*Metrische Studien II. Die hebräische Genesis . . .* [Leipzig, 1904–5]), has done this with any great success for Gen 1.

[5] For a recent discussion of this, see Albright, W. F., *Yahweh and the Gods of Canaan* (London, 1968), chapter 1.

[6] For the literature, see Schmidt, W. H., *Die Schöpfungsgeschichte der Priesterschrift* (Neukirchen-Vluyn, 1964), p. 73, n. 1. An excellent discussion of the whole question of the *Sitz-im-Leben* for Gen 1 may now be found in Westermann, C., *Genesis* (*BKAT*, Neukirchen-Vluyn, 1967–), pp. 127–30.

[7] For the principal arguments over whether to render by "beget, create" or "acquire, possess," see McKane, *op. cit.*, pp. 352 f, and Scott, R. B. Y., *Proverbs, Ecclesiastes* (AB, Vol. 18, Garden City, N.Y., 1965), pp. 71–73.

[8] Dahood, M., "Proverbs 8, 22–31, Translation and Commentary," *CBQ* 30 (1968), 514.

[9] *Ibid.*, p. 515.

[10] Creation by divine exudation is attested primarily in Egypt, certainly as early as the Middle Kingdom (ca 2000 B.C.) in one of the Egyptian Coffin Texts, where Re is said to have brought forth some of the gods from his perspiration, mankind from the tears of his eye. For an English translation of the text in question, cf *ANET*², p. 8. Dahood (*loc. cit.*) suggests the concept of emanation of wisdom came to Israel through Canaanite sources.

[11] Even should *nskty* be derived from the root *skk*, comparing Ps 139: 13, the conceptuality would still be very old.

[12] For my earlier study of these words in Prov 8: 24, see "The Fountain of Jazer," *BASOR* 144 (1956), 32 f. For the occurrences of *nbk/mbk* in Ugaritic, consult the glossary in C. H. Gordon's *Ugaritic Textbook* (Rome, 1965), § 1597.

[13] Dahood, *op. cit.*, p. 517.

[14] Albright, W. F., "Some Canaanite-Phoenician Sources of Hebrew Wisdom," in *Wisdom in Israel and in the Ancient Near East* (*VTS*, Vol. III, Leiden, 1955), p. 8 and n. 4.

[15] *r'šyt*, *thwm*, *'rṣ*, *mym*, *'śh*, *šmym*, and *ym*; possibly *'dm*, if Dahood's emendation is not accepted (*op. cit.*, p. 521), and also *ywm*, though used in an entirely different way.

[16] As does neither *ḥwṣwt* (8: 26) nor *ḥwg* (8: 27).

[17] For rare and/or old forms and expressions in Gen 1, cf *thw wbhw* and *mrḥpt* in 1: 2, the latter best explained in light of Ugar *rḥp*; the use of *l* meaning "from" in *mym lmym* in 1: 6; the verb *qwh* with its noun cognate *mqwh* in 1: 9–10, and the possibility in 1: 9 that *mqwm* should be *miqwēmî*, with final enclitic *mem* (so far neither *qwh* nor *mqwh* has turned up in Ugaritic, to my knowledge); *tnynm* in 1: 21, cf Ugar. *tnn*; the puzzling so-called *waw compaginis* in *ḥytw-'rṣ* in 1: 24, which is usually interpreted as an archaic feature, though still not satisfactorily explained. See p. 290 above.

[18] This is interesting in light of the fact that 'Elohim is often the designation for deity preferred by the wise men, and has been thought one reason Gen 1 should be considered in the orbit of wisdom influence; yet here in Prov 8: 22 ff, we have the most obvious wisdom text using Yahweh and never 'Elohim. Of course in Israelite wisdom circles there was no great hesitation in using the personal name of God, as can be seen in a large number of the proverbs that have been preserved. On this point, see the study of Michael V. Fox, "Aspects of the Religion of the Book of Proverbs," *HUCA* 39 (1968), 55–70.

[19] Following Dahood's interpretation of *b'zwz*, *op. cit.*, p. 518.

[20] Scott, *op. cit.*, p. 68.

[21] Dahood, *op. cit.*, p. 513.

[22] Cf Whybray, *op. cit.*, p. 357 and references.

[23] Dahood, *op. cit.*, pp. 518 f.

[24] We find the same situation in Egypt. In the mythical account of the repulsing of Apophis, the sun god speaks of creating parts of the universe in the primordial waters, Nun, which somehow already exist, and whose origin is not mentioned. Presumably Nun came into being after the sun god, but there is no clear indication the sun god created Nun. Cf John Wilson's translation of this text in *ANET*[2], p. 6, and also one of the versions of the creation by Atum in chapter 17 of the Book of the Dead, *ANET*[2], pp. 3 f.

[25] Cf, e.g., the opening lines of *Enuma elish* (*ANET*[2], pp. 60 f), or the introduction to an incantation that was recited for the purification of Ezida, the temple of Nabû at Borsippa (English translation in Heidel, A., *The Babylonian Genesis* [Chicago, 1951], p. 62). The same motif also appears in Egypt in the so-called Book of Knowing the Creations of Re and of Overthrowing Apophis (translated by John Wilson in *ANET*[2], p. 6) and in one of the versions of the creation by Atum (*ANET*[2], p. 4).

[26] As in the Ugaritic Dan'el texts, where the goddess Anat will make her divine servitor Yatpun into an eagle or vulture, who will then fly and hover over Aqhat at his meal, ready to fall upon him and kill him as an eagle hovers over its prey until it swoops down and takes it. Cf Dan'el III D 1, 20–21, 31–32 (textual references from Virolleaud; referred to as *AQHT* B(iv) in the English translation by H. L. Ginsberg in *ANET*[2], pp. 152 f).

[27] Dahood, M. review of G. Hölscher, *Das Buch Hiob*, *Theological Studies* 13 (1952), 593 f.

[28] *Job* (AB, Vol. 15, Garden City, N. Y., 1965), pp. 266, 272.

[29] Scott, R. B. Y., *op. cit.*, pp. 68, 73.

[30] The whole question of the authorship of Gen 1, and the assumptions underlying it, is in need of a thorough reexamination, not only in light of recent research in ancient Near Eastern creation materials but also in stylistic, grammatical, conceptual motifs that would

seem to challenge both the sixth century B.C. origin of Gen 1 as a literary unit and its original composition by Israelite priestly circles. I hope to treat this matter in a separate study.

[31] Schmidt, *op. cit.*, pp. 45–47.

[32] See Albright's study already cited above (n. 14).

[33] Cf Schmidt, *op. cit.*, p. 27, and n. 4 for literature.

[34] See n. 17, above.

[35] Cf Albright, W. F., "The Refrain 'And God Saw KI TOB' in Genesis," in *Mélanges bibliques, rédigés en l'honneur de André Robert* (Paris, 1957), pp. 22–26.

[36] Cf above, n. 26.

[37] See Freedman, D. N., "Notes on Genesis," *ZAW* 64 (1952), 190 f.

[38] See Bauer, J., "Die literarische Form des Heptaemeron," *BZ* 1 (1957), 273–77.

[39] Cf Albright, W. F., *Yahweh and the Gods of Canaan*, p. 80.

Foster R. McCurley, Jr.
Lutheran Theological Seminary at Philadelphia

The Home of Deuteronomy Revisited: A Methodological Analysis of the Northern Theory

For more than forty years the problem of the provenance of Deuteronomy has been much discussed and debated. The book has been dated in every period from Moses to Ezra. It has been connected to and disconnected from Josiah's reform, and those who have related it to that late-seventh-century-B.C. movement have disputed whether it served as a model for that program or was simply a summary of Josiah's activities. In addition, there continues the debate over the book's place of origin as well as over the group responsible for its ideas and composition. The place has been argued strongly to be northern Israel by some and southern Judah by others. Nominations for the circle responsible for its composition and for the preservation of ideals expressed therein have covered virtually every possible candidate: priests,[1] prophets,[2] kings,[3] and scribes.[4]

While all these questions are integrally related and no one question can be studied in a vacuum, the task of this study is limited to the examination of the major arguments which have been offered for a northern or Israelite theory. It is hoped that, by this analysis, some contribution will be made to the problem of Deuteronomy's origin and development.

The Scope of Proto-Deuteronomy

Most present-day scholars agree that the book of Deuteronomy, as we have it, is not the book purported to have been found in the Jerusalem Temple in 621 B.C. Rather, the original text must be separated from the rest of the book because of: 1) the repetitions, doublets, and contradictions (or at least different viewpoints) in the narrative material surrounding the code of chs 12–26; 2) the repetition of laws and the varying concerns in the laws of the code; and 3) the juxtaposition of sections of address with singular and plural verbs and pronouns. It is a difficult and frustrating—but crucial—task to distinguish what is Proto-Deuteronomy from the remainder of the book. But such an attempt must be made and some stance taken before any conclusions can be drawn on questions pertaining to the home of Proto-Deuteronomy. And yet the difficulties in determining precisely this basic material are evidenced by the variety of positions which have been presented.

The extreme positions on the problem need be mentioned only briefly. In 1889, J. Wellhausen (*Die Composition des Hexateuchs*) stated that the original Deuteronomy consisted only of the law code in chapters 12–26. This position is supported somewhat by Otto Eissfeldt,[5] who argues that the account in 2 Kings 22–23 provides no basis for assuming that the code contained an historical introduction. Moreover, for Eissfeldt the concluding chapters represent two later editions which expanded the brief curses at 22: 16, 19. Quite the opposite of that position, J. Cullen (*The Book of the Covenant in Moab*, 1903) sees Proto-Deuteronomy not at all in the code but only in the hortatory discourses of the framework. The code is simply a summary or deposit of Josiah's reforms rather than the guidelines for those reforms.

Generally held views on the scope of Deuteronomy include sections of both the framework and the legal material. M. Noth[6] and G. von Rad[7] agree that Proto-Deuteronomy did not include the first four or the last four chapters of the present book. E. Nicholson[8] argues that Proto-Deuteronomy consisted of chapters 5–26 and some of 28. Within this corpus, another hand was at work inserting some plural passages within the original singular material, and other chapters were added at the beginning and at the end. Also within the major corpus, Nicholson joins von Rad in omitting the long plural passage at 9: 7–10: 11. It is interesting to note in the matter of 9: 7–10: 11 that G. Fohrer,[9] who regards the code itself as the original work, considers 9: 7–10: 11 to belong (with 1: 1–5; 1: 6–3: 29; and 4: 1–43) to the second of two supplemented introductions. The first introduction, consisting of 4: 44–9: 6; 10: 12–11: 32, was added to the code shortly after 701 B.C., and in that same expansion a conclusion was added with the material at 27: 1–8, 9–10; 28: 1–68. The relationship of the narrative material here is important to note, for in spite of the difference in what constitutes the original, 9: 7–10: 11 does not seem to be related to its surrounding material. Also, there seems to be an agreed break at 28: 68 from the concluding chapters.

A slightly different but also frequently accepted Proto-Deuteronomy is supported by Hartmut Gese, whose convincing analysis is based on a combination of the singular-plural criterion with certain ideological-theological issues.[10] For Gese, the narrative framework of the original book consists essentially of the singular material in 6: 4–9: 6; 10: 12–11: 1; 27: 1–28: 68. In these sections, the word *bryt* is used only for the covenant with the patriarchs (7: 9, 12; 8: 18), the content of which was the promise of the land (see 6: 10 ff, 18, 23; 7: 1 ff, 16 ff; 8: 1, 7; 9: 1 ff). The wilderness experience here is regarded as a time of intimacy with Yahweh (8: 2–5, 15 f; contrast 6: 16 [secondary pl. insert]; 9: 7, 22–24; 11: 5–7; 25: 17 f; 32: 51). And Sinai/Horeb is missing in favor of the Moab covenant, which is nowhere regarded as a renewal of that Horeb situation. Thus, what is essentially different in Gese's view from those cited above is 5: 1–6: 3[11] and 11: 2–32, both of which are plural and which introduce elements nowhere else attested in Proto-Deuteronomy.[12] It would follow, then, that the inclusion of the many references to Sinai/Horeb traditions is the work of a later editor (or editors),[13] whose work explicitly portrayed the Moab covenant as the renewal of the one at Sinai.

The scope of the framework of Proto-Deuteronomy assumed in this study is consistent with that supported by Gese: 6: 4–9: 6; 10: 12–11: 1; 27: 1–28: 68. What the original work contains in the narrative framework is a series of sermons which preserve the covenant as the patriarchal promise, the exodus experience, the favorable wilderness tradition, and some important announcements concerning the nature of Israel's God, the nature of the people as God's own, the gift of the land, and a number of other concepts which will be pointed out in the course of this discussion. But what is omitted from Proto-Deuteronomy are the Sinai/Horeb traditions, the unpleasant wilderness traditions, and other typically Deuteronomistic concerns which will also come to the surface below. As for what is original in the code, this problem is even more complicated. Those laws which are crucial in the present discussion will be studied where appropriate.

Arguments for a Northern Origin

The list of scholars who argue that Proto-Deuteronomy has a northern or Israelite provenance is impressive. Following the lead of A. C. Welch, such men as A. Alt, W. F. Albright, G. Fohrer, A. Weiser, G. E. Wright, F. Dumermuth, H. Ringgren, and others have presented arguments for a northern origin of the book found by Josiah's men.[14] Others admit at least that the book contains a reworking of material from the north,[15] or that it was composed in the south by northerners who had fled after the disaster of 721 B.C.[16] The purpose of this study is to evaluate the major arguments which have been presented for northern concerns in Deuteronomy.

DEUTERONOMY AND HOSEA

Many points of comparison have been made between the book of Deuteronomy and the only northern prophet whose preaching has been collected into a book of the canon. These comparisons have been literary, ideological, and theological. In the first place, specific verses have been compared between the books in terms of style and content. The most impressive list has been put together by H. W. Wolff.[17] He has compared: "forgetting Yahweh" of Hos 2: 10, 15; 4: 6; 13: 4 ff; 8: 14 with Deut 6: 12–14; 8: 11, 14, 18 f; the preaching against alliances of Hos 7: 11; 10: 4, 6; 14: 4 with Deut 7: 2; 17: 16; the view of the *tôrāh* of Hos 4: 1 f, 6 with Deut 17: 19; 31: 9 f; Yahweh as chastiser or disciplinarian of Hos 5: 2; 7: 12, 15; 10: 10 with Deut 8: 5; 21: 18; cf 4: 36; the redemption emphasis of Hos 7: 13 with Deut 7: 8; 9: 26; 13: 6; 21: 8; the life of the true prophet "with God" of Hos 9: 8 with Deut 18: 13 (with which Wolff compares the Deuteronomistic judgment on kings: 1 Kings 8: 61; 11: 4; 15: 3, 14); the brotherhood of the people of Hos 2: 3 with Deut. 3: 18, 20; 10: 9; 17: 15; 18: 2, 7, 15, 18; the *massebah* of the Canaanites of Hos 10: 1 with Deut 12: 3; 16: 22; and, finally, the "corn, wine, and oil" of Hos 2: 10 with Deut 7: 13; 11: 14; 12: 17; 14: 23; 18: 4; and 28: 51. Apart from other issues, which will be discussed below, one could increase the list by adding: the references to God finding Israel in the wilderness (Deut 32: 10 ff with Hos 11: 1 ff; 9: 10); God returning Israel to Egypt because of her unfaithfulness (Deut 28: 68 with Hos 7: 16; 8: 13; 9: 3; 11: 5); and the importance of wisdom and discernment (Deut 32: 28 f with Hos 14: 9).

Such an impressive list should not mislead one into a rash decision on the relationship between Hosea and Proto-Deuteronomy, primarily because many of the parallels cited belong to material which belongs to the work of the Deuteronomistic editor rather than to Proto-Deuteronomy (e.g., probably all those under the "brotherhood" notion as well as the understanding of the *tôrāh*). In addition, some of the parallels are simply too general to be significant (e.g., the *massebah* as well as the "corn, wine, and oil"). Some of the comparisons could be used to show different relationships (e.g., on forgetting God, see the frequency of use at Is 17: 10; 51: 13; Jer 2: 32; 3: 21; 13: 25; 18: 15; 23: 27; Ezek 22: 12; 23: 35; on Yahweh as chastiser, Deut 8: 5 sounds more like the wisdom of Prov 3: 11 f; 19: 18 although the Hosea references may be significant). The most helpful and meaningful of all the comparisons seem to be those which deal with redemption and those which express the rather unusual notion that because of Israel's unfaithfulness God will take the people back to Egypt (to begin all over?).

Second, the notion or motif of love has been cited as a parallel between the two books. However, a study of *'āhēb*, "to love," and *'ahābāh*, "love," demonstrates that the comparison is not as firm as one would like in order to establish an argument for northern provenance. In Hosea, the root *'hb* occurs sixteen times. Some of these passages use the term in a general way, and many employ *'hb* with reference to loving Baal or Baal worship as a harlot loves her lovers (2: 7, 9, 12, 14, 15; 4: 18; 9: 1, 10). In several cases, however, the reference is to Yahweh's love for Israel: 3: 1 (love a woman as Yahweh loves Israel); 11: 1, 4 (Yahweh loves his child); 14: 5 (Yahweh will love repentant Israel, which describes itself in the preceding verse as an orphan). Thus, the kinds of love present in Hosea are: the general references; the people's idolatrous love for idols; and Yahweh's love for the people in terms of the husband-wife analogy and of the father-child type.

In Deuteronomy, the root *'hb* occurs twenty-one times. While only two of these use the term apart from the Yahweh-Israel relationship, six speak of Yahweh's love for people: 4: 37 (God loved the forefathers); 7: 8 (love is the motive for Yahweh's election of Israel); 7: 13 (love is joined with blessing on the people); 10: 18 (Yahweh loves the sojourner); and 23:5 (Yahweh loves his people). In none of these passages is there any reference to Yahweh's love for his people in terms of marriage or paternal love—as in Hosea.[18] As for the people's love for Yahweh, eleven cases speak of a command to love God: 5: 10; 6: 5; 10: 12; 11: 1, 13, 22; 13: 3; 19: 9; 30: 6, 16, 20. The command is directly related to keeping commandments, fearing the Lord, serving him, walking in his ways, and cleaving to him. It is, indeed, not inappropriate to say that love for God in Deuteronomy means primarily obedience to Yahweh and the keeping of his commandments.[19]

Therefore, while one might argue that the election-covenant love relationship can be portrayed in husband-wife or father-son images, the specific use of *'hb* in Deuteronomy is not so clearly or directly related to Hosea that one must think necessarily of a borrowing from Hosea or even of a common tradition underlying both. While for both Hosea and Deuteronomy God's love is unmerited, in Hosea this love is described in intimate, familial terms; in Deuteronomy, in formal covenant categories.

Third, it is argued that in Hosea, as in Deuteronomy, there exists a negative attitude toward kingship, or, rather more specifically, toward the dynastic kingship of Jerusalem. The law at Deut 17: 14–20 is compared with Hosea's polemics on the kings at 7: 3–7; 10: 3 f, 7, 13, 15, and especially 8: 4. About Hosea's attitude there can be no doubt, but the problems with the "royal law" of Deut 17 are, indeed, complex. The arguments center primarily in vss 14–17, 20, for many are of the opinion that vss 18–19 are secondary to the law.[20] First, the negative expression that the people desire to have a king like the other nations is quite reminiscent of the anti-monarchial source at 1 Sam 8: 5,[21] and such a negative attitude was probably northern.[22] Second, the election of the king by the Lord is said to reflect the northern charismatic emphasis rather than the southern dynastic succession principle.[23] Third, the concern about a foreigner becoming king would have been a problem only for the north.[24] Fourth, the prohibition against war chariotry, a multitude of wives, and the heaping up of treasures is said to be anti-Solomonic (reflective of northern attitudes) or a northern concern against the house of Omri.[25] The law is included in this northern anti-dynastic source only because kingship had become a fact of life, which the writers were realistic enough to admit.[26]

Taken all together, these arguments present a formidable case which may, indeed, be correct. However, there are some weaknesses or at least alternative possibilities to this argumentation. First, that vs 14b is reminiscent of 1 Sam 8: 5 (also vs 19) may be explained as the common work of the Deuteronomistic editor,[27] who could have supplied the precise wording into the old anti-monarchical tradition which he had received and then used similar wording to introduce this law which he was incorporating into the code. There is some linguistic evidence to support Deuteronomistic authorship of this verse. The use of the expression *kkl hgwym* is indicative of the editor's fondness for comparing undesirable practices in Israel. The precise expression appears elsewhere only in the narrative at 1 Sam 8: 5, 20, but *kgwym* occurs also and only in the Deuteronomistic passages at Deut 8: 20 (which, with vs 19, bears all the marks of a later addition; see von Rad, *Deuteronomy* p. 73) and 2 Kings 17: 11. In addition, the same style of the editor is demonstrated in his repeated "according to the abominable practices of the nations" at 1 Kings 14: 24; 2 Kings 16: 3; 21: 2; cf also 2 Kings 17: 33 and Deut 18: 9. The other significant expression in the verse concerning the nations "which are round about me" also seems to be characteristic of the Deuteronomist (with *gwym* as here, cf 2 Kings 17: 15; with *ʿmym*, cf Judg 2: 12 and the plural passages at Deut 6: 14; 13: 8; cf also Deut 12: 10; 25: 19 in reference to enemies).[28]

Second, the law does not necessarily refute the dynastic kingship of the Davidic line simply because it employs the term *bḥr*. David, to whom the law may refer, is said a number of times to be chosen by Yahweh both within the Deuteronomistic history (2 Sam 6: 21; 1 Kings 8: 16; cf also 1 Sam 16: 6–13) and without (Ps 89: 4, 20—a psalm which interweaves this election with the promise of an enduring dynasty; see vss 4–5, 20–38). While *bḥr* does not seem to be used in referring to David's descendants, nevertheless, the notion that the initiative comes from Yahweh in their rules can be seen from the reference to the Jerusalem kings as his "anointed" (Ps 2: 2; 18:51;

20: 7, etc.) as well as from the enthronement formula "I have set my king on Zion, my holy hill" (Ps 2: 6).[29] Finally, the use of the adoption formula (Ps 2: 7 and implied elsewhere) may point to an election motif, even though the technical term *bḥr* is not employed.

Third, that a foreigner should not become king presents problems in regard to this passage and with respect to its home. It almost seems inconsistent or illogical that this stipulation should follow the insistence on Yahweh's election; that is, only one chosen by Yahweh may become king, but the people are told that *they* may set over them only one who is from "among your brethren." But as for the question of home, it is difficult to find historical evidence for this problem in the south or in the north.[30] While the possibility of a foreigner becoming king in the north always existed—the only instance in the south which comes to mind is the case of the Syrian Tabeel, whom Syria and Ephraim wanted to put on Jerusalem's throne in place of Ahaz (Is 7: 5 f). It is probable, though, that the stipulation is more religious than historical, and that the real concern was with a ruler who would have little sympathy with Israel's self-understanding as the people of God and who would introduce pagan religions (which happened of course in north and south, without foreigners as kings).[31] Fourth, the polemic against a Solomon-like king could have originated in the south as well as in the north, as is clear from the preaching of Micah (3: 9–12). In addition, such a polemic could, indeed, have come from the pen of the Deuteronomistic editor, who gave unqualified approval to only two kings of Judah, Hezekiah and Josiah.

Thus, while Hosea is quite polemical in his attitude toward monarchy, it is by no means clear that the "royal law" of Deut 17: 14–20 is anti-monarchic (in spite of the negative connotation "like all the nations," it is said, nevertheless, "you may *indeed* set up [infinitive absolute] a king. . . .") or anti-Davidic dynasty. Surely, the passage is against any king who styles himself after Solomon, Omri, or several others, but this polemic could be at home in the south as in the north. Moreover, if one thinks of a writer who takes seriously the Davidic covenant but who harshly judges even the Davidic kings, a writer who elsewhere pointed out the dangers of kingship (1 Sam 8), a writer who elsewhere expresses himself in terms similar to several of the verses of this law[32]—then one brings to mind the Deuteronomist. If the law is, indeed, his work, then of course it is of no use in seeking the home of Proto-Deuteronomy.[33]

In spite of the weaknesses in some of these arguments to demonstrate a relationship between Hosea and Proto-Deuteronomy, however, such a relationship is not to be denied completely. There exist several points of comparison which are probably not accidental. First, there is the deep concern in both works over the dangers of the Canaanite religion and specifically over the apostasy of many Israelites to the cult of Baal. This problem seems to have been particularly acute in northern Israel, as is evidenced also with the prophet Elijah. Second, the exodus tradition plays a major role in both Hosea and Proto-Deuteronomy, and, in spite of the many objections to the thesis, the house of Joseph seems to have had a special concern for preserving that tradition. Third, the positive evaluation of the wilderness in Deut 8, which seems to reflect the attitude of the original work over against the negative editorial insertions, is attested at Hos 2: 14 f.[34] Though the patriarchal covenant-promise—so prominent in Proto-Deuteronomy—is entirely lacking in Hosea,[35] there remains evidence which points toward the possibility of a common home for Hosea and the original Deuteronomy.

DEUTERONOMY AND THE ELOHIST

Parallels between Proto-Deuteronomy and the E source of the Tetrateuch have fallen into linguistic as well as theological-ideological categories. Along the linguistic lines, such phrases as "the Lord, God of [our, their, your] fathers," "to go after other gods," "to hearken to the voice of the Lord," "to walk in his [God's)] ways," "that the Lord may bless you," "to do that which is evil [or right, good] in the eyes of the Lord," the use of the term "Amorite" as a general name for the occupants of the hill country of Canaan, and the use of "Horeb" as the name for Sinai—all these have been cited as indicative of an influence of E on Deuteronomy or of a common northern background.[36]

There are other issues of an ideological-theological nature which are interesting to compare. In the E source, there is a marked emphasis on the distance separating God from man and from the world—a distance evidenced by the necessity for God to approach men through the mediation of angels/messengers (Gen 21: 17; 28: 12, etc.) or through select individuals (e.g., the role of Moses in Ex 20: 18–20). This notion, that God does not walk the earth but dwells in heaven, is attested also in Deut 26: 15, and may be related to the "name theology" (to be discussed below). Moreover, in the E source is the common reference to "fear of God" or "fearing God," which appears frequently with the same meaning of obedience to God's commands and awe in his presence in Deuteronomy.[37] Also the notion of God testing his people appears both in the Elohistic passages at Gen 22: 1; Ex 20: 20[38] as well as in Deut 8: 2, 16; 13: 4.

In addition to these issues, some geography is worth noting. The Elohistic source is well known to be particularly interested in the northern sanctuaries of Bethel and Shechem, and the role of the Shechem area in Deuteronomy is undeniable from the mention of the mountains of blessings and curses: Gerizim and Ebal, respectively (Deut 27).[39]

Finally, it can be argued that the Decalogue of Ex 20: 1–17 and the Book of the Covenant (Ex 20: 22–23: 33), both of which are often assigned to E, must surely be considered in the question of Deuteronomy's origin, for the Decalogue is repeated at Deut 5: 6–18, and many laws in Deut 12–26 are similar to or modifications of many regulations in the Book of the Covenant.[40]

Now to evaluate these comparisons between the Elohist and Proto-Deuteronomy. In the first place, the linguistic arguments are not convincing in every case, because the parallels which are cited could be used to demonstrate any number of relationships. The phrase "to hearken to the voice of the Lord," which is common in Deuteronomy, occurs in the Tetrateuchal material at Ex 15: 26; 19: 5; 23: 21–22; Num 14: 22. While Ex 19: 5 might be E, there is the distinct possibility that the other three cases are Deuteronomistic inserts. Apart from these cases, the expression occurs only in Judg 2: 20; Ps 81: 12; 106: 25; cf also Ps 103: 20. The reference to "going after other gods," which occurs five times in Deuteronomy (6: 14; 8: 19; 11: 28; 13: 2; 28: 14), appears elsewhere at Judg 2: 12, 19; 1 Kings 11: 10; Jer 7: 6, 9; 11: 10; 13: 10; 16: 11; 25: 6; 35: 15. Thus, far from pointing to E, the precise phrase seems, rather, to demonstrate a relationship with the Deuteronomistic historian and with Jeremiah.[41] "To walk in his ways," attested often in Deuteronomy (8: 6; 10: 12; 11: 22; 19: 9; 26: 17; 28: 9; 30: 16; cf also 5: 33; 13: 5, 6), is extremely common in the Deuteronomistic history (Josh 22: 5; 1 Sam 8: 3, 5; 1 Kings 2: 3; 3: 14; 9: 4; etc.), but the only E passage which can be compared is Ex 18: 20, where "the way in which they must walk" sounds more like the wisdom way(s) of Ps 1: 6; Prov 2: 13, 20; cf Prov 3: 23. "To do that which is evil [or right, good] in the eyes of the Lord," common in Deuteronomy (4: 25; 9: 18; 12: 25; 13: 19; 17: 2) appears in the Tetrateuch only at Ex 15: 26, which is probably not E. "That the Lord may bless you," usually introduced in Deuteronomy either by *lmʿn* (14: 29; 23: 21; 24: 19) or by *ky* (14: 24; 15: 4, 10; 16: 15),[42] has no precise parallel. References to the Lord blessing "you" of course appear at Gen 28: 3; 49: 25; Ex 20: 24; 23: 25 (the third of which is E if the Book of the Covenant can be so labeled), but it is doubtful that such a general statement on blessing can be used to establish a relationship with Deuteronomy. The use of the term "Amorites" in referring to the occupants of the hill country of Canaan is difficult to establish as a characteristic of E, since out of the cited cases (Gen 15: 16; Num 13: 29; Josh 24: 8, 15, 18), none can be assigned with certainty to E. As for the phrase "the Lord, God of . . . fathers" and the use of "Horeb" as the mountain of God, both of which are common in Deuteronomy, there can be no question as to their attestation in E. However, that is precious little evidence to demonstrate a relationship between E and the book found in the Jerusalem Temple. The major difficulty in dealing linguistically with this relationship is that in both works there is great debate on what constitutes the source.

As for the theological-ideological comparisons which have been listed above, it is interesting to note that the transcendence of God and the notions that one should fear God and that God tests his people are features which one might expect to find in wisdom literature. In fact, that God dwells in heaven is attested at Eccles 5: 2; Job 16: 19; 22: 12; 25: 2; 31: 2, and for the accompanying notion that man is terrified in the presence of this holy God, see Job 23: 15 f; 42: 1–6. The use of "fear of God" or "fear the Lord" is quite common of course in wisdom literature, and is, in fact, nothing less than "the beginning of wisdom" (Prov 1: 7; 9: 10; cf also 10: 27; 14: 2; 24: 21, etc.). That God tests men is a theme in wisdom traditions can be seen not only in the framework of the book of Job but also at Eccles 3: 18; Prov 17: 3; cf also Prov 16: 2; 21: 2; 24: 12.[43] It may be then that these similarities between E and Deuteronomy are to be explained on the basis of a common wisdom influence, but this judgment does not deny the use of E to argue for a northern origin of Deuteronomy.[44]

The comparison of the law codes presents some problems of a different nature. First, if the scope of Proto-Deuteronomy accepted in this study is correct, then the Decalogues of Ex 20 and Deut 5 cannot be employed in this argument, for Deut 5 has been excluded from the original work. Second, while the Elohistic Book of the Covenant does, indeed, seem to serve as a basis for the Code of Deuteronomy, the precise relationship between the two is not clear.[45] Obviously a different situation had caused the necessity for writing a new code, but that different setting could be explained as geographical as well as sociological (especially in view of the conflicts in regard to the existence of a number of cultic sites) and thus could point to a southern situation. The comparisons between the codes demonstrates only that the writer of Deuteronomy had knowledge of the older Covenant code from the north.

Thus, with E as with Hosea, there are a number of difficulties in the arguments which are presented to show a relationship with the original Deuteronomy. While the linguistic evidence is not as overwhelming as is sometimes argued, there remain some cases which point to a possible common setting for E and Deuteronomy. Much more important and clear, it seems to me, are the theological-ideological features which are common in the two works; even if wisdom is the common influence on these matters, nevertheless a relationship does seem to exist between the Elohistic source and Proto-

Deuteronomy which may be explained within geographical categories. There remains one more issue to be discussed before leaving Hosea and the Elohist.

MOSES THE PROPHET IN HOSEA, E, AND DEUTERONOMY

The emphasis on prophecy and, in particular, the understanding of Moses as a prophet have been argued to be common to all three sources and thus reflective of a common background. In the Elohistic source, the enthusiasm for prophets and prophecy is clear, particularly in E's designation of Abraham as a prophet who would intercede for Abimelech (Gen 20: 7)[46] and in the repeated address by God followed by the response "Here am I" (Gen 22: 1, 11 in reference to Abraham; Ex 3: 6, to Moses), which seems to reflect a prophetic call formula (cf Is 6: 8; 1 Sam 3: 4, 6). Then too, in Hosea, who is obviously interested in prophecy, Moses is specifically called a *nby'* at 12: 14. And in Deuteronomy in two places—18: 15–22 and 34: 10—Moses is regarded as the prophet par excellence. Moreover, to further cement the relationship, the role of prophetic mediator assigned to Moses at Deut 18: 16–17 is tied up directly with the E passage at Ex 20: 18 ff. Thus, it is clear that in all three sources, Moses is regarded as a prophet.

What is questionable, however, is whether the passages in Deuteronomy belong to the original book or are due to the work of the later editors. No one would argue for the originality of 34: 10, and some even consider it to be E.[47] But the passage at 18: 15–22 is a complicated problem. According to some scholars, the entire piece is a later addition, primarily because of the exalted role of Moses, which is uncharacteristic of the Code of Deuteronomy.[48] In addition, if the criteria set down at the beginning of this study are valid, then the passage—or at least vss 16–18, if they can be separated from the rest—is not original, because it is based on Sinai-Horeb traditions which have been excluded from Proto-Deuteronomy. But there are other problems[49] with the originality of the passage. The expressions *nby' . . . yqym lk yhwh* and *nby' . . . 'qym lhm* (vss 15 and 18) betray Deuteronomistic authorship, for *hēqîm* is used in the same way in this history in reference to judges (Judg 2: 16, 18; 3: 9, 15), a priest (1 Sam 2: 35), and a king (1 Kings 14: 14; cf also 2 Sam 7: 12; 1 Kings 15: 4). Also, the effectiveness of the Word of God in vs 22 is characteristic both of the Deuteronomistic historian and of Deutero-Isaiah, who is roughly a contemporary (cf especially Is 55). In addition, the understanding of prophecy applied to Moses in the passage is somewhat different from the prophetic role of Moses in the Elohistic source,[50] and may reflect a later period, when "there has been time to reflect on the analogy between Moses and prophetism."[51]

If this passage is omitted from the original work along with 34: 10, there remains only one place in Deuteronomy where prophets or prophecy is mentioned: 13: 1–5. Though this passage too may be a later addition, with its mixture of singular and plural forms, even its originality in the book would not be sufficient to argue that Proto-Deuteronomy, though apparently influenced by prophetic preaching, demonstrates an explicit enthusiasm for prophets.[52] If this argumentation is legitimate, then there is weakened not only the relationship with E and Hosea but also the theory that the provenance of Proto-Deuteronomy is to be sought in northern *prophetic* circles.[53]

AMPHICTYONIC TRADITIONS

The book of Deuteronomy is said to contain many traditions of the old sacral confederacy—particularly the Sinai covenant and the Holy War—and in this way to reflect northern enthusiasm for the amphictyony. First, the Sinai covenant, which is said to be renewed in Deuteronomy. Now according to the scope of Proto-Deuteronomy assumed in this study, Sinai/Horeb is not mentioned explicitly; rather, the covenant in this book is that made in Moab. Perhaps Sinai/Horeb is not even implicit in the original work. Though the structure of Proto-Deuteronomy—even as it is understood here—corresponds to the suzerain-vassal treaty formula[54] in its general outline, one cannot assume that this structure points to Sinai.[55]

In fact, the more one studies Ex 19–24, the heart of the Sinai theme, the more questionable the presence of the covenant formula becomes. The oldest source, J, apparently speaks primarily of a theophany-Ritual Decalogue tradition (Ex 19; 34: 11–26), unless one can show that 19: 3–8[56] and 24: 3–8 are unquestionably Yahwistic. The Decalogue and the Book of the Covenant are probably Elohistic, but that the latter code belonged originally at Ex 21–23 is questionable. The Book of the Covenant, in spite of the literary connection with 24: 7 (which seems to be secondary), is generally agreed to be inserted from another place. Conjectures on the place from which it came range from just after Josh 24 to just before Deut 27: 2–8.[57] But its original position seems not to have been at Ex 21–23. Now when the remaining Elohistic material is isolated, there remains only a Decalogue which is preceded by a terrifying theophany and perhaps followed by covenant-making rite (24: 1–2, 9–11). Neither combined nor separated into sources, do J and E portray the Sinai tradition along the lines of the suzerain-vassal treaty.[58]

However, it is clear that the formula is present in Proto-Deuteronomy, and it is also obvious that such a covenant pattern was known in northern Israel: at Shechem (Josh 24) and at Gilgal (1 Sam 12). Therefore it can be argued that the amphictyonic tradition of covenant renewal according to the structure of the suzerain-vassal treaty provides the basic outline of Proto-Deuteronomy, and is reflective of northern interests. These interests, however, are probably not to be centered in the Sinai material.[59]

Second, northern interest in amphictyonic traditions is said to be evident in the Holy War ideology,[60] attested in Deuteronomy at 7: 16–26; 9: 1–6; 20: 1–10; 31: 3–8 (probably the first two and parts of the third belong to the original work). It is clear that the Holy War characteristics are present in these passages, but what is now questionable is whether the Holy War was, indeed, an amphictyonic phenomenon. A recent study by R. Smend[61] shows that the Holy War was not a concept of the early amphictyony but an event which led to national status, at first an activity of certain tribes and only later of the confederation. Smend goes on to demonstrate that this "War of Yahweh"—as he prefers to call it, since he does not consider it cultic primarily—was the contribution and concern of the Rachel tribes. If this reasoning is accurate (and there is much to commend it), then one can argue for a northern origin for Proto-Deuteronomy on the basis of the fact that the most influential tribes of the north were the primary practitioners of the Yahweh War. This practice, however, should probably not be labeled amphictyonic.

THE COMPLEX OF CULT CENTRALIZATION, THE NAME CONCEPT, AND DWELLING THEOLOGY

The issues of the centralization of the cult[62] at the chosen place where Yahweh causes his name to dwell are the most complex matters with which to deal in this question concerning the home of Proto-Deuteronomy. Space does not permit a detailed summary and analysis of all the arguments concerning these issues, but such a study would be incomplete without at least pointing to some of the difficulties with the arguments.

The clause "the place which the Lord your God will choose" occurs no less than twenty times in the book of Deuteronomy (12: 5, 11, 14, 18, 21, 26; 14: 23–25; 15: 20; 16: 2, 6 f, 11, 15 f; 17: 8; 26: 2; 31: 11), only one of which lies outside the code. The arguments for the origin of cult centralization in northern Israel generally begin with the notion of a central shrine in the amphictyonic period, for the sanctuaries at Bethel, Gilgal, Shiloh (and Shechem?) seem to have contained the Ark of the Covenant and would thus qualify as cultic centers. These northern sanctuaries might then have served as prototypes for the centralization theme of Deuteronomy, and possibly even one of these four "places" might have been intended in Proto-Deuteronomy.

In nine of the twenty places which speak of the chosen place in Deuteronomy, there is added the notion that Yahweh will "cause his name to dwell there" (12: 5, 11, 14; 14: 23, 24; 16: 2, 6, 11; 26: 2). There are two issues involved in this phrase: name, and dwelling. First, the name of Yahweh is intimately bound up with the cult site. What is unusual about this name concept in Deuteronomy is that, unlike the many prior references to Yahweh's name at this or that sanctuary (Is 18: 7, Ex 20: 24; etc.) or otherwise identifying Yahweh with his name, the concept here seems to be that *only* Yahweh's name dwells in the chosen place. Yahweh himself lives in heaven (Deut 25: 19). Thus, it seems that, in contrast to the general Old Testament usage, where the name *is* the person, for Deuteronomy, the name is Yahweh's *means* of making himself available to his people.[63]

It is argued that this understanding of Yahweh's presence is not consistent with Jerusalem Temple theology, which stressed Yahweh's presence as enthroned on the Ark of the Covenant. Moreover, where the Ark does occur in the book of Deuteronomy, it is considered to be a mere container of the law (Deut 10: 1–9; 31: 9, 24–26). But it is well known that in the Holy of Holies of Solomon's Temple, the Ark played an exalted role as the throne of Yahweh. Now the movement by David of the Ark from the north (where it was housed in the successive central sanctuaries) to Jerusalem had caused a religious vacuum in the north. To compensate for this after the disruption of the monarchy, Israel's King Jeroboam took drastic measures. At the sanctuaries of Bethel and Dan, he established the golden calves (1 Kings 12) as pedestals for Yahweh, thus providing cultic objects comparable to the Ark now in Jerusalem.[64] This much of the situation is fairly well established. But at this point, some of the proponents of the northern theory of Deuteronomy develop the thesis that owing to prophetic condemnation of the golden calf symbol (cf Hosea 8: 4b ff), there developed in the north the name theology as a more exalted notion of explaining Yahweh's presence apart from the Ark. This idea naturally led to devaluing the Ark as the throne of the abiding presence.[65]

Closely related to the name theology and to the polemic against the Ark as the abiding presence of Yahweh in the Jerusalem Temple is the notion that Yahweh "tabernacles" or "dwells" (*škn*) or allows his name to dwell at the central sanctuary. While *yšb* refers to continuing presence, and is used in the sense of enthronement on the Ark, *škn* points, rather, to taking up temporary residence, to pitching a tent. It is argued that the *miškān/škn* "sanctuary" theology, though used mostly by the Priestly writer, goes back to an old sacral tradition of the north. At 1 Chron 16: 39; 21: 29, the sanctuary at the northern city of Gibeon is called the *mškn-yhwh* apparently because it contained the tent of meeting (*'ōhel mô'ēd 'elōhîm*; cf 2 Chron 1: 3). In addition,the sanctuary at the northern city of Shiloh is *mškn* (Ps 78: 60), and the *škn* name theology is assigned to that same city at Jer 7: 12.

On the other hand, the argument continues, the Jerusalem sanctuary is called a *mškn* only in later literature (1 Chron 6: 33; 2 Chron 29: 6; Ps 26: 8; 74: 7), and so the *škn* theology, though present also at 1 Kings 6: 13; 8: 12 f; Is 8: 18, in connection with Jerusalem, does not seem to have caught on in the south. In addition, the use of the *miškān/škn* theology at 2 Sam 7: 5 f is anti-Temple.[66]

It must be admitted in evaluating these arguments in this difficult complex that a good deal of logic prevails. However, sound textual evidence is simply not available to argue these points conclusively. It is, indeed, true that the notion of a central (though not exclusive) sanctuary in the amphictyonic period was prevalent in the north, for several northern cities had made that claim to fame. However, it is clear that in moving the Ark to Jerusalem, David made that city the central cult site, and so after that time the centralization theme could apply to Jerusalem as well as to—in fact, more than —any northern city. As for the name theology, the arguments for northern provenance have little early and reliable textual support. The only passage in which a northern city is said to have possessed the "name" is Jer 7: 12, where Shiloh is the place "where I made my name dwell at first." That a prophet in Jerusalem at the end of the seventh century B.C. should use such an idea for Shiloh may be explained on grounds other than preserving an old sacral tradition. We shall return to this point.

The *mškn/škn* theology has more to commend it. There is evidence concerning the *mškn* notion both at Gibeon and at Shiloh. However, while it is, indeed, possible that these texts preserve an old tradition, it must be said that the earliest one is Jer 7: 12. While the *yšb* Ark as throne concept prevailed in Jerusalem, such texts as Is 8: 18; 1 Kings 6: 13; 8: 13, which connect *škn* to Jerusalem/Mount Zion, cannot be totally ignored; neither can the material from Chronicles cited above.[67] Thus, there is no early conclusive evidence for a northern origin of the *škn* theology.

A larger problem than the attempt to show that the place-name-*škn* complex is northern or southern in Proto-Deuteronomy is the question as to whether all the elements of the complex belong to the original work. With regard to the name theology, several questions arise: 1) Would the notion that *only* Yahweh's name dwelt at the Temple have been useful to Josiah or to anyone else who was attempting to centralize all cultic activity at one site? One would think that to extol one place to the exclusion of others, the theological corrective of the name concept would have been detrimental to Josiah and perhaps removed from the book. 2) Is the concept of the Ark as a law container the development of or simultaneous with the name theology?[68] The only places in the book of Deuteronomy which mention the Ark (10: 1–9; 31: 9, 24–26) are generally agreed to be Deuteronomistic supplements. While it can be argued that the Deuteronomistic editor could have described the Ark in no other way once the name theology stood before him, it might be said that this notion militates against the exalted view of the Temple necessary for the Deuteronomist's criterion for judging every king of Israel and Judah: the purification of the cult at Jerusalem. For such a criterion, the historian needed a Temple view which would not be devalued *simply* because of the name theology's presence in a book which had been handed down to him.

It seems to the present writer that the only legitimate reason for the Deuteronomist's use of the name theology and his devalued description of the Ark is the historical situation which he addressed. It is only in the face of the destruction of the Temple in 586 B.C. that the Deuteronomist could have spoken—in fact, needed to speak—of the Ark no longer as a throne but only as a container of the law. And it was in light of such a situation that he spoke of the Temple as the place where *only* Yahweh's name dwelt.[69] Both these ideas undercut his exalted understanding of the Temple, but his only alternative was to admit that, by the destruction of the Temple, God was dead.

As for the *mškn/škn* theology, it does seem that this dwelling concept could have been present in the north, especially since the tent of meeting seems to belong to the northern sanctuaries at Gibeon and at Shiloh. However, it is not thereby necessary to argue that the northern theology infiltrated Proto-Deuteronomy and then influenced the Deuteronomistic editor. While it is true that the *škn* concept was used by the historian, it does not necessarily follow that he learned of it through Proto-Deuteronomy. At 1 Kings 8: 12 f, 27 ff, and 6: 13 the historian employs the *škn* theology in speaking of the Temple at Jerusalem. The reason for this usage is probably directly related to the historical situation in which he found himself. He would have been committing theological suicide to insist on a *yšb* theology, for if Yahweh were tied up (i.e., permanently enthroned) to a particular place which had been destroyed, then Yahweh was no more. In addition, even if the Temple had been standing in Jerusalem, Yahweh's abiding presence there would have served the exiles in Babylon no use at all. However, to argue that Yahweh only tabernacled (*škn*) at the Temple allowed the exiled people and the remnant in Judah to live in the hope that the God who lives in heaven will again pitch his tent in their midst.

There are two pieces of evidence in particular which can be used to show that the name/*škn* theological complex was employed in connection with the destruction of the Temple, and perhaps was *initiated* because of that disaster. First, there is the testimony at Ps 74: 2, 7. The community lament over the destruction of the Jerusalem Temple speaks of Mount Zion as the place "where thou has dwelt (*škn*)" and as "the dwelling place of thy name *mškn-šmk*)." It is precisely this exilic theology which enables the people to wait in hope for him who "is my king from of old" (vs 12) and who will arise to plead his cause (vs 22).

Second, there is the passage at Jer 7: 1–15, the temple speech of the prophet. In view of the impending disaster which Jeremiah sees coming upon Jerusalem, he points to the false hope in the inviolability of Jerusalem and its Temple, and he calls for repentance. Because he sees the probability of the destruction of the city, Jeremiah employs the *škn*/name concepts throughout the speech. If the people repent, then Yahweh will dwell (*škn*) with them "in this place" (vss 3, 7).[70] Moreover, the place of his "name" he will destroy just as he destroyed Shiloh, "where I made my name dwell at first." The sequence in this argument seems to be 1) the Temple is about to be destroyed; 2) other sanctuaries were destroyed; 3) if there is any hope held out, then not Yahweh's abiding presence but his name as dwelling in the Temple must be proclaimed; 4) Yahweh continued after Shiloh was destroyed, and he will continue even when Jerusalem is destroyed. In other words, if this speech is, indeed, Jeremiah's own, then it seems probable that, rather than receiving a name/*škn* tradition from Shiloh, Jeremiah was faced with expounding a presence theology which would suit the historical situation. In doing so, he used as an illustration the Shiloh sanctuary, because it had been destroyed, and to that sanctuary Jeremiah attached the concepts necessary for his argument. If the passage is not, in its final form, Jeremianic but the editorial result of the Deuteronomist, then it becomes even more probable that the name/*škn* theology was imposed on Shiloh in the exilic period in order to hold out hope for the covenant people of that time. It is possible, of course, to argue that the use of the name/*škn* theology at Jer 7 and at Ps 74 does not point to its origin in the exilic period. However, the only texts which use these concepts in a technical way come from the period after 608 B.C. (if Jer 7 is authentic in its final form) or probably after the destruction of the Temple in 586 B.C.

Conclusion

On the basis of some of the arguments which have been offered over the past several decades, it is probable that the home of Proto-Deuteronomy, or at least of the major traditions of that work, lies in northern Israel. However, the arguments for that provenance are not as firm or as extensive as has sometimes been supposed. Of the points of contact which have been made with the prophet Hosea, those which seem to be most directly related and most legitimate in arguing for a northern home are the parallels between

Deut 28: 68 and Hos 7: 16; 8: 13; 9: 3; 11: 5, in which it is said that God will return Israel to Egypt because of her unfaithfulness, the concern about Canaanism, and the common interest in the exodus and positive wilderness traditions. The similarity of the Elohistic source of the Tetrateuch with Proto-Deuteronomy can be maintained on the basis of a few linguistic parallels, but more important are the role of Shechem and the theological issues of the transcendence of God, the fear of God, and the testing of the people by God. It is probable that these common themes are due to the influence of wisdom traditions on both, rather than to a direct influence of E on Deuteronomy. Even the comparison of Hosea, E, and Deuteronomy on the matter of Moses as a prophet is highly debatable, since the crucial passage at Deut 18: 15–22 seems not to belong to Proto-Deuteronomy.

On the matter of the amphictyonic traditions, the arguments concerning the Sinai material and the Holy War ideology need refinement and restatement in the discussion of this problem, because while the covenant renewal pattern is evident in Proto-Deuteronomy, in Sinai it is not, and that Sinai is at all present in the original work is doubtful; and while the Holy War or War of Yahweh characteristics are attested in several places, this institution is not an amphictyonic phenomenon. In any case, both the covenant renewal pattern and the Holy War point to the north, for the former is known to have been used at Shechem and at Gilgal, and the latter seems to be a particular concern of the Rachel tribes. As for "the place which the Lord your God will choose to make his name dwell there," there is little evidence for finding a home for the name theology in the north, and the chosen place or central sanctuary could, indeed, mean Jerusalem, according to the traditional understanding. While there exists some evidence for the *škn* theology in northern sanctuaries, the presence of this notion in the book of Deuteronomy is more likely to be explained by the historical situation of the Deuteronomistic editor. If some of the elements of this sanctuary-name-*škn* complex do, indeed, belong to the original work, then perhaps a solution along the lines of Nicholson's suggestion, concerning the composition of the work in the south by northerners who had fled south and who saw the hope of the people in Jerusalem, would make a good deal of sense.

Notes

1 Most notably Gerhard von Rad, *Studies in Deuteronomy*, Studies in Biblical Theology, No. 9, trans. David Stalker (London, 1953), pp. 60–69; G. E. Wright, *Deuteronomy*, *IB*, II, pp. 325 f; H. W. Wolff, "Hoseas geistige Heimat," *Gesammelte Studien* (Munich, 1964), pp. 232–50.

2 E. W. Nicholson, *Deuteronomy and Tradition* (Philadelphia, 1967), pp. 58 ff.

3 O. Bächli, *Israel und die Völker: Eine Studie zum Deuteronomium* (Zürich, 1962).

[4] M. Weinfeld, "The Origin of Humanism in Deuteronomy," *JBL* 80 (1961), 241 ff; "Deuteronomy: The Present State of Inquiry," *JBL* 86 (1967), 249 ff; "The Dependence of Deuteronomy upon the Wisdom Literature," (Heb), *Kaufmann Jub. Vol.* (1960), pp. 89–105.

[5] O. Eissfeldt, *The Old Testament: An Introduction*, trans. P. R. Ackroyd (New York, 1965), pp. 231 f.

[6] M. Noth, *Überlieferungsgeschichtliche Studien* I^2 (Tübingen, 1957), pp. 27–40.

[7] G. von Rad, *Deuteronomy*, "The Old Testament Library," trans. Dorothea Barton (Philadelphia, 1966), pp. 11 f. Here von Rad argues for the scope of Deuteronomy proper to run from 4: 44 to 30: 20. In another place, however ("Deuteronomy," *IDB*, I, pp. 831 ff), von Rad seems to regard the introduction as beginning with ch. 6.

[8] E. W. Nicholson, *Deuteronomy and Tradition*, pp. 18–36.

[9] Georg Fohrer, *Introduction to the Old Testament*, trans. David E. Green (New York, 1968), pp. 165–78.

[10] Hartmut Gese, "Bemerkungen zur Sinaitradition," *ZAW* 79 (1967), 137–54, esp. pp. 149–54.

[11] Actually, the block from 5: 1–6: 1 is plural, and 6: 2–3 is singular. However, because of the introductory word *lmʿn* in vs 2, these last two verses cannot be separated from vs 1. Perhaps the singular is employed in 6: 2–3 in order to provide a transition to the singular material beginning with the *šmʿ* at 6: 4.

[12] Gese's conclusions can be supported by another piece of evidence. A study of the vocative use of the name "Israel" bears some interesting results. In the book of Deuteronomy, the vocative *yśr'l* is usually accompanied by the imperative *šᵉmaʿ*, but there is a difference in usage between those passages which are Proto-Deuteronomy and those which are not. In the passages which lie outside the scope of Proto-Deuteronomy, there is always a direct object following the *šᵉmaʿ* (or there is one implied), and that object is statutes and ordinances/commandments: 4: 1; 5: 1; 6: 3. In contrast, the use of the vocative *yśr'l* (usually preceded by *šmʿ*) in Proto-Deuteronomy serves to introduce an important announcement:

6: 4 Hear, Israel: the Lord our God is one Lord.

9: 1 Hear, Israel: you are to pass over the Jordan . . . to dispossess nations great and mightier than yourselves.

27: 9 Hear, Israel: this day you have become the people of the Lord your God.

10: 12 And now, Israel: what does the Lord require of you, but to fear the Lord your God. . . .

Thus, the break between 4: 1–6: 3 and 6: 4 ff is further substantiated by this stylistic device employing the vocative Israel with the imperative *šᵉmaʿ*.

[13] While throughout this study I make some sharp contrasts between what is Proto-Deuteronomy and what is the work of the later Deuteronomistic editor, I do not mean to imply that only two stages of development explain the present book. The Canonical Deuteronomy surely must be the result of a complicated and gradual growth, the major editorial expansions occurring, I believe, at the time of Josiah and in the exilic period under the Deuteronomist (or perhaps Deuteronomistic school). Only in certain cases am I willing to designate one or the other of these revisions / expansions. The task of this study has to do only with what was or was not original, for that question is vital to the question of provenance.

[14] A. C. Welch, *The Code of Deuteronomy: A New Theory of Its Origin* (London, 1924), who argues that only the code is original; W. F. Albright, $FSAC^2$ (1946), p. 241; A. Alt, "Die Heimat des Deuteronomiums," *Kleine Schriften* II (1953), 250–75; G. Fohrer,

Introduction . . ., pp. 174 f; G. E. Wright, *Deuteronomy*, pp. 311–30; F. Dumermuth, "Zur deuteronomischen Kulttheologie und ihre Voraussetzungen," *ZAW* 70 (1958) 59–98; H. Ringgren, *Israelite Religion*, trans. David E. Green (Philadelphia, 1966), pp. 165 f.

15 G. von Rad, *Studies in Deuteronomy*, p. 68.

16 E. Nicholson, *Deuteronomy and Tradition*.

17 Hans Walter Wolff, "Dodekapropheton I: Hosea," *BKAT* 14 (1961), 48 and 294 (forgetting Yahweh), 273 (contra alliances), 176 f (*tôrāh*), 125 (chastiser), 162 f (redemption), 20g (true prophet), 33 (brotherhood), 225 (*massebah*), and 44 (grain, wine, and oil).

18 The father-son relationship does, indeed, appear at Deut 8: 5; 14: 1, but is not attested in these passages. At 14: 1 f, there is a direct relationship between the concept of Israel as "sons of the Lord your God" (vs 1) and the election formula (vs 2). This formula of vs 2 is identical to 7: 6, where there immediately follows in vss 7–8 the use of *'hb* as Yahweh's sole motive for choosing Israel. One might argue therefore that the son relationship of 14: 1 f plays the same role as the love motive in 7: 6 ff. However, it seems to the present writer that the Deuteronomistic editor is responsible for this "sons of the Lord your God" motif (a plural verse) and perhaps also for repeating the formula from 7: 6. If this is correct, then 14: 1 f. cannot be employed against the judgment that there is no father-son love in Proto-Deuteronomy.

19 This understanding of love in Deuteronomy has been shown by William Moran, *CBQ* 25 (1963) 77–87, to have its background in the Amarna correspondence, where *ra'āmu* (the semantic equivalent of *'hb*) is employed: 1) in international treaties to denote friendship among independent and equal rulers (EA 27: 72–73); 2) in faithful relationships between a sovereign and a vassal (EA 123: 23; 53: 40–44); and 3) in the service of a servant to his king (EA 83: 51; 137: 47). This love is defined in terms of obedience, loyalty, and service, and thus is parallel to that in Deuteronomy.

20 G. von Rad, *Deuteronomy*, p. 119; Galling, "Das Königsgesetz in Deuteronomium," *TLZ* 76 (1951), col. 138; E. Nicholson, *Deuteronomy and Tradition*, p. 93; A. Alt, "Die Heimat des Deuteronomiums," p. 264, n. 3.

21 For comparisons between 1 Sam 8 and Deut 17: 14–20, see R. de Vaux, *Ancient Israel: Its Life and Institutions*, trans. John McHugh (New York, 1961), pp. 98 f. Also see E. Nicholson, *Deuteronomy and Tradition*, pp. 49 f. However, Galling argues that since 1 Sam 8 is anti-monarchy per se while Deut 17 is not, the comparison is not helpful.

22 A. Alt, "Die Heimat des Deuteronomiums," pp. 263 ff; E. Nicholson, *Deuteronomy and Tradition*, p. 69; A. C. Welch, *The Code of Deuteronomy*, pp. 117–32.

23 A. Alt, "Die Heimat des Deuteronomiums," p. 265; K. Galling, *TLZ* 76 (1951), col. 135; G. von Rad, *Deuteronomy*, p. 119.

24 K. Galling, *TLZ* 76 (1951), col. 135. Noth suggests the possibility that the law has in mind the case of Omri, whose name is closely related to Arabic roots (*The History of Israel*[2], New York, 1960, p. 230, n. 1).

25 K. Galling, *TLZ* 76 (1951), cols. 135 ff.

26 E. Nicholson, *Deuteronomy and Tradition*, pp. 80 f, 105; A. Alt, "Die Heimat des Deuteronomiums," pp. 263–68.

27 Alt (p. 264. n. 2) believes that 1 Sam 8: 5 is a Deuteronomistic narrative dependent upon Deut 17: 14. However, the linguistic evidence above points to Deuteronomistic authorship of both passages.

28 Elsewhere in the OT, "nations (*gwym*) which are round about" occurs at Lev 25: 44; Ezek 5: 7; 11: 12 (cf also 36: 36); Neh 5: 17; 6: 16. The dating of these passages may be significant for understanding the verse at Deut 17: 14 as Deuteronomistic rather than as belonging to Proto-Deuteronomy.

[29] Even if the passive rendering of this acclamation (so LXX) is correct, the initiative is nevertheless Yahweh's.

[30] But see note 24.

[31] Though *miqqereb* is particularly common throughout Deuteronomy, *miqqereb 'āḥeykā* is quite similar to Deut 18: 15, 18, which may be a supplement to the original work.

[32] In addition to the similarities at vs 14, cf vs 20 with the later material at 30: 17 f.

[33] One more point in particular is of interest. In connection with the prohibition against multiplying horses or causing the people to return to Egypt (as slaves? mercenaries?) in order to multiply horses (Deut 17: 16), there appears the statement that Yahweh promised they "shall never return that way again." Since the only other reference to such a promise occurs at Deut 28: 68, which seems to belong to the original book, it might be argued that this verse (and thus the whole law) is also original. However, the motive clause (the promise) at 17: 16b is plural in the midst of an otherwise singular passage; moreover, it is not clear that this motive is consistent with the stipulation. For these reasons, it has been excluded from its immediate surroundings by Welch, who otherwise regards the law as original. The entire law is regarded as a supplement by G. Fohrer, *Introduction to the Old Testament*, pp. 170, 172.

[34] If George Coats is correct (*Rebellion in the Wilderness*, Nashville, 1968) that the murmuring motif of the wilderness tradition is a Judean polemic against the Northern Kingdom, then the positive wilderness experience might indeed be the North's expression of that period. There are some problems with Coats' arguments, however, particularly in his rejection of Ex 14: 11 f and 17: 3 as E (i.e., the northern source), for on the basis of Num 21: 4–9, such an unfavorable or negative experience does seem to be present in E.

[35] While Hosea does mention some of the peripheral traditions about Jacob (12: 2–6, 12), the theological motifs of the patriarchal covenant and election are not present. This fact may of course be purely accidental.

[36] G. E. Wright, *IB*, II, pp. 318 ff. Wright himself questions whether some of the passages cited in the list taken from Driver (*Deuteronomy*, ICC, pp. lxxviii–lxxxiv) are really E. However, some of those which he adds to the list (p. 320, n. 28), such as the "hornet" (Deut 7: 22; Ex 23: 28; Josh 24: 12) and the reason why some Canaanites were left in the land (Deut 7: 22; Ex 23: 29–30), are probably D rather than E.

[37] In E, cf Gen 20: 11; 22: 12; Ex 1: 17, 21; 3: 6; 18: 21, etc.; in Deut, cf 4: 10; 5: 29; 6: 2, 13, 24; 8: 6; 10: 12, 20; 28: 58; 31: 12 f.

[38] It is possible that Ex 15: 25b is Elohistic, but the testing by Yahweh at 16: 4 seems to be J.

[39] Deut 11: 29–30 locates the mountains as opposite Gilgal near Jericho, but this supplementary material is obscure, to say the least.

[40] It must be admitted that the argument as stated here is a bit more pointed than is usually found, but the implications of various statements would lead logically to this kind of argument. Cf A. Weiser, *The Old Testament: Its Formation and Development* (New York, 1961), pp. 119–25, 127, 130 ff. For the impressive list of comparisons between the Book of the Covenant and the Code of Deuteronomy, see G. von Rad, *Deuteronomy*, p. 13.

[41] To be sure, the concern for worshiping and serving other gods appears in the ethical as well as the ritual decalogues (Ex 20: 3; 34: 14), but this concern, common in Deut (7: 4; 11: 16; 13: 6, 13, etc.), occurs very frequently in the Deuteronomistic history and in Jeremiah (Josh 23: 16; 24: 2, 16; Judg 2: 17; 10: 13; 1 Sam 8: 8; 1 Kings 9: 9; 11: 4; 2 Kings 5: 17; 17: 7, 35, 38; 22: 17; Jer 1: 6; 6: 12; 7: 18; 16: 13; 19: 4, 13; 22: 9; 44: 3, 5).

[42] Also appears without *lmʿn* and *ky* at Deut 1: 11; 7: 13; 30: 16.

[43] Von Rad suggests that this idea may be derived from the Egyptian concept of the judgment of the dead, whose hearts are weighed in the balance by the god Thot; see *Old Testament Theology*, I, trans. D. M. G. Stalker (New York, 1962), pp. 437 f, esp., notes 41, 42.

[44] For wisdom features throughout the book of Deuteronomy, see the works by M. Weinfeld cited in note 4.

[45] Cf. O. Eissfeldt, *The Old Testament: An Introduction*, pp. 220–23; A. Weiser, *The Old Testament: Its Formation and Development*, pp. 130 f; G. von Rad, *Deuteronomy*, pp. 13 ff.

[46] It is of particular importance to note that in the parallel Yahwistic stories at Gen 12: 10–20 and Gen 26, there is no mention of Abraham or Isaac as prophets. Thus, the Elohist's particular interests stand out even more sharply by contrast. However, some E passages often cited to demonstrate Moses as supreme prophet (Ex 4: 16; 33: 11; Num 11: 24–30; 12: 1–8) either fail to use *nby'* for Moses or contrast him with *nby'ym*.

[47] Cf. A Weiser, *The Old Testament: Its Formation and Development*, pp. 113 f; G. von Rad, *Old Testament Theology*, I p. 293.

[48] O. Eissfeldt, *The Old Testament: An Introduction*, p. 225; G. Fohrer, *Introduction to the Old Testament*, p. 171.

[49] In spite of the offices forbidden in the previous passage (vss 9–14), the present "law" which establishes the legitimate office for Israel (if, indeed, it is an office rather than a "Moses to come") is probably not integral to what precedes (contra von Rad, *Deuteronomy*, pp. 122 ff). Elsewhere in Deuteronomy, abomination laws never include an antithesis to what is considered abominable (cf 16: 21–17: 1; 22: 5; 23: 18; 25: 13–16).

[50] See von Rad, *Old Testament Theology*, I, pp. 292–95.

[51] Walther Eichrodt, *Theology of the Old Testament*, I, trans. J. A. Baker (Philadelphia, 1961), p. 290.

[52] The Deuteronomistic history, on the other hand, abounds in the use of *nby'*, especially in the books of Kings. It may be his interest which caused the inclusion of Deut 18: 15–22 (and 13: 1–5?).

[53] In particular, E. Nicholson, *Deuteronomy and Tradition.*

[54] See the works of George Mendenhall: *Law and Covenant in Israel and the Ancient Near East* (Pittsburgh, 1955); "Covenant," *IDB*, I, p. 714–23. Also cf K. Baltzer, *The Covenant Formulary* (Philadelphia, 1970).

[55] For a detailed rejection of the formula from the Sinai tradition, see D. J. McCarthy, *Treaty and Covenant* (Rome, 1963).

[56] Ex 19: 3–8 has more characteristics of E than of J., although some scholars (e.g., Fohrer, *Introduction to the Old Testament*, p. 189) refuse to identify it with any source. Even if it is E, however, the precise relationship of the passage (which does seem to follow the covenant formula) to Sinai can be determined only by its present context.

[57] For a discussion on these suggestions, see A. Weiser, *The Old Testament: Its Formation and Development*, pp. 121 f. Note that if the original context is either Josh 24 or Deut 27, the place involved is Shechem.

[58] The work by W. Beyerlin, *Origins and History of the Oldest Sinaitic Traditions*, trans. S. Rudman (Oxford, 1965), does not really solve the problem.

[59] If Gese is correct that the positive wilderness tradition (*Fundtradition*) of Deuteronomy (as well as of Hosea and Jeremiah) is a reinterpretation of the Sinai tradition because of the formal—i.e., narrative association of the exodus and Sinai traditions in the monarchical period, then of course Sinai/Horeb traditions are implicitly present in Proto-Deuteronomy. That such a reinterpretation is probably northern can be seen in the tradi-

tions concerning Elijah (1 Kings 18 and especially 19) and in the preaching of Hosea (H. Gese, "Bemerkungen zur Sinaitradition").

60 See G. von Rad, *Der Heilige Krieg im alten Israel* (Göttingen, 1958); also in outline form in *Studies in Deuteronomy*, pp. 45–59.

61 Now translated as *Yahweh War and Tribal Confederation*, trans. from 2d ed. by Max Gray Rogers (New York, 1970).

62 For a concise interpretation of the theology of the cult in the book of Deuteronomy, see Jacob M. Myers, "The Requisites for Response: On the Theology of Deuteronomy," *Interp* 15 (1961), 14–31, esp. 19–24. The author provides also sections on Deuteronomy's theology of history and of faith and life, all of which "Converge at one point with several facets—one God, one holy people, one cult place, one prophet—that is, the Covenant community and its several components" (p. 31).

63 For the clearest description of this name theology in Deuteronomy, see G. von Rad, *Studies in Deuteronomy*, pp. 37–44. Also see W. Eichrodt, *Theology of the Old Testament*, II, trans. J. A. Baker (Philadelphia, 1967), pp. 41 f.

64 See W. F. Albright, *FSAC*², pp. 229 f; also W. Eichrodt, *Theology of the Old Testament*, I, p. 117.

65 Fritz Dumermuth, "Zur deuteronomischen Kulttheologie und ihre Voraussetzungen," *ZAW* 70 (1958), 59–98, esp. 70 ff; E. Nicholson, *Deuteronomy and Tradition*, pp. 72 f.

66 This paragraph attempts in an oversimplified way to summarize the gist of Dumermuth (see previous note).

67 In fact, along the traditional lines concerning Jerusalem, one can raise quite sound arguments for a southern theory on the basis of the intertwining of centralization and chosen place. Jerusalem was the only city in which actual reform movements were carried out in order to centralize worship at one place exclusively (under Hezekiah and Josiah in particular), and that actuality must speak strongly to the question at issue. The views on the precise motive for the centralization of worship at Jerusalem have ranged from economic factors (A. Bentzen, *Die josianische Reform und ihre Voraussetzungen*, 1926) to theological ones (the deliverance of Jerusalem from the siege of Jerusalem; see V. Maag, "Erwägungen zur deuteronomistischen Kultzentralization," *VT* 6 [1956], 10 ff.) Moreover, Jerusalem as the elected place has been argued on the basis of the election of David as king; see H. J. Kraus, *Worship in Israel*, tran. Geoffrey Buswell (Richmond, 1966), pp. 179–83. While Jerusalem is mentioned specifically in the Deuteronomistic history as the place where Yahweh caused his name to dwell, the lack of the name in Deuteronomy may be due simply to the fact that the work is supposed to be the speech of Moses in the plains of Moab. It would have been anachronistic to mention the city by name at this point.

68 This question has nothing to do with the ultimate origin of the Ark and its first significance either as a throne (Num 10: 35 f; 1 Sam 4: 4, 5–9, etc.) or as a container (*ʾᵃrôn* = Akk *arānu* and common Semitic meaning "chest").

69 It is important, in this question of the origin of the name theology, to note that the clearest and most comprehensive statement of the concept—and thus perhaps its source—occurs in the Deuteronomistic history at 1 Kings 8: 27–30. In fact, I wonder if the "new" understanding of the name in Deuteronomy would have occurred to anyone without this Deuteronomistic explanation.

70 The reading of the Vulgate, "I will dwell with you" (Heb *wᵉʾeškᵉnāh ʾittᵉkem*), is to be preferred over the Masoretic "I will make you dwell" (*waʾᵃšakkᵉnāh ʾetkem*).

George E. Mendenhall
The University of Michigan

The Shady Side of Wisdom: The Date and Purpose of Genesis 3

Wisdom, it would seem, is as inevitable to human civilization as death and taxes. Yet what it was in ancient cultures that was termed "wisdom" has been grossly obscured by modern scholarly concerns with literary "forms," on the one hand, and by romantic confusion of highly specialized social functions with the rich legacy of quaint folk proverbs in which every simple culture abounds.[1] Paul Volz pointed out decades ago that there is a world of difference between the lowly folk proverb and the highly sophisticated literary productions that we call "wisdom literature,"[2] but the difference in social milieu and social function seems largely to have escaped modern scholarship. The unhistorical or even antihistorical bias of biblical and theological disciplines has resulted in an increasingly sterile mass of irrelevant verbiage about "form criticism" but little insight into the meaning and substance of biblical narratives and literature. The constant concern for the "exegesis" of biblical texts for modern homiletical or theological purposes has resulted in a systematic process of taking texts out of their *own* historical and cultural context—and therefore to a large extent a systematic misrepresentation of the Bible that has come home to roost in the contemporary rejection of it by all sorts of movements, from Women's Lib to radical theologians, and its reduction to mere political propaganda by various secular political ambitions.

Perhaps there is no more dramatic example of the millennia-long distortion and exploitation of biblical narrative than the brief and simple narrative of Genesis 3. It has reemerged into prominence in the news media as a favorite target of Women's Lib and other such movements. One article on the subject quotes a poem of Archibald MacLeish:

The Fall! she said—
From earth to God![3]

The narrative has quite a different thrust when it is seen within the perspective of the cultural and intellectual history out of which it emerged. The problem of recovering that cultural and intellectual history is not an easy one by any means, and it cannot be done at all by treating merely one passage or literary unit of the Bible in isolation. The present treatment of Genesis 3 is, then, merely one episode of a much broader and long-continued concern for the whole problem of ancient Israelite faith, its origins and its history, in the context of the history of ancient civilization in general. At the same time, Genesis 3 is an important element in that intellectual history of biblical times, and to argue, as do some theologians, that such a treatment of biblical texts "loses them in ancient cultural history"[4] is quite the opposite to the truth. It is only by such means that the Bible becomes anything more than merely a mirror or a ground of authority for the arbitrary power or prestige structures of contemporary man, who is and was absolutely irrelevant to the ancient writer or writers. To deal with the Bible as though the real world in which its writers lived was completely irrelevant is just as absurd as the position that the real world of the present is completely irrelevant to the Christian faith. Actually, the ancient and the modern problem are much the same—just what is the connection between faith in God and the course of human experience? On this, Genesis 3 had much to say, until the substance was lost in the forest of theological battles over issues that were originally entirely alien to the author's intention.

The thesis to be presented here is nearly as simple as the story itself—namely, that the apparently naïve and childlike story is actually a work of utmost artistry and sophistication that stems from the "wisdom" tradition of ancient Israel. It is a *mashal*: an "analogy" or, better yet, a "parable" that was told to convey a point, one that could hardly be communicated in any other way with such pathos and sympathy. It is a sad comment on modern civilization that it has become merely a favorite subject for cartoonists, Women's Libbers, and Sunday school lessons for very young children. The narrative does not belong to the J document to which it is universally assigned by the literary critics (except Winnett [*JBL*, 1965, pp. 1–19], who has also seen that the story cannot be tenth-ninth century), but is a part of that enormous ferment of thought and creativity that followed the destruction of the Temple and State in 587 B.C. Like the book of Job, which it closely resembles in ways to be pointed out below, it stems from a wisdom tradition that had been chastened by calamity and that was forced to the conclusion that the old religious tradition was, after all, in the right.

It represents an astoundingly creative transformation of what probably were very old traditions, and therefore offers an engaging illustration of the fact that tradition need not be merely the rust on the bolt of civilization or religion that makes it impossible to remove the nuts. On the contrary, it may well be a source of understanding and inspiration that is otherwise unrepresented in any contemporary society and culture.

The problem of interpreting the original intention of the narrative falls thus into three distinct categories plus a final one of attempting to restate in modern thought patterns what the original author intended to say. It has been a rather curious experience to find that an attempt to understand what the narrator intended to communicate turned out to be inseparable from an understanding of the course of late pre-exilic cultural history, and both, in turn, led to a new concept of narrative forms.[5]

The problems to be dealt with are: 1) the social function of the wisdom tradition, and its connection with Genesis 3; 2) the *mashal* as a thought pattern of antiquity into which category our narrative falls; 3) evidence for the late date of the narrative—over against the general consensus that it is a J document of the tenth century B.C.; 4) the correlation of the narrative with what we know to be true of the enormous changes that took place in biblical thought between Josiah and Deutero-Isaiah—this is, in turn, inseparable from the main purpose, which is to understand what the ancient writer was saying to his contemporaries.

The Social Function of "Wisdom"

As any *philosophiae doctor* is painfully aware, "wisdom," whether it be called *sophia* or *ḥokma* or *ḥikma*, is the presumed product of a long process of training in a specialized field of skills or knowledge. If the major contrast between a primitive culture and civilization is the latter's wealth in specialized occupations, as the anthropologists maintain, then it follows that such specialized training is the only foundation for civilization, and any society without it is necessarily "primitive." It is therefore no accident that our earliest sources indicate a very close relationship between what we blithely label "wisdom literature" and the very ancient pagan educational system by which the children of the elite class of society were trained in the necessary skills that enabled them to compete in the ancient pecking order determined by the ancient states and empires. Those skills were, first of all, literacy itself and, in pre-biblical times, administration. Though it is clear that the various terms translated as "wisdom" included far more than a specialization in scribal arts, nevertheless such works as the Egyptian "Satire on the Trades"[6] certainly places the scribe at the apex of the social scene. Further, the wisdom literature almost certainly functioned as textbooks in the schools for scribes.

As Eissfeldt long ago pointed out,[7] a scribe was far from a mechanical copyist but, rather, was a highly cultured wise man, and often held positions of considerable authority and power. The wise men of antiquity were thus the educated elite upon whom rested the whole structure and function of the political state. Thus the wise man as a political functionary of the late pre-exilic monarchy is also well attested, particularly in Jeremiah. The bitter condemnation of the wise man together with other functionaries such as priests and (false) prophets is a recurrent theme in the prophetic books, building up to a climax just before the destruction. Is it merely a curious coincidence that only a century later Socrates was bitterly excoriating the "Sophists" of his day? Or is it, rather another indication that educated elitism is an international phenomenon, and has similar effects in radically different societies?

As a partial explanation of the problem concerning the crisis of wisdom, I would propose the "law of elaboration." It is an observation that in any society where there is a specialized group with time and resources enough, they will produce an enormously complex body of tradition concerning their own social role, whether it be religious ritual (Leviticus), building of tombs and ideologies to justify them (pyramids to Petra), architecture, theology, or form criticism. The elaboration is then inaccessible to the untrained, whether by virtue of its incomprehensibility to those without technical education or because of a jealous exclusion of those beyond the closed corporation of the elite. As the technical elaboration continues to accumulate, the range of experience, knowledge, and concern of the specialist group becomes more and more restricted, and, in the course of time, the specialist group comes more and more to resemble a primitive tribe whose concern is first to maintain the internal unity, the rigid and secure boundary line against outsiders, and the maintenance of its own power and prestige.

The closed social system becomes increasingly impervious to input from beyond the self-imposed boundary, and the dynamics of the group is characterized by a complex system of feedback. And thus we have the "Grammarian's Funeral"—settling *hoti*'s business—and the "teachers of Israel who do not know these things" (Jn 3: 10). Above all, the closed corporation is most impervious to suggestions from upstart prophets. In time, the specialized elite claim a direct pipeline to heaven, where an important god —Nabu, Thoth, Athena—becomes their divine patron and source.

A well-attested further characteristic of such elite groups is compulsive competitiveness, illustrated, for example, by King Solomon's wisdom that excelled all that of the *b^{e}ne qedem*—usually translated as "sons of the

East," but which almost certainly should be translated as "sons of aforetime," for which compare *malᵉkē qedem* of Is 19: 11. After all, ancient man, during the brief periods of affluence and power, believed in his enormous superiority over the benighted unfortunates who were doomed to live in the pre-modern age too. The competitiveness of the wisdom tradition is also illustrated in the story of Solomon and the Queen of Sheba, who was so overcome that the result was the foundation of the Ethiopian dynasty, according to a tradition that owes more to prestige concerns than to historical fact. However, the tradition does reflect fairly well-established habits of emotional response on the part of women.

For it is true that the products of technical specialization are intended to impress: to neutralize or overcome any possible exercise of critical faculties on the part of those who are not part of the specialized group. It is not surprising, therefore, that the king is *par excellence* the repository of all wisdom, and his regime is that alone which combines the total resources of technology with the monopoly of political and military power. This is the foundation of ancient pagan religion that was confronted with the prophetic spokesmen throughout the period of the Divided Monarchy of biblical history. (In passing, it might be advisable to point out that any similarity between the description of the ancient closed corporation of wise men and a modern university department lies in the eyes of the beholder. What I was thinking of are theological disciplines in which someone is always "going beyond" Bultmann, Barth, or whatever other king figure happens to be the apex of the heap.)

It must be admitted that the combination of the technological and the power factors in the political state is virtually a constant in human civilization. But it is one which has also periodically wrought its own destruction —and out of such a destruction at the end of the Late Bronze age, there emerged suddenly a realization that there is in addition a "transcendent factor" of human history and experience against which both military and technological power are eventually impotent.

To turn to specific biblical passages for illustration of the theoretical structure outlined above, we observe, first, that the oldest narratives of the Bible already illustrate the fact that wisdom has to do with a function in society rather than a mere category of literary form. Note, for example the wise woman of Abel, whose role it was to persuade both Joab and the elders of Abel to accept a course of action that avoided possible destruction of the town and a consequent political albatross on the neck of the king (2 Sam 20: 14–22). But wisdom is also a more than questionable charisma of Amnon's friend, who enables him to find a way to rape his half sister (2 Sam 13). (Luther was only half right; "reason" alias "wisdom" is not only a whore but also a pimp.) English translations often disguise this wisdom by translating with a different word, such as "crafty."

The traditions about King Solomon in regard to wisdom are most eloquent in showing the contrast between the authentic Yahwistic traditions and the neo-paganism of the united monarchy. Wisdom is far from being a divine charisma in the pre-monarchical period. In Deut 32: 29, it is merely a normal human talent that is lacking—an utter inability to see the inevitable consequences of stupidity. In the two cases cited above, wisdom is also an ability to persuade others to courses of action that result in the realization of goals. But what wisdom has never or rarely been able to achieve is a critical evaluation of those goals.

With Solomon's charisma of wisdom, received at the old Gibeonite high place, almost certainly in connection with a pagan incubation ritual, the old pagan tradition of some god as the source of royal or other wisdom was reintroduced into Palestinian politics. And this had nothing to do with the Yahwistic tradition, while the gods as the donors of technical wisdom go back at least to old Sumerian myth. For political reasons, Solomon's gift of wisdom at Gibeon from the pagan Hivvite deity was followed immediately by sacrifices at the ark of the covenant in Jerusalem (1 Kings 3: 15). While his father, King David, was the Constantine of the OT, Solomon was the Kausitoros (the "bull-burner"—an appellative of Julian the Apostate), for which compare 1 Kings 8: 5, 63.

With wisdom thus firmly established as a royal gift derived from the divine world, and therefore immune to critical evaluation from merely historical sources, Solomon proceeds to act as the Supreme Court to solve the legal battle of two prostitutes. In earlier Yahwistic practice, the problem would have been brought "before Yahweh"—either by an oath, by which a perjuror would have placed herself in jeopardy, or by the casting of lots. The case is an excellent example of the mere acceptance of a verdict of power as divinely inspired. One could just as easily argue the opposite—that the true mother would rather see her child killed than give him up to an unscrupulous bitch.

The description of Solomon's wisdom that has recently been questioned by R. B. Y. Scott[8] need not be so facilely dismissed. The organization of wisdom into *mashal*, music, trees and shrubs, beasts, birds, reptiles, and fish[9] corresponds very closely to the Egyptian wisdom tradition of the New Empire, and in some ways is far more sophisticated than the Greek disciple of Aristotle, Theophrastus, several centuries later. Curiously, astronomy, which plays an important part in Egyptian wisdom, is lacking in Solomon's curriculum. It is extremely probable that it was censored by the later tradition—and the rather curious position of the heavenly bodies in the

Creation story of Genesis 1, together with references in Job and Ezekiel, strongly suggests that astrology and its related ideologies were bitterly combated in exilic and post-exilic times. It is perhaps more germane to our present purposes, however, to emphasize the fact that the tradition credited a pagan divine charisma for the accomplishments of Solomon in technical knowledge. When this is compared with the surviving materials, all scholars have admitted that nothing that has survived can be credited to Solomon. There is absolutely no reason to be surprised about this seeming paradox. Solomon's function in the tradition had nothing to do with *content*, but with the social *authority* of the guild of wise men. As in so many other cases, the eminence of his wisdom, whatever it may have been, was much more a product of his social and political power at the time than of any lasting, intrinsic value. Furthermore, all wise men subsequent to his reign would be obligated by the social system to "update" his archaic observations. Whatever conclusions may eventually be agreed upon by biblical scholars, it is at present virtually impossible to conceive of a grandiose power structure of the time of Solomon that did not produce and support a gamut of technical specialists. It is equally impossible to imagine that the king would not have been *ex officio* the "king of the mountain."

The arrogant stupidity of power reinforced by access to, and control of, a wide range of technical wisdom had its logical culmination in the policies of Rehoboam, which resulted not only in the complete disintegration of the empire but also in schism of the homeland itself. Not long afterward, the invasion of Shishak brought destruction to the land, which no doubt indicates that foreign policy was no more tolerable than the domestic policy had been. Such a power structure—that recognized no binding obligation other than its own ambitions and desires—rapidly became intolerable. As in the case of the sorcerer's apprentice, the result was two such structures that limped along on two lame legs for a couple of centuries. After the final destruction, predicted by virtually all the pre-exilic prophets, some anonymous and chastened "wise man" saw the course of history in a new light and used old traditions to construct a new parable of the human plight.

The *Mashal* as a Means of Communication

Though no particular effort has been made to investigate the origin and history of the *mashal*, it can hardly be doubted that such a technique derives from very remote antiquity. It is psychologically—and perennially—much easier to tell a story, completely irrelevant to any existing contemporary vested interests, that brings to bear a principle supposedly shared by the speaker and his hearers than it is to apply the same principle directly to a case at issue. To simplify the historical problem, we may cite only early biblical examples. First is the parable of Jotham in Judg 9 that transfers a real issue to the realm of the trees, that makes ridiculous the prestige and power ambitions of Abimelech.

Another such *mashal* is the case of the woman of Tekoa who thus appealed for the king's amnesty for his exiled son Absalom—with dire results (2 Sam 14: 1–24). Very similar is the *mashal* that Nathan uses to condemn the king himself (2 Sam 12: 1–15). In both the latter cases, a simple example arising out of everyday life, at least in verisimilitude, is used to induce the power-holder to act in accordance with his own decision. It is perhaps not entirely gratuitous to point out that the entire structure of legal thought is based upon such *mashals*: the binding nature of precedent decisions, which applies a legal principle used to decide a case to subsequent cases that are at least conceived to be analogous. One of the best historically attested examples is the trial of Jeremiah, in which he was acquitted on the ground of precedent deriving from the similar case of Micah a century before (Jer 26). Unfortunately, the text indicates very strongly that it was not concern for legal principle but political influence that saved Jeremiah from death.

There can hardly be any question about the importance of the *mashal* as a constant device of ancient thought that is just as alive today in different ways. In addition to the cases cited above, the book of Jonah is a similar type of *mashal*, and there can be no doubt that Hosea's marriage served as a vehicle for a similar thought pattern, regardless of whatever literary or historical purposes it is made to serve. It is not at all surprising that the *mashal* is most unpopular among elite circles and, at the same time, a favorite device of minority movements such as the prophets. The old cliché "comparisons are odious" would no doubt have been just as acceptable in the elite circles of the biblical monarchy as it is today with its parallelophobia. Yet the very title of the book that derives from the ancient elite is *mišlē šᵉlomo* Proverbs (of Solomon). The paradox is easily resolved. Similarities or classifications pointed out and taught by the elite have social status, and it is an affront to respectable society to point out analogies that are in conflict with the accepted social system. It is only when a social system is destroyed that a new value system can make its claim to validity, and this is the historical context of Genesis 3.

It is very tempting to see this form of argument in many other patently unhistorical narratives of the Hebrew Bible, such as many of the stories of the "common ancestors." Since the *mashal* is a form of thought that primarily classifies, such classification can be used for a number of purposes other than upbraiding or persuading, even though this is the clearest usage of the form. A *mashal* may serve as a ground, precedent, or justification of existing reality—similar to the category of myth in ancient pagan cultures. Historical persons and events become *mashal* also, as for example in Deut 28: 37. I would argue, however, that the most elaborate *mashal* in the Bible is the book of Job.

Evidence for the Late Date of Genesis 3

In view of the virtual unanimity among literary critics since the nineteenth century that the narrative belongs to the J document (now dated to the tenth century), it must seem presumptuous and temerarious to suggest that it actually stems from the sixth century. As a matter of fact, the old literary criticism was carried out upon the foundation of such grossly inadequate historical and linguistic presuppositions that it is a wonder that it could even approximate the truth.

Instead of dating or classifying passages by the presence of particular clichés, any sound linguistic method must deal with the entire language of the passage in question. It is true that purely formal elements of language, such as changes in orthography and grammatical elements, have become largely inaccessible because of the long-continued process of editing and standardization to which the text was subjected over a period of many centuries. However, no language stands still for long. Words become archaic and drop entirely out of use, while new words are introduced into the language either by neologism or by borrowing. As passages of the Hebrew Bible are successfully dated with some degree of confidence, those passages, in turn, furnish knowledge of the linguistic inventory of that particular time and increase the total base for reconstructing the history of the language. There is now fairly firm evidence for a systematic archaizing tendency in the exilic period, during which period (as well as perhaps a generation or two earlier) there was a reuse of archaic words and forms that are not attested over a period of perhaps four centuries. The distinction between the archaic language of the tenth century and the preceding period of the Judges and the late imitation of the old language was one which the old literary criticism simply could not cope with. The contention here is that Gen 3 is a parade example of Exilic imitation of archaic language, entirely in harmony with its setting and purpose. The language is no more tenth century than is the prose of the prologue to the book of Job.

Though it is not possible or appropriate here to present what is a very complex and sophisticated technique that perhaps can best be done by computer programming (in which work is being done), a very cursory overview of the distribution of words (*with* their meanings—since the rate of change semantically is much more rapid than morphological change) yields information that should leave no doubt as to the linguistic and historical milieu from which Genesis 3 sprang. That milieu is the pre-exilic wisdom literature—the language of the technically trained specialists of the last generations of the kingdom of Judah. It is incredible that scholars could ever have conceived of the passage as tenth-century prose. Following is a list of linguistic indicators that supports if not proves the present thesis:

ʿarūm: Occurs elsewhere only in Proverbs, always in contrast to *ʾᵉwīl*, "fool," thus a label for a personality trait that is highly admired as the goal of the wise[10]; and twice in Job, where it is definitely pejorative, as here. The feminine abstract form already occurs in the old Covenant Code, Ex 21: 14, where it is equivalent to the legal concept of "malice aforethought." The root shows evolution from "malice" to "cunning" to "sophisticated" to "crafty." Our passage belongs toward the end of the semantic evolution, and illustrates the change of attitude that followed the destruction of Jerusalem caused by the insane political policies of the "wise" condemned by Jeremiah. The word applied to the serpent certainly reflects the common usage of the wisdom literature.

taʾᵃwah: Again a favorite word in Proverbs and Psalms that does not occur in the early sources. Gen 49: 26 is obscure, and probably not this word. The place name *qibrot hat-taʾᵃwah* certainly is a popular etymology. The passage Prov 13: 12 is actually the starting point of our narrative: *ʿēṣ ḥayyīm taʾᵃwah bāʾāh*, "a tree of life is an object of desire realized."

neḥmād: The *nifʿal* form occurs elsewhere only in Prov 21: 20 and Ps 19: 11 outside this narrative (including Gen 2: 9, which is of course closely related).

haśkīl: Infinitive, with meaning "to make wise" occurs only in Ps 32: 8, Prov 16: 23; 21: 11, Nehemiah, 1 Chronicles, Daniel. Pre-exilic uses have quite another meaning—for example, Deut 32: 29.

ʿērummīm: This word occurs elsewhere only in Ezekiel and Deut 28: 48, over against the usual older form *ʿārōm*. There is certainly a play on words intended, referring to the *ʿārūm* that characterizes the serpent.

yitpᵉrū: The word is otherwise exclusively exilic and post-exilic: Ezekiel, Job, Ecclesiastes.

ḥagōrōt: The only word in the chapter that occurs in early sources, 2 Sam 18: 11, 1 Kings 2: 5, 2 Kings 3: 21, Is 3: 24, and then becomes obsolete; outside our passage, it never recurs in exilic and post-exilic literature. The author deliberately chose an archaic or obsolete word to designate the garment of the remote past.

hiššīʾani: Not attested with this meaning before 2 Kings 18: 29 (time of Hezekiah). A favorite word in Jeremiah and Is 36 and 37.

To avoid unnecessary elaboration, further description of the distribution of words may be dispensed with. I had expected that the poetic curses would be older, but the pattern is much the same. In view of the fact that many have expressed skepticism or even hostility to the idea that passages in biblical Hebrew can be dated by such a method as that exhibited above, several observations are in order. First, if an authentic tenth-century passage is dealt with in the same manner, the distribution proves radically different. In other words, if words with particular meanings that have a limited distribution in biblical Hebrew are carefully examined, it seems beyond doubt true that the living, working vocabulary of the time from Jeremiah to Deutero-Isaiah shows a considerable contrast to that of the tenth century. This is precisely what one would expect once the hoary old myth of the "unchanging Orient" is seen to be the nonsense it is. Furthermore, the accepted dating or assignment of passages to the various documents is based merely upon a very amateurish and historically ungrounded similar sort of method but using merely certain key words or phrases. To be sure, the exilic period undeniably did see the reintroduction of archaic linguistic features, but it is usually not difficult to recognize such archaic revivals, for the meaning in context could not be so easily revived—the words are simply used in different ways and sometimes even with different grammatical constructions.

The conclusion from this and further study is that Gen 3 is a work stemming from the period of exile, when there was a great ferment of agonizing and recrimination concerning the question: "What happened—and why?" My impression is that the unknown author was really not much concerned with trying to imitate the old classical prose: his concerns were not linguistic or literary virtuosity but telling his simple and perennial story.

The Context of Destruction and Exile

Pelikan's assessment of the predicament of Protestantism is in part correct when he complains that the Bible is absolutized "as somehow suspended from the historical process,"[11] but when he thinks it is lost "in the cultural-religious history of the Near East," one wonders what is left. His recommendation is the problem, not the answer—namely, the location of the "authority of the Bible in the context of the teaching and praying church. . . " The statement is historically and theologically nonsense: for the church is the product, not the cause, of the proper proclamation of the Gospel. The church is where two or three are gathered who have heard, understood, and responded to that "good news." The reduction of the Bible to a mere authority symbol of ecclesiastical or political power is the basis of the predicament of the church, not its solution. It is precisely the taking of the Bible *out* of its context in the "cultural-religious history of the Near East" that has resulted in the foisting upon it of all sorts of man-made traditions that are increasingly seen to be both absurd and dysfunctional. The obsession with corporate self-preservation is no adequate substitute for faith, particularly when there is no very evident concern for understanding what that faith stands for and how it should be operative in our own historical context. Perhaps the Bible, like any Christian, must lose its life (in that ancient history) in order to find it.

The parable of Gen 3 conveys an insight into the process of history resulting in the destruction of the community and of virtually all its institutions. It is, first of all, to be observed that the scene is placed at the beginning of the history of man—it is not culturally bound, and the unity of all mankind as participating in the same process was correctly seen by Saint Paul. We have an historical phenomenon similar to that of the book of Job, where the event and subsequent dialogue are so successfully removed from the particularistic traditions of ancient Judah that Pfeiffer was led to conclude for a non-Israelite origin.

The breakdown of political parochialisms actually made possible a most highly creative ferment of religious thought, culminating in Job and Deutero-Isaiah. The process is difficult to trace in detail; but, in the first place, the destruction discredited with finality the old political nationalism that the prophets since Amos had protested in vain as no substitute for obedience to Yahweh. The immediate past was painful—and largely irrelevant in exile. The destroyed community had to transcend its own immediate—and grossly inadequate—past if it were to have any continuity at all.

The opposition between the prophets and the wise men, that climaxed in the time of Jeremiah when he narrowly escaped death, is the immediate context for Gen 3. In Jer 9: 22–23, we have a vain plea for the valuation of something other than the big three of the wisdom tradition: power, wealth, and wisdom itself. The message of the prophets from Amos on was that the course bent upon with fanatic determination could lead, lemming-like, only to destruction. In the time of Zephaniah and Jeremiah, the warnings were effectively neutralized: "Yahweh does not do good, nor does he do evil" (Zeph 1: 12). This attitude, illustrated also in the Psalms, underlies the words of the serpent to Eve: "You will not surely die. . ." The wise man is one "who is in control of his environment," who has both knowledge of "the way things are" and the power to carry out his desires, and thus there is an effective negation of the idea that there is a transcendent factor in history—in the process of cause and effect—that must be taken into consideration. Therefore the land is full of "those who fill their master's house with violence and fraud" (Zeph 1: 9)—that is, wealth obtained by such procedures.

Next, we have the description of Eve's desire that is also inseparable from wisdom which itself is able to "discriminate between good and evil." This is a very subtle jibe—a comment upon King Solomon's wisdom that also effectively neutralized the old Israelite covenant theology and ethic in favor of becoming "modern." The result: schism, and destruction at the hands of Shishak. For wisdom as a means of achieving goals has rarely been able to evaluate the goal itself. With no control other than the limitations of technology and power, the possible almost automatically becomes the imperative. If some lasting fears or superstitions are left, they can also be well neutralized by proper ritual—though of this I find no hint in our narrative, and the prophets constantly protested this facile evasion of responsibility. Even the prologue to Job has a mildly ironic reference to the futility of ritual as a means of avoiding calamity (Job 1: 5).

The violation of transcendent obligation—the command of Yahweh—in favor of achieving an immediate and illegitimate goal had consequences that are described again with delightful irony. Adam and Eve became able to distinguish between good and evil, the immediate effect of which new talent was the recognition of their own nakedness. All that the much-desired "likeness to God" had done for them was to add evil to their stock of knowledge and experience. Shame for their own nakedness was soon joined by terror—of God—and the vain attempt to hide. The attempt to read into the narrative a fall "upward," on the one hand, or the discovery of sex, on the other, is a simple illustration of the misuse of biblical narrative.

The old wisdom had proclaimed: "An expectation deferred is a sickness of heart; but a 'tree of life' is an object of desire realized." One is immediately reminded of the case of poor Amnon, wasting away in his incestuous desire for his half sister, until his "wise" ways and means committee found a way for realization—which also turned out to be a "tree of life" for no one (2 Sam 13). The expulsion from Paradise made the "tree of life" inaccessible, and the divine curses constantly reminded Adam's children that the experience of evil is not necessarily being "like God, knowing good and evil."

Though it is not possible to go into all the various ramifications of narrative detail—and no parable can be expected to walk on all fours—the history of the period prior to exile furnishes some very suggestive answers to the question, "Why Eve?" The misuse of the story by contemporary power movements, who seemingly want also to throw out all weightier considerations of love and loyalty in favor of "justice" and of becoming "like men," demands at least some comment on the fact that the narrative represents

Eve as the one who succumbed to the serpent's false promises. One can only point out the unquestionable fact that since Jezebel, most Old Testament prophecy also leveled most serious charges against the upper-class aristocratic females of the time. Rather than indicating a depressed status of women, such charges (e.g., Is 3), as well as Gen 3, indicate rather an utterly unscrupulous competitiveness and unbridled ambition that could not have been without effect upon their equally unscrupulous husbands. And even after the destruction, the final confrontation with Jeremiah (Ch. 44) involves the women's self-willed and compulsive determination to continue the cult of the Queen of Heaven—and their husbands defend it. Our author gently points out that men suffer just as much as do women from the female cult of their own desires— and he cannot place the blame upon the woman.

Possibly some light may be shed upon the matter by observing that women have very often been in the peculiarly dangerous situation of being in a position to exercise enormous influence with virtually no *public* responsibility. This contrast between the public and the private sectors of human life is one of which we seem hardly to be aware, but which seems of crucial importance in understanding the polarization between the sexes that seems to be increasingly exploited for the seizure of power, prestige, and wealth—and therefore the sin of Eve all over again. The lunatic fringe of the feminist movement has at least a potential redeeming social value of reducing the birth rate, but any movement that denigrates and has nothing but contempt for the private sector of life, which must be of primary importance to the young, and probably to the vast majority of the human race, can only be deplored. The concept that the value of any person is merely a function of his income and social role is simply vicious, for it must reduce to nothing not only the vast majority of the human race who are by this definition "nobodies," but, worse, it glorifies precisely those goals and desires that are probably in the long run incompatible with any peaceful society. Over against the Roman empire, where the only respectable occupation for a "gentleman" was politics, the early biblical tradition a thousand years earlier had given the appropriate answer: that it is only the intrinsically unproductive and worthless element of society that *wants* to be in power (parable of Jotham, Judg 9).

There is an intriguing contemporaneity in Is 3: 12, where juveniles and women either are or are to be the dominant powers in society. There is no indication that this is (or was) likely an improvement. It is rather a punishment. The issue is not the age or sex of those in control—but their desires, principles, and value system. To judge from several recent theological references that indicate a bitter hostility if not contempt for "values," since it is not an item in traditional theological vocabulary (and misunderstood by some social scientists as well), an explanation is in order. First, *Random House Dictionary*, under "values" no. 16: "to consider with respect to worth . . ." is of course when made a noun, "worth-ship" = "worship." Second, no. 10: "*Sociol.* the ideals, customs, institutions, etc., of a society toward which the people of the group have an affective [i.e., emotional] regard." These two meanings probably account for the theologians' and perhaps the social scientists' hostility to the term—but for opposite reasons; the first because the complex of such social phenomena (i.e., no. 10) is considered with enormous "respect to worth," and the latter because (unless it is exotic) it seems devoid of worth. But according to no. 16—the verbal usage—valuation is an individual and highly important *act* that has relatively little to do with what the church as an institution calls "wor[th-]ship". A "value" for a person is that which determines his choices when faced with an alternative—and it is his *choice* that exhibits what he "worships" to public view: "By their fruits you shall know them." The "worship" of the church may well be classified as the "ritual labors" of the anthropologist, which have no further significance (as Luther once pointed out) than the fact of going through the ritual—and helping keep the ritual community together, since they often have little else in common as the basis for a real *community*. All the talk about "experimental worship techniques" going around church circles today is prima facie evidence that theological (or at least biblical) illiteracy is present, just as it is when church administrators talk about the "jurisdictional units" of the church.

Both have reduced God to a mere cultural authority symbol, and both are reducing man to a mere "used-people lot." The battle between public-relations techniques and administrative-judicial technology has nothing to do with the Christian (or, originally, the Jewish) faith, but I would suggest they are both very good contemporary illustrations of the perennial validity of Gen 3. Perhaps the cartoonists are right: the idea that there could be something else is merely humorous, but somehow I doubt that the future historians will see much humor in what ensues from the present struggle for publicity and power; Eve and her colleagues are looking for technologies by which they can become gods, while many are looking for a community that will support and encourage them in the belief that honesty, integrity, and refusal to engage in gimmicks for personal ends have at least some chance for survival. The Christian community, if it exists, ought to offer something other than crucifixion. This would really be "good news."

As an epilogue to the history of the wisdom tradition, it may be observed that with its chastening in exile, the reformulation of the tradition, its expurgation, and thorough reorientation resulted in placing at the beginning: "The fear of Yahweh is the beginning of wisdom." Many centuries later, Jesus of Nazareth again broke the identification of the fear and faith in God with the mere teaching of religious traditions when he said, "Call no man father . . . ." Knowledge and love of God cannot be thus absolutely identified with a parochial, technical wisdom or politico-religious tradition—and He lost his life as a consequence.

Notes

1 E. Gerstenberger, "Covenant and Commandment," *JBL* 84 (1965), 38–51, esp. p. 51. The late proverbs he cites derive *from* the covenant form: the prohibitions are followed by the curse.

2 *Hiob und Weisheit, Die Schriften des AT*² (Göttingen, 1921) p. 98 f.

3 Catherine Drinker Bowen, "For American women, again it is the time to move mountains," *Smithsonian* July, 1970, 25.

4 J. Pelikan, "Luther Comes to America," *BLTSG* 52, Feb., 1972, 10.

5 In a recent discussion with a zoological taxonomist, it turned out that we had reached identical conclusions in radically different fields—namely, that classification of phenomena must be based on observations as to how similarities came to be, not merely on formal similarities as such.

6 *ANET*, pp. 432–34.

7 *Sanchunjaton*, p. 51.

8 "Solomon and the Beginnings of Wisdom," in *Wisdom in Israel and the Ancient Near East*; cf the much more defensible position he takes in *Proverbs*, AB, p. 12 f.

9 1 Kings 4: 32 f. This tradition is utilized in Gen 1 also.

10 Prov 12: 16, 23; 13: 16; 14: 8, 15, 16; 22: 3; 27: 12.

11 Cf n. 4.

Carey A. Moore
Gettysburg College

Mark 4: 12: More Like the Irony of Micaiah than Isaiah

There is more humor in the Bible than we sometimes recognize. I first realized this fact the day Professor Myers read interpretively in class selected passages from the story of Samson (Judg 13: 1–16: 31). It became clear to all of us that the writer of the Samson tale, if not Samson himself, had a keen sense of humor. In making a bet with the Philistines, Samson had posed one of the cleverest riddles in the Old Testament: "Out of the eater came something to eat; out of the strong came something sweet" (14: 14). And when Samson's wife tried to coax him into telling her the answer by saying to him, "You only hate me, you do not love me; you have put a riddle to my countrymen, and you have not told me what it is" (14: 16), Samson added insult to injury by countering with, "Behold, I have not told my father and my mother, and shall I tell you?" (14: 16.) And the well-known incident in 16: 6–15, where Delilah tries to wheedle from Samson the secret of his great strength, is really a humorous battle of wits and love-play—until the end. But the playful Samson ultimately had the last laugh against the Philistine captors who had blinded him but neglected to keep his hair trimmed; for in the temple of Dagan he really brought down the house (16: 21–30).

The editor of the Samson story was not the only ancient Israelite who had a sense of humor and delighted in irony, "irony" being "humor, ridicule, or slight sarcasm that adopts a mode of speech the intended implication of which is the opposite of the literal sense of the words."[1] Certainly the prophet Elijah did not intend to be taken literally when at Mount Carmel he said to the four hundred prophets of Baal, "Cry aloud, for he [Baal] is a god; either he is musing, or he has gone aside, or he is on a journey, or perhaps he is asleep and must be awakened" (1 Kings 18: 27). Although Elijah's words could be described as ironic, they are better termed sarcastic; for while both ironic and sarcastic comments mean the opposite of what they literally say, the ironic remark has a lighter tone and tends to prick and reform, while sarcasm tries to wound and destroy.[2]

And it is as obvious to us as it was to King Ahab that Micaiah ben Imlah was being ironic[3] when he said to Ahab, "Go up and triumph; the Lord will give it [Ramoth-gilead] into the hand of the king" (1 Kings 22: 15). Whether it was the twinkle in Micaiah's eye or his slightly sarcastic tone of voice or his past history of opposition to Ahab, the king recognized that Micaiah meant the exact opposite of what he said; for Ahab exclaimed, "How many times shall I adjure you that you speak to me nothing but the truth in the name of the Lord?" (vs 16.)[4]

Irony and its stronger form, sarcasm, are not confined to the stories of Samson, Elijah, or Micaiah; the Old Testament abounds in many such examples.[5] And in the New Testament, there are over two hundred examples of word play and related humor.[6] Jesus himself, it seems to me, had a sense of humor, or at least he deliberately uttered some absurd (see below) and ironical statements.

It is the thesis of this paper that one of Jesus' most misunderstood sayings was deliberate irony—that is, like Elijah and Micaiah before him, Jesus on one particular occasion said the exact opposite of what he actually meant, and was probably correctly understood by his listeners, but was taken, unfortunately, at face value in the oral and written traditions of the apostolic church.

The particular passage in question, which follows immediately after the Parable of the Sower, has given rise to the so-called hardening theory in Mk 4: 10–12 (=Mt 13: 10–15=Lk 8: 9-10).

> 10. And when he was alone, those who were about him with the twelve asked him concerning the parables. 11. And he said to them, "To you has been given the secret of the kingdom of God, but for those outside everything is in parables; 12. *so that they may indeed see but not perceive, and may indeed hear but not understand; lest they should turn again and be forgiven.* (Italics added.)

Few passages in the New Testament have been characterized by such strongly negative adjectives as those used for the hardening theory of Mk 4: 11–12—that is, for the idea that Jesus deliberately used parables to prevent "outsiders" from understanding them, thereby making repentence and forgiveness impossible for them: for example, "strange" (A. T. Cadoux, M. L. Mowry); "notorious" (A. M. Hunter); "cannot be made credible"

(C. H. Dodd); "absurd" (T. W. Manson); "intolerable" (V. Taylor); "preposterous" (W. Bousset); "perverse" (F. C. Grant); "monstrous" (R. Otto).[7]

While a few modern scholars, like Rudolph Otto,[8] T. W. Manson,[9] Joachim Jeremias,[10] and Vincent Taylor,[11] agree with Henry Barclay Swete[12] that Mk 4: 11–12 is a genuine saying of Jesus—albeit misunderstood, contaminated, corrupt, or dislocated—most scholars regard the hardening theory as the complete invention of either the evangelist himself or some other early Christian apologist.[13]

Much of our difficulty in interpreting this passage is rooted in the simple, incontestable fact that we cannot be sure to what question exactly Jesus was responding in vss 11–12. Some scholars, such as Otto[14] and Taylor,[15] go so far as to regard the question *in any form* as secondary—that is, they argue that the question was hypothesized or inferred from the presence of the allegorical explanation of the Parable of the Sower (Mk 4: 13–20) by either Mark or the tradition he drew upon. Certainly Mark's they "asked him concerning the parables" (4: 10) is vague,[16] so much so that both Matthew and Luke made the question clearer but significantly different from one another: "Why do you speak to them in parables?" (Mt 13: 10); and "His disciples asked him what this parable [the Parable of the Sower] meant" (Lk 8: 9). Given this uncertainty as to the meaning of the question asked Jesus, we must frankly concede that any suggestions as to the meaning of Jesus' answer must be quite tentative. (I believe, for instance, that Matthew has correctly clarified the question rather than invented or altered it, but I cannot prove it, especially since in Luke the particular form of both the question and the answer seems quite natural and harmonious [so E. P. Gould][17].)

As noted earlier, the majority of modern scholars regard Mk 4: 11–12 as the invention of either Mark or some earlier Christian apologist. Certainly the arguments for the hardening theory being the product of apostolic teaching are impressive:

1) That Jesus deliberately taught in order to prevent people from gaining understanding, insight, and forgiveness seems so incompatible with Jesus' character[18] as well as with the obvious purpose of teaching per se. Were Jesus' parables intelligible only to his disciples, it is puzzling to understand why "common people heard him gladly" (Mk 12: 37).

2) A priori, Jesus' aim in using parables would not have been basically different from those of his contemporaries the rabbis,[19] who used them to inform, not confound, their listeners.

3) The view that the parables were allegorical mystifications could only have arisen in a non-Jewish setting, such as the pagan Roman society to which Mark addressed himself.[20]

4) It is incontestable that the apostolic church used the hardening theory to explain Jesus' rejection and ineffectiveness among the Jews,[21] neither fact being really evident until after his death.

5) The hardening theory would more naturally have arisen after Jesus' day, when many of his parables were either puzzling or totally unintelligible to Christians who did not know the original context or setting for many of them—that is, their *Sitz im Leben.*

6) Both linguistic[22] and literary[23] analyses clearly indicate that Mk 4: 13–20 (the allegorical explanation of the Parable of the Sower) is the creation of the apostolic age. This fact makes Mk 4: 11–12 all the more suspect, since vss 11–12 are part of the *Sitz im Leben* for 4: 13–20.

7) Although the writers of Matthew and Luke were clearly dependent upon Mark, they somewhat play down his theory, in 4: 11–12, of the secretive or esoteric character of the parables, a theory which was especially appealing to Mark because it was so compatible with his theory of the secret Messiahship of Jesus.[24]

Impressive though the above arguments are, they are not ultimately convincing, since, as will be shown later, there is too much linguistic and psychological evidence for various elements of Mk 4: 11–12 being both old and Palestinian in origin. (To be sure, the allegorical interpretation in Mk 4: 13–20 is certainly an apostolic creation.[25])

With any saying of Jesus, particularly a difficult one, there is always the possibility that it is genuine but corrupt—that is, was altered when translated from Aramaic into Greek or at some time during the transmission of the Greek text. For our particular passage, two quite plausible suggestions, both of which argue for a mistranslation of the Aramaic, have been seriously advanced.

First, while the Greek *ἵνα* used in Mk 4: 12 can only designate purpose —that is, "in order that,"[26] *d*, the Aramaic particle used by the Targum of Is 6: 9, is ambiguous, and can be interpreted either as a conjunction introducing a final clause, "in order that," or as the relative pronoun "who." Thus, according to Manson, Jesus probably said, "To you is given the secret of the Kingdom of God; but all things come in parable to those outside *who* [italics added] 'See indeed but do not know And hear indeed but not understand Lest they should repent and receive forgiveness.'" Linguistically possible, Manson's suggestion has the additional theological merit of making those outside the kingdom, and not Jesus, responsible for their lack of understanding and insight. Such an interpretation is somewhat closer to the view of Mt 13: 13, "This is why I speak to them in parables, *because* [italics added] seeing they do not see, and hearing they do not hear, nor do they understand."

The other plausible suggestion for a mistranslation of the Aramaic underlying the Greek of Mk 4: 12 has been offered by J. Jeremias.[27] The Aramaic word underlying the Greek *μήποτε* ("lest") in Mt 13: 15, and hence also in Mk 4: 12, is *dylm'*, as can be seen from the fact that the Aramaic Targum uses *dylm'* in translating the Hebrew *pn* ("lest") of Is 6: 10, "lest they see with their eyes, and hear with their ears, and understand with their hearts, and turn and be healed." *dylm'*, however, is ambiguous, and can mean "in order that not," "lest perhaps," or "unless." The last meaning was, in fact, the one that later rabbinic exegesis actually chose in interpreting Is 6: 10,[28] thereby transforming Yahweh's words from a sentence of doom to a promise of hope and possible forgiveness. It was with this understanding of Is 6: 10 that Jesus originally used it. What Jesus originally meant was "to you has God given the secret of the Kingdom of God; but to those who are without everything is obscure[29] in order that they (as it is written) may 'see and yet not see, may hear and yet not understand, unless they turn and God will forgive them.'"[30]

It is also possible that Mk 4: 11–12 was a genuine saying of Jesus but had been separated from its original context. As Jeremias has shown,[31] proof[32] that vs 11 is a genuine saying of Jesus, albeit misplaced, is based upon some rather solid linguistic evidence—namely, the presence of antithetical parallelisms (11a and 11b), the redundant demonstrative (*ἐκείνοις* versus *τοῖς ἔξω*), and two circumlocutions for God's activity (*δέδοται* and *γίνεται*). For vs 12, the evidence that the saying is genuine—that is, is old and Palestinian—is even stronger—namely, the greater agreement of vs 12 with the Aramaic translation of Is 6: 10 than with either the MT or the LXX. The most striking form of this agreement is that Mk 4: 12 agrees with the Aramaic of Is 6: 10 in having "it shall *be forgiven* them" [italics added], instead of either "I shall heal them" (LXX) or "it shall be healed to him" (MT).[33] According to both Jeremias and Taylor, the genuine saying behind Mk 4: 11–12 originally referred to *the whole* of Jesus' preaching, not just the parables; but the author of Mark, not realizing that in this separate logion (vs 11) *ἐν παραβολαῖς* meant "in riddles" rather than "in parables," inserted it in its present place.

Persuasive though the above arguments are for the mistranslation, corruption, or dislocation of a genuine logion of Jesus, the most probable explanation is possibly also the simplest. With the exception of *καὶ ἔλεγεν αὐτοῖς* all of vs 11 is a genuine but intrusive saying in Mk 4: 1–12—that is, all of what is now vs 12 originally followed vs 10 and *καὶ ἔλεγεν αὐτοῖς*. Mark's inherited tradition may have run something like this: "And when he was alone, those who were about him[34] asked him concerning the parables [that is, why he used them when they were not always understood by all].

And he said to them, 'That they may indeed see but not perceive, and may indeed hear but not understand; lest they should turn again and be forgiven!'" To the Christians of Mark's day, such an answer was probably cryptic if not absurd. Thus, Mark, in perfectly good faith, attempted to "explain" Jesus' absurd statement by taking another independent but genuine logion, to the effect that "for those outside the kingdom everything" —all Jesus' teachings— "is in *παραβολαῖς*," and inserting it before what is now 4: 12. Mark did not realize of course that *ἐν παραβολαῖς* in the separate logion meant "in riddles" rather than "in parables."[35]

To concede that Jesus' answer (vs 12) to the question (vs 10) is absurd does not rule out its being both genuine and in its original context. In fact, "the very unexpectedness of the saying proclaims it is original."[36] After all, Jesus uttered several hyperboles so absurd that they would hardly have been attributed to him unless he had actually uttered them:

> It is easier for a camel to go through the eye of a needle than for a rich man to enter the kingdom of God. (Mk 10: 25=Mt 19: 24=Lk 18: 25)
>
> Why do you see the speck that is in your brother's eye, but do not notice the log that is in your own eye? (Mt 7: 3=Lk 6: 41)
>
> For truly, I say to you, if you have faith as a grain of mustard seed, you will say to this mountain, "Move hence to yonder place," and it will move; and nothing will be impossible to you. (Mt 17: 20). [Cf Lk 17: 6, where essentially the same point is said about moving a sycamine tree into the sea.]

Mark was quite justified in retaining Jesus' admittedly absurd answer; he erred, however, in failing to understand it as irony. The great danger in using irony is of course that "the ironist depends on his listener or reader for recognition, and therefore risks misunderstanding."[37] But where the total context for a saying is clear, there is little chance of the words being taken literally. When, for example, a young boy sees his father entering the house with his clothes soaking, dripping wet, with the lightning flashing outside and the thunder crashing overhead, and hears his father exclaim, "Beautiful day for a walk," there is little likelihood of the boy's taking those words literally. The details of the total situation—that is, the obvious signs of inclement weather, the father's wet clothes, his facial expression and body posture, his tone of voice, the particular emphasis the father gives the various words—all enable the boy to understand that his father does not really mean what he literally says, but the exact opposite. If, however, we ourselves had not witnessed the actual scene and had only read about it, then the fewer details we knew, the greater the likelihood of our taking the father's observation as literally true, especially if we read only, "The boy went to the door, and his father exclaimed, 'Beautiful day for a walk!'"

It is my contention that in dealing with Mk 4: 12 we are in a roughly analogous situation: the details of the original setting are totally lost to us, the readers. We have only the disciples' question, imperfectly preserved in the Synoptics, and Jesus' answer. The evangelists give us no clue as to the expression in Jesus' eyes or on his mouth, no clue concerning his tone of voice or the particular emphasis given the various words. We have only Jesus' bald answer, and that answer is clearly absurd.

Jesus recognized its absurdity: that is precisely why he said it. After all, the answer to the question was so self-evident. Like the rabbis of his day, Jesus taught in parables simply because the people *could understand* and remember them. Common folk did learn from them; they did see and hear new truths, sometimes at the time the parable was told or when it was pondered later. One of the greatest appeals of Jesus' parables was that one *could see* the religious truths as they were incarnate in everyday objects and people. His parables, in contrast to abstract theological pronouncements, were so graphic and filled with moving images.[38] They never featured the unusual, the esoteric activity, or unbelievable people. His parables concerned commonplace objects and everyday activities and persons—birds and plants, eating and farming, beggars and tax collectors, fathers and sons. Thanks to his mastery of dialogue in his longer parables, one *could hear* the religious truths embodied in the conversations of ordinary people and their experiences.[39]

Thus, when asked why he spoke in parables, Jesus spoke ironically and said, in effect, something like this: "Why do I teach in parables? Why I tell them so that people won't see. I tell them so they won't hear. After all, I wouldn't want to instruct the people or save them." The *Sitz im Leben*—that is, his facial expression, tone of voice, and body posture, the witness of his entire ministry would, it was hoped, have indicated to his listeners that he meant the exact opposite.

But whether or not his disciples understood the saying preserved in vs 12 as irony, the writer of Mark clearly did not. So he took another saying of Jesus, a logion to the effect that for those outside the kingdom everything was a riddle (vs 11), and in perfectly good faith used this independent saying as a prelude to the cryptic saying now in vs 12.

If the above interpretation of Mk 4: 10–12 is essentially correct, then several other considerations or implications are in order. First, and contrary to common consensus, Jesus may not have been alluding to Is 6: 6–10 *at all.* While the Greek of Mk 4: 12 indisputably echoes the Greek of Is 6: 9,[40] this fact may be the result of *Mark's thinking* of Is 6: 9 rather than of Jesus' actually alluding to it. After all, in speaking about unseeing eyes and unhearing ears, Jesus could just as easily have been influenced by

Pss 115: 5–7 (LXX 113: 13–15): "They [the idols] have mouths, but do not speak; eyes, but do not see. They have ears, but do not hear; noses, but do not smell," and 135: 16–17 (LXX 134: 16–17), where idols are spoken of again. Thus, the undoubted allusions to Is 6: 9 in Mk 4: 12 may be more the creation of Mark or some other early Christian apologist than the accurate preservation of Jesus' own words. Second, if Jesus had really intended to advocate the hardening theory, then he should have included the most specific and damning part of Is 6: 10—namely, "Make the heart of this people fat, and their ears heavy, and shut their eyes." Third, the writer of Matthew, recognizing that the hardening theory in Mark was not really credible and yet failing to recognize the saying behind Mk 4: 12 as irony, did the next best thing: he had Jesus say, "This is why I speak to them in parables, because [*ὅτι*, instead of Mark and Luke's *ἵνα*] seeing they do not see, and hearing they do not hear, nor do they understand" (13: 13), thereby making those outside the kingdom themselves responsible for their plight. Luke further "improved" on the difficult saying by totally omitting the most offensive part of Mk 4: 12— namely, "lest they should turn again and be forgiven."

Jesus was evidently a very serious man. But this does not mean that he was devoid of a sense of humor or afraid to resort to the use of irony. Down through the ages prophets, rabbis,[41] and preachers have made themselves more appealing and their views more memorable by the effective use of many kinds of humor, including irony. Sometimes misunderstood by their listeners, they were more often misunderstood by their readers. In this matter, Jesus was no exception.

Notes

1 *Webster's Third New International Dictionary*, unabr. (1961), p. 1195. But not all irony is humorous; it can be quite tragic, as when Jesus said to Judas as the latter betrayed him with a kiss in the Garden of Gethsemane, "Friend, why are you here?" (Mt 26: 50.)

2 So Edwin M. Good, *Irony in the Old Testament* (1951), pp. 26–27.

3 Ironic rather than sarcastic, since Micaiah, in contrast to Elijah at Mount Carmel, wanted to dissuade rather than destroy.

4 The phrase "how many times" implies that, much to the king's annoyance, Micaiah had also employed irony in his past dealings with Ahab.

5 For humor in general, see I. M. Cassanowicz, "Paranomasia in the Old Testament" (1894), a Johns Hopkins University dissertation; for irony in particular, see E. M. Good, *op. cit.* The author of Esther especially delighted in irony; for details see my *Esther* in AB, 7A (1971), p. lvi.

6 E. Russell, "Paranomasia and Kindred Phenomena in the New Testament" (1920), a University of Chicago dissertation.

7 Arthur T. Cadoux, *The Parables of Jesus* (1931), p. 16; M. Lucetta Mowry, "Parable" in *IDB*, 3 (1962), p. 652; Archibald M. Hunter, *Interpreting the Parables* (1961), p. 13;

C. H. Dodd, *The Parables of the Kingdom* (1936), p. 15; T. W. Manson, *The Teaching of Jesus* 2d ed (1951), p. 76; Vincent Taylor, *The Gospel According to St. Mark* 2d ed (1966), p. 257; W. Bousset is so quoted by I. Abrahams, *Studies in Pharisaism and the Gospels*, 1st ser., reprinted with new material (1967), p. 106; Frederick C. Grant, "Exegesis of Mark" in *IB*, 7, (1951), p. 700; and Rudolph Otto, *The Kingdom of God and the Son of Man* rev. ed (1951), p. 91.

[8] According to Otto (*op. cit.*), vs 11a is "an ancient saying original to Christ himself . . . but now likewise misinterpreted in the sense of this theory" (p. 91). Otto thinks Jesus probably said something like this: "To you (i.e., to those who bring seeing eyes) is given the mystery of the kingdom of heaven, but to the others (i.e., to those of dull mind and dim eyes) everything (that I say about the kingdom of heaven) remains a riddle, something not understood or comprehended. Therefore 'he that hath ears to hear, let him hear.'" (*Ibid.*, p. 92.)

[9] *The Teaching of Jesus*, pp. 74–80; see also A. M. Hunter, *op. cit.*, pp. 110–12.

[10] *The Parables of Jesus* 6th ed (1963), pp. 13–18; *Rediscovering the Parables* (1966), pp. 10–14.

[11] "Mark has given an unauthentic version of a genuine saying," *op. cit.*, p. 257.

[12] *The Parables of the Kingdom* (1920), p. 4.

[13] So most scholars since Adolf Jülicher's *Die Gleichnisreden Jesu* (1899), pp. 146–47.

[14] "This [i.e., the disciples' question in Mt 13: 10, which equals Mk 4: 10] is plainly a mere editorial device, for it is artificial to ask why a popular speaker addresses the ''am ha'arez' in parables. He speaks thus, of course, in order and to the extent that simple folk can and should understand him. Everyone knows that; the disciples knew it. Mk iv 33 says it plainly enough." Otto, *op. cit.*, p. 140 f.

[15] *Op. cit.*, p. 255.

[16] For a detailed and well-balanced commentary on the various components of vss 10–12, including those portions not immediately relevant to our present study, see V. Taylor, *op. cit.*, pp. 255–58.

[17] *The Gospel According to St. Mark* in *ICC* (1907), pp. 73–74.

[18] So W. O. E. Oesterley, *The Gospel Parables in the Light of Their Jewish Background* (1936), p. 54. One might even argue that the hardening theory is incompatible with the spirit of a loving God; in any case, as Oesterley has pointed out on p. 52, the LXX softened considerably Is 6: 10 of the Hebrew text by having "For the heart of this people has become gross," instead of "Make fat the heart of this people." While rejecting the hardening theory, G. A. Buttrick correctly observes that in the parables "the hostile received, despite themselves, a story that might germinate in secret, but which did not confirm hostility and deepen guilt, as plainer statement might have done, by provoking enmity to wrath." *The Parables of Jesus* (1930), p. xxi; So also Cadoux: "a parable often hides the truth until it is too late for the hearer to guard himself against it . . . But this is for the sake of getting the truth home to the hearer," *op. cit.*, pp. 16–17.

[19] So Richard C. Trench, *Notes on the Parables of Our Lord*, rev. ed (1880), p. 12.

[20] So C. H. Dodd, *op. cit.*, pp. 14–15.

[21] Cf Rom 9: 6–33; 10: 16–21; and 11: 1–11, 25.

[22] J. Jeremias, *The Parables of Jesus*, pp. 77–79; R. Bultmann, *The History of the Synoptic Tradition*, trans. John Marsh (1965), pp. 187, 199.

[23] Virtually all modern scholars agree that the allegorical explanation of the Parable of the Sower is invented.

[24] First developed by Wrede in *Das Messiasgeheimnis in den Evangelien* (1901).

[25] Since the epochal work of A. Jülicher, *op. cit.*, scholars have tended to regard not

only Mk 4: 13–20 but also the allegorical interpretations in Mt 13: 37–43; 49–50; and Jn 10: 7–18 as creations of the apostolic age. For a fascinating survey of the history of the allegorization of parables, see Jülicher, pp. 203–322.

[26] So Manson, *op. cit.*, p. 78. But some scholars disagree, arguing that the *ἵνα* of Koine Greek has lost the idea of purpose in many places, including this one. Thus C. C. Torrey argues that *ἵνα* can be used to translate the Aramaic *d*, which means, among other things, "who" (*The Four Gospels* [1933], pp. 75–76). Far less convincing is the assertion that *ἵνα* here should be understood as virtually equivalent to *ὅτι* (so W. C. Allen, *The Gospel According to St. Mark* [1915], p. 80), or to *ὥστε*, where, by means of the Hebrew *lmʿn* "the *result* is ironically described as a *purpose*." (Alan H. M'Neile, *The Gospel According to St. Matthew* [1965], p. 192.) (This well-known phenomenon in the Bible of confusing result with purpose is, I think, better explained on psychological, not linguistic, grounds.)

[27] *The Parables of Jesus*, pp. 17–18.

[28] See Jeremias, *op. cit.*, p. 17, n. 26.

[29] Jeremias' use of the word "obscure" in the sense of having the character of a riddle is certainly defensible here, since *παραβολή* is the stock Greek translation for the Hebrew, *māšāl* [Aramaic *m*^e^*tal*], the word meaning riddle as well as parable, e.g., Ps 49: 4 (Heb 5), 78: 2; Ezek 17: 2 f; and Prov 1: 6, where *māšāl* is parallel with *ḥîdāh*, the regular Hebrew word for riddle. See also J. W. Hunkin, *JTS* 16 (1915), 372–91, who suggests "Everything comes to a riddle."

[30] *The Parables of Jesus*, p. 17.

[31] *Ibid.*, p. 15.

[32] Establishing that a saying is old and Palestinian as well as "compatible" with the character and teachings of Jesus as a whole is about the closest one can come to "proving" that Jesus uttered a particular logion.

[33] For details, see Manson, *op. cit.*, p. 77.

[34] Many scholars regard *σὺν τοῖς δώδεκα* as secondary. See V. Taylor, *op. cit.*, p. 255.

[35] See n. 29.

[36] H. B. Swete, *op. cit.*, p. 4.

[37] E. M. Good, *op. cit.*, p. 32.

[38] E.g., from the point of view of vividness and clarity of meaning, cf the Parable of the Good Samaritan (Lk 10: 29–37) with the rather abstract declaration it illustrates in Mk 12: 31: "You shall love your neighbor as yourself."

[39] E.g., the parables of the Prodigal Son (Lk 15: 11–32); the Great Supper (Mt 22: 1–14); and the Last Judgment (Mt 25; 31–46).

[40] Cf *ἀκούοντες ἀκούωσιν* and *βλέποντες βλέπωσιν* of Mk 4: 12 with *ἀκοῇ ἀκούσετε* and *βλέποντες βλέψετε* of Is 6: 9 (*šmʿw šmwʿ* and *wr'w r'w*), where to express emphasis a Greek finite verb is used for rendering the Heb infinitive absolute. Such Greek constructions are hebraisms found only in the Greek of the Septuagint. (That Mt 13: 14–15, Jn 12: 40, and Acts 28: 26–27 are clearly quotes of Is 6: 9-10 may be further evidence that where Is 6: 9–10 is intended, it is clearly quoted rather than alluded to.)

[41] Among his talmudic scholars, Rabbah (third century A.D.), for example, had a reputation for great seriousness; yet even he "used to say something humorous" to cheer his students before he lectured to them (so *Sabbath* 30b in B.T.).

Frederick L. Moriarty, SJ
Boston College

Word as Power in the Ancient Near East

With the steadily mounting discoveries of texts from the ancient Near East and the publication of reliably translated and interpreted literature, we have never been in a better position to examine the concepts, ideals, and institutions of a world so different and yet so like our own. The alien character of that world warns us against a facile, and distorting, modernization of its ethos; yet a cautious and critical use of historical analogy points up elements shared by men of all ages, even though the appropriation of these elements may differ in quality and intensity. As Aristotle noted, man is a "being of the word" (*zōon logon ekon*), and it is the spoken and written word that signalizes man's preeminence amidst the silence of the plant world and the cacophony of sentient life.[1] A common theme in the ancient Near East is the power of the word. The evidence is now clear that the OT is but one of many ancient witnesses to the theme of the word endowed with power.

The Bible no longer stands alone as witness to this concept. In fact, the OT inherited, with only slight modifications, this dynamistic notion of the efficacious word, applying it according to its own theological needs and within the limits of its orthodoxy. Hypostatization of the divine word, for example, played little or no part in the OT, whatever may have been its extraordinary development in the NT.

It seems that at the very beginning, a magical significance was attached to the word in the ancient world. Pronounced under the right circumstances, this word was thought to have irresistible power for good or evil. Studies in comparative religion provide countless examples of the word conceived as a magical power by which men could gain some control over their precarious environment. The spells, rituals, and execrations were so many techniques by which results were achieved. We, who make an essential distinction between an action and a formula, rite, or symbolic act, find it hard to understand the mentality of people for whom such distinctions had little or no meaning, since symbol and reality coalesced.

When the gods of Mesopotamia had conferred kingship upon one of their number, Marduk, they wanted assurance that Marduk's word really had that magical power which brought results. They devised a test:

They placed a garment in their midst
And said to Marduk their firstborn:
"O Lord, thy lot is truly highest among the gods.
Command annihilation and existence, and
May both come true.
May thy spoken word destroy the garment,
Then speak again and may it be intact."
He spoke – and at his word the garment was destroyed.
He spoke again, the garment reappeared.
The gods, his fathers, seeing [the power of] his word,
Rejoiced, paid homage: "Marduk is king."[2]

In Sumerian culture, the basis of Mesopotamian civilization, the dogma of the divine word as creative power became firmly established.

> All that the creating deity had to do, according to this doctrine, was to lay his plans, utter the word, and pronounce the name. This notion of the creative power of the divine word was probably also the result of an analogical inference based on observation of human society: if a human king could achieve almost all he wanted by command, by no more than what seemed to be the words of his mouth, how much more was possible for the immortal and superhuman deities in charge of the four realms of the universe. But perhaps this "easy" solution of the cosmological problems, in which thought and word alone are so important, is largely a reflection of the drive to escape into hopeful wish fulfillment characteristic of practically all humans in times of stress and misfortune.[3]

A bilingual text (Sumerian and Akkadian) containing a hymn to the moon god Nanna, celebrates the power of his word:

Thou ! When thy word is pronounced in heaven the
Igigi[4] prostrate themselves.
Thou ! When thy word is pronounced on earth the
Anunnaki kiss the ground.
Thou ! When thy word drifts along in heaven like the wind
it makes rich the feeding and drinking of the land.
Thou ! When thy word settles down on the earth

green vegetation is produced.
Thou! Thy word makes fat the sheepfold and the stall;
it makes living creatures widespread.
Thou! Thy word causes truth and justice to be,
so that the people speak the truth.
Thou! Thy word which is far away in heaven, which is
hidden in the earth is something no one sees.
Thou! Who can comprehend thy word, who can equal it?
O Lord, in heaven as to dominion, on earth as to valor,
among the gods thy brothers, thou hast not a rival.[5]

A text from the Babylonian Records in the library of J. Pierpont Morgan explicitly associates the word of power with the phenomena of nature.

[*umu*] *a-mat Anu*
umu a-mat Enlil
umu uggat libbi ša Anu rabî
The storm is the word of Anu,
The storm is the word of Enlil,
The storm is the wrath of the great Anu.[6]

A somewhat more sophisticated notion of the word as something conceived underlies a difficult passage in the Sumerian "Exaltation of Inanna." Enheduanna, princess, priestess, and poetess, seems to describe her magnificent creative effort in this hymn to the goddess as something to which she gave birth. The word of this hymn was conceived by Enheduanna.[7]

Over sixty years ago, Stephen Langdon published translations of laments and hymns extolling the word of Enlil, a god of the Sumerian pantheon, and of lesser gods. The following is taken from a service of lament involving the word of Enlil:

Of exalted heaven, lofty is his word.
Of the divine heaven god lofty is his word.
Of Enlil lofty is his word.
If his word be brought to a seer, the seer falters.
If his word be brought to a prophet, the prophet falters.
If his word be pronounced to a youth, the youth
breaks into sobbing.
If his word be pronounced to a maid, the maid
breaks into sobbing.
When his word goes forth in its grandeur, it
brings the land to ruin . . .[8]

The lamentation was a well-established literary form in ancient Sumer. The "Lamentation over the Destruction of Ur," occasioned by the fall of

Ur III and the collapse of the dynasty, pictures the catastrophe as resulting from the decrees (words) of the gods:

> After they [Anu and Enlil] had *pronounced* the utter destruction of my city;
> After they had *pronounced* the utter destruction of Ur,
> After they had directed that its people be killed—
> On that day verily I abandoned not my city;
> My land verily I forsake not . . . .
> Verily Anu changed not his word;
> Verily Enlil with its "It is good; so be it"
>   soothed not my heart . . .
> Me of my city verily they *deprived*;
> My Ur of me verily they *deprived*.
> Anu changes not his command;
> Enlil alters not the command which he had issued.[9]

The verdict was passed in the assembly of the gods, and the word was allowed to run its course. From the viewpoint of the scientific historian, Ur was annihilated by the barbarian hordes which swept in from Elam. For the Sumerian, the invaders were only the outward manifestation and agents of the great storm god Enlil, executor of the decree passed in the assembly. The cosmic were more important than the historical forces in the catastrophe which overwhelmed Ur:

> On that day the word—who knows its meaning?—
>   attacked like a storm,
> The word of Enlil that winds to the right, *knows* the left,
> Enlil who decrees the fates, this is what he did.[10]

The Sumerian lamentation was generally classed as a "*balag*," a characteristic genre in literature which specialized in mourning over great public disasters. The poem had a function beyond that of giving expression to grief. The *balag* was recited to the accompaniment of a drum (*balag*) and a similar instrument (*ùb*), and it was meant to soothe the wrath of the gods who had brought on the disaster.[11]

In the ideology of the Tammuz cult, celebrated at the end of spring and commemorating the death of the vegetation god, it is the word of lamentation which alone can compensate for the loss of the god and the waning vigor of natural life. The power of the word, inhering in its expression of intense human grief and longing, reassures the devotees of Tammuz that the god will return. The mourners will not permit him to sleep in death; they cannot resign themselves to the loss of him, for the life-energies of their world depend on bringing him back from the netherworld.[12]

A consistent characteristic of the word, when uttered by a king or, especially, by a god, was its unalterability. In a Babylonian text from the eighth century B.C., it is said of a god:

> . . . . whose word is favorable, whose utterance
> [cannot be changed], whose command cannot be altered . . . .[13]

In the Epilogue to the Creation Epic (*Enuma Elish*), Marduk's word is praised in these terms:

> Firm in his order, his command unalterable,
> The utterance of his mouth no god shall change.[14]

To these texts may now be added the recently translated supplement to the Sumerian Lament:

> The verdict of the assembly cannot be turned back.
> The word commanded by Enlil knows no overturning.[15]

At this stage of man's thinking, the word appears to be apprehended as a unit of power which has its own independent and fixed existence. The word's function as a term of signification does not seem to have emerged clearly; the line between the concept and the thing is blurred. Instead of pointing to some objective content, the word sets itself in place of this content, becoming a power which exercises its own proper influence upon events. It has an extracommunicative power.[16]

The discoveries at ancient Mari on the Euphrates have illuminated many phases of OT study, but none more than the phenomenon of prophecy. Without questioning the uniqueness of this great spiritual movement in Israel, scholars have become increasingly aware of the analogies existing between Israelite institutions, such as prophecy, kingship, priesthood, and their counterparts in the ancient Near East.[17] The contents of the prophetic texts from Mari range over a fairly broad field. In the first texts to be published, cultic matters, such as the care of a temple or an increase of mortuary offerings for a deceased king, formed the subject matter. The material came from towns other than Mari, such as Aleppo, Tuttul, and Terqa. Subsequent prophetic texts, coming from Mari itself, are almost wholly concerned with the person of the king, his security and prosperity, especially in military matters.

An example of one of these texts from Mari will illustrate the form and spirit of these unusual documents. King Zimri-Lim of Mari is addressed by his wife Šibtu, who reports on a message uttered in the local temple of the goddess Annunītum by a certain Šelebum. He pronounced the message of the goddess (note that he speaks in the strict sense as the mouthpiece of the goddess, *in persona Dei*) while caught up in a trance:

> Speak to m[y] lord: Thus Šibtu your maid-servant. The palace is safe and sound. In the temple of Annunītum, on the third day [of the month] Šelebum went into a trance. Thus [spoke] Annunītum: "O Zimri-Lim, with a revolt they would put you to the test. Guard yourself. Put at your side servants, your controllers whom you love. Station them so they can guard you. Do not go ab[ou]t by yourself. And as for the men who wo[uld p]ut you to the test, I shall deliv[er] these men into your hand." I have now hereby despatched to my lord the hair and the fringe of the cult-[player]. [8]

Making all allowances for the similarities which exist between prophecy in Israel and Mari, extending sometimes even to the phrasing of oracles, it would be an error, methodologically, to conclude that the later was simply a borrowing from the earlier. The science of comparative religion is at its best when, alongside undoubted similarities, it can point up what is specific and unique in a given phenomenon. The differences between the two, Mari and Israel, touch subject matter more than form or style. In the OT, we are moving in a world far removed from that of Mesopotamia. The prophets saw themselves as spokesmen of a transcendent God who, in a mysterious and unique way, had chosen a people as his own by uniting them with him in covenant. The prophet had the task, essentially, of keeping the people faithful to covenant demands; his message grew out of an historical context, with all its attendant ambiguities, but there was in it a transcendent dimension peculiar to Israel.

> The words of the OT writing prophets, in particular, can in no way be compared with the statements of the Mari messengers. They deal with guilt and punishment, being and non-being, the present and the future of the Israelite people as a people chosen for a special service by God; they also seek to explain the present great and stirring world events as taking place according to the will of God, leading to a future goal which is itself also the will of God.[19]

In that other great center of Near Eastern civilization, Egypt, our closest attestation to the dynamic, creative word is found in the Memphite Theology. There is no single, canonical doctrine of creation in Egypt; but the Memphite Theology, so different from other crude creation accounts in Egyptian literature, comes close to an abstract, refined approach to the creation of the world. The extant text in which the Theology is expressed comes from about 700 B.C., but the material itself demonstrably comes from one of the earliest periods of Egyptian history. At this time, the first dynasties established their new capital at Memphis, the city of the god Ptah. The theology expressed in the text was calculated to enhance the national prestige of this new site, Memphis.

Earlier creation texts portrayed the creative act in physical and sometimes repellent terms. In the Memphite Theology, which is unusually intellectual in its orientation, Ptah conceives the gods and the rest of the world through the thought of his heart and the utterance of his mouth. This notion of creation by means of thought and speech undoubtedly had its basis in the everyday experience of the ruler, who decides and then commands. The only relationship that this Theology has to the other, more materialistic, conceptions is the use of "heart" for thought and "tongue" for command.

> Ptah the Great, that is, the heart and tongue
> of the Ennead;
> [Ptah] . . . who gave birth to the gods; . . .
> There came into being as the heart and
> there came into being as the tongue (something) in the form
> of Atum. The mighty Great One is Ptah, who transmitted
> [*life* to all gods], as well as (to) their *ka's*,
> through this heart, by which Horus became Ptah, and
> through this tongue, by which Thoth became Ptah.
> [Ptah's first creation, through thought and word,
> was the creator-god Atum. Horus and Thoth, associated
> gods, stand for the organs of thought and speech.]
> (Thus) it happened that the heart and tongue gained
> control over [every] (other) member of the body, by
> teaching that he is in every body and in every mouth
> of all gods, all men, [all] cattle, all creeping things,
> and (everything) that lives, by thinking and commanding
> everything that he wishes.[20]

Further developments of this concept of the creative word are summarized by Wilson:

> Because the Egyptian thought of the word in physical, concrete terms and because the priesthood was the interpreter of what was divine, this "word of god" came to be treated as a body of literature, the sacred writings, but it was still the directive speech given by the gods. A dead noble was promised "every good and pure thing, in conformance to that writing of the word of god which [the god of wisdom] Thoth made." In another passage one scribe chides another for the impious presumption of his boasting: "I am astonished when thou sayest: 'I am more profound as a scribe than heaven, or earth, or the underworld!' . . . The house of books is concealed and invisible; the council of its gods is hidden and distant . . . . Thus I answer thee: 'Beware lest thy fingers approach the word of God!'" What

> the gods have said is in itself directive and controlling; it sets an order within which man and the other elements of the universe operate.
>
> Thus the "word of the god" is nothing so simple in these contexts as "divine writing" or hieroglyphic. It is the word or concern or business of the gods which applies to the elements which the gods have created . . . Creation was accompanied and directed by a word which expressed some kind of a divine order in order to comprehend the created elements.[21]

At least once, therefore, in Egyptian religious history, thought and word were conceived as instruments of world creation, giving to this act a new spiritual significance. A distinction was made between the spiritual, creative word which expresses thought and the world as an aggregate of observable, material beings.[22]

In connection with the Memphite Theology, it is pertinent to mention two personified deities, Hu, "authoritative utterance," and Sia, "perception," who appear in the earliest Egyptian texts. We have to do here with godlike qualities, perception or understanding, and authoritative utterance or command, which are able to create something new. Together, they added up to the authority to govern. In one of the Pyramid Texts (Pyr. 300), it is said that a ruling god leaves his shrine and hands over his office to the deceased king, because the king "has captured Hu, has control of Sia."

It has been suggested that Hu and Sia, as assistants of the creator god Re-Atum, have provided the model for the Memphite Theology, in which Ptah creates with his heart, seat of intelligence, and his tongue, organ of speech.[23] How similar the two theologies of creation are can be gathered from two texts, the first an obscure Coffin Text, and the second from the Denderah Temple:

> I am Hu; what I said was something good (?),
> which went forth from my mouth,
> and the good that I say is done accordingly.
> For I am Hu, I am Hu.[24]

The Denderah Text mentions both Hu and Sia as creative powers. Of Hu, it is said:

> The tongue of the child [i.e., the king], the judge of
> the Ennead,
> commanding among the gods, nothing has come into existence
> that he has not said (i.e., without his word).

And of Sia:

> Heart of Re, commanding in his beauty, the beloved of the
> Great one, leader of the Eternity, ten thousands live from
> that which he has created.[25]

To sum up, the Memphite Theology, which goes back to the First Dynasty in Egypt, articulates a creation belief in which the god Ptah, by the power of thought and commanding word, brings into being the fundamental elements of the universe. At the dawn of her history, Egypt formulated a cosmology which resembled a much later Logos doctrine.

In the spring of 1928, the ancient Canaanite city of Ugarit was discovered by accident at the small seaport town of Minet el Beida (Ras Shamra) on the coast of Syria. Beginning in 1929, with an interruption during World War II, and continuing up to the present, the French archeologist C. F. A. Schaeffer has excavated the site, which yielded material of primary value for our understanding of Canaanite culture and religion. The impact of the texts upon the study of the OT can hardly be exaggerated. Hebrew poetry and, to a lesser extent, its prose have been brilliantly illuminated in all aspects by the new material. It will take generations before the full significance of these texts for the elucidation of the OT has been realized and their riches adequately exploited.

It comes as no surprise that the Canaanites also shared the idea of a word endowed with power, mysterious and incalculable when it was the word of El or Baal. In the Ugaritic texts thus far published, "word, message" finds expression in three terms: *hwt* II, *rgm*, and *tḥm*.[26] The equivalence of *hwt* and *tḥm* is suggested by the parallelism of KRT A: 305:

> *tḥm* KRT *ṭ*ʿ
> *hwt* [*n*]ʿ*mn* [*ġlm*]
> Message of Keret the Noble
> Word of [Na]aman [the Lad][27]

On the assumption that Ugaritic *tḥm* underlies Hebrew *tanḥūmôt* of Job 15: 11, it may be possible not only to clear up an obscure passage in the biblical text but to provide the evidence for a parallelism between Ugaritic *tḥm* and Hebrew *dbr*. The transliterated and translated text follows:

> *hamᵉʿaṭ mimmᵉkā tanḥūmôt ʾēl*
> *widᵉbārō* [MT *wᵉdābār*] *loʾ ṭaʿᵃmekā* [MT *lāʾa ʿimmāk*]
> Are God's replies inadequate for you,
> Or his word not to your taste?[28]

UT 51.iv.41–42 is a particularly interesting text from the point of view of both style and content. It features an *inclusio*, a stylistic device in which the same word begins and ends the verse. More important, the text joins in parallelism "word," "wisdom," and "life," an early association of concepts which is noteworthy in view of later developments in biblical literature:

tḥmk il ḥkm
ḥkmt ʿm ʿlm
ḥyt ḥẓt tḥmk
Your word, O El, is wise,
Your wisdom is unto eternity,
Lucky life is your word.[29]

Here the word of El has developed into an entity almost distinct from the one who pronounces it, as something close to an hypostasis. The wise word of the god is commensurate with the authority of El.

The biblical concept of thunder as the voice of God (Pss 18: 14; 29: 3 ff; 77: 18) derives from the identical image of Baal thundering in the storm in order to make men hear (obey) his command. In the Baal and Anat Cycle, we read in ʿNT III. 23–25:

abn brq dl tdʿ šmn
rgm ltdʿ nšm wltbn
hmlt arṣ atm
I shall create the thunderbolt in order that the heavens may know,
That men may know the command
That the inhabitants of the earth may understand . . . .

The evidence is thus far too meager for any well-rounded picture of the dynamic word in the culture of Canaan, but there is little reason to doubt that the Canaanites shared with the rest of the ancient Near East a concept of the word endowed with power. The word of El or Baal was a projection of the deity, and served purposes other than that of mere communication. As a unit of power, the word was proportioned to the nature and rank of the speaker.

The texts cited up to now deal almost exclusively with the cosmic power of the word. It was something effective in nature. Both the creation of the world and the maintenance of an established order depended upon the divine and power-laden word. It has been customary for scholars, anxious to save what was thought to be the specifically Israelite conception of the word, to distinguish between the natural world and history when discussing the efficacy of the word. Israel was thought to have made a unique contribution to the ideology of the word in its notion of the word as determining force in history.[30] Whatever the other religions might have professed about the dynamic word and the cosmos, Israel stood alone in her affirmation of the divine word as the controlling force in history.

Whether this is true or not depends upon the published texts. If it can be shown that in areas other than Israel the word of a god was judged to be a determining factor in the sequence of historical events, then the alleged distinction between cosmos and history has no foundation in fact as far as the efficacious word is concerned. It appears that we now have evidence for the contrary view—that the power of the divine word, as understood throughout the ancient Near East, extended to history as well as to nature; in fact, there is reason to question the legitimacy of any such distinction, for it is very possibly due to a refinement in our own thinking, with little basis in ancient belief. While it is clear, especially from cultic texts, that the gods of the Near East were invoked for their indispensable aid in maintaining the life of nature, we can hardly conclude that it was *only* in nature that they operated:

> Yet it is easy to draw a wrong inference from the fact the gods of the ancient Near East may justly be called nature-gods. This knowledge sometimes leads to the conclusion, often drawn instinctively and almost unwittingly, that their only sphere of activity is necessarily nature or that particular realm of nature with which they are closely associated. This may be a very natural inference, but it is nevertheless mistaken. The activities of the so-called nature-gods are by no means restricted to what we call nature. There are a great many other texts to show that they were believed to have power over other spheres of life as well, and history is one section of that manifold reality which the gods are thought to control.[31]

It is through the divine word of Enlil that Ningirsu, the tutelary deity of Lagash, was able to straighten out a boundary dispute between Lagash and perennial rival Umma:

> (Then) did Ningirsu, Enlil's foremost warrior, do battle with (the men of) Umma in accordance with his (Enlil's) straightforward word; by the word of Enlil he hurled the great net upon them (and) heaped up their skeleton (?) piles in the plain in their (various) places.[32]

The cone inscription goes on to describe the continuing strife between the two cities, and then we read the following lines, toward the end of the inscription:

> Entemena, the *ensi* of Lagash, whose name Ningirsu had pronounced, made this (boundary) ditch from the Tigris to the Idnun in accordance with the straightforward word of Enlil, in accordance with the straightforward word of Ningirsu, (and) with the straightforward word of Nanshe, (and) restored it for his beloved king Ningirsu and for his beloved queen Nanshe, (after) he had constructed of bricks the foundation of the Namnunda-kigarra. May Shulutula, the god of Entemena, the *ensi* of Lagash, whom Enlil gave the scepter, whom Enki gave understanding, whom Nanshe chose in (her) heart, the great *ensi* of Ningirsu, the man who had received the words of the gods, stand forever (literally, "unto distant days") before Ningirsu and Nanshe (and plead) for the life of Entemena.[33]

Urukagina, king of Lagash about 2350 B.C., was a socially minded monarch who fortunately left a record of his reforms. In the middle of this extremely valuable document concerned with social justice, we find the following lines:

> He (Urukagina) held close to the word which his king (Ningirsu) spoke to him. He banned (literally, "threw off") the man in charge of the boatmen from (seizing) the boats. He banned the head shepherds from (seizing) the donkeys and sheep. . . .[34]

It detracts nothing from the admirable social consciousness of Urukagina to call attention to the influence of the divine word in his reforming activities.

The "Lament over the Destruction of Ur" bewails the overthrow of the city by the fierce hordes of Elamites who swept down from the eastern mountains. From our historical viewpoint, the downfall of Ur was due to the military superiority of the barbarians who assaulted the city. From the Sumerian viewpoint, expressed in the poignant series of laments which commemorate the disaster, the Elamite warriors are secondary and of little consequence; the city was battered into defeat by Enlil, god of the storm, as he carried out the verdict of the divine assembly. It was, ultimately, the word of the council of the gods which sealed the fate of Ur:

> Enlil called the storm.
> The people mourn.
> Exhilarating winds he carried off from the land.
> The people mourn.
> Good winds he took away from Sumer.
> The people mourn.
> Evil winds he summoned.
> The people mourn.
> To Kingaluda, tender of storms, he entrusted them.
> The storm that annihilates the land he called.
> The people mourn.[35]

In his study of this text, Jacobsen has commented:

> The enemy hordes were but a cloak, an outward form under which that essence (Enlil's) realized itself. In a deeper, truer sense the barbaric hordes were a storm, Enlil's storm, wherewith the god himself was executing a verdict passed on Ur and its people by the assembly of the gods; and as that storm the enemy attack is seen and described. . . .
> In the great catastrophes of history, in the crushing blows voted by the assembly of the gods, there is Enlil, essence of the storm. He is force, executor of the verdicts of the gods.[36]

From the field of ancient law, the Epilogue to the Code of Hammurabi includes a series of curses directed against those who have ignored the law committed by Shamash to the king:

> May Enlil, the lord, the determiner of destinies,
> whose orders cannot be altered,
> who made my kingdom great,
> incite revolts against him in his abode
> which cannot be suppressed,
> misfortune leading to his ruin!
> May he determine as the fate for him a reign of woe,
> days few in number, years of famine,
> darkness without life, sudden death!
> May he order by his forceful word
> the destruction of his city,
> the dispersion of his people, the transfer of his kingdom,
> the disappearance of his name and memory
> from the land![37]

Two things may be noted. The course of history is not seen as something left to free decision, but depends upon the unalterable decision of the gods. Royal prosperity was not something for which the king could claim all credit; it was decreed by the gods. Second, violations of the code were to be punished, not so much by human agencies but by the powerful word of a god wreaking havoc upon the violator of ordinances which expressed the will of Shamash, judge of heaven and earth. History pivoted upon the divine word.

A hymn to Ishtar, written towards the end of the First Dynasty of Babylon, extols the supremacy of Ishtar in the divine assembly and then sings of the blessings, conferred by her word, upon King Ammiditana:

> She [Ishtar] is sought after among the gods;
> extraordinary is her station.
> Respected is her word; it is *supreme* over them.
> Ishtar among the gods, extraordinary is her station.
> Respected is her word; it is *supreme* over them . . . .
> In their assembly her word is powerful;
> it is dominating . . . .
> By her orders she has subjected to him [Ammiditana]
> the four world regions at his feet;
> And the total of all peoples
> She has decided to attach them to his yoke.[38]

As with other Mesopotamian kings, the dominion of Ammiditana is owed to the divine word which directs the course of history. War was waged at the word of a god, probably derived through some divinatory method; victories were credited to the word in whose power the king had swept all before him. The royal inscriptions of Assyria and Babylonia swarm with the standard formula of undertaking a course of action "at the word [command] of a god," using such expressions as *ina qibit, ina pi, ina amat,* all of which are practically synonymous. Let one example suffice, from the annals of Tiglath-Pileser I, recalling his victorious expeditions to the west:

> Tiglath-Pileser, the legitimate king, king of the world, king of (all) the four rims (of the earth), the courageous hero who lives (guided) by the trust-inspiring oracles given (to him) by Ashur and Ninurta, the great gods and his lords, (and who thus) overthrew (all) his enemies; son of Ashurreshishi, king of the world, king of Assyria, (grand) son of Mutakkili-Nusku, also king of the world, king of Assyria.
>
> At the command of my lord Ashur I was a conqueror (lit. my hand conquered) from beyond the Lower Zab River to the Upper Sea which (lies toward) the West.[39]

Twice in the Moabite Stone it is said that Mesha carried out successful campaigns against two cities (Nebo and Hauronen) at the express word of his god Chemosh.[40]

The word of a god was thought to be able to restore a sick person to full health, as is clear from two passages in Hittite prayers. The wife of King Hattusilis says to the goddess Lelwanis:

> If thou, goddess, my lady, wilt grant him life and relay to the gods, thy peers, the good (word), and (if) thou wilt tread under foot the evil words and shut them out—O Lelwanis, my lady, may the life of Hattusilis, thy servant, and of Pudu-hepas, thy handmaid, come forth from thy mouth in the presence of the gods.[41]

In the Prayer of Kantuzilis, probably a member of the royal family, the sick man begs the sun god for restoration to health:

> Were I now to recover, would I not have recovered at the word of thee, my god? Were I to regain my strength, would I not have regained it at the word of thee, my god?[42]

Earlier we pointed out the highly sophisticated creation teaching of the Memphite Theology in Egypt. The text described the whole range of being affected by the heart and tongue of Ptah, the creator god. Who could doubt, then, that Ptah was more powerful than all the other gods? His influence, however, was not limited to the creative act. The power of Ptah extended to all the elements operating in the world—in other words, to ongoing history.

The order which the Egyptian saw in the sequence of events was not haphazard but something planned in the heart of Ptah. J. A. Wilson, to whom we owe the translation of the text, admits that, in his rendition, "the divine order" is something of a free paraphrase of the phrase "the word of god." He defends this in the following way:

> "The word of god" can and does mean "concern of the gods" or what we might call "divine interests." But the phrase "the divine order" implies that the gods have a system into which all the created elements should fit as soon as created. The context enumerates the created elements: gods, fortunes, food, provisions, town, districts, etc. These are summed up in the term "everything," after which we have "as well as the word of the god." What can this mean other than the directive order?
>
> One can argue this same sense in other Egyptian contexts. For example, an assertion that the righteous man is not wiped out by death but has an immortality because of his goodly memory is endorsed with the words: "That is the method of reckoning of the word of god"; in freer sense: "That is the principle of the divine order."
>
> Because the Egyptians thought of the word in physical, concrete terms and because the priesthood was the interpreter of what was divine, this "word of god" came to be treated as a body of literature, the sacred writings, but it was still the directive speech given by the gods. A dead noble was promised "every good and pure thing, in conformance to that writing of the word of god which (the god of wisdom) Thoth made." . . . . What the gods have said is in itself directive and controlling; it sets an order within which man and the other elements of the universe operate.[43]

If the evidence now available shows that others besides the Israelites had the idea of a divine word which was efficacious in both nature (creation and conservation) and history, it does not follow that the uniqueness of Israel's faith has been compromised. But uniqueness must not be purchased at the price of distinctions which cannot be supported in the texts. The specific quality of Israel's belief may not be sought, therefore, in what turns out to be a shared conception of the dynamic word operating in both nature and history. We must look elsewhere, concentrating less on the medium of revelation than on the revelation itself. It is the *content* of the divine revelation, whether in nature or history, which sets Israel apart in the ancient Near East. The message is more significant than the medium. Above all, this revelation in Israel takes place within a strictly monotheistic framework, absolutely unique in the ancient world. The nature and purpose of this God have no parallel elsewhere, for the God of Israel's prophets and psalmists was not enclosed in nature: he transcended nature and, indeed, the whole thrust of mythopoeic thinking.

The uniqueness of Israel's faith, especially in what concerns the word, can be estimated by comparing her basic outlook on the world with that of her pagan environment. In a polytheistic milieu, the literature has accustomed us to see a point of view alien to both the biblical and modern way of thinking. Ancient Near Eastern man felt himself surrounded by threatening and mysterious forces which might engulf him at any moment. One writer has compared this dark, uncomfortable, and complex world to the vast and sometimes frightening world of the subconscious which modern psychoanalysis has exposed.[44] How was man to gain any security in this kind of world? These forces had to be reached in some way and, if possible, controlled. It was this need which drove him to the practices of magic, to the arts of divination. Deut 18: 9–14 has left an unforgettable picture of that eerie world along with the whole vocabulary of pagan superstition; all the while Yahweh solemnly forbids his people to have any truck with this world of the occult. God's will could not be coerced by the magic word or his plan disclosed by the arts of divination; he would reveal his will through the mouth of the prophet. This is the word which Israel was to heed.

Without surrendering its dynamic force, Israel delivered man from the magical concept of the word. This might be described as the shift from the magical to the semantic function of the word, though we cannot lose sight of Israel's belief in the noncommunicative function of the word. The moment when man could no longer put his trust in the magical word has been brilliantly described by Cassirer:

> When man first began to realize that this confidence (in the magic word which the powers of nature cannot resist) was vain—that nature was inexorable not because it was reluctant to fulfill his demands but because it did not understand his language—the discovery must have come as a shock. At this point he had to face a new problem which marked a turning point and a crisis in his intellectual and moral life. From that time on man must have found himself in a deep solitude, subject to feelings of utter loneliness and of absolute despair. He would scarcely have overcome these had he not developed a new spiritual force, which barred the way to magic but at the same time opened another and more promising road. All hope of subduing nature by the magic word had been frustrated. But as a result man began to see the relation between language and reality in a different light.[45]

In the world of magic, distinctions break down between the word and the thing, between the idea and the actuality. All reality becomes, as it were, consubstantial, sharing the same plane of being. It is not possible to classify this situation rationally. One effect, however, is to cover everything with the cloak of the sacred. When the Hebrews broke out of the tight ring of magic, they released man from the pansacrality of life, asserting the qualitative difference between the sacred and the profane. In no other earlier or contemporary religion of the ancient Near East can we find a comparable revaluation of nature and human activity. This desacralization of the world was anything but a profanation; there was no denial of the close relationship between God and his creation. But there was a clear recognition of the infinite distance between the absolute and holy God and the rest of the world, including man.

Notes

1 G. Steiner, *Language and Silence* (1967), p. 36.

2 T. Jacobsen, in *The Intellectual Adventure of Ancient Man* (1946), p. 178. Cf Judg 6: 36–40.

3 S. N. Kramer, *The Sumerians* (1963), p. 115.

4 A group of minor deities in the Sumerian pantheon. For both the Igigi and the Anunnaki, see W. Lambert and A. Millard, *Atraḫasis: The Babylonian Story of the Flood* (1969), p. 146.

5 *ANET*³ (1969), p. 386. Trans. F. J. Stephens.

6 *CAD*, Vol. 1, "A" Part II (1968), p. 36. With this, compare Ps 29.

7 W. Hallo and J. J. Van Dijk, *The Exaltation of Inanna* (1968), p. 61.

8 S. Langdon, *Sumerian and Babylonian Psalms* (1909), p. 59. See also p. xix and Nos. I, II, VIII, and IX. S. N. Kramer reports on a hymn, the text of which has only recently become available, whose opening lines read as follows:

> Enlil, whose command is far-reaching, whose
> word is holy,
> The lord whose pronouncement is unchangeable,
> who forever decrees destinies . . . . *Op. cit.*, p. 120.

9 *ANET*³, p. 458. Trans. S. N. Kramer.

10 *ANET*³, p. 614. Trans. S. N. Kramer.

11 T. Jacobsen, *AJSL* 58 (1941), 219–24.

12 T. Jacobsen, *Towards the Image of Tammuz and Other Essays on Mesopotamian History and Culture*, ed. W. L. Moran (1970), pp. 100–101. For other texts dealing with the "word" in Sumero-Akkadian literature, see under "amatu" in *CAD*, pp. 35–36.

13 W. Lambert, "Literary Style in First Millenium Mesopotamia," *JAOS* 88 (1968), 129. The same writer has published "The Gula Hymn of Bulluṭsa-rabi," *Orientalia* 36 (1967), 105–32, in which we read the following lines:

> My word is not altered,
> the utterance of my mouth is not changed.

14 *ANET*³, p. 72. Trans. E. A. Speiser.

15 *ANET*³, p. 617. Trans. S. N. Kramer. Excerpts from many texts affirming the irreversibility of the divine word, once spoken, may be found in *CAD*, Vol. 4, "E" (1958), p. 175.

16 E. Cassirer, *The Philosophy of Symbolic Forms*, Vol. 2 (1955), p. 237.

17 M. Noth, "History and the Word of God," *The Laws in the Pentateuch and Other Essays* (1966), pp. 179–93; A. Malamat, "Prophetic Revelations in New Documents from Mari and the Bible," *VT(S)* 15 (1966), 207–27; H. B. Huffmon, "Prophecy in the Mari

Letters," *BA* 31 (1968), 101–24; M. J. Buss, "Mari Prophecy and Hosea," *JBL* 88 (1969), 338; W. L. Moran, "New Evidence from Mari on the History of Prophecy," *Bibl* 50 (1969) 15–56.

[18] Translation of W. L. Moran, *op. cit.*, pp. 29–30. Sending of the hair and fringe of the prophet's garment was a common practice in public oracles. Possession of these personal articles gave one a symbolic, though genuinely legal, control over the owner. This was a check upon the authenticity of the oracle, and was calculated to restrain prophets from a too facile exercise of their skill. Once in the hands of the king, these articles made the prophet accountable for the words he transmitted.

[19] M. Noth, *op. cit.*, p. 188.

[20] *ANET*[3], p. 5. Trans. J. A. Wilson.

[21] J. A. Wilson, *Intellectual Adventure of Ancient Man*, p. 60.

[22] J. Zandee, "Das Schöpferwort im alten Ägypten," *Verbum* (Obbink Festschrift, 1964), pp. 33–66.

[23] H. Ringgren, *Word and Wisdom* (1947), p. 12.

[24] *Ibid.*, p. 12.

[25] *Ibid.*, p. 13.

[26] C. H. Gordon, *Ugaritic Textbook* (1965), p. 171.

[27] See also KRT A: 125, 248–49, 268, transliterated and translated by H. L. Ginsberg, *The Legend of King Keret* (1946), pp. 17, 20. In texts 49: iv: 34 and 51: viii: 32–34, *tḥm* is paralleled by *hwt*, as in KRT A: 305.

[28] M. Dahood, "The Phoenician Contribution to Biblical Wisdom Literature," in *The Role of the Phoenicians in the Interaction of Mediterranean Civilizations*, ed. W. A. Ward (1968), pp. 125–26, 144, n. 16.

[29] S. Iwry, "New Evidence for Belomancy in Ancient Palestine and Phoenicia," *JAOS* 81 (1961), 27–34. He points out the double meaning of Hebrew *ḥeṣ* as "arrowhead" and "luck," taking *ḥẓt* of the text to mean "lucky," as in Arabic *ḥaziya*.

[30] O. Grether, "Name und Wort Gottes im Alten Testament," *BZAW* (1934), pp. 127, 139. This distinction has been vigorously challenged in the book of Bertil Albrektson, *History and the Gods* (1967), especially in chap. 4, "The Divine Word and the Course of Events," pp. 53–67.

[31] Albrektson, *op. cit.*, pp. 16–17. F. Nǫtscher, in his book *Enlil in Sumer und Akkad* (1927), p. 45, had said of the chief god of the Sumerian pantheon, "There is hardly anything, with the possible exception of the nether world, which does not somehow belong to Enlil's sphere of action."

[32] S. N. Kramer, *The Sumerians*, p. 314.

[33] Kramer, *op. cit.*, p. 315.

[34] *Ibid.*, p. 318.

[35] T. Jacobsen, *Intellectual Adventure of Ancient Man*, p. 141.

[36] *Ibid.*, pp. 141–42.

[37] *ANET*[3], p. 179. Trans. T. J. Meek.

[38] *ANET*[3], p. 383. Trans. F. J. Stephens.

[39] *ANET*[3], p. 274. Trans. A. Oppenheim.

[40] *ANET*[3], pp. 320–21. Trans. W. F. Albright.

[41] *ANET*[3], p. 394. Trans. A. Goetze.

[42] *ANET*[3], p. 400. Trans. A. Goetze.

[43] J. A. Wilson, *Intellectual Adventure of Ancient Man*, pp. 59–60.

[44] G. E. Wright, *The Old Testament against Its Environment* (1950), p. 44.

[45] E. Cassirer, *An Essay on Man* (1944), p. 110.

Roland E. Murphy, O. Carm.
Duke University

The Old Testament as Word of God

The category "word of God" is only one category under which Sacred Writ can be viewed. Although it has a long and hallowed usage, it is not necessarily the best. The difficulty with the phrase lies in its multiplicity of meanings, ranging from its usc in the Bible itself to its meanings in the writings of Barth and Ebeling. Are we going to understand it in a biblical sense? Then one must conjure with the rich variation of meaning in the *d[e]bar Yhwh* within the Old Testament and the *logos* within the New Testament. It is not our purpose to pursue such an investigation in this paper; nor will we simply adopt a modern theological notion of word under which one might try to fit the Old Testament. Rather, we are understanding the phrase in the broad sense as designating the writings commonly indicated as the Old Testament. Hence, this is a written word. I propose to use "word of God" or "the word of God" without intending any difference; and "word" is in lower case throughout. In order to portray the meaning of the Old Testament as the word of God, we will comment on three basic questions: (1) In what sense is this written word to be called the word of God? (2) What are the static aspects (especially the canonical limits and their implications) of this word? (3) How is this the word of God to the Christian?

This paper was delivered in lectures at Princeton Theological Seminary and Wesley Theological Seminary in 1970, and is here offered as testimony to what has always been a concern of Jacob Myers in his Old Testament studies.

I

It is obvious that there is no pure, naked word of God. We have only what has been transmitted in human language, the result of man's confrontation with the Lord. To speak of God's word is to speak metaphorically in an attempt to describe one aspect of God's communication with Israel: the literature which his encounter with them precipitated. We prefer not to speak of the Old Testament as "indirectly," or as "witnessing to," the word of God, because this only pushes the determination of the phrase another step backward. Rather, we admit that the role of human mediation of the word is quite substantial; we are dealing with the word of God in words of men. But it is the only word of God we have; this word does not exist apart from human response, as enshrined in Holy Writ.

The phrase, "word of God," is applicable in the first instance to the final, written word; it is with the Old Testament in its final form that we are concerned. But at several points in our discussion we will be conscious of the preliterary, oral stage of the Old Testament, and the various phases of its formation. Here too, we are dealing with the word of God. In a sense, the spoken word (oral tradition) might seem to have a greater claim to be the word; it is more direct, it is given immediately to a particular generation. Then, it is preserved, and, as we shall see, often reinterpreted in the light of the growth of the community, and eventually put in writing. The reduction to writing is motivated by the vision of the community which sees in the word more than an immediate application to a given generation. The community's experience proves and approves the relevance of the word for a future generation. This whole process preserves the word—expanded and reinterpreted. Since the word is destined to have such a long and varied life, it cannot be measured merely by its temporal directness, by its pertinence to the first audience. The believing community has always and inevitably wrestled with the tradition or text that has been handed down. The primitive Church did this, in an effort to explain Jesus. The later Church has only this text to refer to as a norm, and it must deal with it in its fullest dimensions.

Thus far, we have stated that the word of God is not to be understood apart from the word of men, and that it has traveled through a long history. These aspects of the word have received proper emphasis only in modern times. Classical Christian theology has traditionally stressed the role of God at the expense of man, as we can see in the writings of the Fathers and medieval theologians, as well as the Reformers. The emphasis on the divine aspect of the word—the word *of God*—goes back to the early Church, and, indeed, the primitive Church itself understood the Old Testament to be somehow *theopneustos* (2 Tim 3: 16). This is not the place to sketch the growth of the doctrine of inspiration, but it would be well to take note of two different theories currently proposed by Catholic theologians—those by P. Benoit and K. Rahner.[1] I think it is correct to say that this is not an area of pressing concern in Protestant circles outside fundamentalism. But I am unwilling to let the question disappear simply because fundamentalists have more or less appropriated it to themselves; it deserves to be treated in a freer manner.

P. Benoit, the noted New Testament scholar, follows the traditional lines of Thomistic theology and psychology. In his view, the inspired writer remains an instrumental cause used freely by God in the production of the written work. The divine influence is centered on the mind and will—the faculties—of the human writer. Benoit has introduced several nuances into this explanation; he recognizes that inspiration and revelation are intimately correlated in fact, although the former bears essentially on the practical judgment (what is to be written). The approach of Benoit is a thoughtful effort to analyze the psychology of the human writer who is influenced by God. But perhaps it has reached the point of no return. The analysis of the pertinent factors is logical, but leaves one with the feeling that the reality remains far too complex.

K. Rahner feels no need to speculate concerning divine and human activity in the composition of the Bible. In fact, he fears that a theory concerning the illumination of the human mind may reify the reality of inspiration. For him, inspiration means that God has willed that the Bible form a constitutive element of the primitive Church; it is nothing else than God's founding of the Church, of which the Bible is an essential part. This is, as it were, "the way it is." A given body of literature came, by a divine and salvific *fiat*, to be a basic factor in the life of the Church. Rahner's judgment upon the Old Testament is not happily conceived; he sees it merely as a prehistory of the Church, deriving its validity and function from the New Testament. It would appear more in harmony with his own theory to recognize the fact that the Old Testament was *the* Bible of the primitive Church, while the New Testament was in the process of formation. But the value of his approach is that it is along historical, rather than speculative, lines. Neither Benoit's nor Rahner's theory opens the door to the old fundamentalistic views of divine inspiration. But neither are they fully adequate. No one has yet developed a theological explanation of inspiration which does justice to the nature of the Bible precisely as word, as literature. If language is seen in its further dimension as word, as structure, as itself an interpretation and not merely a representation of reality, new perspectives on the theological explication of "word of God" will surely emerge.[2]

It might appear that we have walked into the fundamentalism which seems to be the concern of G. Ebeling when he writers:

> The confessional statement, 'Scripture is the Word of God,' can be rightly understood if the full breadth of the hermeneutic task is also included in the explanation of this way of speaking. But it is dangerously confusing, if the hermeneutic problem is left out of account. It cannot of course be corrected by asserting some form of intermingling of God's Word and man's word, but only by affirming that God's Word by its nature is not a written, once-upon-a-time word, but one that is orally spoken and happens. It is not the Bible text, but the proclamation, that is God's Word in the strict sense. In so far as the proclamation is dependent on the text, the exposition therefore serves towards the text proving itself a Bible text, i.e. becoming the source of God's Word.[3]

We should agree with Ebeling that the hermeneutical process is not to be separated from the written word of God; interpretation is surely necessary. But we need not adopt a theory of proclamation at the expense of the "written, once-upon-a-time word." The analysis of the roles of God and man in the production of the written word is worthy of consideration, as the history of Christian thought suggests. One cannot avoid the risk of the "intermingling" of the human and the divine, even if this cannot be precisely captured. Otherwise, one seems to abdicate the task of understanding why the Bible is the word of God in a manner that no other literature is.

In summary, I am understanding the phrase "word of God" as the written word of the Old Testament, formed within Israel and transmitted to the Church. It is not some kind of direct revelation, a speaking or writing of God, but it is the product of divine influence upon the men of Israel—this characteristic constitutes it as God's word. We will now turn to view this word in what may be called its static aspect—its canonical and normative status.

II

The Old Testament has a certain static aspect for the Christian. It is simply a given, accepted as a totality, however varied the contents. It is all the word of God, and with it the Church has lived for centuries, turning to it as a normative source of its own self-understanding. We need not enter here into the problem of exactly where the limits of the canon are to be set, whether or not they include the Apocrypha.[4] Rather, we raise the question whether within the Old Testament one part is more the word of God than another, and whether we are to operate with a kind of canon within the canon.

The point at issue is not merely whether the phrase "word of God" is more truly ascribed to one portion of the Old Testament than to another. (Does the prophet, for example, more than the sage, speak the word?) The importance of the question lies, rather, in the implications that can be drawn from the answer. C. Westermann argues that not every word in the Old Testament is to be understood univocally as the word of God.[5] He discerns three basic elements in the Old Testament: report (*Bericht*), God's address to man, and man's address to God. The report is found in the "history"—that is, in the Torah, the histories of the Deuteronomist and the Chronicler, and in the framework of the prophetical writings. God's address to man is found in the prophetic words and in the commandments and laws. Man's address to God is centred in praise and lament: the Psalms, Lamentations, and the prayers that are scattered throughout the rest of the Old Testament. Only the wisdom writings fail to conform to this schema, as Westermann candidly admits. But they can be accommodated on a different basis. He argues that God's action is not only acts of judgment or salvation in history; it is also the steady action of blessing, as the power of fertility, of growth, of success. Just as the blessing is given to every human being, so wisdom is a gift for all men, without the limitation implied by God's history with Israel. "The word of wisdom is the word that matures in life experience, that grows out of the divine action of blessing."[6] Hence, Westermann concludes that not every word in the Old Testament claims to be the word of God in the same way. Rather, the word of God reaches his people in manifold fashion—within the three directions that have been indicated.

This analysis of the directions of the word is useful, and one can only agree that the word is to be determined from the point of view of its function as well as its content. But this style of classification runs the risk of sorting out something as the word by opposition to something else which is not the word or only very secondarily so. Such a procedure is contrary to the way in which the Israelite community, and the Christian community as well, preserved and received this literature.

For Israel accepted the entire *Tanak* (even though it allowed for the centrality of the Torah) as the word of God. Early in Israel's history, an informal canonization process began to work, when the stories of the Patriarchs and the Exodus took shape and were handed down.[7] As the process accelerated, the whole literature was received by the community as somehow being God's word to them. Even the legal corpora, which modern scholarship has shown to be the cutomary law and legal policy common to the ancient Near East, were so viewed. The Priestly account of the Tabernacle is presented in terms of, "the Lord said to Moses," and this formula is used countless times in the Pentateuch to introduce laws. Hence, one may ask how Westermann can characterize (at least certain) legal narratives as "God's address to men" when he, along with most modern scholars, recognizes that this and similar formulae are merely a literary device and not historical. He simply decides to evaluate positively the "historical" framework of the laws as conveying God's word to the community—perhaps because this is the way in which the community came to understand the laws. It is important to observe that it is the final, community understanding (which historical investigation would not support) which is the hermeneutical principle in this classification. I am in sympathy with this thrust, but it seems arbitrary, then, to group the laws with the prophetic word as "God's address to man" and fail to find a place for the wisdom literature.

As regards the prophetic word, Westermann has argued that the proclaimed word of salvation or judgment is God's word directly, whereas the reason (*Begründung*) joined to it is so only indirectly.[8] Now it would appear literary criticism becomes the touchstone to the (almost pure!) word of God, which is separate from the prophetic expansion of it. It is an illusion to pinpoint the word of God in this manner, and Westermann himself admits that the messenger formula gradually becomes the introduction to the prophetic speech, so that *the whole* is designated as the word of God, or it even comes to indicate speeches that make no claim to be prophetic speeches. This fact should warn us against giving primacy to the word of God, which the prophet was supposedly consciously aware of. If one can thus distinguish between early and late "stages" of the word of God, why should one come down on *one* stage as primary?

Again, "man's address to God" is too narrowly viewed when it is limited to Old Testament prayer. There is a response to God present in all the varieties of literary forms found in the Bible. The initiative of God and the reaction of man, on whatever profound or even minimal level, are inherent to the inspired word. Finally, it is only by a tour de force that wisdom literature is retained by Westermann as some kind of word. He has related the wisdom literature with the notion of the divine blessing; it might be called the word which expresses the power of God's blessing at work in the world. All the more reason, then, to refuse a secondary rating to it. We must take seriously the fact that the community preserved it as part of the total communication of God to his people. The sages did not distinguish between—much less evaluate—revelation and reason, history and human experience, as channels of divine communication. The broad realm of human conduct was the area which they observed, and it was not closed off from the divine, it was not "profane," as we tend to classify it. Israel had no difficulty in accepting wisdom itself as divine and speaking in the name of God. As G. von Rad describes it:

> Nevertheless one can say that she is the form in which Yahweh's will and his association with man (in other words, salvation) comes to him. She is the essence of what man needs for a good life, and of what God gives him. But most importantly, wisdom does not present herself to man as a thing, or teaching, or guidance or salvation, etc., but as a person, an "I" who calls. Hence wisdom is really the form in which Yahweh makes himself present and in which he wants to be sought after by man. "He who finds me finds life" (Prov 8: 35). Only Yahweh can speak this way.[9]

We have been insisting upon Israel's reception and preservation of the word as a totality, over against any literary analysis which might be erected into a touchstone that would categorize or pinpoint the word of God, delimiting it to a specific area of the Old Testament. The same problem appears in another form as the "canon within the canon." The concept of a selective canon has emerged recently in the New Testament context, and it has been asserted for the Old Testament by G. E. Wright.[10]

Wright's presentation is both theoretical and practical. Theoretically, he sees the Torah as holding the rest of the varied literature around it. But he offers no evidence for this. One could possibly point to the eventual identification of wisdom with Torah (Deut 4: 6–8; Sir 24; Bar 4: 1–4) as a measure of proof, but this remains rather slender support. One should, rather, recognize a lack of a synthesizing, classifying principle behind Israel's collection.

Practically, he argues that the actual meaning of the canon cannot be considered apart from the reigning theology of a given period: "The truth is to be found in the actual usage, and here the current theology of the user provides the interpretative principle whereby the canon within the canon can be discerned."[11] This certainly reflects what is happening, but it should not be erected into a principle. It yields too much to the *Zeitgeist*, the constantly changing historical situation of the reader. One must also obey the complex and varied style of the Old Testament word, which provides a corrective to the narrow view of a particular age. The *total* word is the yardstick against which to measure such principles as Law and Gospel, which tend to become the only axis of biblical interpretation. A refusal to delimit the canon means that one can escape partially from the narrow point of view imposed by one's own historicity—an important hermeneutical gain. The acceptance of the total canon brings with it inevitable tensions, such as the particular and jarring viewpoints expressed in books like Proverbs and Ecclesiastes, which are not flattened out because the canon is closed. But the recognition of a total and fixed canon will correct the tendency of each generation to "recanonize" the sacred books.

III

It is in the context of the dynamic aspect of the word that we will ask how the Old Testament is the word of God to the Christian. The dynamic aspect of words in general has been sharply stated by Ebeling: "We do not get at the nature of words by asking what they contain, but by asking what they effect, what they set going, what future they disclose."[12] The Old Testament is an answer to this kind of question, for it is the result of asking what the word of God to his servants has set going. The vitality of the word has been brought home to us through the insights into the Old Testament literature provided by form criticism and tradition history. We now recognize the *movement* within this literature. The saving acts of God in the Exodus event become the basis of Israel's experience of salvation. Deutero-Isaiah sees the liberation from exile as a New Exodus. The Deuteronomistic historian presents a thematic view of Israel's past by taking up sources that are disparate in origin: annals, cycles of prophets, epic stories. The Chronicler does not allow this view of the Deuteronomist to become official for his generation, and so he moves the horizon of history to legitimatization, with the help of Moses and David. The prophets expand the cultic and legal traditions of earlier generations. The authors of Job and Qohelet take their stand against the traditional wisdom which is presented in Proverbs. The author of the Wisdom of Solomon returns to the formula of the sages (wisdom brings life), in order to deepen it (justice is immortal; Wis 1: 15), and he proposes a meditation on the Exodus that is a rarity in the wisdom tradition. The bourgeois sage of Jerusalem, Ben Sira, offers the "praise of the Fathers" (Sir 44: 1 ff), a kind of salvation history, in an age when wisdom has been identified with the Law.

Where is the word of God in all this? It is on the march, being deepened and expanded in the successive generations of Israel as the community lived with and reinterpreted the word.[13] This movement continues into the Christian Church. Heb 1: 1 suggests that it is in virtue of his faith in Christ that the Christian accepts the Old Testament as the word of God to him. It remains for him to work out a relationship between the Old and the New: "In many and various ways God spoke of old to the fathers by the prophets; but in these days he has spoken to us by a Son . . . ." Ultimately, the Christian cannot view the Old Testament apart from the New, although Christian theologians have contested this statement. The nature of the relationship of the two Testaments is far too complex to treat here, but a few basic considerations are in order.[14]

The dynamic aspect of the word of God points up the reality of the history of biblical traditions. The movement of the word perdured into the primitive Church, which reinterpreted the Old Testament in the light of God's eschatological intervention in Christ. Thus, the Christian understanding of the Old Testament as the word of God is a Christian prejudgment (*Vorverständnis*). In terms of our earlier discussion of the canon, we may claim Christ as our ultimate canonical principle (thus, approximately Luther's *was Christum treibet*). We have already noted the limiting factor inherent in the notion of a canon within the canon. The same caution is to be applied when Christ becomes the ultimate canon, lest one lose the total dimension of the word of God. I emphasize *ultimate* canonical principle, for I would not go so far as to say, with N. Lohfink, "that the Old Testament is the 'Word of God' only to the extent that it leads to, and is taken up by and exists in view of Christ, the authentic and final Word of God."[15] This would seem to flatten out the Old Testament, contrary to Lohfink's intention, in the manner of Wilhelm Vischer. It presupposes more unity and continuity between the Testaments than actually exist. Any norm, and especially an ultimate one, has limited application, and usually in a negative way. Christ as canon serves to negate and correct a given thrust of Old Testament thought (e.g., the notion of Sheol, the complaints of the psalmist or Job). Positively, however, it is the structure of my own existence which allows me to appropriate such a thrust as the word of God. The remarks of James Barr supply a needed nuance; he distinguishes between the intended content of a text and its purpose:

> Our use of the texts should relate to the intended content because it was through the intended content that his [God's] purpose moved forward, even if the intended content does not comprehend that purpose. Ultimately, it must be said that this "not yet" is not negative, and for an important (though perhaps controversial) theological reason: positivity in this context is not determined by Jesus Christ solely. The positivity here is that the One God of Israel is proceeding with his purpose. Our Christian faith is that the sending of Jesus Christ is the culmination of this purpose. This does not mean that Jesus Christ becomes the criterion for the meaningfulness of that which is done by God before he is sent.[16]

While the Church has taken over the Old Testament and reinterpreted it, she has never canonized a definitive method for understanding it. The manner in which the relationship is to be worked out has always varied, and it will always vary, according to the needs and the insights of the community of faith. The particular method of exegesis employed by the New Testament writers, or by the Fathers, need not and cannot be adopted in the twentieth century. The relationship between the two Testaments remains complex, and the several lines (e.g., promise-fulfillment) which binds them together must be allowed to stand in the midst of all the discontinuity. It is impossible to forge a conceptual unity of the relationship. The vicissitudes of Israel's history prevent this, but at the same time they present various lines—institutional (e.g., kingship, sacrifice, etc.) and conceptual (messiah, servant of God, etc.)—which can be taken up and pursued. As A. Jepsen notes, the New Testament supplies "the question, the point of view, not the interpretation itself" of the Old Testament text, and thus it has a "heuristic function" in opening up the word of God to its fullness.[17]

There are more points of dissimilarity than of similarity between the two Testaments. But the balance between continuity and discontinuity cannot be judged quantitatively. Rather, the balance is one of tension. Positive and negative points, even if they negate each other logically, do not cancel each other out in the historical development of which the Bible is the written record. They exist together as witness to the variety of God's dealings with men. One lives with this fact only in virtue of the faith in the Lord of Abraham as the Father of Jesus Christ. N. Lohfink has well expressed the balancing of these tensions in the case of Ecclesiastes:

> Similarly, in dealing with the book of Qohelet, one cannot avoid bringing out especially the melancholic and pervasive concern with this world, which encompasses his faith. Then the pros and cons of this traditio-historical discussion concerning a faith that is limited by this world will have to be developed. The New Testament message of the resurrection of the Lord and of all who believe in him will appear as the opposite pole to Qohelet. But then the interpretation is to be continued up into our own time; if the modern reader does not finally have to make his own decision of faith in the resurrection, then the proper role of the "Christian" truth of Qohelet has not been served. Thus the faith of Qohelet is not to be pushed aside and forgotten, as one might like to think, as a kind of preliminary position or indeed as an error. Rather, if the exegesis is correctly done, it remains as an enduring dimension of belief in the resurrection. Were it to disappear, the meaning of the resurrection message would probably be no longer rightly understood.[18]

Finally, any approach to the question of the relationship between the two Testaments can profit from the reaction of Dietrich Bonhoeffer:

> My thoughts and feelings seem to be getting more and more like the Old Testament, and no wonder, I have been reading it much more than the New for the last few months. It is only when one knows the ineffability of the Name of God that one can utter the name of Jesus Christ. It is only when one loves life and the world so much that without them everything would be gone, that one can believe in the resurrection and a new world . . .

I don't think it is Christian to want to get to the New Testament too soon and too directly.[19]

Notes

[1] For a treatment of the recent history of the question, see J. Burtchaell, *Catholic Theories of Biblical Inspiration since 1810* (Cambridge: University Press, 1969). The full bibliography provides also references to the several works of Benoit and the single work of Rahner, *Inspiration in the Bible*, 2d rev. ed. (New York: Herder and Herder, 1964).

[2] As a beginning along these lines, see L. Alonso Schökel, *The Inspired Word* (New York: Herder and Herder, 1965); also "Hermeneutics in the Light of Language and Literature," *CBQ* 25 (1963), 371–86. Schökel has also a general treatment of the Old Testament as word of God in *Wort und Botschaft*, ed. J. Schreiner (Würzburg: Echter-Verlag, 1967) pp. 1–13.

[3] *Word and Faith* (Philadelphia: Fortress, 1963) pp. 428–29.

[4] On this subject, see the symposium in *CBQ* 28 (1966), 189–207, and the thesis and later article of A. Sundberg in *CBQ* 30 (1968), 143–55.

[5] Cf "Zur Auslegung des Alten Testaments," in O. Loretz and W. Strolz, eds., *Die hermeneutische Frage in der Theologie* (Freiburg: Herder, 1968), pp. 190–95.

[6] *Ibid.*, p. 195.

[7] Cf E. Speiser, "The Biblical Idea of History in Its Common Near Eastern Setting," *IEJ* 7 (1957), 201–16.

[8] Cf *Basic Forms of Prophetic Speech* (Philadelphia: Westminster, 1967), pp. 85, 179.

[9] Cf *Theologie des Alten Testaments* (München: Kaiser, 1957) pp. 442–43.

[10] Cf *The Old Testament and Theology* (New York: Harper and Row, 1969) pp. 166–85.

[11] *Ibid.*, p. 182. The position of Ebeling is close to a canon within a canon. For him, the canon is fluid because it must be tested by interpretation (such as Luther's internal criticism of the canon). See *The Word of God and Tradition* (Philadelphia: Fortress, 1968) pp. 113–21, esp. p. 120. But the criterion of criticism remains problematical. One can agree, for example, that there is a difference between Leviticus and Deuteronomy, but the principle of differentiation and the implicit value judgments should be revealed; and even then there is the danger of drawing up a personal canon that may not agree with that of the Spirit. For further details on Ebeling's views, see his *The Problem of Historicity* (Philadelphia: Fortress, 1967), pp. 61–80.

[12] *The Nature of Faith* (Philadelphia: Fortress, 1961), p. 187.

[13] The counterpart of this movement within Israel is the hermeneutical process within the Christian community—and not only the process but also the actual proclamation of the biblical word, the hopes and visions triggered by the word. Historical consciousness has made us ever more aware of the hermeneutical gap between what a text meant and what it means now. The very formation of the word in the Old Testament suggests that there is a continuum that helps to bridge the gap: the understanding and continuous reinterpretation of the word within the believing community. This context is indispensable, whatever the vagaries of interpretation that may arise within the community. Cf Richard E. Palmer, *Hermeneutics* (Evanston: Northwestern University Press, 1969).

[14] For the pertinent literature and a discussion, see R. E. Murphy, "The Relationship between the Testaments," *CBQ* 26 (1964), 349–59, and also The St. Louis University Bellarmine lecture, "Christian Understanding of the Old Testament," *Theology Digest* 18 (1970), 321–32.

[15] "Das Alte Testament nur in dem Mass 'Wort Gottes' ist, in dem es auf Christus, das eigentliche und letzte 'Wort Gottes,' hinführt, von ihm aufgenommen ist, vor ihm besteht." Cf *Bibelauslegung im Wandel* (Frankfurt: Knecht, 1967), p. 210.

[16] Cf *Old and New in Interpretation* (London: SCM, 1966), p. 153; and on p. 140, he writes: "The proper strategy in the Church, then, is not to take Christ as the given and argue from him to the authority of the meaning of the Old Testament; it is rather, taking the Old Testament as something which we *have* in the Church, to ask in what ways the guidance it affords helps us to understand and discern and obey the Christ more truly."

[17] Cf C. Westerman, ed., *Essays on Old Testament Hermeneutics* (Richmond: John Knox, 1963) p. 264.

[18] Cf *Bibelauslegung* . . . (note 15 above), pp. 211–12.

[19] Cf *Letters and Papers from Prison* (New York: MacMillan paperback edition, 1962) pp. 103–4.

Robert North, SJ
Marquette University

Does Archeology Prove Chronicles Sources?

"Archaeological and historical studies have now rendered [Chronicles] more respectable and have shown it to be at times more accurate than some of its parallel sources," wrote honored sexagenarian Professor Myers emphatically at the very outset of his three-volume masterpiece.[1] He here espouses a view which has been most trenchantly set forth and justified by Martin Noth.[2] We feel that a detailed evaluation of Noth's two bedrock cases, plus mention of all minor items which scrutiny can discover, will be an appreciated service not only to Professor Myers but to the lamented German Lutheran master whose admirable methodology we strive to follow even where it may lead to conclusions not bolstering his own.[3]

Here are Noth's words:

> We have in the exposition of the post-Solomonic kings of Judah two individual details not derived from the Deuteronomist [Sam-Kings]. We are in a position to prove from other data that these are historically reliable: so much so that we are forced to suppose the use of a preexilic source by the Chronicler . . . . The question cannot be answered with generalized plausibilities, but only with meticulous demonstration in individual cases. We may assume older sources used by the Chronicler but unknown to us only where we are authorized by solid grounds, taking into account the work's overall character. In less secure cases we will do well to leave open a decision until new evidence is available.[4]

The Tunnel: 2 Chron 32: 3, 30 || 2 Kings 20: 20 [Is 22: 9–11; Sir 48: 17]

The first bedrock case of sources found by Noth in his magisterial Chronicles analysis is Hezekiah's tunnel. The religious reform of 2 Kings 18: 4, greatly amplified in 2 Chron 31 plus 29 f, must doubtless be seen as a veiled project to reassert the independence of United Israel vis-à-vis Assyria (2 Kings 18: 6). Idols like Nehushtan probably included statues of Assyrian divinities set up in sanctuaries, even of Jerusalem, as guarantors of treaty. Such a "protectorate" treaty was sought from Pul by Ahaz of Judah in 735 B.C. (2 Chron 28: 16 ||), and imposed on the northland by Sargon in 721 B.C. (2 Kings 17: 6). The idol purge at Jerusalem involved token representatives of all the northern tribes as part of an "Ecumenical Passover," narrated only by 2 Chron 30: 11; 31: 1.[5] Manpower resources and economic benefits streaming toward Zion in the pilgrimage revival (2 Chron 31: 12) made possible an extensive building of fortifications (2 Chron 32:5; divergingly but more plainly prior to Sennacherib's invasion in 2 Kings 18: 8). Among these defense projects is explicitly included the tunnel from Gihon to Siloam:

2 Kings 20: 20. And the rest of the information about Hezekiah and all his [G *dynasteía* +] *geste*, and his 'building of the pool and the conduit' [G 'spring and aqueduct'] so as to bring the waters toward [G into] the city, are not these written up in the book of annals of the kings of Judah?

Is 22: 9. "You [pl.: Hezekiah and?] collected the waters of the lower pool; you made a sump within the two walls for the waters of the old pool."

Sir 48: 17. Hezekiah fortified his city and brought Gog into their midst [G[B]; [A]water ([S]canal) into its midst]; with iron he excavated the hewn rock, and built up springs for the waters.

2 Chron 32: 2. Hezekiah saw that Sennacherib was on his way to mount a siege of Jerusalem. 3 He took counsel with his princes [G elders] and his power-structure about shutting off the waters of the springs [pl. also G] which [G antecedent 'waters'] stood outside the city, and they promised their cooperation. 4 So they [G he] got together a big crowd and shut off all the water-[G of the] sources, including the wadi [G river] which 'floods over inside the land' [G 'serves as (or passes its) boundary through the *city*]. "Why," it was murmured, "should kings [G the king] of Assyria be able to invade and find water all ready?" [G + *kaì katíschysen* 'and he succeeded' (*ischýō*) or 'shut it off' (*échō*)]. 30 Such was the Hezekiah who stopped up the upper fount of waters of Gihon [G Sion] and directed them to 'a lower point more westerly in relation to' [G pool of] the Davidic city.

Two empirical data of the case are known from modern exploration: the tunnel, and its inscription. The inscription near the Siloam issue at the south end of the tunnel was found by boys at play in 1880. It was on a side wall where the native rock had been smoothed off over an area of 29 by 67 cm, of which only the lower half was occupied by six lines of writing. This block was detached and removed to Istanbul, where it is now on the second floor of the classical (not Near East) museum, and can be visited only with advance permit, difficult to secure, allegedly because of the frailty of the flooring.

Content of the inscription is vivid but tantalizingly laconic. If our reading or translation of the Hebrew strives neither to imply nor to exclude more than the text itself does regarding the idiomatic expression "man to his brother," we may find ourselves forced to corroborate the now universal assumption of two teams working toward each other from opposite ends of the tunnel. But we should ask ourselves whether the text itself contains any expression incompatible with an assumption that the hewers and callers were together and cutting in the same direction. "While 'it' was being cut, the voice of one man calling to another three cubits away was heard . . . the excavators hewed toward one another, axe against axe, and the water flowed from the spring toward the pool, 1200 cubits [1750 ft, 533 m], 100 cubits below the rock surface over the workers' heads."[6]

The inscription does not mention Hezekiah or any historical event even remotely datable. In fact we may generalize that apart from the (Kings) notice that Hezekiah made a canal for the (Gihon) spring, we would have no archeological ground for dating this tunnel any more accurately than we do for the extension of the southern wall to the southwest hill, controverted over a period of 1,300 years.[7] Paleography of the letters fits between the Moabite Stone 830 B.C. and the Lachish Letters 589 B.C. This estimate—taking in stride the fact that the former is in a different dialect and the latter in a different medium—scarcely ties us down to the time of Hezekiah.

The canal itself was excavated and cleared by an expedition under Montagu Parker. His work was never published because it was suddenly and definitively interrupted under suspicion of misdemeanor, presumably the intention of penetrating forbidden areas under the Muslim sanctuary on the nearby Temple area. But Père Hugues Vincent was *au courant* as adviser of the work, and while defending the excavator's integrity he provides a relatively complete account. He narrates vividly how the hardships caused for Siloam villagers by the expedition's blocking up the tunnel flow from Gihon were ended by an acclaim for the renewed pouring forth of the waters, which must have been very like the excitement recorded in the inscription.[8] Barrois considers evident from the present-day appearance of the tunnel itself that it was built by crews working independently from opposite directions.[9] But the only real fact on which this judgment can be based is an unevenness near the midpoint, noticeable enough in itself but not enough to exclude some casual error or obstacle, and in any case trifling in comparison with the incredible accuracy of the supposed independent crews.

The tunnel has remained open to the public—that is, to occasional scholars—naturally with some inconvenience and repugnance for the users of the water. A group can walk in either direction in about twenty minutes; flashlights and sandals are desirable, as well as bathing trunks, though the water rarely reaches above the knees except near the two accesses. The canal floor is remarkably level, with a carefully calculated slight downward slope, and with occasional sharp pebbles strewn about. The ceiling is generally about six feet high, but with notable variations. The canal is S-shaped, and takes 533 m (1,750 ft = 1200 cubits) to cover the 335 m (1100 ft) in a straight line from Gihon to Siloam.[10] In the supposition of two teams working from opposite directions, it was a well-nigh incredible feat of technology to meet head-on so accurately, even if the line had been straight. No hypothesis as to the reason for the S-shape has rallied consensus; there are both interest and difficulty in the claim that some tombs far above were to be avoided.

Infinitely more perplexing is the question of whether the Siloam egress of the tunnel was inside the city wall. This was indubitable, according to Barrois. But most experts find the relevant excavated data exasperatingly ambiguous. The two major recent researches maintain that only around the time of Hezekiah himself was the south wall of the Davidic city extended from the east to the west hill.[11] Some date this as early as David himself or even the Jebusites.[12] But a post-Nehemiah dating has gained wide support.[13] The extreme dating was that of Albright—as late as the time of Herod.[14] But the recent excavations of Miss Kenyon now claim certitude for a date nearly a hundred years later.[15]

Comparing now the facts with the Chronicles report, we find that the name Gihon is explicit only there, along with a less obvious clue that it is "upper" in relation not only to the unnamed egress but also to a second water source available a half mile farther south at Rogel.[16] However, the unlikelihood that "the water source of Jerusalem" could be taken as anything other than Gihon is made clear already in the Chronicler's vs 3. The Kings parallel in fact describes the enterprise more concretely than a proper name could have done, with technical terms like "tunnel" and "pool" not in Chronicles.[17] As for "the wadi which floods over inside the land," this is usually taken to refer to that open-air channel which had already been made earlier to carry Gihon's waters farther southward.[18] No fault can be found with that interpretation, but it adds no information either; if the spring itself was diverted, its waters would no longer flow where they had hitherto flowed. But *naḥal* usually means "wadi," and may well refer to Kidron itself as the location of the spring.[19] *Šāṭap* may indeed mean just "flow," but its nuance of overflow would better fit the rare wadi torrents than the slight variations in volume of water issuing from Gihon.

We will conclude that the essential fact is narrated in Kings concisely and on the whole more informatively. Differences in Chronicles consist in making explicit or rambling or ambiguous what was knowable from the Kings text. Thus, whatever archeological data support the Chronicles variants support a fortiori the Kings narrative from which the whole informational content was or could have been derived. But there is no evidence other than the biblical text itself (if we leave wishful thinking out of account) that the tunnel was built within 500 years on either side of Hezekiah, or that its inscription can be dated more narrowly than within 200 years on either side of him.

This attained, we may fully accept the terms in which Noth proposes three cognate cases to stand or fall with the validity of the tunnel-document supposition. The same or a similar transmitted source would have included also the data on other installations of defensive scope attributed to Judean kings in Chronicles but not in Kings: Rehoboam, 2 Chron 11: 5–10; Uzziah, 2 Chron 26: 9–15; Manasseh, 2 Chron 33: 14a.[20] Noth finds these three examples to be detailed by the Chronicler in a way which distinguishes them from similar observations of military preparedness which he could have glibly supplied from his inner awareness of what normally happens, or generalized from the above "documented" notices: 2 Chron 11: 11 f (with part of vs 10); 14: 5 ff; 17: 2, 12–19; 25: 5; 26: 11–14; 27: 3 f; 33: 14b.

Josiah's Death: 2 Chron 35: 20–24 || 2 Kings 23: 29 f

2 Kings 23: 29. In the days of [Josiah], Pharaoh Neco king of Egypt went up on behalf of [*ʿal* in sense implied by Gadd Chronicle, not 'against'] the king of Assyria to the river Euphrates. So Josiah went to intercept him. But he [G Nechao] killed him at sight at Megiddo [G Magedō]. 30 His retainers drove him away dead from Megiddo [G^B Makedōn]. They brought him to Jerusalem and buried him 'with a funeral' [or 'in a tomb', G *táphos* also ambivalent] of his own.

2 Chron 35: 20. After all these consolidations of the Temple on the part of Josiah, Neco king of Egypt came up to join the battle 'at Carchemish, *ʿal*' [>G^{AB}] Euphrates. Josiah went out to intercept him. 21 He however had sent to him this message: "What affair is this of yours, king of Judah? You are not minding [*ʿal*] your own business [G, S, V: I am not moving against you] today, but 'against the house of' [G to make] my quarrel. Elohim has said [so] to my 'dismay' [or as G 'hastening']. Lay off of Elohim who is with me. Otherwise he will destroy you." 22 But Josiah did not turn back from him. In order to do battle with him,

he 'disguised himself'[21] [G withstood]. He refused to listen to Neco's observations coming from Elohim. On he came, to the battle in Megiddo plain. 23 The archers promptly shot down King Josiah. Then the king said to his retainers, "Bear me away; I am on my last legs". 24 His retainers transferred him from his chariot and drove him in the spare chariot he had brought along. They brought him to Jerusalem. There he died, and was buried amid the tombs of his fathers. All Judah along with Jerusalem bewailed Josiah.

Noth admits frankly that the Chronicler's genuine additions to the Kings report are here harder to detect amid much that is mere paraphrase. Everything about the mode of the king's wounding can be dismissed as a perhaps subconscious echo of the similar situation of Ahab's death in 2 Chron 18: 33 = 1 Kings 22: 34. Similarly, the Chronicler's own musings can be seen in the curious moralizing about Josiah's punishment for not obeying a message transmitted by pharaoh from Elohim. We may admit that the factual details are "supplied by theological reasoning" from the Chronicler's own imagination.[22] In that case, we need feel no concern about who this alleged "god" was: the Elohim of the Hebrews or some one of the many gods of the pharaohs. It may have been the divine symbols on standards of the Egyptian army.[23] Venerable authorities even suspect the Assyrian king (= *ilani*) involved here.[24]

Strangely, Noth does not single out the Chronicler's detail that only after reaching Jerusalem did Josiah expire, which others hold to be historically factual.[25] Ultimately his only real talking point is the purpose of Neco's expedition, which is given by the Chronicler so vaguely that it escapes the positive inaccuracy which Noth attributes to Kings as disproved by the Gadd Chronicle.[26] Insofar as the Chronicler frequently garbles the concise Kings data by rotund rhetoric, we can hardly be surprised to see his vagueness occasionally diverging less palpably from some known minor detail than the Deuteronomist's exactness. But Noth can scarcely have overlooked that *'al* may equally well mean "for" (as Gadd) or "against" (as G), exactly like our deplorably ambiguous English "fight *with*."[27] Presuming that Josephus *Antiquities* 10 (74 ff) 5, 1 has before him the Greek text of both Kings and Chronicles, we find even less reason for Noth's further supposition that Josephus was using a third source distinct from that of either biblical report.[28]

Here again, supposing as proved the existence of a factual documentation underlying the Chronicler's report, Noth adds minor battle reports which gain likelihood from it for the reason that "they just don't *look* like the Chronicler's inventions": 2 Chron 13: 3–20 (omitting the adverse judgment of 1 Kings 15: 3–5); 14: 8–14; 26: 6–8; 27: 5; 28: 18. Noth reckons loyally with the fact that these instances, and especially the first two, may owe their lifelikeness to the Chronicler's recollections of a real battle which took place near his own time. He can project it back into a historic situation which he deems similar, just as the author of Jubilees attributes Maccabee battle traits to Jacob.[29] Gladly we agree with Noth that there is something realistic about these battle descriptions; this would not indeed be beyond the literary skill of a counterfeiter, but simply does not fit into this particular author's creativity. Yet the point at issue, highlighted by Noth himself, remains: whether the minor episodes gain historical reliability from the archeologically proved force of the test case freely chosen by him.[30] We here find the data for the test case less cogent than for the daughter cases.

TOPONYMY: 2 CHRON 20: 1–30 (NOT || 2 KINGS 3: 4–27)

This chapter is quite emphatically claimed by Noth to be a transformation of 2 Kings 3: 4–27, though that Jehoram-Jehoshaphat campaign is located elsewhere by Vannutelli and related back, rather, to 2 Chron 18: 1–34, which has its own parallel in 1 Kings 22: 1–40.[31] Noth's book does not cite his own lengthy article spelling out details of the same conclusions, except perhaps for a more vague equating with 2 Kings 3.[32] He formally excludes this passage from his test cases, and indeed from any relevance to the search for the Chronicler's written sources at all, because he thinks that the variants from Kings here are due to a tradition known indeed to the Chronicler but local and oral.[33] But we must take into account the extent to which the whole Bible was composed normatively in oral form (for which the early written equivalent served chiefly as a memory aid, like our systems of musical notation).[34] In any case, much of the detective work which would enable us to intuit in the variants empirical information not drawn from the Chronicler's own head would be just as relevant to oral as to written source determination.

The main factual empirical content is found to be in 2 Chron 20: 2, "Hazazon-Tamar which is En-Gedi." Though the Chronicler "had no more idea than we do where the *real* Hazazon-Tamar of Gen 14: 7 was located," he in fact rightly associated with En-Gedi this name preserved in wadi Haṣâṣa of Nabatean Ma'ôn, which constitutes the upper origins of the wadi Yassâra (176.108 Israel Survey grid), north of En-Gedi. In vs 27 of the same chapter may be noted also the toponym Beracah, "blessing": representative sample of the "etiology" for which Noth's *Josua* has become normative.[35]

Toponymic reasoning like the foregoing may serve as a model for the type of archeological topography that has characterized the century between Robinson and Abel.[36] To locate an unidentified toponym related in a biblical passage to a known metropolis, a noncommittal list is made of all discoverable Arab place-names in a wide circuit around that area. If one turns out to have the same consonants (taking into account normal ablaut between Hebrew and Arabic), then a check is made at the spot: not necessarily the exact spot, but within a radius to which toponyms are known to "migrate." If there are found features of terrain and artifacts compatible with the biblical episode and chronology, then a working hypothesis is laid down. Further inferences regarding either that episode or other occurrences of the name are then drawn, and gradually, as "it all hangs together" with no contradictions creeping in, the hypothesis is taken to be a fact. It then is no longer important how frail the original guess was, because the assurance now lies in a convergence of empirical compatibilities: a sound and normal procedure of the inductive sciences.

Here are similar geographical details divergently given in Chronicles from its parallels, and recently clarified by archeology. Moriah ("mountain;" Gen 22: 2 "land") is attested only by 2 Chron 3: 1 (relevant to Solomon; not David, 1 Chron 21: 15) as name or fortuitous homonym of the Jebusite crest acquired as temple area. Vincent upholds with rabbinic tradition that Abraham from near Beersheba could have gone with Isaac as far as Jerusalem.[37] Glueck denies it.[38] It may be noted that (*har*) *ha-môriyyâ* (Aram *amoriyy-â*) could mean "mountain of the Amorite," which may well be what the Chronicler intended to write.[39] In payment of temple materials, Solomon gave Hiram some cities near the Tyre-Dan border (1 Kings 9: 10). But 2 Chron 8: 2 knows only cities given not by Solomon but to him by "Huram." Maybe Hiram, either dissatisfied (1 Kings 9: 13: followed by Hiram's implausible compensation to Solomon) or otherwise indemnified, just gave back the cities. The border towns seem related to the other "Huram son of a Tyrian father and Danite mother" sent by King Huram as architect in 2 Chron 2: 14. The "Valley of Salt" where David defeated Edom (1 Chron 18: 12) and Amaziah massacred hordes of Seir and Sela (both = Petra; 2 Chron 25: 11) is too similar to the parallel (2 Sam 8: 13; 2 Kings 14: 7) to shed light on whether we are here dealing with "Salt-City" of Josh 15: 62 = Qumran.[40] This Seir is doubtless distinct from the one near Baalah [and] Kiriath-jearim.[41] The Greek of 1 Chron 18: 17 omits the "Cherethites" or Cretans cognate to (?Philistine) Pelethites in David's bodyguard.[42]

Other examples abound in the "genealogical vestibule" 1 Chron 1–9, recently treated (with Gen parallels) as an artificial production in support of David's claims.[43] Noth devotes many pages to this prologue under the heading "post-Chronicler insertions," which might blind us to the fact that he firmly makes the essential lines of an "Adam-to-David history by cue-names" in Chapter 1 an indispensable part of the Chronicler's overall plan. It gathers up incidentally much of the biblical ethnography.[44] The verses 2 on Kenan, 5 Javan, 7 Kittim, 8 Canaan, and 17 f Shem-Eber are prominent in recent researches beyond our present scope.[45] We have treated elsewhere relation of Ophir (1: 23) and the man Tarshish (7: 10) to the "Tarshish (i. e. far-)sailing ships" sent by Solomon to "Ophir" (2 Chron 8: 18 = Parvaim, 2 Chron 3: 6).[46] "Ophir gold for Beth-horon" is attested at excavations near Joppe, alleged to corroborate also the unparalleled 2 Chron 2: 16 as base for cedar transshipment though north of the Yarqon River.[47] Israel's northeast boundary *Lᵉbôʾ-Ḥamat* under David (1 Chron 13: 5; cf 18: 3) and Solomon (2 Chron 7: 8; 8: 3; cf 9: 26) is unduly stretched by the reading Tadmor (Palmyra, 8: 3): the vaguely parallel 1 Kings 9: 18 reads Tamar (near Baalah, probably that of Kiriath-jearim in 1 Chron 13: 6).[48]

A link with the Essenes and Qumran may be provided by Rechab of 1 Chron 2: 55 (2: 44 Rekem; 4: 12 Recah) and Jer 35: 2.[49] This Rechab is related to Cain and the Kenites, thus also to Kenaz (Teman, Edom, 1: 51; ?Nebaiot 1: 29), Midian (1: 32, 46), Amalek (4: 43).[50] This Kenite background adds another link of David's Bethlehem to Calebite Hebron; the seven different genealogies given for "somebody named Caleb" in 1 Chron 2–4 may perhaps be homogenized by supposing Jephunneh to be a village rather than a patronym, as in 2: 50 ff.[51] Caleb's congener Mareshah occurring in the second half of 1 Chron 2: 42 is replaced in the first half by Mesha (G variants: Mousa, Marousa), a name too momentous in 2 Kings 3: 5 to be dismissed as just a slip.[52] The Ephraim towns in 1 Chron 7: 28 curiously include Gezer and even Gaza (ʿAzza for ʿAyya) in the Talmud variant adopted in the earliest printed Bibles. The Ḥuppim of 1 Chron 7: 12 (with Šuppim) corroborates the reading of Gen 46: 21 (with Muppim) against Num 26: 39 Ḥuppam [with Šup(p)am], if plausibly equated with the modern-sounding Akkadian *ḫipi* = "so-and-so." Gozan is a river in 1 Chron 5: 26, or a town on a river, but distinct from Ḥabor, which in 2 Kings 17: 6; 18: 11 is the "river of Gozan" at Tell Ḥalaf, Oppenheim's epochal excavation.[53]

Manasseh's Salvific Arrest: 2 Chron 33: 10–17 (2 Kings 21: 10–16; 20: 18).

We add as the fourth test case one which Noth intentionally excludes (except for half of vs 14 allotted to the tunnel document above). The first half of the chapter devoted to Manasseh in both Kings and Chronicles narrates the same sordid vices, syncretist idolatry, and "passing his sons through fire."[54] But the latter part differs radically in the two reports:

2 Kings 21: 10. YHWH by means of his servants the prophets spoke thus: 11 Because Manasseh king of Judah has committed these abominations, piling up evil beyond the measure of the Amorites before him, and seducing Judah into sin with his idols, 12 therefore thus has YHWH God of Israel said: "See, I am bringing evil upon Jerusalem and Judah, such evil as will make both ears ring for anyone who hears of it. 13 I will stretch over Jerusalem the line by which Samaria was measured, and the plumb-line which was hung over Ahab's house. I will wipe out Jerusalem the way a man wipes off a plate, wipes it and turns it upside down. 14 I will abandon the remnant of my inheritance; I will turn them over to their enemies; they shall be plunder and prey to all their foes: 15 because they have done evil to my face, and have spited me ever since the day their fathers fared forth from Egypt and right down to this day. 16 Manasseh has shed innocent blood, far too much; it has filled Jerusalem from one edge to the other, quite apart from the outrage which he had done to my face by leading Judah into sin."

20: 18. [Isaiah to Hezekiah] "Your sons will be seized and castrated in the royal palace of Babylon."

2 Chron 33: 10. YHWH spoke to Manasseh and his people, but they would not listen. 11 So YHWH brought upon them the generals of the Royal Assyrian Army. They seized Manasseh with halberds and flung him in irons. Thus they brought him all the way to Babylon. 12 He however in his crisis besought the face of YHWH his God. He was humbled indeed in the sight of the God of his fathers. 13 To him he prayed, and was heard. God hearkened to his plea. All the way back to Jerusalem he brought him, back to his royal throne. Thus Manasseh realized that YHWH is indeed God. 14 He thereupon rebuilt the outer wall of the Davidic city, on the slope west of Gihon along the access to the Fish Gate. It continued on around Ophel; he increased its height considerably. He furthermore installed armed guards in all the fortified cities of Judah. 15 Naturally he got rid of the gods of the foreigner. Their statues he flung out of the Temple. As for all the altars which he himself had built upon the very Temple crest and elsewhere in Jerusalem, he had their rubble dumped outside the city. 16 The altar of YHWH however he refurbished, to offer upon it sacrifices of communion and gratitude. Judah too he invited to the cultus of YHWH God of Israel. 17 Nevertheless the people went right on sacrificing on the high-places, only claiming it was in honor of YHWH their God.

For many commentators, this passage is better than either of Noth's as touchstone of the Chronicler's use of factual documentation beyond his parallels. Myers and Randellini see no escape from postulating for the Babylonian repentance a free invention of the Chronicler. But, like Robert, they would call this a warranted theological syllogism rather than, as Pfeiffer and Torrey have, a blatant hoax. For the Chronicler, it is simply impossible that evil should be rewarded with longevity; hence, somewhere along the line the longest-reigning of all Judah's monarchs must have mended his ways, and ("as everybody knows") downfall is the likeliest occasion for tears of remorse. The invented repentance is commonly held to have prompted the equally fictitious "Psalm of Manasseh."[55] Only Cazelles has hazarded the intriguing observation that the psalm had already come into existence first, from the meditations of a theologian with views on retribution similar to the Chronicler's, who then could lift it from him ready-made.[56]

The willingness of Myers and Randellini to admit some creativeness in the Chronicler's use of the data in this chapter is the more noteworthy since they, like Noth, feel that at least part of the later Judah rebuilding comes from a reliable document.[57] They both (like Galling and Rudolph) point to Assyrian sources which attest temporary arrest of vassal kings for briefing at the palace.[58] But be it noted that all these allegations reinforce rather than diminish the likelihood that the fact of Mannasseh's own arrest is learned by the Chronicler by theological inference rather than from the materials in his sources or in historical reality.[59] Rudolph rather confidently rejects the possibility that the major premise of his syllogism was precisely Isaiah's threat to Manasseh's father cited in 2 Kings 20: 18.[60] Short shrift is made also of several Catholic attempts to vindicate the historicity of the repentance and Jerusalem purge by supposing it to have been quickly abandoned.[61]

Moreover, Manasseh is mentioned by name in an Ashurbanipal fragment, as Myers had noted. It is one of those reconstructed as "Cylinder A" supplementary to the Rassam Cylinder.[62] Rassam 1, 25 gives the name and domain of each of the twenty-two kings mentioned anonymously in Rassam 1,65 as forced to accompany Ashurbanipal (668–633 B.C.) on a punitive expedition to Egypt; he then returned (? still taking them along) to Nineveh. Meanwhile Ehrlich pointed out that the unexpected naming of Babylon in 2 Chron 33: 11 corresponds to the fact that in the year 648 B.C. Ashurbanipal, after a two-year siege, had crushed his rival Šamaš-šum-ukin there and had sent to summon Manasseh from Jerusalem as one of the vassals supporting the uprising.[63] Only in the years 652–48 B.C. could Manasseh have had any chance to act otherwise than with that loyalty he is otherwise attested showing toward Assyria. Ehrlich does not mention the Cylinder A inscription, and bases himself rather on policies of Assyrian kings generalized from other examples, including even the Rassam Cylinder, concerning pardon granted to an arrested king (Neco) after he had been suitably enlightened in Assyria. Ehrlich's historical intuition is interesting, but is based on no documented mention of Manasseh; the mention of Manasseh which is found in Esarhaddon-Ashurbanipal records says nothing of his being brought to Mesopotamia. So there is no real confirmation of the historicity of the deportation, much less of a written source from which the Chronicler drew it as a fact.

We thus conclude our exposition of the four passages which have best claim to be normative in proving a dependence of the Chronicler upon extracanonical written sources either already or foreseeably corroborated by excavation and exploration. Like Manasseh's repentance and Josiah's fatal flaw, the following details are often such that their relevance to archeology could only be secondary, via inference or inscriptions.

Temple Materials, Zadok, and Wise Chant

The Temple is in general far more the achievement of David for the Chronicler than in Kings, and it is much more the focus of his life's interest. David is called the seventh son of Jesse in 1 Chron 2: 15, whereas in 1 Sam 17: 12 he is the eighth; it has been proposed that Elihu of 1 Chron 27: 18 is omitted because he had no descendants. Randellini concludes rather with Rudolph to an extrabiblical source, "since if he was just inventing the names he could easily have invented an eighth." Saul's suicide upon his squire's refusal to kill him is told in 1 Sam 31: 4 as in 1 Chron 10: 4, though, in hope of benefit, the squire reports the episode differently to David in 2 Sam 1: 10: only Saul's head is put on the Dagon temple in 1 Chron 10: 10; in 1 Sam 31: 9 it is his headless trunk. The whole "crime *does* pay" chapter of necromancy in 1 Sam 28 is summarized in the single verse 1 Chron 10: 13.[64] If a similar reference to the occult lurks in 1 Chron 12: 32 "skill in knowing the times" (astrology: Targum), it has been expressed vaguely enough to suggest rather political savvy (Rudolph).

David begins his reign over the northern kingdom, and moves from Hebron to Jerusalem, immediately after Saul's death in 1 Chron 11: 4, though 29: 27 does not ignore the seven-year lag at Hebron filled with fascinating episodes in 2 Sam 2–4. Then in the siege of Jerusalem, 1 Chron 11: 6 omits the *ṣinnôr*, which, despite well-grounded archeological acclaim for the "water-shaft" (RSV), is more objectively rendered "pipe" ("grappling-hook," *NEB*; G *paraxiphís*).[65] Details from real but separate episodes [1 Chron 11: 23, 26 (= 2 Sam 23: 21, 24); 20: 5 (2 Sam 21: 19)] involving an Elḥanan son of Dodo or Jair, also David himself and his nephew, a (Beth-) Lehemite, and giants of Egypt and Gath: all seem to have been contaminated intc the David-glorifying narrative of 1 Sam 17, omitted by the Chronicler because it shows David a killer. The list of 1 Chron 11 which furnishes part of the above evidence is claimed to betray in vss 41–47, after Uriah, an East Jordan origin.[66]

To a general prudishness of the Chronicler is traced his omission of David's nudity as the source of Michal's contempt (2 Sam 6: 20; not in 1 Chron 15: 27 ff).[67] Vital to the allegation of a "Third Source" used more faithfully by the Chronicler than by the Deuteronomist are the dynastic promise of 1 Chron 17, with its parallels in 2 Sam 7 and Ps 89: 19–37, and the suppression of 2 Sam 7: 14 conditions and threats in 2 Chron 6: 10.[68] David's census in 1 Chron 21: 1 is prompted by Satan; in 2 Sam 24: 1, by angry YHWH as a trap; its close relation to the plague of 1 Chron 21: 14 = 2 Sam 24: 15 is ingeniously and, with surprising naturalness, related by Myers to an epidemic caused by germ-laden census takers trudging from one town to another. In this same census, as is later noted in 1 Chron 27: 23 f without Kings parallel, David made no effort to count minors under the age of twenty; this may perhaps reflect the age of liturgical service in 1 Chron 23: 27 (Ezra 3: 8) and the curious variants this undergoes at Qumran.[69]

David may have bought the Temple site from a Hittite.[70] The Temple stones were hewn: 1 Chron 22: 2 not in Kings and against Ex 20: 25. Height of the Temple pylon in 2 Chron 3: 4 (180 feet) is not mentioned in 1 Kings 6: 2, but the building itself is said only there to have been forty-five feet high; such a towering pylon does not seem disproportionate to Egyptian standards surviving at Karnak and Idfu from earlier styles generally held to have guided Solomon.[71] Free standing sphinxes (*k^e^rûbîm*, 2 Chron 3: 10 = 1 Kings 8: 7) with wings outspread over the Ark surely seem better than lid scratchings (1 Sam 4: 4; Ex 25: 17; perhaps by analogy with other cherubs carved on the *walls*, 2 Chron 3: 7); these and the seraphim of Is 6: 2 carry forward a long tradition of "God rushing into battle on cloud-wings of unemployed *elohim* drawing his ark-throne chariot."[72] We are famished to know what was really inside the Ark; "the ten commandments and nothing else," says 2 Chron 5: 10 in agreement with 1 Kings 8: 9; Deut 10: 1; but Heb 9: 4 and plausible Arab *qubba* parallels lead us to suspect that the contents may have been either ephod-urim or sacral emptiness.[73]

The "3000 baths contained in the priests' washing-tub called Bronze Sea" is inexorably confusing in the English of 2 Chron 4: 5. Bath is a liquid measure of some twenty-four quarts corresponding to the dry measure called ephah.[74] Only two thousand baths are given for the same vessel in 1 Kings 7: 26, which may be the result of calculating its three dimensions as a hemisphere ($V = \frac{1}{3} Cr^2$) while the Chronicler calculates them as a cylinder ($V = \frac{1}{2} Crh$).[75] Hiram agreed to float timbers (1 Kings 5: 6) of cedar and pine and algum (added in 2 Chron 2: 8 along with "via Joppe = ?Qasila" in vs 16).[76] The Temple area was to be 60 × 20 "old standard" cubits (2

Chron 3: 3). This was rather small if meant as 17.5 inches, in contrast to the "royal cubit" known from Herodotus 1,178: possibly understood also in Ezek 40: 5 as "a (normal) cubit plus a palm"—some twenty inches. Responsibility for the whole archeological crux of weights and measures is thrown on the Levites by 1 Chron 23: 29, not in Kings.

Metallurgy too, at this critical threshold of transit from the Bronze Age to the Iron Age, is prominent in relation to the "bath"-tub called "the sea". The bronze for the tub came from Zobah cities conquered by David (1 Chron 18: 8); vs 10 adds that fringe benefits from the conquest of Zobah were gifts of gold and silver and copper from relieved Hamath. The bronze for Huram's art work was cast at Solomon's foundry between Succoth and Zeredah (2 Chron 4: 17; G: Anamesirdathai; 1 Kings 7: 46 Zarethan, G: Seira). All this time the Philistine monopoly of iron (1 Sam 13: 20; not in Chron), only recently noticed, has been taken as a key factor pushing the Israelites from judgeship-anarchy into kingship.[77] However, the Tyro-Danite Huram sent by his homonymous king in 2 Chron 2: 14 is called an experienced worker in iron (as well as in bronze, 1 Kings 7: 2). David in fact had stored up tons of iron to make nails and hinges for the Temple doors, imagines 1 Chron 22: 3, 14 f without Kings parallel. This was in addition to the hundred thousand talents of iron gathered up from the families within Israel (1 Chron 29: 2, 7). Already in his previous military operations, David had set the defeated Ammonites to work with iron picks (1 Chron 20: 3; also in 2 Sam 12: 31). On that occasion he took a one-talent gold crown from the statue of Milcom in the Ammonite capital; this doubtless came in handy when he paid Ornan six hundred shekels of gold (1 Chron 21: 25; only fifty of silver in 2 Sam 24: 24).[78] The shekel weighed only half an ounce, or twelve grams; used as money in doubtless baser metal, it amounted to a half-dollar in current values. Solomon paid 150 shekels each ($75) for his horses from Egypt (2 Chron 1: 17; only $25 in 1 Kings 10: 33); the going rate in other lands is not noted. Among the free local contributions of gold, David got ten thousand anachronistic darics in 1 Chron 29: 6; that coin, worth five dollars in modern terms, was invented by Darius five hundred years later (Ezra 8: 27; ?2: 69). The Ophir from which David got gold in 1 Chron 29: 4 we above claimed to be identical with Parvaim 2 Chron 3: 6 (neither name is in the Kings parallel).

Seizure of Jerusalem as eventual Temple site is related to the mysterious eclipse of Abiathar's priesthood by Zadok. In 1 Chron 16: 39, Zadok is called priest "left" rather than "installed" by David at Gibeon, or rather at its High Place (? Nebi Samwîl; = ? Nob of Ahimelech, 1 Sam 21: 1). This Gibeon, founded by Benjamite Jehiel (1 Chron 9: 35; cf 8: 29; no ||) served as semiofficial sanctuary (2 Chron 1: 3, expanding 1 Kings 3: 7) between the floruits of Shiloh and Zion.[79] Hence there was good reason for maintaining that the Zadok "confirmed for Israelite cult" in place of high priest Abiathar of the Ithamar line was in fact a Canaanite through whom a politically influential sanctuary could be exploited for theocratic worship of YHWH.[80] In this Zadok's genealogy, only summarily hinted in 2 Sam 8: 17, Ahitub should be not his progenitor but Abiathar's along with Ahimelech, as in 1 Sam 22: 11 (Wellhausen).[81] Ahimelech is Abiathar's son in 1 Chron 18: 16. The combination "Zadok ben-Ahitub" is indeed given twice elsewhere and traced back to Phinehas-Eleazar-Aaron-Levi in 1 Chron 6: 8–12; 24: 3, but at several removes both before and after the priest of Solomon's temple explicitly declared to be one Azariah (but Ahitub grandfather of Zadok in 9: 11). These genealogical quirks are rightly seen to show that Zadok is "without genealogy," which, according to Heb 7: 3, he has in common with Melchizedek.[82] Indeed that name is identical or dynastically similar to "king Zadok, *melek Ṣadoq*"; and Melchizedek was worshiper of "God most high" (Ps 9: 3), acknowledged by Abraham at "(Jeru-)Salem," Gen 14: 18. Hence Rowley's further conclusion is warranted: Zadok was the pre-Israelite priest not at Gibeon but at Jebus = Zion.[83] To this we have added that the defense of Jebus crag only by "blind and lame" (2 Sam 5: 8) is best explained as Zadok's token resistance in exchange for a secret deal with David assuring to his descendants a dynastic dignity second only to the king's. Both the promise of eventual priesthood to Phinehas in Num 26: 11 and the specific names relating him to Zadok are thus a legitimate "legal adoption." Similarly, the genealogy of Moses (1 Chron 6: 22; 6: 3 = Num 26: 58 f) is a juridical straightening out of his enigmatic relation to Aaron and Miriam ("Aaron's sister," not his, in Ex 15: 20).[84] Moses' grandsons are called priests in Judg 18: 30; but few would follow the consistency of making Moses himself (Ex 18: 12) a priest.[85] Moses is further involved in the Davidic rise to power insofar as Caleb lost Hebron to "Aaron's grandfather Kohath" (1 Chron 6: 55; Ex 6: 18 ff).[86]

Zadok in 1 Chron 16: 41 is closely associated with Heman and Jeduthun, whose genealogy links the Chronicler's own family to David's psalmody, Solomon's wisdom, and Job's topography. Music directors for the temple were already appointed by David himself (2 Chron 5: 12): Asaph, Jeduthun, and Heman (1 Chron 25: 1, 6), and their sons, especially Heman's (whose names make up a little poem in 25: 4).[87] These are of Levite descent in 1 Chron 15: 17 ff. But in 2: 6 there is a Heman descendant of Judah, brother of Ethan, Calcol, Dara, all nephews of Hamul.[88] These (Darda for Dara) are the pre-Solomonic paragons of wisdom in 1 Kings 4: 31, but their father is (? by metathesis) Mahol.[89] Heman and Ethan are named authors of Ps 88 and 89; Asaph, of 73–83 and 50.[90] Ethan is commonly taken to be a variant of Jeduthun, and is called *ezraḥi*. This is equated with the local or proper name of 1 Chron 2: 6, but may mean just "the native." Albright maintains this to mean Canaanite.[91] But there is an Edomite Zerah in Gen 36: 17, and the place-names of Job are linked in tenuous traditions to East Jordan; hence there has been launched a hypothesis of "Edomite Wisdom."[92] Thus there seems to be more to link the Psalmody and Wisdom traditions together than the blood of David in Solomon. The psalm of Asaph in 1 Chron 16: 25 "YHWH is more to be feared than all gods" is echoed in Solomon's letter to Huram (2 Chron 2: 5) "our god is greater than all gods" (6: 13: "O YHWH, there is no god like you"), whereas Huram replies with a much more acceptable theology, "Blessed is YHWH the God of Israel, the maker of heaven and earth" (2 Chron 2: 12). Solomon's pious explanation of the palace he built for Pharaoh's daughter—"No woman of mine shall live in the house of David, because any place where the Ark has entered is holy"—suggested Myers' charming subtitle, "Moving Day for the Daughter of Pharaoh." *Whose* daughter she was continues to agitate the Bureau of Missing Persons.[93]

The Split Kingdoms and Their Arithmetic Problems

Jeroboam's social-justice strivings against Solomon's corvée are ignored by the Chronicler. The Samaria whose independence gets reasserted in Jeroboam (2 Chron 10: 16) had been entrusted to David only to administer as a second fief, and the offer would have been continued if Rehoboam had shown some sense. To intercept politico-economic aspects of YHWH-pilgrimage flow southward to Zion, Jeroboam set up at Bethel and Dan the normal YHWH-throne bull sphinx (= "cherub"), whose implications were distorted by 1 Kings 12: 28 describing it in terms borrowed from the golden calf of Ex 32: 4.[94] 2 Chron notes only in passing these demonic calves (11: 13; 13: 8), along with the theologumenon that not only all priests and Levites in Jeroboam's domain, abandoning their livelihood, but also all nonapostate laymen came to live in Judah and thus strengthened Rehoboam's reign.

Huge numbers are attributed to southern victories in skirmishes with the north; in 2 Chron 13: 17, Abijah felled 500,000 picked Israelites, "and the rest were reduced to submission" (inference from 16: 12?); in 17: 14, Jehoshaphat had a standing army of a million crack troops in Jerusalem alone plus others in the provinces. Refusal of burial with the other kings to Jehoram, Joash, Uzziah, Ahaz (21: 20; 24: 25; 26: 23; 28: 27) is coupled with clear insistence on burial of kings within the urban area (21: 20, Jehoram, as 1 Kings 15: 8, Abijam); popular convictions to the contrary are not confirmed by archeology.[95] Authenticity of the Uzziah gravestone has been claimed defensible only in the rather ad hoc supposition of a reburial monument.[96] The name of this king is given sometimes as Azariah, perhaps because of a transfer from his priest-regent.[97]

The chronology of Asa in 16: 12 (along with his Christian Science sin of seeking medical assistance) is claimed superior to 1 Kings 20: 34.[98] (Variants of 2 Chron 17–24 concern only indirectly a new Jehoash chronology inscription.[99]) But such claims can hardly stand except in an overall theory of the thorny monarchy dating norms.[100] Asa's reported destruction of dowager Maacah's Ashera idol (2 Chron 15: 16; as Josiah in 2 Kings 23: 6, 15) is the type of thing on which illuminating archeological finds might be hoped.[101] Jehoram's Judah domination in Edom (21: 8), "in imitation of Ahab up North," we might say, sheds an interesting light on the Mesha inscription noted above, which makes Ahab the unsuccessful suzerain of nearby Moab.

Athaliah, with operatic villainy, instigated her husband Jehoram's murder of all his brothers (21: 4); she is "daughter of Ahab" and of Jezebel (21: 6) and (grand)daughter of Omri in 22: 2 = 2 Kings 8: 26, despite escape from some chronological tangles gained by supposing her Omri's own daughter.[102] Jehoram has brothers whose Persian style names Jehiel and Michael also raise minor chronological suspicions. Athaliah herself also "destroyed all the family of the king" who succeeded Jehoram, his son Ahaziah (22: 10 = 2 Kings 11: 1). Despite the time lag, these two massacres may both refer to a single continuing murderousness, from which, however, as by a Dumas plot, Joash escaped. But he, despite his virtue, lived so short a time that idolatry and sacrilege had to be supplied for him (24: 18, 25; not in Kings).[103]

Hezekiah's reign is a free field for archeological solutions in addition to the tunnel and southwest wall.

The invasion of Sennacherib connected with the tunnel in 32: 2 (but not 32: 30 or its probable source 2 Kings 20: 20) is generally held to have occurred only once, in 701 B.C. But the brief surrender of Hezekiah in 2 Kings 18: 14 ff, omitted in the Isaiah 36: 1 f parallel but corroborated by the chronology of Tirhakah (2 Kings 19: 9) and by Sennacherib's own account (*ANET*, p. 287), induces Bright to postulate a *second* campaign in 688, unmentioned in Assyrian records.[104] It is noteworthy that in 2 Chron 32: 12 (= 2 Kings 18: 22) the foreign agent Rabshakeh ascribes quite explicitly to Hezekiah the cult monopoly long claimed to have been the Deuteronomic (12: 13 f) innovation of Josiah (2 Chron 34: 7, 21; 2 Kings 23: 3 f). No real empirical information or error (van den Born) is involved in making Josiah's reform already well under way when the book was found; he was a child submissive to priests from the beginning of his rule. Excavated objects in

Egypt and Assyria show musicians setting the beat for masons at work; for Temple work it is plausible that such musicians should be Levites, and that this fact should be mentioned by a chronicler who is apparently a Levite musician.[105]

Our principal conclusions may be summarized as follows. Extrabiblical sources of the Chronicler's factual variants may be admitted as a general rule if two or more cases can be empirically proved to correspond to his data better than to the parallels. Four test cases emerge.

The tunnel of Hezekiah is described at greater length in 2 Chron 32: 3, 30 but with no additional information not implicit in 2 Kings 20: 20. Thus neither the inscription nor the exploration of the tunnel corroborates Chronicles better than Kings, or affords a genuine proof that this tunnel was made by teams working from opposite ends or in Hezekiah's time.

The place of Josiah's expiring, given differently in 2 Chron 35: 24 and in 2 Kings 23: 30, and its theological justification, typical of the Chronicler, have received no archeological corroboration despite indecisive details about the "god" Josiah disobeyed; better conformity of 2 Chron 35: 20 to the Gadd Chronicle is due only to its greater vagueness along with misinterpretation of Hebrew *ʿal* in 2 Kings 23: 29.

Geographical precisions like 2 Chron 20: 2; 1 Chron 2: 55; 18: 12, even if due to local traditions known orally to the Chronicler, might justly be attributed to an extrabiblical source; but the numerous interesting cases do not so far pass the bounds of working hypothesis.

A Babylon captivity of Manasseh in 2 Chron 33: 10 is proved neither by his forced accompaniment of Ashurbanipal in Palestine-Egypt nor by Esarhaddon's penchant for bringing refractory vassals to Nineveh; and whatever likelihood of a captivity these Assyrian documents do create is negated rather than supported by the Chronicler's assertion of divine liberation and consequent repentance.

In similar but minor Chronicles variants, we neither found nor expected to find any more cogent proof of source than the four test cases. Unless we have some of our facts wrong or have interpreted them more tendentiously than is done by current consensus, it would follow as a fact that no single use of extrabiblical sources by the Chronicler has ever been proved. From this further follows not the fact but the undeniable possibility that any information communicated to us only by the Chronicler may be due in every case to his own legitimate theological inference or paraphrase from the canonical Scripture.

NOTES

[1] Jacob M. Myers, *I Chronicles* [*II Chronicles, Ezra-Nehemiah*], *AB* 12 [-14] (Garden City: Doubleday, 1965), p. xv; but see also pp. xlix, xxiv, xviii, xx: cited in our appreciation in *CBQ* 28 (1966), 520.

[2] How the dozen sources explicitly cited by the Chronicler can be reduced to a single "Midrash on Kings," whether or not identical with the canonical Sam-Kings [or known to the Chronicler only as already cited in Kings: A. van den Born, *Kronieken* (*De Boeken van het Oude Testament*, 5/3; Roermond: Romen, 1960) 9], must here be presumed from our *Jerome Biblical Commentary* "Chronicles" (Englewood Cliffs, N.J.: Prentice-Hall, 1968), p. 403, or Myers, or any other recent commentary; or the OT Introductions of O. Eissfeldt (Oxford: Blackwell, 1965) pp. 532 ff, and G. Fohrer (London: SPCK, 1970), p. 241; A. Burnet, "Le Chroniste et ses sources," *RB* 60 (1953), 481–508; 61 (1954), 349–86.

[3] "On Right and Wrong Uses of Archaeology," see Roland de Vaux in the Nelson Glueck Festschrift, *Near Eastern Archaeology in the Twentieth Century* (ed. J. Sanders; Garden City: Doubleday, 1970), pp. 64–80; also pp. 268–76, "The Megiddo Stables: a Reassessment," by James B. Pritchard.

[4] Martin Noth, *Überlieferungsgeschichtliche Studien: Die sammelnden und bearbeitenden Geschichtswerke im Alten Testament*[3] (Tübingen: Niemeyer, 1967 = [1]1943) p. 139; p. 133 (our translation). In more specific justification of our limiting the source problem here to the books of Chronicles without the same author's Ezra-Nehemiah, see Frank Michaeli, *Les livres des Chroniques, d'Esdras et de Néhémie* (*Commentaire de l'Ancien Testament*, 16; Neuchâtel: Delachaux, 1967) [Footnotes p. 1], p. 24.

[5] "Unity Passover": W. A. L. Elmslie, "Chronicles," *IB* (Nashville: Abingdon, 1954), 3, p. 537.

[6] Guido Berardi, *Inscriptio Siloam* (facsimile, with explanations of Pietro Boccaccio; Rome: Pontifical Biblical Institute, 1956); trans. of W. F. Albright in *ANET*[3], p. 321; Sabatino Moscati, *L'epigrafia ebraica antica* (*Biblica et orientalia*, 15; Rome: PBI, 1951) pp. 40 ff; Raymond P. Dougherty, "Sennacherib and the Walled Cities of Judah," *JBL* 49 (1930), 160–71.

[7] R. North, "Ḥômôt Yᵉrušalayim lᵉ-pî ḥᵃqîrôt ḥᵃdašôt," in *Judah and Jerusalem* (Jerusalem: Israel Exploration Society, 1957), pp. 59–64; *Stratigraphia geobiblica*[3] (Rome: PBI, 1970), p. 118; see notes 11–15, below.

[8] L.-Hugues Vincent, *Jérusalem de l'Ancien Testament: Recherches d'archéologie et d'histoire I. Archéologie de la Ville* (Paris: Gabalda, 1954), pp. 269-79; *Underground Jerusalem* (London, 1911); "Les récentes fouilles d'Ophel," *RB* 20 (1911), 567-77; 21 (1912), 105–11, 424–41.

[9] Georges Barrois, "Siloam," *IDB*, 4, p. 354; his map on p. 352 shows well the relation of the tunnel to earlier channels.

[10] G. Ernest Wright, *Biblical Archaeology* (Philadelphia: Westminster, 1957), p. 169.

[11] Jan Simons, *Jerusalem in the Old Testament: Researches and Theories* (*Studia Scholten*, 1; Leiden: Brill, 1952), p. 238; on tunnel, pp. 157–94. To Hezekiah in 2 Chron 32: 5 is falsely ascribed the work of Manasseh (33: 14; note 57 below), according to Johann Fischer, "Die Mauern und Tore des biblischen Jerusalem," *TTQ* 113 (1932), 287; 221–88; 114 (1933), 73–85.

[12] Gustaf Dalman, *Jerusalem und sein Gelände* (Gütersloh: Bertelsmann, 1930), p. 83. David's occupation of the west hill, Urusalim of the Amarna letters, while Jebus was the east hill, is maintained by Pierce S. Hubbard, "The Topography of Ancient Jerusalem," *PEQ* 98 (1966), 130–54.

[13] A. H. Sayce, "The Topography of Pre-Exilic Jerusalem," *PEQ* 15 (1883), 215–23; M. Avi-Yonah, "The Walls of Nehemiah: A Minimalist View," *IEJ* 4 (1954), 239–48 [18 (1968), 98–125]; Millar Burrows, "Nehemiah 3: 1–32 as a Source for the Topography of Ancient Jerusalem," *AASOR* 14 (1934), 115–40; "The Topography of Nehemiah 12: 31–43," *JBL* 54 (1935), 29–39; retracted in "Nehemiah's Tour of Inspection," *BASOR* 64 (1936), 12; and *IDB* 2, p. 854 [referring to 3, p. 533 map]. A Maccabean dating was favored by Kurt Galling, "Jerusalem," *Biblisches Reallexikon* (*HAT*, 1; Tübingen: Mohr, 1937), p. 302; "Die Baugeschichte Jerusalems," *ZDPV* 54 (1931), 85–90; "Die Nekropole von Jerusalem," *PJ* 32 (1936), (73–) 95–101; following A. Alt, "Das Taltor von Jerusalem," *PJ* 24 (1928), 79–98.

[14] W. F. Albright, *Archaeology of Palestine* (Pelican, 1951), p. 154, with J. Germer-Durand, *Topographie de l'ancienne Jérusalem* (Paris, 1925; *Guide N. D. de France* 1932, p. 82).

[15] Kathleen M. Kenyon, *Jerusalem: Excavating 3000 Years of History* (New Aspects of Antiquity; London: Thames, 1967), p. 144; "Excavations in Jerusalem, 1966," *PEQ* 99 (1967), 65–71, and preceding campaigns [*BA* 27 (1964), 33–52]; Glueck Festschrift (note 3 above), pp. 232–53, "Israelite Jerusalem"; her excavations are incorporated into an overall reappraisal of Jerusalem's topography by Ernst Vogt, "Das Wachstum des alten Stadtgebietes von Jerusalem," *Bibl* 48 (1967), 337–58.

[16] Since "Springs" is plainly plural [not also singular as in English, or as the Hebrew word for "water(s)"], not only Gihon but also Rogel and even "the dragon spring" of Neh 2: 13 are meant, according to Wilhelm Rudolph, *Chronikbücher* (*HAT*, 21; Tübingen: Mohr, 1955), p. 311. On p. 315, he suggests that vs 30 is taken from 2 Kings 20 "and amplified from the Chronicler's immediate personal experience of the local situation"; but its anticipation in vs 4 is anachronistic. The Rogel and (dubiously) dragon springs are admitted also by Lino Randellini, *Il libro delle Cronache* (S. Garofalo, *Sacra Bibbia*; Torino: Marietti, 1966), p. 462. But on p. 467 he feels surprisingly sure that the later allusion forms part of an addition "entirely due to the Chronicler" (32: 27–30, plus "a personal reflection" in vs 31) "possibly due to a special source listing Hezekiah's wealth"; p. 468 "his mode of describing the tunnel in divergence from the canonical source confirms the hypothesis that he was using a special document, yet does not exclude that an acquaintance with local conditions would have been adequate for him" (! ?).

[17] Hence we cannot admit Noth's too casual observation that the Chronicler adds to Kings three *genaue Angaben* (presumably empirical details, as distinct from verbal paraphrase): "occlusion of the upper issue," "deviation downwards," "toward west of Davidic city" (*ÜS*, 139, n. 3). He adds in the text that there can be no question here of a local Jerusalem tradition known orally to the Chronicler *because* (!) his vs 30 gives essentially the same fact as his vs 4, which is "all too plainly far removed from a local tradition."

[18] Kurt Galling, Die Bücher der Chronik (*ATD*, 12; Göttingen: Vandenhoeck, 1954) p. 165; he holds 2 Chron 32: 3 an interpolation not agreeing with 32: 30.

[19] F. X. Rodríguez Molero, "Los dos libros de las Crónicas," in *La Sagrada Escritura: Texto y comentario*, ed. J. Leal (Madrid: Biblioteca de Autores Cristianos, 281, 1968), pp. 2, 934.

[20] Noth, *ÜS*, 140; G. Beyer, "Das Festungssystem Rehabeams," *ZDPV* 54 (1931), 113–34; on Manasseh, see note 57 below. We may note here some titles whose apparent relevance to our theme is fallacious: Elias Auerbach, "Die grosse Überarbeitung der biblischen Bücher," VT(S), 1 (Copenhagen volume, 1953), 1–10 relates to D and P sources; H. W. Hertzberg, "Die Nachgeschichte alttestamentlicher Texte innerhalb des ATs" (*BZAW* 66, *Werden und Wesen des ATs*, 1936), 110–21.

[21] Godfrey R. Driver, "L'interprétation du texte masorétique à la lumière de la lexicographie hébraïque," *Ephemerides Theologicae Lovanienses* 26 (1950), 347, "applied himself."

[22] André Robert, "Littéraires (Genres)," *DBS* 5, pp. 418; 405–21; (with A. Tricot), *Guide to the Bible*[2] (New York: Desclée, 1960), 508; cf A. Robert, A. Feuillet, *Introduction to the OT* (New York: Desclée, 1969), "Chronicles" by H. Lusseau. Millar Burrows, "Ancient Israel," in R. Dentan, *The Idea of History in the Ancient Near East* (New Haven, 1955), p. 126, the Chronicler "interprets the whole past in terms of individual retribution, even though this sometimes involves a radical reconstruction of what could be known from the more ancient sources." It must be recognized that in the search for *sources* there is no essential difference between such "theological reasoning" and what other authors call "pure fiction": Robert H. Pfeiffer, *IDB*, 1, p. 577; C. C. Torrey, *Ezra Studies* (University of Chicago Press, 1910) p. 231; *The Chronicler's History of Israel* (1954); though it is hard to see what is gained by considering the Chronicler "as fantastically unhistorical as possible" [Hugo Preller, *Geschichte der Historiographie unseres Kulturkreises: Materialien, Skizzen, Vorarbeiten; I, bis 330 a.D.* (Aalen: Scientia, 1967), p. 104].

[23] B. Couroyer, "Le litige entrė Josias et Nechao," *RB* 55 (1948), 388–96.

[24] Bernard Alfrink, "Der Schlacht bei Megiddo und der Tod des Josias," *Bibl* 15 (1934), 180; 173–84.

[25] James A. Montgomery, *Kings*, in *ICC* (New York: Scribner, 1951), p. 537, notes grounds for a "detailed and probably true tradition preserved in Chron."

[26] Noth, *ÜS*, 140; *ANET* 305 [with insertions by A. Oppenheim]; C. J. Gadd, *The Fall of Nineveh: The Newly Discovered Babylonian Chronicle* (London: Longmans, 1923), p. 35, "Ashur-uballit, king of Assyria, much E[gy]pt, crossed the river to conquer Harran"; Donald J. Wiseman, *Chronicles of Chaldaean Kings* (London: British Museum, 1956); David N. Freedman, "The Babylonian Chronicle," *BA* 19 (1956), 50–60; Ernst Vogt, "Die neubabylonische Chronik über die Schlacht bei Karkemisch und die Einnahme von Jerusalem," *VT(S)*, 4 (Strasbourg volume, 1957), pp. 67–96; A. C. Welch, "The Death of Josiah," *ZAW* 43 (1925), 255–60.

[27] The combination *ʿālâ ʿal* can only be hostile, according to Arthur Hjelt, "Die Chronik Nabupolassars und der syrische Feldzug Nechos," *BZAW* 41 (Festschrift K. Marti, 1925), 145; 142–47.

[28] The Chronicler misunderstood as Megiddo that *Migdol* near Qadeš which Herodotus 2, 159 calls *Mágdolos*, according to T. H. Robinson, *History of Israel* (Oxford: 1932), 1, p. 424, n. 2, following an unpublished lead of R. H. Kennett.

[29] S. Klein, "Palästinisches im Jubiläenbuch," *ZDPV* 57 (1934), 16; 7–27.

[30] J. Mulcahy, "1 and 2 Chronicles," in Nelson's *New Catholic Commentary on Holy Scripture* (ed. R. Fuller; London, 1969), p. 356, seems to hold with A. Bea, *Bibl* 27 (1946), 145, that every report similar to the corroborated ones must be ascribed to factual sources until proved otherwise. [His citation of Bea's "Neuere Arbeiten zum Problem der biblischen Chronikbücher" in #297a should be *Bibl* 22 (1946), 46–58; while *Collationes Gandavenses* 33 (1950), 205–27, is H. van den Bussche, "Het Probleem van Kronieken."] But on p. 355 he says "we are justified in making the general statement that [the Chronicler's] changes of Sm-Kgs are based on literary and theological grounds, rather than on historical information."

[31] Primo Vannutelli, *Libri synoptici Veteris Testamenti, seu librorum Regum et Chronicorum loci paralleli hebraice graece et latine* (Rome: Pontifical Biblical Institute, 1931), pp. 428, 442 referring to 410.

[32] Noth, *ÜS*, 142, n. 3; "Eine palästinische Lokalüberlieferung in 2 Chr. 20," *ZDPV* 67 (1945), 52, 45–71.

[33] Professor Myers in *II Chronicles*, p. 114, not rejecting the view of Benzinger that this chapter is "a beautiful example of an historical midrash," adds, "the essence of the story is not pure fabrication, although much of it is couched in terms drawn from the period in which the author was writing . . . certain features have been magnified somewhat out of proportion."

[34] Adolphe Lods, "Le rôle de la tradition orale dans la formation des récits de l'Ancien Testament," *RHR* 88 (1923), 51–64; W. H. Gispen, *Mondelinge overlevering in het Oude Testament* (Meppel, 1932); H. S. Nyberg, "Das textkritische Problem des ATs am Hoseabuche demonstriert," *ZAW* 52 (1934), 243; 241–54 and *Studien zum Hoseabuch* (Uppsala, 1935); Geo Widengren, "Literary and Psychological Aspects of the Hebrew Prophets," *Uppsala Universitets Årsskrift* 1948/10, pp. 61 and 11–34. The objections of J. van der Ploeg, "Le rôle de la tradition orale dans la transmission du texte de l'AT," *RB* 54 (1947), 5–41, "must be reappraised," according to H. Stoebe, *BZAW* 77 (1958), 243.

[35] M. Noth, *Das Buch Josua*[2] (*HAT*, 7; Tübingen: Mohr, 1953 [1]1937); Brevard S. Childs, "A Study of the Formula 'Unto This Day,'" *JBL* 82 (1963), 279–92; Johannes Fichtner, "Die etymologische Ätiologie in den Namengebungen der geschichtlichen Bücher des ATs," *VT* 6 (1956), 372–96; J. L. Seeligmann, "Aetiological Elements in Biblical Historiography," *Zion* 26 (1961), 141–69.

[36] Edward Robinson, *Biblical Researches in Palestine (1838)*[2] (Boston, 1856); F.-M. Abel, *Géographie de la Palestine* (Paris: Gabalda, 1967 = 1933–38).

[37] L.-Hugues Vincent, "Abraham à Jérusalem," *RB* 58 (1951), 360–71.

[38] Nelson Glueck, *Rivers in the Desert: A History of the Negev* (New York: Farrar, 1959), p. 63.

[39] Noted with disfavor by Samuel Krauss, "Moriah-Ariel I," *PEQ* 79 (1947), 46.

[40] M. Noth, *Josua*[2], p. 100, abandons the view of *Josua*[1] on the basis of G. Harding *PEQ* 84 (1952), 104 (no pre-Roman sherds at Qumran), but reespouses it in "Der alttestamentliche Name der Siedlung auf chirbet ḳumrān," *ZDPV* 71 (1955), 111–23.

[41] R. North, "Three Judean Hills in Josue 15, 9 f," *Bibl* 37 (1956), 209–16. This Baalah is equated rather with that of Jos 19: 44 on a ridge south of Beersheba by Mordechai Gichon, "The Defences of the Salomonic Kingdom," *PEQ* 95 (1963), 113–26. On Petra-Seir as the stronghold of Ḥorim but not Ḫurrians, see R. de Vaux, "Les Ḫurrites de l'histoire et les Horites de la Bible," *RB* 74 (1967), 481–503; otherwise our "Some Links between the Ḫurrians and the Language of the Exodus," *Jahrbuch für kleinasiatische Forschung*[2] (H. Bossert volume, 1965), pp. 349; 343–57.

[42] The Carians/Cretans in 2 Sam 8: 18 are called centurions and given Jewish names in 2 Chron 23: 1. Egyptian *Keftiu* was Caphtor=Crete until 1370, then applied to Cilicia, according to J. Prignaud, "Caftorim et Kerétim," *RB* 71 (1964), 215–29; somewhat similarly, G. A. Wainwright, "Caphtor-Cappadocia," "Some Early Philistine History," *VT* 6 (1956), 199–210; 9 (1959), 73–84. Hanniba'al the PLTY is linked with Phoenician Cirta of Algeria by Hermann Schult, "Ein inschriftlicher Beleg für 'Plethi'?", *ZDPV* 81 (1965), 74–79.

[43] Abraham Malamat, "King Lists of the Old Babylonian Period and Biblical Genealogies" [J. J. Finkelstein, "The Genealogy of the Hammurapi Dynasty," *JCS* 20 (1966), 95–118], *JAOS* 88 (Speiser issue, 1968 = *AO* Series, 53), 163–73.

[44] J. Simons, "The 'Table of Nations' (Gen. x): Its General Structure and Meaning," *Oudtestamentische Studiën* 10 (1954), 155–84; cf 5 (1948), 92.

[45] N. A. van Uchelen, *Abraham de Ḥebreeër: een literair- en historisch-kritische studie naar aanleiding van Genesis 14: 13* (Studia Semitica Neerlandica, 5; Assen: van Gorcum, 1964), reviewing theories of Albright (note 83 below) and others on Abraham as merchant,

concludes he was rather a warrior hero like the Ḫabiru. S. N. Kramer, "Sumerian Literature and the Bible," *Studia Biblica et Orientalia* (Analecta Biblica, 12; Rome: PBI, 1959), pp. 203; 185–204, holds with Poebel that Šem comes from Sumer like *šem* "name" from *šummu*.

[46] M. Noth (also ed.), *Könige* (*Biblischer Kommentar*; Neukirchen: Verein, 1964), p. 232, rejects as "forced" the interpretation "*foundry*-ships" by W. F. Albright, "New Light on the Early History of Phoenician Colonization," *BASOR* 83 (1941), 17 [and J. M. Solá Solé, "Tarshish y los comienzos de la colonización fenicea en Occidente," *Sefarad* 17 (1957), 23–35]; R. North, "Ophir/Parvaim and Petra/Joktheel," *Fourth World Congress of Jewish Studies* (Jerusalem, 1967), 1, pp. 197–202; other interpretations of Parvaim in *VT* 11 (1961), 30–38 and 14 (1964), 155–63 (Hyperborea: P. Grelot); 13 (1963), 158–86 (Hesperides: H. E. del Médico).

[47] Benjamin Mazar (=Maisler), "The Excavation of Tel Qasileh," *IEJ* 1 (1950), 209.

[48] Eugene Maly, *The World of David and Solomon* (Backgrounds to the Bible, 2; Englewood Cliffs, N. J.: Prentice-Hall, 1966), p. 151; R. North, "Phoenicia-Canaan Boundary *Lebô'-Hamat*," *Mélanges de l'Université Saint-Joseph de Beyrouth* 46 (M. Dunand volume, 1971), 71–103.

[49] S. Abramsky, "The Qenites," "The House of Rechab: Genealogy and Social Character"; S. Talmon, "*Hemmâ ha-qēnîm ha-bā'im mê-ḥammat* [= "relatives"] *ābî bêt Rekab*": *Eretz-Israel* 3 (1954), 124; 8 (1967), 255–64; 5 (Mazar volume, 1958), 111–13.

[50] R. North, "The Cain Music," *JBL* 83 (1964), 373–89 [p. 377, correct to "Breadville" the *third* "Forestville," of 1 Chron 2: 54 (*not* 53)].

[51] R. North, "Caleb," *Bibbia e Oriente* 8 (G. Rinaldi issue, 1966), 167; W. Beltz, *Die Kaleb-Tradition* (Budapest, 1966; *ZAW* [1967], 117).

[52] G. Berardi, P. Boccaccio: facsimile, *Inscriptio Meša Regis* (Rome: Pontifical Biblical Institute, 1956); Albright translation and bibliography in *ANET*, p. 320.

[53] Barthel Hrouda, *Tell Halaf IV: Die Kleinfunde aus historischer Zeit* (Berlin: de Gruyter, 1962); our review in *Orientalia* 39 (1970), 579.

[54] On this practice attributed to Israelites only here and 2 Chron 28: 3 = 2 Kings 16: 3 Ahaz, see R. de Vaux, *Ancient Israel* (tr. J. McHugh; London: McGraw, 1961), pp. 445 f and bibliography, p. 548.

[55] Text and concise critical exposition in Randellini, *Cronache*, p. 475 ff; Herbert E. Ryle in R. H. Charles, *Apocrypha and Pseudepigrapha of the Old Testament in English* (Oxford University Press, 1968 = 1913), 1, pp. 612–24; L. Gry, "Manassé dans les légendes midrashiques," *Mélanges L. Podechard* (Lyons, 1945), pp. 147–57.

[56] Henri Cazelles, *Les livres des Chroniques* (Bible de Jérusalem; Paris: Cerf, 1954), p. 56; Eissfeldt's *OT Introduction*, p. 588, finds a similar implication in 2 Chron 33: 12; but it is rejected in the English Jerusalem Bible (ed. A. Jones; Garden City: Doubleday, 1966), p. 565 n.

[57] J. Simons, "The Wall of Manasseh and the 'Mišneh' of Jerusalem," *Oudtestamentische Studiën* 7 (1950), 191, 179–200; *Jerusalem in OT*, p. 328.

[58] D. J. Wiseman, "The Vassal-Treaties of Esarhaddon," *Iraq* 20 (1958), 1–99; R. Borger, "Die Inschriften Asarhaddons, König von Assyrien," *AfO*, Beiheft 9 (1956), 60; *ANET*, p. 291.

[59] Eissfeldt's *OT Introduction*, p. 536, in admitting Manasseh's captivity "no doubt historical but clearly improperly interpreted," does not take issue on whether the Chronicler got this from a documented source.

[60] Rudolph, *Chronikbücher*, p. 316. He here rejects even more bluntly the view that the Chronicler erroneously applies to Manasseh what was true of Jehoiachin (36: 10; 2 Kings

24: 15) as hinted in the "halberds" of Ezek 19: 9; Cazelles, *Chroniques*, p. 227 [also rejected in the English Jerusalem Bible, p. 565 n]; R. Fruin, "De gevangenschap van Koning Manasse te Babel," *Nieuw Theologisch Tijdschrift* 19 (1930), 3–9.

[61] Johann Goettsberger, *Die Bücher der Chronik* (Bonner Bibel 4/1; Bonn: Hanstein, 1931), p. 369; following Carl F. Keil, *Chronik* (Biblischer Commentar; Leipzig: Dörffling, 1870), p. 365; Franz X. Kugler, "Zur Glaubwürdigkeit der Chronik," *Von Moses bis Paulus: Forschungen zur Geschichte Israels* (Münster: Aschendorff, 1922), pp. 224–300; 282 [and *Stimmen der Zeit* 109 (1925), 367–82].

[62] Maximilian Streck, *Assurbanipal und die letzten assyrischen Könige bis zum Untergange Ninivehs* (*Vorderasiatische Bibliothek*; Leipzig: Hinrichs, 1916), 2, p. 139; 1, p. xvii.

[63] Ernst E. Ehrlich, "Der Aufenthalt des Königs Manasse in Babylon," *TZ* 21 (1965), 281–86. He declares that Noth's first edition of *ÜS*, on p. 183, holds the deportation unhistorical. But the only allusion on p. 282 of the later edition is less clear. The Esarhaddon prism A 5,57 is in *ANET*, p. 291; F. Michaeli refers to it also on p. 69 of his *Textes de la Bible et de l'Ancien Orient*. Esarhaddon's date is 680–669 B.C.; and Manasseh's 696 [Jepsen; 687 Bright]–642 B.C.

[64] Francesco Vattioni, "La necromanzia nell'Antico Testamento 1 Sam 28, 3–25," *Augustinianum* 3 (1963), 474; 461–81.

[65] Hans-J. Stoebe, "Die Einnahme Jerusalems und der Ṣinnor," *ZDPV* 73 (1957), 73–99; Vincent and Simons as notes 8 and 11 above.

[66] Charles C. Torrey, "The Chronicler as Editor and as Independent Narrator," *Ezra Studies* (Chicago, 1910), ch. 10 = *AJSL* 25 (1909) 157–73; 188–217; otherwise Benjamin Mazar, "The Military Elite of King David," *VT* 13 (1963), 319; 310–20.

[67] A. van Selms, "Preutseid in Kronieke," *Hervormde Teologiese Studies* 4 (1948), 136, 133–44; Hans-J. Stoebe, "David und Mikal: Überlegungen zur Jugendgeschichte Davids," *BZAW* 77 (Festschrift for O. Eissfeldt, *Von Ugarit nach Qumran*, 1958), 224–43; R. A. Carlson, *David, the Chosen King* (Uppsala: Almqvist, 1964), p. 93.

[68] H. van den Bussche, "Le texte de la prophétie de Nathan sur la dynastie davidique, II. *Sam.*, VII—I. *Chron.* XVII," *Ephemerides Theologicae Lovanienses* 24 (1948), 393; 354–94; a common source, not necessarily better preserved in Chronicles, is also maintained by [J. Wilhelm Rothstein] Johannes Hänel, *Kommentar zum ersten Buch der Chronik* (*KAT*; Leipzig: Deichert, 1927), p. 385; denied by Noth, *ÜS*, 132–37; G. Johannes Botterweck, "Zur Eigenart der chronistischen Davidgeschichte," *TTQ* 136 (1956), 402–35. Van den Bussche bases his view largely on Arno Kropat, *Die Syntax des Autors der Chronik verglichen mit der seiner Quellen* (*BZAW*, 16; Giessen: Töpelmann, 1909); but a third source behind Kings and Chron can *not* be determined by textual criticism, according to Martin Rehm, *Textkritische Untersuchungen zu den Parallelstellen der Samuel-Königsbücher und der Chronik* (Alttestamentliche Abhandlungen, 13/3; Münster: Aschendorff, 1937), 128; see now Gillis Gerleman, "The Chronicles and Their Sources," *Synoptic Studies in the Old Testament* (Lund: Gleerup, 1948), pp. 8–23; and *Studies in the Septuagint II: Chronicles* (Lund, 1946). On the 2 Sam 7 parallel, further: Marcel Simon, "La prophétie de Nathan et le Temple," *RHPR* 32 (1952), 41–58; on van den Bussche and Sigmund Mowinckel, "Natanforjettelsen, II. Sam. kap. 7," *Svensk Exegetisk Årsbok* 12 (1947), 220–29; now Artur Weiser, "Die Tempelbaukrise unter David," *ZAW* 77 (1965), 153–68; Hans Gottlieb, "Die Tradition von David als Hirten," *VT* 17 (1967), 190–200; John L. McKenzie, "The Dynastic Oracle: II Samuel 7," *Theological Studies* 8 (1947), 190; 187–218.

[69] Myers, *I Chronicles*, p. 146; R. North, "'Kittim' War or 'Sectaries' Liturgy?" *Bibl* 39 (1958), 90 [84–93] on Qumran *Milḥāmâ* scroll 2, 4; 7, 1, ed. Yigael Yadin (Jerusalem: Bialik, 1957), p. 72.

[70] M. D. Goldman, "From Whom Did David Buy the Temple Area?" *Australian Biblical Review* 1 (1951), 138 f; H. B. Rosen, "Arawna—nom hittite?" *VT* 5 (1955), 319 [*arawanni* = "free"]; Arawna was the last Jebusite king, according to Shemuel Yeivin, "Social, Religious, and Cultural Trends in Jerusalem under the Davidic Dynasty," *VT* 3 (1953), 149 (–166), citing his "Beginnings of the Davidids," *Zion* 9 (1944), 63 f, and Mazar, "The Scribe of King David and the Problem of the High Officials in the Ancient Kingdom of Israel," *Bulletin of the Israel Exploration Society* 13 (1947), 105. But see notes 80–83 below.

[71] Shemuel Yeivin, "Was There a High Portal in the First Temple?", *VT* 14 (1964), 331–43, holds that Chronicles gives only the height of the *porch after repairs* (implied in 2 Chron 24: 6 ff; 34: 8 = 2 Kings 12: 5; 22: 3), while Kings gives only the height of the *building before repairs*; at both times, building and porch would have had similar height.

[72] 1 Sam 4: 4; 2 Chron 7: 41 = Ps 132: 8; Ps 138: 1 (angels = *elohîm*); 99: 1; 104: 3 f; 18: 10; Ex 13: 21; 23: 23; R. de Vaux, "Les Chérubins et l'arche d'alliance; les Sphinx gardiens et les trônes divins dans l'ancien Orient," *Mélanges de l'Université Saint-Joseph de Beyrouth* 37 (R. Mouterde issue, 1961), pp. 94; 93–124.

[73] Henri Lammens, "Le culte des bétyles et les processions religieuses chez les Arabes préislamites," *Bulletin de l'Institut français d'archéologie orientale* 17 (1919), 39–101 = his *L'Arabie occidentale avant l'Hégire* (1928), 101–79; Julian Morgenstern, "The Ark, the Ephod, and the 'Tent of Meeting,'" *HUCA* 17 (1943), 185 (beautiful girl inside); 205 (copies of Qor'an inside); 153–265; 18 (1944), 39; 1–52; Frank Cross, "The Tabernacle: A Study from an Archaeological and Historical Approach," *BA* 10 (1947), 60; 45–68; Eduard Nielsen, "Some Reflections on the History of the Ark," *VT(S)*, 7 (Oxford volume, 1960), 61–74; Edward Robertson, "The 'Ūrīm and Tummīm: What Were They?", *VT* 14 (1964), 67–74; 73, contained in Ark; denied by Leonard A. Bushinski (N. Greitmann) in L. Hartman (A. van den Born), *Encyclopedic Dictionary of the Bible* (New York: McGraw, 1963) 134 f following L. Dürr, "Ursprung und Bedeutung der Bundeslade," *Bonner Zeitschrift für Theologie und Seelsorge* 1 (1924), 17–32; further H.-J. Kraus, "Archäologische und topographische Probleme Jerusalems im Lichte der Psalmenexegese," *ZDPV* 75 (1959), (125–40); Gerhard von Rad, "Zelt und Lade," *Neue Kirchliche Zeitschrift* 42 (1931), 476–98 = *Gesammelte Schriften* (München: Kaiser, 1965) pp. 109–29; *OT Theology*, 1, 237 f.; G. Henton Davies, *IDB*, 1, pp. 222–26.

[74] R. North, "Measures" (chart), *New Catholic Commentary on Holy Scripture* (London: Nelson, 1969) p. 106 f (#86g). G. Barrois in *IB*, 1, pp. 152–57, calculates the *bath* at double this amount; excavated samples bear marks ranging from 20 to 50 quarts.

[75] C. Wylie, "On King Solomon's Molten Sea," *BA* 12 (1949), 86–90.

[76] See note 47 above; and Hannes Mayer, "Das Bauholz des Tempels Salomos," *BZ* 11 (1967), 53–66.

[77] Harry C. Richardson, "Iron, Prehistoric and Ancient," *AJA* 38 (1934), 555–83; 41 (1937), 441–47; G. Ernest Wright, "Iron: The Date of its Introduction into Common Use in Palestine," *AJA* 43 (1939), 458–63; R. J. Forbes, "The Early Story of Iron," *Studies in Ancient Technology*, 9 (Leiden: Brill, 1964), pp. 175–290; 7 (1963), 67–191; *Metallurgy in Antiquity: A Notebook for Archaeologists and Technologists* (Leiden: 1950); M. Noth, *The History of Israel*[2] (tr. P. Ackroyd; London: Black, 1960), p. 171; John Bright, *A History of Israel* (Philadelphia: Westminster, 1967), p. 164.

[78] William F. Stinespring, "Eschatology in Chronicles," *JBL* 80 (1961), 213, 209–19.

[79] Shemuel Yeivin, "The High Place at Gibeon," *Revue de l'Histoire Juive en Égypte*, 1 (the only volume, 1947), pp. 143–47.

[80] Elias Auerbach, "Die Herkunft der Ṣadoḳiden," *ZAW* 49 (1931), 327 f; Henri Cazel-

les, "David's Monarchy and the Gibeonite Claim," *PEQ* 87 (1955), (162–)172; J. M. Grintz, "Aspects of the History of the High-Priesthood," *Zion* 24 (1959), 124–40; J. Dus, "Gibeon, eine Kultstätte des šmš und die Stadt des benjaminitischen Schicksals," *VT* 10 (1960), 353–74; James B. Pritchard, *Gibeon Where the Sun Stood Still* (Princeton, 1962).

81 W. Rudolph, *Chronikbücher*, p. 53, citing the unsuccessful refutation of Wellhausen by Kurt Möhlenbrink, "Die levitischen Überlieferungen des Alten Testaments," *ZAW* 52 (1934), 204; L. Waterman, "Some Repercussions from Late Levitical Genealogical Accretions in P and the Chronicler," *AJSL* 58 (1941), 49–56.

82 Harold H. Rowley, "Melchizedek and Zadok," in *Festschrift für A. Bertholet* (Tübingen: Mohr, 1950), pp. 461–72; "Zadok and Nehushtan," *JBL* 58 (1939), 113–41; Karl Budde, "Der Herkunft Ṣadoḳs," *ZAW* 52 (1934), 42–50; H. G. Judge, "Aaron, Zadok and Abiathar," *JTS* 7 (1956), 70–74.

83 Christian E. Hauer, "Who Was Zadok?" *JBL* 82 (1963), 89–94: not king but deserting soldier-priest of Jebus; see his "Jerusalem, the Stronghold and Rephaim," *CBQ* 32 (1970), 571–78; J. R. Bartlett, "Zadok and His Successors at Jerusalem," *JTS* 19 (1968), 1–18; on Salem = Jerusalem, M. Noth, "Jerusalem und die israelitische Tradition," *Oudtestamentische Studiën*, 8 (1951), pp. 29; 28–46; Joseph (Ignatius) Hunt, "Recent Melchizedek Study," Memorial for M. Gruenthaner, *The Bible in Current Catholic Thought* (ed. J. McKenzie; New York: Herder, 1962) pp. 25; 21–33; denied by W. F. Albright, "Abram the Hebrew: a New Archaeological Interpretation," *BASOR* 163 (Oct., 1961), 52; 36–54.

84 Leroy Waterman, "Moses the Pseudo Levite," *JBL* 59 (1940), 397–404; denied by T. J. Meek, "Moses and the Levites," *AJSL* 56 (1939), 113–20.

85 C. Hauret, "Moïse était-il prêtre?", *Bibl* 40 (1959), 509–21.

86 André Lefèvre, "Note d'exégèse sur la généalogie des Qéhatites," *Recherches de Science Religieuse* 37 (1950), 287–92.

87 Harry Ṭur-Sinai (Torczyner), "A Psalm by the Sons of Heman," *JBL* 68 (1949), 247–49; Edward L. Curtis and Albert A. Madsen, *Chronicles*, in ICC (Edinburgh: Clark, 1910), p. 281.

88 Hartmut Gese, "Zur Geschichte der Kultsänger am zweiten Tempel," Festschrift for O. Michel, *Abraham unser Vater* (ed. O. Betz; Arbeiten zur Geschichte des Spätjudentums und Urchristentums, 5; Leiden: Brill, 1963), pp. 225, 226–34.

89 Albrecht Alt, "Die Weisheit Salomos," *TLZ* 76 (1951), 139–44; M. Noth, "Die Bewährung von Salomos 'Göttlicher Weisheit,'" *VT(S)*, 3 (Rowley volume, 1960), 225–37.

90 M. J. Buss, "The Psalms of Asaph and Korah," *JBL* 82 (1963), 382–92.

91 W. F. Albright, *ARI*[2] (Baltimore 1953), pp. 197, 210; holding *māḥôl* = "dancer"; see also his "Some Canaanite-Phoenician Sources of Hebrew Wisdom" *VT(S)*, 3 (Rowley volume, 1960), 1–15.

92 Robert H. Pfeiffer, "Edomitic Wisdom," *ZAW* 44 (1926), 19; 13–25; *Introduction to the Old Testament* (New York: Harper, 1941), p. 676, rejecting the apocryphal addition to Septuagint Job which makes him the Edomite Jobab of Gen 36: 33.

93 Abraham Malamat, "Aspects of the Foreign Policies of David and Solomon," *JNES* 22 (1963), 11, 1–17; favoring Siamun. Shishak is a more intriguing but less likely candidate: B. Mazar, "The Campaign of the Pharaoh Shishak to Palestine," *VT(S)*, 4 (Strasbourg volume, 1957), 57–66, finds 2 Chron 12 an amalgam of a prophetic and a Kings source.

94 Roland de Vaux, *Ancient Israel* (New York: McGraw, 1961), p. 333, and "Le schisme religieux de Jéroboam Ier," *Angelicum*, 20 (Vosté volume, 1943), 77–91.

95 Shemuel Yeivin, "The Sepulchers of the Kings of the House of David," *JNES* 6 (1948), (30–) 45; Samuel Krauss, "Moriah-Ariel II: The Sepulchres of the Davidic Dynasty," *PEQ* 79 (1947), 102–11; J. Simons, *Jerusalem in the OT*, pp. 274, 309; both *IDB*,

1, p. 475; and *Encyclopedic Dictionary of the Bible*, p. 2452, preserve the no-city-burial view.

[96] Eleazar L. Sukenik, "An Epitaph of Uzziahu King of Judah," *Tarbiẓ* 2 (1931), 288–92; W. F. Albright, "The Discovery of an Aramaic Inscription Relating to King Uzziah," *BASOR* 44 (1931), 8–10, suggesting that the reburied bones were not those of Uzziah.

[97] R. North, "The Qumran Reservoirs," in M. Gruenthaner Memorial, *The Bible in Current Catholic Thought* (New York: Herder, 1962), pp. 112 n; 100–32.

[98] H. Neil Richardson, "The Historical Reliability of Chronicles," *JBR* 26 (1958), 10, 9–12, citing W. F. Albright, "A Votive Stele Erected by Ben-Hadad I of Damascus to the God Melcarth," *BASOR* 87 (1942), 27.

[99] Stephanie Page, "A Stela of Adad-nirari III [810–783] and Nergal-ereš from [David Oates excavation] Tell al Rimah," *Iraq* 30 (1968), 139–53; best explained as a co-regency of Jehoash with his father dating from 806 B.C., according to Aelred Cody, "A New Inscription from Tell āl-Rimah and King Jehoash of Israel," *CBQ* 32 (1970), 333; 325–40.

[100] A. Jepsen [R. Hanhart, *Makkabäer*], *Untersuchungen zur israelitisch-jüdischen Chronologie* (*BZAW*, 88; Berlin: Topelmann, 1964), updating of J. Begrich, *Die Chronologie der Könige von Israel und Juda und die Quellen des Rahmens der Königbücher* (*Beiträge zur historischen Theologie*, 3; Tübingen: Mohr, 1929); V. Pavlovský, E. Vogt, "Die Jahre der Könige von Juda und Israel," *Bibl* 45 (1964), 321–47, and Vogt "Zeittafel," in *Wort und Botschaft* (ed. J. Schreiner; Würzburg: Echt, 1967), pp. 389–402; Edwin R. Thiele, *The Mysterious Numbers of the Hebrew Kings*^{2} (Grand Rapids: Eerdmans, 1965), our review in *CBQ* 29 (1967), 181–83; W. F. Albright, "The Chronology of the Divided Monarchy of Israel," *BASOR* 100 (1946), 16–22; see also the 1961 Albright Festschrift articles on chronology by D. Freedman and E. Campbell, pp. 203–88.

[101] Gerhard von Rad, "Die levitische Predigt in den Büchern der Chronik, in *Festschrift für O. Procksch* (Leipzig: Deichert, 1934), pp. 113–24; A. S. Herbert, "Chronicles," in *Peake's Commentary on the Bible* (London: Nelson, 1962), p. 358, distinguishes deuteronomic from priestly influences in the Chronicler; W. Rudolph, "Der Aufbau der Asa-Geschichte," *VT* 2 (1952), 367–71.

[102] Myers, *II Chronicles*, p. 120, lends tacit support to J. Begrich, "Atalja, die Tochter Omris," *ZAW* 53 (1935), 78 f and H. J. Katzenstein, "Who Were the Parents of Athaliah?" *IEJ* 5 (1955), 194–97.

[103] Similarly 1 Chron 15: 13 augments the punishment of Uzzah, 2 Sam 6: 7, according to A. George, "Fautes contre Yahwé dans les livres de Samuël," *RB* 53 (1946), 161–84.

[104] John Bright, *History of Israel*, pp. 282–87; denied by H. H. Rowley, "Hezekiah's Reform and Rebellion," *BJRL* 44 (1961), 417, 395–431; Herbert Haag, "La campagne de Sennachérib contre Jérusalem en 701," *RB* 58 (1951), 356; 348–59.

[105] 2 Chron 34: 13; Rudolph, *Chronikbücher*, p. 323, against G. von Rad, *Das Geschichtsbild des chronistischen Werkes* (*BWANT*, 54; Stuttgart: Kohlhammer, 1930), p. 104.

Michiko Ota
Pontifical Biblical Institute

A Note on 2 Sam 7

In Jerusalem, in the capital he chose for his kingdom, David wanted to build a temple for his God. The word of God concerning the matter, spoken through the mouth of Nathan and recorded in 2 Sam 7, has been a puzzle to many biblical scholars, and innumerable attempts at its explanation have been made.[1] Whether of the opinion to see there an expression of absolute denial of a temple in the religion of Israel,[2] or to find there the tension between the Ark and the tent,[3] or to feel David's attitude toward the temple building problematic,[4] or to try to explain it from a political viewpoint,[5] or whatever else,[6] none of those numerous attempts seems really to offer the solution of the puzzle.

The Old Testament itself offers two explanations outside the text of 2 Sam 7: that David shed too much blood, and the temple building should not be undertaken by such a hand;[7] and that he was too busy because of the wars he had to fight.[8] In the first we have a glimpse into the current temple theology,[9] and in the second we find the simple historical fact: David just could not do it. It seems, from the above, that it did occur to the people of the Old Testament to wonder why David, of all their kings, did not build the temple. It does not seem, however, to have occurred to them to wonder why the temple was built at all.[10]

The purpose of this paper is very modest. It is not another attempt to solve the difficult literary and historical problems that are involved in 2 Sam 7. It will try only to put the biblical text in the wider context of ancient Near Eastern religious thought. It might very well be—as we hope—that this very shift of perspective will shed no little light on the text and show that some of the problems that have been found in it are automatically solved.

In the world of ancient Mesopotamia, the relationship god–king–temple was clear. A king was a mediator between the divine and the human worlds and, as such, he carried an immense load of responsibilities in two directions: heavenward to assure the gods of the devotion of the people, and earthward to confirm the fertility thus resulting from the gods' pleasure. One of the most important of the royal duties was to build, rebuild, and repair the gods' earthly abodes—the temples—and to keep them and their functions in good condition.[11] None of those activities, however, could be undertaken at a king's own will or whim. The sole authorizing power rested with gods. That it was no casual matter for a king to undertake one of those activities, especially the (re)building of a temple, can be seen in many Mesopotamian inscriptions. The classical examples are Gudea, Esarhaddon, and Nabonidus. Esarhaddon states quite simply:

> For the renewal of that temple I was agitated and was struck with awe, and was quite at a loss. But through the *X* (some divination utensil) of the divination Shamash and Adad answered me with a reliable affirmative, and concerning the building of that temple and renewal of its cells they caused a liver-omen to be written (to show their will).[12]

Discovery of the foundation inscription of any former kings being considered a favorable omen for an affirmative divine will for the renewal of that temple, Nabonidus had the foundation of the ruined temple excavated thoroughly until such was found. Upon coming across one, he says:

> The inscription of Hammurapi, an ancient king, who, 700 years before Burnaburiash, had built Ebarra and the ziggurat for Shamash upon the ancient foundation, I found therein, and was struck with awe, agitated with fear, and was troubled. Thus I said to myself: the wise king Burnaburiash built the temple and had Shamash the great lord dwell within it. [. . . . .] me that temple, in its place [. . . . .] I raised my hand and prayed to the lord of lords: "O, Lord, foremost of the gods, Prince Marduk, without you no dwelling is founded, no foundation is laid; without you who can do anything! Lord, by your exalted command let me do what is pleasing to you!"[13]

But by far the most elaborate is the account concerning the renewal of the temple of Ningirsu by Gudea, preserved for us by the famous *Gudea Cylinder A*. Ningirsu reveals to Gudea in a dream his wishes for the renewal of his temple. Though the dream seems rather clear to modern readers, Gudea insists that he does not understand the meaning. How he confirms and reconfirms that will by many and repeated means, how he is worried and then overjoyed, at one and the same time, at the revelation of that divine will—all these are told in the somewhat exaggerated literary composition of the first twenty columns of the *Cylinder*, followed by the detailed description of how he then set out for the undertaking.[14]

We sense in the above examples those kings' feeling of agitation at the revelation of the divine will concerning the renewal of the temples. They made repeated efforts to confirm the divine will and to assure themselves of their own capacities to engage in the task. Not only were the physical and spiritual preparations made with utmost care, but the tension and excitement during the construction work seem to have been nationwide. It certainly presupposed an historical moment when a king felt assured of his people's united attention as well as favorable physical conditions.

As to who should be nominated for the task, the gods reserved the right of the decision to themselves. For a king to be chosen for such a task or to have secured the divine permission for it no doubt meant his uncontested position and power over his kingdom, and he seldom failed to boast of it. We may quote, as an example, some passages from the inscription of Nebukadnezar written at his renewal of the temple of Shamash:

> At that time, Ebarra, the temple of Shamash, which was in Sippar, which since long before me had been in ruins, was like a flat land. Shamash, my great lord, had not showed favor toward any of the former kings nor had he commanded (any of them) to build; he desired me, his servant, the devout one, reverent of his divinity, for the building of the shrine. I waited for the sun, raised my hand, and prayed to the sun. I prayed for the building of the temple Ebarra . . . .[15]

It must have happened, as we may deduce from the above, that there were cases when a king was denied the task. Relevant records usually being the so-called building inscriptions, it is difficult to find a text explicitly mentioning such a denial. We may still be able to see in the following examples that such did happen once in a while. In the famous Sumerian poem "The Curse of Akkad," Naram-Sin seeks permission from Enlil to renew his temple Ekur. It is denied him, and, according to the poem, the denial caused very serious consequences.

> Concerning the temple he sought for an oracle—
> To build the temple, there was no oracle.
> Again concerning the temple he sought for an oracle—
> To build the temple, there was no oracle.[16]

Among the Mari Letters we may find a similar example, though the letter in question is broken, and, not knowing the circumstances of the correspondence too clearly, we must admit that the rendering of the word *bītu* presents some problems:

He saw the following (dream): "You (pl.) shall not (re)build this *deserted* house. If the house is (re)built, I will make it collapse into the river." The day he saw this dream, he said nothing to anyone. The next day he again saw the following dream: "It was a god. 'You (pl.) shall not (re)build this house. If you (re)build it, I will make it collapse into the river.' "[17]

From these few passages, though presented neither systematically nor exhaustively, it will have become clear that a positive divine command and a divine appointment of a specific person were absolute requirements for the building (rebuilding or repairing) of a temple. If we now return to 2 Sam 7, we will see that similar religious ideas underlie Nathan's prophecy concerning the building of the temple in Jerusalem. There is no question in our text of a denial of temple building. Nor is there any hint at theological streams in Israel that were opposed to the building of any temple for Yahweh. The real issue is that both the initiative to build a temple and the choice of the person for the task must come from God and not from an individual king. The prophecy stresses these two points. First, God has not commanded the building of a temple either to any of the past leaders or to David himself (vss 6–7). Second, the choice of the person is God's affair. God's denial—put in the interrogative form (vs 5)—concerns the person of David and not the temple itself. The emphatic position of the pronoun (*h'th*) makes this point more than clear. Moreover, this denial of David results in the positive choice of his successor in vs 13, where the emphatic *hw' ybnh* is to be noted as a counterpart of the emphatic denial in vs 5.

There still remain many problems, both literary and historical, in the text. But we hope that the similar texts presented here have made it clear that 2 Sam 7 falls into the category of divine revelations concerning temple building, which is so common in the ancient Near East, and that, like those similar texts, Nathan's prophecy is positive in tone—that is, it does not imply any criticisms of temple building as such but, on the contrary, expresses the positive choice of one person for the task of building a temple for Yahweh.[18]

Notes

1 The main suggestions and discussions were summarized by J. Schreiner, *Sion-Jerusalem. Jahwes Königssitz* (*SANT* 7), München, 1963, pp. 80–89; cf R. E. Clements, *God and Temple*, Oxford, 1965, pp. 56–60.

2 R. de Vaux, *Ancient Israel*, London, 1961, pp. 329 f; idem, "Jerusalem et les Prophètes," *RB* 73 (1966), 485.

3 G. von Rad, "The Tent and the Ark," in *The Problem of the Hexateuch and Other Essays*, Edinburgh and London, 1966, p. 119.

[4] J. Schreiner, *op. cit.*, pp. 89–94, maintains that divine refusal was caused because David used the verb *yšb* but not *škn*, which is supposed to show the misconception of what a temple should be; cf H. W. Hertzberg, *I and II Samuel*, London, 1964, pp. 284 f; A. Weiser, "Die Tempelbaukrise unter David," *ZAW* 77 (1965), 158–60.

[5] According to G. W. Ahlström, "Der Prophet Nathan und der Tempelbau," *VT* 11 (1961), 113–27, the real cause of Nathan's rejection of David's wish is to be found in the politico-religious conflict between the Jebusite and Israelite parties in Jerusalem.

[6] According to M. Simon, "La Prophétie de Nathan et le Temple," *RHPR* 32 (1952), 41–58, enmity against the temple at Jerusalem; according to J. Dus, "Der Brauch der Ladewanderung im Alten Israel," *TZ* 17 (1961), 1–5, the text was originally against the temple at Shiloh and was utilized in this context as against that in Jerusalem.

[7] 1 Chron 22: 8; 28: 3.

[8] 1 Kings 5: 17.

[9] Cf J. M. Myers, *I Chronicles* (*AB*, vol. 12), New Kork, 1965, p. 154.

[10] It seems problematic to suppose the existence of the anti-temple trend in ancient Israel from the very few and difficult passages: 2 Sam 7: 5–7; Is 66: 1; and the story of the Rekabites in Jer 35; cf R. de Vaux, *Ancient Israel*, p. 330. The total rejection of the temple in the New Testament (Mk 14: 58; Jn 4: 21; Acts 7: 48; 17: 24) may be considered as a late sectarian development.

[11] Cf H. Frankfort, *Kingship and the Gods*, Chicago, 1948, pp. 267–74.

[12] R. Borger, *Die Inschriften Asarhaddons Königs von Assyrien*, (*AfO* Bh 9), Osnabrück, 1967², p. 3, Col. III 42–IV 6.

[13] S. H. Langdon, *Die Neubabylonischen Königsinschriften* (*VAB* 4), Leipzig, 1911, p. 238, Col. II 20–40.

[14] F. Thureau-Dangin, *Les Cylindres de Gudéa* (*TCL* VIII), Paris, 1925; for translation in German, see A. Falkenstein and W. von Soden, *Sumerische und Akkadische Hymnen und Gebete* (*BAW*), Zürich and Stuttgart, 1953, pp. 137–57.

[15] S. H. Langdon, *op. cit.*, p. 100, Col. I 25–II 10.

[16] A. Falkenstein, "Fluch über Akkad," *ZA* NF 23 (1965), 43–124; the relevant passages are on p. 55, lines 96–99.

[17] *ARMT* XIII, No. 113, rev. 1–14; English trans. by W. L. Moran, "Divine Revelations," *ANET*³, pp. 623 f (the passages quoted are on p. 624, rev. 1'–14').

[18] For the detailed discussion on the prophecy of Nathan in the light of the texts from Mesopotamia, see the forthcoming doctoral dissertation, "The Royal Dynasties in Ancient Israel," by Tomoo Ishida, Hebrew University of Jerusalem.

Jesse B. Renninger
Muhlenberg College

A Study of Selected Isaianic Passages in the *Wormser Propheten Übersetzung* of 1527 and Luther's *Isaiah* of 1528

It is intriguing to compare works coming from approximately the same time and place, especially Bible translations. Because of the influence of various forces, personalities, and earlier versions, one can learn from their translations a great deal about the men who translate and how they respond to their environment.

We would like to compare the German Bible translations of Ludwig Haetzer and Martin Luther. Some things well done are often overlooked when overshadowed by subsequent efforts. This is the case with these two translations. Haetzer's translation, known to Martin Luther, has been completely obscured by Luther's.

We have a twofold purpose here: to contrast the vocabularies and literary merits, and to examine Isaiah 9: 1–9 and the Servant Songs in order to reexamine a conclusion reached some time ago in a seminar paper on Deutero-Isaiah at the Hartford Theological Seminary.[1] That conclusion was that the translator of the *Wormser Propheten* deliberately mistranslated on christological grounds.

Now specifically about the translations: The *Propheten Übersetzung* appeared at Worms April 13, 1527, in folio and octavo editions. The title page was inscribed: "Alle propheten nach Hebraischer sprach verteuscht. O Gott erloss die gefangenen MDXXVII Peter Schaffern in Worms." The work, according to the introduction, was done by Johannes Denck and Ludwig Haetzer. The latter was responsible for Isaiah. The translation found favor, and no fewer than a hundred editions appeared in the five years following its publication. Five folio and five octavo editions appeared before Luther's translation of Isaiah appeared in 1528.

This work, according to Eberhard Nestle, is an "achtungswerten Arbeit."[2] M. Reu described it as "On the whole a creditable translation which Luther praised as well as criticized. The translators really knew Hebrew, and at the same time had caught the spirit of Luther's German."[3] Luther, in a letter to his friend Wenceslaus Link in May, 1527, writes: "Prophetes vernacula donatus Wormatiae non contemno nisi quod Germanismus obscurior est forte natura illius regionis. Fecerund diligentiam quis autem omnia attingit? Ego tamen iam accingor et ipsos vernacula extrudere lecturus simul Iesiam, ne otiosus sum."[4]

Ludwig Haetzer, the translator of Isaiah in the *Propheten Übersetzung*, was born in Bischofzel near St. Gallen at a date unknown. He studied at Freiburg im Breisgau, where the mysticism of Tauler was very strong. He later served as "Kaplan" in Wadersil, near Zurich, and was a friend of H. Zwingli.

In 1523, as the leader of the "Bildsturmer," he published "*Tübschen Büchli*," and in the same year wrote the protocol of the "Zweite grosse Züricher Religionsgespräch." He also participated in the "Religionsgespräch" of January 17, 1525, which centered on infant baptism. On January 21, he was given eight days to leave the city.

In 1526, he met Johannes Denck, the schoolmaster of Nuremberg, at Worms and with him translated the Prophets. Denck helped clarify Haetzer's thought, which up until this time had been rather characterless.

Theologically it might be said that he embraced the sacramental teaching of Karlstadt, and would have summed up his christological thought as: "Gott ist nur einer. Christus aber nur Bruder bis zur Herrlichkeit." He was put to death at Constance in 1529, on the charges of bigamy and adultery.

For the text of the *Wormser Propheten*, we have used a folio first edition in the Schwenckfelder Historical Library at Pennsburg, Pennsylvania. This volume measures 10 5/8 by 7 1/4 inches, is bound in leather with metal adornments, and once had clasps.

For Isaiah 9: 1–6, we have used the Christmas Sermon of Luther for 1525, which appeared in print early in January, 1526, at the printery of N. Schirlentz in Wittenberg. We also made use of the *Luther Handschrift*, the Pal. Ger. 731 of the University of Heidelberg, as printed in the Weimar Edition of *Luthers Werke* (*Die Deutsche Bibel*, vol. 2).

For the Servant Songs, we have used a microfilm of *Der Prophet Isaiah Deutsch*, 1528, from the printery of Hans Luft in Wittenberg, courtesy of the British Museum.

For the textual work, we have used Kittel's *BHK*[3], the *Göttinger Septuaginta*, ed. by J. Ziegler, and *Biblia Sacra Vulgata*, ed. by Fischer.

Isaiah 9: 1–6

1525

Das volck das ym finstern wandelt sihet eynn grosses liecht, uber die da wonen ym finstern lande, scheinet es helle. Damit machstu der freuden wenig weil du der Heiden so viel machst, doch fur dir werden sie sich freuen, wie man sich freuet ynn der erndte, wie man frolich ist, wenn man beute austaylet, denn das joch yhrer last, und die rute yhrer schulder, und den stecken yres treibers hastu zubrochen, wie zu zeit Midian, denn aller krieg mit ungestum und blutig kleid wird verbrand durch feur verzeret werden, denn uns ist eyn kind geboren, der son ist uns gegeben, wilchs Hirschaft ist auf seiner schulder und heyst, wunderbar, rad, kraft, held, ymmer vater, friedefurst, auff das seine Hirschaft gros werde, und des friedes keyn ende, auff dem thron Dauid und seinem Konigreich, dass ers zurichte und stercke mit gericht und gerechtigkeyt von nu an bys ynn ewigkeyt. Solchs wird thun der eyver des Herrn Zebaoth.

1527

Das volck das im finsteruss wandelt sihet ain gross liecht und es scheint hell uber die im finstern land hausen. Un dieweil du die hayden meerest so machest auch der freuden vil denn sy werden sich ja wol vor dir erfrewen wie man sich in der ernd frewet unnd als man guts muts ist so man die beutten ausstailet. Ursach das joch jres last un die rut jrer schulter und den stab jres treibers hast du zerbrochen alss zum tagen Midian. Dann aller krieg mit ungestume und blutig klaid wirdt verbrendt und durchs fewr zerzert werden. Dan uns ist ain kind geborn, uns ist ain sun geben dess herrschaft auff seiner schulter ist unnd er haisst wunderbar, rath starck, held, allwegvatter, Fridfurst darmit sein herrschaft gross werde und sein frid unendtlich auf dem thron Dauids und seinem Kunigreyche das ers zurichte und stercke mit gericht und gerechtigkait von von yetz an biss in ewigkait. Dies wirt der eyfer des HERRN Zebaoth thun.

1528

Das volck so ym finstern wandelte sihet ein grosses liecht und uber die da wonen ym finstern lande scheinet es helle. Du machst der heiden viel damit machstu der freuden nicht viel fur die aber (werden sie) wird man sich frewen wie man sich frewet ynn der erndte wie man frolich ist wenn man beute austeilet. Denn du hast das joch yhrer last and die rute yhrer schulter und den stecken yhres treibers (hastu) zubrochen wie zur zeit Midian. Denn aller krieg mit ungestum und blutig kleid wird verbrand und mit feur verzeret werden. Denn uns ist ein kind geboren ein son ist uns gegeben welchs herrschaft is auff seiner schulter und (er) heisst Wunderbar, Rat, Krafft, Helt, Ewigvater, Fridfurst, auff das seine herrschaft gross werde und sein frides kein ende auff dem stuel Dauid und seinem konigreiche das ers zurichte und stercke mit gericht und gerechtigkeit von nu an bis ynn ewigkeit. Solchs wird thun der eiver des HERRN Zebaoth.

This Christmas lection, used by Luther as the basis of his sermon in 1525, provides us with a third translation: two by Luther, and one by Haetzer. When the three are compared, we discover that the two translations of Luther differ in only 15 percent of the 160 words. The percentage is somewhat smaller for the Haetzer translation and Luther's 1528 version. There undoubtedly was a two-way borrowing.

The first thing to note is that Luther begins the ninth chapter with "Das volck" whereas Haetzer begins it with the preceding verse. Here Luther follows the Hebrew text and Haetzer follows the LXX and Vulgate.

The first verse brings a problem in word order. Luther says, "über die da wonen ym finstern lande scheinet es helle"; Haetzer says, "und es scheint hell über die im finstern land hausen." Luther agrees with Hebrew, LXX, and Vulgate. "Wonen" and "hausen" must be regarded as synonyms.

The word *hhlkym* is translated "wandelt" by Luther in 1525, and also by Haetzer; but in 1528, Luther changed this to "wandelte." This is a different tense. The LXX has a present participle, and the Vulgate has the imperfect. Did this influence Luther?

The word order of Luther's earlier translation is found in neither the Hebrew nor the versions. Luther has "viel machen"; Haetzer, "meerest." Luther, "der freuden nicht viel"; Haetzer, "der freuden vil." The first is merely a difference in expression, while the second suggests different Hebrew texts. "Nicht viel" renders the Heb *l'*, while Haetzer has a text reading *lw*, with which twenty MSS agree.

In 1525, Luther translated "der son," but changed it in 1528 to "ein son." The Heb is *bn*. The LXX omits the article. Luther at one time contemplated inserting "er" before "heisst," as Haetzer did.

The Heb *'l* may have been troublesome. Haetzer has "starck"; Luther, "Kraft." LXX has *aggelos*; the Vulgate, "Deus." Hebrew *'by ʿd* was translated "Allweg vatter" by Haetzer, and "Ewig vater" or "ymmer vater" by Luther; Haetzer uses an Allemanic word here.

In vs 6, Luther says, "stuel D"; Haetzer, "thron D." The Hebrew *ks'* is translated "solium" by the Vulgate, but the LXX has *thronon*. Here Haetzer follows the LXX; Luther, the Vulgate.

The Servant Songs

Isaiah 42: 1–5

Sihe das ist mein knecht	Nimwar er ist mein knecht
ich erhalte ihn Und mein	ich will jn erhalten. Er

auserweleter an welchem meine seele wolgefallen hat. Ich habe ihn meinen geist gegeben Er wird das recht unter die heyden bringen. Er wird nicht schreyen noch ruffen und seine stymm wird man nicht horen auff den gassen. Das zustossen rhor wird er nicht zubrechen und das glymmend tocht wird er nicht ausslesshen. Er wird das recht mit warheit erfur bringen. Er wird nicht murrisch noch grewlich sein auff das er auff erden das recht an richte. Und die Insulen werden auff seine gestzt warten.

ist main auserwelter an dem mein seel ain wolgefallen hat. Ich will mein gaist auf jn geben und er soll den Haiden das gerecht furtragen. Er wirdt weder schryen noch zancken und sein stymm wird er auf der gassen nit horen lassen. Ain zerstossen ror wirdt er nit zerknischen unnd ain riechendes docht wirdt er nit ausslaschen. Er wirdt das gericht nach der warhait furtragen. Er wirdt am gesicht und stercke nit abnemen bisz er das gericht auff erden auffricht und die Inseln werden auf sein gesatz verhoffen.

Vs 1. *hn*: Luther, or L *Sihe*, Haetzer, or H *Nimwar*. L *das*, H *er* not in Heb. *'tmk*: incomplete: L present, H future. *ntty*: L *habe gegeben*, H *will geben*. H *Gerecht* MHG for *Recht*. *furtragen* NHG *vortragen*, L *bringen*.

Vs 2. L *nicht . . . noch*, H *weder . . . noch*. ys': L *ruffen* (*rauffen*), H *zancken*. Luther stresses the physical; Haetzer, the verbal. *yšmy'*: LXX *anēsei* future, H is the more literal.

Vs 3. *yšbwr*: LXX "breaks," Vulg "bruise," "grind," H *zerknischen* religious usage, *niederdrucken*, *von Reue gebrochen*. *khh*: "expiring," L *glymmend*—"eye," H *riechend*—"nose." LXX "smoking," Vulg *fumigans*.

Vs 4. *ykhh*: L *verzagen*, H *nachlassen*. L *auf . . . das*, H *bisz*; the one is consecutive, the other temporal. L *murrisch—unwillig sein*, *grewlich* from *grauen-schrecken*. *yyḥlw*: L *warten*, H *verhoffen*; Heb has both meanings.

Isaiah 49: 1–6

Hoeren mir zu yhr Insulen unnd yhr volcker yn der ferne mercket auff. Der HERR hat mir geruffen von mutter leib an. Er hat meines namens gedacht da ich noch in mutter leib war und hat meinen mund gemachet wie eyn scharff

Loset mir jr Insulen und jr volcker merket auf. Mich hat der HERR von der geburt an berufft unnd meins namens von muterlayb her gedacht. Er hat meinen mund gemacht wie ain scharpff schwerdt und mich under seiner hand schatten verborgen. Er hat

schwerd mit dem schatten seiner hand hat er mich bedecket. Er hat mich zum hubschen pfeil gemachet und mich ynn seinen kocher gestecht. Und spricht zu mir Du bist mein knecht Israel durch welchen ich will gepreiset werden. Ich aber dacht ich erbeitet vergeblich und brachte mein kraft umbsonst und unnutzlich zu. Wiewol meine sache des HERRN und mein ampt meines Gottes ist. Und nu spricht der HERR der mich von mutter leib an zu seinem knecht bereitet hat das ich sol Jacob zu yhm bekeren Auff das Israel nicht weg gerafft werde. Darumb bin ich fur dem HERRN herlich und mein Gott ist meine sterke, Und spricht Es ist geringes das du mein knecht bist die geschlecht Jacob auff zurichten und das verwarloset ynn Israel widder zu bringen. Sondern ich hab dich auch zum liecht der Heiden gemacht das du seyest mein heil bis an der welt ende.	mich zu ainem ausspolierten pfeyl gemacht und mich in seinen kochen geschoben und zu mir gesagt: Du bist mein knecht Israel in welchem ich eer einlegen wird. Da saget ich: Ich hab vergebens gearbaitet und mein vermogen layter umsonst abgelegt yedoch ist mein recht mit dem HERRN dran und mein werck mit meinem Gott. Nun aber sagt der HERR der mich von mutter leib her jm zu aim knecht geschaffen das ich Jacob widerum zu jm furte aber Israel wolt sich nit versamlen lassen. Noch bin ich teuer in den augen des HERRN und mein Gott ist mein sterck. Er aber sprach: Es ist mir zu wenig das du mein knecht seyest die stammen Jacobs auffzurichten und der verwustet Israel widerumb auffzyfuren hierumb hab ich dich auch zu aim liecht der heyden gesetzt das mein hail biss zu end der erden raiche.

Vs 1. *šmʿw*: H *loset* MHD—*oberdeutsch lose* is NHG *lauschen.*

Vs 2. *brwr*: L *hubschen*—related to *hofisch*, H *auspolierten.*

Vs 3. *b . . . bk*: L *durch*, H *in. ʾtpʾr*: L "be glorified," "to glory," H *eer einlegen wird.*

Vs 4. *mšpṭy*: L *Sach*, H *Recht. wpʿlty*: L *ampt*—follows LXX; H *Werck*—follows Vulg.

Vs 5. L *zu seinem knecht*, H *zu aim knecht* (definite versus indefinite). *ysry*: L *bereitet*, H *geschaffen. lšwbb*: L *fuhren*, H *bekeren. yʾsp*: L *weggerafft*, H *wollt sich nit versammlen lassen. yʾkbd*: L *herlich*, H *teuer.*

Vs 6. *šbṭy*: L *geschlecht*, H *stammen.*

Isaiah 50: 4–9

Der HERR HERR hat mir eine
gelerte zunge gegeben das
ich wisse mit den muden
zu rechter zeit zu reden.
Er wecket mir das ohr das
ich hore wie ein junger. Der
HERR HERR hat mir das ohr
geoffenet und ich bin
nicht ungehorsam und gehe
nicht zu rucke. Ich hielt
meinen rucken dar den die
mich schlugen und meine
wangen den die mich rauften.
Mein angesicht verbarg ich
nicht vor schmache und
speichel denn der HERR Herr
hilfft mir darumb werde ich
nicht zu schanden. Darumb
hab ich mein angesicht dar
geboten als einen kisel-
stein. Denn ich weiss das
ich nicht zu schanden werde.
Er ist nahe der mich recht-
fertiget. Wer wil mit mir
hadern? Lasst uns zusammen
tretten. Wer ist der recht
zu mir hat? der kome her
zu mir. Sihe der HERR HERR
hilfft mir wer ist der mich
wil verdammen? Sihe sie
werden allzumal wie ein
kleid veralten mottenn.

Mir hat der herrschend HERR
ains jungers zung geben hie-
mit ich wisste mit dem muden
zu rechter zeyt zureden und
hat mirs or alle morgen umb-
geriben das ich hort wie ain
junger. Das herrschend HERR
thet mirs or auff und ich
widerte mich sein nicht und
hab nit hindersich gezaufet.
Ich hab mein rugken den
schlahenden dargebotten und
meine wangen den rupffenden.
Mein angesicht hab ich vor
schmach und spaichel ver-
borgen. Und der herrschend
HERR wirdt mir helffen der
wagen ich nit zuschenden wird.
Darumb hab ich mein angesicht
gesetzt wie ain kysslingstain
und waisst das ich nit zu-
schanden wird. Mein recht-
fertiger ist nahe wer ist der
mit mir zancken woll? Lasst
uns gegenainan der steen
wer ist der recht zu mir hat?
der kome her an mich. Nimwar der herrschend HERR wirdt
mir helffen wer ists der
mich zu ainem boswicht
machen will? Schaw sy
werden allsamt wie ain
klayd verwesen und die
schaben werden es fressen.

Vs 4. *ʾdny yhwh*: L *HERR HERR*, H *herrschend HERR*. L adj. "trained," "disciplined," H noun "disciple," LXX *paideias*, Vulg *eruditam*. *dbr* verb. adds *zu rechter zeyt*. *yʿyr*: H omits first one, L takes with following, as Vulg second L *wecken*, H *umgeriben*. (*drehen*).

Vs 5. *mryty*: L "rebellious," "refractory," H "oppose." *swg nswgty*: L *gehe nicht zuruck*, H *hindersich gezaufet*, LXX *ouk apeithō oude antilegō*, Vulg *non contradico retrorsum non abii*.

Vs 6. *ntty*: L *hielt*, H *dargebotten*. *mkym*: L *die mich schlugen*, H *den schlahenden*, LXX *mastigas*, Vulg *percutientibus*. *imrṭym*: "pluck," "pluckers," L *rauffen-reissen*, *kratzen*, H *rupffenden-ausreissen*, LXX *rapismata* "those striking." *hstrty*: L preterite; H past perfect.

Vs 7. *y'zr*: L present, H future, LXX *boēthes*, Vulg *auxiliator*. *'l-kn*: L *darumb*, H *darumb*, LXX *alla*, Vulg *ecce*. *śmty*: L *dargeboten*, H *gesetzt*. *kḥlmyš*: *stein ohne metallischen gehalt*. *w*: L *denn*; H *und*. *'bwš*: L *werde*, H *wird*.

Vs 8. *yrby*: L *hadern*—"legal proceeding," H *zancken*—"face to face encounter." *n'mrh yḥd*: L *lasst uns zusammen tretten*. L uses *'md* in same sense as used in Damascus Document. H *lasst uns gegenanender steen*—this may reflect the LXX. *'ly*: L *in*; H *an*.

Vs 9. *yrs'ny*: L *wil verdammen*, H *mich zu aim boswicht machen will*. *Boswicht* is "a worthless fellow", LXX *kakōsei*. *yblw*: L *veralten*, H *verwesen*, LXX *palaiō-thesesthe*, Vulg *conterentur*. *'š*: L *motten*, H *schaben oberhochdeutsch*, LXX *sēs*, Vulg *tinea*. L *sie*, H *es*, LXX *umas*, Vulg *eos*.

Isaiah 52: 13–53: 12

Sihe mein knecht wird kluglich faren und wird erhohet
und ser hoch erhaben sein.
Das sich viel uber dir er-
gern werden weil seine gestalt hesslicher ist denn
ander leute und sein ansehen
denn der menschen kinder.
Aber also wird er viel
Heiden besprengen und auch
kunige werden yhren mund
gegen yhm zuhalten. Denn
welchen nichts davon verkundiget ist die selbigen werdens mit lust sehen und die
nichts davon gehort haben
die werdens mercken. Aber
wer glaubt unser predigt? Und
wem wird der arm des HERREN
offenbaret?
Denn er scheusst auf fur yhm
wie eyn reys und wie eine
wurtzel auss durrem erdreich.
Er hat keine gestalt noch
schone wir sahen ihn aber
dawar keine gestalt das
wir sein hetten mogen be-
geren. Er war der aller
verachtest und unwerdest
voller schmertzen und
kranckheit. Er war so

Sihe mein knecht wird ver-
stendig erhocht erhaben und
ser empor sein und wie sich
vil ab dir verwunderen also
ist sein angesicht verderbt
das es nyemandt gleich sihet
und sein gestalt kainem
menschen. Dargegen wirdt er
vil haiden besprengen und die
kunig werden jren mund uber
jm beschliessen. Denn denen
es nit verkundiget ist die
werden es sehen und die es
nit gehort haben die werden
sich sein anneman.
Wer hat unnserm gerucht
glaubt und welchem ist der
arm ser HERRN geoffnet? Und
er ist vor jm auffgangen wie
ain schoss unnd wie ain
wurtzel auss ainem durren
erdtrich. Er hett weder
gestalt noch zierd wir sahen
er hatt aber kain ausehen
das wir ainen lust zu jm
hetten. Er war der verachtest
unnd verworffnest man ain
schmertzhafftiger man da
er waisst was kranckhait ist.
wir haben jn verschmahet und
so gar nicht geachtet als

veracht das man das angesicht fur yhm verbarg darumb haben wir yhm nichts geacht.
Furwar er trug unser krangkheyt und lud auff sich unser schmertzenn. Wir aber hielten ihn fur den der von Gott geplagt und geschwecht were. Aber er ist umb unser missethat willen verwundet und umb unser sunden willen zuschlagen. Die straf ligt auff yhm auff das wir friede hetten. Und durch seine wunden sind wir geheylet. Wir giengen alle ynn der yrre wir schaffe ein iglicher sahe auff seinen weg. Aber der HERR warf unser allen sunde auff yhn. Da er gestraffet und geschwecht ward thet er seinen mund nicht auff wie ein lam das zur schlachtbanck gefurt wird und wie ein schaff das erstummet fur seinem scherer und seinen mund nicht aufftthut.
Er ist aber aus der angst und gericht genomen. Wer wil seines lebens lenge ausreden? Denn er ist aus dem land der lebendigen weggerissen da er umb die missethat meines volcks geplagt war. Und er ist begraben wie die Gottlosen und gestorben wie ein reicher wiewol er niemand unrecht gethan hat noch betrug ynn seinem mund gewesen ist. Aber der HERR wolt yhn also zerschlahen mit krangheit. Wenn er sein leben zum schuldopffer gegeben hat so wird er samen haben und ynn die lenge leben. Und des HERREN furnemen wird

ainen vor dem man das angesicht verbirgt. Warlich er hat er hat unsere kranckhaiten auff sich genomen und er hat unsere schmertzen getragen und wir haben in darfur gehalten. Got hat jn geplagt und genidert. Aber er ist von unserer bosshaiten wegen biss auf dem tod verwundt und von unserer missthaten wegen ist er geschlagen worden. Die zuchtigung unnsers frids ist uber jn und durch seine beylen seind wir gesund worden.
Wir irrten allsmet wie ain schaff ain jeder lugt seines wegs aber der HERR hat all unnser missthaten auff jn geleget. Er ist dargeben und gepeinigt worden noch hat er seinen mund nit auffgethon. Er ward gefurt wie ain lamb zyr metzgung und ist wie ain schaff vor seinem bescherer stumm gewesen und hat seinen mund nye auffgethon. Noch ist er von der angst und dem recht genomen und jm kompt sein plag von der schalckhait meines volcks. Er hat jm die gottlosen fur sein begrabnis und die reychen fur seinen tod gegeben daumb das er sich kaines raubs gebraucht unnd in seinem mund kain betrug gewesen ist.
Aber der HERR hett lust jn mit kranckhait zu schlahen und so er sein seel zu ainem schuldopfer gibt wirdt er ainen somen saen und lang leben und den willen des HERRN wirdt jn gelingen.
Er wirdt sein aigne arbeit saen und satt werden. Mein gerechter knecht wirt mit seinen kunst vilen gerech-

durch seine hand fortgehen. Darumb das seine seele gearbeitet hat wird er seine lust sehen und die volle haben. Und durch sein erkentnis wird er mein knecht der gerechte vil gerecht machen. Denn er tregt yhre sunde. Darumb wil ich yhm grosse menge zur beute geben und er sol die starcken zum raube haben. Darumb das er sein leben ynn den tod gegeben hat und den ubelthettern gleich gerechent ist und er viler sunde getragen hat und fur die ubelthetter gebetten.

tigkait schaffen und er wirdt jre missthat tragen darumb will ich jm tail geben mit vilen unnd mit dem starcken wirdt er die beyt ausstailen derwegen das er sein leben zum tod aussgeschutt hat unnd zu den bosswichten bezelt ist. Dann er viler sund auf sich genomen und die bosswichtigen hat er vertretten.

Note division of chapters. L begins the chapter here.

Vs 13. *yśkyl*: L *kluglich fahren*, H *verstandig* (Heb is hiphil). L takes *wgbḥ hoch* as an adj.; H as a noun. May have been influenced by the LXX.

Vs 14. *šmmw*: L *argern, bebend, zittern*; H *verwundern*. *kn*: L *weil*, H *also*. *msḥh*: "disfigurement," H verb *aussehen*, Vulg *inglorius*. *m'yš*: L *den ander leutte*, H *nyemand gleich*, LXX *anthrōpōn*, Vulg *inter viros*. *mr'ḥw*: L *gestalt*, H *angesicht*, LXX *eidos*, Vulg *aspectus*. *wtarw*: L *ansehen*, H *gestalt*, LXX *doxa*, Vulg *forma*. *mbny 'dm*: L *menschen Kinder*, H *kainem menschen*. LXX *apo anthrōpōn*, Vulg *filios hominum*.

Vs 15. *kn*: L *aber also*, H *dargegen*, LXX *outōs*, Vulg *iste*. *spr*: L *gehort haben*, H *verkundiget*. *r'w*: L *werden mit lust sehen*, H *werden es sehen*. *htbwnnw*: L *merken*, H *sein annemen*, LXX *sunēsousi*, Vulg *contemplati*.

Vs 1. *lšm'tnw*: L *predigt* (*Verkundigung*), H *gerucht* (*Hilfgeschrei*), LXX *akoē*, Vulg *auditur*. *nglth*: L *offenbart*, H *geoffnen*.

Vs 2. *kywnq*: L *reis*, H *schoss* (*junger trieb*) LXX *paidion*, Vulg *virgultam*.

Vs 3. *yḥdl*: L *umwerdest*, H *verworffnest*. L seems to think of the man himself, whereas H seems to have in mind the attitude of others. L omits *'yšym* and *'yš. nbdh* difference in word order.

Vs 4. *'kn*: L *furwar*, H *warlich*; LXX omits; Vulg *vere*. L *drangheit*, H *kranckhaiten*, LXX *amartias*, Vulg *languores*. *nś'*: L *trug*, H *auffgenomen*, LXX *pherei*, Vulg *tulit*. *sblm*: L *lud auff*, H *getragen*,

Vulg *portavit. ngwʿ*: omitted by both L and H. *wmʿnh*: L *geschwecht*, H *genidert*, LXX *kakōsei*, Vulg *humiliatum.*

Vs 5. *mpšʿnw*: L *missethat* (*schandliche Tat*), H *bosshaiten* (*wertlosigkeit*), LXX *anomias*, Vulg *iniquitates.* L *wunden*, H *beylen* ("contusion," "swelling"), Vulg *livore.*

Vs 6. *kṣʾn*: L *schaff*, H *ain schaff*, LXX and Vulg have plural. *pnynw*: L *sihe*, H *lugt* (*ausschauen*), LXX *eplanēthē*, Vulg *declinavit.*

Vs 7. *ngš*: L *gestrafft* ("idea of punishment"), H *dargeben*, LXX *kekakōsthai* ("maltreat"), Vulg *oblatus. lṭbh*: L *schlachtbank*, H *Metzgung.*

Vs 8. *wmmšpt*: L *gericht*, H *recht* (MHG for *Gericht*), LXX *krisis*, Vulg *iudicio. dwrw*: L *seines lebens lenge*, H *sein geschlecht*, LXX *tēn genean*, Vulg *generationem. mpšʿ*: L *missethat*, H *schalckhait* (*arghait, boshait*) Vulg *scelus.*

Vs 9. *wytn*: L *ist*, H *hat gegeben. ʿšyr*: L *ein reicher*, H *die reychen*, LXX *plousious*, Vulg *divitem. bmtyn*: L *gestorben*, H *fur seinen tod*, LXX and Vulg agree with H. *ḥms*: L *niemand unrecht getan hat*, H *darumb das er sich kaines raubs gebrauch*, LXX *oti anomian ouk epoiēsen*, Vulg *iniqitatem non fecerit.*

Vs 10. *npšw*: L *leben*, H *seel*, LXX *psuchē*, Vulg *animam suam. yrʾh*: L *haben*, H *sehen*, LXX and Vulg agree with H.

Vs 11. *bdʿtw*: L *erkenntnis*, H *kunst*, Vulg *scientia.*

Vs 12. *ʾḥlq*: *ist*, L *zur Beute geben*, H *teil geben*, LXX *klēronomēsei*, Vulg *dispertian.* 2nd. L *haben*, H *austailen*, LXX *meriei*, Vulg *dividet. hʿrh*: L *gegeben hat*, H *aussgeschutt*, LXX *paredothē*, Vulg *hadidit* ("to give oneself up"). *ypgyʿ*: L *gebetten*, H *vertretten*, LXX *paredothē*, Vulg *rogavit.*

Both Luther and Haetzer produced good, though not identical, translations. The former is from a background of a Middle Eastern dialect, and the latter from the Allemanic High German. They differ in vocabulary, but one must remember that when they were intended for South Germany or Switzerland, the first printings of Luther's translations were always provided with a glossary of Middle German terms and their equivalents. Both translations are from the Hebrew, although there are indications that the texts used differed at several places both from each other and from the text we have today.

As to the translations themselves, Haetzer's seems to be more concrete, with strong rhythm, and with structure that mirrors the parallelism of the Hebrew text, though admittedly the language is more archaic and perhaps academic. On the other hand, Luther's translation is more abstract, has no such vigorous rhythm, and is what Luther intended it to be—expressed in the language of the marketplace.

Both take liberties with the Hebrew text, and seem more interested in content than in literal fidelity to words.

One intriguing problem is that of the definite versus the indefinite article or demonstrative. No stable pattern appears. Sometimes Haetzer used the indefinite, and Luther the definite; sometimes the reverse is true. I believe there are three possible explanations. One, we may assume that their knowledge of the Hebrew language was rather meager, and the irregularity is therefore to be explained as due to their lack of knowledge. Two, it is a deliberate mistranslation on christological grounds. Three, the reason is to be found in the use of *der* and *ein* in the Middle High German and the New High German periods.

Since there is no definite pattern, it cannot be the first. The second must be eliminated, because it is not always the same one using the definite rather than the indefinite. The third seems to be the most likely explanation.

What shall we say about the hypothesis we started to investigate? In the texts studied, we have seen that both men have presented credible translations of the Hebrew text. There have been times when we may have felt that one or the other presented eisegetic paraphrase rather than a translation—but both do this, and there is no consistent pattern. Consequently, we are compelled to reject the thesis which we have investigated.

It was unfortunate that Luther's translation so overshadowed Haetzer's that the latter's is so little known. It deserves more—it is a good piece of work.

Notes

1 Foster, Naomi, "Comparison of Messianic Passages in Luther and the *Propheten-übersetzung*," Unpublished Seminar paper submitted at Hartford Theological Seminary, n.d.

2 *Realencyclopedie f. prot. Theol. u. Kirche.* 3d ed., vol. 3, Leipzig, 1899 ff, p. 77.

3 Reu, M., *Luther's German Bible.* Columbus, Ohio, 1934, p. 206 f.

4 Enders, *Luthers Briefwechsel*, 6, 46.

Alfred von Rohr Sauer
Concordia Seminary at St. Louis

Ecological Notes from the Old Testament

The 1970s bid well to become the decade of ecological and environmental concern. The opening year of the decade offered ample evidence that the nation and the world are becoming obsessed with the problem that concerns all: how to preserve the earth's natural resources. The dangers of DDT, mercury, oil, nuclear radiation are being recognized by industry and government throughout the Americas, Eurasia, and Africa. The craving for pure water, clean air, and good soil is common to all the peoples of the "civilized" world. And there is evidence that the longing for rivers and lakes, forests and fields, mountains and skies that are free from man-made pollutants will intensify as the decade advances. State and local communities are resolved to resist with greater tenacity the march of industrial progress which threatens to deplete more and more of their natural beauty.[1]

The Sacred Scriptures, especially the Old Testament, have some significant references to ecology and environment which may be useful in arriving at solutions for our contemporary problems. Throughout the Old Testament, man is given such a position of authority over the entire natural world that one might almost be inclined to say that there is a tendency to underestimate the importance of the earth's natural resources. For example, God made man in his own image and likeness, so that he might rule the fish and the birds, the cattle and wild animals, and all the reptiles (cf Ps 8: 5–8). But men took advantage of their divine-like status and exploited their unique position. They made themselves selfish lords over the entire creature world. They set out to extract from it everything that would benefit them. God gave them light (Ps 118: 27; 36: 9). But men have so abused this gift of God that the light is all but shut out, and men are constrained to walk through a valley that is as dark as death itself (cf Ps 23: 4). God gave men the pure sky (Ps 19: 1). But men have so saturated the atmosphere with their putrid gaseous products that the earth is practically enveloped by a vast blanket of smog. God gave men the oceans, with their great whales and other varieties of marine life (Ps 104: 25–26). But men have so exploited and polluted the seas that many varieties of sea life are in danger of becoming extinct. At creation, God filled the earth with beautiful sounds when the morning stars sang together and all the sons of God shouted for joy (Job 38: 7). But men filled the earth with a cacophany of jets, SSTs, and industrial din and reduced it to a screeching pandemonium.[2]

As a sampling of what the Old Testament has to say concerning ecology, the present study will survey the Psalter, the Deuteronomic Corpus, Wisdom Literature, and some of the Prophets, with an eye on environment. Both parts of the paper will have to do with relationships, first the relationship between Yahweh and the earth, then the relationship between the people and the land. In the brief conclusion, attention will be called to the need for action in all areas of ecological concern.

Yahweh and the Earth, or God's Gift to Man

That the universe belongs to God is a basic affirmation of the Old Testament. In a number of poetic sections, Yahweh himself makes this claim. He asks Job, for example, in the whirlwind vision, whether Job was there when Yahweh laid the foundation of the earth (Job 38: 4). In the same vision, Yahweh asks Job caustically who it was that shut in the sea with doors when it burst forth out of the womb, who it was that made clouds the garments of the sea, and who wrapped the sea with thick darkness as its swaddling band (Job 38: 8–9). In a prophetic Psalm that takes issue with sacrificial rites, Yahweh makes the blunt claim that every beast of the forest belongs to him, also the cattle on a thousand hills; He is familiar with all the birds of the air, and everything that moves out in the field belongs to him (Ps 50: 10–11).

The Universe is God's

In one form of response, man acknowledges reverently that the universe is, indeed, God's own. The psalmist addresses Yahweh, and affirms that the heavens belong to him, the earth also is his, everything in the world is His, because he has founded the universe (Ps 89: 11). Both the prelude and the postlude of Psalm 8 echo the praises of Yahweh: "Oh Yahweh, our Lord, how majestic is Thy name in all the earth!" (Ps 8: 1, 9). One poet acknowledges Yahweh's lordship in the brief comment that with him is found the fountain of life (Ps 36: 9).

In another type of response, men acknowledge to one another and to their fellow creatures that the earth belongs to Yahweh. Through countless generations men have been saying to one another, "The earth is the Lord's and the fullness thereof, the world and those who dwell therein" (Ps 24: 1; 50: 12). Music lovers are fond of hearing Haydn's creation motif echo in their ears, "The heavens declare the glory of God and the firmament showeth His handiwork" (Ps 19: 1). In a spirit of loyalty and devotion, Deuteronomy has Moses remind his people that the heaven of heavens belongs to Yahweh their God, along with the earth and all that is in it (Deut 10: 14). In the only passage in the Joban dialogue (i.e., chs. 3–31) which uses the name Yahweh, Job urges his friends to turn to the beasts and the birds, to the plants and the fish for an acknowledgment that it is the hand of Yahweh which has given life and breath to every living thing (Job 12: 7–10). The above examples show that, for the Old Testament, it is widely assumed and generally recognized that the universe with all its resources belongs to Yahweh.

GOD ENTRUSTED THE CARE OF THE UNIVERSE TO MAN

What does the poet mean when he observes that the heavens belong to Yahweh, but that he has turned over the earth to the sons of men (Ps 115: 16)? A literalist might be inclined to argue that this text speaks against the space efforts of the USSR and the USA, because the heavens are Yahweh's area of control and man has no business there. But it must be noted that this psalmist shared the world view of his day—namely, that Yahweh resides in the heavens, living men inhabit the earth, and dead men find their place of residence in Sheol. The text is intended to say simply that while Yahweh resides in the heavens, the earth with its resources is his gift to men to be administered responsibly by them. Such a turning over of the earth to the sons of men is also implicit in the priestly concept of the image of God in Gen 1: 26 as well as in the truck garden ecology of the Yahwist in Gen 2: 8, 15.[3]

The picture of man as God's viceroy on earth has been taken up especially in a number of creation hymns in the Psalter. In his amazement that Yahweh pays any attention to man and that he cares about him at all, the author of Psalm 8 can say: "Yet Thou hast made him little less than God . . . . Thou hast given him dominion over the works of Thy hands; Thou hast put all things under his feet, all sheep and oxen, and also the beasts of the field, the birds of the air, and the fish of the sea" (Ps 8: 4–8). In another creation tribute, the Song of the Seven Wonders, the poet praises his God for putting at man's disposal the sky, the earth, the water, the produce, the sun and moon, and the sea; above all, Yahweh has bestowed upon man the gift of life itself (Ps 104: 1–30). In typical Gunkelian terms, the earth is like one vast farmyard, over which Farmer Yahweh presides: when Yahweh exhales, the entire creature world, including man, comes to life (Ps 104: 30); when Yahweh inhales, all creatures breathe their last and return to the dust whence they came (Ps 104: 29).

Yahweh not only turned the earth over to man, he also made, and still makes, rich provision for man's well-being on the earth. He continually visits the earth, and greatly enriches it, crowning each year with his wonderful bounty (Ps 65: 9–11). He gives directions to the skies above, and opens the doors of heaven as a blessing for man (Ps 78: 23). Like the great river at the end of time, the rivers and streams on the earth are there to gladden the people of God (Ps 46: 4). Even such a gift as sound, sustaining sleep comes from God as regularly as day and night (Ps 3: 5; 4: 8). In the light of such assurances, man should, indeed, be inclined to say, "God is in His heaven, all must be well among the sons of men on earth!"

MAN DESPOILED THE UNIVERSE

If, as Elihu argued, "God teaches us (men) more than the beasts of the earth, and makes us wiser than the birds of the air" (Job 35: 11), then one might be justified in affirming with the closing sentence of the last paragraph that all ought to be well with man on earth. Unfortunately, however, such optimism is unwarranted. One of the poets is quick to point out the mess that man has made of God's earth. He observes, "But man who is of the earth strikes terror in it" (Ps 10: 18). Those words summarize all that the Old Testament has to say about the ecological abuses of homo sapiens. One can find many similar references to the corruption of men whose portion in life is of the world (Ps 17: 14). The wisdom poet of Ps 14: 1 calls them impious fools who are incapable of doing any good. The many outbreaks of man-made terror on earth moved the pious poets to raise their voices in righteous lament. When the foundations of society (and these include its ecological conscience) are destroyed, what are the righteous to do (Ps 11: 3)? The righteous protest that help is needed, because the godly are gone, the faithful have disappeared (Ps 12: 1). There are cries of distress out in the streets (Ps 144: 14). In Deborah's day, terror inflicted by men was so bad on the earth that caravans had stopped functioning, travelers had taken to byways, and the peasantry had ceased (Judg 5: 6, 7). What timely tips for exposing the terror that is man in its modern form!

The reign of terror caused by human corruption was bound to have a destructive effect upon all nature. When the psalmist, for example, speaks of the wearing out of the heavens and the earth like a garment (Ps 102: 26), that may be applied, at least in part, to what earthy man has done to the heavens and the earth. Yahweh created the "great wide teeming sea" (Ps 104: 25), but what happened when some of the corrupt terror-striking men went down to the sea in ships doing their business (Ps 107: 23)? Yahweh formed Leviathan to sport in the great wide sea or for Yahweh to play with as his beach ball (Ps 104: 26). But what happened to Leviathan and the sea monsters? Recent reports speak of a fearful decline in the whale population of the world's oceans, the results of decades of overfishing. Although the International Whaling Commission set annual quotas of whales for its twelve member nations, the established quotas are too large—and, even so, are scarcely enforced. Fortunately, our own Interior Department has prohibited the import into the United States of oil from any of the chiefly threatened species of whales. Since the United States uses a quarter of the world production of whale oil, the restriction may help to alleviate the problem, and whales may begin to increase.[4] Recently, something like a million gallons of fuel oil were spewed into the waters of San Francisco Bay as the result of a collision of two tankers in the area of the Golden Gate Bridge, spelling fearful disaster for marine life. During the same week, New Haven's harbor, on the east coast, was contaminated by a lesser dose of lethal diesel oil.[5]

There were still great stands of cedar for Yahweh's voice to shatter in Lebanon at the time of the Thunder Psalm (29: 5). But where have all the cedars gone? Destruction-dealing people had to be asked whether the trees were men, that they were being besieged (Deut 20: 19)? Ephraim and Manasseh were bidden to clear the forested hill country of Palestine and thus to deforest it (Josh 17: 15, 18). At the time of the Covenant Code, men grasping to exploit nature had to be forbidden to stew the flesh of a kid in its own mother's milk (Ex 23: 19; cf Deut 14: 21). It was also ruled that either the mother bird sitting on eggs or the baby birds that she had hatched needed to be released, so that grasping humanity might not take both mother and young (Deut 22: 6–7). By the very command of Yahweh, the invading Hebrews hamstrung the horses of the enemy at Merom, cruel and inhumane as that was (Josh 11: 6, 9). Because of human abuses, the sheep may long in vain for the green pastures and the still waters, with which the shepherd renews their lives (Ps 23: 2). At the time of the Thunder Psalm, there were still enough deer in Palestine for them to be intimidated by the thunderstorm (Ps 29: 9). But what has happened to all the panting hinds?

Terror strikes at its worst when man becomes inhumane toward man himself. Sensitive souls are still shocked that, by the command of Yahweh himself, the men, women, and children of Sihon and Og east of Jordan were destroyed at the hands of the invading Hebrews (Deut 2: 34–35; 3:

6–7). Similar examples of the practice of *ḥērem* occur at various points in Israel's early history. The peace-loving poet of Ps 120: 4–7 could cry out that when he favors peace, the opponents are for war; he is even constrained to compare their sharp tongues to the broom tree that burns with such intensive fire. Was man ever more alienated from his fellows than that poet who cried out in deep dejection, "I have passed out of mind like one who is dead" (Ps 31: 12), or than that most lonely of all souls in the psalter, who said, "No man cared for my soul" (Ps 142: 4)? Job charged his brethren with being as treacherous as a torrent bed, as freshets that pass away (Job 6: 15; cf Jer 15: 18). In the presence of his friends, Job also insisted that anyone who denies kindness to a friend has actually given up the fear of God (Job 6: 14). When Jael violated the basic code of desert hospitality by pinning Sisera's head to the ground within the sacred precincts of her own tent (Judg 4: 21), it is small wonder that the Deuteronomic historian would say of the times before the monarchy that "everyone did as he pleased" (Judg 17: 6). The sensitive ecologist has a question to raise even about nature's cruelty to nature. When the lions pray for prey in Ps 104: 21, one certainly must ask whether the terror-stricken victims of the lion are not subjected to great suffering? The biological scientists may counter that only the fittest survive, but that still does not justify the suffering that is caused when nature terrorizes nature.

In the light of man's abuse of the heritage entrusted to him by God, it is understandable that Pascal describes man as a chaoslike monster, because this greatest of God's creatures cannot overcome evil within himself. Man's lordship over nature has so deteriorated that he has become little more than a ruthless tyrant. Being like God is only a small step from aspiring to be God and thus upsetting the entire creator-creature relationship between God and the earth. In his relationship to nature, man is, indeed, as powerful as God himself; but in his own microcosm, he falls far short of demeaning himself as God does.[6]

The People and the Land, or Yahweh's Gift to Israel

Although earth and land are not distinguishable in the Hebrew word *ʾereṣ*, there is ample reason to point out the distinction between them theologically and ecologically. Even as God entrusted his earth to mankind so that man might be his caretaker, so the land of promise was Yahweh's gift to his people Israel as far back as the original promise to Abraham in Gen 12. The land plays an important role in Israel's ancient narrative sources, but it comes into full flower and prominence in Deuteronomy and the Deuteronomic History. It is there that the basic ecological concern for the land is to be sought. As above, we shall therefore occupy ourselves, first, with

Yahweh's gift of the land to his people, then, with his exhortation to the people not to forget him when they have settled in the land, and, finally, with his urgent exhortation to them to take care of the land which will be in their charge.

YAHWEH GAVE ISRAEL THE LAND OF PROMISE

In the opening chapter of Deuteronomy, Yahweh took up the ancient promise given to Abraham, Isaac, and Jacob, and bade his people to receive their inheritance. He set the land before them; they were to go in and take it: both the hill country and the Arabah, the Negeb as well as the sea coast (Deut 1: 6–8). This was the land described elsewhere in the Old Testament as extending from Dan in the north to Beersheba in the south or, in its wider dimensions, the land stretching from the River Euphrates to the Wadi Arish on the Egyptian border. Poets and Prophets were fond of comparing this land to a luxurious grapevine or to a choice vineyard. The psalmist, for instance, paid tribute to Yahweh, who brought a grapevine out of Egypt, made it take deep root and fill the land of promise, its branches extending all the way to the sea and the river (Ps 80: 8–11). Isaiah included in his message an ancient love song concerning Yahweh and his vineyard. Yahweh planted his vineyard on a verdant hill, cultivated it, and cleared it of all foreign objects. He planted only choice vines in it, and built a watchtower in its midst. He even carved out a wine vat for the processing of the grapes (Is 5: 1–2).

The gift of the land was accompanied by Yahweh's promise to make ample provision for his people's well-being. Deuteronomy made much of the fact that in Egypt, the Israelites watered the ground with their feet (as one can still readily see it done on the banks of the Nile today), but in Canaan, the land of Yahweh's people was able to drink water by the rain of heaven (Deut 11: 10, 11). During historical times, the climatic conditions of Palestine did not change. Yahweh continued to give the early and the late rains, and the staple products remained the same: corn, wine, and oil (Deut 11: 14). When the land, for example, became weary, Yahweh refreshed it with rain (Ps 68: 9). Even as Yahweh had been favorable to his land in the past (Ps 85: 1), so he would continue to give what was good, and the land would yield its increase for his people (Ps 85: 12). Who, if not Yahweh, could tilt the water skins of the heavens for the benefit of the land (Job 38: 37)? Even as the sea fled, the Jordan turned back, Sinai skipped, and the rock became a water pool for Israel's benefit (Ps 114), so the seas and rivers, the mountains and the rocks would continue to respond to the God of Jacob and bring blessing to his people.

Of special ecological significance are the scattered references to winter precipitation. The psalmist rejoiced that Yahweh provided snow like wool, spread out hoarfrost like ashes, tossed out ice like morsels (Ps 147: 16, 17). In Elihu's classic "Lord of the Seasons" speech, Yahweh gave orders to the snow to drop gently to the earth; it was the breath of God whereby ice was given and whereby the wide-open waters were frozen over (Job 37: 6, 10). It should be noted in this connection that snow has always been the "poor man's fertilizer," because during and after snowfall it is possible for the nitrogen which it brings to soak into the ground slowly. On the other hand, Yahweh told Job in the whirlwind vision that he had reserved the snow and the hail for the time of trouble, for the day of battle and war (Job 38: 22–23). The ancient Song of Moses paid tribute to Yahweh because he gave his people curds and milk, the finest wheat, together with the blood of the grape (Deut 32: 14). It is significant that the only exception among the recipients of land grants were the Levitical priests; they were charged not to take possession of any portion of ground, because Yahweh himself was their inheritance (Deut 18: 1–2).

Yahweh's directive to his people to go in and take the land was underwritten by the guarantee that he would drive out the indigenous population of Canaan. Historically, Israel's Lord did break down the opposition of the Canaanites, but scholarship continues to wrestle with the question of whether there was an infiltration, an uprising from within, a gradual or a sudden take-over of the land. According to the suddenly completed conquest tradition, the land lay subdued at an early date (Josh 18: 1). Yahweh gave rest to Israel from all her enemies (Josh 23: 1). But on the basis of the differing tradition in Judges, one might ask whether it was not the seven nations who had rest from Israel. This record states specifically that the Canaanites persisted in occupying the plain of Jezreel. When Israel grew strong, they put the Canaanites to forced labor, but did not utterly drive them out (Judg 1: 19, 21, 28–33). The full realization of the gift of the land took place somewhere between an initially successful thrust and a subsequent gradual elimination of continuing opposition until the very time of the monarchy.

YAHWEH EXHORTED HIS PEOPLE NOT TO FORGET HIM

Successive warnings against forgetfulness were given in the early chapters of Deuteronomy. When the people had all that they needed of food and drink in the land, they were to beware lest they forget Yahweh their God (Deut 6: 10–12). After all their physical needs had been met, after they had taken up residence in the fine homes that they had built, after their flocks and herds had increased, they were to take care lest their hearts become lifted up and they forget Yahweh their God (Deut 8: 11–14). The words of Yahweh which his people were to lay up in their hearts, bind on their hands, and write on their doorposts—these words referred primarily to the people's obedience to all Yahweh's directives (Deut 11: 18–19). But they might also be applied to the manner in which Israel used the gifts of the land that Yahweh had bestowed upon her.

There are some examples which indicate that the people took Yahweh's warning seriously and remembered it. For instance, at the conclusion of Israel's most ancient credo (Deut 26: 5–10), the individual Israelite who had brought his gift to Yahweh was bidden to say, "And behold, now I bring the first of the fruit of the ground, which Thou, Oh Lord, hast given me" (Deut 26: 10). Many a pious Israelite must have spoken these words and thus indicated his remembrance of Yahweh's exhortation. Many an Israelite must also have joined in the psalmist's affirmation that he would call to mind the deeds of Yahweh, that he would remember his wonders of old, that he would meditate on all Yahweh's work and muse on his mighty deeds (Ps 77: 11–12). But the great majority did succumb to forgetfulness, as the Old Testament clearly indicates. Their response is described most poignantly in the Song of Moses. Jeshurun, who should have shown his "straightness" by remembering, rather, waxed fat and kicked because he was so filled with the abundance of honey, oil, curds, wheat, and grapes provided by Yahweh (Deut 32: 13–15). Is there a lesson to be learned here—namely, that environmental abuses are often the worst in the most prosperous countries? In one of his great outbursts on the problem of theodicy, Job saw the wicked flourishing so contentedly in their families, in their farmyards, on their feast days, that they thought they could do without God. Job summarized their attitude in the rhetorical question, "Behold, is not their prosperity in their hand" (Job 21: 16)? The psalmist too begged to be delivered from men "whose portion is of this world." He gave assent to their being filled, but his satisfaction would be found in seeing Yahweh's face (Ps 17: 14–15).

YAHWEH URGED HIS PEOPLE TO TAKE CARE OF THE LAND

It is again a chapter in Deuteronomy that pinpoints the basic idea. Yahweh said to his people, "Take care that the land be able to support you, when your days and your children's days are multiplied" (Deut 11: 16–21). The words "take care" call to mind Yahweh's directive to man in the garden that he should "till it and keep it" (Gen 2: 15). These words are also a reminder of the work, sweat, and hard toil which came to be associated with man's cultivation of the soil (Gen 3: 17–19). Moreover, in the Song of the Vineyard, Yahweh took great pains with his grapevine; the fact that it yielded bad grapes instead of good grapes indicates that Israel failed to do her part in taking care of the land (Is 5: 2).

The words "take care," however, must also be understood in the light of another poet's plea that the work of our hands may be established by Yahweh's favor (Ps 90: 17). And therein lies a lesson for contemporary man and his ecological concerns. It may be difficult to take care of the land so that it may be able to support us, but we do have the Lord's promise that he will bless the efforts of our hands. The question is: Are we preserving the pleasant places into which the lines have fallen for us? Are we cherishing the goodly heritage that is ours (Ps 16: 6)? Even if many ecological foundations appear to be in the process of being destroyed (Ps 11: 3), even if those who care about preserving a good environment be few (Ps 12: 1), the few have often carried the day, even at the expense of being frowned upon and laughed at by the great mass of their contemporaries. There might even be some basis for answering the question of Ps 15: "Who shall dwell on Thy holy hill?" with such a quasi-ethical and highly ecological requirement as, "He who takes proper care of the land, he who preserves the atmosphere, the rivers, and the seas from pollution and contamination and thereby shows his devotion and obedience to Yahweh."

The words "that the land be able to support you" raise the question of pollution and related problems in the Old Testament. One of the earliest examples of pollution recorded in the biblical tradition was the action of Moses performed by divine directive when he turned the waters of the Nile into blood so that the fish died (Ex 7: 20–21). It is historically attested that the land of Egypt is unable to support its inhabitants if the waters of the Nile fail. The Mosaic disturbance of the lifeline of Egypt has its modern counterpart in the recently dedicated high dam at Assuan in Egypt. It must of course be granted that the dam eliminates the age-old phenomenon of high and low waters with which Egypt's fortunes rose and fell. But such elimination also introduced some serious ecological problems. Backed up behind the Assuan Dam are huge quantities of rich silt that used to provide nourishment for marine life not only in the lower Nile but even in the Mediterranean itself. Without the annual spill-over of such alluvial silt on their land, the farmers down river are forced to use costly and sometimes questionable chemical fertilizers. Upstream too, complications have set in. Above the dam, Lake Nasser has been infested by parasite-carrying snails that constitute a serious health threat to Egypt's population. The balance of nature is being seriously jeopardized by the dam in yet another way. With the dam causing lower freshwater levels near the sea, the briny seawater is moving more and more upstream, not only affecting marine life but also depriving the river of its irrigation potential. Granted, Egypt may no longer experience its circle of seven fat and seven lean years (Gen 41: 25–31), but it remains to be seen whether the land of the Nile will still be the bread basket which was a haven for Palestinians ever since patriarchal days (Gen 12: 10; 42: 1–3).[7]

According to the biblical account, Moses never had an opportunity to contaminate the streams of the Holy Land. Could he be charged with pollution, however, when he cast the dust from the golden calf into the brook (Deut 9: 21)? The ancient inhabitants of Jericho feared that their land would be unable to support them. Complainingly, they said to Elisha, "The situation of this city is pleasant . . . but the water is polluted and the soil is unproductive" (2 Kings 2: 19). Their complaint finds its counterpart in many a community today. Job denied that he ever abused the soil, stating under oath, "If my land has cried out against me, and its furrows have wept together; if I have eaten its yield without payment . . . let thorns grow instead of wheat" (Job 31: 38–40). Job also recognized that overflowing rivers have a way of washing away the rich soil of the earth (Job 14: 19). In his effort to establish Job's guilt, friend Bildad asserted that one does not expect papyrus to grow where there is no marsh and that neither does one expect reeds to flourish if there is no water (Job 8: 11).

With the psalmist, contemporary man is recognizing more and more how the panting of the hart after the water brooks is being intensified by the rapid disappearance of clear-flowing streams (Ps 42: 1). Jeremiah may have been certain that the cold-flowing streams from the mountains would not run dry (Jer 18: 14). But he did not consider what men might do to stop such a flow. He could not yet know what Wisdom's Song in Job has to say about men mining silver, gold, iron, and copper, about their opening subterranean shafts and putting an end to darkness, about their overturning mountains by the roots and binding up streams to stop the trickle (Job 28: 1–4; 9, 11). Dams that stop the natural flow of water can hurt nature just as strip mines that efface the beauty of the countryside and superhighways that cut a standard swath through mountains and valleys (Is 40: 4) with little, if any, concern for nature's loveliness that is destroyed. Our president's ecological proposals of mid-February, 1971, recognized that man has not known the way to environmental wisdom (Job 28: 12–13) and therefore needs something like the Environmental Protection Agency (EPA) to arouse his ecological conscience. The president sought to put teeth into the EPA's program by giving it authority to levy fines of $25,000 to $50,000 a day against industries that pollute the nation's waterways.[8] That sounds very much like the sanctions imposed upon a recalcitrant Israel in Deut 28.

The entire sacrificial system of the Old Testament as outlined, for example, in Lev 1–7 could be subject to question on ecological grounds. A modern environmentalist would not only think of the huge numbers of animals that needed to be slaughtered for these sacrifices but would also have reservations about the many sacrificial fires that would add seriously to the pollution of the air. On the other hand, there may be some ecological merit in the fact that Israel was bidden to pour gazelle's blood on the ground like water (Deut 12: 15–16; 15: 23). The Old Testament recognized that blood is life, and the Hebrews had ritual reasons for disposing of it. But today it is being recognized more and more that blood meal qualifies as a contributor to the soil. As a good fertilizer, it puts new life into the earth. Job did not want the earth to cover his blood, because he felt the blood would testify to his innocence (Job 16: 18); but may we not acknowledge today that covering blood with earth may be a direct benefit to the earth?

Like blood, excrement is a long-established medium for making the land able to support its population. Sanitation may not have been the only reason for the regulation in Deut 23: 13, "When you squat outside, you shall scrape a hole with it [a trowel] and then turn and cover your excrement" (NEB). The ground also needed such fertilization. It appears that more modern plumbing facilities may have been known to ancient Moab. While the servants of King Eglon of Moab were waiting for him, they thought he was relieving himself in the cool of the closet (Judg 3: 24 NEB). In our cities, a few sewage disposal plants are doing a creditable job today of treating human excrement before it is reused as fertilizer. But far more remains to be done. Anyone who has worked on an archeological mound in Palestine will recall the agony and distress that are caused when untreated human excrement is used for fertilization or simply deposited on the side of the mound. The multiplicity of germ-carrying flies and the frequent bouts with dysentery caused by contaminated food and/or water have brought no end of discomfort to workers and travelers in the Near East. Finally, it should not be forgotten that one psalmist even wished that the corpses of his enemies would become fertilizer for the earth because of their aggressive behavior (Ps 83: 10).

Yahweh's directive in Deut 11: 21 calls for care of the land "when your days and your children's days are multiplied." That involves not only greater longevity for the Israelites but also an increase in their population. It also raises the question of the relationship of population control and limited parenthood to matters of environmental concern today. Our conservationists are telling us that more fertile soil and better water distribution are only part of the solution of our ecological problems. The other part must be a sharp reduction in the rate of growth of the world's population. In the past, however, such population control has run into considerable opposition from churches which based their objections on certain texts of Scripture. Ecclesiastical opponents of planned parenthood have pointed to the statement in Ps 127: 3 that "sons are an heritage of the Lord," to the divine directive in Gen 1: 28 "to be fruitful and multiply," and to the death penalty for Onan because "he spilled the semen on the ground," Gen 38: 9–10, to show that manipulation of the birth process is contrary to the Scriptures. It is therefore to be welcomed that recently the voices of the church, with some exceptions, have been less vehement in their opposition. It is being recognized more and more that the Scriptures simply do not have anything to say about limiting the number of births in the human race.

What is to be done to stop the despoiling of God's good earth and to make sure that proper care will be taken of its resources? The federal government's program, as outlined by the president in February, 1971, is certainly a major step in the right direction. Special taxes are to be sought on such pollutants as coal smoke and the exhaust fumes from leaded gasoline. Federal outlays running into ten figures are deemed necessary to bring a halt to water pollution by municipal waste-processing plants. A national policy for the most effective use of our country's land resources is being established, but it will need to be implemented by effective action on the part of individual states. Pesticides will be more rigidly controlled than ever before. A great number of bills involving ecological sins have been submitted to the congress for action. So there are hopes that our goodly heritage may yet be preserved.[9]

But other nations must also become involved in similar programs, as many of them are. And, above all, individual action is also called for. That is what the above tips in biblical ecology are intended to achieve. It will therefore be well if these directives drop down upon contemporary humanity as the gentle rain falls upon the tender grass (Deut 32: 2). If a man has no good apart from God, if he keeps the Lord always before him, then he will want to act responsibly to preserve the good earth that God has entrusted to him (Ps 16: 2, 8). He will get busy preserving the earth's rivers, lest the Lord turn them into deserts because of man's misuse of them (Ps 107: 33–34). Although his portion in life may not be of this world, it is up to him while he is in it to help preserve that world, so that the next generation may have a goodly heritage in it (Ps 17: 14; 16: 6). He still has time to look after the vineyard that has been entrusted to him. If he does not, he will be responsible for its being trampled down and made a wasteland (Is 5: 5–6).

Moreover, the Lord will summon him as he once summoned Job: "I will question you, and you declare to me!" (Job 38: 3; 40: 7). "What have you done with the Garden that I turned over to you?" (Gen 3: 13). "I gave you a good earth! What have you made of it? I brought order out of chaos for you! Why have you brought the good earth back to the brink of chaos? I gave you the birds and the fish, the cedars and the lilies! But where has all of nature gone? I made you my stewards, I entrusted all of creation to you! You exploited my property, you used up the rich resources, you wasted all that I gave you! Give an account of your stewardship!" (Lk 16: 2).

NOTES

[1] *Time Atlantic Edition* (Amsterdam, Netherlands) 97: 1 (Jan. 4, 1971) 34–35.

[2] May, Edward C. *That Thy Saving Health May Be Known among All Nations.* Chicago, Wheatridge Foundation, 1967, pp. 13–15.

[3] For a more detailed treatment of this theme, see the author's article "Man, the Steward of Creation. The Biblical Concept of the Image of God," *St. Louis University Magazine* 43: 1 (Spring, 1970). 43–48.

[4] *Newsweek Atlantic Edition* (London) 77: 4 (Jan 25, 1971), 54–55.

[5] *Newsweek*, 76: 5 (Feb. 1, 1971) 40.

[6] Terrien, Samuel. *The Psalms and Their Meaning for Today.* Indianapolis and New York: Bobbs-Merrill Company, 1952, pp. 48–49.

[7] *Time* 97: 4 (Jan. 25, 1971) 27. *Newsweek* 72: 4 (Jan. 25, 1971) 10–11.

[8] *Time* 97: 8 (Feb. 22, 1971) 48.

[9] *Newsweek* 72: 8 (Feb. 22, 1971) 40.

Frank H. Seilhamer
Hamma School Of Theology

The Role of Covenant in the Mission and Message of Amos

One of the main problems that traditionally has surrounded the assessment of the role which covenant played in the theology and preaching of the prophets of Israel has been the establishment of how much of the religious tradition of the Bible was made or developed by them and how much of it was preexistent and was simply transmitted by these divinely appointed spokesmen.

In the past, some biblical scholars asserted that the prophets were the principal architects of Israel's faith.[1] They held that it was the prophets who originated, rather than passed on, some of the great theological-ethical cornerstones of Israel's religious system.[2] The prophets, said they, took the crude raw material of a nomadic, or seminomadic, primitive religion, and through their personal experience and insight, individual genius, and divine inspiration, shaped the faith of Israel into a sophisticated and highly ethical moral-religious system.[3]

The moral-covenant concept was, some scholars asserted, one of these ideas originated by the prophets. Covenant was too highly complex and sophisticated a concept to have come from the desert.[4] The great national covenants of the Pentateuch came into Israelite life only after the prophets had laid the groundwork for them.[5] Hence, to look for any well-developed, and centrally crucial, covenant theology in any prophet earlier than Jeremiah was to read back into that material ideas that could not have been there originally.[6]

This assigning to the prophets of the role of innovator has been carried over, to some extent, to the present day. C. F. Whitely[7] and J. Jocz,[8] as late as the present decade, still support such views. Yet much of the more recent research done by biblical and Near Eastern scholars, and evidence turned up by archeologists have tended to temper the innovative role once assigned to the *nby'ym.*[9] New texts from many ancient and allied cultures and the decipherment of languages far predating the founding of the Israelite nation have shown that many of the ideas assigned late dates because of their complexity actually were ancient by the time Abram left Ur.[10]

As is well known, treaty-covenant texts were found to be in use in the Near East before the twentieth century B.C. Cultures with which the Israelites had to have had, and were shown to have had, contact used covenant concepts, forms, and formulations which, in some cases, are almost identical to those contained in the national covenants of the Pentateuch. Moreover, it has been demonstrated that these concepts, forms, and formulations were reflected, to varying degrees and with various emendations, in each of the Israelite covenant documents, including those covenantal texts that may be assigned Mosaic dates. Hence, while the prophetic genius may have had much to do with the sharpening of the religious consciousness of Israel's covenantal responsibilities, it seems probable now that even the earliest of the canonical prophets presupposed and built on a covenant concept already known and acknowledged as normative by the people to whom they were sent.[11]

The basis for the mission of most of the canonical prophets seems to rest on the existence of the covenant relationship between God and Israel. The main preaching emphasis of many of these prophets was the assailing of the people of the nation for breaking covenant law.[12] Recent studies have emphasized that the prophetic books of even the eighth-century prophets are laced with covenant references and technical covenantal terminology, even though the word *bryt* appears only infrequently in their texts. Terms like *twrh,*[13] *ḥq,*[14] *mṣwt,*[15] *ḥsd,*[16] *ṣdqh,*[17] *mšpṭ*[18]—all of which were employed by the prophets to convict, challenge, and influence the people to whom God sent them to speak—have been shown to have strong covenantal roots and points of reference.

Indeed, in the opinion of some contemporary scholars, without the covenant relationship between God and the nation, and the nation's frequent disregard for that relationship's demands and responsibilities, the prophets would not have been needed by God so often. It was as divinely appointed champions of covenant keeping that they found their purpose in Israelite society and history. For as W. J. Phythian-Adams has pointed out, the prophets "never saw themselves as sent to proclaim a new vision or a new conception of God: they came, as messengers with strict and definite orders, to recall revolting Israel to Yahweh who had chosen it."[19]

The prophecy of Amos gives evidence of having been provoked precisely by such a need as Phythian-Adams described. When Amos came out of the hills of Tekoa to deliver his message to the populace of Israel (Amos 1: 1), its thrust was centered upon the nation's repeated transgressions of the covenantal stipulations and upon the consequences those transgressions were going to bring.

This covenantal basis for Amos' charges against the nation is to be seen in his oracles against both the southern and northern kingdom in the second chapter of his book:

> Thus says the Lord:
> "For three transgressions [*pš'y*] of
> Judah, and for four, I will not re-
> voke the punishment [*l' 'šybnw*];
> because they have rejected the law of
> the Lord [*'l-m'sm 't-twrt yhwh*],
> and have not kept his statutes
> [*wḥqyw l' šmrw*],
> but their lies have led them astray,
> after which their fathers walked.
> So I will send a fire upon Judah,
> and it shall devour the strong-
> holds of Jerusalem."[20]

The indictment of Israel, which immediately follows, while more specific and not mentioning either *twrh* or *ḥq*, is based on the same grounds as his condemnation of the southern sister:

> Thus says the Lord:
> "For three transgressions [*pš'y*] of
> Israel, and for four, I will not re-
> voke the punishment [*l' 'šybnw*];
> because they sell the righteous for
> silver,
> and the needy for a pair of shoes—
> they that trample the head of the poor
> into the dust of the earth,
> and turn aside the way of the afflicted;
> a man and his father go in to the same
> maiden,
> so that my holy name is profaned;
> they lay themselves down beside
> every altar
> upon garments taken in pledge;
> and in the house of their God they
> drink
> the wine of those who have been
> fined." (Amos 2: 6–8)

The premise that the rebukes made by Amos are covenant-backed is based on two factors. First, the *terminology* used to describe the nation's corruption is frequently employed in Near Eastern and biblical technical covenantal parlance. Second, the sins of which the people are guilty are actions proscribed by covenantal texts or covenantal traditions.

In the first of the two indictments, Amos specifically states that the reason for God's displeasure with Judah is that she has rejected the *twrt yhwh* and has not kept or fulfilled *ḥqyw*. Both *twrh*[21] and *ḥq*[22] are used repeatedly in the OT to describe the provisions of the covenant which the nation is to observe because she has bound herself to the Lord. In these passages in Amos, they apparently refer to the stipulations embodied in the *bryt* which God made with Israel at Sinai, a fuller form, or more complete description, of which was later included in the Deuteronomic account of Josiah's reaffirmation of that covenant in the seventh century B.C.[23]

As James Muilenberg has said, *twrh* is "the revealed law implementing the covenant."[24] Even when the term is used in a broader context, where it refers to the whole body of God's teaching or instruction, *twrh* is rarely devoid of this essential covenant rooting. Likewise, *ḥq*, which is sometimes linked with *twrh* (Deut 17: 19) and in other instances is used in covenantal texts and traditions in conjunction with *mṣwh*,[25] often has the same point of reference as the former. It too usually encompasses the body of stipulations delineated in the *bryt* itself.[26]

Just which of these specific obligations from their covenant with God the people of Judah were violating is not pointed out in the text of the oracle against them. They are simply charged with trampling the covenant in general. But in the condemnation of Israel, the blanket indictment gives way to a delineation of covenant infidelities. "The specific violations of the Covenant fall like sledge-hammer blows upon the heads of the guilty."[27] One by one, the acts of disobedience are enumerated in a lengthy catalog.

The injustice shown to, and the oppression of, the poor and righteous as condemned in vss 6–7a are infractions of injunctions against the same in the stipulations set forth at Sinai. The nation had been bound by its acknowledged and sworn covenant with God to deal fairly with such innocent and defenseless individuals.[28]

The sexual aberration of a father and his son having intercourse with the same woman (vs 7b), which many scholars believe is a direct reference to some variety of sacred prostitution,[29] is prohibited by the covenantal stipulations as repeated in Deut 23: 17.

To use "garments taken in pledge" for religious carousing (vs 8a) when they should have been returned to their owners for their use at sunset, transgressed the Sinai dictum to the opposite (see Ex 22: 26). God would hear their voice when the ones so wronged cried to him for redress (Ex 22: 27).

Drinking wine gathered by fine "unjustly extorted"[30] and "laying down beside every altar" were to make light of God's majesty and violate the sovereignty which the Lord demanded in the first stipulation of the Decalogue (Ex 20: 2).

Further evidence that these indictments, as well as others which are made at various places in the text, are proclaimed within a covenant framework is to be found in the term used to describe the activities condemned by the prophet.

The people's actions are termed *pšʿy*, "acts of rebellion." In Near Eastern treaty language, the term "to revolt," "to transgress," "to rebel" means to throw off the authority of an acknowledged suzerain by violating the stipulations of the pact that bound the parties together.[31] *pšʿ* has a similar connotation in various biblical texts as well. There are instances where it refers specifically to the breaking of existing alliances or to the overthrowing of a previously accepted sovereign.

The term is used in this sense in the account of the fracture of the union between Israel and Judah (1 Kings 12: 1 ff). When Rehoboam sends his taskmaster into Israel, where he is stoned to death by the populace (1 Kings 12: 18), the murder of the king's official, and therein the rejection of the royal authority, is described as *pšʿ*.[32] The same verb is similarly employed in the narratives concerning the rejection of their vassalage by two kings who had been made *ʿbdym*, "servants," by David.[33] Both the severance of its vassal status to Israel by Moab[34] following the death of Ahab and the setting up of its own king by Edom during the reign of Jehoram in Judah[35] are denoted by the verb *pšʿ*.[36] Such usage supports the assertion of such scholars as Gerhard von Rad that the term "belongs preeminently to the language of politics,"[37] especially the politics of treaty-covenant relations.[38]

In Amos 2: 4–8, the relationship which has been broken by the nation's "revolt" is the one that was forged in the covenant made between God and his people.[39] Such negating of their sworn obligations to the treaty and its Master threatened to bring down the consequences of the curses which had been framed for just such eventualities. Not only had such protection been built into the agreements forged by such men as Suppiluliumas[40] and Esarhaddon,[41] but the biblical covenants contained similar provisions to guard against the violation of their stipulations:

> You shall have no other gods before me. You shall not make for yourself a graven image, or any likeness of anything that is in heaven above, or that is in the earth beneath, or that is in the water under the earth; you shall not bow down to them or serve them; for I the Lord your God am

a jealous God, visiting the iniquity of the fathers upon the children to the third and fourth generation of those who hate me, but showing steadfast love to thousands of those who love me and keep my commandments.

You shall not take the name of the Lord your God in vain; for the Lord will not hold him guiltless who takes his name in vain.[42]

Drawing upon such provisions in the treaty-covenant tradition, Amos declares that the rebellion of the nation will be dealt with by God according to the *mutually accepted* covenant agreement. Disobedience to that bond's stipulations will be punished. Those who disregard their *sworn* allegiance to God, with the covenant loyalty which that entails, must expect to be visited with the consequences of their acts:

"Behold I will make it tremble [*m'yq*][43]
beneath you as a cart
trembles [*t'yq*] loaded with
sheaves.
Flight shall perish from the swift,
and the strong shall not retain
his strength,
nor shall the mighty save his life;
he who handles the bow shall not
stand,
and he who is swift of foot shall not
save himself,
nor shall he who rides the horse
save his life;
and he who is stout of heart among
the mighty
shall flee away naked in that day,"
says the Lord. (Amos 2: 13–16)

What is especially significant is that this punishment is given to the people *because* the nation has accepted a covenantal relationship with God. The populace is not being chastised for failing to keep obligations to God about which they knew nothing or which they had not committed themselves to observe in the first place. The thrust of Amos' message is that it was precisely because they *had* entered into a covenant with the Lord, and *had* pledged themselves to live by an accepted religio-ethical standard delineated in the stipulations of that pact, a standard which they had ignored repeatedly, that divine punishment would be meted out to the nation:

Hear this word that the Lord has
spoken against you, O people of Israel,
against the whole family which I

brought up out of the land of Egypt:
"You only have I known [*rq 'tkm yd'ty*]
of all the families of the earth;
therefore will I punish you
for all your iniquities" (Amos 3: 1).

The key to understanding the covenantal import of this passage is to be found in Amos' use of the term *yd'ty*, "I have known." Its use here does not mean the usual "to learn", "perceive," "experience," "discriminate," etc.[44] As Herbert Huffmon has shown, *yd'* is used in this instance in a more formal legal sense.[45] In a pattern common to the Near Eastern treaties and earlier biblical usage, "know" is employed by Amos as a technical term for the recognition of the covenant stipulations as binding by the covenanting partners.[46]

"Know" is often used to "indicate mutual legal recognition on the part of suzerain and vassal, i.e. Yahweh and his servant(s) . . . in the Bible."[47] In a number of the prophetic books,[48] including that of at least one other eighth-century prophet,[49] *yd'* must be understood within this legal frame of reference if one is to grasp the full implications of the text. The *covenant recognition* of Israel by God is the couching for Amos 3: 1–2:

> Comparison with Am. 9:7, with its mention of the Ethiopians, the Philistines, and Aram, should make it clear that Am. 3: 2 has reference to that peculiar relationship between Yahweh and Israel expressed by the covenant, and that *yada'* in this context means more than "care for"[50] or "take notice of"[51] as is evident from the common translation "choose." The passage calls for the technical sense, viz., "You only have I recognized by covenant,"[52] from which it follows that the covenant-breaking invokes the curses, i.e., punishment for iniquity.[53]

The covenantal frame of reference for Amos' proclamation is also evidenced in his rhetorical question in the following verse, where two of the key words or phrases have strong covenantal overtones and implications:

Do two walk together
unless they have
agreed ['*m-nw'dw*]

The phrase "walk together" is a figure of speech used in some of the Near Eastern treaties to describe the keeping of the covenantal obligations by the treating partners.[54] In the letter of Rib-Addi to Pharaoh contained in the Amarna correspondence, the same metaphor is used, there describing the vassal's loyalty to his overlord in the face of a conspiracy against the suzerain.[55] Rather than throw in with the conspirators in their designs against the Egyptian throne, Rib-Addi held fast to his treaty obligations to his lord. Despite the reported pressure of the populace of Byblos, who pressed him to "walk after (follow) the son of Abdiashirta, and let us make a treaty of peace between us,"[56] the vassal in Canaan stood firm. For "to walk after" or "to follow after" another ruler would have meant that Rib-Addi had broken his sworn treaty obligations to serve only the pharaoh.

In the treaty between Abban and Iarimlim, a similar metaphor is used to convey the same idea. The vassal is specifically warned by the suzerain against any action that would allow the subject to stray from the relationship to which his superior had bound him:

> If ever Iarimlim says to Abban, vizier of Hattusa: "Abban [is not . . . ."] and he lets go out (deserts?), then to another king he will not go out. If he lets go the horn (hem?) of Abban's garment and seizes the horn of another king's garment, he shall f[orfei]t the towns and territories.[57]

In both cases, the implication of the texts is clear. The treaty stipulations bound the vassal to complete allegiance and obedience to his lord. Any departure from that prescribed responsibility and obligation, such as leaving the suzerain to attach oneself to, follow after, or serve another, was considered a sign of open revolt on the part of the subject who did so.[58]

The same concept is contained in *each* of the national biblical covenants, where to go after other gods and serve them is to violate both the stated terms and the spirit of the bond with Yahweh.[59] Thus, when Amos uses this metaphor in 3: 3 he stands within this treaty-covenant tradition and usage. Both the nation and God should be "walking together" because they had bound themselves in the covenant at Sinai.

The people should not let go of God to go after any other as a new sovereign, be it a human one or an idol, because both they and God had ruled out such conduct when they had "agreed" (*nw'dw*).[60] While this term in Amos 3: 3 is usually taken to be part of a wisdom saying,[61] and is interpreted by some scholars as referring to "two men making their way across the horizon of Judah's empty hill country" to meet at an appointed time and place,[62] it may very well refer to the covenant-making event when God and Israel acknowledged—that is, "knew," or "agreed with"—each other at Sinai. It could be a play on the word *yd'*, "to know," in the sense that both Yahweh and the nation had recognized the covenant and its stipulations as binding on themselves and each other.[63] Such a frame of reference would not only fit it in well with the two verses which precede it but would carry out the covenantal implications of the "walking together" metaphor in the first half of the verse—that is, because two parties *have* covenanted, they *should* walk together, each fulfilling his role and its responsibilities as delineated by the stipulations of that agreement. "The basic idea, the relation between Yahweh and Israel as a bond between partners, and details of formulation all suggest . . . [the] concepts and terms having to do with the covenant."[64]

But the nation has totally forgotten this "agreement" and its responsibilities. They no longer know how "to do what is right" [*nkḥh*] (Amos 3: 10), but, on the contrary, "store up violence [*ḥms*] and robbery [*sd*] in their strongholds" (3: 10). The norms which should have governed the affairs of the Israelites have been put out of mind. Yahweh's demands had "dropped out of sight and consciousness among Samaria's leading citizens."[65]

The term *nkḥh* has the essential meaning of "to walk straight forward," "to go directly toward [a goal]." At times, it is used in the Bible to mean that which is "straight," as well as that which is "honest [true]."[66] In some cases, it is used in contrast to that which is deceptive and false (cf Is 30: 40). It is also used as a synonym of "justice," "righteousness," and "faithfulness" in Is 59: 14 in a sequence dealing with the theme "justice is far from us."[67] It appears in a legal framework in Prov 24: 26 and 2 Sam 15: 3; in the former instance, being used in a wisdom saying concerning conduct in legal affairs; and in the latter, being applied to a legal appeal.

In Amos' indictment, *nkḥh* appears to be used in this legal sense. It points to what was desired to be the style of justice observed in the legal proceedings in the nation. "What is alone of moment to him is the departure from an order of society which was formed according to Yahweh's will and which maintained every Israelite one with the other in a system of mutual responsibility."[68]

That all such covenantal norms have been completely forgotten by his contemporaries is to be seen in the fact that while the poor are trampled (Amos 8: 4), as dishonesty is rampant in the marketplace (vs 5), and as the defenseless are sold into slavery (vs 6), the debauched lie on their beds of ivory (6: 4) and demand more luxury for themselves (4:1). Moreover, in the place of covenant obedience, the populace attempts to substitute religious ceremonialism. But their empty ritual and hollow pilgrimages cannot atone for the breaking of the covenantal stipulations. Through biting sarcasm in the mouth of his prophet, God pours out his abhorrence of such religious sham:

"Come to Bethel, and transgress;
to Gilgal, and multiply transgression;
bring your sacrifices every morning,
your tithes every three days;
offer a sacrifice of thanksgiving of
that which is leavened,
and proclaim freewill offerings,
publish them;
for so you love to do, O people of
Israel!"
says the Lord God.[69]

Because the covenant has been broken, Amos declares that the punishment entailed in the bond's curse clauses is going to be unleashed. In three chapters (7, 8, 9) Amos delineates some of the forms that chastisement will take.

In the first prophecy, the people are told that the high places and sanctuaries will be destroyed, and that God is going to set himself against the kingdom:

He showed me: behold the Lord
was standing beside a wall built
with a plumb line, with a plumb
line in his hand. And the Lord
said to me, "Amos, what do you
see?" And I said, "A plumb line."
Then the Lord said,
"Behold, I am setting a
plumb line in the midst
of my people Israel; I
will never again pass by
them; the high places of
Isaac shall be made desolate,
and the sanctuaries of Israel
shall be laid waste,
and I will rise against the
house of Jeroboam with the
sword." (7: 7–9)

In the second oracle, the prophet declares that the people within the northern kingdom will personally feel the consequences of their rebellion. Even though the sentence was spoken to Amaziah for his contradiction of God's command to Amos, the whole nation of covenant breakers will suffer the same consequences as he:

> Therefore thus says the Lord:
> "Your wife shall be a harlot in
> the city and your sons and
> daughters shall fall by the
> sword,
> and your land shall be parceled
> out by line;
> you yourself shall die in an un-
> clean land, and Israel shall
> surely go into exile away
> from its land." (7: 17)

The third prophecy tells of the extensiveness of the punishment that is to come, and announces that the moment for its breaking forth is at hand:

> Thus the Lord showed me: behold
> a basket of summer fruit. And he
> said, "Amos, what do you see?"
> And I said, "A basket of summer
> fruit." Then the Lord said to me,
> "The end has come upon my
> people Israel;
> I will never again pass by
> them.
> The songs of the temple shall
> become wailings in that day,"
> says the Lord God;
> "the corpses shall be many;
> in every place they shall be
> cast out. Hush!"

Other punishments, including some directly connected with the curse clauses in the biblical covenantal tradition and their Near Eastern parallels, are threatened by Amos at various points within his book.[70] Together with what is forecast here, they are to comprise the chastisement for the nation's rebellion.

As in every national covenantal text preserved within the Bible, as well as in almost every complete Near Eastern treaty document, the covenantal texts themselves had provided for such a punitive response by the Deity, or deities, against those who broke their oaths and bolted the covenant's stipulations. As J. L. Mays has commented, it is "clear that Israel is to be judged precisely in her identity as the covenant people."[71]

This is what God has sworn to do (cf Amos 6: 8). Three times the phrase *nšbʿ adny yhwh bnpšw* is used by Amos, each time to introduce a divine decree of punishment.[72] The total force of God's personal integrity is invested in this solemn oath, the ancient Near East's most binding form of personal commitment.[73] Since Israel had thrown over God's lordship, she had to take the covenantal consequences.

To smash the nation was, however, not what God *wanted* to have to do. His desire was for the people to assume a responsible and obedient posture in keeping with their covenantal ties. If that were done, then all the predicted calamity could be averted. The people had only to reverse their pattern of disobedience and "seek" the Lord, in the sense of "going after" him (5: 5–6). In the Near Eastern tradition, such an action implied not only a "search" for the Lord, but a "following after" him—that is, it entailed obedience to that Lord as the supreme partner in a covenant relationship as well.[74] If that were done, the covenantal relationship could be restored, and the people would "live" (cf Amos 5: 6) rather than perish:

> Seek good, and not evil,
> that you may live;
> and so the Lord, the God
> of hosts, will be with
> you,
> as you have said.
> Hate evil, and love good,
> and establish justice
> in the gate;
> it may be that the Lord, the God of
> hosts will be gracious
> to the remnant of Joseph. (5: 14–15)

The "good" which Amos envisioned was a return to living covenantally. The whole of Chapter 5 of his book, where the sins of Israel are lamented, is laced with covenantal language and allusions. The sins attacked are almost always those prohibited in the covenantal stipulations themselves.[75] His remedy for that sinfulness involves a reacceptance of their covenant responsibilities by the people:

> Let justice [*mšpṭ*] roll down
> like waters; and righteousness
> [*ṣdqh*] like an ever-flowing
> stream. (5: 24)

The people had agreed to do that when they entered the pact with God that made them his peculiar people.[76] Though they had repeatedly refused to carry out the covenantal terms they swore to perform, the assumption on which the prophecy of Amos is based is that if they acted positively on them at once, the God-Israelite breach could be healed. While the possibility for that to happen was left open by God, on the basis of the people's past obstreperousness and obstinacy, Amos apparently anticipated no change in the nation's moral-religious course.

Since the people did not acknowledge the "right" they were to live by (cf 3: 10), then there was little hope that it might become the norm for their activity. They had denied the very basis for any such God-dictated covenantal obedience by repudiating, by their *pš'y*, God's authority over them (cf 2: 4, 6). The patience that God had shown in the past as he waited for that rebellion to end had finally reached its limits. He would no longer continue to forgive their sins. The day for reform had come, and its rejection would be dealt with:

> The end has come upon my people
> Israel;
> I will never again pass by them. (7: 8; 8: 2)

In the eyes of Amos, this combination of the end of the divine patience and the persistent rebellion and callousness of the leaders and upper classes of Israel foreboded doom for the nation. Nevertheless, the premise that man had within himself the power to change his stance toward God and the covenant *was never denied* by the prophet. Man did have within himself the capacity for obedience. He could have—indeed, should have—been keeping the covenant all along. It was *because* the Israelites had the potential to do so, and did not use it, and *because* they had sworn to be obedient, and had then refused to perform what they were capable of accomplishing, that they were going to be punished by God. The covenant's stipulations were possible to fulfill; the problem was that God's people had chosen to break them rather than to obey them.[77]

Thus, the assumption of an existing covenantal bond between Yahweh and the nation is apparent in the prophecy of Amos. The presence of at least three important factors lead clearly to such a conclusion. Briefly summarized, they are these:

First, Amos made repeated use of terms which were part of the reservoir of formal treaty-covenant parlance. Words like *yd'*, *pš'*, *twrh*, *ḥwq*, *šb'*, *mšpṭ*, *ṣdqh* recur often in the text of the book. While each one of these roots can be interpreted to have more than one meaning or point of reference, all of them have been shown by various scholars and textual evidence to have strong grounding in the Near Eastern and biblical treaty-covenant tradition and practice.

Second, the basis for most of the prophet's charges against the nation is their violations of specific covenant stipulations. As has been shown, in numerous instances the sins pointed out by him are those prohibited in one or another of the extant biblical covenantal texts.

Third, the curses which Amos either invokes or alludes to as being ready to befall the nation for the violation of the covenant's demands are also, for the most part, attested in the treaty-covenant texts. Even where no specific quotes or parallels to Amos' threats can be found in any biblical or Near Eastern religio-legal corpus, his maledictions clearly fit into that genre of literature.

The presence of any one of these factors, or the appearance of any single element or component of them, would not of itself be sufficient evidence to prove that Amos had presupposed and built his message on an existing covenantal relationship between God and Israel. However, the clustering of such factors, coupled with the central role they play in this biblical book, points to the conclusion that not only was there a covenant concept known to, and appreciated by, Amos and his contemporaries but that without it he may have had no mission to the nation at all. It was because the people had revolted against their divine Suzerain and the bond which he had consummated with them that Amos was taken *m'ḥry hṣ'n* and was sent to tell his fellow countrymen that the covenant's curses were about to fall upon them.

Notes

1 Cf J. Wellhausen, *Prolegomena to the History of Ancient Israel*, Menzies and Black, trans. (New York, 1957), pp. 399 f; S. A. Cook, *The Old Testament: A Reinterpretation* (London, 1936), p. 168; see also his *The Truth of the Bible* (London, 1938), p. 63.

2 Cf W. A. Irwin, "Revelation in the Old Testament," in *The Study of the Bible Today and Tomorrow*, H. R. Willoughby, ed. (Chicago, 1947), p. 258; W. C. Graham, *The Prophets and Israel's Culture* (Chicago, 1934), p. 45.

3 J. Wellhausen, *op. cit.*, pp. 417 f.

4 *Ibid.*, p. 417, where Wellhausen attributes this transformation of the basis of Israelite religion from a "natural bond" to a "relation depending on conditions of a moral character" to "such prophets as Elijah and Amos." Although Wellhausen became the great popularizer of this theory, he was not the one with whom many of the bases for this position originated. Scholars who preceded him, such as W. M. L. de Wette, *Beiträge zur Einleitung in das Alte Testament* (1806–7), Wilhelm Vatke, *Die biblische Theologie Wissenschaftlich dargestellt: Die Religion des Alten Testaments nach den kanonischen Büchern entwickelt* (1835), and K. H. Graf, *Die geschichtlichen Bücher des Alten Testaments: Zwei historisch-kritische Untersuchungen* (1866), among others, argued that much of the covenantal-legal legislation of the Pentateuch was of late origin. They declared that many of the laws included in these texts were the products of a long process of development and could not therefore be attributed to the age of Moses or even to the early monarchical period. Such a complex religious system as the covenant documents portrayed was to be dated in the period after the time of the prophets. Cf also B. Duhm, *Die Theologie der Propheten als Grundlage für die innere Entwicklungsgeschichte der israelitischen Religion* (Bonn, 1875).

5 Cf W. A. Irwin, *The Old Testament: Keystone to Human Culture* (New York, 1952), p. 206; I. I. Mattuck, *The Thought of the Prophets* (London, 1953), pp. 36 f.

[6] Cf R. H. Pfeiffer, "Facts and Faith in Biblical History," *JBL* 70 (1951), 2, n. 3; also his *Introduction to the Old Testament* (New York, 1941), pp. 221 ff.

[7] *The Prophetic Achievement* (Leiden, 1963), pp. 24 ff.

[8] *The Covenant: A Theology of Human Destiny* (Grand Rapids, Mich., 1968).

[9] Cf N. W. Porteous, "The Basis of the Ethical Teaching of the Prophets," in *Studies in Old Testament Prophecy*, H. H. Rowley, ed. (Edinburgh and New York, 1950), pp. 143–56, and his "Prophecy," in *Record and Revelation*, H. W. Robinson, ed. (London, 1939), p. 217; A. C. Welch, *Prophet and Priest in Old Israel* (London, 1936), pp. 148 f.; G. Mendenhall, *Law and Covenant in Israel and in the Ancient Near East* (Pittsburgh, 1955), p. 19; W. F. Albright, *FSAC*, p. 239.

[10] Cf G. Mendenhall, *op. cit.*, pp. 3 ff; D. McCarthy, *Treaty and Covenant* (Rome, 1963), pp. 7 ff; K. Baltzer, *Das Bundesformular* (*WMANT*, 4; Neukirchen, 1960), pp. 12 ff,

[11] Cf G. E. Wright, *The Old Testament against Its Environment* (London, 1950), p. 29; W. J. Phythian-Adams, *The Call of Israel* (London, 1934), p. 23.

[12] W. J. Phythian-Adams, *op. cit.*, p. 23.

[13] Cf J. Muilenberg, *The Way of Israel* (New York, 1961), p. 68; N. W. Porteous, *op. cit.*, pp. 147–51.

[14] Cf G. Schrenk, "entellomai," *TWNT*, II, p. 546.

[15] *Ibid.*

[16] N. Glueck, *Ḥesed in the Bible* (Cincinnati, 1967), pp. 56–101.

[17] Cf J. Muilenberg, *op. cit.*, p. 60; J. Bollier, "The Righteousness of God," *Interp* 8 (1954), 408–10.

[18] J. Bollier, *op. cit.*, pp. 404 f.

[19] *Op. cit.*, p. 23.

[20] Amos 2: 4–5. Some critics are of the opinion that this oracle against Judah did not belong to the original series; cf O. Eissfeldt, *The Old Testament: An Introduction* (Oxford, 1965), p. 200; G. Fohrer, *Introduction to the Old Testament*, D. Green, trans. (New York, 1965), p. 579. As J. L. Mays points out, however, such a conclusion may be unwarranted. Ultimately such critics must "call on psychological presuppositions which cannot be established," *Amos: A Commentary* (Philadelphia, 1965), p. 41.

[21] Cf Ex 24: 12; Deut 4: 44; 17: 11; 27: 38; 28: 58; 29: 29. See also Josh 24: 26.

[22] Cf Deut 6: 17, 24; 7: 11; 11: 32; 12: 1; 16: 12; 17: 19; 26: 16, 17; 27: 10. See also Josh 24: 25.

[23] Cf W. R. Harper, *Amos and Hosea* (*ICC*; Edinburgh, 1905), p. 49. Because of the inclusion within these passages of phrases which have strong similarities to the terminology, usage, structure, and so on, employed in the book of Deuteronomy, some scholars delete some portions of this material as not having come from Amos, declaring them to be later additions. Cf J. Wellhausen, *Die kleinen Propheten übersetzt und erklärt* (Berlin, 1892); and K. Marti, *Dodekapropheton* (Berlin, 1903), *in loci*; C. C. Torrey, "Notes on Am 2^{7} 6^{10} 8^{13} $9^{8\text{-}10}$," *JBL* 15 (1896), 151–54. For those opposed to this view, see S. R. Driver, *Joel and Amos* (*Cambridge Bible*; Cambridge, 1897), and H. J. Elhorst, *De Profetie von Amos* (Tübingen, 1901), *in loci*; A. Alt, "Ursprünge des israelitischen Rechts," *Kleine Schriften zur Geschichte des Volkes Israel* (München, 1953), I, pp. 278–332; W. F. Albright, *The Biblical Age from Abraham to Ezra* (New York, 1963), pp. 19 f.

[24] *The Way of Israel*, p. 60.

[25] Cf Deut 26: 17; 27: 10.

[26] Cf Deut 4: 45; 5: 1; 6: 17, 24; 11: 32; 16: 12; 26: 16; Josh 24: 25.

[27] J. M. Myers, *Hosea-Jonah* (*Layman's Bible Commentary*, 14; Richmond, 1959), p. 110.

[28] Ex 23: 6–8. For a Near Eastern parallel, see the votive inscription of Urukagina

as translated in S. N. Kramer, *The Sumerians: Their History, Culture, and Character* (Chicago, 1963), p. 319.

29 Cf H. Bauer, *Der Prophet Amos erklärt* (Berlin, 1847); S. R. Driver, *op. cit.*; H. Ewald, *Commentary on the Prophets of the Old Testament* (1875–81); H. J. Elhurst, *op. cit.*; *W. Nowack, Die kleinen Propheten übersetzt und erklärt* (*HAT*; Berlin, 1903); W. R. Harper, *op. cit., in loci*; J. M. Myers, *op. cit.*, p. 111. By the change of one consonant, however (*hnʿrh* to *hnʿdh*), the text could read "a man and his father act by agreement," making it fit very well with the preceding charges of the people defrauding the poor. Cf W. R. Harper, *op. cit.*, p. 51; J. M. Myers, *op. cit.*, p. 11. In either case, it would be a violation of the covenant stipulations, as in the footnote above.

30 J. M. Myers, *op. cit.*, p. 111.

31 Cf D. J. Wiseman, 'The Vassal-Treaties of Esarhaddon," *Iraq* 20 (1958), Part I, 34, 36, 46, 52, etc.

32 1 Kings 12: 19. In Hebrew, the vs reads: *wypšʿw yśrʾl bbyt dwd ʿd hywm hzh.*

33 Cf 1 Chron 18: 2, 13, where the term is used in connection with both Moab and Edom. In these contexts, *ʿbd* appears to carry the connotation of "vassal," *BDB*, p. 712. Cf 2 Kings 3: 4; 2 Sam 10: 19. The designation "servant" is used in Near Eastern treaty parlance in this sense. Cf D. J. Wiseman, *op. cit.*, pp. 34, 52.

34 2 Kings 1: 1; 3: 2 ff.

35 2 Kings 8: 20–22 (parallel 2 Chron 21: 8, 10). Such an act is prohibited in both Near Eastern and biblical treaty-covenant texts. Cf D. J. Wiseman, *op. cit.*, p. 34; Ex 20: 3; Deut 6: 13 f; Josh 24: 20.

36 See also 2 Kings 8: 22b, where the same term is used in reference to Libnah.

37 *Old Testament Theology* (Philadelphia, 1963), I, p. 263. See also J. L. Mays, *op. cit.*, p. 28.

38 Cf W. Eichrodt, *Theology of the Old Testament*, J. A. Baker, trans. (Philadelphia, 1961), II, pp. 381 f.

39 J. A. Bollier, *op. cit.*, p. 407.

40 Cf the treaty between Suppiluliumas and Mattiwaza, *ANET*, p. 206.

41 Cf D. J. Wiseman, *op. cit.*, pp. 60–80; *ANET*, p. 534. See also the treaties between Niqmepa of Alalakh and Ir-Im of Tunip, *ANET*, p. 531, and Ashurnirari V of Assyria and Matiʾilu of Arpad, *ibid.*, p. 532.

42 Ex 20: 3–7; see also Deut 27: 15 ff; Josh 24: 19 ff.

43 The meaning of *mʿyq* is uncertain. The root *ʿwq* has been translated as "press," "totter," by *BDB*, p. 734, and as "behindert sein," "schwanken lassen," by *KB*, p. 690. H. Gese, "Kleine Beiträge zum Verstandnis des Amosbuches," *VT* 12 (1962), 421, translates the word as "ausholen" ("to excavate, groove"), "eingraben ("to dig in, furrow"). See also W. R. Harper, *op. cit.*, pp. 60 f.

44 *BDB*, pp. 393 f.

45 "The Treaty Background of Hebrew *YĀDAʿ*," *BASOR* 181 (1966), 34 f.

46 *Ibid.*, p. 33.

47 *Ibid.*, p. 34. Cf Gen 18: 19; Ex 33: 12; 2 Sam 7: 20; 1 Chron 17: 18.

48 Cf Is 45: 3–4; Jer 1: 5, 12: 3; 31: 34.

49 Cf Hosea 2: 22; 4: 1; 5: 4; 8: 2; 13: 4–5.

50 J. Lindblom, *Prophecy in Ancient Israel* (Oxford, 1962), p. 326.

51 S. R. Driver, *Joel and Amos, in loci*, and his *Deuteronomy* (*ICC*; Edinburgh, 1895), p. 425.

52 For similar opinions for the covenant rooting of this passage, see B. Vawter, *The*

Conscience of Israel (New York, 1961), p. 95; W. Harrelson, *Interpreting the Old Testament* (New York, 1964), p. 346.

53 H. Huffmon, *op. cit.*, pp. 34 f.

54 D. R. Hillers, *Covenant: The History of a Biblical Idea* (Baltimore, 1969), p. 131; W. J. Moran, "The Ancient Near Eastern Background of the Love of God in Deuteronomy," *CBQ* 25 (1963), 83, n. 35.

55 J. A. Knudtzon, *Die El-Amarna-Tafeln* (*VAB*; Leipzig, 1915), II, 135: 11 ff.

56 *Ibid.*

57 D. J. Wiseman, "Abban and Alalakh," *JCS* 12 (1958), 129.

58 For other examples of this use of "to follow after" in other Near Eastern treaties, see J. A. Knudtzon, *op. cit.*, 149: 46; 280: 20.

59 Ex 20: 3; 23: 13; Deut 6: 14; 8: 19; 11: 28; 13: 2; 28: 14; Josh 24: 2, 16.

60 Amos 3: 3.

61 Cf H. W. Wolff, "*Amos' geistige Heimat,*" *WMANT* 18 (1964), 3–12.

62 J. L. Mays, *op. cit.*, p. 60.

63 H. Huffmon, *op. cit.*, pp. 34, 35, 37.

64 D. R. Hillers, *op. cit.*, p. 131.

65 J. L. Mays, *op. cit.*, p. 65.

66 *BDB*, p. 647.

67 J. L. Mays, *op. cit.*, p. 65.

68 *Ibid.*

69 4: 4–5; for the place of Gilgal and Bethel in Israelite worship, see H. J. Kraus, *Worship in Israel*, G. Buswell, trans. (Richmond, 1966), pp. 146–65.

70 See especially Amos 4: 8, 11; 5: 11; 8: 8, 10, 12; D. R. Hillers, *Treaty Curses and the Old Testament Prophets* (*Biblica et Orientalia*, 16; Rome, 1964), discusses each of these verses and their treaty-covenant curse rootings on pp. 29, 76, 29, 71, 58, 29 respectively.

71 J. L. Mays, *op. cit.*, p. 132.

72 4: 2; 6: 8; 8: 7.

73 Cf J. L. Mays, *op. cit.*, p. 118; J. Pedersen, *Der Eid bei den Semiten* (Strassburg, 1914); F. C. Fensham, "Maledictions and Benedictions in Ancient Near Eastern Vassal-Treaties and the Old Testament," *ZAW* 74 (1962), 1–9.

74 See W. J. Moran, *op. cit.*, p. 83.

75 Compare Amos 5: 7, 10 with Ex 23: 1–8 and Deut 16: 18, 20; Amos 5: 11 with Ex 22: 22; 23: 6 and Deut 10: 18; 24: 17; 27: 19; Amos 5: 12 with Ex 23: 7–8 and Deut 15: 7–11; 16: 18–20; 24: 14–15.

76 For the covenantal exhortations to justice, cf Ex 23: 6; Deut 16: 18–19; 17: 9; 23: 17; 27: 19. For an example of stipulation calling for *righteous* behavior or actions, see Lev 19: 15.

77 G. von Rad, *The Message of the Prophets* (London, 1968), p. 107.

John Alexander Thompson
American Bible Society

The Date of Joel

The purpose of this paper[1] is to classify and evaluate some of the discussions of the date of Joel since the appearance of Kapelrud's *Joel Studies* in 1948.[2] Kapelrud's work is taken as a starting point because he broke new paths by using Ugaritic parallels and by analyzing the liturgical elements of the book. The reason for choosing this subject for the present volume is that J. M. Myers[3] has given a fresh approach to the dating of Joel by citing recently discovered archeological evidence. In 1962, W. Neil[4] summarized the opinions on Joel's date as follows: "Critics have ranged from the ninth century to the second century B.C. in seeking to determine a date for the prophecies, either as a whole or in part. The modern consensus, however, regards them as post-exilic and narrows the range of time to the period ca. 400." Though most of the scholars surveyed below do date Joel about 400 B.C. or soon thereafter, examples will be given of those who maintain earlier or later dates.

Advocates of a Pre-exilic Date

During the minority of King Joash of Judah, about 830 B.C.

The basic argument of J. Ridderbos[5] for this early date is the position of Joel in the Hebrew canon as the second of the Minor Prophets. It is not certain, however, that the order of the Minor Prophets in the Hebrew Bible is chronological throughout; for example, Zephaniah certainly prophesied about a century before Nahum and Habbakuk, which precede Zephaniah in order. Furthermore, the LXX lists Joel as the fourth of these prophets. Ridderbos sees the background of 3 [4]: 19 in Shishak's invasion (1 Kings

14: 25) and in Edom's revolt against Joram (2 Kings 8: 20). Since this Egyptian and Edomite hostility to the Israelites could be remembered after the exile and was actually continued after the exile, it is therefore no proof of a pre-exilic date. Ridderbos explains the failure to mention any king in Joel by suggesting that Joash was still a minor and Jehoida was really reigning. In 2 Kings 11: 21 [12: 1]; 12: 1 [2] and 2 Chron 24: 1, the reign of Joash, beginning in his seventh year, is treated like any other reign. The absence of the reigning king's name in the introduction of Joel is still contrary to the analogy of the introductions mentioning the king in most prophetic books during the monarchy Is 1: 1; Jer 1: 1–2; Ezek 1: 2; Hos 1: 1; Amos 1: 1; Mic 1: 1; Zeph 1: 1). Even stronger evidence that Joel prophesied after the monarchy had ceased is the absence of king, princes, nobles, and royal officials from Joel's lists of those classes who mourn the devastation caused by the locusts (1: 5–14; 2: 16). If Joel had prophesied about 830 B.C., a reference to the high priest Jehoiada would also be expected, since the latter would presumably have issued the call to public repentance and since he was even more important than the Joshua mentioned in Hag 1: 1, 12, 14; and Zech 3: 1–8. Ridderbos rightly recognizes that 3 [4]: 2–3 sound like some destruction of Jerusalem. He identifies the attackers as either the Chaldeans or (if it is predictive) the Romans. He suggests that this passage may be predictive (which is certainly not to be expected from the Hebrew perfects) or a later addition. A simpler solution is to understand this passage as referring to the capture of Jerusalem in 587 B.C., which had already taken place when Joel prophesied.

M. Bič[6] uses Ugaritic parallels to support dating Joel in the time of Joash. He interprets Joel's prophecy as a polemic against Baalism. He sees in 1: 8 a reference to the Ugaritic myth of Anat weeping for the dead Baal, and in 2: 9 a reference to the Ugaritic myth of Mot entering the temple of Baal. The context of the first passage lists those who mourn the locust plague, and the context of the second is a description of the coming of the locusts to the city. These contexts hardly prepare for mythological references. If the book is a polemic against Baalism, one would expect clear references to Baal, to idols, to idolatrous altars, to the high places, to idolatrous rites, or to idol priests. These features of idolatry are clearly denounced by pre-exilic prophets (e.g., Hos 2: 8 [11]; 4: 13; 9: 10; Jer 2: 8; 7: 9; 19: 5), and the absence of such denunciations is a probable indication of origin after the exile, when idolatry had practically ceased among the Jews. Bič speaks of parallels to Elijah and Hosea, but closer are the parallels to later prophets, including exilic Ezekiel, Joel 2: 28 [3: 1] = Ezek 39: 29; Joel 3 [4]: 17 = Ezek 36: 11; Joel 3 [4]: 18 = Ezek 47: 1–12) and post-exilic Malachi, Joel 2: 11 = Mal 3: 2; Joel 2: 31 [3: 4] = Mal 4: 5 [3: 23].

E. J. Young[7] recognizes some of the arguments for a post-exilic date but upholds a pre-exilic date under Joash. One of Young's arguments, in addition to those mentioned above, is that the style of Joel is different from that of post-exilic Haggai, Zechariah, and Malachi. But from the post-exilic standpoint, since Joel borrowed phrases from pre-exilic prophets, it is not surprising that he equals the vivid poetic style of some of them in his description of the locust plague. Young thinks that it was Joel that influenced Amos in the parallels (Joel 3 [4]: 16 = Amos 1: 2; Joel 3 [4]: 18 = Amos 9: 13). Recently H. W. Wolff[8] has given reasons for thinking that Amos influenced Joel. Young recognizes that "Israel" in Joel is a synonym for "Judah," and he maintains, without giving examples, that such a usage is proper before the exile. There are, however, many clear pre-exilic examples where "Israel" definitely means the Northern Kingdom (e.g., 1 Kings 12: 16; 15: 9; Amos 1: 1; 2: 6). The most obvious conclusion from Joel's use of "Israel" is that the Northern Kingdom had ceased to exist. Young says that there was no occasion for Joel to mention the "high places." The call to repentance in 2: 12–13 would have been a suitable occasion to denounce the "high places," if they really existed in Judah in Joel's day. Pre-exilic prophets denounced the "high places," which were associated with idolatry (Jer 7: 31; 19: 5; Ezek 6: 3; Hos 10: 8); but Haggai, Zechariah, and Malachi do not mention them after the exile, when they had ceased to be used by the Jews.

D. Deere[9] favors a pre-exilic date under Joash. He rightly points out that the phrase in Joel 3 [4]: 1 translated in KJV, "I shall bring again the captivity," can be correctly interpreted, "I restore the fortunes" (RSV, and similarly JB, NEB, NAB). In this context, however, this meaning could well include return from the exile. About Joel 3 [4]: 4 6, Deere remarks that these verses refer to the events described in Obadiah, who he evidently thinks is pre-exilic. G. H. Livingston,[10] however, writing in the same volume with Deere, concludes that that the capture of Jerusalem mentioned by Obadiah is that of 587 B.C. No known capture of Jerusalem before this date produced the scattering of the Jews and the dividing of their land described by Joel 3 [4]: 2. Deere observes that Phoenicia and Philistia were pre-exilic enemies of Judah, but, it should be noted, they were also post-exilic enemies.

R. A. Stewart[11] argued plausibly that a reference to making ploughshares into swords (3 [4]: 10), would probably precede the hope of the reverse process (cf Is 2: 4). In the same year, L. H. Brockington[12] argued that Joel here parodies the earlier expression of Is 2: 4 and Mic 4: 3.

ABOUT 600 B.C.

A. S. Kapelrud brought fresh elements into Joel studies by using Ugaritic parallels and by arguing for a date of the original prophecy about 600 B.C., then a period of oral transmission, and writing in its present form in the fourth or third century. Kapelrud's strongest argument for a date about 600 B.C. consists in Joel's parallels with Jeremiah. Joel does have such parallels; but it also has, as pointed out above, striking parallels with exilic Ezekiel and post-exilic Malachi. Kapelrud's contention that Joel did not consciously copy other prophets but used common expressions may be right in some cases; but in 2: 32 [3: 5], Joel expressly states that he is quoting, probably from Obad 17, and most scholars consider Obadiah post-exilic. Kapelrud suggests the possibility that Joel 3 [4]: 2, with its reference to the scattering of the Jews and the dividing of their land, may be a post-exilic addition. This verse, however, fits with other features of the capture of the city in 3 [4]: 2–6, 17: the taking and selling of slaves, the plundering of the Temple, and the occupation of Jerusalem by foreigners.

J. Steinmann[13] was influenced by Kapelrud to advocate also a date about 600 B.C. In addition to noting similarities in Joel to Jeremiah, Steinmann points out that Joel's phrase "the day of Yahweh" (1: 15; 2: 1, 11, 31 [3: 4]; 3 [4]: 14) also occurs in pre-exilic Zephaniah, Jeremiah, and Ezekiel. Advocates of a post-exilic date can point out that the expression also occurs in post-exilic Zech 14: 1, and that "the day" for the time of judgment is often found in Zechariah and Malachi. Steinmann frankly admits that 3 [4]: 1, 3, 7 must come after the fall of Jerusalem, but he thinks that these verses are later additions to an essentially pre-exilic Joel. But it is difficult to take these verses away from their context with vss 2, 6, and 17, which also imply the fall of Jerusalem. It is simpler to leave these verses in place and recognize that the prophecy is post-exilic.

C. A. Keller[14] places the ministry of Joel between 630 and 600 B.C., and he adduces careful and comprehensive arguments. Because no mighty empire is mentioned, Keller places 3 [4]: 1–8 after the decline of Assyria and before the rise of Babylonia and Persia—that is, between 630 and 625 B.C. An advocate of a post-exilic date could point out that the dominant Persian empire is not mentioned in post-exilic Malachi, except by implication in the reference to the governor (Mal 1: 8), and Joel may come from the same period of benevolent Persian administration. Keller associates 3 [4]: 19 with Pharaoh Neco's invasion of Palestine and killing of Josiah in 609 B.C. It may well be that this Egyptian invasion was the attack or one of the attacks referred to by the prophet, but it cannot be assumed that the prophecy was delivered immediately after the attack. The people of the Near East have long historical memories. Keller interprets 3 [4]: 1–3 as referring to raids by the Philistines and Phoenicians. However, the scattering of the Jews and the dividing of their land imply something more serious than raids. Furthermore, Joel does not accuse the Philistines and the Phoenicians of an attack on Judah, but only of receiving plunder and selling Jewish slaves (3 [4]: 5, 6). Keller rightly maintains that the style of Joel is not like that of post-exilic Nehemiah, Ecclesiastes, Esther, and Daniel, but, with the exception of some portions of Ecclesiastes, these are prose works and Joel is mostly poetry. Keller's opinion that a message for the people after the days of Nehemiah would have been in Aramaic is controverted by the composition of Sirach in Hebrew about 190 B.C. Keller gives a careful list of Joel's words and expressions which are also found in prophets of the later seventh and early sixth centuries. This is not surprising in a prophet who has so many parallels to other prophetic books of all periods. One must also consider Joel's words and phrases which are found elsewhere only in post-exilic writings (see below).

W. Rudolph[15] gives justified criticisms of some of the arguments used for a post-exilic dating, and opts for a date soon after the Chaldeans took Jerusalem in 597 B.C. without destroying it. Rudolph is right in using the analogy of Jer 26 and 36 to prove that the gathering of the people in the forecourt of the Temple (Joel 2: 16) does not necessarily mean every single member even of a small community. He considers Joel as one of the prophets of peace rather than of judgment for Jerusalem who are condemned by Jeremiah (Jer 28). It is questionable, however, whether a prophet of peace would have interpreted the locust plague and the drought as God's judgment on Israel calling for repentance. With Rudolph's dating, it is strange that Joel does not specifically mention the Chaldeans, as Habakkuk, Jeremiah, and Ezekiel do. Rudolph argues that Joel would have referred to the destruction of the Temple if this event connected with the capture of Jerusalem in 587 B.C. had already taken place. Joel 3[4]:5 seems to imply that the Temple had been looted and therefore presumably destroyed. Rudolph thinks that Joel 2: 11, 31 [3: 4] precede the parallels in Mal 3: 2; 4: 5 [3: 23], but recently G. F. Wood[16] has argued to the contrary.

Exilic Dating

soon after 587 B.C.

L. Mariès[17] is strongly influenced by Kapelrud, and places Joel shortly after the fall of Jerusalem to the Chaldeans. He considers Joel a contemporary of Ezekiel, because of the resemblances between the two prophets. For a later date, Joel's parallels to post-exilic Malachi can again be cited. Mariès envisions Joel as prophesying in Jerusalem to the remaining Jews who had not gone into exile. A difficulty for Mariès's dating is that the Temple was destroyed by the Chaldeans in 587 B.C., but Joel implies an intact, standing Temple in which sacrifice was being offered (1: 9, 13; 2: 17).

Post-Exilic Dating

post-exilic, but no specific dates

The first of L. H. Brockington's arguments (cf n. 12) for a post-exilic date is that the Jews have been scattered in exile (3 [4]: 2).

W. T. Smith and J. Mauchline[18] list the main arguments for a post-exilic date: 1) The Northern Kingdom—Israel—is not mentioned. Israel has become a synonym for Judah (2: 27; 3 [4]: 16). 2) There is no mention of royalty or aristocracy. 3) The Temple (1: 9, 13, 14, 16; 2: 17; 3 [4]: 5 and its ritual (1: 9, 13; 2: 14) are regarded as very important elements of religion, in contrast to pre-exilic prophets who criticized ritualism. 4) The call to repentance (2: 12) does not mention the specific sins denounced by pre-exilic prophets: idolatry, formalism, sensuality, and oppression. 5) The foreign peoples mentioned (Phoenicians, Philistines, Egyptians, Edomites, Greeks, and Sabeans) do not include the Assyrians or the Chaldeans, which pre-exilic prophets mention. 6) A national catastrophe has occurred; the people of Yahweh are scattered, and the land of Yahweh has been divided among foreigners (3 [4]: 2). 7) There are at least twenty-seven parallels to other Old Testament writings, and it is likely that in some of these Joel was the borrower. 8) The vocabulary of the prophet is late, including such Aramaisms as *'ly*, "lament" (1: 8), and *swp*, "rear" (2: 20).

O. Eissfeldt[19] places 1: 1–2: 27 in the post-exilic period, but does not further specify the date. He notes the failure to mention the royal court and the Aramaisms in Joel. He also argues that the daily offering in the Temple (1: 9; 2: 14) indicates a post-exilic date. As Kapelrud (on 1: 9) points out, 1 Kings 18: 29 and 2 Kings 3: 20 show that the daily offerings were already practiced in pre-exilic times.

about 520 or 500 B.C.

J. M. Myers, in his commentary on Joel (1959) and more fully in his article of 1962 (see n. 3) on the dating of Joel, has argued for a date about 520 B.C. One of the important contributions of Myers' study is the use of archeological evidence from the ancient Near East.

Myers has assembled a wealth of archeological evidence for Greek commercial relations with the Near East from the eighth century onward. After Myers' study, it should be unnecessary to say, as did L. H. Brockington (see n. 12), without the benefit of seeing Myers' evidence, that the selling of Jews to the Greek (3 [4]: 6) was unlikely before the fourth century, "when Greek contact with Palestine began." Myers argues that the prediction of selling Tyrian and Philistine slaves to the Sabeans points to the sixth century rather than to the fifth or fourth century, when the leadership in South Arabia passed to the Mineans. On the other hand, the Sabeans had been known to the Israelites since the time of Solomon, and Sabean royal inscriptions,[20] published since Myers wrote, show that the Sabean kingdom continued in the fifth and fourth centuries B.C., and even into the fifth century A.D.

Myers argues that Joel 2: 7, 9, referring to Jerusalem's wall, may be dated before Nehemiah. The book of Nehemiah, however, states that before Nehemiah's repairs the wall of Jerusalem was broken down (1: 3; 2: 13), and so locusts could have come through the breaches (Neh 4: [1] 7) without scaling the wall (Joel 2: 7). Therefore a date after Nehemiah's restoration of the wall in 445 B.C. seems more likely. Haggai and Zechariah make many references to Zerubbabel and Joshua, and it is strange that Joel does not mention these leaders, even in the lists of all the classes who join in the mourning, if he also prophesied about 520 B.C. Also in 520 B.C., the Temple was not yet completed, but Joel implies that the vestibule and the Temple have been standing for some time (1: 13, 14, 16; 2: 17). One reason that Myers prefers a date early in the post-exilic period is that he wants to bring the references to the fall of Jerusalem closer to the time of the event in 587 B.C. The memory of great events like the Exodus and the fall of Jerusalem remained, and still remains, fresh among the Jews. Therefore prophetic comment on such events long after their occurrence is not surprising.

Myers gives a careful analysis of similarities in the religious situation in Joel and in Haggai-Zechariah; these similarities help to establish a post-exilic date for Joel. Attention should be called, however, to some significant differences in the temper of religious life reflected in Haggai-Zechariah and in Joel. Myers rightly says that in Haggai-Zechariah, the priest and prophet joined to reestablish the religious community. In Joel, on the other hand, the religious community is already established, and the priests are in full control of the religious life. Hag 1: 9–11 chides the people for their indifference to the Temple; but in Joel, the people are much concerned with reestablishing regular sacrifices after they have been interrupted by the locusts and the drought (1: 13, 16; 2: 14). Probably between the people's indifference to the cult shown in Haggai and Mal 1: 1–14 and the people's zeal for the cult shown in Joel came the reforming activities of Ezra and Nehemiah and the reestablishment of religious law.

D. R. Jones[21] gives good arguments for a post-exilic dating, and places Joel about or soon after 500 B.C. He puts Joel after the completion of the Temple in 516 B.C. and after Haggai and Zechariah, because Joel shows a concern for the Temple similar to theirs. Joel, he suggests, came before the popular laxity in sacrifice denounced in Mal 1: 1–14. It is more likely that Joel, who reflects popular zeal for proper sacrifices, came after Malachi and after the religious reforms of Ezra and Nehemiah.

ABOUT 400–350 B.C.

T. H. Robinson[22] briefly adduces arguments for a post-exilic dating of Joel, and places Joel 1: 1–2: 27 not before the fourth century B.C.

T. Chary[23] votes for a date about 400 B.C. He criticizes some of Kapelrud's use of Ugaritic material, pointing out that some Hebrew cultic terms similar to Ugaritic were used by the Israelites long before any of the dates suggested for Joel. Therefore Joel's use of these terms does not prove a pre-exilic date. Chary thinks that Kapelrud underestimates the force of Joel's parallels to exilic and post-exilic prophets. For example, Joel's "I am the Lord your God and there is none else" (2: 27) is almost certainly a reflection of one of the dominant themes of Deutero-Isaiah (Is 45: 5, 18, 22; 46: 9), and Joel 2: 11, 31 [3: 4] probably derive from Mal 3: 2; 4: 5 [3: 23].

J. A. Thompson[24] adds the following to the items already given as bearing on the date of Joel: 1) The reference to Sidon as yet to be judged (3 [4]: 4) argues for a time before 345 B.C., when Artaxerxes III Ochus destroyed the city and sold its inhabitants into slavery (so Diodorus Siculus, XIV.45). 2) The omission of any mention of Persia, as in Malachi, may indicate a time during the benevolent Persian administration before Artaxerxes III's expedition in 345 B.C. suppressed revolts in Syria. 3) Another late word used by Joel is *šlḥ*, "weapon" (2: 8, and elsewhere in 2 Chron 23: 10; Neh 4: 17, 23 [4: 11, 17]; Job 33: 18; 36: 12). 4) In a full treatment of Joel's parallels to other prophets, Thompson points out that variations of the expression "and you shall know that I am the Lord your God" occur over fifty times in Ezekiel, and therefore Joel 3 [4]: 17 is probably the borrower and is post-exilic. 5) Since both Obadiah and Malachi, whom Joel seems to quote (see above), come probably from the mid-fifth century, allowing time for Obadiah and Malachi to be accepted would likely place Joel about 400 B.C. at the earliest.

J. Bourke[25] agrees with Chary in dating Joel about 400 B.C. Bourke thinks that Joel's eschatology was influenced by Amos, Jeremiah, Deuteronomy, and also exilic Ezekiel.

J. Trinquet[26] states the main arguments to establish a date for Joel in the period 400 to 350 B.C.

W. Neil (see n. 4) gives an excellent list of reasons for a post-exilic date at the end of the fifth or the beginning of the fourth century.

E. G. H. Kraeling (1966)[27] dates Joel 1: 1–2: 27 late in the Persian period—that is, in the fourth century.

A. Weiser[28] places Joel after Nehemiah, at the earliest about 400 B.C.

G. F. Wood (see n. 16) gives strong and comprehensive reasons for dating Joel between 400 and 350 B.C. He rightly points out that the reference to the Greeks as far away and as buyers of slaves, not conquerors, requires a date before the battle of Issus in 333 B.C., after which Alexander began his conquests of Syria-Palestine.

R. K. Harrison[29] recognizes the difficulties of dating Joel, and tends to favor a post-exilic date, somewhat before 400 B.C. Most scholars would agree with his conclusion for a post-exilic dating, but they would disagree with his concession that no element of Joel's thought is incompatible with a pre-exilic date. Joel's zeal for the cult, his eschatology, and his exclusiveness fit into the religious pattern of the post-exilic rather than of the pre-exilic period.

F. R. Stephenson[30] uses astronomy to support a post-exilic date for Joel. Stephenson assumes that Joel 2: 31 [3: 4] and 3 [4]: 15, mentioning the darkening of the sun, refer to an eclipse that had recently taken place. He finds that between 1130 B.C. and 300 B.C. there were only two total eclipses visible in Jerusalem: on February 29, 357 B.C. and July 4, 336 B.C. The eclipse of 763 B.C., probably referred to in Amos 8: 9, was only partial in Israel, and there was an eclipse in 402 B.C., which was total in Galilee, not Jerusalem. Stephenson is probably right that Joel's references to the darkening of the sun were influenced by eclipses. It should be noted, however, that Joel predicts the darkening of the sun as a future sign of the day of the Lord, and that Isaiah also refers to the darkening of the sun as a sign of God's judgment (13: 10; 24: 23; 50: 3). Therefore we cannot be sure that Joel was directly influenced by an eclipse which he himself saw.

H. W. Wolff (see n. 8) gives careful and logical arguments for dating Joel after Nehemiah's rebuilding of the wall in 445 B.C. (Joel 2: 7, 9) and before Artaxerxes III's destruction of Sidon about 345 B.C. He would place the ministry of Joel in the first half of the fourth century B.C. Wolff suggests that Joel is before Amos in the Hebrew canon, not for chronological reasons but because of the literary parallels: Joel 3 [4]: 16 = Amos 1: 2; Joel 3 [4]: 18 = Amos 9: 13. He also points out that the LXX order making Joel the fourth of the Minor Prophets brings together three prophecies which are not dated in the headings: Joel, Obadiah, and Jonah. To Joel's words with only post-exilic parallels, Wolff adds *ṣḥnh*, "foul smell" (2: 20, elsewhere Sir 11: 12, Heb).

R. A. Cole[31] agrees with a date about 400 B.C.

LATE FOURTH OR THIRD CENTURIES

T. H. Robinson (see n. 22) dates Joel 2: 28–3: 21 [3: 1–4: 21] in the third century. He suggests that 3 [4]: 2 may reflect the carrying away of Jews into captivity by Artaxerxes III in 344 B.C., but such a date is incompatible with the address to Sidon, 3 [4]: 4, which Artaxerxes' army destroyed in 345 B.C. Robinson is certainly right that this part of Joel precedes the Seleucid control of Palestine (beginning in 198 B.C.), because in 3 [4]: 6 the Greeks are not yet conquerors. The Greek conquests, however, took place in the latter part of the fourth century, and a third century dating of this part of Joel is therefore eliminated.

M. Treves[32] argues for a date soon after 312 B.C. He gives nine of the arguments mentioned above for the general post-exilic dating of Joel. Treves further proposes that 3 [4]: 2, 3, 19 refer to Ptolemy I Soter's capture of Jerusalem in 312 B.C. and the deportation of Jewish captives to Egypt as described by Josephus (*Jewish Antiquities*, XII, ch. 1). Treves associates this capture with Ptolemy's second occupation of Palestine in 312 B.C., but it should be noted that some associate it with his first occupation of Palestine in 320 B.C. (see Kraeling below). There are several difficulties with Treves' dating. In the first place, Joel does not state or even imply that it was Egypt that scattered the Jews and divided their land (3 [4]: 2). Furthermore, as Jones points out (see n. 21), the Greeks in 3 [4]: 6 are faraway people who buy Jewish slaves through the Phoenicians and the Philistines, not present conquerors who take Jewish slaves for themselves directly, as Ptolemy did. With this dating, Alexander had already taken Sidon and Tyre and had killed or enslaved the people of Tyre, and a reference to future punishment for these two cities becomes difficult (3 [4]: 4–8). Egypt's shedding innocent Jewish blood (3 [4]: 19) could refer to Pharaoh Neco's victory over Judah and killing of Josiah in 609 B.C., an event which was still lamented by the Jews in post-exilic times (2 Chron 35: 25).

G. M. Rinaldi[33] suggests that Joel prophesied at the end of the Persian period or, better, at the beginning of the Greek period. As pointed out above, the reference to Sidon (3 [4]: 4) disagrees with such a late dating, and the reference to the faraway Greeks (3 [4]: 6) cannot be squared with a date after Alexander's conquests. Rinaldi gives a valuable critical survey of some recent writers on the date of Joel (Kapelrud, Treves, Chary, Bourke).

O. Eissfeldt (see n. 19) places Joel 2: 28–3: 21 [3: 1–4: 21] in the fourth or third century. Arguments against a late fourth or third century dating are given above.

E. G. H. Kraeling's (see n. 21) dating of Joel 2: 28–3: 21 [3: 1–4: 21] about 300 B.C. is open to the objections given above. Kraeling thinks that the enslavement of the Jews and the partitioning of their land (3 [4]: 2–6) took place in connection with Ptolemy I Soter's first occupation of Palestine.

After considering the above variety of opinion on the date of Joel, some may be tempted to agree with the medieval Jewish commentator Ibn Ezra, who said that we have no way of knowing Joel's time. Although a few uphold a pre-exilic date, and—at the opposite extreme—a few date Joel in the Greek period, the majority of scholars in the past twenty years place Joel in the post-exilic period. Even those who disagree with Kapelrud's conclusion will agree with his principle: "Only a collective view of the whole, particularly against the religio-historical background, can constitute a foundation for the placing of Joel in history."[34] If one considered the factor of vigorous poetic style alone, one might place Joel in the pre-exilic period. All factors considered—the historical allusions, the religious situation, the vocabulary, and the parallels which probably influenced Joel—have led most recent scholars to date Joel between 400 and 350 B.C.

NOTES

[1] I thank my colleague S. L. Morris for some of the items used below. When the book is not cited with the Scripture references, it is the book of Joel. Scripture references are given according to the chapter divisions in the RSV and most English translations, and when the Hebrew chapter or verse differs, then the reference in Hebrew is in square brackets. (In Joel, the difference in chapter divisions is as follows: RSV 2: 28–32 = Heb 3: 1–5; RSV 3: 1–21 = Heb 4: 1–21.)

[2] A. S. Kapelrud, *Joel Studies* (*Uppsala Universitets Årsskrift*, 1948: 4), Uppsala: A. B. Lundequista Bokhandeln, 1948; on date of Joel, see pp. 181–92.

[3] J. M. Myers, *Hosea, Joel, Amos, Obadiah, Jonah* (*The Layman's Bible Commentary*, 14), Richmond: John Knox Press, 1959; on date of Joel, see pp. 72–73; "Some Considerations Bearing on the Date of Joel," in *ZAW* 74 (1962), 177–95.

[4] W. Nell, "Joel, Book of," in *IDB*, ed. G. A. Buttrick, Vol. II, New York: Abingdon, 1962, pp. 926–29; on date, see p. 928.

[5] J. Ridderbos, *Hosea, Joel, Amos*, in *De kleine Propheten*, Vol. I (*Korte Verklaring der Heilige Schrift*), Kampen: J. H. Kok, 1952; on date of Joel, see pp. 122–26.

[6] M. Bič, *Das Buch Joel*, Berlin: Evangelische Verlaganstalt, 1960; on date of Joel, see pp. 9, 106–8.

[7] E. J. Young, *An Introduction to the Old Testament*, rev. ed., Grand Rapids: Wm. B. Eerdmans, 1960; on date of Joel, see pp. 271–73.

[8] H. W. Wolff, *Dodekapropheton 2 Joel und Amos* (*BKAT*, XIV, 2), Neukirchen-Vluyn: Neukirchener Verlag, 1969; on date of Joel, see pp. 2–4.

[9] D. Deere, "Joel," in *The Wycliffe Bible Commentary*, eds. C. F. Pfeiffer, E. F. Harrison, Chicago: Moody Press, 1962; on date of Joel, see p. 819.

[10] G. H. Livingston, "Obadiah," in *The Wycliffe Bible Commentary*, ed. C. F. Pfeiffer, E. F. Harrison, Chicago: Moody Press, 1962, p. 839.

[11] R. A. Stewart, "Joel, Book of," in *The New Bible Dictionary*, ed. J. D. Douglas, London: Inter-Varsity Fellowship, 1962, pp. 638–39.

[12] L. H. Brockington, "Joel," in *Peake's Commentary on the Bible*, eds. M. Black, H. H. Rowley, London: Thomas Nelson and Sons, 1962, p. 614.

[13] J. Steinmann, "Remarques sur le livre de Joël," in *Études sur les prophètes d'Israël* (*Lectio Divina*, 14), Paris: Éditions du Cerf, 1954; on date of Joel, see pp. 172–73.

[14] C. A. Keller, "Joël," (*Commentaire de l'Ancien Testament*, XIa), Neuchâtel: Delachau & Niestlé, 1965; on date of Joel, see pp. 103–4.

[15] W. Rudolph, "Wann wirkte Joel?" in *Das ferne und nahe Wort, Festschrift Leonhard Rost* (Beihefte zur *ZAW* 105), Berlin: Alfred Töpelmann, 1967, pp. 193–98.

[16] G. F. Wood, "Joel," (*The Jerome Biblical Commentary*), Englewood Cliffs: Prentice-Hall, 1968; on Joel, see pp. 439–43.

[17] L. Mariès, "A propos de récentes études sur Joël," in *Recherches de science réligieuse*, XXXVII (1950), 121–24.

[18] W. T. Smith and J. Mauchline, "Joel, Book of," in *HDB*, rev. ed. by F. C. Grant, H. H. Rowley, New York: Charles Scribner's Sons, 1963, pp. 505–6.

[19] O. Eissfeldt, *The Old Testament: An Introduction*, tr. by P. R. Ackroyd, New York: Harper and Row, 1965; on date of Joel, see pp. 394–95.

[20] A. Jamme, *Sabaean Inscriptions from Mahram Bilqîs* (*Mârib*), Baltimore: Johns Hopkins University Press, 1962.

[21] D. R. Jones, *Isaiah 56–66 and Joel* (Torch Bible Commentaries), London: SCM Press, 1964; on date of Joel, see pp. 135–38.

[22] T. H. Robinson, *Die zwölf kleinen Propheten Hosea bis Micha* (*HAT*, erste Reihe, 14), zweite Auflage, Tübingen: J. C. B. Mohr, 1954; on date of Joel, see pp. 55–56.

[23] T. Chary, *Les prophètes et le culte à partir de l'exil*, Tournai: Desclée & Cie, 1955; on date of Joel, see pp. 190–96.

[24] J. A. Thompson, "The Book of Joel," *IB*, ed. G. A. Buttrick, Vol. VI, New York: Abingdon Press, 1956; on date of Joel, see pp. 732–33.

[25] J. Bourke, "Le jour de Yahve dans Joël" in *RB*, LXVI (1959), 5–31, 191–212.

[26] J. Trinquet, "Habaquq" "Abdias" "Joel" (*La Sainte Bible traduite en français sous la direction de l'École Biblique de Jérusalem*), 2d ed., Paris: Éditions du Cerf, 1959.

[27] E. G. H. Kraeling, *Commentary on the Prophets*, Vol. II, Camden: T. Nelson, 1966; on date of Joel, see p. 125.

[28] A. Weiser, *Das Buch der zwölf kleinen Propheten I: Die Propheten Hosea, Joel, Amos Obadja, Jona, Michia* (*ATD*, 24), 5. verbesserte Auflage, Göttingen: Vandenhoeck & Ruprecht, 1967; on date of Joel, see p. 106.

[29] R. K. Harrison, *Introduction to the Old Testament*, Grand Rapids: Wm. B. Eerdmans, 1969; on date of Joel, see pp. 876–79.

[30] F. R. Stephenson, "The Date of the Book of Joel," in *VT*, XIX (1969), 224–29.

[31] R. A. Cole, "Joel," in *The New Bible Commentary*, rev. ed. by D. Guthrie and J. A. Motyer, Grand Rapids: Wm. B. Eerdmans, 1970; on date of Joel, see p. 716.

[32] M. Treves, "The Date of Joel," in *VT* VII (1957), 149–56.

[33] G. M. Rinaldi, *I Propheti Minori, Fasicolo II, Osea—Gioele—Abdia—Giona* (*La Sacra Bibbia*, ed. S. Garfalo), Turin: Marietti, 1959; on date of Joel, see pp. 129–31.

[34] *Op. cit.*, p. 189.

John C. Trever
Baldwin-Wallace College

The Future of the Qumran Scrolls

Tourists from all over the world continue to flock to the unique, cave-simulated Shrine of the Book situated on the southwest extension of modern Jerusalem opposite the new Hebrew University. They go to see the famed Qumran Scrolls. I have noticed that many a visitor stands in almost reverent silence before the glass-enclosed, soft-lighted cases where the ancient inscribed leather scrolls and fragments have been beautifully displayed.

Centered directly beneath the shrine's dome, which is shaped like one of the fifty jar covers discovered in Qumran Cave I in 1949, and dominating the entire exhibit is a great cylinder more than twenty-five feet in circumference for displaying the great Isaiah Scroll (1QIs[a]), the oldest extant book of the Bible. The mounting is so designed that should an emergency arise, the cylinder could be lowered into a rock-cut cave below. One is immediately impressed by the prodigious lengths to which scholars and builders have gone to exhibit with artistic decor and academic dignity this priceless heritage from biblical history.

On entering the shrine in June, 1966, I was shocked rather than impressed by the exhibit. It was not, however, for lack of appreciation of the architectural and scientific artistry, but because of an immediate awareness that the scrolls, especially the great Isaiah Scroll, revealed distinct evidences of marked deterioration. Even though many years had elapsed since my previous close study of the scrolls, I became alarmed over the distinctly apparent darkening of the leather, over which I had labored in 1948 and 1949. The text was by no means as readable as I remembered it then.

Through the examination of the condition of many of the Qumran documents, it has become clear that as leather deteriorates, it darkens until it is reduced to a deep amber-colored gelatinous mass not unlike hardened glue. Then, when subjected to high humidity or excessive moisture, it begins to act like glue and, finally, gradually evaporates. It was this advanced state of disintegration of some of the leather fragments that was mistakenly called "pitch" in the early days of the scroll discovery.[1] The oldest fragment from all eleven Qumran caves, 4QEx[f], to judge from its paleography,[2] is so darkened that its text cannot be seen at all with the naked eye. It can, however, be seen by holding it before a strong light, for the leather is somewhat translucent. Infrared film, fortunately, produced a fairly readable photograph of the text, according to Frank Cross, who is preparing its publication.[3]

If deterioration of the scrolls is so marked after less than two dozen years since the first discovery in the winter of 1946–47,[4] the future of the Qumran Scrolls becomes a matter of major concern. Will all the scrolls in time be reduced to a blackened gelatinous mass that will gradually evaporate into thin air?[5]

During an interview with Yigael Yadin in Israel, I expressed my concern; and Yadin agreed that many others shared this same alarm. Many consultations with scientific experts had already been held to discuss and analyze the problem. A larger effort was even then being planned for the fall of 1966 to bring together experts from all over the world to focus their technical knowledge on this archeological riddle. Thus, I left Israel with the assurance that if modern science possesses the skills, the Qumran Scrolls will be assured preservation for future generations to view in the Shrine of the Book.[6]

To trace the history of the disintegration of the scrolls, it is necessary to recall at least two factors which preceded the deposit in ancient times: 1) The long usage of 1QIs[a] in the Qumran Community left its special impact upon that scroll in the form of darkening of the back of the scroll from the many hands that held it during reading; then too, there were the many ancient repairs. These were features noted in the earliest reports.[7] 2) The evidence of violent treatment of many of the scrolls prior to their deposit has also been noted with: 1QH, one section of which was discovered in a severely twisted condition; 1QIs[b], the condition of which may have been the result of violent abuse[8]; 1QDan[a, b] and 1QPrayers, which reveal clearly violent treatment in ancient times[9]; and numerous cases among the Cave IV fragments.[10]

During nineteen centuries in the caves, the scrolls seem to have suffered proportionately less disintegration than either before their deposit or since their discovery. The exact degree of loss from the ravages of time cannot, of course, be known, as a result of the conditions under which the discovery was made by those unconcerned with academic matters. Those scrolls which had the good fortune to remain in their jars apparently suffered the least. It is my opinion that the only way to account for the splendid condition of 1QIs^a, 1QS, and perhaps 1QpHab, 1QM, 11QPss, and a few others over so many years is that the jars in which they were stored remained intact. The fact that many large rocks fell from the ceiling of Cave I during the centuries may account for the unfortunate condition of many of the other scrolls from that cave.[11] It is reasonable to suppose that the serious condition of those which display violent treatment (such as 1QH, 1QDan$^{a, b}$, 1QPrayers) may have resulted from hasty and unprotected deposit in the cave about A.D. 70, thus exposing them more fully to the elements. It is difficult, to be sure, to go much beyond speculation concerning the causes of the condition of each piece when discovered, but the variations are extensive.

It will doubtless never be known how many scrolls and fragments have been lost for all time as a result of the discovery and handling of most of them by the Ta'amireh Bedouins and the merchants who were consulted or acted as mediators. Only a few details about their condition in this period of the history of the scrolls have been documented. From my interviews with the three Bedouins who discovered the first three scrolls,[12] I was able to confirm that 1QIs^a had a sheet of uninscribed leather which formed a cover and that it was broken apart and lost during the time the scroll was carried about.[13] From examination of the many lacunae along the lower edge of 1QIs^a, it was clearly apparent that most of those breaks occurred during the time the scroll was in their hands and prior to February 19, 1948, when I first examined it. The Bedouins readily admitted that they had stretched the scroll to its full length in one of their tents on at least one occasion. Beyond these meager bits of evidence, however, very little could be gleaned from the Bedouins.[14] John Allegro has claimed that some large fragments of scrolls from Cave I were buried by Khalil Eskander Shahin (Kando) in his backyard in Bethlehem, only to find later that the damp soil had reduced them to worthless gluey lumps.[15] If this undocumented story is reliable, it would demonstrate the rapidity with which moisture may affect the disintegration of these documents, for they could not have remained in Kando's backyard longer than six months, judging by the rapidly developing scroll events at the end of 1948 and following.[16]

Once the first four scrolls reached the hands of the Assyrian Orthodox Community of Saint Mark's in Jerusalem in July, 1947, a somewhat better handling can be assumed. At least, they were wrapped in newspapers and kept together in a leather satchel.[17] Nevertheless, some fragments along the lower margin of 1QIs[a] crumbled away from that scroll, for I found numerous pieces in the satchel when I began to repair the scroll preparatory to photographing it on February 21, 1948.[18] Apparently some attempts to repair the Isaiah Scroll had been made by either Kando or the Assyrians, for at several points pieces of paper had been attached on the back of the scroll to strengthen particularly fragile areas.[19]

Despite all the care that was exercised with the scrolls from February, 1948 on, at least one small piece crumbled away unnoticed even at the time 1QIs[a] was being photographed. When studying the color transparency of col. XLVIII recently, I discovered a stray bit of leather with an upside-down *'aleph* obscuring the final *taw* of *ntybwt* in line eight of the column. The fragment measured only 3 by 8 mm. Tracing it through earlier photographs, I found it on one negative on the left margin of col. XLVI between lines 7 and 8,[20] and finally discovered it on the negative made on February 21, 1948, folded over and partly obscuring a *yodh* in the third line of col. LII through which ran a crack. It thus proved to be the *'aleph* from the word *'š* in Is 65: 5.[21] One very small gap in the great Isaiah Scroll can therefore be restored from photographs, though it is missing from the original.

Some concerns were felt for the preservation of the Cave I scrolls as they were carried about to several exhibitions during 1949 and 1950 and during their stay in a bank vault in New Jersey, where variations in temperature and humidity could be encountered.[22] With the sale of the Saint Mark's scrolls to Israel in 1954, they were returned to Jerusalem; but variations in temperature and humidity were destined to continue to affect the scrolls, even there, despite the greater care given them. It is my conviction, on the basis of the evidence, that high and varying humidity has been the primary cause of the obvious disintegration of the scrolls. The authorities in Israel claim that it is light and exposure to air (oxidation?) that have been primary offenders, but the evidence is persuasive that moisture changes have been the major cause.[23]

Any traveler to the Qumran cave area is immediately aware of the extremely low level of humidity encountered there, except during the very short and sporadic rainy season during the winter months.[24] Considering the orientation of Caves I and XI, from which the best-preserved MSS have been recovered, it is understandable why moisture would affect the contents of those caves less than it would the others with more exposed entrances. Destruction from vermin, however, is quite another matter, and apparently was a major loss factor for scrolls in all the caves.[25]

I have no frame of reference for judging the effects of the past two decades on the multitude of fragments housed in the Palestine Archeological Museum and the Amman Museum, but Frank Cross has mentioned in private conversation that evidence for disintegration of these fragments is an equal cause for concern. The problems relative to the discovery, retrieval, and probable losses of this material from Caves I, II, IV, and XI are well known.[26]

Before 1QIs[a] was mounted on the cylinder in the Shrine of the Book, it was strengthened against crumbling with a very fine nylon netting, which was apparent to the viewer only on close examination. It doubtless served an important function, but would have no value against damage caused by humidity, air, or light. In the meantime, however, the whole shrine has been air-conditioned and humidity-controlled, which should contribute significantly to assuring a future to the scrolls contained therein. Since it is believed by the experts that light is an important factor, that problem has also been carefully studied and adjusted, according to the curator.[27]

Having become aware of the problem of accelerated disintegration of the scrolls since their discovery, I was prompted to seek ways to preserve all the negatives, and especially the color transparencies, of the Cave I scrolls and fragments which I had recorded in 1948–49. Even negatives are vulnerable, unless "archival quality" treatment is given them at the time they are processed.[28] But the dyes used in color films, as indicated by their manufacturers on every package, are far more vulnerable to the ravages of time than are leather documents. The preservation of color films therefore poses another problem for the future of the scrolls.

On a recent examination of the color transparencies made in Jerusalem in 1948 from three Cave I scrolls, I detected evidence of some loss of color, especially in those transparencies which had been occasionally removed from their storage container and subjected to light. Efforts to preserve these materials have therefore been vigorously pursued. Each color transparency has now been duplicated on fresh color film by a process aimed at restoring whatever loss of color could be detected. In addition, a set of color negatives has been produced from the transparencies.[29] A new set of black-and-white negatives has also been produced from them by a special process to be described elsewhere.[30] Several sets of "archival quality" natural-sized enlargements have been prepared, and all the photographic materials have been housed in a special safe under controlled humidity conditions.[31] No longer will any of the original color transparencies be released to publishers for reproduction, but, instead, color duplicates will be provided as needed.[32]

Ultimate preservation of the color reproductions of the scrolls as they appeared in 1948, however, can best be accomplished only through high quality publication, using separation negatives and four-color plates printed on the best and most durable papers. It was for this goal that I pressed

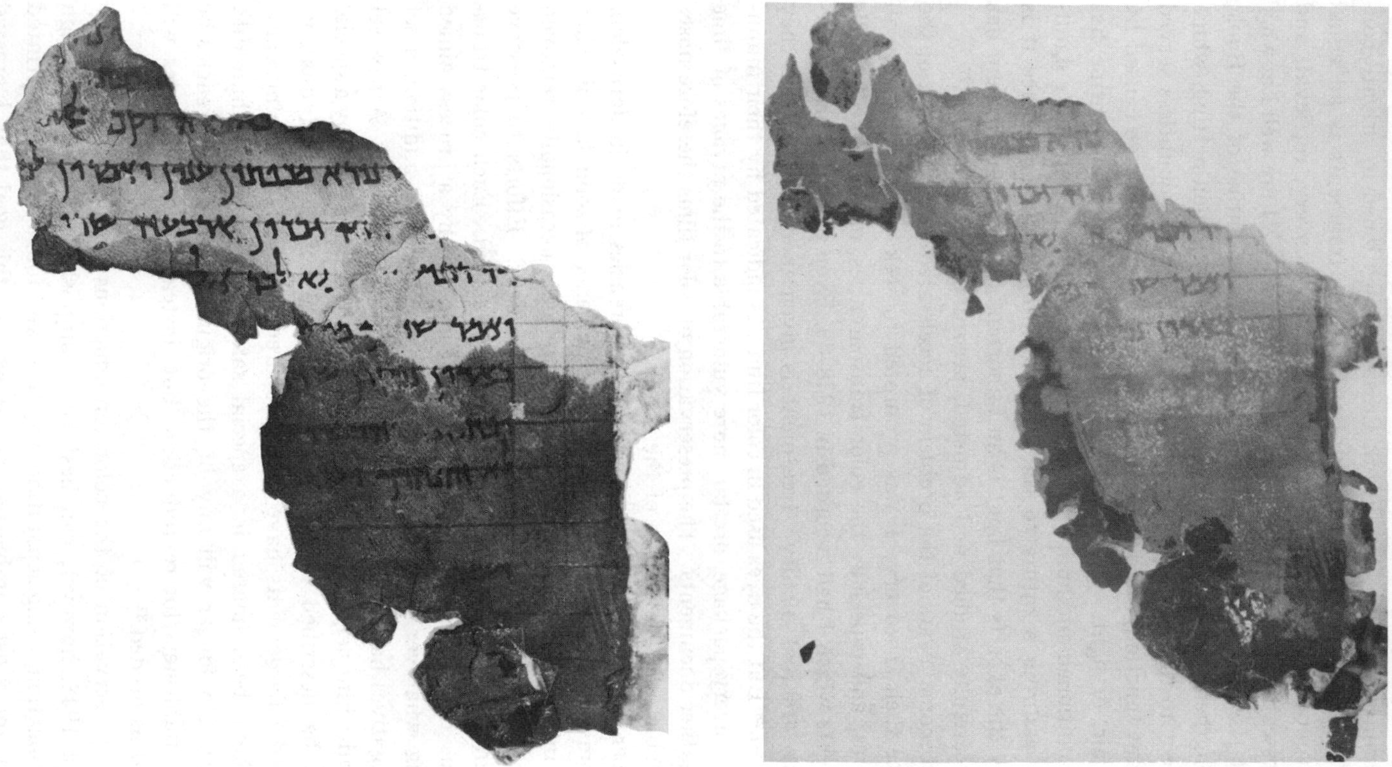

Two photographs of the same section of 1QDan^{b}. The left one was taken by the author in 1949 (© John C. Trever, 1964). The right one, taken about 1965 and reprinted here by courtesy of his Grace, Archbishop Athanasius Y. Samuel, was published in A. Y. Samuel, *The Treasure of Qumran*, Philadelphia, Westminster, 1966, p. 205.

the ASOR on my return from Palestine in 1966. It is good to report that such a volume, entitled *Scrolls from Qumrân Cave I: The Great Isaiah Scroll, The Order of the Community, The Pesher to Habakkuk*, appeared in late 1972. A companion volume, to include many additional color reproductions from my Qumran Cave I materials, will be issued later from the Dead Sea Scroll Research and Preservation Center recently established at Baldwin-Wallace College to pursue these matters in the future.[33] Despite the splendid series of *DJD* published by Oxford University and the volumes produced by the Hebrew University, it should be the objective of those who control the rest of the Qumran materials to follow a similar publishing procedure in full color with at least the most important of all the other Qumran Scrolls.[34] Obviously, such a procedure would involve great expenditures, for which budgets are lacking, but worldwide concern could solve that dilemma.

The most startling and yet instructive illustration of Qumran Scroll deterioration became evident with a publication by the former owner of some of the Cave I scrolls, A. Y. Samuel.[35] In an appendix to his autobiography, he included reproductions of some Qumran fragments which he has continued to retain in his possession—namely, 1QDan^{a,b}, 1QPrayers, 1Q19^{bis} (a fragment of the "Book of Noah" material related to Enoch), and p1Q70^{bis} (the largest piece of papyrus recovered from Cave I).[36] Having labored patiently to separate the matted mass of nine layers of leather, in which form most of these same fragments were first handed to me in February, 1949,[37] I was immediately struck by the severe extent of deterioration the intervening seventeen years had produced. From photographs taken in both black-and-white and color at each step in the process of separating and assembling the fragments in April, 1949, it is now apparent that large gaps have developed in the original pieces where previously the text had been extant. Fortunately, these areas are preserved on the photographs. Notice the striking difference, produced by exposure over a period of time, in two photographs of the same fragment in the illustration opposite.

There were several points on these fragments, however, where no attempt was made to separate them, because of the lack of time and technical resources. Through the years it was hoped that further details might be recovered from these fragments with more careful treatment. All these points have now disintegrated away, with complete loss of these details.[38]

Deterioration of the scrolls which is beyond the control of modern technology is one thing, but the kind of deterioration exhibited in the Samuel volume is a warning about what may be expected for the future of the scrolls if scientific attention to their care is not provided. In view of the fact that these fragments have not been exhibited often or extensively and thus not subjected to light and air, but have been kept largely in a bank vault, it seems likely that the cause of their disintegration is high humidity, for which the New Jersey area, where they are kept, is well known. From their photographic reproduction in the Samuel volume, it is apparent that not only have many areas of these fragments been further reduced to the state of gelatinous "glue" but also other areas have now evaporated away, leaving only gaps where before there had been darkened leather. Since I returned the fragments to Samuel on December 3, 1949, and at that time they revealed no sign of new disintegration, all this radical change took place between then and whenever the photographs were made that were published in 1966—or less than seventeen years.

It will be noted that the piece of papyrus which was published on page 208 of Samuel's book shows no change from the photograph made by me in April, 1949,[39] which may indicate that papyrus is far less affected by moisture—or whatever the basic cause of disintegration may be—than is leather.

The evidence from Samuel's volume should serve as a warning to any traveler to the Near East who may have secured fragments of Qumran materials through devious channels in order to secure unique "souvenirs," that their future is short-lived except with the most exacting attention to technical matters of their preservation. Those who do possess such fragments should, rather, turn them over to competent authorities. The future of even the best-cared-for scrolls, indeed, may be problematic without even better and probably extremely costly techniques of storage and exhibition.

Notes

1 The only evidences of which I am aware that an actual "glue" was used by the men of Qumran are those which appear at the joining point of columns XLIII and XLIV of 1QIs[a] and the less apparent adhesive used for the repairs on the back of the same scroll (cf cols. I–IV, XVIII–XIX, XXV, etc.). For a scientific note on the disintegration of the leather, see D. Barthélemy and J. T. Milik, *DJD*: I, Oxford, Clarendon Press, 1955, p. 40. For some illustrations of disintegrated leather, see J. C. Trever, "Completion of the Publication of Some Fragments from Qumran Cave I," *RQ* 19 (Nov., 1965), 336 and plates II and VII: b, c.

2 Frank M. Cross, "The Development of the Jewish Scripts," in G. Ernest Wright, ed., *The Bible and the Ancient Near East*, Doubleday, Anchor Books edition, 1965, p. 179 and p. 175, fig. 1, line 3.

3 The next oldest fragments—4QSam[b] and 4QJer[a]—reveal their script fairly well despite their very dark leather. Since infrared photographs recover the text remarkably well from these very disintegrated fragments, their publication fails to reveal the actual state of the leather on which they are inscribed. Frank Cross' publication of 4QSam[b] in *JBL* 74: 3 (Sept., 1955), opp. p. 151, for instance, hardly reveals the almost black condition of the originals at the time of their discovery (but compare John M. Allegro, *The People of the Dead Sea Scrolls*, Garden City, Doubleday, 1958, plate 64). A good way to observe the process of disintegration of leather is to examine the entire 1QIs[a] Scroll

and 1QM. Both scrolls are very dark at the beginning, which formed the outside layers of the scrolls during the centuries in the cave; toward the center of each, the leather is lighter, until it becomes a cream white or light tan toward the end. It is obvious that the nearer the leather was to exposure to air in the cave, the more rapid was its disintegration.

[4] For the evidence regarding this date for the discovery, see J. C. Trever, *The Untold Story of Qumran* (hereafter *USQ*), Old Tappan, Revell, 1965, pp. 103–4, 194–96. The information given there modifies somewhat that which appeared in J. C. Trever, "When Was Qumran Cave I Discovered?", *RQ* 9 (Feb., 1961), 135-41.

[5] See above, pp. 471 f.

[6] Since 1966, various reports have reached me about the presence or absence of the Isaiah Scroll in the shrine exhibit. Some have said they saw a facsimile there; others claim to have seen the original. A letter, dated September 28, 1970, from a friend just returned from Israel, says, "Unfortunately, the Isaiah Scroll was not on exhibit, but there was a note that it had been removed for repairs." A letter, dated December 23, 1970, from Magen Broshi, curator of the shrine, says that the Isaiah Scroll is being kept in "a safe storage." He continues by saying that "in a few weeks we intend to return one sheet for exhibition."

[7] See *BASOR* 111 (Oct., 1948), 5–6. As has already been pointed out in my "1QDan^a, the Latest of the Qumran Manuscripts," *RQ* 26 (April, 1970), 285, it is more than likely that 1QIs^a was deposited in Cave I long before the demise of the community about A.D. 70, judging from these evidences of disintegration in ancient times and other factors.

[8] E. L. Sukenik, *The Dead Sea Scrolls of the Hebrew University*, Jerusalem, Magnes Press, 1955, figs. 14 and 10, respectively.

[9] See J. C. Trever, *RQ* 19 (Nov., 1965), 326 f. and plate II.

[10] See John M. Allegro, *op. cit.*, plates 47–48.

[11] The appearance of 1QApocGen may be accounted for on such a basis, since one part of the tightly rolled scroll appears to have been exposed to air and humidity, perhaps as a result of its jar having been broken.

[12] *USQ* (see fn. 4), pp. 103–6, 169–71 and indicated notes.

[13] *Ibid.*, p. 196, note 19.

[14] Just when 1QS was divided into two parts between cols. VII and VIII could not be determined from the interviews. See *ibid.*, p. 196, note 20.

[15] *The Dead Sea Scrolls*, Baltimore, Penguin Books, 1956, p. 19.

[16] See *USQ*, pp. 146 and 204, note 9, where I challenge Allegro's chronology for this event. G. L. Harding, in *DJD*: I, p. 4, assumes that the additional fragments secured by Yusef Saad from Kando were a part of the original find, thus ignoring the Assyrian "clandestine excavation" in the fall of 1948, when much additional material apparently was secured from Cave I.

[17] They also reversed 1QIs^a, so that its more fragile beginning was at the center of the roll. For the record of these scrolls during this period see *USQ*, pp. 107–10, 112–13.

[18] These bits of uninscribed fragments, some thread and repair material, mostly from 1QIs^a (one tiny piece from 1QS, and four pieces of 1QApocGen, plus one gelatinous mass with some linen cloth attached) have been carefully preserved by me.

[19] See *USQ*, plate facing p. 49 (reproduction of 1QIs^a, cols. XXXII–XXXIII), where such a repair appears at the extreme left on the back of col. XXXIV.

[20] This was the 13 × 18 cm negative made on outdated portrait film (cf *USQ*, pp. 78 f.).

[21] The fragment failed to appear at all in *The Dead Sea Scrolls of St. Mark's Monastery*, New Haven, ASOR, 1950; for there col. LII was printed from a negative made in April, 1949, after the scroll had arrived in the United States and the fragment had disappeared entirely.

[22] The Isaiah Scroll was frequently unrolled for publicity purposes in connection with the exhibits, sometimes without proper caution. See frontispiece to A. Y. Samuel's *Treasure of Qumran*, Philadelphia, Westminster Press, 1966; also pp. 188 and 190.

[23] See below.

[24] H. J. Plenderleith, a renowned expert on the preservation of antiquities, once told me that he believed the humidity conditions at the Qumran Caves were equal to, or even lower than, those in the Faiyûm of Egypt, whence such an abundance of ancient papyrus has been recovered. Yigael Yadin remarked facetiously at the close of an interview with me in 1966 that perhaps the only solution to the preservation of the scrolls was to return them to the caves. The projected plans of the Jordanians to build a museum for the scrolls near the site of Khirbet Qumran held real merit in this regard.

[25] The deep scallops which are so prominent along the edges of 1QS, 1QpHab, 1QM, and 11QPss were apparently the result of this cause.

[26] John Allegro, *op. cit.* (1964 ed.), pp. 27–51.

[27] I do not know whether or not similar precautions have been applied to the vast collection of Cave IV fragments and the other materials in the Palestine Archeological Museum, but the authorities are now alerted to the needs. The materials in the Amman Museum may have an advantage, since the problem of high humidity is not so serious there. Jordanian officials should be alerted, if they have not been already, to the factor of the effect of light upon inscribed fragments in their exhibit.

[28] The ASOR has returned all the negative materials to me for proper attention to their preservation.

[29] Color negatives, technically called "internegatives," are valuable for producing better quality display color prints.

[30] See *Scrolls from Qumrân Cave I*, p. 8, n. 9.

[31] While the scrolls and fragments themselves need a humidity range of about 5 to 10 percent for best preservation, the photographic materials survive best in a range of 30 to 40 percent.

[32] Unfortunately, this policy was not applied soon enough, for the original transparency of 1QIs[a], col. XLIX was lost while in the hands of a publisher in 1951. With every duplicate made from a color transparency, there is a slight loss in definition, which increases in succeeding generations of duplicates. This procedure is therefore by no means a permanent solution for preservation. A few black-and-white negatives also were lost and/or damaged during the years. Substitute negatives have been prepared from the color transparencies in these cases.

[33] The first project of the new center has been to produce a high quality microfilm which includes all the texts from Cave I whose photographs are under my control. On a good microfilm reader, the texts can be read from this film with great ease, for they project to twice the size of the originals.

[34] Admittedly, some of the scrolls that can be recovered only with infrared film would not make satisfactory color reproductions.

[35] *The Treasure of Qumran: My Story of the Dead Sea Scrolls*, Philadelphia, Westminster Press, 1966.

[36] Apparently the photographs reproduced there were made about 1965.

[37] See J. C. Trever, *RQ* 19 (Nov., 1965), plates II and VII.

[38] Compare the photograph on page 190 of A. Y. Samuel's book, which illustrates the condition of the fragments when exhibited at the Oriental Institute of the University of Chicago in December, 1950, with the appearance of the same fragments in the appendix to the book.

[39] See J. C. Trever, *RQ* 19 (Nov., 1965), plate VII.

Bruce Vawter, CM
De Paul University

History and Kerygma in the Old Testament

Recently, in criticizing a book dealing with some aspects of the contemporary theological posture, a reviewer[1] commented on its author's alleged

> preoccupation . . . with trying to make sense out of biblical passages for modern man. A common reaction among the young would certainly be: "So what? If it makes sense, fine; but if it doesn't say anything to us, don't try to twist it for the sake of saving it." . . . Instead of "reinterpreting," why not move on?

This kind of question is being raised more and more these days, and—such is the erosion of the common ground on which theology once stood—it is becoming increasingly harder to answer in terms that are mutually intelligible. The biblical theologian—by which I mean here simply the theologian who takes the biblical word as his *point de départ*, who would define the theological task as having an initial stage at least in "trying to make sense out of biblical passages for modern man," —will no doubt be puzzled as to what he is supposed to move on to: what has displaced Scripture as the *norma normans* which will now only tolerate Scripture if it "makes sense," and which indulges "reinterpreting" more as a concession to nostalgia than as a necessary step in methodology? If he is told that the social and behavioral and phenomenological sciences constitute this norm, he may be old-fashioned enough to inquire whether the roles of philosophy and theology have not been dramatically reversed. A decent and dynamic humanism suitably illustrated by biblical parallels—the sort of thing that Erich Fromm, for one, has done very well—can faithfully depict a world of man which theology must take into account; but it is not theology itself, not Christian theology, unless the humpty-dumpty school of linguistics now prevails and words mean what we choose to make them mean, no more and no less.

There is little point in belaboring this issue. Most of those who consider themselves theologians working within the (Judeo-)Christian tradition will mainly agree that "the Bible is in a peculiar way the foundation of all theology, of all thinking about Christianity. No form of Christianity can afford to dispense with the Bible . . . the foundation document of the Christian faith."[2] Such an affirmation will be made by Catholics as well as by Protestants and, along with conservatives, by those who believe that the Bible must be radically de-mythologized and/or that its canon must be sharply circumscribed. Even those whose theology *de facto* was or is not biblical—the medieval scholastic for whom *scriptura* was in reality patristic tradition, the post-Tridentine Roman Catholic who began with conciliar or papal formulas and eisegeted biblical tags to fit them, the present-day philosopher of religion whose conclusions turn out to be corroborated by the Scripture rather than inspired by it—did and do believe themselves to be biblical theologians in the sense defined above. Theoretically at least, it is agreed that theology is subject to the judgment of the biblical word, however minimal this word may be conceived to be, and it is not at all a question of twisting the word to accommodate it to something else of whatever provenance.

At the same time, what so-called radical theologians are prepared to deny to the Bible as a whole, many of those who qualify eminently as biblical theologians in the above sense are cheerfully prepared to deny to the OT in particular. That is to say, they view OT history and/or its kerygma as having nothing whatever to do with NT faith.[3] The reasons for this attitude are various and not invariably Marcionist. One of the more respectable of them, which has also suggested the topic of this present paper, is the disparity which critical study of the Bible has revealed to exist between the *bruta facta* of ascertainable history and the kerygmatic version of that history.[4] The disparity is not of course confined to the OT; it also poses an acute problem for the NT, as, most recently perhaps, the discussion provoked by the Pannenberg-*Kreis* has made very clear. The OT difficulty, however, is compounded by associated factors: exotic literary forms, the extreme distance that separates us from most of Israel's formative experiences, and—above all—the new direction into which NT faith has shunted the OT kerygma. Research into the kernel of fact that may lie hidden in a cult legend or in the saga of a thirteenth-century tribal chieftain can much more readily be made to appear meaningless for Christian faith than can research into the circumstances of the historical Jesus, though, to be sure, the latter appears equally meaningless to many Christians. In any case, and whether or not one is disposed to make a point of it, the disparity between what Abraham, let us say, was according to his putatively contemporary lights—at last account, a donkey trader (and smith?) resembling the Ibsha of the celebrated wall painting from Beni Hasan—and what he is in the book of Genesis, not to mention Galatians and Romans, is more than considerable.

So much more, in fact, that the discovered discrepancy readily encourages both ridicule and caricature. In a rather gloomy view of the prospect of OT studies, Morton Smith has indicted biblical faith as the culprit responsible for a perverse approach to what he characterizes as a "body of documents from the ancient Mediterranean world."[5] His approach is obviously that of an historian who sees his discipline threatened by the aprioristic view of so many who deal with this body of documents, who are ideologically committed to making the biblical construction of events square anyhow with the history of scientific method: *die Bibel hatte doch recht!* With fine impartiality, he scores the conservatism displayed in reproducing biblical texts, some desperate efforts that have been made to wrest meaning from a corrupt textual tradition through recourse to comparative linguistics, romanticizing biblical history on meagre archeological evidence while failing to acknowledge how thoroughly archeology has vindicated the substance of Wellhausen's hypothesis (an ingratitude of which I believe OT study is really guilty), claiming uniqueness to the OT of religious motifs that are not unique at all, and so forth. Only about OT theology does he not speak, because it is "unspeakable." As we will recall, most of these points were given attention in a much milder fashion several years ago at separate stages by that valuable gadfly James Barr.

Smith's article is often incisively witty and of course often quite on the target. No one is unaware of the effort that has been made to prove the Bible right by the naïve use of archeological and other evidence. It is part of the price that has had to be paid to the concerns that made those Mediterranean documents objects of study in the first place, that endowed the chairs of learning and underwrote the publication of the texts and funded the digs. Without those concerns, and despite their incidental aberrations, it is very doubtful that there would have ever been the resources, let alone the occasion, for either Morton Smith or me to be writing at this juncture. Critical method, after all, has not been something lately imposed on biblical studies after having been tested and proved in alien areas. It was the study of the biblical texts that only later led to the idea of extending textual criticism to other literature.[6] It is at least arguable too that it was biblical archeologists who did the most to convert what began as a treasure hunt into an organized discipline making sense out of—*faute de mieux*, perhaps—shards and walls and queer scratchings. It is true they have dug by the Book, as Schliemann, for example, dug by his book rather than look for Troy in, say, the forests of Swabia. But I do not really find with Smith the unmasking of a sinister plot in "Solomon's copper foundry that turned out to be a granary, Solomon's stables that were built by Ahab, a Maccabean fortress that turned out to be Solomonic," and the rest. No more sinister, at least, than the canals of Mars that disappeared with better telescopes or that extra pair of human chromosomes that float about in limbo now that microscopes have improved. It might be remembered too that Nelson Glueck, who, after all, corrected his own mistake—a thing that is not lightly done in scholarship—went looking in the Ghor for neither smelters nor granaries, but for the docks of Ezion-geber, which he never found.[7]

At all events, on both sides we are being urged to cease trying to find religious meaning in the OT, either because the quest leads nowhere, as far as the presuppositions of Christian faith are concerned, or because it interferes with the serious study of an otherwise significant corpus of written materials. On the contrary, however, I believe the quest to be both legitimate and necessary—necessary too not only for faith but for basic and minimal human understanding. If Morton Smith is serious when he sums up the OT portrayal of Yahweh as "a North-Arabian mountain god who traveled in thunderstorms and liked the smell of burning fat"—the late Colonel Robert Ingersoll lacked the erudition to phrase it quite this well—I must conclude that either his collection of the documents is missing some folios that are in mine or he has gravely misconstrued the character of the literature to whose study he has dedicated his scholarly life.

For the God whom Jesus revealed was very different from this, while at the same time he was the God of Israel, the very God of the OT. "Revelation of God in Christ" cannot but be meaningless unless it takes into account both a prior knowledge of the God whose fullness came to be seen in Jesus and the expectation of his manifestation which was the sum of Israel's history and the substance of Jesus' proclamation.[8] This is true not only of the situation of Jesus' original preaching to the Jewry of his time and place (or of the perhaps comparable situation of a later Jew who hears the kerygma of the gospel), it is likewise true of that of most Christians, who come to a knowledge of Israel's God and its expectation only through the Jesus of the church's preaching: there is always a logical if not a temporal "prior." It is true too, even when it is conceded that Judaism has legitimately retained its own interpretation of the OT based on the Torah which "by no means leads to the companion of taxgatherers and sinners, to the Pauline doctrine of justification, or to the Johannine assertion of the divinity of Jesus."[9] It is not necessary to denigrate Judaism in order to affirm that for Christian faith the prior of the OT and the direction of its history have found in Jesus an interpretation that is its own, an interpretation, however, that the earliest church considered to be an extension rather than a denial of Judaism's. At least, what is of key concern in the one acceptation of the OT kerygma is of key concern in the other:

> The New Testament does not deny that the Jews pray to the same God as the Christians. Even if we are children of Abraham in a special sense, we are yet subject to the same God and represented by the obedience of the same patriarch. At the same time that Abraham was promised a son and heir, he was also assured that he would become father of many nations. His faith is set before the Romans and Galatians as the decisive type of the faith by which men are justified.[10]

The promise and the God of the promise constitute the one inspiration of both Judaism and Christianity.

Now the one God common to Christians and Jews, the God whom Jesus revealed in fullness, is the God who first came to be known in Israel's history. Lately we have been warned against making too much of this historical factor,[11] to the detriment of revelation through the spoken word, which is likewise attested to by the OT; but it still seems to be an unassailable fact that history throughout has been the determinant of OT revelation in a way that nothing else has, and to it everything else has been subordinate.[12] The earliest bearers of the prophetic word in Israel of whom we have any firsthand acquaintance already presuppose the decisive deeds of Yahweh in history—basically the kerygma of the Pentateuch, in fact—as having revealed the God in whose name they speak: prophecy is a consequent, not the determinant, of this historical process of revelation (Amos 3: 9–12; Hos 9: 10; 11: 1–4; etc.). It may be rejoined that the prophetic word was required to give interpretation to the historical event in the first place before it could become a medium of revelation, and this in a sense may be true; but if it is true, it is unverifiable from the prophecy we know: as with all history, event and interpretation have come down together and are encountered together in the ancient "cultic credos." A prophet may, indeed, give a prior interpretation to a coming event,[13] but, whatever may be the source of his word, it is intended to set that event in corroboration of a primary one that is presupposed: *ky ʼny yhwh.* There is no purpose in denying that the OT represents God as being encountered other than through the indirect mediation of history. Yet it is doubtless not without significance that even the priestly Torah has at all turns been worked into the framework of Israel's history. Neither is the wisdom literature, with its alleged lack of interest in history, usually concerned with the God of Israel's revelation. However, wisdom did display an interest in the history of Israel. Not only has it strongly influenced the didactic, so-called secular histories of Joseph and the Davidic succession narrative,[14] its motifs have probably entered into the portrayal of sacred history as well.[15] It is worthy of note too that the apocalyptic view of eschatology which, after much reluctance, present-day scholarship is willing to ascribe to Jesus as well as to the early church, a perspective which gave Israel's history universal and cosmic dimensions,[16] is with some probability attributed to the wisdom tradition as having played a predominant role in its formation.[17] In its end as in its beginning, therefore, the OT presupposition of NT faith has had a strong historical orientation.

And thus we are brought back to the question of the tension between the data of history as we are able to know them and history as it has been told in the kerygma. To be concerned about the facts of OT history as relevant to biblical faith, to find other than philological significance in literary and historical criticism and what is turned up by the archeologist's spade, is not, as some seem to take it, the reversion to a religious historicism. It is, simply, to take the Bible seriously in its claim to represent a history of revelation—to take that claim seriously, that is, with the same critical approach and resources one is expected to bring to bear on other claims to credence. The claim is not taken seriously in the existentialist *als ob* acceptance of the OT kerygma seemingly favored by, among others, Gerhard von Rad, much in the manner of Martin Kähler's repudiation of historical criticism in relation to the kerygmatic Christ. History and interpretation are inseparable—granted—and the one comes to us only by means of the latter; but to exhibit no curiosity over what has been interpreted is hardly to enter into the spirit of the OT, which from first to last is concerned with things that happened or would happen. No necessary distinction between the historic and the merely historical should be allowed to obscure the fact that, in the biblical view, history always contains something that is *einmalig*, and that something cannot be dispensed with.

Morton Smith has justly praised an article by Roland de Vaux on historical method in which, it should be observed, de Vaux, qualifying von Rad's *Theology of the OT* as rather a history of Israel's religion, maintains:

> The theologian takes for his starting point the conclusions of the historian of religions, and he judges of their validity, not only according to the criteria of rational science, but according to their conformity to the established truths of his faith. He then goes beyond these conclusions by integrating them into the whole of revelation. The connection between religious history and objective history, between the history believed by Israel and

> the true history of Israel, is apparently more difficult to establish; however, it must be established in the eyes of the believer, for if the historical faith of Israel is not in a certain way founded in *history*, this faith is erroneous and cannot command my assent.[18]

I see no realistic option to this one. It involves what Helmut Thielicke has called "the irrevocability of anti-criticism."[19]

By this expression, Thielicke designates the task of historical research in relation to faith as not to define the territory in which faith can settle down but, rather, to come to grips with those historical-critical considerations that would, if validated, deprive faith of any ground on which to settle. Oscar Cullmann has recently seen the force of this kind of argument in his response[20] to the (unconscious) challenge thrown down by, among others, S. G. F. Brandon's *Jesus and the Zealots*.[21] There must be no mistake about it: if Brandon's (re)construction of the Jesus of actual history is peremptory as well as merely plausible, then Christianity has lost the basis of its kerygma. There can be no talk of adjustments or of reinterpretations or of higher truths; it must only be admitted that the doctrine of the cross, behind which, as a *brutum factum*, lies the event which Brandon calls "the most certain thing known about Jesus of Nazareth," was, by a colossal mistake or by one of the most successful deceits known to history, a groundless myth created out of the routine execution of a convicted *λῃστής* by a second-string civil servant in one of the backwaters of the Roman empire. (I am by no means denying the undoubted contribution which Brandon has made to *Leben Jesu-Forschung* but, rather, acknowledging, as he has not explicitly, that the conclusion he has drawn from it quite negates the Christian gospel.) The historical validity of Israel's kerygma is of course not as intimately connected with NT faith as is the person of Jesus, but the connection is no less real for being of relatively less importance. If historical research should force us to acknowledge that there had never been those *ṣdqwt yhwh* in which Israel had found its God, it is not merely that Jesus addressed himself to a mythical Father; there simply was, by definition, no God for him to reveal, no God reconciling us to himself in Christ in culmination of a *Heilsgeschichte* that never was.

It is not, obviously, that we are called upon to make history out of the cult-inspired recitals of the conquests of Jericho and Ai, or whatever literary form we are supposed to assign these perennially interesting etiologies, or to ask ourselves whether the axe head really floated. Solomon's granary is all one with his foundry, which is to say that it matters neither more nor less nor at all. Considerations of this kind are irrelevant to the question of whether we may continue to regard the OT as a record of historical revelation, and no service is paid to the cause of reasonable discussion when such considerations are dragged in as though they were entirely germane to that issue. Neither is the issue changed in the least because earlier Christians, who lived in an uncritical and unhistorical age, did mistakenly believe such considerations to be germane to it. We know, as they usually did not, that the OT, like history in the mass, contains its share of myth and legend, and we have learned, in part through their mistakes, to disengage the question of historical revelation from the outmoded category of biblical inerrancy.

Neither is there question of historical criticism being expected to confirm that God covenanted with Israel, thereby somehow proving right the prophets and the pentateuchal histories in the moral and religious implications they discovered in his having revealed his mercy and loving-kindness. Historical criticism cannot do such a thing; as we have said, its task is the much more modest one of ascertaining the facts, as best it can recover them, of which history has been fashioned. History itself is not facts but the interpretation of facts. The best—or worst—that historical criticism can do is to establish that the interpretation is or is not, as the case may be, compatible with the facts. This is not to reduce the function of historical criticism to a purely negative one, as though it served its purpose only by not coming up with data that would make a peremptory judgment against biblical history inevitable. Its business is with facts, and the more facts we have the better we are able to understand how the history came about and what are its virtues and shortcomings, how we must qualify it if we still choose to accept it. But even if we should someday find a record from, let us say, the nineteenth Egyptian dynasty telling of a flight of Asiatics through the Sea of Reeds, though for some reason we might think that our biblical history had been proved to be more "factual" than we had hoped it to be, actually we should be not much affected in regard to our disposition to accept or reject the history of the exodus. I have chosen an example which, though highly unlikely, is not entirely inconceivable: there was a time, after all, when far more recent happenings, such as the Babylonian captivity, and the Ezran-Nehemian restoration, and the prophet Ezekiel, could all be written off as so much romanticizing provoked by theology, until the Babylonian chronicles turned up to present their own version of certain facts that were indisputably the same. Facts again, not history. To have the Babylonians confirm independently that King Jehoiachin was, indeed, one of their guests in exile did clear the air a bit. It did not, however, speak to the evaluation of Jehciachin made by Jeremiah or Ezekiel or the Deuteronomic historian, or to the meaning of the exile ventured by any of these or by the Second Isaiah or Ezra and Nehemiah and the Chronicler. We have Sennacherib's version of his siege of Jerusalem and his bottling up of Hezekiah in the capital (probably recounting the first of two campaigns which the OT has united into one). It is good to have this agreement on facts; yet what could be further removed than the separate interpretations that have been given the facts? The excavator of an Israelite town of the age of Amos and Hosea may be able to show, by the mute evidence of archeology, the glaring contrast of rich and poor that called forth the prophetic denunciations of these eighth-century spokesmen for human rights,[22] but the evidence, which is undoubtedly far less abundant than that which will be available to the same effect to the remote archeologist of twentieth century America, must have been as ambiguous to men of good will then as it remains to men of good will now. Who wrote the proper commentary on the agreed facts? Historical criticism, it seems to me, can mainly offer interesting suggestions, the value of which should not be minimized; but it can offer no final solutions. And thus we must reluctantly conclude that its findings, in any positive sense, are usually of far more interest to the biblical scholar in his capacity as student of Near Eastern culture and religion than as biblical theologian.

Still, since history is an interpretation of facts, the facts are always a comforting thing to have, and thus must be of interest to the biblical theologian. Has the possession of the facts damaged, in any way that we now know, their interpretation as offered by the OT? I am not aware of any, or at least of any that is significant. Recognition that the facts are patient of interpretations other than that of the Bible, even that a contemporary interpretation of them, as in some instances mentioned above, would have inevitably differed from it, constitute no apodictic argument against the OT kerygma. Not, first of all, in point of principle. As Alan Richardson has correctly stated, history does not automatically become "truer" the closer it is brought to the events it chronicles and interprets. He uses as an example the meaning of Bismarck in history, which could be accurately appraised only in the light of what happened in 1933 and 1945.[23] The thing is, history simply cannot be written by contemporaries, a fact that seems to be generally accepted by practically everyone except biblical critics.[24] It is probably the most respectable of the reasons for the *loi de cinquante ans* governing access to the French national archives, a provision understandably frustrating to a journalist like William L. Shirer in his recent inquiry into the 1940 collapse of the Third Republic, yet indirectly given some sort of justification by Shirer's own decision to make the first act in his drama the Dreyfus case of 1894.

Neither in point of principle nor in point of specific detail do I conceive of the facts' having dislodged the biblical interpretation. Certainly we know that the history of Israel was a far more complicated one than the kerygmatic version of it we find in the Bible. We have learned to separate the exodus tradition from the wilderness tradition, and both of them from the tradition of Sinai, and to trace the paths by which they came to be united.[25] Or, alternatively, we have left Sinai with the exodus complex but separated it from the cultic credos and the promise of the land, stressing in the process the importance and the complexities of the patriarchal traditions.[26] We have agreed that the major components of what came to be the people Israel were three or perhaps four, that for all practical purposes this people came to be in the land of Canaan, that the *Landnahme* might with some justice be better termed an insurrection than a conquest. In many ways, therefore, our reconstruction of what happened must be quite different from the story which Israel told of itself. Yet when we reconstruct, we go back to the same facts that Israel presupposed in its story. So far as I know, no responsible research into biblical origins has done other than confirm that there was an exodus, that there was a wilderness experience, that something important took place at Sinai. Is the historical reality of these events diminished by their being assigned to only one element or other of the forebears of the covenant people Israel? I do not see how, unless at the same time we must deny any relevance of the events of 1776 to other than the relatively few descendants of certain Dutch and English colonists who now inhabit thirteen of our southern and eastern states. In the biblical view of history, Israel was created by covenant granted it by its God. I do not know of any finding of critical history that invalidates such an interpretation; I do know of some that support it, to the extent that they suggest Josh 24 as a scene taken from life, even though what is represented there as a renewal may well have been a beginning. Here as well as elsewhere in scholarship, there have been false starts and necessary corrections. Albrecht Alt's seminal work on Israel's laws has been modified by the studies of Erhard Gerstenberger, and George Mendenhall's pioneer recognition of the relevance of the treaty form has had to undergo numerous refinements. But it would be hard to think of an area where research has been more rewarding,[27] offering a realistic alternative to the Wellhausenian synthesis of the past century. More and more too, it is taking us back to the kernel of historical fact which underlies the patriarchal legends, which may in the long run prove to be a more fruitful field for biblical understanding than the Nuzi parallels have been.

When I say that historical criticism, thus far at least, has served the study of the Bible not by validating the history of the OT but, rather, by not invalidating it, I recognize that I am subject to various objections. The discrepancy between interpreted event and the often recoverable facts that have been mentioned above has to be admitted by even the most conservative biblical theologian. It is a question, I presume, as to whether the discrepancy has become so wide that the one must exclude the other. I do not see that it has become so wide in any significant instance, but others may well disagree. Some scholars there are of course whose concept of the discrepancy is far more radical than the majority of their peers, and it is safe to assume that they would consider the scientific evidence to have ruled out rather thoroughly the biblical construction. The late and great Martin Noth, for instance, to all practical purposes eliminated the not inconsiderable figure of Moses from his purview of the history of Israel. I doubt that most OT scholars would agree with Noth in this respect, but his and other extreme positions do tell us of the continuing need we have for rigorous critical study of Israel's traditions. Would the OT interpretation have to go if we had to discard Moses as an historical character? In his brief study of the Moses question of a few years back, which in my view demonstrated the need of common sense as the climate required to save scholarship from absurdity, Rudolf Smend[28] concluded, if I read him rightly, that Moses could be dispensable: he contrasted his case with that of Jesus, who is identified with the gospel in a way that Moses is not with the OT kerygma. Certainly critical study has forced us to reduce the figure of Moses, though not so much the Moses of the OT as the one of later legend and mysticism. Not Moses but the exodus is represented in the OT as the event in which God was revealed, just as the conquest—or whatever we are to call it, in fidelity to the facts—of the land is represented as the fulfillment of divine promise, not the Ephraimite chieftain Joshua, whom the biblical historian has transformed into Moses' successor and leader of a united Israel. Moses' case is somewhat different from that of Joshua, it is admitted, but I think it fair to say that the OT kerygma is never concerned with persons or dates or geographical routes to any of the degree that it is definitely concerned with the deeds of the Lord. The deeds of the Lord certainly involved all these, but in ways that the biblical traditions had often forgotten and which we may sometimes rediscover only with difficulty. Even where in the OT revelation is presented as separated from historical event (the prophets serve as a partial example here just as they serve as a partial exception to what follows), the characteristic of the divine "inbreaking" into human consciousness is remarkable for its anonymity.

Another objection may be that historical criticism has, indeed, invalidated much of the OT historical kerygma, and that I am simply refusing to acknowledge the fact by taking refuge in an idealized and selective anamorphosis of the OT that bears little resemblance to the real article. I do not believe this to be the case, however. When I speak of the OT kerygma, I mean the kerygma of the OT canon. To accept a canon of Sacred Scripture is to make an act of faith, but, as an historical phenomenon, the formation and composition of the Biblical canon are matters for critical study. It has become a truism to say that the biblical canon testifies to a unity of diversities. Those who hold to a canon-within-the-canon principle have stressed the undeniable diversities, contradictions, indeed—at least incompatibilities—to conclude to the necessity of taking one's stand on one or another enunciation of the canon at the expense of the rest. That this stand may not appear to be merely an arbitrary choice, appeal has been made to the hermeneutical principle[29]—resulting, however, in what many will judge to be a choice which, if not arbitrary, is still highly personal. I think that the argument may fairly be turned in the opposite direction. What is wrong with the assumption that the hermeneutical principle was operative in the formation of the canon, that it is this that accounts for what unity the canon possesses? For a unity of some kind, the canon demonstrably is: a selected body of materials gathered of set purpose with full awareness of its inner tensions. Earlier, I objected to the caricature of the God of the OT as "a North-Arabian mountain god who traveled in thunderstorms and liked the smell of burning fat." If such were the kerygma of the OT, I doubt very much that its word would have much to say to me. But it is not the kerygma of the OT, or even of one part of the OT, though I am perfectly aware that all the terms of this composite portrait are to be found in its pages. Many years ago, Otto Eissfeldt made some sound observations on the interaction of OT theology and historical criticism which seem to be entirely applicable at this point.[30] Historically considered, the OT is a corpus of writings produced over many years and subject to all the changes that time and, it is hoped, the development of the human spirit inevitably bring. Within this historical perspective, it is not hard to see how the patriarchal legends, or the Davidic theology of the Yahwist, or the Chronicler's retrojection of post-exilic Judaism into the era of David and Solomon, could have had meaning and significance proper to the age of their devising and have lost them in a subsequent generation. The same history that first made them relevant might also later declare them superseded. This is not simply to decide in favor of the most recent, but to submit the canon as a whole to the judgment of history. The early prophets had already in principle examined and rejected the more naïve kind of covenant theology manifested in the doctrine of holy war or the schematic outline imposed by the D author on the portrayal of Israel's past in the book of Judges. Historical criticism, no less than the balance of the OT canon, rules in favor of the prophets: history does not recur in the cyclic fashion described in Judges, however useful it may have been at the time to think of it so doing. In the same way, when the canon of the OT is seen as the record of an historical process, the God who emerges from its kerygma has assumed more subtle attributes than those once ascribed to Baal Zaphon. The fault of the rabbis and the fathers of the church was not, as I see it, their acceptance of the whole OT canon, which they then felt obliged to interpret as having uniform weight throughout, despite all its internal tensions. Living in an uncritical and unhistorical age, they simply did not have the impulse to read the OT historically, to see what by the historical nature of the case was residual and what had been merely provisional.

Neither is it a question, as far as I can see, of having to take the NT as the standard of interpretation of the OT—of beginning with the OT from the standpoint of its position in the church's canon, in other words.[31] In the first place, while the NT presupposes an OT scriptural canon, it is not of one mind concerning either the dimensions of that canon or, except in general terms, the details of its kerygmatic message. There is more about the OT that the NT presupposes than that it attempts to define and assimilate, so that its invitation is for us to seek the meaning of the OT with the means at our disposal rather than to find a ready-made interpretation of it at hand. Further, as Eissfeldt pointed out, it is not through the NT, but rather through historico-critical method, that much of the authentic message of the OT has been recovered. For example:

> The prophets as personalities, as religious figures in their own right, remained unknown to Christianity for eighteen centuries. They lived and functioned—one need only think of the frescoes of the Sistine Chapel—as those who had prophesied Christ, and thus a few of their words were of significance. But as personalities they remained not understood and inoperative. It was the historical research of the 19th century which taught us to understand the grandeur of the prophetic figures by entering into a living experience of their proclamation. And who would deny that this newly discovered value in recognition has also enriched the life of faith?[32]

We do not, as I see it, take our interpretation of the OT from the NT, even though we take a general direction from it, just as Judaism has proceeded to the OT from another general direction. Our understanding of much of the kerygma of the OT and of what is really central to it depends on interests and means that were not always those of the NT and its age. This is the more positive side to the function of historical criticism in relation to OT understanding, and one which can often reach conclusions acceptable to Jew and Christian alike.

I would like to conclude on this note. Far from being superfluous or detrimental to the faith which approaches the OT seeking to hear a word, historical criticism serves the dual function of setting its critical affirmations in credible relief and of bringing to its text the resources necessary for the better understanding of its message. Without destroying its value for faith, historical research helps us to define the kind of history, and its limitations, that has been made the vehicle of revelation. It has become a commonplace to designate this as history become myth: "The Exodus from Egypt is a historical datum, it becomes a matter of religion only when myth has portrayed it in paradigmatic terms."[33] I remain not entirely convinced of the aptness of this category. It is true that by now we have long been schooled away from a simplistic conception of myth as stories about disreputable goings on among the gods; we have learned that this is a distortion of myth, that myth is in fact a genuine, if not an empirical or strictly rational way of attempting to get at a truth. There are, we are told, good as well as bad myths, and even just harmless myths which, nevertheless, give men direction and motivation: myths of race and of nationhood, the American dream and Yankee know-how, the lost Eden to be regained or the utopia to be achieved, and so forth. It may be that in this sense we will have to understand kerygmatic history as myth—that is, all history that man lives by as a faith can be called myth.[34] But it seems to me that we are in danger of taking away myth's distinctive meaning by making it mean too many different things. Also, I would prefer a term for biblical history other than one which, to the extent that the Bible uses it at all—which is rarely—it sets precisely in opposition to its kerygma.[35] Nor is this usage merely a reflection of an unsophisticated appreciation of myth, since the same wealth of meanings now attached to myth was available to the biblical authors as well. I would prefer, in other words, a term that did not apply equally well to the biblical kerygma and to those cleverly concocted tales (2 Pet 1: 16) that the Bible sets against it. If myth is to be the phrase, we no longer have a means of distinguishing what the Bible calls myth—and is myth, by anyone's definition—from that which it sets in the most profound opposition to it, and we set on one and the same level an historical faith in election with its caricature in *Blut und Boden* superstition. Faced with the same option some years ago, G. E. Wright preferred to define the OT idea as one of history interpreted by faith.[36] This is the way I believe the Bible would want to describe itself, and that I believe is what historical criticism assists us in defining more precisely.

The scholar who is being honored in these present pages has, among the many other contributions he has brought to biblical studies, always evinced a concern for theological interpretation, pointing out the enduring value of biblical meaning once it has been wrested from the text. (I think, for one thing, of his work on the Chronicler's history in the AB series, dealing with material that has not always been judged to hold much promise for the Christian reader.) Whether or not he will approve of the views expressed in the article preceding, I trust that he will accept them as having been uttered in appreciation of and in the same spirit with which he has always approached the OT.

Notes

[1] *Mary Daly*, on Gregory Baum's *Man Beginning*, in *National Catholic Reporter*, July 10, 1970, p. 12.

[2] R. P. C. Hanson, in *The Pelican Guide to Modern Theology*, Volume 3, *Biblical Criticism* (Penguin, 1970), p. 15.

[3] Rudolf Bultmann ("To Christian faith the OT is no longer revelation"), "The Significance of the OT for Christian Faith," in B. W. Anderson, ed., *The Old Testament and Christian Faith* (London: SCM, 1964), p. 31. Friedrich Baumgärtel ("The OT is a witness out of a non-Christian religion; its self-understanding is not identical with evangelical prior understanding"), in Claus Westermann, ed., *Essays on OT Interpretation* (London: SCM, 1963), p. 135. Franz Hesse ("Der alttestamentliche Zeugnis ist in seinem Selbstverständnis ein fremdes Wort aus einer fremden Religion, ein Wort ausserhalb des Evangeliums"), "Kerygma oder geschichtliche Wirklichkeit," *ZTK* 57 (1960), 17–26. See the discussion in my "History and the Word," *CBQ* 29 (1967), 512–23. See also the sensitive study of G. E. Wright, "Historical Knowledge and Revelation," in *Translating and Understanding the Old Testament*, Essays in honor of Herbert Gordon May, ed. by H. T. Frank and W. L. Reed (New York and Nashville: Abingdon, 1970), pp. 279–303.

[4] Hans-Joachim Kraus is not extremely helpful on this point in the revised edition of his *Geschichte der historisch-kritischen Erforschung des Alten Testaments* (Neukirchener Verlag, 1969). After bringing the discussion only to the point of von Rad's *Theology* and its sequelae, he asks (p. 509): "Wird ein Weg gefunden werden, auf dem die Spaltung überwunden kann? Das ist jetzt die Frage."

[5] "The Present State of OT Studies," *JBL* 88 (1969), 19–35.

[6] Cf C. F. Evans, "The Inspiration of the Bible," *Theology* 59 (1956), 11–17.

[7] For a much more balanced and informative assay of the role of archeology in controlling "tradition," and *vice versa*, see the article of one who is well informed of both: Roland de Vaux, "On Right and Wrong Uses of Archaeology," in *Near Eastern Archaeology in the Twentieth Century*, Essays in honor of Nelson Glueck, ed. by J. A. Sanders (Garden City: Doubleday, 1970), pp. 64–80.

[8] Cf Wolfhart Pannenberg, "The Revelation of God in Jesus," in James M. Robinson, John B. Cobb, eds., *Theology as History*, New Frontiers in Theology 3 (New York: Harper & Row, 1967), pp. 102–5.

[9] Ernst Käsemann (critique of the 1967 report of the Dutch church on the authority of the Bible), in *Das Neue Testament als Kanon* (Göttingen: Vandenhoeck & Ruprecht, 1970), pp. 347 f.

[10] Markus Barth, *Israel and the Church* (Richmond: John Knox Press, 1969), p. 16.

[11] Notably by James Barr, "Revelation through History in the OT and in Modern Theology," *Interp* 17 (1963), 193–205; then in his *Old and New in Interpretation: A Study of the Two Testaments* (New York: Harper & Row, 1966). Barr is much better at puncturing exaggerated claims and conclusions—a valuable function—than he is at articulating positively what he believes the fair assessment of the situation to be. However,

it seems evident that he does not intend to deny that history has been *a* chief vehicle of the knowledge of God in the OT.

[12] Cf Hans Lubsczyk, "Die Einheit der Schrift. Zur hermeneutischen Relevanz des Urbekenntnisses im Alten und Neuen Testament," in *Sapienter Ordinare*, Festgabe für Erich Kleineidam, ed. by F. Hoffman *et al.* (Leipzig: St Benno-Verlag, 1969), pp. 73–104.

[13] Cf Walther Zimmerli, "Das Wort des göttlichen Selbsterweises (Erweiswort), eine prophetische Gattung," in *Mélanges Bibliques rédigés en l'honneur de André Robert* (Paris: Bloud & Gay, 1956), pp. 154–64.

[14] See, most recently, R. N. Whybray, *The Succession Narrative: A Study of II Sam. 9–20 and I Kings 1 and 2*, Studies in Biblical Theology, Second Series 9 (Naperville: Allenson, 1968).

[15] See Martin J. Buss, "The Meaning of History," in *Theology as History*, p. 149.

[16] Cf Jürgen Moltmann, *Theologie der Hoffnung*, 5th ed. (Munich: Kaiser Verlag, 1966), pp. 120–24.

[17] Cf Gerhard von Rad, *Theologie des Alten Testaments* (Munich: Kaiser Verlag, 1960) II, 319 f. Without sharing all of the author's assumptions (e.g., his conviction of an absolute dichotomy between prophetic and apocalyptic eschatology), one can nevertheless agree that he has made a good case for wisdom influence.

[18] "Method in the Study of Early Hebrew History," in J. Philip Hyatt, ed., *The Bible in Modern Scholarship* (New York and Nashville: Abingdon, 1965), p. 16. Parallel in "Les patriarches hébreux et l'histoire," *RB* 72 (1965), 7: "Si la foi historique d'Israël n'est pas fondée dans l'histoire, cette foi est erronée, et la nôtre aussi."

[19] "The Resurrection Kerygma," in *The Easter Message Today* (New York: Nelson, 1964), p. 82.

[20] *Jesus und die Revolutionären seiner Zeit* (Tübingen: J. C. B. Mohr, 1970).

[21] Manchester University Press, 1967. Also in articles and books previously and subsequently.

[22] Cf Roland de Vaux, "La quatrième campagne de fouilles à Tell el-Farʿah, près Naplouse," *RB* 59 (1952), 566. Parallel in "The Excavations at Tell el-Farʿah and the Site of Ancient Tirzah," *PEQ* 88 (1956), 133 f.

[23] *History Sacred and Profane* (Philadelphia: Westminster, 1964), p. 222.

[24] *Ibid.*, p. 235.

[25] See, most recently, Brevard S. Childs, "A Traditio-Historical Study of the Reed Sea Tradition," *VT* 20 (1970), 406–18.

[26] So Horst Seebass, *Der Erzvater Israel und die Einführung der Jahweverehrung in Kanaan* (*BZAW* 98 [Berlin: Töpelmann, 1966]).

[27] See, among recent studies, Gene M. Tucker, "Covenant Forms and Contract Forms," *VT* 15 (1965), 487–503; and M. Weinfeld, "The Covenant of Grant in the OT and in the Ancient Near East," *JAOS* 90 (1970), 184–203. Also the interesting work of R. E. Clements, *Abraham and David*, Studies in Biblical Theology, Second Series 5 (Naperville: Allenson, 1967).

[28] *Das Mosebild von Heinrich Ewald bis Martin Noth* (Tübingen: J. C. B. Mohr, 1959).

[29] Käsemann, *op. cit.*, pp. 355 f.

[30] "Israelitische-jüdische Religionsgeschichte und alttestamentliche Theologie," *ZAW* 44 (1926), 1–12 = *Kleine Schriften* (Tübingen: J. C. B. Mohr, 1962) I, pp. 105–14. For a much more negative view of Eissfeldt's article, cf Norman W. Porteous, "Old Testament Theology," in H. H. Rowley, ed., *The Old Testament and Modern Study* (Oxford University Press, 1951/61), pp. 318 ff.

[31] Despite my basic agreement with Brevard S. Childs, I much prefer to his idea of the OT as emerging from the Christian canon my notion of its canon as validated by its own internal history. See his *Biblical Theology in Crisis* (Philadelphia: Westminster, 1970), pp. 99 ff.

[32] *Loc. cit.*, 7 = 10. Eissfeldt goes on to argue that historical criticism also helps in other ways to separate the perennially valid from the unacceptable in the OT—for example, by pointing out the kind of narrow nationalistic motivation which Israel itself outgrew.

[33] Theodor H. Gaster, *Myth, Legend, and Custom in the Old Testament* (New York: Harper & Row, 1969), p. xxxvi. Also Joseph Jensen, in "What Happened to Moses?" *CBQ* 32 (1970), 404–17 (an article with which I am in almost total agreement), ends by accepting "myth" as a valid designation of the kerygmatic history of the OT.

[34] So, apparently, R. A. F. MacKenzie, "The Problem of Myth and History," in his *Faith and History in the Old Testament* (New York: Macmillan, 1963), pp. 69–81.

[35] In the NT, *μῦθος* occurs late in 1 Tim 1: 4; 4: 7; 2 Tim 4: 4; Tit 1: 14; 2 Pet 1: 16, always in the sense of fable, deceptive story, the very opposite of what is historically true. In the intertestamental literature, it might seem to have been given a more neutral sense: Sir 20: 19 has it equal *mšl* (cf Gustav Stählin in *TWNT* (IV), 787); still, the fact that it is here ascribed to a fool has doubtless determined the translation. The *μυχός* reading at Wis 17: 4 B S is doubtless preferable to the A *μῦθος*. In Bar 3: 23, *μυθολόγοι* occurs in the sense of sloganists, manufacturers of empty tales.

[36] *God Who Acts*, Studies in Biblical Theology 8 (London: SCM, 1952), pp. 126 ff.

Hans Eberhard von Waldow
Pittsburgh Theological Seminary

Israel and Her Land: Some Theological Considerations

Discussion of Israel and her land puts us in a peculiar situation. On the one hand, the topic has great historical interest. Hence, the question of the occupation of the land as dealt with by Albrecht Alt and his followers and, in a different way, by John Bright and others[1] is at present of central concern in the study of the early history of Israel. On the other hand, to examine the topic theologically is another matter. In Old Testament study, it was never really the center of interest,[2] although this topic occurs throughout, from the earliest to the latest layers of the book. When it was possible to write an Old Testament theology centering in the idea of the covenant,[3] the question could also be raised of whether it would not be possible to make the concept of Israel and her land the main idea of an Old Testament theology. Setting aside the legitimacy of taking a single so-called proposition of faith as the central idea in a theology of the Old Testament, should one wish to make the attempt, one can well select the theme of Israel and her land. Certainly it is much more dominant than the covenant idea. To examine it thoroughly throughout all layers of the Old Testament tradition cannot of course be done in a short article. We simply draw attention to its theological importance to show how dominant it is and to suggest some ways in which it can be dealt with.

Yahweh the Owner of the Land

In Lev 25: 23, we find within the context of ordinances concerning the Year of Jubilee the following passage:

> The land shall not be sold in perpetuity, for the land is mine, for you are strangers and sojourners with me.

This verse consists of a prohibition and two sermonlike extensions. The first extension gives the idea justifying the prohibition, and the second points out its meaning when it is applied to Israel.[4] The idea is that Yahweh owns all the land. The same idea is found in Jer 2: 7 and 16: 18, where the land is called *naḥ^a^lat yhwh* (cf 2 Sam 20: 19; 21: 3). The basic meaning of *naḥ^a^lāh* is "landed property apportioned to an individual."[5] Clearly, here the term is not used in its original meaning. Nobody could apportion land to Yahweh. This does not imply, however, that the idea, "Yahweh is the owner of the land," is late. Rather, just the opposite seems to be true. The idea is the first attempt of the Israelite tribes and clans who had invaded Palestine to relate their God, Yahweh from Sinai, to the new land they had just occupied. The idea that a god owns all the land where his worshipers live is actually an old Canaanite concept, where Baal or the Baalim are the owners of all the landed properties, fields, vineyards, orchards, together with all the springs, trees, hills, and the like. They give rain and fertility to the land, and thus make possible the living of their worshipers.[6] Accordingly, the Baalim receive worship to assure rainfall and fertility. When, however, the Israelite tribes and clans entered the Canaanite world by settling in Palestine, their religion of Yahweh from Mount Sinai or of the Gods of their Fathers[7] was not related to a way of life on arable land. Consequently, when the Israelites first turned the sod of Canaan, they became dependent upon the blessings of its gods. This means that the change of the culture by the newcomers in Canaan was necessarily a move toward syncretism unless a way was found to relate the new life, with its dependence on rain and fertility, to Yahweh. The simplest way to cope with this crucial problem was for them to follow the Canaanite example and to conceive of Yahweh as the owner of the land and the giver of its fertility.

That they did so is indicated by the many cultic practices related to agrarian life, which the Israelites adopted from the Canaanites and related to their God Yahweh. All these practices must be seen against the background that Yahweh is the owner of the land: the sacral fallowness every seven years, Ex 23: 10 f; Lev 25: 1 f;[8] the offering of the first fruits, Ex 23: 19; 34: 26; Lev 23: 10; the custom of not harvesting the fruits of newly planted trees, Lev 19: 23 ff;[9] the tithe, Ex 22: 28; Num 18: 21 ff; Deut 14: 22; or the practice of not gleaning the fields completely, Lev 19: 9 f; 23: 22.

Such assimilation of the Yahweh religion to the needs of a rural society through introduction of a new proposition of faith—that Yahweh is the owner of the land—could not be done overnight. It was easier to leave the traditional picture of Yahweh as it was and to worship Yahweh and Baal together. The resultant struggle is reflected in Hos 2: 4 ff. The prophet accuses in the name of Yahweh, "She did not know that it was I who gave her the grain, the wine and the oil . . . ." (2: 8).

In the light of all this, it can be said that it was a fundamental necessity for the Israelites to relate their God Yahweh to the basic needs of daily life, which in this case meant to relate him to the land where they now lived and to their new way of making a living—that is, in an agricultural environment. A religion is doomed when it no longer answers the fundamental questions of life. So it was quite natural for the Israelites in their new home to conceive of Yahweh as the owner of the land and the giver of its yield. And it was also quite natural that it was here where the struggle between Yahweh and Baal began.

Two ideas complementary to the concept that Yahweh owns the land were developed by the Israelites. The first looks rather peculiar within Old Testament theology. It introduces a strange limitation, and therefore never played a major part in Israelite thinking. It is the idea that since Yahweh's land is Canaan, the other countries are owned by the gods of the Gentiles. Accordingly, the Israelite who has to leave his homeland also leaves his God (1 Sam 26: 19). Furthermore, whoever wanted to worship Yahweh in a foreign country had to take with him a certain amount of Israelite soil. No fugitive like David, rather, only a rich person who traveled in a caravan, could do that (2 Kings 5: 17). The same idea could be expressed in cultic terms. Yahweh's land is considered clean; the countries of the Gentile gods, unclean. The idea sometimes occurs in the earlier prophets (Hos 9: 3 f; Amos 7: 17).

The other complementary idea is characteristic of Israelite thinking. Once the land of Israel was called *naḥ^a^lat* Yahweh, the term *gēr* ("sojourner," "alien") entered the picture. Because of the realities of life, both terms are closely related to one another. Wherever there are people living within their natural family communities on their landed property allotted to them, there are also people who have come from other places, where they have left their natural communities and their inheritance. Where they are living now, they are strangers or sojourners and can lay no legal claim on protection from their host communities or on their *naḥ^a^lāh.*[10] So once the idea—the land where Israel lives is the *naḥ^a^lat* Yahweh—was introduced (Lev 25: 23; Ps 79: 1; Jer 2: 7), the complementary idea could be developed: Israel is the *gēr* permitted to live on Yahweh's property. The phrase "You are strangers and sojourners with me" (Lev 25: 23) is certainly one of the latest developments of the idea that Yahweh owns the land. It reveals a deep and fine understanding of the Yahweh-Israel relationship much more sublime than the old Canaanite concept. Israel can claim nothing. Instead, her existence, livelihood, and security depend completely on her God, the true owner of the land.

Some Israelites disapproved of the new features ascribed to Yahweh with the new idea that Yahweh owns the land. But to disapprove actually meant not to make the change of culture from a nomadic to an agricultural way of life; there was no other way to avoid the rule of the Canaanite fertility gods. Thus the Rechabites, in order to sustain the traditional Yahweh-religion, tried to continue the nomadic way of life, even after the occupation of the land (Jer 35).[11] Such a backward radical conservatism could hardly expect broad support; so its representatives were considered outsiders.

Another consideration is needed in this context. When Yahweh was conceived as the owner of the land and giver of the yields, something was taken away from Baal and ascribed to the God of Israel. This meant that both gods were seen as competitors more or less on the same level. In the long run, the outcome of their struggle would have been highly uncertain. But Israel was able to take the new concept of Yahweh as the owner of the land and describe it in categories unknown to the Canaanite world of thought. The God of Israel who, as the owner of the land, gives the yield of the fields is the God of history. That understanding is clearly reflected in a relatively late passage, Deut 6: 10 f, where it is stated that Yahweh brought Israel into the land which he had promised to the patriarchs, a land with

> Great and goodly cities, which you did not build, and houses full of good things, which you did not fill, and cisterns hewn out, which you did not hew, and vineyards and olive trees, which you did not plant. . . .

Here the essential gifts of nature, water, wine, and oil are related to Yahweh as the Lord of history. This made Yahweh so far superior to Baal that over the centuries Baal disappeared and the God of the Old Testament became the God of two world religions.

The Inheritance of Israel

There is a second theological concept in the Old Testament concerning Israel and her land. It is found primarily in the narrative tradition, especially in the Pentateuch, where it is one of the dominating topics. It appears in the phrase referring to Canaan as "the land which Yahweh your God gives you for an inheritance." Even though the phrase does not occur prior to Deuteronomy (Deut 4: 21, 38; 12: 9; 15: 4; 19: 10; 20: 16; 21: 23; 24: 4; 25: 19; 26: 1), it is representative of the whole concept. Again we have the term *naḥ^a^lāh* ("inheritance"), but now related to Israel. Yahweh, who owns all the lands, allots them to individual people as an inheritance, (Josh 23: 4). Canaan is Israel's inheritance.

This idea was developed within the categories of history. The older idea described above—that Yahweh owns the land, and accordingly the land is the *naḥ*ᵃ*lat yhwh*—was part of the concept that he is the lord of nature. This is Canaanite in origin, since it reflects the cultural situation of a sedentary population tilling the soil. Beliefs that a god owns the land and gives the blessing of the soil are not related to a particular country; they can be developed anywhere. So they are not confined in a special way to Palestine; they can apply to any productive land. But a specific Israelite development is that the concept of Yahweh as the Lord of nature was connected with the concept of Yahweh as the Lord of history.[12] History, however, takes place in areas that can be geographically localized, and deals with peoples who can be identified. Within this context of Yahweh the Lord of history, Israel could move to much more specific statements concerning her relationship to her land than within the concept of Yahweh as the Lord of nature. Speaking in historical categories, Israel could say that the land was promised and given to her by Yahweh. She could then describe how the promise was fulfilled. The land could be identified and its boundaries described, and finally she could face the problem that before she occupied the land it was not without population; rather, it was owned by other peoples.

Probably the oldest text in the Old Testament dealing with the land of Israel as a gift of God is the old creed in Deut 26: 5–9. According to Israel's way of thinking, which is to explain conditions of the present as results of happenings in the past, this text states the following: Israel is enjoying the yields of the fields of the land Canaan because Yahweh brought her "into this place" and gave her "this land" (vs 9). It is the culmination of a long history, which began with the forefather, who was a wandering Aramean (vs 5). This creed was recited with the annual dedication of the first fruits to Yahweh on the occasion of the Feast of Weeks.[13] What was, within the concept of Yahweh as the owner of the land, during and immediately after the period of the occupation, a gift of thanksgiving for the yields of nature is now, within historical categories which lead to the concept of Israel as the owner of the land, a gift of thanksgiving returned to Yahweh for the gift of the land. A gift of nature is returned for a gift of history. The God of nature and the God of history have become one.

The allusion to the "father" who was "a wandering Aramean" is broadly expanded in the Pentateuch. It is dominated by the two promises, to make Israel a great nation, and to give her land (Gen 12: 1–4; 24: 7; 26: 3). The promise of national greatness and the promise of a land belong together. Since there is no great nation without a land, the fulfillment of the promise of the land must precede the fulfillment of the other promise to make a great nation. Although in the schematic reconstruction of salvation history in Deut 26: 5–9 this order is reversed, the fulfillment of the one promise remains necessary to the fulfillment of the other.

Once Israel believed that her land was promised and given to her by her God, it was essential to describe the land geographically and to define its boundaries. The land which Yahweh promised to show to Abraham (Gen 12: 1) had to be identified. In this respect, however, the Old Testament gives us no clear picture. The descriptions of boundaries reflect the situation of different periods, and include territories actually possessed or territories not possessed but claimed. To discuss all this in detail is neither possible nor necessary.[14] It is sufficient to point out that in various passages in the Old Testament, within the context of the idea of the promise of the land, rather general boundaries are given. The promised land stretches from the Sea of Suf (or the River of Egypt) in the south to the Euphrates (or the Gateway to Hamath) in the north; and from the sea in the west to the banks of the Jordan River in the east.[15] It is important to observe that Transjordania was not included. It was considered foreign soil (Gen 31: 3), and the construction of an altar east of the Jordan River was regarded as a defection from Yahweh (Josh 22: 10 ff).[16] This is land Yahweh does not own, and so it was considered "unclean" (vs 19). In full agreement with this, the system of Israelite tribal boundaries given in the book of Joshua includes no tribal territories east of the Jordan.[17] This, however, was incompatible with the facts. According to the historical evidence, at least the tribes Gad and Machir occupied territories in East Jordania[18] and, according to the Pentateuch, the traditional tribes of East Jordania were Reuben, Gad, and Half-Manasseh.[19]

The story in Num 32 shows that this was considered a problem. When the representatives of these tribes asked Moses to have East Jordania assigned to them, Moses considered it an act of noncompliance with the promise of the land. Clearly, Transjordania was originally not part of the promised land. Later, according to the story, after Reuben and Gad had promised Moses to help the majority of the tribes with the occupation of West Jordania, their request was met. Moses assigned to them Transjordania (vs 23 ff; Josh 22: 1–9). Here the original understanding is corrected. Since Israelite tribes were well established in East Jordania, that area was later included in the promised land. All this accurately reflects the historical events. The East Jordanian country was colonized only in a second move from the west by parts of Ephraim and Machir when they had difficulties in finding land in West Jordania. Gad, a later arrival from the desert, on discovering the west banks of the Jordan already occupied, settled in the east from the beginning.[20]

A rather late description of the boundaries of the promised land is included in Ezekiel's program of the future (Ezek 47: 13–20).[21] Here the original picture is restored; East Jordania is excluded—which may have been due to the fact that, with the destruction of the northern kingdom in 722/1 B.C. by the Assyrians, this area was definitely lost.[22]

In agreement with the belief that the land described in the boundary lists is a gift of God, the narratives concerning the occupation emphasize that the land was given to Israel—she did not take it herself. Deut 31: 3 says: "The Lord your God himself will go before you; he will destroy these nations before you, so that you shall dispossess them."[23] The statement is a guideline for interpreting the stories in Josh 1–12 concerning the occupation. These begin with the story of the crossing of the Jordan River (Josh 3 and 4). The event is described in the imagery of the crossing of the Red Sea,[24] a fact indicating the importance attached to the occupation. As Yahweh brought Israel out of Egypt, so he brought her into the promised land. The same line is continued in the subsequent war stories. They belong to the genre of the narratives concerning the holy war,[25] and emphasize the idea that Yahweh was the one who gave the victory. This is strongly indicated by the stereotyped phrase "Yahweh gave Jericho in your hand" (Josh 6: 2) and the mention of a miracle in favor of the Israelites during the battle (Josh 6: 20; 10: 10–13). On the other hand, when Israel tried to occupy the land all by herself, she could not succeed (Num 14: 39 ff; Josh 7). This is enough evidence to underscore the idea that the land was given to Israel—she could not take it.[26]

God's gift is praised with enthusiasm. It is called "a land flowing with milk and honey" (Ex 3: 8; 13: 5; Lev 20: 24; Num 13: 28; 14: 8; Deut 6: 3; 26: 9), a phrase reflecting the yearning of people living in the desert for arable land. Almost hymnlike praises of the land surpass this stereotyped phrase in Deuteronomic sermons (Deut 8: 7–10; 11: 10–12; cf Num 13: 23). In the exuberance of that praise, the land is described as even superior to Egypt, where the Israelites once enjoyed the "fleshpots" of the country (Ex 16: 3). The land gives its yield almost by itself: "The eyes of the Lord . . . are always upon it" (Deut 11: 12). In such language, the land of Israel becomes almost a kind of paradise. It did not bother the Israelites that the reality fell considerably short of that. Canaan appeared to them a paradise not because of its character as a land but because it was a gift of Yahweh. For that the Israelites expressed their gratitude by exuberantly praising the land.

There was another area where the religious language of the faithful and reality were in conflict, and this was considered a real problem. According to the promises to the patriarchs, Canaan was to be given to Israel, but the

Israelites never held it completely or alone. Before their coming, Palestine was populated by the Canaanites and representatives of various other peoples. How much attention was given to that fact is indicated by the frequent and almost stereotyped lists of the original inhabitants.[27] In the period of the occupation, Israel was too weak to expel them;[28] and later, during the period of the kingdoms, she did not intend to do so.

The gap between the theory of Israel's full ownership of the land and the political reality in the country became subject to reflections of various kinds. Rather rationalistic answers explained why Canaanites and others remained. It was "because they had chariots of iron" (Judg 1: 19; cf Josh 17: 16). It was because "the generations of the people of Israel might know war, that he might teach war to such at least as had not known it before" (Judg 3: 2). It was "lest the land become desolate and the wild beasts multiply against you" (Ex 23: 29). It is clear that among a people that used to interpret historical facts in the light of their faith, such answers could hardly suffice. Hence, other answers were given on a more theological level. A relatively early passage in the Book of Covenant says:

> Little by little I will drive them out before you, until you are increased and possess the land . . . . For I will deliver the inhabitants of the land into your hand, and you shall drive them out before you. You shall make no covenant with them or with their gods. They shall not dwell in your land, lest they make you sin against me; for if you serve their gods, it will surely be a snare to you. Ex 23: 30–33).[29]

Vs 30 exhibits impatience with the unsatisfactory situation in the country, and offers an explanation. Then follows a new promise—Israel will drive out the original inhabitants—and a prohibition against any kind of agreement or settlement with them.[30] That the promise and the prohibition could develop shows that Israel still hoped to reach a final solution with the original population in the near future.

How difficult, however, the situation was with the Canaanites still in the promised land is indicated by the offering of additional theological explanations: "They shall be a snare and a trap for you, a scourge in your sides, and thorns in your eyes" (Josh 23: 13); it is a punishment of Yahweh for Israel's attempts to come to terms with the original population (Judg 2: 1 ff); it is Yahweh's anger with Israel's idolatry (Judg 2: 11–19, 20 f); Yahweh wanted to test Israel's loyalty (Judg 3: 4 f). Such a variety of answers shows that none of them was completely satisfactory. There was actually no solution to the problem of the Canaanite's continuance in the promised land.

David, in his time, offered at least a political solution. He incorporated the hitherto independent Canaanite city-states into the territories of Judah and Israel.[31] Later his successor Solomon called on the non-Israelite population to supply forced labor for his various building activities.[32] This too, however, could not solve the theological aspect of the problem that the Canaanites were still there.

Thus, in the Deuteronomic tradition, the Israelites preparing for the crossing of the Jordan River were instructed: "You must utterly destroy them; you shall make no covenant with them, and show no mercy to them" (Deut 7: 2; 20: 17).[33] From the Deuteronomic point of view, and against the historical background of this theological movement, it is quite clear that such ordinances were used as the reason for all the problems which arose over the centuries from the cohabitation with the Canaanites, because they were not followed.[34] On the other hand, with the collapse of the Assyrian empire, hope arose that King Josiah of Judah could reunite the two kingdoms and have full control of the promised land.[35] Even though that did not happen, hope continued that sometime the land would be fully possessed, as had been promised. In the description of the redistribution of the land following the return from the exile (Ezek 47: 13 ff,) land (*naḥ*ᵃ*lāh*) was also to be allotted to the *gērîm*. It is certainly presupposed that those *gērîm* would now be worshipers of Yahweh.[36]

Certain theological considerations are related to the concept that the land of Canaan is the *naḥ*ᵃ*lat* Israel.

It can be shown that in the Old Testament the two promises to Israel—that it would become a great nation, and that it would possess the promised land—belong inseparably together. The promise to a group of seminomadic clans and tribes that they would become a great nation makes no sense without the hope that sometime they would possess a land where they could become a great nation. And, vice versa, they would not need a promised land if they had no hope of becoming a great nation. Consequently, wherever there are Israelites who believe themselves to be the people of God, they cannot conceive of the idea of their being or becoming a great nation without the idea of their possessing a promised land; and the idea of their possessing a promised land makes no sense to them without the hope of their becoming a great nation to hold and populate it.

The idea of the promised land was developed within the belief of Yahweh as the Lord of history. Of necessity, then, the land had to be identified. The promised land is not any country. It is the land of Canaan, the borders of which could be identified, given to Israel in the thirteenth century B.C.

Accordingly, whoever thinks of Israel as the people of God must associate them with Canaan—not with another land. Israel and Canaan, the promised land, belong together. The existence of Israel can be described only in a triangular relationship:

Yahweh
/ \
Israel —— Canaan

No point can be left out. Without Yahweh, there would be no promise of a great nation, no promise of a land, and no fulfillment. The nation Israel, without claim of being the people of God, would be without any special interest in world history. Canaan, without assignment to the people of God, would be just another area of contention in the power game of world politics.[37] It was certainly with a lack of theological understanding that, in the very beginning of the Zionistic movement, men like Leon Pinkser or Theodore Herzl, for reasons of suitability or expediency, discussed Argentina, Uganda, or other countries as new homelands for the Jews.[38] Either there is a people of God—Israel—related to Canaan; or there is just another powerful ethnic minority group trying to invade the territory of a foreign nation.

The historian might say that Canaan was invaded and taken by the Israelites, as lands were invaded and taken by other peoples at different times in different areas of the ancient Near Eastern world. But the theological reflection of the Old Testament tradition clearly indicates that Israel firmly believed this land was given her by an act of her God. It was not taken forcefully, but was bestowed by God upon his people in an act of mercy. Here two things belong together: the idea of the promised land, and the idea of its bestowal. A promised land taken by force would be self-contradictory.

In her cult, Israel confessed that the promise of the land was fulfilled (Deut 26: 9); and yet the original inhabitants were not completely exterminated or expelled. Israel was not able to do so. The result was tension between the confession of fulfillment of the promise and the reality, which constantly needed correction by a "not yet total." Even though, in her historical retrospection, Israel pointed out that everything that was promised was fulfilled, the "not yet" of the reality left open the possibility of further acts of Yahweh in the future.

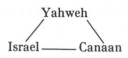

Our investigation has now reached a point where another question should be introduced. Are these biblical ideas in any way applicable to the present situation in the Middle East, where today Jews have returned to the country which in the Bible is called the promised land? It seems that the greatest caution is needed here. Is contemporary Israel just a secular nation or state, or is she more? Is she still the chosen people of God, again trying to live in the promised land? Can a direct line be drawn from Old Testament Israel, to New Testament Judaism, to all the different factions of later world Judaism, and—finally—to the Israel of our day? Only if positive answers can be given, would it be theologically justifiable to apply theological conclusions drawn from the biblical evidence to the present situation in Palestine. It would be wrong, however, to try to establish such a connection historically. Statements like "Israel is the people of God" and "Canaan is the promised land" are theological statements and propositions of faith. Hence, the question with reference to the present situation in the Middle East is: Does the Israel of today still represent the people of God? An affirmative answer would be another proposition of faith important for both the Jewish religion and Christianity.

Israel's Responsibility in the Promised Land

The promise and bestowal of the land constituted only one aspect in Israel's concept of the land. Here Israel was dealing with her past. But there was something more. When Israel received the gift of the land, a heavy responsibility was placed upon her. She was to do everything necessary to keep and maintain this gift and not to lose it.

In Lev 18: 24 f (cf 20: 22) we have a rather archaic-looking passage:

> Do not defile yourselves by any of these things, for by all these the nations I am casting out before you defiled themselves; and the land became defiled, so that I punished its iniquity, and the land vomited out its inhabitants.

The basic idea behind this quotation seems to be a very old one belonging to the world of natural religion and mythology. A natural relation exists between men and the land they live on. If they violate the order of nature, they defile both themselves and the land also—which is why the land vomits out the transgressors. The land is spoken of here as a mythological entity with its own power. Israelite thought differs. The mythological power of the land is suppressed, and Yahweh is introduced as the one who casts out the transgressors and punishes them. But the archaic phraseology that the land is acting is still sustained.

This shows that in the Code of Holiness, of which Lev 18 is a part, there is more than merely a relationship between Israel and her land in categories of theological history. The new dimension added here is that, with the bestowal of the land, a heavy responsibility was laid upon Israel. Now she has to act and to behave in the land in a way that she can keep it or stay in it.[39] The same idea is even more strongly developed in Deuteronomy, and certainly under the impression of the exile in the Deuteronomistic literature. Two areas are to be briefly discussed in this context: cult, and law.

If Canaan was Yahweh's gift to Israel by which her existence as a great nation became possible, then Israel's first duty in the promised land was to worship Yahweh. Accordingly, the Yahwist relates that one of the first things Abraham did after arriving in the promised land was to build an altar (Gen 12: 7 f), as also did Isaac and Jacob after the promises were renewed to them (Gen 26: 25; 28: 18 ff; JE). The obligation of worship is again recognized when, according to Josh 4 and 5, Israel began the Yahweh cult immediately after the tribes had set foot on Canaanite soil. As soon as the people of Yahweh enter Canaan, regular worship of Yahweh shall begin. Deuteronomy emphasizes this by declaring that in the promised land is "the place which the Lord your God will choose out of all your tribes to put his name and to make his habitation there" (Deut 12: 5). The place is not identified, but, it is important to see, it is in the promised land (Deut 12: 1).

Again we see that Yahweh, Israel, and Canaan belong together inseparably, this time for cultic reasons. It is probably not an overstatement to say that the destiny of Canaan is to be the place where Yahweh is worshiped. There can be no worship of Yahweh by his people other than in the promised land. An altar in East Jordania is considered illegitimate (Josh 22: 10 ff); or when the exiles worship in the land of their captivity, they turn to Jerusalem to pray (1 Kings 8: 48). P adds that in order to make legitimate worship possible later in the promised land, a model of the temple and all the equipment was prepared by Moses on Mount Sinai (Ex 25 ff).

According to all this, Canaan is the land where the people of God are to worship Yahweh.[40] Accordingly, it is decreed in Deuteronomy that Israel must destroy in Canaan all the places where the original inhabitants worshiped their Gods (12: 1 ff). Only the single place designated for the worship of Yahweh is left. No worship other than that paid to Yahweh at that particular place is permitted (Deut 4: 25; 6: 14; 12: 30). Only in this way can the promised land be what it is intended to be—the one land in the world where Yahweh receives worship from his people. To fulfill its destiny, Canaan needs Israel. Or, in other words, Israel can be the people of God only if it worships Yahweh in Canaan. Israel needs Canaan to be the people of God.

A rather archaic-looking formulation is found in Lev 25 in the introduction to the laws concerning the Sabbatical Year: "When you come into the land which I give you, the land shall keep a Sabbath to the Lord" (vs 2).[41] Strangely enough, not Israel but the land appears here as the subject of a cultic activity directed to Yahweh. This shows again that the land has a special obligation to Yahweh, and that when Israel enters the promised land she assumes the responsibility to respect that obligation.

The fact that the cultic regulations of the Old Testament are part of the Old Testament law tradition allows us to go one step further. Not only is worship to Yahweh related to the promised land, but so is the entire law. To be a great nation, Israel needs a land—there can be no great nation without land. Similarly, to be the people of Yahweh, Israel needs the law of Yahweh (Deut 4: 5 ff). There can be no people of Yahweh without his law. So Canaan is the land where the law of Yahweh is complied with. All this plays again a major role in the theology of Deuteronomy. The law is given to Israel as a rule of life for her stay in the promised land (4: 1; 5: 31; 6: 1–3). In Deut 12: 1, the Deuteronomic law code is introduced with the formula: "These are the statutes and ordinances which you shall be careful to do in the land which the Lord, the God of your fathers, has given you to possess all the days that you live upon the earth." It is important to see that the land is not given to Israel as recompense for her compliance with the law of Yahweh. To consider it a recompense would be to misunderstand passages like Deut 11: 8: "You shall therefore keep all the commandments which I command you this day, that you may be strong, and go in and take possession of the land which you are going over to possess."[42] Accomplishment and recompense are not the categories to be applied. Rather, we have a theological order of thought: If Canaan is the land where Israel is to comply with the law of Yahweh, then Israel needs that law in advance so that she can enter the promised land. That is why, according to Deuteronomy, the law (Deut 12–26) was given at Mount Nebo, on the doorsteps of the promised land. Says Deut 11: 31 f: "For you are to pass over the Jordan to go in to take possession of the land which the Lord your God gives you; and when you possess it and live in it, (then) you shall be careful to do all the statutes and ordinances which I set before you this day."

The land was not given to Israel as recompense (Deut 9: 4 f; 12: 30); Israel was chosen, the patriarchs had received the promises, and the land was bestowed upon Israel without any special merit. The only reason that is given is "Yahweh loved her" (Deut 6: 8). In return, Israel is expected to show gratitude. An instruction intended for the children is devised accordingly (Deut 6: 20 ff).[43] The children ask, "What is the meaning of the testimonies and the statutes and the ordinances which the Lord our God has commanded you?" The fathers are to answer with a creed, referring to the acts of God beginning with the liberation from Egypt up to the occupation of the land. Here it is quite clear: gratitude for the gracious acts of God culminating in his gift of the land is the motivation behind Israel's compliance with God's law. On the other hand, without God's gift of the land, Israel would have no reason to respect his law.

As the people of Yahweh, Israel was unique among the nations of the world (Deut 4: 6), and she lived in a special country of the world. She was responsible for maintaining her special character and that of the land by living in the land according to the "testimonies and statutes and the ordinances" that Yahweh her God had "commanded her" (Deut 6: 20). Israel could easily fail and, as a matter of fact, often did. As a violation of her relationship to her God, her failure was spelled out in detail by the Old Testament prophets—for instance, in the accusations of their announcements of judgment against her.[44] But her failure was also an offense against the special character of the land as Yahweh's own country. Violation of the law of Yahweh in the land where the order of Yahweh is to be respected or worship of other gods in the land where Yahweh is to be worshiped would sever Israel's relationship to the land, and the logical result would be expulsion.

This brings us back to the archaic formulation in Lev 18: 25 f (cf 20: 22), which we discussed before. Because of their conduct, even though they did not know what they were doing, the original inhabitants of Canaan defiled the land, so that it "vomited them out," and the people of God entered it to fulfill its destiny. The same fate could easily befall Israel and, as a matter of fact, it did (Lev 26: 32 f). The same idea is widely expressed by both the Deuteronomic-Deuteronomistic literature[45] and the pre-exilic prophets.

In a rather peculiar way, the idea is also expressed at the end of the Code of Holiness (Lev 26: 33–35). Here the idea of expulsion is given in cultic categories. The background is the archaic idea mentioned above: the land is under obligation to "keep a Sabbath to the Lord" (Lev 25: 1). But a disobedient Israel could interfere and not allow the land to do so. In that case, Yahweh "will scatter them among the nations," and "then the land shall enjoy its Sabbaths" (Lev 26: 33 f). In this context, the expulsion of Israel seems to be a cultic necessity.

There is, however, a decisive difference between the expulsion of the original inhabitants and the expulsion of the people of Yahweh. The expulsion of the original inhabitants was definite and final, and the land was given to Israel forever.[46] But the expulsion of Israel does not annul the promise and bestowal of the land; it is only temporary.

Consequently, two exilic passages, which certainly reflect the influence of the message of the prophets, deal with the possibility of Israel's return to the promised land (Deut 30: 1 ff, and 1 Kings 8: 46 ff).[47] Israel may return if she returns to Yahweh and repents. Then Yahweh will restore her fortunes, gathering her from all the peoples where he had scattered her and bringing her back to her land. Two things are important in this development: 1) Israel's return to the promised land is possible if—and only if—Israel returns to her God and repents. This means, in turn, that there can be no return to the promised land without repentance. 2) If Israel repents, then Yahweh promises to act. He it is who restores Israel to the promised land, giving the land to her again, as he did the first time under Joshua. Israel may not return on her own to retake the land.

Here our investigation must be concluded. Again, we observe that it was not intended to give a full picture of the Old Testament concept of Israel and her land. That is impossible within the limitations of such a short article. Instead, it was intended simply to show how important and far-reaching the idea is in the Old Testament tradition—indeed, that it has a much more important place in Israelite thinking than recent works on Old Testament theology seem to indicate.

A broader discussion of our topic should certainly put much more emphasis on the prophets. The prophets of the seventh and sixth centuries in particular made a major contribution, especially on the subject of "expulsion and return to the homeland." So, for example, Deutero-Isaiah would deserve a closer look, since it is he who announces the return of Israel to the promised land at the beginning of the eschatological age. Then God leads his people back to Jerusalem (Is 40: 9–11; 52: 7–12), in an event equal to the exodus from Egypt.[48]

Notes

1 Albrecht Alt, "The Settlement of the Israelites in Palestine," in *Essays on Old Testament History and Religion*, trans. by R. A. Wilson (1968); John Bright, *A History of Israel* (1959); George E. Mendenhall, *The Hebrew Conquest of Palestine, BA* XXV (1962), 66–87.

2 Noteworthy are the following contributions: Hans Wildberger, "Israel und sein Land," EvT (1956), 404–22; Gerhard von Rad, "The Promised Land and Yahweh's Land in the Hexateuch," in *The Problem of the Hexateuch and Other Essays*, trans. by E. W. Trueman Dicken (1966), pp. 79–93; Gerhard von Rad, *Old Testament Theology*, trans. by D. M. G. Stalker, Vol. I (1962), pp. 296–305.

3 Walter Eichrodt, *Theology of the Old Testament*, trans. by J. A. Baker (1691).

4 Cf Henning Graf Reventlow, *Das Heiligkeitsgesetz, WMANT* 6 (1961), 133 f.

5 See *KB*.

6 Ulf Oldenburg, *The Conflict between El and Baʿal in Canaanite Religion* (1969), p. 76.

7 *Ibid.*, pp. 176 f; Albrecht Alt, *op. cit.*

8 H. J. Kraus, *Worship in Israel*, trans. by Geoffrey Boswell (1965), pp. 70 ff.

9 See Karl Elliger, *Leviticus, HAT*, 1/4 (1966), pp. 260 f.

10 Roland de Vaux, *Ancient Israel: Its Life and Institutions*, trans. by John McHugh (1961), pp. 74 ff.

11 *Ibid.*, pp. 14 f.

12 See Martin Buber, *Israel und Palästina* (1950), pp. 22 f.

13 See Gerhard von Rad, *The Problem of the Hexateuch*, pp. 32 ff; Martin Buber, *op.cit.*, pp. 15 ff.

14 See Yehezkel Kaufmann, *The Biblical Account of the Conquest of Palestine*, trans. by M. Dagut (1953), pp. 48 ff.

[15] Gen 15: 18; Ex 23: 31; Num 13: 21 f; 34: 2–12; Deut 1: 7; 11: 24; Josh 1: 4; cf Ezek 15–20.

[16] It is not likely that Josh 22: 10 ff presupposes the Deuteronomic centralization of the cult. It is probably older. Shiloh—not Jerusalem—is named here as the only legitimate sanctuary in Canaan.

[17] See Albrecht Alt, "The Formation of the Israelite State in Palestine," in *Essays on Old Testament History and Religion*, p. 294, 141; Martin Noth, *Das Buch Josua, HAT*, 2d ed (1953), pp. 73 ff.

[18] Cf the term "Machir the Father of Gilead," Josh 17: 1; 1 Chron 7: 14; see Martin Noth, *The History of Israel* (1960), pp. 63 f.

[19] Num 32; cf Deut 3: 12 ff; Josh 13: 8 ff.

[20] See Martin Noth, *op. cit.*, p. 63.

[21] Cf Num 34: 3 ff.

[22] Actually already eleven years earlier; see Martin Noth, *op. cit.*, pp. 260 f.

[23] Cf Josh 4: 13 f and the earlier passages Ex 23: 23, 27 f; 34: 11.

[24] H. J. Kraus, *op. cit.*, pp. 154 ff.

[25] Gerhard von Rad, *Der heilige Krieg im alten Israel*, 2d ed (1958).

[26] She cannot say: "My power and the might of my hand have gotten me this wealth" (Deut 8: 17).

[27] See Yehezkel Kaufmann, *op. cit.*, pp. 49 ff.

[28] See Götz Schmitt, *Du sollst keinen Frieden schliessen mit den Bewohnern des Landes, BWANT* 91 (1970), 46 ff, 76 ff.

[29] Cf Ex 34: 11 f; see Götz Schmitt, *op. cit.*, pp. 13 ff.

[30] Cf the narrative Josh 9; and Schmitt, *op. cit.*, pp. 30 ff.

[31] Martin Noth, *op. cit.*, pp. 191 ff.

[32] *Ibid.*, p. 211; cf Judg 1: 27 ff; 1 Kings 9: 15a, 20–22.

[33] The question as to whether Ex 23: 20–33 was an older model cannot be discussed here; cf on this Götz Schmitt, *op. cit.*, pp. 13 ff.

[34] *Ibid.*, pp. 131 ff.

[35] Martin Noth, *op. cit.*, pp. 269 ff.

[36] Walter Zimmerli, *Ezechiel, BKAT*, Vol. XIII/2 (1969), pp. 1218 f. He, however, thinks only of proselytes who joined the exiles in Babylon.

[37] Martin Buber, in *op. cit.*, brings into the picture the third promise to the patriarchs: "Only in connection with this soil, with this land, the people can become, what they are supposed to become: 'A blessing' (Gen 12: 2)," p. 39 (my translation).

[38] Cf Martin Buber, *ibid.*, pp. 155 ff.

[39] Not so expressed in the Book of Covenant.

[40] Cf also the cultic harvest ordinances, which are related not to soil or to arable land in general but to the land of Canaan (Lev 19: 23 f; 23: 9) (25: 1). Concerning the Passover, see Ex 12: 25.

[41] See Karl Elliger, *op. cit.*, pp. 349 ff.

[42] Cf Deut 8: 1; 16: 20.

[43] See Gerhard von Rad, *Deuteronomy*, trans. by Dorothea Barton (1966), p. 63.

[44] See Claus Westermann, *Basic Forms of Prophetic Speech*, trans. by Hugh C. White (1967), pp. 169 ff.

[45] Deut 4: 27 f; 11: 17; 28: 63 ff; 29: 28.

[46] So already in J, Gen 13: 15; in P, Gen 48, 4. Ex 32: 13 is an addition to E.

[47] Gerhard von Rad, *Deuteronomy*, pp. 183 ff; and Martin Noth, *Könige, BKAT* IX/1 (1968), p. 188 f.

[48] See H. Eberhard von Waldow, "The Message of Deutero-Isaiah," *Interp* 22 (1968), 276 f.

G. Ernest Wright
Harvard University Divinity School

The Conquest Theme in the Bible

The gap between a popular understanding of the book of Joshua and the biblical understanding is so wide that one may well wonder whether it can ever be eliminated or even narrowed. Since the Enlightenment, Joshua has seemed to many people as so primitive, as so gross an example of man's inhumanity to man, using God's word as the excuse for indiscriminate killing, that many have queried how the book can be considered sacred Scripture. All one can do with it, it has often been said, is to consider it the earliest and lowest point in Israel's history, out of which she emerged with her prophets and wisemen to become the conscience of the Western world. Theologically, this emergence has been dealt with as a spectacularly vivid example of what used to be called "progressive revelation."

On the other hand, the introduction of history of tradition methods has overcome the technical fragmentation of source criticism. Thus, now we have been taught to see that Israel's ancient epic is confessional in nature, centering on the themes: God's promise to the Patriarchs; the deliverance of the newly created and chosen people from Egyptian slavery; and the gift of the Land of Promise to those who had no power, for whom the world's powers would provide no justice or righteousness. These themes are set in the context of a view of the world (Gen 1–11) in sordid disarray, in violent rebellion against the conditions of creation. Hence, God's actions with Israel are his positive answer to the problem of man and his civilization. And man's warfare on earth, in the context of his life as rebellion, can, from the larger perspective, be viewed as God's warfare, his use of human agency for his own purpose, to the end that the world become his Kingdom.[1]

This recalling by the new scholarship of the classic Old Testament themes means that the book of Joshua can no longer be considered an ugly and fanatical primitivism. It is squarely at the center of Israel's most "advanced" confessional theology. The tradition centers in God's deliverance from bondage, with its accompanying themes of crossing the sea and leading through the wilderness, and finally the entrance into the Promised Land.

At this level, Old Testament scholarship has finally come abreast of what the historian has all along seen to be the formative influence of these traditions of Israel, so understood and interpreted, on the Western world, and especially on America. The sociologist Robert N. Bellah has written about an American "Civil Religion" that exists in certain formal public documents from the Puritans through Washington to Johnson. It is a religion that is precisely in neither church nor synagogue, but exists beside them. The God of this religion

> has much less to do with natural law than with ancient Israel; the equation of America with Israel in the idea of the "American Israel" is not infrequent . . . . [This, always implicit] becomes explicit in Jefferson's second inaugural when he said: "I shall need, too, the favor of that Being in whose hands we are, who led our fathers, as Israel of old, from their native land and planted them in a country flowing with all the necessaries of life." Europe is Egypt; America, the promised land. God has led his people to establish a new sort of social order that shall be a light to the nations.[2]

Theodore P. Greene, professor of American history at Amherst College, in assessing the history of higher education in this country, affirms that the full dimensions of the present student unrest "are fundamentally religious impulses and that neither the categories of Enlightenment liberalism nor those of Marxist radicalism can do full justice to them." Nineteenth-century colleges had at the center of their education certain impulses, biblically centered, which can be summarized as: a sense of community, a sense of mission, a strong sense of vocation, and an intimate concern for salvation, which with all its variations of meaning meant, and still means, at its center "a state of wholeness, a sense of being at one not only within one's self but with the whole universe and society in which one lives . . . ." In the words of a certain Reverend David Clark, at the dedication of the first building of Amherst College, all this endeavor was "to fertilize the boundless wastes of a miserable world."[3] Here again, the basic themes were drawn from the Bible, with Joshua as central with Exodus to Israel's confessional epic: a chosen community to be a blessing to the world, each individual called by God's "Thou shalt" to labor for the common good, until the weapons of war become those of peace.

From Israel's prose narratives, von Rad, as is well known, separated a number of pericopes which narrate God's mighty acts, or saving activity, in the formation of the new people. The conquest of Canaan is always the climax, but it is not a tale of heroes and great acts of bravery. Joshua and Israel are simply God's instruments, but the work is God's work. He is the only hero, and the only one to receive full praise and credit. The land was not won by Israel; it was won by God. It is a Promised Land which God gives to Israel. One result in Jerusalem regulations was the forbidding of land profiteering: "The land must not be sold in perpetuity; the land belongs to me" (from the Holiness Code, Lev 25: 23).[4] The Apostle Paul's sermon, as summarized in Acts 13: 16–19, is simply the epitome of an age-old manner of confession:

> Men of Israel and you who fear God, hear [this]: The God of this people Israel chose our fathers and exalted the people during their time in the land of Egypt. Then with great power he led them from it . . . . And when he had destroyed seven nations in the land of Canaan, he allotted them the land . . . .

In Israel's Psalms and hymns, the recital of the *magnalia Dei* may be used in two basic ways: On the one hand, God's acts may be sung as a paean of praise and worship whereby he is magnified and blessed by the community. On the other hand, the recital may be made, but God's powerful goodness to Israel then becomes the background for the story of Israel's infidelity, the hymn thus serving the purposes of confession. The prophets frequently used the second manner as one of their forms of speech (cf Hos 11 and Jer 2). In the Exilic or post-Exilic trilogy (Pss 104–106) Ps 105 is an example of the first type, and Ps 106 is an example of the second.

Here, however, we have space to call attention only to certain hymns which have special features to be observed. Ps 78 is, in its overall form, a meditation on the fall of Shiloh to the Philistines *ca.* 1050 B.C. and the reasons for God's rejecting the people of Joseph but, instead, choosing David and Jerusalem of Judah for leadership and the seat of his temple. The Jerusalem Psalmist of the royal court explains that Ephraim failed to keep God's covenant:

> (11) They forgot his deeds,
> His marvels which he had shown them.

Reciting God's great deeds in the Exodus on Israel's behalf, the Psalmist continues:

(54) He brought them to his holy territory
(To) this mountain his right hand created.
(55) He drove out nations before them;
He allotted them (land) in a measured inheritance;
He settled the tribes of Israel in their tents.[5]

One thing to be noted in this early pre-Exilic Psalm is that the land is God's allotment to Israel. The Hebrew words strongly suggest that God not only gave the land to Israel but distributed it among the tribes. The only way at the time the tribes of Israel could have known about their portions is on the presumption that the land had been surveyed and parceled out by lot. This Psalm, then, gives strong support to the supposition that what has seemed to scholars in Joshua as late and artificial is, indeed, very old—that is, the tradition that each tribe and clan had received its "inheritance" from God. To this tradition, the affirmation of the lottery in Josh 13–19 seems also to testify. Can those chapters therefore be a gloss on the book by a post-Exilic priesthood, as literary criticism has commonly supposed? Would the Deuteronomic historian of Israel in the Promised Land be expected to compose a book out of old sources which narrated God's victories and not God's gift of "inheritances"? It seems to this writer hardly a likely hypothesis.

A second theme is one of great sophistication—that is, the reference to the conquest as God's bringing of his people to the holy mountain which he has created (vs 54). This is a mythological allusion; the holy mountain is that one of Canaanite mythology existing in the far north at the juncture of heaven and earth where the gods abide. The conquest of Canaan—what does the poet mean by referring to it as God's creation of the holy mountain? For explanation, let us turn to an even older poem, the Passover Hymn found in Ex 15 and now often referred to as the Song of the Sea.

My colleague Frank M. Cross, Jr., has written about this poem as follows:

> We have argued elsewhere[6] that the language of Exodus 15 is more consistently archaic than that of any other prose or poetic work of some length in the Bible. The poem conforms throughout to the prosodic patterns and canons of the Late Bronze Age. Its use of mixed metrical structure, its baroque use of climactic parallelism, internal rhyme and assonance, place it alongside of the Song of Deborah [Judg 5].[7]

Cross' argument is that this is one of the earliest poems in the Bible, though it may not have been put into writing until the tenth century B.C.

After celebration of Yahweh's deliverance of Israel from pharaoh and his hosts at the Egyptian Reed Sea, the poet turns to the conquest of Canaan as follows:[8]

(13) You have faithfully led
The people whom you have delivered.
You have guided [them] in your might
To your holy encampment.
(14) The peoples heard, they shuddered;
Horror seized the dwellers of Philistia . . . .

(16c) When your people passed over, Yahweh,
When your people passed over whom you created,
You brought them [in], you planted them
In the mount of your heritage,
The dais of your throne
Which you made, Yahweh,
The sanctuary, Yahweh,
Which your hands created.
Yahweh will reign
Forever and ever!

In these forceful words, we have a mixture of Israel's historical experience, expounded partly in her ordinary language of event and partly in the language of Canaanite myth. The conquest is God's bringing his people into the Promised Land. Yet that event has cosmic significance. It is his planting them there on the mountain of his "heritage," the place of his temple (probably both cosmic and earthly in replica), all of which he has created and from which he will exercise his sovereignty forever. The holy mountain at earth's centrally crucial point, where his people live, gathered about his throne, and from which he will forever reign—this is precisely the central theme of that beautiful hymn quoted in both Is 2: 1–4 and Mic 4: 1–4. There the temple mountain will become the highest and central point of earth, to which the peoples of the world shall stream to learn the ways of the sovereign Judge of all the earth. Only then will there be universal peace, so that a man may lie down under his vine or his fig tree and "none shall make them afraid" (Mic 4: 4).

The peculiarity of the early employment of this mythical language is twofold: On the one hand, it demanded a high degree of sophistication on the part of both Israelite poet and his hearers if they were to comprehend both the allusions and the high degree of complexity in the prosody. On the other hand, at the very time when Israel was battling for her distinctive life against Canaanite religion, Israelite poets were free to make such use of Canaanite mythical expressions and to expect to be understood. So deeply rooted is the Yahwism of these passages that we cannot for a moment suppose that the Israelite poet believed the myth he was quoting. Nor does the old pattern of argumentation that Israel was historicizing myth or was mythicizing history seem quite appropriate for this usage. Instead, we must suppose that the symbolic power of the mythic pattern was fully understood. Thus, to speak of the conquest as God creating his holy mountain and the temple upon it, and planting his people there to observe and to obey his eternal sovereignty—all this was to set these seemingly minor events in a tiny corner of world history and place them apart from all other earthly happenings. The conquest was a deed of cosmic and eternal significance, the mythical expressions revealing the truly transcendent meaning of the event without any loss of its historical nature.

Another Psalm, later but actually undatable, though surely pre-Exilic, interprets the crossing of the Jordan (Josh 3) in the personalized terms of the Canaanite creation myth. The power of order overwhelming chaos was told as Baal's triumphant conflict with Sea (or Sea dragon of chaos, sometimes called Rahab or Leviathan). Ps 114 sees the crossing of the Jordan as Yahweh's victory over Sea—thus the creative event of universal history without parallel. A translation of the Psalm is as follows:

(1) When Israel went forth from Egypt,
    The household of Jacob from a foreign-tongued nation,
(2) Judah became his holy [place],
    And Israel his royal dominion.
(3) The Sea looked and fled;
    The Jordan turned backwards.
(4) The mountains danced like rams,
    Hills like the young of sheep.
(5) What is the matter, O sea, that you flee,
    O Jordan, that you turn backwards,
(6) O mountains, that you dance like rams,
    O hills, like the young of sheep?
(7) Before the Sovereign tremble, O earth,
    Before the God of Jacob
(8) He who transforms the rock into a pool of water,
    Flint into a spring of water.

In vss 3 and 5, Sea and Jordan are in synonymous parallelism, and are addressed as a person who fled, turned backward, in fear at Yahweh's approach.

Ps 66: 5–7 has another reference to this personalizing of Sea, which is made to serve God's purposes:

(5) Come and see the deeds of God,
    The Awesome One in his work among the sons of men.
(6) He turned Sea to dry land;
    Through the Stream they passed on foot;
      There we rejoiced in him.

(7) He is ruler by his power forever.
His eyes watch over the nations—
Let not the rebellious exalt themselves.

At this point, we cannot be sure whether the Sea referred to is the Jordan or the Egyptian Reed Sea, for God's victory over Sea, in language of myth, is used of both (cf Ps 106: 8–9; Is 51: 9–11). Yet it makes little difference, because by the principle of synecdoche, one major element in the complex of recital events brings to mind the whole story. If in the later period the crossing of the Jordan was absorbed into the crossing of the Reed Sea, the basic point remains. Israel's rescue and implanting in the Land of promise are in Biblical theology events in the life of earth equally important with creation itself.[9]

Furthermore, the old events became the ground of hope and interpretation for both present and future. In both prophetic and apocalyptic eschatology, God's power and purpose as shown in the old events become the promise of a Second Exodus and a Second Conquest.[10] Even at Qumran, the people of the Scrolls possessed a book about *The War between the Children of Light and the Children of Darkness*, while awaiting God's creation of the new heavens and the new earth.[11] In addition to the explicit references to these final events by the Apostle Paul, in the defense of Stephen (Acts 7: 45), and especially in Revelation, we should note the more generalized interpretation of the Exodus-Conquest cycle as God's mercy and salvation in 1 Pet 2: 9–10:

> Indeed, you are an elect race, a royal priesthood, a holy nation, God's own possession,[12] in order that you may proclaim the wondrous deeds of him who called you out of darkness into his marvelous light, [you who] once were no people but now are God's people, [you who] had not received mercy but now have received mercy.

Here again, the Exodus-Conquest cycle is God's gracious gift to those who had been outcast.

If this, then, is the true story of the book of Joshua as biblical people understood it, how are we so to read it when we repeatedly see after major battles, such statements as this: "Then Israel placed under *ḥērem* [the sacred ban or taboo, the verb then meaning "killed"] all in the city, men and women, young and old, cattle, sheep and donkeys, by the sword" (Josh 6: 21). A proper commentary on the book is a task which deals with the very heart and core of biblical faith, but to my knowledge no such commentary has been produced in modern times. The best literature on war has generally been written by pacifist humanists and Christians, to whom Joshua—and, for that matter, most of the Old Testament—makes poor reading indeed. In one of the best modern surveys, Roland H. Bainton concludes a few paragraphs on the Deuteronomic school with the words: "War is more humane when God is left out of it."[13] This may well be true with regard to the fanaticism of a holy war crusade, but it exhibits no understanding whatever of Israel's own views on the subject, which are anything but simplistic and are the very antithesis of doctrinaire pacifism. The latter has its roots in modern idealism (in the technical philosophical sense of that term), rather than in biblical "realism," which insists upon seeing the providence of the Divine Suzerain in the mixed good and evil of human activity on earth.

Hence, by way of conclusion, a few words suggest the framework of conception within which the biblical views of Joshua's conquest might conceivably make sense to the modern mind:

There is at work in the world a mysterious creative power that is experienced on the human scene in both positive and negative, redemptive and judgmental ways.[14]

The negative side of this power is most commonly seen in conflict, not only of individual wills but when evolutionary processes going in different directions—one advancing, the other decaying—intersect. In that intersection, innocent suffering also takes place because we are all "bound in the bundle of the living" together and there is no escape to a secure hideaway.

Our world is in disorder because it has not surrendered to the will of its Creator and Lord. Conflict as war takes place only in this rebellious world. It is fought by sinners who employ their structures of power to their own ends in the complex advance, defense, retreat of the human lust for power.

God works in this world by *mediate* means—that is, through human agents, whether or not they realize it. Yet because one is an agent does not mean that one is therefore automatically good and holy. God uses us as we are; his righteousness does not automatically make his agents righteous (cf Deut 9 or the contest between Jacob and Laban). Certainly Israel is not to think of herself as more righteous in God's sight than those she defeats.

The special institution of holy war, which still breathes through the books of Deuteronomy and Joshua and which had such a profound influence on the conception of "faith" in prophecy, can be handled by us today if we see it from the standpoint of agency. God used Israel as she was. To the prophets, the Arameans, Assyrians, and Babylonians were the instruments of God's "holy" war against Israel, the language of the old institution reappearing in part, only under different agency. Yet the foreign ruler was certainly not deemed righteous. His problem was self-deification, which meant that he, in his turn, would suffer judgment.

Early Christian pacifism is again to be viewed from the standpoint of agency. It was the tactic to be used by Christians in the vast Roman empire—until the time of Constantine, when Christians suddenly had to take part in government and the search for world order. Then Christian views changed, and Augustine was the first to attempt to set down certain guidelines for the use of force by Christians.

Because there is at work in the world a Power determined on righteousness and the Kingdom of God, mankind may have hope, even in our time. The sickness in our present is not eternal; Satan has been defeated, and will be again and again, though the outcome of any one moment is never certain.

Such a standpoint requires a view of human life as vocational. We were not born into Paradise, but into this world. Our lives achieve meaning only as they are engaged in God's conflict to make the world his Kingdom.

Notes

1 Cf Gen 12: 3 and parallel passages; for the new approach, see Gerhard von Rad, *The Problem of the Hexateuch and Other Essays*, tr. by E. W. T. Dicken from the German monograph first published in 1938 (London and New York, 1966), pp. 1–78; and *Genesis*, tr. by John H. Marks (Philadelphia, Westminster's Old Testament Library, 1961).

2 Robert N. Bellah, "Civil Religion in America," *Daedalus* (Winter, 1967), 1–21, later reprinted in various publications. Quotations are from pp. 7–8.

3 Theodore P. Greene, "The Crisis in the Colleges and the Role of the Churches," 1970, an as yet unpublished paper, quoted by permission of the author.

4 Note Isaiah's charge of flagrant violation of this principle, Is 5: 8.

5 For defense of details of translation, see the forthcoming Anchor Bible Commentary on *Joshua*.

6 See his treatment (with David Noel Freedman) in "Studies in Ancient Yahwistic Poetry" (a Johns Hopkins University dissertation, 1950, Microfilm-Xerox reprint, Ann Arbor, 1963) pp. 5–127; and Cross and Freedman, "The Song of Miriam," *JNES* 13 (1955), 237–50.

7 Cross, "The Song of the Sea and Canaanite Myth," *Journal for Theology and Church* V (1968), 1–25.

8 Translation is that of Cross, except for modernizing the English from the King James pattern.

9 Space and time do not permit a further elaboration of the Conquest theme in Biblical theology through the citing of specific passages. For more detail, see the Introduction to the writer's work on *Joshua*, forthcoming in the Anchor Bible Commentary; and especially to the 1971 Harvard dissertation of Phyllis Bird, "Studies in the Use of the Conquest Theme." It may be remarked that such a complete study of the use of either of the confessional themes of Exodus or Conquest in the Bible to my knowledge has never been done. Cf also the writer, *The Old Testament and Theology* (New York, 1969), Chap. V.

10 For a "ritual conquest" as a part of Israel's life or worship, see Frank M. Cross, Jr., *op. cit.*; and his "The Divine Warrior in Israel's Early Cult," *Biblical Motifs: Origins and Transformations, Studies and Texts*, Vol. III (Cambridge, Mass., 1966), pp. 11–30.

For brief reference to the Divine Warrior and the Conquest theme as the pervasive background of the New Testament, see the writer, *The Old Testament and Theology*, pp. 124–25, 141–44.

[11] The final eschatological war and the detailed rules for it form the chief subject also of the fourth and last section of the Temple Scroll, recovered during or following the Six-Day War in 1967: see Yigael Yadin, "The Temple Scroll," *BA* XXX: 4 (Dec., 1967), 139.

[12] Quoting here in part from Ex 19: 5.

[13] Bainton, *Christian Attitudes toward War and Peace: A Historical Survey and Critical Re-evaluation* (New York, 1960), p. 49.

[14] See Gordon D. Kaufman, *Systematic Theology: A Historicist Perspective* (New York, 1968), pp. 51–56; and "On the Meaning of 'Act of God,'" HTR 61 (1968), 175–201.

Bibliography of Jacob Martin Myers

Carey A. Moore
Gettysburg College

Bibliography of Jacob Martin Myers

1932

"A Survey of Recent Old Testament Literature (1923-31)," *LCQ* 5, 202–9

1933

"A Review of Old Testament Literature (1932)," *LCQ* 6, 328–35

1935

"Old Testament Literature (1933-34)," *LCQ* 8, 72–79

Reviews

Barton, G. A., *Semitic and Hamitic Origins*, *LCQ* 8, 75–76

1936

"Old Testament Literature (1934-35)," *LCQ* 9, 78–86

Reviews

Dodd, C. H., *The Bible and the Greeks*, *LCQ* 9, 82–84

1937

"The Significance of the Covenant." Unpublished S.T.D. dissertation, Temple University

"Old Testament Literature (1936)," *LCQ* 10, 74–83

"Form Criticism and the Socio-Historical Method," *LCQ* 10, 295–311

1938

Reviews

Reider, J., *The Holy Scriptures: Deuteronomy with Commentary*, *LCQ* 11, 93–94

Cooke, G. A., *The Book of Ezekiel*, *LCQ* 11, 213–14
Leslie, E. A., *Old Testament Religion*, *LCQ* 11, 434–35

1939

Reviews

Beer, G., and K. Galling, *Exodus* (*HAT*), *LCQ* 12, 443
Caiger, S. S., *Archaeology and the New Testament*, *LCQ* 12, 444
Filson, F. V., *Origins of the Gospels*, *LCQ* 12, 112–13
Frey, H., *Die Botschaft des Alten Testaments*, *LCQ* 12, 333

1940

"The Enrichment of Bible Study by Recent Discoveries and Methods," *LCQ* 13, 27–43

Reviews

Goodspeed, E. J., *Christianity Goes to Press*, *LCQ* 13, 313–15
Hewitt, A. W., *Highland Shepherds*, *LCQ* 13, 98–99
Kenyon, F., *Our Bible and the Ancient Manuscripts*, *LCQ* 13, 313–14

1941

Reviews

Kenyon, F., *The Bible and Archaeology*, *LCQ* 14, 107–8

1942

Reviews

Adler, C., *I Have Considered the Days*, *LCQ* 15, 98–99
Pfeiffer, R. H., *Introduction to the Old Testament*, *LCQ* 15, 193–94

1943

"The Old Testament Today," *LCQ* 16, 363–81

Reviews

Wallis, L., *The Bible Is Human*, *LCQ* 16, 102–3

1944

Reviews

Fritsch, C. T., *The Anti-Anthropomorphisms of the Greek Pentateuch*, *LCQ* 17, 318

1945

Reviews

Lamsa, G. M., *New Testament Commentary: From the Aramaic and the Ancient Eastern Customs*, *LCQ* 18, 434–35

1946

"Elijah and the Yahweh-Baal Conflict," *LCQ* 19, 393–402
A History of St. Luke's Union Church; Mt. Pleasant Twp., Adams County, Pa., 1846–1946. Hanover, Pa., 42 pages

Reviews

Torrey, C. C., *The Apocryphal Literature, LCQ* 19, 324–25

1947

Reviews

Frankfort, H. et al., *The Intellectual Adventure of Ancient Man, LCQ* 20, 352–54
Heidel, A., *The Gilgamesh Epic and Old Testament Parallels, LCQ* 20, 109–10
Hyatt, J. P., *Prophetic Religion, LCQ* 20, 229–30
Simpson, C., *Revelation and Response in the Old Testament, LCQ* 20, 458

1948

"Law in the Old Testament," *OTC*, pp. 43–52
"The Psalms" (with H. C. Alleman), *OTC*, pp. 82–91
"The Book of Jeremiah," *OTC*, pp. 699–732
"The Message of the Prophets," *LCQ* 21, 351–68

Reviews

Gebhard, A. L., *Rural Parish, LCQ* 21, 192–93
Matthews, I. G., *The Religious Pilgrimage of Israel, LCQ* 21, 100–102
Waterman, L., *The Song of Songs, LCQ* 21, 289–90
Willoughby, H. R., ed., *The Study of the Bible Today and Tomorrow, LCQ* 21, 81–82

1949

"The Discovery of New Hebrew Manuscripts," *LQ* 1, 195–200
"Helpful Hints in Studying Hosea," *Christian Living* 1, no. 4, 10–13
"Old Testament Literature 1948," *Interp* 3, 96–105

Reviews

Bewer, J. A., *The Book of the Twelve Prophets*, Vol. I, *LQ* 1, 341
Robinson, H. W., *The Cross of Hosea, LQ* 1, 337–38

1951

Reviews

Bewer, J. A., *The Book of Isaiah*, Vol. II, *LQ* 3, 98

1952

Reviews

Bewer, J. A., *The Book of Jeremiah*, Vol. I, *LQ* 4, 218
Cunliffe, J. H., *Deuteronomy: Introduction and Commentary, LQ* 4, 114–15

1953

"Introduction and Exegesis on Judges," IB, II, 677–826
"In Memoriam: Herbert C. Alleman Who Discussed with Us the Scriptures," *BLTSG* 33, 14–18
"The Word of God and the Teacher," *BLTSG* 33, 18–25

Reviews

Rowley, H. H., *The Zadokite Fragments and the Dead Sea Scrolls*, *BLTSG* 33, 27
Swain, J. C., *Right and Wrong Ways to Use the Bible*, *BLTSG* 33, 19

1954

Reviews

Leslie, E., *Jeremiah*, *BLTSG* 34, 18–19
Simon, U. E., *A Theology of Salvation: A Commentary on Is 40–55*, *Interp* 8, 248

1955

The Linguistic and Literary Form of the Book of Ruth, Leiden: Brill, 69 pages
"Joshua" and "Judges" in *Twentieth Century Encyclopaedia of Religious Knowledge*, L. A. Loetscher, ed. Grand Rapids, Michigan: Baker Book House, pp. 614–15, 619

1956

Reviews

Burrows, M., *The Dead Sea Scrolls*, *BLTSG* 36, 18–19
Lewy, I., *The Growth of the Pentateuch*, *LQ* 8, 172–73
Parrot, A., *The Flood and Noah's Ark*, and *The Tower of Babel*, *LQ* 8, 285–86

1957

"Books on the Dead Sea Scrolls," *BLTSG* 37, 10–11

Reviews

Bright, J., *Early Israel in Recent Historical Writing*, *LQ* 9, 277–78
Köhler, L., *Hebrew Man*, *BLTSG* 37, 14
Laetsch, T., *Bible Commentary: The Minor Prophets*, *LQ* 9, 72–73
Ringgren, H., *The Messiah in the Old Testament*, *LQ* 9, 278–79
Sloan, W. W., *A Survey of the Old Testament*, *BLTSG* 37, 14
Wright, G. E., *Biblical Archaeology*, *LQ* 9, 363–64

1958

Reviews

Burrows, M., *More Light on the Dead Sea Scrolls*, *BLTSG* 38, 16–17
Creager, H. L., *Basic Hebrew with Some Supplementary Studies*, *BLTSG* 38, 14

Cross, F. M., *The Ancient Library of Qumran and Modern Biblical Studies*, *BLTSG* 38, 17
Gordon, C., *Adventures in the Near East*, *BLTSG* 38, 14
Kenyon, K., *Digging Up Jericho*, *BLTSG* 38, 15
Moscati, S., *Ancient Semitic Civilizations*, *BLTSG* 38, 17
Noth, M., *The History of Israel*, *BLTSG* 38, 16
Tur-Sinai, N. H., *The Book of Job*, *BLTSG* 38, 14–15
Würthwein, E., *The Text of the Old Testament*, *BLTSG* 38, 15–16

1959

Hosea to Jonah, *The Layman's Bible Commentary*, Vol. 14. Richmond: John Knox Press, 176 pages
"I Kings" and "II Kings," in *The Holy Bible, The Berkeley Version in Modern English*. Grand Rapids, Mich.: Zondervan, pp. 347–411

Reviews

Allegro, J. M., *The People of the Dead Sea Scrolls*, *BLTSG* 39, 22
Glueck, N., *Rivers in the Desert*, *BLTSG* 39, 19–20
Avi-Yonah, M., and A. Malamat, *Views of the Biblical World, I: The Law*, *BLTSG* 39, 19
Gottwald, N. K., *A Light to the Nations*, *BLTSG* 39, 23–24
Grant, F. C., *Ancient Judaism and the New Testament*, *BLTSG* 39, 22
Harding, G., *The Antiquities of Jordan*, *BLTSG* 39, 24–25
Herbert, A. S., *Worship in Ancient Israel*, *BLTSG* 39, 19–20
Köhler, L., *Old Testament Theology*; and Vriezen, T. C., *An Outline of Old Testament Theology*, *BLTSG* 39, 19
McCown, C. C., *Man, Morals, and History*, *BLTGS* 39, 22
Mowinckel, S., *The Old Testament as Word of God*, *BLTSG* 39, 20–21
Neher, A., *Moses and the Vocations of the Jewish People*, *BLTSG* 39, 21–22
Pritchard, J. B., ed., *Archaeology and the Old Testament*, *BLTSG* 39, 20
Rabin, C., and Y. Yadin, *Scripta Hierosolymitana: Vol. IV: Aspects of the Dead Sea Scrolls*, *BLTSG* 39, 21–22
Schubert, K., *Die Gemeinde vom Toten Meer*, *BLTSG* 39, 20–21
Strong, K., *Old Testament Portraits*, *LQ* 11, 84
Thompson, J. A., *Archaeology and the Old Testament*, and *Archaeology and the Pre-Christian Centuries*, *BLTSG* 39, 20–21
Vriezen, T. C., *An Outline of Old Testament Theology*, *Interp* 13, 333–36
Yadin, Y., *The Message of the Scrolls*, *BLTSG* 39, 22–23

1960

Biblical Studies in Memory of H. C. Alleman, eds. J. M. Myers, O. Reimherr, and H. N. Bream. New York: J. J. Augustin, 224 pages

Reviews

Allegro, J. M., *The Treasure of the Copper Scroll*, *BLTSG* 40, 31
Andrae, T., *Mohammed: The Man and His Faith*, *BLTSG* 40, 20
Avi-Yonah, M., and A. Malamat, *Views of the Biblical World, II: Former Prophets*, *BLTSG* 40, 32–33

Bright, J., *A History of Israel*, *BLTSG* 40, 18–19
Gödan, H., *Christus und Hippokrates*, *BLTSG* 40, 29
Ibn Kahldun, *The Muqaddimah: An Introduction to History*, tr. F. Rosenthal, *BLTSG* 40, 19
Kaufmann, Y., *The Religion of Israel*, *BLTSG* 40, 30–31
Kenyon, K., *Archaeology in the Holy Land*, *BLTSG* 40, 32
Keyes, N. B., *Story of the Bible World in Map, Word, and Picture*, *BLTSG* 40, 18
Kuhl, C., *The Prophets of Israel*, *BLTSG* 40, 33–34
Morgan, G. C., *The Minor Prophets*, *BLTSG* 40, 18
Moscati, S., *The Face of the Ancient Orient*, *JBL* 79, 384–85; also in *BLTSG* 40, 27–28
Smend, R., *Das Mosebild von Heinrich Ewald bis Martin Noth*; and Rad, G. von, *Moses*, *BLTSG* 40, 28–29
Wheeler, M., *A Second Book of Archaeology*, *BLTSG* 40, 20–21
Wright, G. E., *The Rule of God*, *BLTSG* 40, 29–30

1961

"The Requisites for Response," *Interp* 15; 14–31

Reviews

Dietrich, S. de, *God's Unfolding Purpose*, *BLTSG* 41, 29
Fakhry, A., *The Pyramids*, *BLTSG* 41, 25
Gardiner, A., *Egypt of the Pharaohs*; and Kees, H., *Ancient Egypt: A Cultural Topography*, *BLTSG* 41, 27–28
Kuhl, C., *The Old Testament: Its Origins and Composition*, *BLTSG* 41, 26
Kuhn, K. G., *Konkordanz zu den Qumrantexten*, *BLTSG* 41, 30
Moriarty, F., *Introducing the Old Testament*, *BLTSG* 41, 30
Owen, G. F., *Archaeology and the Bible*, *BLTSG* 41, 25–26
Rad, G. von, *Genesis: A Commentary*, *BLTSG* 41, 26
———, *Theologie des Alten Testaments*, *BLTSG* 41, 27–28
Thompson, J., *The Old Testament View of Revelation*, *BLTSG* 41, 31
Wright, G. E., *Biblical Archaeology*, abr. ed., *BLTSG* 41, 28

1962

"Some Considerations Bearing on the Date of Joel," *ZAW* 74, 177–95
Foreword to *The Royal Psalms* by Keith R. Crim. Richmond: John Knox Press, pp. 7–11
Contributions to *IDB* (4 vols.), ed. G. A. Buttrick. New York: Abingdon Press:

Anklets I, 137
Apron I, 176
Armlet I, 227
Array, Holy I, 231
Bag I, 339–40
Bandage I, 345–46
Bands, Magic I, 346
Beaten Oil I, 369
Bell I, 378
Bleach I, 445
Boot I, 454–55
Bracelet I, 460
Breeches I, 465
Broach I, 467
Collar I, 657
David I, 771–82
Design I, 829
Dress and Ornaments I, 869–71
Earring II, 2
Embroidery & Needlework II, 96–97
Festal Garment II, 265
Figured Stone II, 267

Finery II, 368
Fringe II, 325–26
Frontlets II, 326
Garland II, 354
Girdle II, 399
Haircloth II, 512
Headband II, 541
Headdress II, 541
Linen III, 134–35
Linen Garment III, 135
Mantle III, 261
Napkin III, 510
Nose Ring III, 561
Oak of the Pillar III, 575
Pendant III, 711
Powders of the Merchant III, 854
Purse III, 971
Ring IV, 100
Robe IV, 102
Sandals and Shoes IV, 213–14
Saul IV, 228–33
Script IV, 248
Sewing IV 296
Shuttle IV, 342
Silk IV, 352
Skirt IV, 382
Sleeves IV, 391
Solomon IV, 399–408
Stuff IV, 448–49
Tassel IV, 520
Turban IV, 718
Twined Linen IV, 720
Veil IV 747–48
Vestment IV, 784
Waistcloth IV, 796

Reviews

Eichrodt, W., *Theology of the Old Testament*, Vol. 1, *BLTSG* 42, 24
James, E. O., *Sacrifice and Sacrament*, *BLTSG* 42, 31–32
Noth, M., *Exodus: A Commentary*, *BLTSG* 42, 32–33
Muilenburg, J., *The Way of Israel*, *BLTSG* 42, 23
Payne, J. B., *The Theology of the Old Testament*, *BLTSG* 42, 30–31
Weiser, A., *The Old Testament: Its Formation and Development*, *BLTSG* 42, 24–25

1963

Reviews

Finegan, J., *In the Beginning: A Journey through Genesis*, *BLTSG* 43, 34
Hastings, J., ed., *Dictionary of the Bible*, rev. by F. C. Grant and H. H. Rowley, *Interp* 17, 334–36
Newman, M. L., *The People of the Covenant*, *BLTSG* 43, 35–36
Thompson, J. A., *The Bible and Archaeology*, *BLTSG* 43, 34–35

1964

"Jeremiah: Old Testament Hero," *Resource* 5, 22–25
"Choice Vessels," *BLTSG* 44, 3–9

Reviews

Amsler, S., *David, Roi et Messie*, *JBL* 83, 98–99
Bruce, F. F., *Israel and the Nations*, *BLTSG* 44, 25
Carlson, R. A., *David, the Chosen King*, *JBL* 83, 440–42

1965

Theological and Missionary Studies in Memory of John Aberly, eds. J. M. Myers, H. N. Bream, and O. Reimherr, Gettysburg: Gettysburg Times & Publishing, 152 pages
I Chronicles in AB. New York: Doubleday, 239 pages
II Chronicles in AB. New York: Doubleday, 268 pages
Ezra-Nehemiah in AB. New York: Doubleday, 268 pages

Reviews

Hertzberg, H. W., *I and II Samuel*, *Interp* 19, 357–60

Mowinckel, S., *Studien zu dem Buche Ezra-Nehemia I, Die nachchronische Redaktion des Buches; II, Die Nehemia-Denkschrift*, *JBL* 84, 94–95

Watts, J. W., *A Survey of Syntax in the Hebrew Old Testament*, *LQ* 17, 88–89

1966

Invitation to the Old Testament. New York: Doubleday, 252 pages

"The Kerygma of the Chronicles," *Interp* 20, 259–73

"Is Paul Also among the Prophets?" (with E. D. Freed), *Interp* 20, 40–53

Reviews

Noth, M., *Leviticus.* The Lutheran World 13, 330

Randellini, Lino. *Il libro delle Chronache. CBQ* 28, 527–29

Thiele, E. R., *The Mysterious Numbers of the Hebrew Kings*, *LQ* 18, 281

1968

The World of the Restoration. Englewood Cliffs, N. J.: Prentice-Hall, 182 pages

Reviews

Aharoni, Y., *The Land of the Bible*, *LQ* 20, 97-98.

Michaeli, F., *Commentaire de l'Ancien Testament xv: Les Livres des Chroniques, d'Esdras et Néhémie. Interp* 22, 224–25

1969

Search the Scriptures: New Testament Studies in Honor of Raymond T. Stamm, eds. J. M. Myers, O. Reimherr, H. N. Bream, Leiden: Brill, 196 pages

Reviews

Ackroyd, P. R., *Exile and Restoration*, *Interp* 23, 243–45

Hals, R. M., *The Theology of the Book of Ruth*, *Interp* 23, 483–84

Heaton, E. W., *The Hebrew Kingdoms*, Vol. 3, *CBQ* 31, 257–58

Liver, J., *Chapters in the History of the Priests and Levites* (in Heb.) *CBQ* 31, 579–581

Plöger, O., *Theocracy and Eschatology*, *Interp* 23, 105–7

1970

"Sanka-coffee Hour at Faber's," *BLTSG* 50, 6–8

Reviews

Bornkamm, H., *Luther and the Old Testament*, *CBQ* 32, 436–38

Gaster, T. H., *Myth, Legend, and Custom in the Old Testament*, *Christian Century* 87, 638

Smith, W. R., *Lectures on the Religion of the Semites, 3d ed., with Prolegomenon by J. Muilenburg*, *CBQ* 32, 634–35

1971

Contributions to Encyclopedia Judaica (16 vols.), Jerusalem: Keter; New York: Macmillan:
Ezra 6, 1104–6
Ezra and Nehemiah, Book of 6, 1111–23
Nehemiah 12, 936–37

Reviews

Pohlmann, K. F., *Studien zum dritten Esra*, *JBL* 90, 344–46
Torrey, C. C., *Ezra Studies, With Prolegomenon by W. F. Stinespring*, *CBQ* 33, 468–69

1972

I and II Esdras in AB (in press). New York: Doubleday.

Reviews

Sehmsdorf, E., *Die Prophetenauslegung bei J. G. Eichhorn*, *CBQ* 34, 112–13